Bubonic Plague in Early Modern Russia

The Johns Hopkins University Studies in
Historical and Political Sciences
Ninety-eighth Series (1980)

1. Bubonic Plague in Early Modern Russia: Public Health and Urban Disaster
   By John T. Alexander
2. Reckoning with the Beast: Animals, Pain, and Humanity in the Victorian Mind
   By James C. Turner

Bubonic Plague in Early Modern Russia

Public Health & Urban Disaster

JOHN T. ALEXANDER

THE JOHNS HOPKINS UNIVERSITY PRESS
Baltimore and London

This book has been brought to publication with the generous assistance of the Andrew W. Mellon Foundation.

Manufactured in the United States of America

The Johns Hopkins University Press, Baltimore, Maryland 21218
The Johns Hopkins Press Ltd., London

Library of Congress Catalog Card Number 79-3652
ISBN 0-8018-2322-6

Library of Congress Cataloging in Publication data will be found on the last printed page of this book.

To Maria, Michal, and Darya,
with sweet and sour memories
of Moscow and the Hotel "Pekin"

Contents

ILLUSTRATIONS

Figures

Maps

Graphs

TABLES

Preface

This study explores a catastrophe which, though now half forgotten, darkened the reign of Empress Catherine the Great of Russia (1762-96) and horrified Europe in the age of the Enlightenment. Accustomed (as we are) to dismiss bubonic plague as a historical relic fortunately confined to backward regions of the world, the Empress and her contemporaries watched in disbelief the widening ravages of an immense epidemic that caused one of the worst natural disasters of the eighteenth century. To recapture some inkling of their consternation, we might recall the anguished response to "Legionnaire's disease" in Philadelphia in 1976 or the alarm about a swine flu epidemic in 1976-77. Two centuries ago the shattering experience of massive pestilence challenged comfortable assumptions that Russia and Europe were safe from the mysterious disease lurking in the Middle East. As the plague's last major invasion of Russia and of Europe beyond the Balkans, the epidemic of 1770-72 coincided with a widespread, meteorologically induced subsistence crisis that aggravated the political crisis culminating in the Russo-Turkish War of 1768-74 and the First Partition of Poland in 1772-73. Moscow substained the worst local manifestation of this international epidemic, a spectacular outbreak that deranged the entire metropolis in 1771.

The present account seeks to present a total picture of this complex phenomenon from multiple perspectives—local, imperial, and international—by recreating the epidemic as contemporaries experienced it and by analyzing its vagaries in the light of modern epidemiology and in comparison with other plague epidemics in Russia and elsewhere. In particular, this presentation studies the evolution of public health institutions in Russia and reinterprets the role of the medical professionals in an effort to move beyond simplistic or nationalistic concerns about personal responsibility for the plague's reaching and ravaging Moscow. Previous historiography has been pitifully distorted by the widespread contemporary accusation, based upon mistaken assumptions about plague, that officials and physicians were both delinquent, jointly or individually, in their failure to protect the metropolis from the awful visitation. Modern epidemiology can lead the way in exposing such crude indictments. Thus narrative and analysis are combined to provide a synthesis that substantially revises previous scholarship.

Beyond the inherent drama of a great social calamity, study of the Moscow plague offers an unusual opportunity to elucidate trends and events that affected the gamut of Russian society, from the Empress at the top to chimney sweeps and convict gravediggers at the bottom. The prolonged and perplexingly sporadic epidemic threatened all levels of society. Many normally inarticulate groups and individuals impressed their actions and aspirations upon the abundant documentation produced by the crisis. Indeed, the Moscow plague left an enormous quantity and variety of records that allow it to be examined in greater depth than most epidemics before 1800.

Scholarly study of the plague of 1770–72 began almost as soon as the epidemic ended and has made fitful progress over two centuries, but the subject remains poorly known even to most specialists because Russian medical history never achieved independent stature inside or outside the Russian Empire or the Soviet Union. After a promising start in the nineteenth century, Russian medical historiography suffered general disruption and neglect after 1917. The three most important Russian publications about the Moscow plague, for example, all date from 1905 or earlier. The official account compiled by Dr. Afanasii Shafonskii in 1775 presented a valuable selection of governmental documents. In 1884, Alexander Brückner, an eminent historian and biographer of Catherine II, synthesized in a long two-part article the published sources, including the physicians' plague tractates. Franz Dörbeck's doctoral dissertation of 1905 surveyed plague epidemics in Russia over a period of ten centuries; the next year a severe abridgement of his book in German made Russian scholarship available to a wider audience. Yet all three of these works, albeit excellent in their time, exhibit basic flaws in their outdated conceptions of plague etiology, one-sided documentation, and narrowly national focus. To provide a fuller account of the Moscow plague in a broader context, this book employs modern epidemiology, marshals fresh documentation—mainly unpublished sources from archives in the Soviet Union—and reinterprets events in Russia from an international, comparative perspective of several centuries. The comparative and long-term dimensions have benefited greatly from recent studies of plague and other epidemics in other regions and periods by Jean-Noël Biraben, Carlo Cipolla, Michael Dols, Roderick McGrew, William McNeill, Charles Mullett, John Norris, John Post, and J. F. B. Shrewsbury.

The foregoing considerations account for the structure of this book. The introduction summarizes modern understanding of bubonic plague, and Part I establishes the historical background, medical context, and local setting of the epidemic. Part II offers a largely narrative explication of the plague's evolution in the Russian Empire, focusing upon Moscow and its hinterland. These chapters also pursue several particular themes: the influence of weather on the plague's erratic emergence, the disputes within the medical community over the nature of the disease, the interaction of medical practitioners with governmental authorities in Moscow and Petersburg and between the two capitals, and the reactions of the population to the authorities' antiplague precautions. Part III analyzes the plague's impact on Moscow, examines the continuing discussions among medical thinkers about the nature of plague as revealed in the recent epidemic, and compares the plague of 1770–72 to others in the seventeenth and eighteenth centuries. Withal, the study aspires to contribute to several fields of history: Russian and European, social and economic, medical and urban, demographic and meteorological.

Acknowledgments

It is a pleasant obligation to record the generous financial, institutional, and personal support that made possible the completion of this project during a period of almost ten years. This publication was supported in part by NIH grants 1 R01 LM 01664-01 and 1 R01 LM 02359-01 from the National Library of Medicine, U.S. Public Health Service. Two grants from the International Research and Exchanges Board underwrote a total of eleven months of research in Moscow and Leningrad in 1971 and 1975, in conjunction with reciprocal grants from the USSR Ministry of Higher and Specialized Secondary Education. An award from the Penrose Fund of the American Philosophical Society in 1971 (grant no. 5890) assisted in the acquisition of research materials and defrayed travel expenses. Numerous grants from agencies of the University of Kansas—from the General Research Fund, the Small Grants Subcommittee, the Faculty Development Fund, the Biomedical Sciences Support Grant Subcommittee (grant RR07037), the Graduate School Research and Travel Fund, and the sabbatical leave program—financed summer and sabbatical research, travel, purchase of materials, and clerical expenses. The KU Cartographic Services prepared the maps.

This work is substantially based on unpublished sources gathered through the cooperation of the following Soviet research institutions: the Chief Archives Administration, the Central State Archive of Old Documents, the Central State Archive of the City of Moscow, the Central State Historical Archive of the USSR in Leningrad, the Manuscript Department of the State Lenin Library in Moscow, the Department of Written Sources and the Graphics Department of the State Historical Museum in Moscow, the Manuscript Division of the State Public Library in Leningrad, and the Museum of the Chief Geophysical Observatory at Voeikovo near Leningrad. Microfilm copies of British diplomatic dispatches were obtained from the Public Record Office in London, and a microfilm copy of Dr. Georg von Asch's journal of the Russo-Turkish campaigns was kindly provided by the manuscript department of the Niedersächsische Staats- und Universitätsbibliothek in Göttingen with the permission of Dr. Heinz Müller-Dietz, who plans to publish the manuscript in translation. Published sources were collected in the following libraries: the State Lenin Library, the library of the Kirov Military-Medical Academy, the University of Leningrad Library, the Gor'kii Library of Moscow State University, the Library of the Wellcome Institute of the History of Medicine, the Library of Congress, the National Library of Medicine, the New York Public Library, the library of the New York Academy of Medicine, the Columbia University Library, the University of Illinois Library, the Indiana University Library, and the Watson, Spencer, Medical, and Clendening History of Medicine libraries of the University of Kansas. The Inter-library Services Department of Watson Library facilitated the borrowing of materials from other libraries.

Soviet colleagues provided valuable advice and guidance to materials, particularly M. T. Beliavskii, my principal consultant in Moscow, and M. I. Avtokratova, S. R. Dolgova, V. L. Ianin, V. M. Kabuzan, V. V. Mavrodin, R. V. Ovchinnikov, N. I. Pavlenko, L. N. Semenova, S. M. Troitskii, and A. A. Vasil'ev. This book profited greatly from the critical readings of preliminary drafts by Edward Alexander, Nancy Frieden, Clifford Griffin, Robert Hudson, John Klier, John Norris, Kasimir Papmehl, John Post, Marc Raeff, and David Ransel. Other colleagues at the University of Kansas offered helpful comments on chapters presented to our department discussion group, the Hatchet Club, and scholars at other institutions at home and abroad responded to presentations at local, regional, national, and international scholarly conferences. Those small portions of the study that have appeared in article form have all been reworked for this synthesis. The secretaries of the Department of History kindly typed early drafts of the work, and Judi Janzen typed the final draft with exemplary efficiency. Henry Y. K. Tom and Nancy M. Gallienne of The Johns Hopkins University Press furnished tactful editorial guidance. Despite all this assistance, I alone retain responsibility for the final text.

Note on Dates and Transliteration

Except for British periodicals and some diplomatic dispatches designated new style (NS), all other dates are given according to the old style Julian calendar, which in the eighteenth century lagged eleven days behind the Gregorian calendar. Russian terms have been transliterated by means of the Library of Congress system, with a few small variations for the sake of readability. Diacritical marks have been omitted in the text but retained in the notes.

Bubonic Plague in Early Modern Russia

INTRODUCTION

Bubonic Plague, Fleas, and Rats

To facilitate fuller understanding of the erratic course of the epidemic in eighteenth-century Moscow, some appreciation of modern knowledge about bubonic plague is essential, for this infamous disease has inspired abundant myths and half-truths. If modern epidemiology has clarified most of the plague's mechanics, that knowledge has emerged fairly recently and has not resolved all ambiguities, especially at the practitioner's level. In the United States, for example, occasional cases evade detection or defy diagnosis, as happened to a young girl in Denver, Colorado, in 1968.[1] Furthermore, of 7 confirmed cases in New Mexico in the 1960s (none fatal), plague figured in the initial diagnosis just once.[2] These facts alone ought to elicit sympathy for the plight of medical practitioners and officials who confronted plague in the centuries before anybody understood the mysterious affliction.

The changed status of this formerly fearsome disease represents an extraordinary achievement of modern microbiology—an achievement the more astonishing when one recalls that the causative agent, the bacterium *Yersinia (Pasteurella) pestis,* was isolated only in 1894, and that plague's full etiology —the rodent-flea nexus—was definitely established about 1910.[3] Vaccines and antibiotics presently enable health workers to limit outbreaks and to save the majority of those infected. Of 31 cases recorded in the United States in the 1960s, just 7 proved fatal.[4] Despite some recent resurgence of the disease in this country, morbidity and mortality rates remain low: 20 cases with 4 deaths in 1975 and 16 cases with 3 deaths in 1976.[5] Even though isolated cases and small outbreaks still afflict scattered, mainly underdeveloped regions of the world, great epidemics or pandemics of bubonic plague no longer threaten most of human society under peaceful conditions. Thermonuclear war, terrorist attack, or some other disruption of the social fabric could conceivably puncture this relative security, however.[6]

An ancient disease, bubonic plague possibly afflicted the Philistines in the well-known Biblical account.[7] It may also have caused the famous "Plague of Athens," in 431 B.C., described by Thucydides, although several other diseases have also been suspected.[8] It certainly engendered the disastrous pandemic of the early Middle Ages—a whole series of epidemics from 541 to

767—and triggered at least two others: the "Black Death" of the mid-fourteenth and subsequent centuries, and the global outbreaks of the period 1890–1930.[9] The bacterium shows great stability. Although two or three subtypes have been distinguished, strains of *Y. pestis* "recovered from man, rats, wild rodents and fleas from every corner of the earth are biologically identical and remarkably homogeneous in virulence and infectiousness."[10]

As presently understood, bubonic plague is an insect-borne bacterial disease that occurs in nature as an internal parasite of rodents and *Lagomorpha.* One of more than 100 *zoonoses*—diseases transmitted between vertebrate animals and people—it is not primarily a human affliction. In biological terms, plague epidemics reveal an explosively unstable parasitism. Permanently settled or *enzootic* among remote colonies of burrowing rodents, plague periodically spreads erratically among them as an *epizootic* which, if it should reach a dense population of commensal rodents, may provoke human cases. Despite its dreadful reputation, bubonic plague cannot infect human communities quickly or easily. Usually it requires intermediaries in order to spread from rodent to rodent, from rodent to people, or from person to person. Fleas act as the primary transmitters.

Fleas pick up the bacteria from their rodent hosts, some of which are resistant to the disease and harbor the bacteria in their bloodstream. More than 200 species of rodents are susceptible to *Y. pestis* by flea bite or, more rarely, by consuming infected rodent carcasses. When fleas suck blood from rodents infected with *Y. pestis,* some of the ectoparasites become engorged with the bacteria, for the growth of which their gullets offer ideal conditions. The bacteria block the feeding mechanism of a small proportion of the fleas. Ravenously hungry and threatened by desiccation as a result, these "blocked" fleas strive desperately to feed and, in the process, regurgitate bacteria-laden matter into their hosts—25,000 to 100,000 bacilli each time. The blood of a highly susceptible rat dead of plague may contain up to 100 million bacilli per cubic millimeter.[11] Once the host rodent sickens, dies, or is otherwise disturbed, its fleas seek other nearby warm-blooded hosts and infect some of them in the same manner. If the rodents and fleas are numerous and natural conditions are propitious, an epizootic results. If the rodents—house rats, for example—live close to humans, some starving "blocked" fleas attack them, too, once their preferred rat hosts have died. If the flea, rat, and human populations are large enough and live close together, an epidemic may ensue. Fleas transmit the disease from rats to humans, but not from person to person, because humans rarely develop sufficient concentrations of bacteria to infect fleas. Neither age nor sex nor race protects individuals against plague. Because it afflicts humans infrequently, no natural, lasting immunity seems to exist. Recent experience suggests that younger persons may be more susceptible and liable to develop more severe symptoms.[12]

Bubonic plague, the most common form of the disease, derives its name from the bubo, a swelling of the regional lymph glands. Buboes commonly occur in the groin—the word comes from the Greek for groin—but they also appear in the armpits, neck, or elsewhere. Among a group of 40 plague patients in South Vietnam in 1970, for example, all presented buboes, nearly two-thirds on the thigh.[13] The bubo "may remain small, hard and tense, but more frequently enlarges to the size of a walnut or goose egg and is embedded in boggy edema [swelling]."[14] Buboes arise when the bacteria, injected through the skin by flea bite, multiply and flow to the nearest lymph glands, which become swollen as they attempt to disarm the intruding microorganisms. Unless destroyed by the body's natural defenses, or drugs, *Y. pestis* attacks the circulatory system and associated organs, and death results from heart failure within a period of 5 days or more. The case mortality rate of untreated bubonic plague may vary widely, but during severe epidemics it usually reaches 60 to 90 percent. Occasionally, if immunity is inadequate or virulence is high, the bacteria proliferate so rapidly as to overwhelm the body's resistance and cause death within twenty-four hours—the so-called septicemic form of plague.[15]

Sometimes, bubonic plague involves the lungs by inciting or exploiting secondary pneumonia, which may then infect other persons directly in the form of air-borne primary pneumonic or pulmonary plague. How this happens remains uncertain. Perhaps bloodclots from lesions in lymph nodes, liver, or spleen become embedded in the pulmonary capillaries.[16] This form of plague looks and behaves quite differently from the bubonic type. Transmitted by interpersonal, droplet infection—coughing, spitting, or vomiting—pneumonic plague is one of the deadliest diseases known, with a case mortality rate of nearly 100 percent unless treated with antibiotics within hours of its onset. Fortunately, the pneumonic variant rarely occurs, and it tends to be self-limiting because many of the stricken perish before they can infect others. An outbreak in Los Angeles in 1924 killed only 30 persons in several square blocks within 2 weeks.[17] Probably the widespread coincidence of pneumonic, bubonic, and septicemic plague during the Black Death pandemic of the mid-fourteenth century gave rise to the popular conviction of plague being acutely infectious.[18]

Besides the bubo, plague symptoms may include severe headache, fever, rapid pulse, bloodshot eyes, skin lesions such as carbuncles, hemorrhagic spots (petechiae), nausea, vomiting, prostration, slurred speech, staggering gait, and delirium. These symptoms may appear separately or in diverse combinations at various stages of the malady. Indeed, plague may dispatch victims before any external signs can be observed. "Sporadic cases of primary septicemic plague are particularly difficult to recognize because there are no specific findings."[19] Doubtless septicemic plague, in conjunction with concealed bubonic cases, caused the sudden deaths—corpses in the streets, persons dying overnight—mentioned in many accounts. Other comparatively rare types of plague include the carbuncular, tonsillar, vesicular, and anginal.[20] Without modern laboratory assistance the multifarious symptoms of plague render diagnosis extremely difficult, for it may resemble many other diseases and conditions. For the 7 cases examined in New Mexico in the 1960s, physicians offered the following preliminary diagnoses: tularemia, cat scratch fever, streptococcal adenitis (swollen glands), venereal disease, viral meningitis, rickettsial infection, cellulitis, gastroenteritis, appendicitis, and incarcerated hernia. Yet laboratory findings confirmed plague in all but one instance.[21] Small wonder, then, that physicians of the eighteenth century and earlier frequently misdiagnosed plague.

"The progress of plague is affected by the habits of man and the nature of his commerce and communications, and by the density of population and habits of a vast variety of species of rodents and their fleas, and they in turn are influenced by climate, harvest, weather, and a number of other changes in the general environment."[22] An epidemic of bubonic plague represents an ecological disruption. Four radically different organisms come into unwonted contact. Thus, "seemingly minor differences in the habits of rats and fleas may have major reflections in the spread of epizootic and epidemic plague."[23]

To launch the epidemic cycle, plague bacteria must multiply in enough rodents to infect enough fleas to produce an epizootic. Highly sensitive to changes of temperature and humidity, *Y. pestis* flourishes in moderate humidity within a temperature range of 50–80° F. Temperatures above and below this range halt the disease's progress. Furthermore, the main flea species involved, *Xenopsylla cheopis,* multiplies best in the temperature range 68–78° F. Rats and other rodents also breed most actively in moist, moderately warm conditions, which generally produce the best harvest of grain, their main diet. Finally, warmth and humidity shorten the incubation period of *Y. pestis* in fleas, promote the blockage phenomenon, and prolong the survival of infective fleas. An unusually frequent feeder, *X. cheopis* quickly leaves ailing hosts. "A vicious circle is thus set up, but undoubtedly momentum is added to this through the mass attacks of recently contaminated fleas."[24]

All these relationships influence the plague's distinctive seasonal periodicity and spatial irregularity. In temperate regions, such as Europe and most of the United States, plague ordinarily occurs in the spring, summer, and early fall. Nevertheless, heat and drought may shift the disease to late fall and early winter, a pattern that occurred in New Mexico in 1974.[25] Cold weather usually checks outbreaks, inactivity of the fleas and hibernation of the rodents breaking the chain of transmission. Pneumonic plague, by contrast, sometimes appears in cold weather, probably not so much from any biological cause as from the crowding together of people indoors. Plague-afflicted fleas may survive for long periods, months or even years in some cases, although they usually live only about 14 days and can probably only transmit the disease during half or less of that period.[26]

The transmission and preservation of *Y. pestis* involve, worldwide, more than 200 species of rodents and *Lagomorpha.* In the United States, some 38 species of rodents have been found infected with plague bacteria, and they cause occasional isolated human cases—termed sylvatic, campestral, or wild rodent plague. The recent cases in Colorado, New Mexico, and other western states mainly afflicted hunters and rural inhabitants who handled rabbits, squirrels, chipmunks, marmots, and prairie dogs.[27] Domestic pets, dogs and cats, have been linked to some cases, either becoming infected themselves or carrying infective fleas.[28] Several species of fleas may transmit plague, among them the eclectic and sometimes human flea, *Pulex irritans.* From this fact some writers have hypothesized that the epidemics of the medieval and early modern centuries spread directly from person to person by human fleas, which they assume to have infested the population at large. Modern research, however, has shown that *P. irritans* is a poor plague vector, and most authorities therefore deny it any substantial role in epidemics, even in earlier, less hygienic centuries. Neither do lice, the main transmitters of typhus fever, play an important role in the spread of plague.[29] The reason rodents other than rats do not ordinarily cause plague epidemics relates less to their inherent efficiency as vectors than to their habits. Large numbers do not live close to congregations of people. Mice enjoy closer association with humankind, but they carry fewer fleas than do rats, and the kind they bear are less efficient transmitters than *X. cheopis.*

While many species of rats are susceptible to plague, the two most common types are the black, house, roof or ship rat *(Rattus rattus);* and the brown, field, Norway or sewer rat *(Rattus norvegicus).* The house rat is smaller, more timid, and has a more localized life pattern than its larger, stronger, more adventurous cousin. House rats established themselves in Europe and Russia quite early. They predominated until the eighteenth century, when *R. norvegicus* became noticeable in many areas that it had already infiltrated covertly. "At any rate, although rats sometimes emigrate in substantial numbers over short distances, the spread of *norvegicus* over Europe and other parts of the world must have been a fairly slow process."[30] Apparently, *R. norvegicus* entered Russia from the west in the seventeenth and eighteenth centuries.[31] Thus, assertions that the Norway rat migrated westward en masse from Central Asia in the 1720s, largely displacing its smaller rival, oversimplify a more complex, fluctuating, and long-term phenomenon. One may also doubt that this allegedly wholesale change of rat species largely delivered western Europe from epidemic plague. For, if *R. norvegicus* at first supplanted *R. rattus* in some places, the latter proved "not only capable of retaining or regaining a foothold in the seaports, into which it was incessantly imported by ships, but also of reestablishing itself to a greater or lesser extent inland."[32] Comparative numbers of the two species shift over time and space, as changing conditions dictate their local balance. At present, the two coexist rather easily because they prefer different habitats.[33] But was this always so?

R. rattus and *R. norvegicus* are equally susceptible to plague.[34] Their habits differ markedly, however, and these differences may distinguish their roles in particular epidemics. Both species depend heavily on human communities for food and shelter.[35] Both are highly exploratory and are mainly active at night or under cover. An excellent climber, *R. rattus* usually nests above ground, sometimes in trees, but in cold climates it prefers buildings. It avoids burrowing or swimming. *R. norvegicus,* by contrast, burrows easily and swims well. It "lives readily in hedgerows, earth banks, haystacks and the ground near sewers and streams. . . . In ports such as London both species sometimes live in the same building—*norvegicus* in the basement and *rattus* in the attic."[36] In the large cities of the present-day Soviet Union, too, Norway rats "usually live in shops and warehouses, mainly in lower stories."[37] By climbing, gnawing, or burrowing, the two species can infest almost any building.

Norway rats spend more time outside and in the fields, especially in summertime at the height of the usual plague season. They might thus cause scattered cases of plague on farms, in villages, and in agricultural towns. Field rats might also convey plague from agrarian suburbs into cities. Major epidemics, however, require a plentiful population of house rats carrying large numbers of infective fleas and living among urban congregations of people. Though abundant, house rats may elude observation by infesting wooden walls, attics, and thatched or shingled roofs (from where their plague-ridden fleas and feces might fall on the people and livestock below).[38] Studies of two English villages in 1948–49 found almost as many rats as people and, before a recent poisoning campaign, Rome's rat population was estimated to be 15 million.[39] For a large-scale epidemic of bubonic plague to occur, the rats must be sufficiently numerous and widespread to enable *Y. pestis* "to be distributed rapidly over the area of the epidemic by haphazard rat-contacts."[40] Irregularity in the local distribution of rats and fleas, together with changing weather conditions and human movements, govern the uneven territorial incidence of bubonic plague. Contrary to popular belief, bubonic plague cannot wipe out entire communities overnight. Most plague epidemics (and epizootics) develop gradually, devastate some areas, barely touch others, and bypass still others.[41]

These facts should make clear, too, that bubonic plague does not arise from insanitary conditions, except insofar as dirt implies the presence of rats and fleas. Neither is plague necessarily associated with poverty and the lower strata of society, except insofar as poor people commonly live in crowded dwellings more accessible to rat infestation. "Throughout its long history epidemic bubonic plague has been preeminently a disease of the dwelling-house, with a familial incidence that no other *bacterial* disease of man has ever equalled."[42] Accordingly, population density, modes of house construction, and residence patterns comprise three critical variables in the study of any plague epidemic.

For an epidemic to surmount local boundaries, infected rats and, even more, infective fleas must be imported into urban communities. The passive voice is used here advisedly, because in normal circumstances neither rats nor fleas can venture widely enough under their own power to cause more than sporadic local outbreaks. Typically, infected rats or fleas arrive in grain shipments, bales of raw textiles (fleas are attracted by white), and in other goods wherein they can conceal and, possibly, feed themselves. Hence, bubonic plague can spread only as fast as the prevalent means of transport. When introduced into a new urban complex, the fleas in infected merchandise might cause a few human cases among goods-handlers. Then, depending upon weather conditions, a lag of ten days or more would ensue while the local rat population became infected, whereupon a larger epidemic would begin.[43] Rat plague was rarely noticed before the 1890s and often escapes detection even today; yet field studies show that enzootic plague is much more widely spread than human epidemics.[44] "In every instance of an epidemic of bubonic plague in human history an epizootic of the disease in a domiciliary rat population must have preceded and progressed concurrently with the human disease."[45] Sanitary cordons and quarantines would be unlikely to stop the progress of plague, therefore, unless they took account of the rat-flea nexus—a concept unknown before the early twentieth century, as indicated earlier by the failure of most observers even to mention rats.[46]

Modern epidemiological knowlege thus provides important guideposts to understanding plague epidemics of the past. We now know how bubonic plague epidemics begin, expand, and decline. Nevertheless, epidemiology cannot solve all the historian's problems; he cannot be certain that past occurrences of plague corresponded in all particulars to its present behavior. The virulence of the bacterial agent changes over time, whereas local physical and cultural conditions influence the behavior patterns of all four living participants: ectoparasite and rodent, microbe and man. "It is a significant possibility that the characteristics of the plague bacillus may be altered in an epidemic affecting man."[47] Also, the disease still preserves etiological puzzles, such as the factors that determine its different clinical types. If epidemiology indicates the relevant variables to be considered, it neither enables the historian to make rodent- and flea-counts nor elucidates for him the social context of a specific epidemic. For all these reasons, a historian armed with modern knowledge about bubonic plague should be cautious in analyzing epidemics of earlier epochs.

To apply the findings of modern epidemiology to a past epidemic, one must demonstrate conclusively that bubonic plague was the principal disease involved. Because the bacteria responsible for an epidemic in the eighteenth century could not be isolated then and cannot be recovered now, the historian must marshal evidence beyond symptoms to show that the disease in question behaved like bubonic plague. Consideration of ecological circumstances and careful correlation of mortality rates with seasonal conditions, temperature and rainfall, above all, can furnish crucial proof in identifying any past plague epidemic. One should not accept uncritically the explanations of contemporary observers about the nature and causation of the epidemic they encountered.[48]

PART ONE

Historical Background, Medical Context, and Urban Setting

CHAPTER ONE

Plague Epidemics and Antiplague Precautions in Russia to 1770

The epidemic that devastated central Russia in 1770–72 had many predecessors. To gain a perspective on Moscow's calamitous experience with communicable disease, earlier outbreaks should be reviewed in comparison with the social responses and the institutional precautions that plague generated in Russia and elsewhere. Many difficulties attend this enterprise, however, for the sources are often few, laconic, and ambiguous; problems of nomenclature abound. The Slavs usually referred to epidemic disease as *mor*—plague or pestilence, a generic term indicating only that the malady was considered communicable. Some terms implied contagion by roots related to air: for example, *morovoe povetrie* (pestilential contagion or lethal air), *vetrennaia nechist'* (air-borne contamination), and *zapovetrie* (miasm or impestation). Communicability was also expressed by *zaraza* and *prilipchevaia bolezn'*, "affliction" or "catching disease." The roots of other terms alluded to external symptoms, like *morovaia iazva*, a fairly literal rendering of *pestis bubonica*, which was frequently translated in early modern English as "pestilential distemper." Distemper connoted a violent systemic affliction, whereas *iazva* denoted exanthemata—sores, swellings, spots, and the like. Obviously, such vague terms could subsume many different diseases, some infectious and some not.[1]

Institutional and cultural disparities compound the terminological confusion. Russia's vast and expanding territory, dispersed population, low literacy rate, and the rudimentary administration of most localities guaranteed that some epidemics either would not be recorded or that their description would be too meager to identify the diseases at work. One cannot easily ascertain the incidence of a particular epidemic from reports originating in widely separated localities. Depending on the level of natural immunity among a population, some diseases might have acted differently in the past than they do today. Measles, for instance, posed a far more serious threat to health in past centuries.[2] Additional uncertainty concerns chronological definition: When does one epidemic stop and another begin? A recent tabulation of epidemics in Russia enumerates about 60 for the period 1060–1760, of which some 27 are identified as plague.[3] Doubtless other outbreaks could be added to this total, many of which might have involved more than one disease. The coincidence of many epidemics with natural calamities and warfare could conceal the impact of disease alone. Then, too, when mortality and morbidity are given for early epidemics, both must often be discounted. Chroniclers frequently muddled numbers and counted as victims many persons who had fled. All these ambiguities obscure the centuries before 1700, when Russia's embryonic medical administration focused upon the sovereign and the court, the capital and the army.

An epidemic in 979 was the first to be recorded in Kievan Russia. The new state's numerous towns and villages, growing commercial contacts, and continuous interaction with nomadic peoples all invited infection from abroad. The Eurasian steppes and the extensive waterways afforded open access to the region from several directions.[4] No doubt the fledgling East Slavic principalities soon spawned local or regional epidemics of their own, but many outbreaks probably lasted so briefly and affected so few people that they left no trace. From 1060 onward, however, the newly begun chronicles regularly mentioned epidemics and, sometimes, epizootics.[5] Annalists recorded widely scattered outbreaks in the eleventh and twelfth centuries. The thirteenth century witnessed the first recorded epidemic of wider scope, in 1229-30, which ravaged Novgorod and Smolensk especially, though the chronicle's figure of 32,000 deaths in Smolensk must either be inflated or encompass the entire region. Another widespread visitation took place in 1237–40, sparing only Pskov and the Polotsk-Minsk regions. Oddly, chroniclers did not link this pestilence to the Mongol-Tatar invasion of those years, which may have broadened the avenue for the importation of infection direct from the Orient.[6] Substantial mortality from disease also occurred at Pskov in 1265, across northeastern Russia in 1278-79, at Suzdal in 1282, in the southwest in 1283–84, in the northcentral regions in 1286, and at Pskov again in 1299.[7]

In the first half of the fourteenth century, epidemics of undefined character and scope touched northeastern Russia in 1309, 1318, 1341, 1344, and 1349-50. One can only guess which diseases caused these early epidemics, perhaps typhus in 1229-30 and dysentery in 1286.[8] If these outbreaks exerted merely temporary and localized effects, they prefigured the three main accesses or foci of subsequent pestilence: across the western border via Polotsk, Pskov, Novgorod, and Smolensk; from the southwest via the Pontic steppes; and up the Volga from the Caucasus, Central Asia, and points east.

The Black Death and Its Aftermath

With the Black Death pandemic beginning in the 1350s, one can at last determine the main disease involved. The chronicle accounts become more detailed, more graphic too, even though chronological and geographical puzzles persist. In fact, nobody has established precisely when and how the disease reached Russia. A common version has the plague arriving in the Crimea from India or China in 1346, spreading to western Europe via the Mediterranean in 1347–48, afflicting northern Europe in 1348–49, and finally striking Pskov and Novgorod through the Baltic in 1351–52.[9] The sequence springs from the pandemic's course as observed in western Europe and from the assumption that it followed the main trade routes.

Several considerations challenge this version. First, fourteenth-century Russia was not so isolated from the southeast as some have assumed. The northeastern Russian principalities enjoyed frequent intercourse with the Golden Horde and the other oasis trading centers of the steppe zone. Indeed, the chronicles recorded a second wave of plague in 1364–65 as having come up the Volga.[10] Perhaps these contacts were too infrequent earlier to facilitate the spread of plague in merchandise, or maybe the Turkic and Russian towns lacked the rodent and human populations necessary to sustain a major epidemic. Seasonal conditions in 1346 and the following years might also have interdicted a direct leap northward. Pending fuller study, it seems unwise to discard the possibilities that the plague either reached Russia earlier than 1351—from Poland via Polotsk in 1350, say, or from local sources left by earlier, unidentified epidemics—or that it arrived directly from the southeast. Second, as to the pandemic's following trade routes, additional circumstances should be kept in mind. "Blocked" fleas or infected rats could be transported in merchandise and thereby spread plague. The arrival of alleged "plague-goods," however, might simply coincide with the appearance of *Y. pestis* from contacts with local rats.[11] It is not necessary to accept literally the chronicles' contention that the disease came from the west. Finally, the Black Death could have come from indigenous plague foci of great antiquity embracing the Pontic steppes, the Caucasus, and northern Iran. If tapped perchance by the caravan trade that benefited from the Pax Mongolica of the thirteenth and fourteenth centuries, these reservoirs of pestilence might have supplied rodent-flea conduits northward to the Russian principalities.[12] Indeed, recent research has discounted the east Asian origins of the Black Death and argued persuasively that the strain of plague now found in the Eurasian steppes originated in northern Persia.[13]

Another fact complicates the picture: the initial onslaught of the Black Death in Russia, as elsewhere, brought both bubonic and pneumonic plague. "These were the symptoms of that death," commented the Novgorod chronicle for 1352: "a man would spit blood and after three days he was dead."[14] These observations indicate pneumonic plague and, although observers did not mention buboes, bubonic plague nearly always accompanies the pneumonic form. Because pneumonic plague spreads directly from person to person through coughing or spitting blood, its incidence depends less on the domestic rodent population, urban agglomerations of people, and warm weather. Without pneumonic plague, therefore, the Black Death could not have struck medieval Europe so powerfully, for the population still lived mainly in dispersed villages. This was even more true of fourteenth-century Russia where, except for a few sizable towns like Novgorod and Pskov, the bulk of the population consisted of peasants engaged in extensive forms of agriculture and primitive gathering. Hence rural communities would have been relatively safe from bubonic plague alone, whereas the pneumonic form threatened villagers almost as much as urban dwellers. Pulmonary plague would also compromise the possibility of avoiding the disease by flight to the countryside.

If the presence of pneumonic plague obscures the mechanics and course of the Black Death in Russia, it also beclouds its social impact. Clearly, mortality soared in certain localities at certain times. The chronicles of Novgorod and Pskov speak of hundreds dying daily, of mass graves, of abandoned fields. Remote Beloozero suffered such devastation that it had to be relocated. Neither social status nor wealth, age nor sex protected people from the pestilence. The archbishop of Novgorod and, perhaps, the metropolitan of Moscow fell victim; the dynasty of the Moscow principality nearly died out as a result.[15] Possibly the Black Death assisted the growth of absolutism in northeastern Russia by decimating the aristocracy when it still enjoyed political parity with the dynasties of the leading principalities.[16] Plague may have contributed to the political turmoil in the republic of Novgorod in the 1350s.[17] Although the pandemic must have been less catastrophic than in western Europe, it caused similar social and economic dislocation. As elsewhere, in Russia the Church subsequently received manifold bequests from the dead and the conscience-stricken. A frequent popular reaction to thwart pestilence was to erect a church to a favorite saint, often within 24 hours; so scores of new chapels dotted the country, particularly in the Novgorod region. Moreover, the disease spurred the process of colonization of northeastern Russia, monk and peasant alike seeking sanctuary from the plague-ridden towns.[18] Unlike medieval western Europe, Russia had no Jewish population to serve as scapegoats for these unfathomable visitations of "God's wrath." Instead, popular opinion sometimes blamed the Tatars—possibly with some justice, for several epidemics must have come from the east—as well as sorcerers, witches, and wizards. In Pskov at the end of the fourteenth century, eleven "women soothsayers" were burned during an epidemic, an episode that was repeated in 1411.[19]

The effects of the Black Death on Russia extended beyond the losses of its initial onslaught. Thenceforth, the disease became enzootic for a century or more, as outbreaks recurred at gradually lengthening intervals. Until the nineteenth century, the expanding Russian state seldom enjoyed respites from plague of a decade or more. In northern Russia, place-names with roots derived from the term for pestilence (*iazva*), such as Iazvetsovo and Iazvishche, recall the ubiquity of infectious disease.[20] After the violent eruptions of the fourteenth century, plague rarely afflicted more than one region or locality, but its periodic recurrence compounded the pervasive insecurity of Russian life and sapped demographic growth, especially in urban areas. A chronological sketch of the various outbreaks will emphasize the longer-term impact of the plague, while illustrating the variety of its manifestations.

Bubonic and pneumonic plague reappeared in Pskov in 1360, but apparently did not spread further. Then, in 1363–65, a second pestilential wave rolled over central Russia from the southeast via Nizhnii-Novgorod. Moscow and its environs suffered again in 1366, as did Lithuania, possibly from a "trailer" epidemic that continued in some areas until 1369–70. Scattered outbreaks in 1374–77 hit the Golden Horde and the regions of Tver, Kiev, and Smolensk. Pskov, Novgorod, and Smolensk felt the scourge once more in 1387–90. The last outbreak of the century, in 1396, spared Russia in two respects: it convulsed the Golden Horde and supposedly dispersed a Tatar attack on Moscow.[21]

The fifteenth century as a whole marked some diminution both in the severity and the frequency of plague epidemics. Its first quarter, however, was punctuated by numerous eruptions: in Smolensk (1401), Pskov (1403–04, 1406–07), all Russia (1408), and nearly continuously from 1417 to 1428.[22] The Novgorod chronicler described the epidemic of 1417 in terms that suggest pneumonic and bubonic plague: "First of all it would hit one as if with a lance, choking, and then swelling would appear, or spitting of blood with shivering, and fire would burn one in all the joints of the body; and then the illness would overwhelm one; and many after lying in that illness died."[23]

During these decades influenza and typhus visited some of the same localities. Russia's long, cold winters and frequent famines invited typhus or famine fever, the symptoms of which may closely resemble bubonic plague. Presumably, the two diseases sometimes alternated seasonally, the lice-borne fever appearing in the winter and early spring, the flea-borne in late spring through autumn. Crop failures might also have provoked afflictions such as ergotism and other so-called mycotoxicoses (fungi-produced poisoning) of man and beast alike. One of these maladies, known as alimentary toxic aleukia (A.T.A.), caused epidemics in the Soviet Union during World War II and can produce symptoms like those of bubonic and pneumonic plague. The heavy reliance of the Russian diet upon cereals, rye being the peasants' staple, would have sharpened the threat of such diseases, especially in time of famine, when traditional milling and storage techniques might break down.[24] Then too, the action of mycotoxicoses may explain the chronicles' frequent association of epidemics with epizootics and, equally, their linkage of some epidemics to famine.[25] As the Novgorod annalist reported of 1420–21: "During these two years there were great famine and plague, and three public graves were filled with the dead, one behind the altar in St. Sophia and two by the Nativity in the field."[26] An outbreak of "scabrous disease" (*bolezn' korkotnaia*) in 1422, the third year of dearth, could have signified an ergotism-like disease, not plague. Depictions in illuminated manuscripts support this diagnosis.[27] Famine fostered epidemics in two other respects: by weakening bodily resistance and neglecting personal hygiene because of malnutrition, and by promoting an extraordinary migration of people and animals. Warfare instigated epidemics by similar means.[28]

Longer lulls separated the Pskov epidemic of 1442–43 from its predecessors and from its own successor of 1465–67, which afflicted Novgorod too. The Muscovite conquest of Novgorod took advantage of another pestilence there in 1478. Plague racked Pskov again in 1487–88. Henceforth, plague became mainly bubonic and largely confined to the towns. After a century and a half, the Black Death began to wane. Longer intervals spaced the outbreaks, most of which remained localized. In the interim, Muscovy supplanted the defunct Golden Horde, itself a frequent target of pestilence, to assume hegemony over all of northern Russia, even as it grew into a Eurasian empire.[29]

Plague in Muscovy, 1500–1700

Plague continued to decline in frequency during the next two centuries. If the cooler weather of the Little Ice Age (1550–1850) militated against enzootic pestilence, Muscovy's territorial, demographic, and economic expansion rendered it more vulnerable to imported epidemics.[30] Pskov fell prey again in 1506, and Novgorod allegedly lost 15,396 dead in 1508 during the finale of a three-year visitation. Both towns endured severe outbreaks of an undetermined disease, possibly the "English sweating sickness," in the 1520s and further ravages, probably from smallpox, in 1532–33.[31] Yet central Russia in these decades looked unusually healthful to Sigismund von Herberstein, who opined that "no plague has raged there in the memory of man. They sometimes, however, have a disorder of the bowels and head, not unlike the plague, which they call 'the heat': those who are seized with it die in a few days. That disorder was very prevalent when I was in Moscow [in 1517 and 1526], and took off one of my servants."[32]

Quiescent for more than four decades, plague assailed Novgorod and Pskov afresh in 1552–53. In Novgorod, the clergy sustained heavy casualties, and the whole region supposedly lost nearly 280,000 souls (doubtless an inflated total), whereas Pskov buried 25,000 (evidently an exaggerated figure too). In 1563 and 1566–68, Polotsk and other towns across the Lithuanian border sustained epidemics of undefined scope and nature, perhaps typhus in view of the wartime conditions then prevailing. While being sacked in 1570–71 by Ivan the Terrible's terror brigade, Novgorod reeled under the combined assault of plague and famine. This is one of the earliest outbreaks to yield some credible mortality figures. Of 241 heads of homesteads or messuages (*dvory*) recorded as having died in Novgorod in 1571, more than half (136) were attributed to "the contagion." Since the whole town comprised 3,312 messuages in that year, only 4 percent felt the epidemic directly. Assuming 10 persons per messuage, however, deaths from disease could have surpassed 1,000—a heavy loss for a town already sliding into long-term economic decline.[33]

This epidemic smote central Russia, too, in association with natural calamities, civil war, and the burning of Moscow by the Crimean Tatars; "thus many thousand people died in the country and were eaten by dogs." Heinrich von Staden, the eyewitness just quoted, depicted a terrible crisis in 1570-71: "Then there was a great famine and plague, and many houses and monasteries were abandoned. Many rich merchants left their homes and fled here and there in the country." Moscow underwent pestilential horrors the like of which the rapidly growing metropolis had not seen for more than a century. "When the plague got the upper hand, large pits were dug around the city of Moscow," von Staden reported, "and the dead were thrown in them without coffins, two hundred, three hundred, four hundred, five hundred in a pile."[34] Nevertheless, estimates of 250,000 to 300,000 plague victims in Moscow seem grossly inflated and probably encompassed the whole region or subsumed deaths from all causes. If losses among the clergy were unusually high and visible, one must doubt that 2,703 priests succumbed in Moscow within 8 days of August 1570.[35] Plague revisited sixteenth-century Muscovy for the last time in 1592, when it struck Pskov and its region as well as Ivangorod.[36]

Seventeenth-century Muscovy received even fewer visitations of plague, but what they lacked in frequency they recouped in severity. In combination with other epidemics, plague contributed to the "Time of Troubles" at the start of the new century. Severe famine in 1601-03 set the scene for an epidemic in 1602, probably of typhus. Uprooted by hunger so intense that cannibalism was reported to be rampant, throngs of starving peasants converged on Moscow, where 127,000 corpses were buried within 28 months. In 1605, disease, perhaps dysentery, riddled the contending armies of Tsar Boris Godunov and the false Dmitrii.[37] The next year plague appeared in Novgorod for the last time. Another epidemic, possibly typhus, hit the Moscow region the same year; 3,000 corpses were interred at the Trinity-St. Sergius Monastery alone.[38] Although major epidemics missed Muscovy until mid-century, in 1630 an unidentified malady struck Pechory, northwest of Pskov, killing 1,700 persons in 5 months. Perhaps this was an offshoot of a broader pestilence that apparently came out of the southwest to ravage the Pecherskii Monastery at Kiev in the summer of 1630.[39]

The plague that burst over central Russia in 1654 displayed several parallels to the outbreaks of 1570-71 and 1770-72. Unfortunately, the published accounts, though more specific than for previous epidemics, contain many contradictions. Its origins remain vague. The infection may have come up the Volga from Astrakhan and beyond, from the Crimea where an outbreak occurred in 1653, or from the Ukraine.[40] Muscovy's war against Poland-

Lithuania for Smolensk and the Ukraine might have facilitated the epidemic. The disease surprised Moscow, just as it had in 1570 and would again in 1770. "In the Moscow region and neighboring areas, the air is generally fresh and healthy," commented Adam Olearius, the Holstein emissary who visited Muscovy in the 1630s and 1640s. "As every one writes, and as the Russians themselves say, little is heard here of epidemic diseases or great plagues; moreover, one meets many very old people. It is therefore very surprising that this year (1654), at the time of the campaign at Smolensk, a great, virulent plague broke out in Moscow. They say that people who leave their houses believing themselves healthy fall down in the streets and die. Therefore Moscow is now closed to entry and departure."[41]

Plague reached Kazan by July 1654 and hit Moscow about the same time, its seasonal amplitude approximating the epidemic of 1771. By July the epidemic caused the tsaritsa, tsarevich Aleksei, and Patriarch Nikon to leave Moscow—Tsar Aleksei was then with the army besieging Smolensk. The garrison and the populace fled en masse. By early September, the city virtually collapsed. A crowd of distraught Muscovites protested Nikon's abandonment of his flock, alleged that he patronized heretics and allowed the defacement of icons, and threatened violence. Tales of miraculous phenomena floated about.[42] Looters pillaged abandoned houses, convicts broke out of prison, wild dogs and pigs tore at the multitude of corpses that littered the streets "like cordwood."[43] Left in charge of the city, Prince Mikhail Pronskii died on September 11; his chief assistant, Ivan Khilkov, perished the following day. But troops quickly restored order. They sealed off the Kremlin from the rest of the city and belatedly established a cordon around Moscow to prevent refugees from spreading the infection. Nevertheless, the pestilence blanketed the countryside.[44]

From early August, plague gradually enveloped most of the towns of central Russia, from Nizhnii-Novgorod in the east to Torzhok in the west, and from Shatsk in the south to Vologda in the north. Perhaps in testimony to the decline of both towns, Vladimir and Novgorod somehow escaped. At Vologda, however, "people died a sudden death: whether walking or standing or sitting, if somebody forgot himself for a moment, he soon died; while others went to bed in the evening and turned up dead in the morning."[45] By 10 October the epidemic began to abate in Moscow, doubtless from the advent of cold weather, and some of the sick began to recover. The horror ceased in Moscow by the end of the year, but Tsar Aleksei only reentered his capital in February 1655. Elsewhere the plague died out early in 1655, reappearing along the lower Volga in 1656–57.[46]

The total and proportional mortality from this epidemic are disputed. Some contemporary foreigners believed as many as 400,000 died in Moscow and 800,000 in central Russia, while Kazan allegedly lost 48,000.[47] Such estimates are fantastic—far above the total population of either city at the time. Moscow was no larger than 200,000 and Kazan no more than 25,000.[48]

By contrast, figures as low as 6,095 for Moscow and 18,928 for the other localities have been suggested, which seem closer to reason.[49] Septicemic plague must have accounted for the many sudden deaths. But pneumonic plague remained absent and scarcely appeared anywhere in the seventeenth century.[50] The clergy, the garrison, and the house-servants of the aristocracy suffered heavily, a fact probably explained both by their crowded living quarters and their relative inability to flee. Unlike the elite of seventeenth-century Venice, the Moscow aristocracy largely escaped; besides, many of the service nobility were away with the army.[51] Just as debatable as the figures for Moscow are those for provincial towns. Contemporaries estimated that 11 towns lost 13,000 persons; in Kostroma only 1,895 of 5,356 taxable males survived, more than half of the houses standing empty.[52] As much as half the population of Yaroslavl allegedly perished.[53] Yet such figures, even if accurately reported, require at least three qualifications. Many of the victims could have been refugees from elsewhere, some probably died from causes other than plague, and many of those listed as dead had doubtless fled.

Other instances cast further doubt upon the enormous mortality estimates for provincial towns. For the period from 10 September to 20 December 1654, Vologda reported the death of 532 persons, including 212 adult males: barely 5 percent of the taxable population and an even smaller fraction of the whole town. A roster of the 86 deaths recorded in Kashin from 6 September to 12 November 1654, reflected another mild, selective outbreak. Half of the victims came from only a dozen families, less than 5 percent of the town's total. Ten individuals died "quickly," but just 7 presented markings. Since nearly one-third of the dead were young children or persons who perished after more than a week's illness, many of them probably succumbed from less exotic causes than plague. All these considerations make it unlikely that Moscow, or central Russia, underwent a demographic cataclysm in the mid-seventeenth century.[54]

After the incursion of 1654–56, Muscovy escaped epidemic plague for three decades. In most of Europe, the last third of the seventeenth century witnessed a gradual subsidence of the disease. While reports of epidemics abroad perturbed Muscovite officialdom, southward expansion brought the Russian Leviathan closer to enzootic foci and prolific transmitters alike. Raiding expeditions and ordinary commerce, colonization and warfare among the contending imperial and local powers, offered preconditions and ample occasion for the propagation of plague beyond local limits and across national borders. The Muscovite administration recognized the threat and took precautions against epidemics reported in Vilna in 1657, in Livland in 1658, among the Zaporozhian cossacks in 1664, in Warsaw in 1677, in Cracow in 1681, in the Crimea and its hinterland in 1669, 1673, 1677, and 1681.[55] That none of these outbreaks reached Russian territory can hardly be credited to Muscovite administrative efficiency; the same precautions failed to stop an extensive incursion in 1690.

Since numerous variables govern the progress of any eruption of plague, one cannot be certain why it spread farther in one instance than another. Still, one may suggest that the return of plague in 1690 derived primarily from territorial expansion and colonization. By the 1680s, Muscovy pushed its southern border to within about a hundred miles of the Crimean peninsula, which Muscovite armies unsuccessfully attacked in 1687 and 1689. One of the bases of the latter campaign was Fort Novobogoroditsk, built in 1688 on the southern Samara River. Situated far south of the general limits of Russian colonization, Novobogoroditsk furnished a fateful link between local or imported sources of plague and the Russian settlements farther north.

Disease ravaged Novobogoroditsk and its environs from 22 February to 16 June 1690, killing 522 of the 762-man garrison, including the commander. More than 100 other soldiers fell ill but survived; the townspeople fled en masse. The epidemic began slowly, 71 persons dying in 5 weeks, from 22 February to 31 March. It exploded in April, with 325 more deaths by 2 May, as well as 76 in nearby Novosergievsk, and then subsided, claiming 126 more victims by mid-June. Cotton cloth and other wares from the Crimea were thought to be the means of importation, although local foci might have been involved too. Typhus might have been present, expecially at the beginning, but the clinical picture and territorial spread of the disease strongly resembled bubonic plague. Colonel Vasilii Borkov, who later perished in the epidemic, reported on 2 May that his musketeers (*strel'tsy*) were dying "from the previous sickness, they suffer headache, and diarrhea, and swelling of the chest, and they go out of their minds during the sicknesses, and their loins ache, and from this the glands fall away." The last two phrases apparently describe buboes of the groin, the best known external sign of plague. Another eyewitness spoke of high fever and observed: "with some the glands have fallen away from recurring sickness, and with others the glands have suppurated, and such people have recovered."[56]

The establishment of successive cordons north of the stricken locality failed to prevent the epidemic from penetrating westward and northward. Fugitives from Novobogoroditsk may also have propagated the plague by the same means as freebooters who, heedless of the danger, pillaged the residences and persons of those stricken. Some refugee soldiers and cossacks even tried to fight their way past the military cordons, which could not intercept everybody coming from the south and which were sometimes ineffective when the troops manning them fell ill or fled. Kodak, on the Dnieper south of Novobogoroditsk, reported cases in mid-June, as did the Zaporozhian cossacks. Some two hundred miles north, the *voevoda* (district governor) of Khotmyshsk learned of an outbreak at the village of Krasnoe on 12 June. Investigation disclosed that of 30 stricken, 26 had died in the period 7–17 June, mostly within 2 or 3 days. Further inspection uncovered another site at the hamlet of Sankova. On 17 June, 5 persons had suddenly died at the house of Stepan Yudin, where 2 others had recently perished. Checking revealed that Yudin had visited Krasnoe in late May. The authorities sealed the infected house and mustered local landowners to mount guard around the hamlet, which nobody was allowed to enter or leave. The same measures were taken at Krasnoe, where by 21 June the death toll had reached 38. A villager described the symptoms: "scabs [*boliachki*] appear, and they die from those scabs"—apparently a reference to the necrosis of the skin that plague may produce, or an indication of ruptured buboes. The villagers linked the outbreak, understandably, to the arrival of 8 persons from the Novobogoroditsk region. Evidently these local outbursts soon abated.[57]

The epidemic reached northward as far as the *strel'tsy* settlements at Kursk in late June. Amid panic and massive flight some local officials and clergymen denied the peril. Between 21 June and 10 October 1690, however, 851 persons were listed as plague victims, with isolated cases appearing until January 1691. In concert with the government's strict quarantine, the epidemic paralyzed Kursk; the cordon was only removed in October 1691. From desperation some *strel'tsy* threatened to strike out for Moscow and elsewhere in search of food and salvation. The authorities responded with threats of death to anybody who trespassed the barriers and ordered the protesting *strel'tsy* to be publicly lashed. *Strel'tsy* would have been unusually vulnerable to plague because of their commercial-artisan pursuits and their living in compact communities. Neither medical practitioners nor medicaments were employed to help the victims of this epidemic, though hetman Ivan Mazepa of the Ukraine promised to send 10 barrels of spirits.[58]

Plague Epidemics and Alarms in the Eighteenth Century

Except for an outbreak in the Astrakhan region in 1692-93 that supposedly killed 10,000, plague receded again for nearly a decade. This was a fortunate lull for Russia. Widespread pestilence could have disrupted the Azov campaigns of 1695-96 and impeded Peter the Great's shipbuilding and colonization activities along the lower Don. As it was, disease (typhus?) hit the dockyards at Voronezh and afflicted the soldiers and laborers building the new port of Taganrog where, in December 1703, 60 persons died in 2 weeks, 18 with markings and 42 "suddenly" without markings. Other minor flare-ups in the south from 1701 to 1706 hinted that the disease was not extinct, but they were mere sparks compared to the pestilential conflagration that scorched the Balkans, central and eastern Europe, and the Baltic nations in 1709-12.[59] Danzig, Stockholm, and Copenhagen suffered horribly. The epidemic impinged on warfare and politics, sapping the power of Sweden, where the disease raged till 1713 and claimed about 100,000 victims. It obstructed King Charles XII's attempts to return home from Turkey after his defeat at Poltava in 1709 and facilitated the Russian conquest of Livland, Estland, and part of Finland.[60]

The disease imperiled Russian military operations on the northeastern Baltic seaboard, in Poland and the Ukraine. When Field Marshal Boris Sheremetev reported cases among his troops blockading Riga in May 1710, Tsar Peter ordered the army to pull back across the Dvina, behind a sanitary cordon. Unlike earlier outbreaks when no medical assistance had been provided, Peter took a more active view and sent Dr. Christian Wiel to supervise antiplague measures. The Tsar recommended Dr. Wiel because he was "skillful for such putrid diseases and has been in those places where such diseases frequently occur." Simultaneously, Peter dispatched medicines to the army and directed Sheremetev to isolate sick soldiers, "and order the doctors to use simple medicines for the [sick] soldiers and to give the healthy extra wine with camphor," as Dr. Johann Dohnell had advised. Healthy regiments were to be kept far apart during the "fever seasons" of spring and summer. When plague hit Kiev and Chernigov, the cordon was extended to the southwestern border. On 8 June 1710, the medical administration hurriedly dispatched a 5-man medical team and cartloads of medicaments to Kiev.[61]

At Riga, the plague speeded capitulation to the Russians on 3 June 1710. Sheremetev reported that 60,000 persons died inside the city, while his forces lost 9,800 men from 14 May to the end of the year. In the first instance, the toll was obviously inflated—a diarist of the siege estimated only 22,000 victims—and, of course, starvation and other diseases must have swelled the total. Still, the losses on all sides were heavy. Peter had to levy additional recruits to refurbish his plague-thinned soldiery.[62] As apprehended, the epidemic worsened in the summer and infected new localities. Reval and its hinterland supposedly lost about 40,000 dead to the plague. From Chernigov a field surgeon reported on 10 August 1711, that 31 persons had fallen ill there, 13 of them with "sores [buboes] and with blue spots and carbuncle[s]." The population had been evacuated to a field outside town and surrounded by troops.[63]

Compared to the Baltic region and the Ukraine, central Russia largely escaped the plague, which only brushed some towns along its western border. An outbreak in 1710 at one village in the Insar district of Tambov province appears to have been unrelated and probably resulted from local foci, a separate importation, or another disease.[64] So many died in Pskov, however, that every church had to bury 40 to 60 victims daily. Yet neither Novgorod nor the newly founded St. Petersburg experienced an outbreak.[65] The epidemic gradually dissipated by 1712, probably more from natural reasons—cold weather, population dispersion, extinction of the rodent population—than from human action, although the cordons may have inhibited its spread through infected merchandise and from person to person if, as seems likely, pneumonic plague was also present. In any event, this was the last time

Map 1 European Russia and northern and eastern Europe, with main towns and rivers.

plague spread so far north, and the last incursion to reach northwestern Russia across its western frontier.

Aside from localized outbreaks in the south in 1718–19 that probably sprang from enzootic sources, plague shifted eastward for two decades.[66] A temporary occupation of Persian territory along the Caspian Sea in 1722–35 recapitulated Russia's disease experience with the Crimea, encroaching upon and multiplying intercourse with plague-ridden provinces. Astrakhan fell prey to an epidemic in 1727–28. Either plague reached the port city in the effects of troops returning from Persia or through the silk trade, or it arose from local foci.[67] Cognizant of outbreaks further south, Astrakhan officials took alarm in July 1727 when a soldier with suspicious symptoms arrived by ship from Gilian. Three field surgeons examined the stricken man. A bubo in the groin spurred precautions, but when the soldier did not die until August 27 and the practitioners discovered no other cases they concluded that he had perished from dropsy and leg wounds, not plague.[68] A week later, however, a cossack recently returned from garrison duty in Persia succumbed with "two carbuncles, one on the right hand and another on the right side, and a swelling on the chest and left side that has not burst, as well as a bluish bloodshot inflammation under the right eye."[69] The corpse was burned immediately and the dead man's companions were rushed out of town. Even so, a sporadic epidemic survived the unusually mild winter (the ice on the Volga broke up in mid-December 1727 and unseasonable warmth, rain, and mists continued until at least mid-January 1728) and then engulfed the city in April, when 411 persons died with "buboes, malignant fever, and petechiae" and 315 were isolated in pesthouses.[70]

Summer-like heat and the crowds of barge-haulers and merchants detained in town caused the governor to advise everybody to move to the suburbs or the hinterland, to evacuate the garrison, and to close all government offices. The infection worsened because few heeded this advice, the governor observed on 3 July; "for when a house is impested, then they clandestinely remove impested belongings from that house to healthy houses, to their relatives or friends, and they buy necessities with impested money, and therefore all the healthy houses without exception have been impested, [and] not understanding that they infect themselves, people clandestinely haul out the dead without informing the surgeons assigned for that purpose, and they live in those very houses, and therefore this disease has shown itself more than heretofore."[71] Maximum mortality occurred in June, with 1,300 deaths by 21 June. Heavy casualties among the itinerant workers prompted their evacuation, and on 30 June the governor ordered everybody out of town. By early August, the death toll returned to normal. Still the imperial court, then in Moscow for the coronation of Peter II, banned all movement from the south until June 1729, a policy that apparently exacerbated a subsistence crisis in Astrakhan.[72] Total mortality from this outbreak remains uncertain, but one may confidently discount claims that half the population perished.[73] If the clergy and the merchants suffered disproportionately, the town as a whole quickly recovered its losses, which probably did not surpass 3,000 out of a total population of 20,000.[74] Many victims must have been outsiders—workers and merchants, soldiers and sailors—and malnutrition must have aggravated the toll. The medical debate that preceded this epidemic became a ubiquitous feature of subsequent outbreaks in the Russian Empire, just as it has been elsewhere before and since. Closer acquaintance with plague does not necessarily facilitate its timely diagnosis.

In racking the empire's southern marches and menacing its center, the plague epidemic of 1738–39 resembled those of 1690 and 1727–28. More ominously, it prefigured the catastrophe of 1770–72 by coinciding with aberrant weather, a protracted Russo-Turkish war over the Pontic littoral, and pestilence in Constantinople, the Danubian Principalities, Transylvania, and southern Poland. The massive albeit temporary Russian presence in the far south, trespassing among primordial plague foci, amplified the number of pestilential targets and transmitters alike. The disease first appeared in the spring of 1738 among the Russian garrison at Ochakov, a Turkish fortress captured the previous summer. Either it sprang from local sources—the plague "never fails to be at Oczakoff every summer," noted the British envoy to Russia—or it arrived from the Balkans or the Kuban, where epidemics had broken out in 1737.[75] Perhaps famine in the Ukraine in 1732–36 heralded the plague by spurring rodent migrations. At any rate, "bad weather" in the fall of 1737 obstructed the movement of supplies to Russian occupation forces in desolate regions, inciting both famine and disease. When the Turks attempted to regain Ochakov in late October 1737, "continual rains" and rampant disease reinforced the Russians' successful defense. A mild winter in 1737–38 set the stage for the plague's spring debut.[76]

Like the epidemic at Astrakhan a decade earlier, the new outbreak showed its character slowly. From the start of the Turkish war in 1736, disease steadily depleted the Russian army of Field Marshal Münnich. At Ochakov, the corps of General Stoffeln sickened and died by the hundreds throughout the fall and winter of 1737–38.[77] Informed that more than 1,000 of Stoffeln's men died in January 1738, the Petersburg authorities ordered Münnich to increase provisions and medicines, but accepted his explanation of the mortality as mainly the product of scurvy brought on by bad quarters, short rations, and impure water.[78] The continuously high death rate at Ochakov amid wartime conditions obscured recognition of the plague, which gradually surfaced in the spring of 1738. By mid-June, however, General Stoffeln admitted the death of 1,722 men within 6 weeks.[79] With other diseases plague "made terrible havoc" at Ochakov and nearby Kinburn; the troops "died like rotten sheep." After razing both fortresses in September 1738, General Stoffeln "brought scarcely one-third of his men back to the Ukrain." Indeed, plague undercut the indecisive campaign of 1738, killed many of the 30,000 regular troops Russia lost that year, and hastened the war's inconclusive end in 1739.[80]

Besides afflicting frontline troops, the epidemic hit the capital of the Zaporozhian cossacks and pummeled the Ukrainian garrison towns. At Izium, crowds gathering for the annual summer fair may have worsened the regional impact of the plague's surprise visit. Instances of "spotted fever" appeared there by 18 June, and army surgeon Erhart Egidi discovered buboes by 6 July. For the next two months plague terrorized Izium and its environs. Many townspeople fled, others settled in the abandoned houses, human corpses and dead livestock dotted the streets. The whole region supposedly lost 6,610 persons to pestilence that year.[81]

Khar'kov, the largest town of the southern Ukraine, lost about 800 victims to plague, 500 of them in October 1738. Cold weather cut off the epidemic there by December, as it had done earlier elsewhere. In fact, the timely arrival of winter effectively contained the pestilence by late 1738. The next year plague erupted at Azov and settlements along the Don; small flareups caused alarm as far north as Kursk. Fortunately, the winter of 1739–40 proved to be extraordinarily severe in southern Russia, the river ice exceeding three feet in thickness. Frigid weather thus curtailed the epidemic's territorial spread and forestalled its early recurrence.[82]

Because the plague of 1738–39 afflicted the armed forces and compromised Russian foreign policy, the imperial authorities instituted unusually vigorous countermeasures. Münnich established a cordon along the Dnieper, but when the epidemic soon crossed into the Russian Ukraine, Petersburg dispatched emissaries to oversee cordons between the Ukraine and Russia, and between southern and central Russia, respectively. Assisted by many medical practitioners mobilized for the purpose, this impromptu "plague commission" coordinated administrative and medical precautions in every stricken or suspect locality. Special measures were taken to protect Moscow. Checkpoints were established a hundred miles south of the city, the Moscow post office created a special department in the suburbs to rewrite dispatches from the south, and medicaments for 100,000 persons were stockpiled. Providentially, plague did not reach the metropolis on this occasion. The cordon guarding Moscow lasted till mid-1739, however, while Azov remained closed till July 1740. This epidemic sparked consternation out of all proportion to its actual incidence, for it struck no large towns and mainly affected a vast, sparsely populated borderland.[83]

The three decades after 1740, like the lull from 1657 to 1690, registered no epidemic plague within Russia. Even so, almost annual outbreaks in neighboring polities lapped ever closer to the expanding Russian presence in the south. An epidemic raked Transylvania and southern Poland in 1756–57, killing 360 persons in the town of Vinnitsa and its environs.[84] Each year thereafter, to the mid-1760s, recorded scattered pestilence in Constantinople, the Balkans, southern Poland, the Crimea, the Caucasus, and the Caspian provinces of Persia—sometimes in all these regions at once. Such activity kept Russian officials constantly on the alert. The Russian embassy in Constantinople regularly reported the many local outbreaks, as did representatives in the Crimea and Persia.[85] Thus the Kiev authorities in September 1765 sent word that plague had spread northward into Poland from the Turkish fortress of Bender on the lower Dniester. The threat recurred the next spring and summer in the same localities, other outbursts afflicting Constantinople and the Crimea. Plague supposedly entered Russian territory at Fort St. Dmitrii (Rostov on the Don), but this proved to be a false alarm, just as an epidemic in the Moscow district in September 1765 proved to be smallpox.[86] Another plague scare that seized a locality of Tver province in May 1767 prompted the Moscow authorities to send a medical inspection team. Either the report was spurious or the disease was mild, for nothing came of the incident.[87]

Doubtless the cessation of warfare between Russia and Turkey facilitated localization of the frequent epidemics on Ottoman territory in the three decades after 1740. Concurrently, Russian administrators strove to block the importation of plague by establishing quarantine stations along the southern frontier, but their efforts alone could not have been consistently effective, as the events of 1770–72 would show. The tremendous extent and irregular delimitation of the southern border, the acquisition in 1739 of new territory between the southern Bug and Don rivers, the administrative instability of the region and its sparse settlement, all hindered efficient sanitary surveillance of the contiguous plague-enzootic lands. Furthermore, the presence of autonomous communities, such as the Zaporozhian cossacks and the military colony of New Serbia, fragmented governance of the region, reorganized in 1764 as the guberniias of Slobodsko-Ukraina and Novorossiia—New Russia.

Two incidents will illustrate the problems that frontier officialdom encountered. First, the commandant of Fort St. Elizavet (later Elizavetgrad and now Kirovograd), the capital of New Serbia, founded in 1752, complained in January 1760 that Serbian hussars had violated the quarantine the previous autumn by driving 1,400 sheep across the border from suspect Polish localities. Troops sent after the trespassers had been driven off by gunfire.[88] Second, in March 1765 a Russian observer in the Crimea accused merchants from Ukrainian towns of importing Turkish wares despite the pestilence then raging in the peninsula. Not only did the commerce originate from pestiferous regions, he warned, but officers at remote border posts admitted the cargoes without quarantine precautions. Outraged, Petersburg reaffirmed the necessity to inspect all merchants entering the empire from that direction, quarantining persons and airing merchandise and clothing.[89] But the local authorities could not implement these procedures any more effectively after 1765 than before. Incidentally, the Russian-Ukranian term for drover, *chumak*, took on a folk derivation from the Turkish for plague, *chuma*, and originally denoted traders of Crimean salt who smeared pitch on their clothing as protection against pestilence.[90]

Meanwhile quickening colonization of the steppe lands nearly tripled the male population of Novorossiia guberniia within two decades, by 1763, and this movement accelerated into the 1770s.[91] The influx of population accompanied an expansion of international trade across the region, opening new entries and paving potential thoroughfares for the importation of plague from the south. By mid-century, Moscow had blossomed into a major center of textile fabrication that extensively utilized wool and silk from Ottoman and Persian sources. Greek merchants brought finished and unfinished textiles to Russia and the Ukraine, where sizable Greek communities took root, especially at Nezhin on the main road from Kiev to Moscow.[92] As textiles ranked high among known "plague goods," the imperatives of Russia's industrial and commercial growth persistently raised the threat of imported pestilence. The senate, the empire's top administrative council, grappled with this dilemma in 1764. With plague active in Constantinople, the Russian ambassador there forbade Russian merchants to export textiles to Russia; "but the Turkish silk has always been brought to Moscow in substantial quantities by Greek merchants," to whom the embargo did not apply, objected Senator Dmitrii Volkov. As president of the Collegium of Manufactures, Volkov opposed the embargo as discriminatory and harmful to Russian commercial and industrial interests. Moscow's textile mills needed more raw materials to expand, he contended, yet foreign importers were charging high prices for silk and wool of inferior quality. The senate endorsed Volkov's proposal to repeal the prohibition so long as precautions were taken at the points of entry.[93] Commerce and colonization in the south received additional impetus from warfare after 1768 as Turkey and Russia renewed their armed contest for the Pontic steppes, inadvertently abetting another invasion of plague.

For more than four centuries before 1770, then, recurrent epidemic plague exerted multiple effects on Russian society. Extensive outbreaks repeatedly caused enormous social and economic disruption, sometimes influencing political and military events. Population growth and replacement, particularly in urban areas, evidently stagnated during the initial onslaught of the Black Death, roughly 1350 to 1450. Wastelands proliferated as the population died or decamped.[94] The frequent repetition of pestilence cultivated widespread dread among the population, stifling initiative and enterprise. Epidemics believed to have come from abroad stirred xenophobia. After the early sixteenth century, however, plague became less frequent and less widespread: an occasional and regional, instead of a constant and national, menace. Thenceforward all plague epidemics originated in the south, and after the incursion of 1654–56 none reached central Russia.

By 1770, although the disease periodically threatened Russia's advancing southern frontier, few persons in the Russian Empire had ever seen it firsthand. Just as western Europeans had not experienced plague since the epidemics in Provence in 1720–22 and in Sicily in 1743, so Russians also began to think of it as a remote peril confined to the backward fringes of southeastern Europe. Mikhail Lomonosov (1711–65), the versatile man of science and letters, commented in 1761 that plague mostly occurred along Russia's southern border, and he called upon the medical profession to compile a handbook of precautionary measures based on the best authorities. His own conception of plague reflected the age's theoretical eclecticism. Solar eclipses often foreshadowed epizootics and epidemics, Lomonosov speculated, through interruption of the flow of electrical energy to the earth. "Time will show how much the electrical force can operate as concerns pestilence." Since astronomers could predict eclipses, the authorities should forewarn the people to take precautions, keeping livestock inside and neither harvesting nor consuming food or fodder crops contaminated by the "poisonous dews" thought to fall during eclipses.[95] Lomonosov's remarks illustrate the growing confidence of the European scientific community that plague could be averted and, perhaps, controlled. In the case of Russia, however, such confidence proved premature.

Social Responses and Precautions against Plague

Considering the frequency of plague in Russia before 1770, what reactions did it inspire? The most obvious one was flight. Just as in western Europe, the Black Death, with its high frequency of pneumonic plague, convinced people that the disease was highly contagious. Even after pneumonic plague became less common, by the mid-fifteenth century in Russia, people persisted in believing in the danger of contagion. Besides, plague was not always seen as a single entity; it was often thought to be the apogee of a general infective process. Such beliefs conditioned varied modes of behavior. During the Black Death's early visitations an attitude of fatalistic resignation apparently prevailed, a reaction buttressed by the notion of pestilence as a manifestation of the "wrath of God." Possibly flight became more common from the fifteenth century onward, with tacit encouragement from the authorities. Should pestilence impend, a seventeenth-century leechbook counseled, "seek out a healthful place and a pure air or live in remote forests for a time, so that the noxious wind not kill a person."[96] Such advice repeated the sense of the traditional European adage: run swiftly, go far, and return slowly.[97] Indeed, during the epidemics of the mid-seventeenth century, Patriarch Nikon advised that it was not a sin for Christians to flee from pestilence, but rather a fulfillment of God's will.[98]

Belief in the contagiousness of plague also spurred attempts to prevent its spread. These assumed two forms: appeals for divine intervention, and administrative measures directed against the movement of people and goods. Viewing pestilence as an expression of God's wrath at man's sinfulness, people naturally turned to spiritual mentors. Community prayers, fasting, processions with icons, blessings by local or outside clerical hierarchs, sprinkling with holy water, construction of specially dedicated churches—all exemplified customary religious responses to disaster.[99] If Russian Orthodoxy cultivated a spirit of patient endurance amid pestilential crises, it shunned the passive fatalism that pervaded Muslim conceptions of plague. The disease might be seen as a punishment for the unfaithful, but not as a martyrdom or mercy for the Orthodox.[100]

Governmental authorities generally endorsed these traditional religious responses well into the seventeenth century, but thereafter some officials began to doubt their efficacy. The schism within the Russian Church in the middle of the seventeenth century, together with the accelerating secularization and westernization of Russian society that culminated in the reign of Peter the Great, made officialdom wary of "superstitious" and "fanatical" religiosity that might incite public unrest in time of crisis. The near riot in Moscow during the plague of 1654 suggested the explosive potential of religious dissidence. Similar concern for social control motivated the persecution of an alleged sorceress, Agafa Dmitrieva, at Izium during the plague of 1738. Under torture she confessed to charges of transforming herself into a dog or a goat, killing several persons by the invocation of evil spirits, and proselytizing others. Even though several supposed accomplices died with Dmitrieva after this inquisition, the imperial authorities approved further investigation.[101]

From the mid-fourteenth century, if not earlier, communities also undertook secular precautions. At Novgorod and Pskov the authorities expelled outsiders and prohibited their entry during epidemics. They appointed special personnel to bury the dead in mass graves, marked and isolated stricken houses, instituted pyres to cleanse the corrupted atmosphere, confined the sick to their homes or placed them in isolated quarters that clergymen were forbidden to visit.[102] In sum, local governments gradually developed a panoply of prophylactic measures much like those used in Europe at the time. Before 1700, neither local nor central authorities created any equivalent to the public health boards of northern Italy and other advanced regions of Europe in the sixteenth and seventeenth centuries, if only because Russia lacked the medical professionals to support such institutions.[103] By the sixteenth century, with the territorial consolidation of Muscovy and its creation of a highly centralized administration, the antiepidemic policies of previous centuries and localities were extended to the whole nation. Enforcement increasingly assumed a military character, partly because of the frequency of war and its close connection with epidemics in many instances. Cordons of checkpoints (*zastavy*) manned by troops or militia became the ubiquitous instrument of attempts to confine epidemics. Threats of extreme penalties, even death, were announced for those who circumvented these sanitary cordons.[104]

Contrary to some Russian claims of the greater humanitarianism of these practices than of those employed in Europe at the time, panic on the part of government and people could cause brutal enforcement.[105] Thus a government order of 1654 directed that plague victims in Moscow be buried in their clothes, and that infected houses be segregated and their occupants forcibly detained inside.[106] "During the famine and plague" of 1570–71, averred Heinrich von Staden, "whoever was seized on the Polish border was impaled."[107] And he sketched this harrowing picture of precautions taken:

> Whatever court or house the pestilence visited was immediately nailed up, and if a person died within, he had to be buried there. Many died of hunger in their own courts and houses. Throughout the country, all cities, monasteries, settlements, and villages, as well as all the roads and highways, were guarded so that a person could not pass from one to another. And if a person were caught by the guard, he was immediately thrown into the fire that was next to the guard [post] along with everything he had with him—wagon, saddle, bridle.[108]

Yet these remarks exaggerated the efficacy of such sanitary cordons. In practice, many persons evaded the checkpoints, and trespassers, even when caught, often avoided the stated penalty. Several persons condemned to death for violating cordons during the epidemic of 1738–39, for instance, had their death sentences changed to corporal punishment once the plague passed. Furthermore, the instructions of 1728 to governors and voevodas provided for the exemption of noblemen from the death penalty in such cases—a provision the authorities evidently honored in 1738–39.[109]

Recognizing the danger of importation from abroad, the central government watched border points closely and occasionally solicited information about epidemics in neighboring countries from agents abroad. When epidemics did occur, efforts were made to detain merchants and goods from suspect regions. Indeed, trade sometimes remained paralyzed for months at a time, and starvation might overshadow the plague in threatening sequestered localities. Dispatches to the sovereign and the central authorities received special treatment. They were passed between fires, dipped in vinegar, and rewritten on fresh paper up to 6 times, this process being repeated several times as the message approached the capital. Money was subject to the same precautions, presumably because it might touch many hands and could imperil the governmental and mercantile elite.[110]

The resurgence of plague after 1690, coupled with the government's greater concern for public health, intensified efforts to safeguard Russia's expanding territory. In the eighteenth century, antiplague precautions evolved from the customary ad hoc procedures into standardized practices prescribed by law; these in turn gradually took shape in permanent institutions. The new policies consolidated past experience, consulted foreign practice, and introduced two striking innovations: medical inspection and treatment of plague victims. Pioneered under Peter the Great, the dispatch of professional medical personnel to supervise antiplague measures received authoritative formulation in the instructions of 1728 to governors and voevodas, which simultaneously codified the traditional policies of isolating infected localities. Orders of 1718 and 1722 obligated the householders of St. Petersburg and Moscow to report any death from fever on their premises. The instructions of

1728 extended this obligation to provincial officialdom, requiring them to send doctors or field surgeons to investigate all cases of suspected communicable disease and to inform the senate immediately. Once an epidemic appeared, the provincial authorities were to seal off the area, alert neighboring governmental units, quarantine persons from stricken houses, and burn or air out infected dwellings and articles. Couriers and travelers from suspect regions should be inspected and interrogated under threat of death, quarantined up to six weeks, and their dispatches passed over flames and rewritten three times before forwarding.[111]

Numerous reports to the senate from 1730 onward demonstrate consistent attempts to implement these antiepidemic policies, which also applied to newly incorporated regions.[112] A set of instructions for district commissars of Slobodsko-Ukraina guberniia in 1766, for example, contained an article "Concerning the Pestilential Distemper" that prescribed immediate investigation of all communicable diseases, medical examination of the stricken, and imposition of the precautions described in the instructions of 1728.[113] Both central and local officials routinely obtained professional medical opinion in cases involving unusual mortality or suspicious symptoms.

If the instructions of 1728 followed tradition in emphasizing detection and isolation rather than treatment of the stricken, the medical professionals themselves showed greater initiative during the plague of 1738–39. Dr. Johann Fischer, the chief imperial physician, dispatched unprecedented numbers of medical practitioners to supervise the antiplague campaign. He issued instructions for treatment of plague victims, recommended amulets to encourage the population—many assumed that depressed spirits could engender disease—and polled the field practitioners for additional suggestions. He and Dr. Aruntius Azzariti both prescribed special antipestilential powders. Perhaps Fischer also inspired a government order of 30 July 1738, advising that the common people, whether sick or well, should drink a spoonful of liquid pitch to ward off pestilence. At Khar'kov, Dr. Johann Lerche established a pesthouse or lazaret, and surgeon Erhart Egidi at Izium dissected some corpses in searching for the cause of plague.[114] Egidi carefully described the symptoms of the sick, whom he tried to save by the generally approved means of promoting the suppuration of buboes and lancing carbuncles. Other practitioners used different treatments. Surgeon John Cook described a plague patient who "had been blooded, vomited, and his back, arms, and legs blistered, of which he had no manner of feeling." Predictably, the man died. Cook recounted, too, a false alarm at Voronezh in 1739, when an apothecary blamed plague for the death of a woman who suffocated in a bathhouse. Two military surgeons en route from Moscow to the army proved that the dead woman's symptoms were venereal not pestilential. Concerning their knowledge of plague, "they said, that they never had seen that disease, but acknowledged that they had read about it, and that they also had heard several lectures by Dr. Blumentrose [Blumentrost], physician, by the Great Hospital in Moscow, concerning it, and the various methods of cure."[115]

Several foreign physicians in Russian service wrote accounts of this epidemic. Although most of their descriptions were not published, some may have circulated in manuscript; and Dr. Johann Schreiber's *Observationes et cogitata de pestilentia, quae annis 1738 et 1739 in Ukrainia grassata est* (St. Petersburg, 1740) went through four Latin editions by 1752, the same year it appeared in German. Other practitioners transmitted their observations orally to professional colleagues and students. Medical men and officials alike believed that their activities prevented the epidemic from penetrating central Russia. As a reward, practitioners who fought the plague received at least an extra half year's salary.[116]

With plague menacing the southern frontier almost annually after 1690, the frequent imposition of cordons eventually grew into a network of inspection and quarantine stations at the main points of entry. Such a facility functioned intermittently at Vasil'kov near Kiev as early as 1729. Others guarded Astrakhan, Taganrog, and Kizliar in the Caucasus. Medical personnel staffed these places from the start. In 1742, Dr. Johannes Fabri was appointed border-physician (*Grenze-medicus*) with two surgeon-assistants and authority over the newly built quarantine at Vasil'kov and others further south. These institutions devoted special attention to merchandise, basing their procedures upon previous experience and the policies recommended by a translated treatise about the famous quarantine at Venice in 1756. The Admiralty also secured copies of British and Dutch maritime precautions against plague in 1728, and island quarantines protected Petersburg and Reval.[117]

The troubles at the Vasil'kov quarantine in the 1750s and 1760s exemplified the larger problem of protecting the empire against infectious disease from abroad. From 1750 the senate leased the Vasil'kov station to a Greek manager, Yurii Tomazin, for 600 rubles per year. Tomazin soon found it an unprofitable concession, however, for many merchants circumvented Vasil'kov to cross the border without fees or inspection. To avoid delay, some caravan-masters used a clever ruse. They sent servants ahead to request that the quarantine officials begin counting the isolation period for an approaching caravan and when, some weeks later, the caravan actually reached the border the waiting period might already have expired and the shipment might enter without delay. Tomazin urged the establishment of additional checkpoints on the lower Dnieper to inspect merchants bringing Turkish goods from the Crimea and other Pontic ports. The senate answered Tomazin's complaints in October 1751 by ordering all merchants from Ottoman territory to enter only at Vasil'kov, to submit to medical inspection, and to secure bills of health. Three years later the senate proposed construction of a network of quarantines in Smolensk guberniia and New Serbia, with field surgeons, lazarets, and storage barns at each. The medical administration reviewed the project, added details from foreign quarantine legislation, and the senate ordered the plan implemented in June 1755.[118]

All the same, building a comprehensive system of sanitary surveillance remained merely an aspiration, constantly postponed by practical difficulties.

financial constraints, and conflicting priorities. In 1764, the imperial authorities revived the project, evidently in connection with the administrative reform of the Ukraine after the abolition of the hetmanate. Empress Catherine II earmarked funds for the construction of quarantines in Smolensk, Kiev, and Novorossiia guberniias, and she detached Senator Aleksei Mel'gunov, president of the Commerce Collegium, to supervise the program. But this effort accomplished little besides relocating some checkpoints in the Ukraine in 1765. No quarantine was built in Smolensk guberniia along the Polish border; neither was the Vasil'kov station refurbished. Luckily, the danger of plague seemed on the wane. None of the outbreaks abroad had touched Russian soil by 1765, and the next few years saw the peril recede even further.[119]

The continuing deficiencies of the Vasil'kov quarantine were reported to the Petersburg authorities in 1765 by the local medical officer, Dr. Ivan Poletika. Upon assuming his post in 1763, Dr. Poletika found that none of the storage and quarantine facilities proposed in the senate project of 1755 had been built. The station comprised just 3 buildings: 2 small houses, for merchants and for embassies, and an open-sided barn with a thatched roof for airing merchandise. The shortage of storage room and the lack of goods-handlers, remarked Poletika, caused wares to be aired outdoors. Worse yet, baled goods were not unpacked, in blatant violation of the inspection regulations. No lazarets had been constructed, nor had any provision been made for quarantining livestock in case of epizootics. The Kiev authorities ignored repeated appeals for assistance, Poletika charged. Furthermore, when alerts were proclaimed because of plague in Constantinople and in Poland, the guberniia administration routinely authorized border guards to permit crossings by local people hauling grain, hay, and timber.[120]

Poletika's criticism overlooked another factor that further compromised the effectiveness of the border quarantines: the inspection fees, customs duties, and bribes collected at Vasil'kov all gave merchants great incentive to cross the border elsewhere. In fact, allegations of corruption at Vasil'kov almost cost the doctor his post in 1765–67. Accused of sanctioning bribery, Poletika spent more than a year in St. Petersburg arguing his innocence, until the Empress personally reinstated him over the objections of the head of the medical administration.[121] This imbroglio further postponed any reform of the Vasil'kov quarantine, the defects of which became manifest when the plague arrived in 1770.

The imperial authorities soon discovered how ineffective their antiplague defenses were. In any event, neither cordons nor quarantines could repulse the unseen invader. Both proved to be unenforceable in practice, and well-intentioned attempts to impose them could actually unleash social dislocation. During the decades before 1770, the imperial government formulated antiplague policies based upon Russian tradition and European norms. These policies presupposed intervention by the newly consolidated medical profession. By 1770, both the government and the practitioners were more willing than ever to respond vigorously to the threat of plague. Yet a more activist antiplague policy endangered the lives of practitioners and risked provoking even more violent social reactions if it failed. Ignorance of the disease virtually guaranteed failure.

CHAPTER TWO

Medical Professionals and Public Health in Russia to 1770

The Russian medical profession in 1770 was only half-prepared to cope with any public health emergency. Nevertheless, in fighting the plague of 1770-72 professional medical practitioners were more numerous, more active, and more influential than they had ever been in Russia. Their vigorous antiplague efforts exemplified the comparatively recent, rapid introduction to Russia of European standards of public health and professional medical care. Beginning in the seventeenth century, two powerful stimuli, incessant warfare and recurrent epidemics, expedited the formation of public health institutions in Muscovy and its Europeanized successor, the Russian Empire. War and disease often interacted to cause widespread crises. By threatening the armed forces in particular, epidemics imperiled Russia's foreign and domestic policies in general, as seen in the coincidence of plague, warfare, and internal disarray in 1654-56, 1709-12, 1727-28, and 1738-39. Military needs and military personnel therefore dominated Russia's new medical institutions. In the eighteenth century, the bureaucratized medical administration and profession devoted even greater attention to communicable disease as it affected the reorganized, standing army, the newly created navy, and the population at large. All these institutional developments enabled medical professionals to assume prominent roles in the Russo-Turkish War of 1768-74 and the plague that it provoked. Together, the plague and the war assaulted the empire's emergent public health institutions, disclosing weaknesses that temporarily overshadowed the many medical developments since 1700.

Peter I personally initiated enlarged state commitments to public health that his successors, Catherine II, above all, steadily elaborated for the whole empire. This involvement in public health reforms prior to 1770 predisposed Catherine to take an unusually active part against the plague. In sum, the intervention of medical practitioners in the plague of 1770-72 resulted from the consolidation of a distinctive medical profession in Russia, as manifested in the rapid increase of practitioners who trained and worked under a centralized state medical administration, and whose professional roles were expanding through recent health reforms and experience in the Russo-Turkish War.

Doctors, Surgeons, and Apothecaries

Before the reign of Peter the Great (1689–1725), the Muscovite government rarely sent medical professionals to fight epidemics. This passive policy derived from two considerations: medical professionals were few, and most were either prominent foreign physicians hired to attend the court or surgeons attached to the army. The authorities hesitated to squander scarce and expensive medical talent on dangerous diseases for which there were no known remedies. From this perspective, Peter's deployment of medical professionals against pestilence signified a remarkable departure from tradition. Twin developments permitted the innovation: heightened state concern for public health, and recruitment of much larger cadres of practitioners, both foreigners and Russian subjects. Throughout the eighteenth century, the number of medical professionals in Russia continuously increased. By 1803, they totaled at least 2,053 persons, excluding apothecaries, midwives, and paramedics, as compared to less than 200 in 1700.[1] Although the rate of growth varied over time for the different ranks, and although the territorial distribution of medical professionals remained extremely irregular, the enormous increase in numbers of practitioners sharply distinguished imperial Russia from Muscovy.

Atop the medical profession in Russia stood the *doktor,* whose title required the M.D. degree and therefore necessitated study at a foreign university. Doctors enjoyed considerable social status. The Table of Ranks instituted in 1722 placed doctors in the ninth class, which conferred nonhereditary noble status, and in 1762 they rose to the eighth class, which entailed hereditary nobility. Without an M.D., the rank of staff-surgeon (*shtab-lekar'*) was the highest that a practitioner could attain. In the regular army, staff-surgeons belonged to the tenth class of the Table of Ranks and, in the Guards regiments, to the ninth class. Extremely few practitioners, mostly men of foreign background, reached this rank until late in the century. Indeed, most medical professionals remained outside or at the bottom of the Table of Ranks until 1762, when the positions of apothecary (*aptekar'*), surgeon (*lekar'*), and surgeon's mate (*podlekar'*) were incorporated into the bottom rungs of the service hierarchy. The humble posts of surgical apprentice (*uchenik*) and barber (*tsyriul'nik*) continued to be unranked.[2]

The different medical ranks varied greatly in numbers, service status, salaries, nationality, and social origins. Surgeons and surgeon's mates outnumbered doctors, staff-surgeons, and apothecaries many times over. As in western Europe, surgical practitioners were equated to more or less skilled craftsmen, depending upon their experience, whereas doctors were presumed to have theoretical as well as practical knowledge. Unlike British practice, however, apothecaries in Russia were forbidden to treat patients or to prescribe medicine independently.[3] Because of the scarcity and high social standing of doctors in eighteenth-century Russia, their numbers can be determined rather precisely. By contrast, fragmentary statistics yield only rough estimates of the numbers of surgical personnel. Yet statistical deficiencies should not preclude a tentative, quantitative reconstruction of the formation of the medical profession in early modern Russia.

Tabulating biographical information compiled by Wilhelm Richter and Iakov Chistovich, Alexander Brückner prepared an index of M.D.'s in Russia from 1600 to 1800. For the period to 1730, the index registers the term of service by counting each decade of a doctor's activity. Though based on admittedly incomplete data, Brückner's index sketches some dynamics of the growth in Russia of a medical elite (table 1). This elite emerged in three discrete periods. The first phase, 1600–90, recorded a mere handful of M.D.'s as European-style academic medicine gained entry to the court of Muscovy. Roughly coterminous with the Petrine era, the second phase (1690–1730) reflected an influx of foreign-trained doctors and their employment in the armed forces, hospitals, surgical schools, and the Academy of Sciences. The post-Petrine decades constituted a third phase of steadily accelerating growth that, after 1760, also eroded the monopoly of foreign physicians. Under Catherine II (1762–96) and Paul I (1796–1801) the top medical ranks proliferated with increases in the size of the armed forces, the growth of civilian medical institutions, and the extension of medical services to regional administrative units.

Most doctors in Russia before 1800 were foreigners or russified foreigners. Of the few Slavic physicians, about 70 percent were Ukrainians educated abroad. Although the central medical administration received authority in 1764 to grant the M.D. degree, it seldom did so. The empire's single university medical faculty, organized at Moscow University in 1764, awarded its first M.D. only in 1794.[4] Among the foreign physicians who made their careers in Russia, primacy belonged to Germans, who can be grouped into 4 types: natives of Germany, Baltic Germans, russified Germans, and persons with German names but of undetermined national origin. Of the approximately 500 M.D.'s in Russia to 1800, Brückner estimated that at least 175 (40 percent) were Germans from Germany, the other 3 Germanic subgroups together constituting another 20 percent. Thus some 60 percent of all M.D.'s in early modern Russia were of German origin. Other foreign physicians arrived from Britain and the Netherlands, Italy and Greece, France and Poland, and at least one—the well-known Antonio Ribeiro Sanchez—from Portugal via the Netherlands. Since the social origins of these foreign physicians have not been studied, one must hazard the guess that they came largely from middle-class, especially ecclesiastical and professional, backgrounds.[5] Approximately half of the doctors in Russia before 1770 held their

Table 1 Growth of M.D.'s in Early Modern Russia

Period	Total number of physicians	Russians and Ukrainians
To 1600	12	
1600–50	22	
1650–90	28	
1690–1730	125	
1730–40	46	
1740–50	58	
1750–60	76	
1760–70	94	21
1770–80	124	25
1780–90	229	34
1790–1800	236	38

Note: The figures to 1730 represent doctor-decades, index numbers that count both the number of individuals and each decade of their activity in Russia; the number of physicians did not suddenly decline after 1730.
Source: Brückner, *Die Aerzte in Russland*, pp. 13, 68.

degrees from Leyden University. The others mainly trained at German universities, especially Halle and Göttingen.[6]

Only a few dozen men of Slavic nationality and Russian citizenship earned M.D. degrees before 1800. Because knowledge of Latin was required for formal medical study, Ukrainians enjoyed a considerable advantage over Great Russians, owing to the Ukraine's longer tradition of classical learning. Furthermore, the Ukraine's fluid social structure facilitated educational expansion of a kind not possible in the agrarian, serfdom-dominated Russian core of the empire. The Ukrainian clergy conspicuously surpassed their Great Russian counterparts in education and relative social status, dominating the hierarchy of the Russian Orthodox Church and furnishing numerous recruits to the new medical profession.[7]

The 94 M.D.'s in Russia in the 1760s greatly outnumbered their predecessors of the seventeenth century and, since the 1730s, their ranks had doubled (table 1). In the same period, surgical cadres expanded at a similar, if not faster pace, although nobody has detailed the process. Richter counted 300 surgeons and apothecaries in Russia between 1689 and 1761, but recent research indicates much higher totals: about 400 practitioners by 1725 and perhaps as many as 800 by the 1760s.[8] Slavs and russified foreigners comprised a steadily rising proportion of these surgical cadres. Nevertheless, foreign names still predominated among the Moscow medical community at the time of the plague (appendix 1), an indication of the profession's cosmopolitan composition and of the greater professional opportunities available in the metropolis. By 1800, however, the surgical schools begun in Petrine times trained about 2,000 surgical personnel, the great majority of whom were Slavs or thoroughly russified, as shown by the names of the surgical students in Moscow in 1771 (appendix 2).[9] Natives virtually monopolized the lowest level of medical practice as barbers, bonesetters, and folk healers, but their numbers remain problematical.

An exact count of all medical personnel in Russia on the eve of the plague is not available, but their numbers probably did not exceed 1,000, for the medical administration in 1780 reported a total of 1,038.[10] Whatever their numbers before 1770, Russia's medical professionals could not satisfy the growing state and private demand for their services. In wartime, the demand soared. For example, during the Seven Years' War (1756–63) the main Russian army fighting in Prussia in 1760 deployed 53 surgeons, 89 surgeon's mates, and 526 barbers to serve some 40,000 men. Additional surgeons were hired in East Prussia and Livland.[11] A much wider gap separated medical professionals from the civilian population. With a population of about 26 million in 1782 (excluding the Baltic Provinces and the territory gained from the First Partition of Poland), the Russian Empire had a ratio of practitioners per capita of roughly 1:26,000—far less than the professional medical care available in northwest France at the time, or in northern Italy and other advanced regions of western Europe in the seventeenth century.[12] But the actual availability of professional medical care to the rural population was even less. Most practitioners served the armed forces or worked in St. Petersburg and Moscow. In the Baltic Provinces, moreover, European cultural and educational traditions supported higher ratios of practitioners per capita. At least 244 medical men practiced in Estland in the eighteenth century, 177 in Livland, and 438 in Kurland.[13] By comparison, thinly populated regions like Siberia and around Orenburg received their first practitioners in the 1730s and 1740s, but just a few towns and garrisons maintained any permanent medical facilities.[14]

The State Medical Administration

The tsars of Muscovy sponsored the introduction of European academic medicine as early as the reign of Ivan III (1462–1505). In the absence of an independent church and higher educational institutions, the close association of medicine with the tsarist court facilitated the early development of a highly centralized state medical administration. The sovereigns' patronage lent social respectability to the emergent medical profession, while molding it to suit state purposes. Until the late eighteenth century, in consequence, most medical professionals in Russia worked primarily for the state, which reserved the right to mobilize even private practitioners in case of need.

State supervision of medical affairs became institutionalized around 1620, in the Apothecary Bureau, an outgrowth of the office of the tsar's apothecary. This office rapidly evolved into the central administration of medical affairs, gaining jurisdiction over all medical personnel, military and civilian, foreign and native alike. By 1692, 39 medical professionals of all types were serving under its auspices.[15] Nominally headed by a nonprofessional administrator, the Apothecary Bureau operated under the sovereign's chief physician, invariably a foreign M.D. The various Petrine administrative reshuffles formally recognized the higher stature of medical professionals and their broader functions by placing the chief physician, now styled archiater, at the head of the Apothecary Chancery in St. Petersburg in 1718 (renamed the Medical Chancery in 1721). The facilities of the former Apothecary Bureau in Moscow retained prominence as the single regional branch of the Medical Chancery, which usually accompanied the court on its visits to Moscow. The Moscow Office, as it was called, was subordinated to the Moscow *shtat-fizik* or city-physician in 1763.[16]

Understaffed and underfinanced, the Medical Chancery employed only fourteen officials in 1755, lacked bureaucratic status, suffered from favoritism and discontinuous leadership, and struggled to coordinate the growth of the medical profession and the expansion of public health facilities. The archiater's dual responsibilities as director of the Medical Chancery and chief body-physician to the sovereign overburdened the foreign medical professionals named to the post, resulting in administrative confusion and neglect. Highly paid, the archiater might become highly influential in court politics, but he faced commensurate risks. Several fell from political intrigues and palace revolutions. Thus, surgeon Count Hermann Lestock (1692–1767), though he lacked a degree, displaced Archiater Johann Fischer in 1742 after engineering Elizabeth's coup d'état, but accusations of treason and of intent to poison the Empress brought about his disgrace, imprisonment, torture, and exile in 1748.[17]

Several archiaters proved to be quite capable. Johann Blumentrost (M.D., Halle, 1702) consolidated the Medical Chancery between 1718 and 1730. As archiater from 1735 to 1742, Johann Fischer (M.D., Leyden, 1705) organized the system of military hospitals and surgical schools. Pavel Kondoidi (M.D., Leyden, 1733), a russified Greek, managed the Medical Chancery under Lestock until 1747 and later became archiater himself from 1754 to 1760. He established libraries at the surgical schools, redefined their program of study, and bolstered their faculties with new personnel and specialties. Like Fischer, whose abortive project to send six Russians abroad for advanced training aimed at the promotion of native medical instruction, Kondoidi planned to train native professors of medicine by the same means. This plan was finally implemented in 1761, after Kondoidi's death. Although James Mounsey, a Scottish army doctor, served just six months as Peter III's archiater, from January to July 1762, he sponsored important legislation providing higher ranks, pensions, and definite duties for medical professionals in state service. Relieved of his post "for weak health" at the start of Catherine II's reign, Mounsey proved to be Russia's last archiater.[18]

The new German-born Empress, who seized the throne in June 1762 by a coup d'état tinged with antiforeign and antiwar overtones, left the post of archiater vacant, perhaps to avoid appointing another foreigner (she vividly remembered Lestock's fall).[19] Because Russia's recently concluded participation in the Seven Years' War had strained all branches of administration, the Medical Chancery included, Catherine courted popularity through civilian-oriented, patronage-dispensing bureaucratic reforms. Interested in public health from reading cameralist and physiocratic works, the Empress investigated medical reform in the early months of her reign. Dr. Johann Lerche, acting head of the Medical Chancery, reported the current status of the medical profession and suggested means to multiply the medical cadres in state service. He proposed to increase the number of students at the surgical schools and at the military hospitals, recruiting aspirants from seminaries and universities; he recommended sending up to 6 students abroad for training as operators and prosectors, i.e., surgical and anatomical instructors. He noted the need for better quarters for the teaching staffs of the surgical schools. To boost morale among state medical servitors, Lerche advised reconfirmation of the ranks, salaries, and pensions proposed by Mounsey.[20]

Among the other advice Catherine received, an unidentified commentator criticized the Medical Chancery's cramped quarters and deplored its lack of a library and archive. He wanted it moved to a special building and made independent, reporting directly to the senate. Like Dr. Lerche, this critic favored greater financial support for the surgical schools, estimating their current enrollment at 200 students and recommending that all students and teachers receive salaries through the Medical Chancery. Hospitals should be reimbursed for medicaments sent to the army, and the civilian population of Petersburg should have health facilities—a public hospital or lazaret and an insane asylum. "If there would be such institutions in Moscow, too, at which there would also be established surgical schools with professors of surgery, apothecaries, and other instructors with the requisite number of students, then in time there would no longer be a deficit of capable surgeons in the state." Finally, this adviser suggested that the Medical Chancery should operate a press to publish useful medical works and should establish a facility in Voronezh guberniia to prepare medicinal plants.[21]

Catherine delegated two officials familiar with medical affairs, Baron Alexander Cherkassov and State Secretary Grigorii Teplov, to fashion these proposals into a new medical administration. By 18 October 1763, Cherkassov and Teplov had drafted guidelines that a panel of eight high-ranking practitioners unanimously approved. The draft proposals urged the separation of routine administration and financial accounting from professional medical concerns, a reform that would abolish the office of archiater. Because foreign physicians were neither trained for administration nor understood the Russian language and laws, they could not "be master either of regulations or of great state expenditures." The new administration should therefore have a collegial structure, with separate medical-scientific and administrative-accounting departments, the whole to be presided over by a

Russian layman conversant with the natural sciences. Other draft proposals advocated increasing the number of native medical professionals and bringing them into closer contact with the medical administration. Doctors and surgeons should periodically submit journals of their practice, enabling the administration to evaluate each practitioner and to assign them on the basis of merit instead of chance recommendations, self-seeking, "and sometimes (as reported) for bribes, with the bad ones taking precedence over the good." To encourage research and initiative, the medical administration should publish original medical treatises in Latin, the international language of the medical profession.[22]

Catherine's decree establishing the Medical Collegium, on 12 November 1763, incorporated most of the draft proposals, but significantly recast a few. The bifurcated collegial structure was adopted, for example, but the requirement that the president be a Russian was dropped, presumably to conciliate the high-ranking foreign practitioners; nevertheless, Catherine appointed her friend Cherkassov to the office that same day. Having abolished the position of archiater, she excluded all court practitioners from the collegium's purview and placed them under her personal jurisdiction. An expanded preface also justified the new institution as a restoration of Petrine administrative principles. Noting that, despite 60 years of medical development, the empire still possessed "an extremely small number of doctors and surgeons who are Russians," the decree censured the hiring of expensive foreign-trained practitioners of questionable competence. In cooperation with Moscow University, the Medical Collegium was to devise means for the training of Russian doctors. Six months later Catherine empowered the Medical Collegium itself to grant the M.D. degree to worthy candidates after examination, whether or not they had studied at foreign universities.

Precautions against plague also figured in the duties of the Medical Collegium. "As soon as the collegium receives a report from anywhere about an outbreak of pestilence, it should immediately employ those methods already prescribed by decrees or devise new ones according to the circumstances and thereby prevent and avert its spread." The president should know, furthermore, "what decrees there are or can be concerning cases of the pestilential contagion, horse and cattle plague, or infectious diseases."[23]

The reformed medical administration consisted of 2 departments: a business office and the Collegium of Physical and Surgical Art, which supervised professional matters and set general policy. In addition to the president, 7 voting members comprised the medical department: 3 doctors, one staff-surgeon, one surgeon, one operator, and one apothecary. They were assisted by 2 secretaries and a translator, none of whom had votes. The president directed the business office with the help of 2 secretaries and one Russian assistant. The budget approved in January 1764 listed a staff of 92 persons, including 28 in the Moscow Office, with total salaries of 13,655 rubles.

Baron Cherkassov, president of the Medical Collegium until 1775, had received a broad education, including study at Oxford, and Catherine authorized him to select the first members of the Medical Collegium. He chose General-Staff Dr. Georg von Asch (M.D., Göttingen, 1750), Dr. Christian Pecken (M.D., Wittenberg, 1751), Dr. Andreas Lindemann (M.D., Göttingen, 1755), staff-surgeon Johann Wolf, surgeon Johann Bloch (who died in 1766 and was succeeded by Friedrich Garloff), and apothecary Johann Modell (no operator seems to have been nominated). From 1764, Dr. Pecken also served as the collegium's scholarly secretary. All the professional members of the collegium had been educated abroad. Native members only entered in the last decades of the century.[24]

The Medical Collegium had three main duties: to promote professional medical care of the population at large, to train more native practitioners, and to oversee apothecary shops. In the early years of his presidency, Baron Cherkassov supplied Catherine with monthly reports of the collegium's efforts to expand public health facilities and to increase native medical cadres.[25] He assisted with projects to upgrade the system of border quarantines and to regularize the army medical service.

Catherine often consulted Cherkassov directly, sometimes bypassing the other members of the collegium. One such instance occurred in 1766 and reveals her candid thoughts about medical training and practice. In March 1766, a Hungarian, Franciscus Jaellatchitsch—Elachich in Russian—applied for permission to practice obstetrics in Moscow, but a board of examiners found him totally unqualified. Since the seventeenth century, the Russian medical administration had exercised licensing authority and certified all medical personnel before they could legally practice. This procedure was intended to guard against charlatans and incompetents. It was discovered that Elachich had been practicing since 1742 and had attained the rank of collegial assessor in 1763, qualifying for hereditary noble status. Though he called himself a surgeon and operator, he had neither medical training nor skill.

Catherine reacted to the imposture by sending Cherkassov a confidential note in which she quoted the famous Boerhaave (1668–1738) upon the disparity between the study and the practice of medicine. Such cases persuaded her "that the doctor's art for the most part depends upon boldness, and that there will be found many such Elachichs, of whom some are already practicing without having studied, while others who have practiced are still studying; and in my opinion both sorts, until they make themselves skillful, will bury many of their mistakes in the ground." The Empress could not condemn the impostor; "only it seems to me that Elachich is not the only one in the world guilty of having undertaken a profession without knowing anything." Having reviewed the case, the Medical Collegium returned it to Catherine, who forwarded it to the senate. Ten years later the senate finally exonerated Elachich and awarded him back pay.[26] Insignificant in itself, this incident demonstrates Catherine's pragmatic approach to medical affairs, her concern with results rather than professional qualifications, and her private reservations about the efficacy of academic medicine.

Despite Catherine's hopes for the Medical Collegium, it produced neither consistent policies nor efficient administration. Sometimes the professional members clashed with Cherkassov. When the president tried to dismiss Dr. Poletika on charges of bribe-taking, for instance, the other members blocked summary dismissal, appealed to Catherine, and saved the doctor. By contrast, when surgeon Gustav Orraeus sought an M.D. degree from the Medical Collegium in 1765, Cherkassov and Catherine had to override the stubborn resistance of the professional members before the collegium granted its first degree, in 1768.[27] Starved for funding, the Medical Collegium lacked the resources and bureaucratic muscle needed for the rapid implementation of Catherine's ambitious schemes for public health reform. By 1768, its finances became so tangled that the Empress appointed a 3-man commission to investigate, but no improvement resulted.[28] The empire's massive medical deficiencies could not be solved by administrative reforms alone.

Medical Education and Hospital Service

Training more native practitioners ranked first among the tasks assigned to the Medical Collegium. Sovereigns, officials, and practitioners all recognized the need. Recruitment of medical personnel abroad, albeit essential for the introduction of modern academic medicine to Russia, could not sustain a permanent, comprehensive empire-wide program of medical care. Foreign practitioners were too unreliable, often departing when their contracts expired, and too expensive—double or triple the cost of training medical cadres in Russia, according to Catherine's advisers.[29] Unless foreign medical professionals learned Russian they could not possibly treat large numbers of patients or hope to inspire confidence in the general population. European-style medicine would remain a luxury confined to the social elite, but suspect in the eyes of most Russians. Besides, no matter how many foreigners were hired, their effective employment demanded auxiliary personnel and services, hospitals in particular.

Peter I's accelerated conversion of the armed forces from a conglomeration of noble militia and their retainers into a standing army and a new navy, both recruited by centrally controlled conscription, necessitated the provision of regular medical services on a greatly expanded scale. At first, the Tsar recruited additional foreigners, but this expedient could not meet the extraordinary demand arising from the Great Northern War (1700-21). Moreover, it offended national pride. The alternative was to establish native institutions for medical instruction: no mean task in a country that lacked a tradition of scientific inquiry, that had few educational facilities of any kind and not a single permanent secular hospital, where the literacy rate was minuscule, printing presses were few, and the language was ill-adapted to the study of science. In sum, it is amazing that the dual-purpose institution founded in Moscow in 1706 ever amounted to anything. Yet the Moscow *Gofshpital'* and surgical school became Russia's first permanent, secular medical treatment and training facility. Rebuilt and expanded many times, it still occupies the same site on the bank of the Yauza River in northeastern Moscow.[30]

This institution owed its existence to the determination of the Tsar and his personal physician, Dr. Nicolaas Bidloo (1674–1735). A native of Amsterdam and medical graduate of Leyden University who came to Russia in 1702, Bidloo soon tired of Peter's constant travels to the front, but when he asked to go home the Tsar persuaded him to found a hospital and surgical school in Moscow.[31] The Dutchman planned, built, and directed both institutions from their opening in 1707 until his death. His institutions survived many trials; the main building burned down in 1721 and again in 1737. As welfare and educational facilities the hospital and surgical school operated under the Monastery Bureau (later the Collegium of Economy) of the Holy Synod until 1754, when military and financial exigencies converted them to exclusively army institutions under the War Collegium. In practice, the military and the medical authorities constantly wrangled about their respective shares of administrative and financial responsibility. Military imperatives often conflicted with the hospital's therapeutic and educational missions. Besides, the assignment of a permanent military inspector in 1754 muddled an already confused situation, resulting in frequent disputes between the military authorities and the medical professionals who administered the hospital and the surgical school.[32] Bidloo and his successors labored to find staff, supplies, and the scarcest resource of all—qualified students. The surgical school was supposed to enroll fifty students, but Bidloo could never assemble that many at once. Still, the first contingent graduated in 1712–13, 10 men in all. By 1730, at least 65 others joined the military medical service.[33]

Most surgical students came from undistinguished backgrounds. Since Latin was the main language of instruction, many students were from the Ukraine and western Russia. The Slavo-Greco-Latin Academy in Moscow furnished some students, and its provincial counterparts, the seminary schools, also sent contingents of aspirants, mainly the offspring of churchmen. The clergy's higher literacy rate, traditional service ethic, and semicorporate social organization all made it a likely source of budding medical practitioners. Some low-ranking medical professionals also sent their sons. In 1758, the senate even decreed that the male progeny of surgical personnel who died in service should remain under the Medical Chancery, to be prepared for surgical and apothecary careers. Threatened with forfeiture of pension rights, widows of surgeons were also charged to train their sons for medical service. In consequence, a relatively closed social stratum of surgical personnel evolved in eighteenth-century Russia. Only a minute fraction became doctors or staff-surgeons.[34]

Until mid-century, the term of instruction at the Moscow surgical school varied from 5 to 10 years, summers included. Archiater Kondoidi shortened the program in 1754 to 7 years, which in practice usually meant 4 to 5 years: 2 or 3 to become a surgeon's mate, and one or 2 more to become a surgeon. Both surgery and internal medicine were taught, with the emphasis on practical application. The Dutch manner of bedside instruction, made popular by Boerhaave at Leyden, was widely employed and partly compensated for the dearth of written instructional materials. Cadavers were often used for demonstration purposes. Predictably, the school's early graduates were of mixed quality. Bidloo praised his best pupils as the equals of surgeons anywhere, yet admitted that many could serve only as surgeon's mates and apprentices because of their meager knowledge.[35]

The success of the Moscow school inspired the creation of others. During Peter's reign, at least 7 more hospitals were built, 3 of which, the twin Petersburg Admiralty and Infantry hospitals and the Kronstadt Naval Hospital, employed surgical apprentices and formally added schools in 1733. Though expanded in the 1750s, all 3 remained smaller and produced fewer practitioners than the Moscow school. By 1800, the Moscow facility trained about 800 surgical personnel; the 2 Petersburg schools, which amalgamated in 1786, together prepared another 800; while the Kronstadt school graduated only about 200. Unlike the Moscow school, where the student body comprised mostly Slavs, the Petersburg and Kronstadt surgical schools enrolled many foreigners, a natural result of Petersburg's cosmopolitan population and westward orientation. Additional surgical cadres received training through apprenticeship in the military hospitals.[36]

Russia's surgical schools concentrated upon the transmission of rudimentary medical and surgical knowledge. They sponsored no research, and their instructional program suffered at times, though it also benefited, from the involvement of the teaching staff in the hospitals' therapeutic functions. Stingily financed, the schools experienced chronic shortages of staff and equipment, students and books. Living conditions at the hospitals were harsh, salaries and stipends were low, the students were subject to corporal punishment, and many were dismissed or dropped out. Surgical careers attracted few students from the higher social strata. Programs and instructors changed frequently and, since the schools were subordinate to both the military and the medical administrations, teachers and students were often assigned to other duties at a moment's notice, particularly in time of war and epidemics.[37]

Language problems also impeded instruction. By the 1760s, when the first native instructors began teaching at the Moscow school, they encountered the same difficulties at their foreign predecessors. Thus, Dr. Konstantin Shchepin (M.D., Leyden, 1758), who taught there from 1762 to 1764, complained that he could more easily read ten lectures in Latin than one in Russian. Perhaps this dilemma aggravated the heavy drinking that brought about his dismissal.[38] Shchepin's successor, Peter Pogoretskii (1740–80), a headstrong young Ukrainian graduate of the Petersburg Admiralty school with an M.D. from Leyden in 1765, found the Moscow school in dreadful condition. In December 1765, he informed the Medical Collegium that the school had numerous vacancies, proposed to fill them with Russians who knew Latin, and lamented the shortage of books. Receiving no response, Pogoretskii, in August 1766, complained anew and criticized the students' copybooks for transmitting errors. He wished to publish the Latin edition of the late Dr. Schreiber's medical textbook. But when he asked for a raise and a new position as well, the Medical Collegium summoned him to Petersburg for an explanation and rejected both requests. Exasperated, Pogoretskii returned to Moscow grumbling about his low salary and the lack of assistance. In 1768, he published Schreiber's textbook in Latin with a preface berating the Medical Collegium, which then assigned him to Siberia. Pogoretskii declined the transfer and the collegium sought to send him under arrest, but Catherine intervened and allowed his retirement from state service in 1769. He entered private practice in Moscow, where he soon faced the plague. Another Ukrainian graduate of the Petersburg Admiralty school, Kas'ian Yagel'skii (M.D., Leyden, 1765), succeeded Pogoretskii at the Moscow school in 1768. Yagel'skii avoided Pogoretskii's troubles, however, and also participated in the antiplague efforts.[39]

Russian commentators frequently blame the deficiencies of the surgical schools on the empire's foreign medical establishment. Viewed from this perspective, Dr. Pogoretskii's travails at the Moscow surgical school assume the proportions of a nationalistic struggle pitting an heroic, progressive, democratic, and patriotic Russian (Ukrainian) physician against a malevolent, reactionary, aristocratic, and alien medical bureaucracy. One need not ignore antagonism between Russian and foreign medical professionals in the eighteenth century, but such clashes should be seen in a wider context, considering personal and institutional factors as well as the dynamics of Russia's emergent medical profession. From this point of view, Pogoretskii's experience seems rather ordinary—the common plight of a young, self-confident, newly trained scientific professional who, upon returning home from advanced study abroad, encounters immense difficulty in applying his new skills to a traditional environment. His complaints, his attempts to remedy the situation overnight naturally provoked animosity from colleagues and superiors alike. Frustrated, he incited further hostility by seeking a higher salary and another position. The medical bureaucracy, beset by myriad problems of its own, decided to transfer an apparent troublemaker. This is not to argue that all Pogoretskii's actions were short-sighted. The Medical Collegium obviously treated him shabbily, but then both foreign and Russian medical professionals often criticized the negligence of the medical administration. None of the problems Pogoretskii confronted was new; the surgical schools perpetually lacked students, books, and equipment. In short, conditions not personalities underlay many of Pogoretskii's difficulties, while his own combative character inflamed the imbroglio.

One should not exaggerate the general quality of surgical training in Russia. Some Russian commentators have lauded these schools as the most progressive of the era, their graduates exemplifying the preventive, humanist orientation that allegedly characterizes the Russian medical tradition. Their graduates supposedly enjoyed medical instruction superior to, because more "practical" than, the "scholastic" medicine of western and central Europe.[40] Such claims seem overblown. For one thing, the picture of medical education outside Russia is as crudely oversimplified as the portrayal of the Russian surgical schools is blatantly idealized. For another, such contentions disregard contemporary Russian criticism of the surgical schools and forget that alternative modes of medical instruction, such as apprenticeship and study abroad, persisted despite the existence of such allegedly superior medical training. Charges of prejudice against the surgical schools on the part of the foreign physicians who dominated the medical profession in collusion with their aristocratic Russian patrons, simply avoid the issue and smack of chauvinism as well. In fact, the gradual russification of the instructional staffs at the schools did little to solve the deep and manifold problems inhibiting faster growth.[41]

The Academy of Sciences and Moscow University might have compensated for some of the surgical schools' deficiencies. Founded in 1725 with chairs in anatomy and physiology, the academy sponsored research in both fields. Yet a recent appraisal opines that the academy "never really played the role of a Faculty of Medicine."[42] The Moscow University charter of 1755 provided for a medical faculty, and Professor Johann Kerstens (M.D., Halle, 1749) began lecturing on physics, chemistry, materia medica, and hygiene in 1758. Kerstens alone taught a mere handful of students until 1764, when the medical faculty opened with the appointment of Professor Johann Erasmus (M.D., Jena, 1747) to teach anatomy, surgery, and obstetrics. The anatomical theater that Erasmus established employed a Hungarian prosector who had graduated from the Moscow surgical school, Ferenz Keresturi (1735-1801). Two young Slavic doctors joined the faculty in 1765, Semen Zybelin (1735-1802) and Peter Veniaminov (1733-75), both recent graduates of Leyden. Zybelin lectured on theoretical and practical medicine, physiology and pathology, anatomy, surgery, and pharmacy. In 1768, he gave the faculty's first lecture in Russian. Veniaminov taught botany, materia medica, chemistry, and medical practice.[43]

In theory, creation of the new medical faculty promised to train larger numbers of native medical professionals. Despite an impressive faculty, however, Moscow University attracted few medical students. Only 16 enrolled for medical lectures in 1765-66; 2 years later just one remained.[44] In any event, the new medical faculty only gained the right to award the M.D. in 1791, and it trained few if any surgeons. Professors Erasmus and Kerstens ceased teaching there in 1769, evidently for lack of students. Since the university had neither laboratory nor clinical facilities, its instructors provided "too theoretical and bookish training."[45] Still, its professors achieved some influence through their research, other state duties, private practice, and popularization of medical controversies. Although Kerstens left Russia in 1770, Erasmus, Zybelin, Veniaminov, and Keresturi all actively fought the plague in Moscow.

Beyond the opportunities for formal medical study and training through apprenticeship at home, some Russian subjects acquired such knowledge abroad. As early as 1692, the government dispatched a Russian youth, Peter Posnikov, to the University of Padua, where he earned an M.D. in 1694. Yet linguistic, educational, and financial barriers combined to limit such training mainly to the sons of foreigners or officials, at least 25 of whom studied medicine at Leyden by 1760.[46] In the same period, Russian medical students matriculated at other European universities, especially Halle and Strasbourg. The senate in 1723 proposed regularly sponsoring 4 surgical students for study abroad, and Archiater Fischer in 1738 planned to improve instruction at the surgical schools by sending 6 students to Paris for advanced training; but war and lack of funds put an end to both projects. Finally, in 1761 the Medical Chancery financed study at Leyden for 10 Slavic graduates of the surgical schools. Attending Leyden at the same time were Semen Zybelin and Peter Veniaminov, the future professors at Moscow University, and Afanasii Shafonskii, subsequently a graduate of Strasbourg in 1763, who headed the Moscow hospital and surgical school throughout the plague of 1771.[47] All these men earned their degrees, and upon returning to Russia they constituted an important Slavic segment of the medical elite. Many of them battled the plague in 1770–72. Peter Pogoretskii and Kas'ian Yagel'skii served in Moscow; Sila Mitrofanov survived the epidemic in Kiev, but later perished in Moldavia, as did Matvei Kruten in 1771; and Koz'ma Rozhalin countered it in the Ukraine. Another Leyden graduate, Konstantin Shchepin, the first Russian instructor at the Moscow surgical school, died of plague in the Ukraine in 1770. For Russia's first generation of native M.D.'s the Turkish war and the plague provided a searing professional baptism.

Public Health Reforms under Catherine II

In the delivery of professional medical care to early modern Russia, the court and the armed forces held top priority until the mid-eighteenth century. But the very frequency of warfare, focusing state interests as it did, tended to impose military imperatives upon other spheres of policy, sometimes effacing civilian-military distinctions in the process. Military practitioners treated the civilian population during epidemics, for instance, and in their spare time. In peacetime, some medical professionals established private practices; others served in nonmilitary capacities, particularly those who attended the court. Before 1754, the Moscow hospital functioned primarily as a civilian institution. The example of the military medical service highlighted by contrast the need for public health institutions to serve the population as a whole. By reorganizing the medical administration and creating a medical faculty at Moscow University, the government of Catherine II prepared to extend health care to broader segments of the population. The first six, comparatively peaceful, years of Catherine's reign witnessed a reorientation of public health policies that devoted much greater attention to the civilian population.

Catherine's personal interest in medical affairs revived several precedents and activated public discussion of general health policies. The European institution of the city-physician, an office that combined functions of medical police and of a physician for the poor, appeared in Moscow and Petersburg in Petrine times and became permanent in both capitals in 1733. As the empire's largest city in its most populous region, Moscow received two public physicians and one surgeon in 1756, assigned to the guberniia chancery and the municipal administration, respectively. In 1763, the Moscow city-physician assumed control of the Medical Office, which cooperated with the Medical Collegium in the implementation of national health policy and which exercised primary jurisdiction over the central region.[48]

Starting in 1737, the Medical Chancery began to assign retired military practitioners to the main provincial towns. Instead of pensions, these men received free quarters and a salary of 12 rubles per month from the municipal administrations (*magistraty*). By 1756, when the Seven Years' War redirected medical resources to military needs, just 26 of the projected 56 posts had been filled.[49] Following Russia's withdrawal from the war, Archiater Mounsey, in June 1762, reiterated the urgent need for medical personnel in the countryside; he proposed to institute rural practitioners (*landfiziki*) at the guberniia and province levels, a plan that would have assigned about 90 more practitioners to civilian duties. The paucity of local practitioners in relation to the empire's vast expanse and dispersed population, remarked Mounsey, precluded the timely detection of epidemics.[50] His suggestions reappeared a year later in Catherine's provision that the Medical Collegium assign practitioners to guberniias and provinces, where hospitals and pharmacies were to be founded as well. Decrees in 1764 provided for the construction of military hospitals near the main towns and designated funds for their construction and maintenance, but few treatment facilities resulted from this legislation.[51]

Not only medical officials criticized the lack of health services for the bulk of the population. In November 1761, Mikhail Lomonosov privately deplored the high death rate: "a great multitude of people fall into various diseases, for the cure of which there are still few proper institutions, . . . and only for the most part simple, illiterate muzhiks and old women heal by guesswork, often combining natural means, as much as they know, with fortune-telling and mumbo-jumbo." Horse-doctors and bone-setters might occasionally help the sick, Lomonosov admitted, but he advocated the diffusion of professional medical science through adequate numbers of doctors, surgeons, and apothecaries in every town.[52]

Besides the human losses to epidemic and endemic disease, the scarcity of medical services contributed to the scandalously high mortality rate among infants. Lomonosov blamed the death of thousands of infants annually on general ignorance and negligence. "How many are there of such unfortunate parents who have given birth to as many as 10 or 15 children, and yet not a single one remains alive?" He suggested establishing foundling homes and publishing instructions about midwifery and infant diseases, "so that priests and literate persons by reading may themselves know how to treat others by instruction."[53] To train midwives, the Medical Chancery in 1757 recruited two professors of obstetrics, Dr. Andreas Lindemann in Petersburg and Dr. Johann Eramus in Moscow. Neither had many students, however, and both had difficulty lecturing in Russian. When Dr. Erasmus died in 1777 he had trained a total of 36 midwives, mostly women of non-Russian origin. Still, Erasmus in 1762 published in Russian a pamphlet about the proper diet for pregnant women. Two years later his assistant, surgeon Johann Pagenkampf, issued a Russian translation of a Swedish textbook on obstetrics.[54] In 1763, moreover, Catherine approved the project of Ivan Betskoi for the establishment of a foundling home and lying-in hospital in Moscow. Opened in 1764, the Moscow Foundling Home sprouted a branch in Petersburg which began receiving infants in 1770.[55]

Catherine herself publicized these issues in her *Great Instruction* to the Legislative Commission, which opened in Moscow in July 1767. The commission, in turn, offered a public forum for wide-ranging criticism of the empire's health deficiencies. At the Empress's invitation a plethora of governmental agencies, local and regional estate groups, and individual spokesmen discussed medical problems in written instructions (*nakazy*) submitted to the commission and in debates at its plenary sessions. Like Lomonosov, Catherine implicated the deficit of health care in the high death rate, especially among infants.[56] The instruction of the Medical Collegium acknowledged the general neglect of the civilian population and supplied its delegate, Dr. Georg von Asch, with projects for increasing medical professionals at the regional level. Doctors should serve in each guberniia capital; surgeons and barbers should practice in the provincial seats and other populous towns. All these urban centers should have apothecary shops and lazarets, whereas the larger cities should provide facilities for the insane, the destitute, and abandoned infants. Midwives should be appointed in guberniia capitals. If each midwife trained several pupils, then they might soon serve provincial towns as well. Condemning the sale of universal remedies and uncertified drugs, the Medical Collegium reaffirmed its duty to prohibit unlicensed practitioners "as well as all sorts of ignorant persons who practice with impunity in almost all towns and estates, to the utter ruin of human health."[57] Thus, the Medical Collegium's proposals of 1767 attempted to answer criticism like that of Lomonosov and to realize Archiater Mounsey's recommendations of 1762.

Many other instructions censured the absence or inadequacy of medical care in town and country. Even the nakazy from St. Petersburg and Moscow lamented the insufficiency and maldistribution of medical practitioners. According to the Chief Police Administration, St. Petersburg needed at least 3 more doctors and 12 more surgeons, while Moscow should have 6 more physicians and 18 more surgeons. The police nakaz urged that every town employ a midwife. St. Petersburg required at least 6; Moscow needed double that number. Nearly all the instructions and the spokesmen at the commission's plenary sessions wished to increase medical personnel and to construct treatment facilities by means of private or public initiative or both combined.[58]

Outside of the Legislative Commission some individuals advocated more ambitious measures. In an essay submitted in 1768 to the prize competition of the newly established Free Economic Society, Aleksei Polenov, a commoner who had studied at Strasbourg and Göttingen, urged the Medical Collegium to assign surgeons to large villages. In time, doctors should be delegated to oversee designated country districts. "As regards the establishment of skillful and trained midwives, although this would be extremely useful," Polenov confessed, "one ought not think of it, when it's still impossible to find them not only in villages, but even in the towns." He later suggested that wealthy landowners might select promising serf youngsters for medical training. At the Legislative Commission others recommended basic medical instruction for the parish clergy.[59]

Several nakazy cited the danger of epidemics in advocating medical services for rural localities. Because there were so few practitioners in the countryside "people die without assistance, especially during any kind of infection," explained the senate's instruction; "hence for the assistance of people in such misfortunes, no less than for precaution against infectious diseases, necessity demands that localities be supplied with doctors and surgeons as well as pharmacies and hospitals."[60] More ominously, the nakaz of the Pustorzheva nobility warned that, should pestilence appear, nobody would know what precautions to take. Meanwhile the police nakaz reiterated the duty of all citizens to report every instance of infectious disease or sudden death, so that police surgeons could investigate. In consultation with the Medical Collegium, the police should take the necessary precautions "and leave signs upon [suspect] houses for the information of all inhabitants."[61]

This criticism of public health at the Legislative Commission helped

Catherine push for further reforms. On 10 January 1768, she directed Baron Cherkassov to arrange for more apothecaries and pharmacies in provincial towns because local surgeons lacked medicaments. Each guberniia ought to have a doctor, Catherine reasoned; the Medical Collegium should therefore ascertain whether the provincial nobility would agree to defray the expenses of such physicians, or what other sources of support might be tapped.[62]

Concerned about possible epidemics near Petersburg, the Empress, in September 1769, appointed Dr. Dominicus Crutta, a Greek from Constantinople, to assist the local city-physician. The Medical Collegium gave Dr. Crutta special instructions, "in case of widespread and communicable diseases, and most especially putrid fevers of every sort with and without spots." He was to inform the Medical Collegium immediately of all epidemics and suspicious symptoms, to employ quarantines in doubtful cases, and to prevent contacts between the sick and anybody employed at court. He was also charged to investigate instances of disease outside Petersburg, so that the capital's other doctors need not leave their posts except for an emergency.[63] Issued on 16 November 1769, these instructions reaffirmed the activist policy expected of practitioners who encountered epidemics; they also revealed a rising apprehension of infectious disease in the heart of the empire. Within a year such apprehension proved all too justified.

In the 1760s, Catherine's administration moved to provide treatment for two epidemic diseases—syphilis (i.e., venereal disease in general) and smallpox. In Moscow on 30 December 1762, the senate directed the Medical Chancery to formulate plans for a network of "secret" hospitals, where those suffering from venereal disease might receive professional care for a fixed payment without questions. Within a month the medical authorities planned such facilities for Petersburg, Novgorod, and Moscow guberniias. The Medical Chancery recommended, moreover, that the poor and the infirm be treated free of charge. Before organizing these centers the Medical Chancery ordered all surgeons in provincial towns to report how many were suffering from contagious diseases. Whatever the response to this inquiry, the project was not fully implemented. Syphilitic homes sponsored by the police appeared in Moscow and St. Petersburg by 1765, but little is known about either. Both were impromptu institutions, housed in secluded quarters on the outskirts of the capitals and served by medical personnel from the military hospitals. In 1767–68, surgeon Danilo Samoilovich, a recent graduate of the Admiralty surgical school, oversaw the Petersburg syphilitic facility; he subsequently won prominence during the plague in Moscow.[64]

No network of syphilitic homes emerged outside the capitals, nor did the disease abate noticeably. In 1766, Dr. Lerche and staff-surgeon Johann Chemnitser visited Finland to assist surgeon Johann Wilckens in the treatment of 96 persons suffering from venereal disease.[65] The next year Catherine's *Great Instruction* indicted syphilis as a prime cause of the high mortality rate.[66] But her advice availed nothing, and venereal disease persistently impaired public health, particularly among the armed forces. Of 417 patients at the Moscow General Infantry Hospital in September 1769, for instance, 45 were suffering from syphilis, and the 1,070 sick at the Kronstadt Naval Hospital included 49 syphilitics.[67] Judging from the subsequent publication of several medical tracts about venereal disease and the remarks in Alexander Radishchev's *A Journey from St. Petersburg to Moscow* (1790), the last decades of the eighteenth century witnessed no reduction in the incidence of such maladies.[68]

Better publicized and, possibly, more effective was Catherine's sponsorship of inoculation against smallpox. The fading of plague from eighteenth-century Europe made smallpox the most dreaded affliction of the era. Indeed, smallpox seemed more threatening than plague in certain respects. It exhibited less tendency to follow social class and occupational lines, striking high and low alike, and often disfigured those who survived. Thus, the male branch of the Romanov dynasty became extinct when Emperor Peter II succumbed to smallpox in 1730. Empress Elizabeth repeatedly ordered that anybody exposed to that disease, or exhibiting exanthemata, must not attend court for a stipulated period.[69] During Catherine's 16 years as grand duchess under Elizabeth, she experienced numerous ailments—pleurisy or pneumonia, measles, various fevers—but never smallpox, for which she possessed a vivid horror. Catherine's apprehension extended as well to her son and sole heir, Grand Duke Paul, a sickly child from birth. For greater safety in the summer of 1768, when smallpox raged in Petersburg, the Empress accompanied Paul from one suburban estate to another. Meanwhile the recent death from smallpox of Countess Sheremeteva, a young lady-in-waiting and the fiancée of the leading minister of state, Count Nikita Panin, deepened Catherine's fears.[70] Beyond the imperial palace smallpox caused nearly annual epidemics that reaped a large share of the huge infant mortality rate. The disfiguring disease claimed so many victims in Siberia that a team of surgical personnel went there in 1763 to organize a "smallpox house" in Tobol'sk.[71] Thus, Catherine's personal and maternal aversion to smallpox, her general concern for public health and special desire to lower the infant death rate, and her shrewd grasp of public relations all impelled her in 1768 to set an example by seeking inoculation.

Before Edward Jenner's discovery of cowpox vaccination, published in 1798, inoculation against smallpox was accomplished through the technique of variolation. Healthy persons would receive matter from the pustules of a smallpox patient, contract a mild case themselves, and thereby gain immunity. An ancient folk practice, variolation became known in western Europe early in the eighteenth century through the efforts of Lady Mary Wortley Montagu. Giacomo Pylarino, a Greek physician at Constantinople who popularized variolation, also practiced in Muscovy where, it has been alleged, he learned the technique from native practitioners.[72] Whatever the origins of variolation in Russia, it received little public attention until German practitioners experimented with the technique in Livland in the 1750s—about the time it began to be discussed in Petersburg. Lomonosov, for one, recommended variolation in 1761 as the best way to lower the infant death rate.[73] In western Europe and north America, variolation provoked much dispute because it was not foolproof; patients sometimes died and, besides, they might infect nonimmune segments of the community.[74]

At Catherine's request, Count Panin and Baron Cherkassov arranged for a British specialist, Dr. Thomas Dimsdale, to perform the controversial procedure. Dimsdale had made his reputation in 1767 with an improved method of variolation. By elaborating techniques developed by Robert Sutton and Sutton's sons, which simplified the procedure and cut its cost, Dimsdale claimed to have minimized the risks involved. He carefully prepared his patients for inoculation and assiduously treated them afterward. His tract explaining the method achieved popular success and went through four editions in 1767 alone.[75]

Despite Dimsdale's own qualms, Catherine had herself secretly inoculated on 12 October 1768. Nine days later she proclaimed the success of the operation with great fanfare and made Dimsdale the toast of Petersburg society. He next inoculated Grand Duke Paul on 2 November 1768 and, assisted by his son Nathaniel, repeated the procedure on some 140 aristocrats in Petersburg and Moscow. His tract appeared in Russian translation in 1770. He also supervised the establishment of variolation clinics in both capitals, which served as prototypes for similar facilities elsewhere. By 1780, more than 20,000 persons in the Russian Empire had been inoculated. Lavishly rewarded and styled a baron, Dr. Dimsdale returned to England to become a fellow of the Royal Society and a medical celebrity. He revisited Russia briefly in 1781 to inoculate Catherine's grandsons, Alexander and Konstantin. If the practical effects of Catherine's sponsorship of variolation remain debatable, the favorable publicity embellished her image as the enlightened sovereign of a progressive nation. Voltaire lauded her foresight and exemplary fortitude.[76]

Ironically, Catherine's triumph over smallpox occurred shortly before her empire confronted an equally fearsome disease—bubonic plague. Contemporaries generally distinguished between the two maladies, but many thought that both spread by the same means, and some believed that inoculation might work against plague as it did against smallpox. Still others suspected that plague was not so much a specific disease as the apogee of a general infective process. It was believed that various maladies might, under certain conditions, transform themselves into plague. Hence, Dr. Johann Schreiber's book about the epidemic of 1738–39 in the Ukraine argued that plague was "fulminant syphilis," while syphilis was simply "slow plague."[77] Neither the authorities' practical measures against smallpox and syphilis, nor the analogies that practitioners drew between those diseases and plague, would avert the frightful epidemic of 1770–72. Nevertheless, both the measures and the analogies shaped the policies adopted, sometimes with disastrous results.

Military Medicine and the Russo-Turkish War of 1768–1774

The reorientation of health policy undertaken at the start of Catherine's reign proceeded from a broadened conception of public health. No demotion of military medicine was implied in principle. In fact, the imperial government began reorganizing the military medical service on the basis of proposals formulated under Elizabeth and Peter III. The general reform of the medical administration in 1762-64 addressed problems of health care common to soldiers and civilians alike, the foremost being the scarcity of medical professionals. All the plans for training more native medical cadres and for improving the status of the medical profession assumed that most practitioners would serve the armed forces first. Furthermore, the outbreak of hostilities with the Ottoman Empire in the fall of 1768 refocussed, temporarily, Russia's slender medical resources upon the armed forces. With huge Russian forces fighting in the south, from 1769, the appearance of plague there in 1770 redoubled official concern for the military's medical needs.

Just as the Seven Years' War disrupted the empire's economy and administration on the eve of Catherine's takeover, so it revealed deficiencies in the armed forces. In November 1762, Catherine appointed a military commission to reform the army. The medical service urgently needed refurbishment, the Empress declared as she condemned shortages of personnel, surgical skill, instruments, and medicaments for the needless suffering, mutilation, and loss of life in the recent Prussian campaigns. The military commission and the Medical Chancery should jointly draft reforms for health care in the army. Professional medical services must be available to the troops at all times, Catherine insisted; military practitioners should wear distinctive uniforms to facilitate recognition amid the confusion of battle.[78]

Catherine's critique expressed at the highest level of government problems that had preoccupied the medical authorities for decades. The army was perennially short of medical personnel, the deficit always widening in wartime. After 1762, the shortage of military medical cadres apparently worsened. The peacetime army needed fewer medical professionals, many of whom preferred civilian practice to military careers. Indeed, for most military practitioners—i.e., all those below the rank of staff-surgeon—social status and service conditions were abominable. Their mortality rate exceeded the normal civilian death rate, expecially in wartime, while the duties of field surgeons and surgeon's mates continually exposed them to the danger of infection. Their salaries remained minuscule: 180 rubles per year for a surgeon, 120 for a surgeon's mate. Even if one survived the rigors of service, there was no assurance of a pension. Many military practitioners therefore retired as soon as possible.[79] Others angled for safer and softer posts in the capitals or provincial towns. The contrast between military and civilian medical careers became even sharper after 1762, for the expansion of civilian medical services opened new opportunities, while the abolition of compulsory service for the nobility allowed practitioners to retire at will in peacetime.

To forestall the loss of scarce and expensive medical talent to civilian careers, Archiater Mounsey in 1762 proposed upgrading the ranks and salaries of military practitioners, providing pensions, and specifying the duties of regimental surgeons. Mounsey's proposals won Peter III's approval and influenced Catherine's medical reforms as well.[80] Cognizant, for example, of the disparity in earning potential between army surgeons in the provinces and practitioners in the capitals, the Medical Collegium prohibited the appointment of regimental surgeons to Petersburg and Moscow until they had served 6 years in the field. The collegium coupled this prohibition with a promise to supplement the salaries and reserve future vacancies for 10 to 15 regimental surgeons who served their term in the provinces with distinction. Furthermore, doctors who distinguished themselves in military or civil service might become honorary members of the Medical Collegium. They would enjoy precedence in consultations with the medical authorities, and the physician who held seniority among the honorary members might enter the Medical Collegium when a vacancy opened.[81]

The architects of the Medical Collegium, Baron Cherkassov and State Secretary Teplov, projected a reorganization of the military medical service on the basis of Catherine's instructions of 1762. With Count Zakhar Chernyshev, head of the War Collegium, they drafted "An Institution concerning Medical Servitors" on 26 November 1765. Essentially, their program repeated Mounsey's and Catherine's calls for more medical professionals. It proposed to regularize the basis of the military medical service, to raise salaries, and to improve surgical instruction by regularly sending 4 native surgeons abroad for advanced training. To underscore that military surgeons enjoyed officer status, they should wear officers' uniforms with distinctively colored collars and carry officers' sword-knots.[82] The proposed reforms were quite modest, however, and remained mostly aspirations. Salaries did not improve, for example. During the 1760s, the number of military doctors increased with the return of contingents of new M.D.'s from study abroad, but surgical cadres probably declined. The shortage of surgical personnel became critical with the outbreak of the Russo-Turkish war in October 1768.

Comprising about 120,000 men, the Russian armies that marched southward against the Turks in the spring of 1769 employed just 15 medical professionals above the rank of surgeon's mate.[83] By regulation, each of the 78 regiments should have enrolled at least one surgeon and one surgeon's mate, and both armies together should have deployed 186 medical professionals.[84] Dr. Georg von Asch, the top-ranking member of the Medical Collegium, who became chief medical officer for both armies, immediately demanded more surgical personnel. But the Medical Collegium ignored his plea, unable as it was to fill even the regular complement. To mobilize all available practitioners, the collegium announced on 24 March 1769, that it would no longer honor requests for retirement or reassignment for reasons other than ill health.[85] All the same, by mid-August the medical corps with the First Army amounted on paper to just 13 professionals, not counting apothecary servitors and 33 barbers.[86] Fewer than a dozen practitioners were actually present. Asch was the single doctor with the main army; Dr. Ivan de Theyls only assumed his post at the end of 1769. Staff-surgeon Johann Rendler, appointed at the same time as Dr. de Theyls, arrived even later, in January 1770. Not only were military practitioners in short supply; within a year at least 9 died, 6 retired because of illness, and 2 were dismissed for chronic drunkenness.[87] As Dr. von Asch summed up the year's campaign at the end of October 1769: "of sick with the First Army there have occurred extraordinarily many, while of medical men there have been extremely few."[88]

Fortunately, the Russian armies spent the summer of 1769 maneuvering more than fighting, so the shortage of medical personnel caused little inconvenience beyond overworking the few practitioners in the field. Before the First Army could assault the fortress of Khotin on the Polish-Moldavian frontier, for example, supply deficits and disease forced out the Turks on 9 September. As the main Turkish forces withdrew south of the Danube, detachments of the First Army quickly occupied the Danubian Principalities. But overextended supply lines and an early winter prevented the Russians from exploiting their advantage any further in 1769. Thus, General Count Peter Rumiantsev, named commander of the First Army on 13 August, battled constant delays and bad weather to join his troops near Khotin on 17 September. "The present rainy, severe and most unbearable weather not only continues unceasingly," Rumiantsev complained on 4 October, "but even covered the earth with snow today, accompanied by such a frost that, according to the declaration of local inhabitants, happens extremely rarely here at the present not very late autumn season."[89] He therefore halted operations and prepared his army for winter quarters.

The advent of winter hampered the delivery of supplies from the army's magazines in southern Poland and the Ukraine. Accordingly, the risk of disease rose among the ill-supplied and idled troops, quartered upon the local population or huddled in makeshift shelters. In the eighteenth century, it was axiomatic that soldiers in the field during the normal spring-to-fall campaigning season enjoyed better health than stationary troops crowded into winter quarters. The winter of 1769–70 confirmed this rule for the First Army. In mid-November 1769, Rumiantsev personally complained to the Medical Collegium about the dearth of medical cadres to serve his widely dispersed regiments; many detachments "do not possess a single practitioner, even though they are operating for the most part against the enemy and in localities frequently subject to contagious diseases." Widespread sickness that winter foretold worse suffering the next summer, when operations would encroach upon southern regions "full of various distempers."[90]

For the summer campaign, in 1770, Rumiantsev therefore demanded quadruple the medical ranks provided in 1769.[91] In response, the War Collegium assigned him a total of 26 medical professionals. The imperial authorities satisfied only one-third of Rumiantsev's demand because of the shortage of practitioners, a shortage that increased with the assignment of 31 to the Second Army under General Count Peter Panin.[92] Indeed, Panin's chief medical officer, Dr. Conrad Dahl, requested 15 surgeons and 30 surgeon's mates before the opening of the spring campaign. The Medical Collegium also fulfilled only part of this request, dispatching 15 more surgeons and authorizing the promotion of surgeon's mates to fill the other vacancies as the Second Army marched against the Turkish fortress of Bender in the summer of 1770.[93]

The army's sudden, extraordinary need for medical professionals exceeded the manpower readily available in Russia, the more so as the dispatch of the Baltic fleet to the Mediterranean in 1769–70 further depleted the medical corps. Following precedent, the government recruited 40 surgeons in Germany. Hired at salaries considerably above the Russian norm (300–500 rubles as compared to the usual 120–180), these men began joining the armies in the spring of 1770, just in time to encounter plague in the Danubian Principalities.[94] The epidemic compounded the medical menace to the Russian armies, for Petersburg's strategy envisaged a 2-pronged invasion of Bessarabia, the First Army advancing southward from Khotin while the Second attacked Bender from the northeast. Hence, the army leadership insistently demanded more medical professionals to protect the soldiery from plague. Pressed for more practitioners, the Medical Collegium squeezed the surgical schools, hastily promoting students to surgeon's mates and the latter to surgeons, so that both might fill the many new positions and the anticipated vacancies. Surgical personnel assigned to the interior were transferred to the front. The imperial government thus reenacted the medical mobilization of 1738–39 on a larger scale and supplied the 2 armies by the end of 1770 with a total of 110 medical professionals—nearly double the number deployed at the start of the year, but still short of the army's stipulated requirements.[95] Well before plague touched Russian territory in mid-1770, the Turkish war was straining the empire's limited medical resources.

CHAPTER THREE

Catherine II and Moscow on the Eve of the Plague (1762–70)

By 1770, Moscow had not recorded a case of bubonic plague for more than a century. As the world's most northern giant city, Moscow seemed relatively safe from warm weather diseases, such as plague, which Europeans increasingly relegated to backward regions like the Middle East. Although the epidemic of 1770–72 surprised the city, some observers had foreseen the threat of communicable disease. Indeed, whether viewed from the perspective of the eighteenth or the twentieth centuries, Moscow in 1770 presented an ideal setting for massive infection.

What kind of city was Moscow on the eve of the plague? What features attracted disease? What urban problems did contemporaries see as critical, and how were those perceived as dangerous being resolved? To fathom the reactions of contemporaries to the epidemic, one should understand their perceptions of the city. Catherine's opinions hold special importance, because they shaped the policies that Petersburg devised for Moscow in the context of the imperial government's general domestic program. Yet since the Empress loathed Moscow and rarely visited there, her views require comparison with local and foreign perspectives.

In the sphere of domestic policy, Catherine spent the first eight years of her reign cultivating public confidence in her government's ability to lead Russia toward full and equal membership in the European community. Coincidentally she calculated that prudently progressive policies would solidify her doubtful claim to the throne. Thus, her government instituted piecemeal reforms that pursued administrative efficiency and uniformity, promoted economic advance and fiscal growth, and propagated enlightenment through expanded educational facilities, cultural activities, and religious tolerance. For example, Catherine rejuvenated the senate in 1762–63, expanded the functions and personnel of the office of procurator-general in 1763–64, and incorporated the Ukraine into the empire by abolishing New Serbia in 1762 and the hetmanate in 1764. The Legislative Commission of 1767–68 focused public concern upon recodification of the empire's laws on the basis of recent

European social philosophy, as outlined in Catherine's *Great Instruction*, and in the light of proposals and grievances from all free estates. To stimulate the economy, the Empress abolished most state monopolies in 1762, invited foreign colonists in 1763, sanctioned grain exports in 1764, sponsored foundation of the Free Economic Society in 1765, and established a commission on commerce that formulated a new tariff in 1766. Finally, Catherine secularized ecclesiastical estates in 1764, the same year that she founded the Smol'nii Institute for the education of young women, and she also eased restrictions on the schismatic Old Believers. The foreign policy crisis of 1768 slowed the pace of domestic reform, but Catherine maintained the initiative by encouraging public discussion of social issues through the new media of satirical journals.[1] All in all, the 1760s witnessed sweeping change or the promise of change in virtually every field of internal policy. Many of these changes impinged upon Moscow, which to the young Empress epitomized traditional Russian backwardness.

Catherine's disdain for Moscow stemmed from her unpleasant experiences there during the frequent visits of Elizabeth's court and, once she became empress, from her growing conviction that the city violated every tenet of orderly administration. It was in Moscow in 1744 that the future Empress contracted a severe respiratory ailment only a few weeks after her arrival in Russia. There, too, she endured many indignities and several frights, such as when her quarters burned down in 1753.[2] Still, unlike her inept predecessor Peter III, who had planned to be crowned in St. Petersburg, Catherine grasped the national pride embodied in Moscow, "the first-crowned capital of the Russian Empire."[3] Having gained power by the coup d'état of 28 June 1762, she went to Moscow the following September for her coronation in the Kremlin's Assumption Cathedral. She stayed until June 1763 and meanwhile gained insight into the city's shortcomings. Thenceforth she made only two other extended sojourns in the old capital, each time for specific political purposes: in 1767–68 for the Legislative Commission and in 1775 for the celebration of victories over the Turks and the rebel Pugachev. The plague of 1771 inflamed her animus against Moscow. Anything might happen there, she confided to Voltaire; "Moscow is a world of its own, not just a city."[4] Several of her satirical comedies, notably *O Time!* (supposedly "written in Yaroslavl during the plague of 1772"), mocked Muscovites for their gullibility, hypocrisy, and rumor-mongering.[5] The last two decades of her reign recorded brief visits in 1785 and again in 1787, on the latter occasion to mark the twenty-fifth anniversary of her rule. She deliberately avoided the city and even chided noblemen who retired there.[6]

Like many European visitors, Catherine deplored Moscow's sprawling layout and teeming streets, its Eurasian architecture and disorderly appearance. And like her predecessors from Peter the Great onward, she wished to renovate Moscow after the fashion of the new, European-style, and planned imperial capital of St. Petersburg. Her reading of cameralist and physiocratic theory reinforced an apprehension that huge cities threatened orderly governance and social development. The cameralists Bielfeld and Justi, whose treatises Catherine consulted and ordered translated into Russian, warned that excessive enlargement of a capital city would engender social abuses in the metropolis and stunt the growth of provincial towns, deforming the national organism.[7] Moscow exemplified these very problems.

Unlike the Empress and her advisers, who were beginning to look upon towns as functional entities, few Muscovites conceived of the city as a whole. Most residents thought in terms of church parishes, particular neighborhoods, occupational groups, or governmental institutions. Houses were not numbered before 1785, so addresses were customarily given by church parish and neighborhood.[8] One had to specify the neighborhood, because many of the city's 269 Orthodox parishes, which were grouped into 6 territories known as "forties" (*soroka*), centered upon churches with the same name. More than 40 churches were named after St. Nicholas the Wonderworker.[9] Whatever Muscovites thought of their city, they had few means to publicize their views. The single newspaper, the officially published *Moskovskie vedomosti*, appeared 2 or 3 times a week after 1756 and carried mainly international, governmental, and business news borrowed from its Petersburg namesake. In the absence of public media of expression and city-wide representative institutions embracing all social strata, local initiative primarily took the form of petitions to state agencies. These petitions usually addressed particular concerns and seldom broached subjects such as public health.

In 1767, however, representatives chosen by the householders of Moscow devoted much attention to sanitary and health deficiencies in their instruction to the Legislative Commission. Signed by 98 electors, the Moscow nakaz was neither a democratic expression of public opinion nor a product of local initiative alone. Barely 7 percent of the small fraction of the population that owned land participated in the elections, and the subcommittee of electors that compiled the nakaz evidently consulted officialdom beforehand. Nevertheless, such qualifications about the provenance of the nakaz need not invalidate its usefulness as an informed, primarily local, appraisal of Moscow's main problems. The imperial government wished to know what was wrong with Moscow; the nakaz respectfully recounted the city's needs. The compilers enjoyed considerable latitude to formulate their criticisms, to borrow and to adapt suggestions from various sources. They drew liberally upon the Petersburg nakaz; for the new capital was the only metropolis in the empire of comparable size and with similar problems, and they could assume that proposals advanced there would reflect the imperial government's latest aspirations. Much of the Moscow nakaz was eventually enacted into law and implemented in practice, which indicated both the importance of the issues it raised and the government's endorsement of the solutions proposed.[10] Furthermore, the plague dramatized many of the shortcomings mentioned in the Moscow nakaz, affirming the accuracy of its analysis.[11]

Even for a sovereign as energetic and resourceful as Catherine, the transformation of Moscow posed immense obstacles. Foremost was the sheer size of the city, which defied territorial and administrative definition alike. Some 26 miles in circumference, Moscow's "prodigious extent" so impressed William Coxe, who toured the city in 1778 and 1785, that he pronounced it "the largest town in Europe."[12] After a visit in 1765, Giacomo Casanova joked that "my carriage was for four horses, for the city of Moscow is made up of four cities, and one has to drive great distances through unpaved or badly paved streets if one has many visits to make."[13] Muscovites knew the problem equally well. "The excessive extent of the city, which from time to time is constantly increasing," commented the Moscow nakaz, "is known to everyone, as are the inconveniences that stem therefrom." It proposed setting limits that would prevent further sprawl by promoting denser settlement; it favored more public conveyances too. The nakaz also blamed Moscow's "tremendous expansion" for widespread encroachment upon municipal pasturelands, requesting supplementary land from the state.[14] Indeed, Moscow had outgrown itself and presented a microcosm of eighteenth-century Russia: a congeries of traditional societies in the throes of rebirth into the modern world. Though Coxe's description postdated the plague, he captured the city's transitional state, its double aspect of growth and decay.

> I was all astonishment at the immensity and variety of Moscow, a city so irregular, so uncommon, so extraordinary, and so contrasted, never before claimed my attention. The streets are in general exceedingly long and broad: some are paved; others, particularly those in the suburbs, formed with trunks of trees, or boarded with planks like the floor of a room; wretched hovels are blended with large palaces; cottages of one story stand next to the most stately mansions. Many brick structures are covered with wooden tops; some of the timber houses are painted, others have iron doors and roofs. Numerous churches present themselves in every quarter, built in the oriental style of architecture; some with domes of copper, others of tin, gilt or painted green, and many roofed with wood. In a word, some parts of this vast city have the appearance of a sequestered desert, other quarters, of a populous town; some of a contemptible village, others of a great capital. Moscow may be considered as a town built upon the Asiatic model, but gradually becoming more and more European; exhibiting a motley mixture of discordant architecture.[15]

Since the sixteenth century, Moscow had been Russia's largest industrial and commercial center, as well as its administrative and ecclesiastical capital.[16] Despite the transfer of the seat of government, the court, and the Church to St. Petersburg, the old capital retained administrative parity, demographic superiority, and economic preeminence throughout the eighteenth century. The Collegium of Manufactures, which from 1719 to 1779 supervised nonmetallurgical industry, was located in Moscow. So was the Chief War Commissariat, the central supply administration of the armed forces. The sovereign personally appointed the governor-general of Moscow, and when Catherine divided the senate into 6 departments in 1763 she placed 2 in Moscow. More than 40 other central government agencies had offices there. In addition, Moscow functioned as the regional capital of Moscow guberniia, an enormous territory that comprised eleven provinces and had its own civil governor.[17]

The antithesis of a planned city, Moscow disconcerted a French visitor in 1774, who found it "a conglomeration of a great number of villages arranged without order and where everything is in such confusion that it is like an extremely vast labyrinth, in which it is not easy for a foreigner to find his way."[18] The Kremlin, with its government and Church buildings, formed the city's physical hub. Alongside it, *Kitai-gorod*, the walled commercial quarter, enclosed numerous markets, residences, governmental and Church buildings. Bordering these two enclosures on three sides lay *Belyi Gorod* ("White Town"), a tangle of residential and commercial districts formerly bounded by a brick wall. "This Circle, the Houses of which are very mean," remarked a contemporary gazetteer, "contains two Palaces, two Markets, a Magazine of Provisions, a Brew-House, the Basil Garden, the Salt-fish Harbour, a Cannon Foundry, seventy-six Parish Churches, seven Abbeys, and eleven Convents."[19] Between the crumbled wall of Belyi Gorod, which traced the line of the present-day interior boulevards, and the *Zemlianoi Val* ("Earthen Wall"), which ran along today's Sadovoe *Kol'tso* ("Garden Ring"), stretched *Zemlianoi Gorod*. Its connecting link, across the Moskva River from the Kremlin and Kitai-gorod, completed the encirclement of the city center and was known as *Zamoskvorech'e*, literally "area beyond the Moskva River." A broad band of former settlements and villages ringed these inner-city districts, clustering along the radial thoroughfares. These suburbs had long been linked to the city and lay within its official limits, which reached to the *Kompaneiskii* or *Kamerkollezhskii Val*, a moat-and-parapet customs barrier that had deteriorated since the abolition of internal duties in 1754.[20] Even so, Muscovites commonly thought of the Zemlianoi Val as the city limits, thereby excluding many suburbs from the city proper.

The decrepitude of the Kompaneiskii Val typified the vagueness of Moscow's territorial and administrative delimitation. Only a century earlier the city comprised some 140 separate communities. By the eighteenth century, however, nearly all of these subdivisions had shed their communal endogamy, territorial integrity, and specialized occupations; just 33 remained as administrative-fiscal groupings of the merchants and burghers.[21] By 1770, Moscow was divided into 14 police districts, but these did not encompass all the communities within the Kompaneiskii Val. In 1752, for instance, the imperial authorities proposed that the "village" of Pokrovskoe, a community of crown peasants in the northeastern sector of the city, be taken under the jurisdiction of the Moscow police. Either this proposal was not implemented at all or it was later revoked, for in March 1766 Catherine issued a similar order in connection with a violent incident involving illegal workshops in

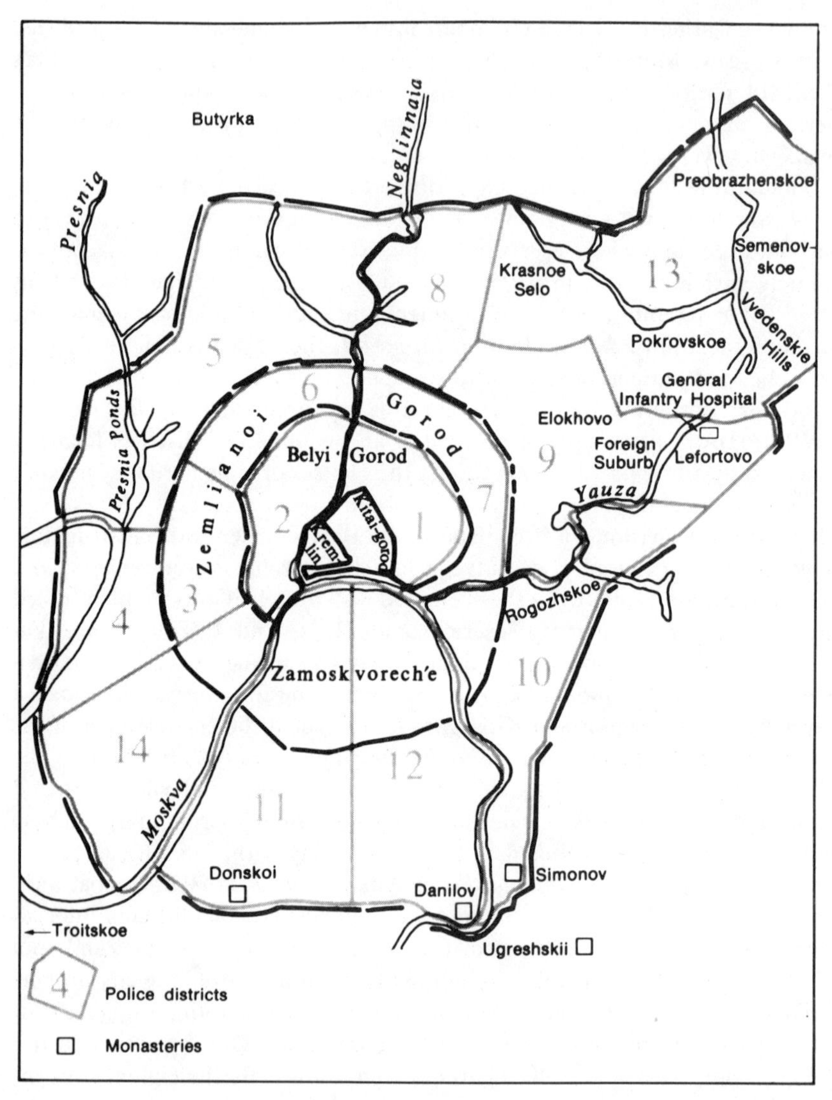

Map 2 Moscow, showing the fourteen police districts, watercourses, and main suburbs.

Pokrovskoe. In 1770, Pokrovskoe was still not considered fully a part of Moscow and only became so in 1782. Several other communities within the Kompaneiskii Val were administered not by city authorities but by government agencies, like the Collegium of Economy, the Admiralty, the Artillery and Fortification Office, the Stables Chancery, the Postal Office, and the Palace Chancery.[22]

Given a loose definition of urban space, Moscow in the mid-eighteenth century surpassed all other European cities in the extent of its territory. Such sprawl presented a large target for the importation of communicable disease. Contemporaries recognized the peril, as seen in the frenzied efforts to protect Moscow from the epidemic of 1738–39. This sprawling layout, when combined with a fragmented administration, offered the further possibility that infective agents might infiltrate remote quarters of the city before anyone noticed anything amiss. This characteristic of the city might invite any communicable disease. For a city to suffer a major incursion of bubonic plague, however, four other sets of variables exercise greater weight: the ecological setting, population density, housing conditions, and the economic infrastructure, especially the location of industry and the nature of commercial intercourse with the hinterland. Because these four elements largely predetermine the parameters of any plague epidemic, they require special elaboration.

Rats, Rivers, and Grain

A massive epidemic of bubonic plague presupposes an enormous rodent population living in close proximity to dense groups of people. The spatial and temporal evolution of the epidemic of 1771 suggests that Moscow harbored immense numbers of rats, several hundred thousand if one assumes they exceeded the human population. Yet this critical fact has not been directly documented. The Moscow nakaz, for example, said nothing about rats or any other rodents. As was true of most plague epidemics before the twentieth century, observers of the Moscow outbreak missed the rat epizootic that must have accompanied its beginning. Nor have later researchers attempted to reconstruct the size of Moscow's rat population. Archeologists would be hard pressed to distinguish rat skeletons from the myriad bones unearthed at sites in Moscow.[23] Nevertheless, both topography and modern knowledge of rat habits argue for a huge rodent population in eighteenth-century Moscow.

Straddling a broad valley sculpted by the Moskva River and its numerous tributaries, the city encompassed a riverine topography with large expanses of low-lying ground. The multiplicity of watercourses traversing Moscow was more obvious in the eighteenth century, for most of the 20-odd smaller streams presently flow underground. Thus the Neglinnaia River, which bisects central Moscow from the north and washes the west wall of the Kremlin before joining the Moskva, has been completely enclosed; so has the Presnia River, its memory clinging to the Krasnopresnenskii district of west-central Moscow and to the ponds of the present-day Moscow Zoo.[24] Two centuries ago, by contrast, the filthy state of Moscow's watercourses caused official anxiety. The nakaz of the Chief Police Administration, which directly influenced the Moscow nakaz, deplored the pollution of the city's water supplies, suggested constructing public wells, and recommended cleaning the main

Figure 1 View of the Moscow Kremlin and the Stone Bridge across the Moskva, with the Zamoskvorech'e area to the right; a good illustration of the Kremlin's central position and of the low-lying topography of Zamoskvorech'e. Oil painting by F. Ia. Alekseev, 1790s, reproduced in *The Art of Russia 1800–1850* (Minneapolis, 1978), p. 88.

rivers. "As far as the Neglinnaia River is concerned, both it and the ponds along it not only are of no use to the city, but are a real menace to human health from the consumption of that water, for during a great part of the year there is an unbearable stench from it, so that inhabitants living close to it are in danger from the corruption of the air."[25] Citing the same dangers, the Moscow nakaz proposed to seek springs nearby and to augment the waters flowing through the city. It insisted, too, that dumping garbage into the Moskva and other waters be forbidden, and that tanneries "or other manufactories that render the water unclean" be prohibited from locating upstream from the city.[26]

Contemporaries did not know that the abundance of waters in Moscow would be a prime attraction for *Rattus norvegicus*, which established itself in Russia by the mid-eighteenth century. Hardier than the black or house rat (*Rattus rattus*), Norway rats require plenty of water and swim readily, habitually infesting sewers and drains. This rodent's "outstanding prowess in burrowing," in conjunction with its habitat and nocturnal habits, would partly account for the low visibility of Moscow's rat population.[27] Only 600 oil lanterns illuminated the central districts in the 1760s.[28] Another reason for the failure of eighteenth-century Muscovites to mention rats must have been simple familiarity; commensal rodents were so common that nobody thought them worthy of comment.

Unlike house rats and mice, which are relatively dainty feeders and therefore depend heavily on food supplies destined for human consumption, Norway rats eat whatever is available.[29] These nocturnal scavengers would have found abundant food amid the littered courtyards of Moscow, in the outbuildings where livestock was kept, around markets, in slaughterhouses, and in the ubiquitous dung-hills—all ideal areas for harborage too. As the empire's leading grain market, Moscow constantly received, stored, and shipped huge amounts of rats' favorite food. Grain shipments from the south probably arrived with veritable rodent convoys. The central grain market on Bolotnaia (literally "Swamp") Square, spilling across the frequently flooded south bank of the Moskva opposite the Kremlin, must have drawn multitudes of rats to the very middle of Moscow. Heavily settled and the site of constant deliveries and dispatches of grain, spirits, and textiles, this bustling district could easily sustain a rat epizootic and distribute it over the city.[30]

By 1770, Moscow probably sheltered hordes of Norway rats along the rivers, streams, and ponds. At the same time the predominant wooden construction must have concealed thousands of house rats. In 1753, for instance, the Chief Palace Chancery reported that "mice" were damaging the Amusement Palace in the Kremlin; the vermin had gnawed at wallcoverings and through the bottoms of doors. Described as "numerous" and "large," the rodents in question doubtless included rats as well as mice.[31] That same year, during a fire at the Golovin Palace in suburban Lefortovo, Catherine herself observed "an amazing number of rats and mice, which descended the staircase en masse, not even hurrying much."[32] Thus, a combination of large numbers of house rats and sewer rats, the former infesting Moscow's crowded wooden buildings and the latter congregating along watercourses and swampy areas, provides the rodent component necessary to explain the gradual spread of bubonic plague through Moscow and its environs in 1770–72. Furthermore, the presence of two different kinds of rats, with different habits and habitats, partially accounts for the slow emergence and uneven incidence of the plague in Moscow.

Though oblivious or inured to the infestation of rats, some Muscovites perceived a health danger in polluted air. At Moscow University on 22 April 1765, professor of physics Johann Rost discussed "the penetrating action of the smallest particles which emanate from bodies, especially of animals." His public lecture cited foreign, historical, and personal observations that corrupted air could be harmful, even deadly, to people. Because human bodies, corpses in particular, exuded dangerous "vapors," Rost suggested forbidding burials within city limits. If such burials must continue, he advised gravediggers to dig deeper and to pile up the dirt, packing it firmly "so that deadly vapors cannot escape freely and afflict adjacent people through inhalation."[33] More boldly, the Moscow nakaz proposed to transfer slaughterhouses outside the city, to move the fishmongers' row from Kitai-gorod to a peripheral location, and "to appoint places, especially outside built-up areas, for the disposal of sewage and garbage." Because "the many cemeteries here throughout the city also cause the air to be dirty," the nakaz requested their removal too.[34]

In short, contemporaries discerned an epidemic potential in Moscow, although their fears about corrupted air missed the mark as concerned bubonic plague. If, however, one reads their admonitions against filth and polluted water as a shorthand for conditions that favored massive rat infestation, then Muscovites vaguely sensed some of the main preconditions for plague. But their exhortations to clean up the city went largely unheeded.

Residents and Transients

The human population of Moscow proved almost as difficult to count as the resident rodents. Population statistics for the period are therefore scanty and imprecise, produced as they were by the imperfect administrative machinery of Church and police. Moscow then as now contained a large unregistered "floating" populace, in the suburbs especially. With the easing of restrictions upon the Old Believers that Peter III inaugurated in 1762, many returned to Moscow from the provinces and abroad, yet still avoided contact with the authorities and inscription on the tax rolls. The city also experienced substantial daily and seasonal fluctuations in the number of its residents and lacked clearly defined urban limits. Consequently, contemporary estimates of the population vary from a low of 152,190, according to Church and police statistics of 1770, to a high of 500,000 reported by Joseph Marshall in 1769 and an official gazetteer in 1773.[35] The first total probably meant permanent residents only, excluding the non-Orthodox and transients, while undercounting the suburbs. The second figure seems obviously inflated, but might refer to the entire metropolitan area at the height of the winter social season. Half a million would have been far too many for 1773 in particular, considering the massive loss 2 years before. William Coxe thought the figure for 1770 too low and endorsed police estimates of 250,000 to 277,000 for 1780; whereas, two other official enumerations yielded 161,101 for 1776—a year that might still reflect the plague losses—and 184,478 for 1781.[36] (If these last two totals were consistent, they implied speedy replacement of the population killed by the plague; perhaps the difference between these two figures and those reported by Coxe arose from different territorial bases, Coxe counting more of the suburbs.) Comparing the various estimates, it seems reasonable to support the view of Dr. Charles de Mertens, who concluded that Moscow before the epidemic had a population of 250,000 to 300,000 in the period December–March, or 25 percent more than during the rest of the year.[37] Subsequent calculations in this study will therefore employ a working figure of 250,000.

Evidence of substantial demographic growth in the 1760s deepens the uncertainty about the size of Moscow's population on the eve of the plague. Contemporaries believed the population of the city was increasing, and several joined the Empress in condemning the fact. Indeed, much of the legislation that Catherine issued during her first visit to Moscow as empress derived from the assumption that the old capital was becoming overpopulated. Beyond the usual crush of pedestrians and conveyances in the streets, Catherine and her advisers deduced a burgeoning population from the multiplication of industry, rising food prices, and rampant beggary. All three phenomena evoked legislative responses. On 23 October 1762, the Empress prohibited the establishment of new industry in Moscow and Petersburg; thenceforth industrial expansion was to proceed elsewhere.[38] In practice, the new policy was scarcely enforced, because it conflicted with efforts to stimulate the national economy. Soaring food prices and beggary posed more immediate dangers. Even before Catherine's coronation, on 22 September 1762, she ordered the senate to provide all towns with grain magazines, "in order that the price of bread always be in MY hands." On 3 September 1762, the senate acted to restrain rising prices for oats and hay in Moscow.[39] Nonetheless, the situation worsened in the next 2 months, owing to the arrival of the court, much of the imperial administration, seven regiments of troops, and a multitude of the nobility, the clergy, the merchantry, and their retainers.[40] Moscow temporarily became sole capital of the empire. Fearing that local food prices would skyrocket, the Empress personally solicited monthly tabulations of the population and weekly reports of local food prices. Unfortunately, the records of these censuses have not yet been found, but since price data have, the order must have been implemented for a time. Catherine obviously blamed Moscow's growing population for the inflation of food prices. The continuous rise of grain prices throughout the 1760s reinforced her worries.[41]

Another sight that appalled the new Empress was the crowd of beggars and cripples roaming about Moscow shrieking for alms. She probably linked this phenomenon to unchecked population growth, too, as it illustrated the cameralist axiom that too many people would overburden a bloated city and harm the state.[42] Moscow's governmental and economic functions brought in masses of convicts, beggars, invalids, and "soldier's wives"—military dependents who enjoyed the right to choose their place of residence when their husbands were on campaign; many were impoverished widows. Catherine feared that such declassed, unemployed groups contained explosive ingredients that rising bread prices might goad into crime and disorders. As palliatives for these social problems she pardoned some convicts, paid the obligations of petty debtors, and reviewed digests of those imprisoned. Like her predecessors, she abhorred beggary and ordered the police to suppress it. Ablebodied vagrants were dispatched to the Collegium of Manufactures for temporary assignment to factory labor; the aged and the infirm were returned to their villages or placed in monastic poorhouses. In 1764, the Empress summoned the Holy Synod to remove mendicant monks from the streets of Moscow, and she secretly sent a Guards officer to investigate rumors that destitution was forcing many retired soldiers into beggary. The next year she urged the senate to expedite the settlement of invalid soldiers on suburban pasturage.[43]

These modest attempts to stabilize the population of Moscow had little effect. When Catherine revisited the city in the spring of 1767, she still thought it "populous to the point of tedium."[44] At the Legislative Commission in Moscow that very summer others voiced similar opinions. The nakaz from the Chief Police Administration echoed cameralist premises in requesting legislation that would empower the police to banish from Moscow and St. Petersburg anybody without an art or trade; such persons should lose the right to own houses in either capital.[45] Several proposals of the Moscow nakaz implied that the size of the population exceeded the city's capacity. It called for continuing government supervision of food prices and asked for the establishment of grain magazines, indicating that Catherine's order of 1762 had not yet been implemented in Moscow. Wood prices had also risen steeply, the nakaz explained, because Moscow's growing industry had depleted the nearby forests; it recommended a ban on new manufactories in the city. Acknowledging that helpless mendicants and cripples should be assisted, the nakaz advocated construction of a workhouse for the dissolute and the disorderly. The police should arrest anybody found intoxicated on the street and consign them to at least a week of hard labor. Sources of population influx were hinted in the nakaz's proposals to forbid private building on state lands, where "outsiders" might be illegally harbored, and to free the householders of Moscow from the obligation to quarter unliveried court servants.[46] In the latter regard, Moscow undoubtedly absorbed a substantial increment of population in 1767-68 from the lengthy presence of nearly 600 delegates to the Legislative Commission, as well as the Empress and her court. At the commission itself and in print various spokesmen lamented the imminent depopulation of the countryside from peasants' going off to the city.[47] Bustling Moscow exemplified this very trend.

Who were the people flocking to Moscow in the 1760s? It is easier to indicate some sources of population growth than to determine the total numbers or the proportional shares of the various social strata. What the nobility lacked in numbers, for instance, they recouped in social visibility and relative wealth. With the cessation of compulsory state service for the nobility in 1762, bolstered by the period of peace following Russia's withdrawal from the Seven Years' War that same year, the nonserving elite enjoyed greater opportunities to sample Moscow's social attractions, which Catherine's lavish coronation so amply displayed—the government alone spent 32,585 rubles upon the celebration.[48] Since 1755, the city boasted the empire's single viable university, together with two *gimnazia* and some private schools, and, from

1758, foreign and native theatrical companies offered regular performances.[49] Impecunious noblemen visited Moscow to obtain loans from the Noble Bank, founded in 1754; others came to secure paper currency (*assignats*), 2.6 million rubles of which were printed in 1769.[50] Noblemen found so few comforts on their isolated estates that many settled permanently in Moscow or brought their families for the winter social season. Legions of servants accompanied some aristocrats.[51] The more numerous middling and lesser nobility hired temporary quarters or lived with relatives. Some bought rental properties.[52] In the 1760s, this migratory social convention was becoming so firmly entrenched that two decades later it would swell the population of Moscow in the wintertime by nearly 100,000.[53]

The influx of nobility constituted only a part of the demographic growth that mirrored the city's enlarging role as a marketplace and production center. The abolition of internal customs duties in 1754 stimulated commerce generally and with the Ukraine especially. Economic expansion attracted many newcomers to Moscow, demonstrating Justi's contention that if diverse crafts and industries flourish in a city, its population will automatically increase.[54] Merchants from provincial towns, even some from abroad, strengthened their ties with Moscow's markets; many frequently visited or permanently settled there.[55] Masses of peasants followed suit, pushed by the commercialization of agriculture and lured by the growth of industry and crafts. In 1764, Governor Yushkov of Moscow guberniia commented that the peasantry of the region preferred crafts to cultivation; "they serve as drovers, [working] in Moscow as bakers, peddlers, gardeners, stonemasons, bootmakers, and in other crafts and labors."[56] Few of these people joined the merchant guilds and artisan corporations. Indeed, Moscow became a focal point for the gradual formation of a new socioeconomic category of "trading peasants," who retained residence in the countryside while pursuing gain in the towns of central Russia. Urban censuses only recorded them late in the century, but their activities were evident by the 1760s in Moscow, where they approximated 13 percent of the merchantry.[57] With the final secularization of ecclesiastical estates in 1764, about one million male peasants came under the jurisdiction of the Collegium of Economy. Such "economic" peasants comprised about 20 percent of the population of Moscow guberniia, and their new status facilitated opportunities to seek urban employment. In the period 1742–82, they furnished two-thirds of the 1,506 persons newly enrolled in the merchantry of Moscow guberniia, more than four-fifths of whom were registered in Moscow.[58] The number hired at Moscow's manufactories more than doubled in 1763–69, as compared to the previous 9 years (see table 7).

Crown villages near Moscow, like Pokrovskoe within the city limits, also funneled recruits into the city's entrepreneurial groups. The years 1763–69 saw a rapid increase in the number of crown peasants hired at Moscow's manufactories (table 7). By 1782, the entire population of Pokrovskoe had become either merchants or burghers. In the period 1720–80, some 1,512 adult males from crown properties around Moscow enrolled in the merchantry, burghers, and artisan corporations. More than 75 percent of these men changed their legal status in the 1760s and 1770s.[59] Unfortunately, these statistics do not specify how many of these "peasants" gained urban citizenship prior to the plague, nor do they distinguish between individuals and families or between Moscow residents and recent immigrants. Still, these data suggest that the twin processes of in-migration and urban expansion were accelerating prior to the plague.

Employment opportunities in Moscow opened wider in the late 1760s, when, as a result of Russian military involvement in Poland and against the Ottoman Empire, large new government contracts rescued the city's military suppliers from the economic doldrums they had endured since the end of the Seven Years' War. By serving as the army's chief supplier and provisioner, Moscow augmented its already vigorous commerce with the southern guberniias. This development fueled the economic boom underway and added to its permanent and transient population. Moscow grew despite a murderously high death rate and a low birth rate, both of which caused a rapid turnover of population and meant that many Muscovites were "yesterday's provincials."[60]

If the old capital's total population for this period remains uncertain, its social composition is equally problematical. Official statistics for the 1780s, though suggestive (table 2), suffer from the limitations mentioned above, and they reflect the impact of the plague and later trends. Several of the categories were also ill-defined and revealed little about the social status and economic functions of the persons classified. For instance *raznochintsy*—literally, "various statuses"—represented a social catch-all subsuming persons who were neither nobles nor peasants nor enrolled in urban merchant guilds or artisan corporations. Many were government functionaries, clerical workers, members of professions, retired noncommissioned officers, soldiers, and their dependents.[61]

A similar vagueness beclouded the legal class or estate termed merchants (*kuptsy*). Two sets of statistics for 1764 provided different breakdowns of this group (table 3). Column A showed that persons legally classified as merchants actually performed many different kinds of labor. At least one-third of them—those listed as artisans, state servants, and laborers—were not merchants in the usual sense. Column B suggested, moreover, that elements that might roughly be labeled entrepreneurial and laboring groups constituted only about one-fifth of the total population. Of course, the latter groups did not include the increasing number of newcomers—full- and part-time, seasonal and permanent, adolescents and children, state peasants and private serfs, Orthodox and Old Believers—who were joining the Moscow labor market in the 1760s (table 7). Fragmentary and imprecise as the statistics on total population and social groupings are, they portray the human di-

Table 2 The Social Structure of Moscow's Population in the Late Eighteenth Century (males and females)

1781[a]		1788–95[b]	
Nobility	10,857	Nobility	8,600
Clergy	4,775	Clergy	3,600
Military	18,386	Military	7,000
Raznochintsy	76,760	Officials and *raznochintsy*	17,600
Serfs	73,700	House serfs	61,300
Total	184,478	Peasants	53,700
		Merchants	11,900
		Burghers and artisans	9,100
		Foreigners	2,200
		Total	175,000

[a]"General'naia vedomost', uchinenaia v Moskovskoi politsii v 1781 godu, o chisle v Moskve nakhodiashchikhsia zhitelei. . . ," ORGBL, f. 129, no. 22, d. 15:1.
[b]*Istoriia Moskvy*, 2:307.
Note: Obviously, *raznochintsy* is used in two different senses. In 1781, it seems to include peasants, artisans, foreigners, merchants, burghers, and perhaps some officials; the meaning in 1788–95 is clearly much narrower.

Table 3 "Middle" Population Groups in Moscow in 1764

A (males only)		B (males and females)	
First guild	622	Merchants	15,687
Second guild	3,259	Burghers	3,868
Third guild	3,104	Bondaged workers	22,370
Artisans	1,345	Drovers and suburban residents	2,814
Servitors	343		
Laborers	1,848	Registered artisans	178
Total	10,520	Total	44,917

Sources: G. L. Vartanov, "Moskovskoe i inogorodnoe kupechestvo vo vtoroi polovine XVIII v.," *Uchenye zapiski Leningradskogo gos. ped. instituta im. A. I. Gertsena* 278 (1965): 276–78; F. Ia. Polianskii, *Gorodskoe remeslo i manufaktura v Rossii XVIII v.* (Moscow, 1960), pp. 38, 138.

mension of Moscow as a mirror image of its physical appearance: a jumble of contrasts in the process of accelerating change.

For the immediate purpose of understanding why the plague struck Moscow so hard, however, three facts stand out. It was the empire's most populous city, its population was growing rapidly, and its booming industrial and handicraft production stimulated large-scale foreign and domestic, military and civilian commerce. Plague in the south might reach Moscow through commercial channels, and once there it would find hospitable rodent and human hosts.

Hovels, Barracks, and Mansions

Just as commercial intercourse and a substantial population are necessary to introduce and sustain an epidemic of plague, so the incidence of an urban outbreak largely follows the territorial distribution of the population and its housing conditions. Statistics from 1765, 1770, 1771, and 1775 give some idea of proportional housing for the main social groups (table 4). These data did not reflect residence directly, however. Some property owners—aristocrats, wealthy merchants, and manufactory operators—possessed more than one messuage or homestead (*dvor*), which usually comprised several detached structures. Many people lived in rented quarters, and multifamily dwellings were very common. Although Kitai-gorod and Belyi Gorod housed a dense population in a small area, most Muscovites resided in the smaller, dispersed dwellings of Zemlianoi Gorod and the suburbs. Much of the new construction since 1745 was located in Zamoskvorech'e and beyond the Zemlianoi Val. Comparison of housing statistics for 1765 and 1771 revealed a rapid tempo of new and larger construction: 897 new messuages with 4,265 rooms, an average of 4.75 rooms per message, as against the city-wide figure of 2.66 in 1765. Though not a very sensitive measure of social trends, these data hinted that noblemen, merchants, and manufactory operators built most of the new structures, whatever social strata inhabited them. By 1775, the nobility alone owned more than one-quarter of all messuages (26.2

Table 4 Ownership, Distribution, and Composition of Messuages (*Dvory*) before and after the Plague (number of habitable rooms in parenthesis)

1775	Total Messuages	Kremlin, Kitai-gorod, and Belyi Gorod	Zemlianoi Gorod	Suburbs
Nobility	2,384 (17,422)	429 (4,962)	1,209 (7,917)	751 (4,543)
Clergy	1,168 (2,267)	406 (1,000)	462 (782)	300 (485)
Raznochintsy	3,544 (6,650)	151 (391)	981 (2,248)	3,412 (4,011)
Merchants	1,627 (4,756)	99 (624)	743 (1,742)	776 (2,390)
Manufactory operators	164 (1,838)	31 (124)	69 (826)	64 (888)
Totals[a]	8,887 (32,933)	1,116 (7,101)	3,464 (13,515)	4,293 (12,317)
Totals in 1770[b]	12,538 (34,155)	1,399	4,383	6,756
Totals in 1771[c]	12,522 (35,230)			
Totals in 1765[d]	11,625 (30,965)			

[a]Sytin, *IPZM*, 2:81–82.
[b]Sytin, 2:52, and TsGADA, f. 199, d. 367:266.
[c]Chicherin to C., 1 Jan. 1771, TsGADA, f. 16, d. 481, pt. 3:151.
[d]*SA*, 15:486.
Note: no further breakdowns of the data for 1765, 1770, and 1771 are available.

Figure 2 In Zamoskvorech'e, a good illustration of the contrast between simple wooden structures and larger masonry palaces and churches. Painted etching by F. Dürfeldt, 1800, reproduced in *Moskva: Pamiatniki arkhitektury XVIII-pervoi treti XIX veka* (Moscow, 1975), p. 68.

percent) and more than half the rooms (52.9 percent). Merchants and manufactory operators held about one-quarter of each.[62]

Except for the noble and merchant elite, most residents of Moscow lived and worked either in small dwellings (two rooms or less) or large, barracklike structures. Assuming a total population of 250,000 on the eve of the plague, its density averaged about 20 persons per messuage and more than 7 persons per room, based upon an average of 2.81 rooms per messuage in 1771. Many homesteads in the suburbs, like those "wretched hovels" Coxe mentioned after the plague, must have been smaller and more crowded than these averages indicate. The fuller statistics of 1775 recorded the clergy, *raznochintsy*, and merchantry as owning 4,488 messuages with only 6,866 rooms in the suburbs, i.e., 1.53 rooms per house. Yet the sparser figures for 1770 enumerated just 1,222 more rooms in all Moscow as compared to 2,463 more messuages in the suburbs, implying an even lower ratio of rooms per suburban homestead; so did the city-wide average of 2.81 rooms per messuage in 1771 as against 3.70 in 1775. Floorplans of common dwellings and of rental quarters confirmed these statistics. Peasant-style single-room huts and single-room apartments for families housed a large portion of Moscow's population in the mid-eighteenth century.[63] Small cheap houses predominated in the military and manufacturing suburbs of Semenovskoe and Preobrazhenskoe. Of 93 real estate sales in both communities in 1763–67, for example, 86 structures cost no more than 50 rubles, and 58 buildings just 5 rubles or less.[64] In 1767, manufactory workers of these suburbs complained that they received neither state salaries nor provisions and therefore petitioned to be relieved of quartering obligations.[65] By contrast, the structures belonging to manufactory operators, with an average of 11.2 rooms per messuage, could have housed nearly 80 persons each if the city-wide average of 7 persons per room held true for them. Several industrial complexes actually sheltered much larger aggregations, as will be seen. Whether Muscovites resided in large or small dwellings, then, they lived very close together.

The homesteads of the social elite, albeit roomier than the quarters of the unprivileged, also encompassed large numbers of people in crowded conditions. For that very reason the residences of the Moscow nobility disgusted Catherine. She scoffed at "useless servants in the houses—what houses, what disorder there is in the houses, where the lots are immense and the courtyards are filthy swamps. Usually each noble has not merely a house but a small estate in the city."[66] As examples of Moscow's large noble properties, Count Peter Apraksin sold Ivan Golovin a messuage in the Foreign Suburb in 1763 for 6,000 rubles that encompassed 92,855 square feet, and Princess Agrafena Kantemir bought one from Count Moisei Vladislavich in Belyi Gorod in 1764 for 11,000 rubles.[67] The composition of such houses may be seen from the following sales notice in the *Moskovskie vedomosti* in the spring of 1771:

> The wooden house of Court Councilor Mikhail the son of Afanasi Ustalkov, situated beyond the Moskva River on Bol'shaia Kaluzhskaia Street in the parish of the Church of the Most Holy Virgin of Kazan in Zemlianoi Gorod, in which [there are] 7 living rooms on a stone foundation, an eighth storeroom, [the walls] inside are all covered with paper wallcoverings, the ceilings are decorated with plasterwork, [and there are] 2 vestibules with closets, a carriage barn, a stable with 6 stalls, a cellar with a cold pantry, a kitchen, a bathhouse, 2 servants' rooms, a regular garden with fruitbearing trees, a carpenter shop: in this homestead with the garden the land is more than 50 *sazheni* deep, and 21 *sazheni* across along the street [350 × 147 feet].[68]

A great many people could inhabit such homesteads. Naturally their rural character, extensive grounds, orchards, kitchen gardens, artisan shops, granaries, stables, and servants' quarters would have attracted rodents in abundance, both house and field rats.

The overwhelming majority of Moscow's cramped housing was built of wood (table 5). Though generally larger than wooden buildings and increasing in number, brick edifices were concentrated in the central city, where in 1770 they still constituted less than a third of all messuages. This mass of wooden buildings made Moscow a fireman's nightmare. The constant fire hazard prompted Catherine to establish, in December 1762, a high-level commission for the rebuilding of St. Petersburg and Moscow in brick. The

Table 5 Brick and Wooden Messuages by City Regions

	1770		1775	
	Wooden	Brick	Wooden	Brick
Kremlin, Kitai-gorod and Belyi Gorod	993	406	577	539
Zemlianoi Gorod	4,076	307	2,985	473
Suburbs	6,756	Unknown*	4,091	207
Totals	11,825	713	7,653	1,219

*A. F. Büsching, who lived four years in Russia (1761-65), counted 11,840 wooden and 708 brick messuages in Moscow in 1770; the latter figure implies the absence of brick structures in the suburbs, a fact difficult to credit. *Neue Erdbeschreibung* (7th ed.; Hamburg, 1777), vol. 1, pt. 1:841.
Source: Sytin, *IPZM*, 2:33-34, 81-83.

commission surveyed Moscow by 1767 and eventually produced a plan in 1775. Meanwhile, fires wrought further havoc, as the Moscow nakaz dolefully noted.[69] Conflagrations in May and July 1773, for example, consumed 1,231 messuages—more than 10 percent of the city. Thousands of small wooden dwellings were burned in 1771-72 as an antiplague measure, which, in conjunction with spontaneous fires, caused the decrease of 4,172 wooden messuages between 1770 and 1775 shown in table 5. Efforts to catch and punish alleged incendiaries achieved nothing. Worse still, Moscow's fire-fighting organization remained rudimentary until 1784 and unsatisfactory until after 1812.[70]

Muscovites complained about the fire and health hazards inherent in their crowded, often filthy and decrepit, wooden housing. Yet they overlooked one attribute of wooden construction that twentieth-century epidemiology would underline: its invitation to rodent infestation. Moscow's myriad wooden houses offered a mecca to rats. The one- and two-room hovels that predominated in the suburbs, where thatched roofs could still be seen, must have harbored hordes of rats and mice.[71] Even the larger masonry structures included plenty of plaster and wood construction, as well as generous cellar and attic space, rendering them equally vulnerable to rodent infestation. The centuries-old preference for wooden housing in Moscow stemmed from the low cost and easy workability of wood as compared to the limited local supply of building stone and the high price, low quality, and more complicated use of brick and plaster.[72] Warmer and drier than brick buildings, wooden houses also were thought to be healthier.[73]

Textile Workshops and Manufactories

Economic expansion in the 1760s magnified the potential for communicable disease in Moscow by channeling streams of laborers and artisans, merchants and peasant traders, into the already crowded metropolis. Textile fabrication led the industrial boom, compounding in the process several preconditions for pestilence. Indeed, Moscow's textile mills and workshops interwove an exceptionally dangerous fabric of circumstances conducive to the importation, gestation, and propagation of bubonic plague. Rats and fleas could easily hide in the bales of silk and wool that the textile industry constantly brought to Moscow from the southern guberniias and from plague-enzootic regions of Persia and the Ottoman Empire. Every district, except the Kremlin, encompassed textile manufactories and workshops, but both types of enterprise were larger and more numerous in Zemlianoi Gorod and the suburbs than in the center (see table 4 and map 3). The Zamoskvorech'e region enclosed an unusually dense complex of fabricating facilities that rivaled the largest cloth manufactories of Europe. Usually built of wood, generally located near watercourses, and hence accessible to river-haunting Norway rats, the many textile manufactories sheltered dense congregations of people working and living amid insanitary conditions. Hundreds of ordinary dwellings, mainly in the suburbs, contained small textile workshops that suffered from rat infestation and all the perils of Moscow's cramped wooden housing, besides the crowding and pollution characteristic of industry. Since many enterprises functioned both as production sites and residences for large clusters of workers, their families, and others not employed in the textile industry, an outbreak of plague at such places would inexorably afflict other social strata and occupational groups. By the same token, workers living outside the manufactories might bring plague home to nonindustrial locations and social groups. Because economic ties connected many of the city's textile enterprises, an epidemic at one might soon reach others. Finally, if bales of wool and silk could convey *Y. pestis* to Moscow and facilitate a city-wide epidemic, the multiplying links between cloth production in the city and related facilities in the hinterland opened potential channels for the outward spread of plague to the provinces.

Statistical measures of industry in Moscow on the eve of the plague share many of the deficiencies of the population data: incomplete territorial coverage, imprecise terminology, inconsistent economic trends, and inconstant government policies. Official statistics frequently overlooked small enterprises in the suburbs. Contemporaries made no consistent distinction between a manufactory (*zavod*) and a workshop (*fabrika*), or between manufacturing and crafts in general.[74] Furthermore, industry reflected the fluctuations of the Moscow economy in the 1760s, growth in some sectors masking stagnation or decline in others. Coincidentally government policy toward industry underwent fundamental changes that affected economic trends, industrial morphology, and the collection of industrial statistics. State patronage of large-scale, privileged manufactories, most of which depended upon bondaged labor, yielded to promotion of small-scale enterprise manned by hired workers. From 1767, a series of senate decrees gradually eliminated the

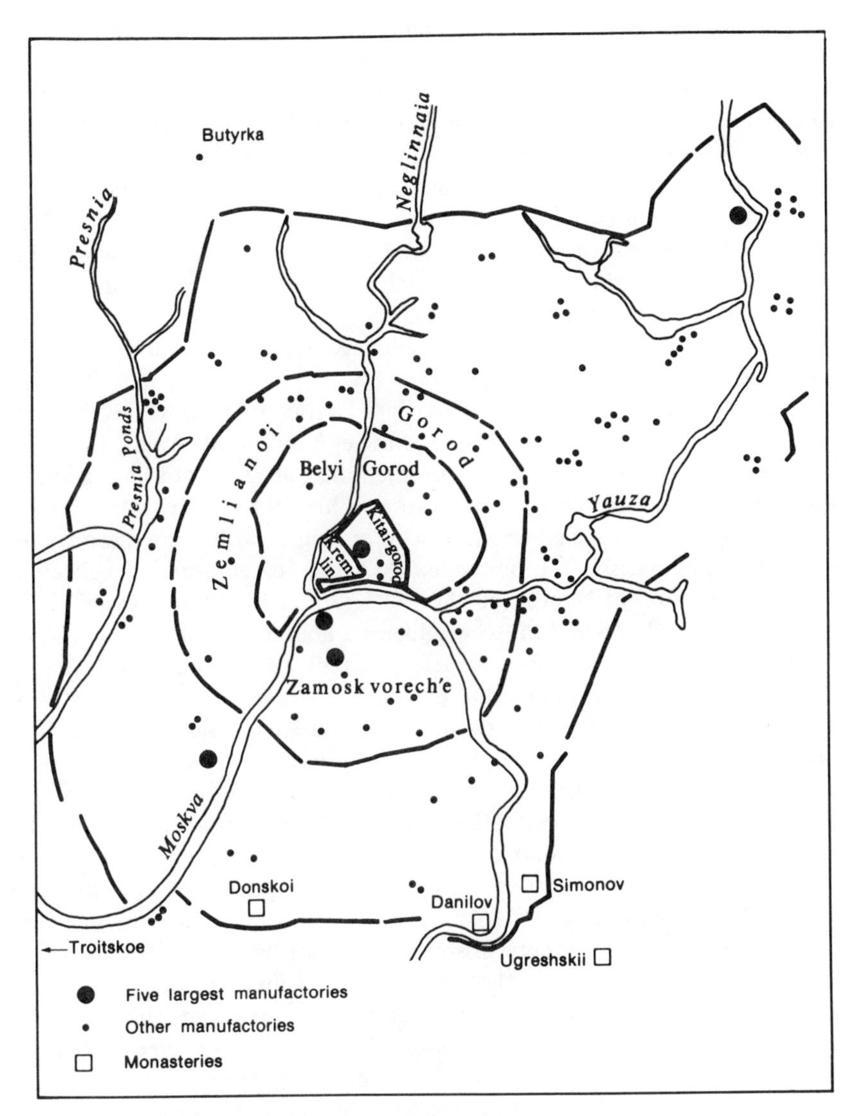

Map 3 The textile industry in Moscow in 1773.

mercantilistic distinction between registered or "decreed" (*ukaznye*) enterprises regulated by the Collegium of Manufactures and illegal or "nondecreed" *(neukaznye)* concerns. The new policy eventually legalized the existence of hundreds of small-scale enterprises that had proliferated for decades on the periphery of Moscow.

Before 1767, the Collegium of Manufactures neither recognized nondecreed industry, which it fitfully and vainly sought to suppress, nor collected statistics about such enterprises, although their growth was apparent to everyone. Nor did legalization of nondecreed concerns bring about their wholesale registration, the more so as the government in 1769 temporarily doubled the yearly licensing tax of one ruble per loom on production for sale, an imposition that had the effect of encouraging small entrepreneurs to conceal their operations. To cloud the statistical record further, there is evidence that nondecreed enterprises formed the fastest growing portion of Moscow's industry on the eve of the plague. Inasmuch as the statistics collected prior to 1767 excluded nondecreed enterprises, they failed to give a full picture, whereas later tabulations remained equally incomplete as a result of registration no longer being compulsory.[75]

Whatever the measure of industrial production in Moscow, the city and its region accounted for a major share of the empire's total output. Peter III discovered this fact in 1762 when he ordered the Collegium of Manufactures transferred to St. Petersburg, only to reverse his decision two months later "as all manufactories are either in Moscow or near it, while here there are so few that no comparison can be made."[76] Of the 567 enterprises registered with the Collegium of Mines and the Collegium of Manufactures in 1767, Moscow contained 116 and Moscow guberniia another 37. Since the Petrine era textiles dominated the city's industry, 72 mills turning out in 1767 more than 80 percent of the total value of goods produced there by registered enterprises. Moscow mills comprised between one-third and one-half of the country's registered textile enterprises. They produced a similar proportion of all textiles, in terms of value, and employed a like share of the total work force engaged in cloth production. Of the 3 main branches of textile manufacturing—woolens, silks, and linens—Moscow's dominance rested on the first 2, although it also supported 2 of the largest linen mills in the empire. In 1769, Moscow housed 27.4 percent of Russia's woolen manufactories and 48.5 percent of its silk enterprises, but only 7.1 percent of its linen mills (all these statistics excluded the Ukraine). Measured by the number of looms, the city's woolen mills in 1771 boasted more than one-third, its silk enterprises nearly two-thirds, of the empire's total.[77] If nondecreed concerns could be enumerated for this period, their multiplying numbers would reconfirm Moscow's commanding position in the Russian textile industry.

The distinction between decreed and nondecreed enterprises mirrored differences of status among their operators. Persons of merchant origin ran the bulk of Moscow's registered textile mills. Exempt from the taxes and service obligations borne by the rest of the variegated merchant estate, these so-called *fabrikanty* or *soderzhateli* (literally "holders" rather than owners) constituted a small, privileged, largely ingrown elite. A few even gained noble rank by government order.[78] Although noble entrepreneurship had grown rapidly since 1740, their enterprises were usually small and generally located on provincial estates; many functioned only during the winter to supply household needs. Nondecreed industry, by contrast, grew out of rural and urban crafts, and engaged a hodgepodge of social groups. Persons of peasant status manned most of the small workshops, sometimes with noblemen and ordinary merchants as silent partners. Naturally, these unprivileged entrepreneurs resented the special status enjoyed by registered industry. Some of their resentment surfaced in a proposal of the Moscow nakaz that *fabrikanty* bear the same obligations as other city residents. Before the change of government policy toward industry in 1767, however, the *fabrikanty* constantly accused nondecreed concerns of unfair competition for materials, markets, and manpower.[79]

Registered industry in Moscow, as elsewhere in Russia, differed from nondecreed enterprise most of all in the size and character of its labor force. Decreed enterprises possessed extensive legal authority over large numbers of unfree workers and their dependents. Bondaged labor consisted of several types. Some workers had been "eternally committed" (*vechnootdannye*) to factory labor by particular government decrees, especially that of 7 January 1736; others had been purchased by nonnoble entrepreneurs on the basis of the decree of 18 January 1721. These two groups later amalgamated into the category known as "possessional" workers, bound to an enterprise rather than a person. Still other bondaged workers were owned by entrepreneurs of noble rank. On the eve of the plague, the 113 registered enterprises in and around Moscow held claim to 12,681 bondaged persons. More than 90 percent of these people were concentrated in the textile industry, with 11,835 bound to 68 enterprises, an average of 172 each (table 6). These registered manufactories quartered large detachments of a small army of industrial conscripts.

Registered industry in Moscow also employed growing numbers of hired workers (table 7). Hence the number of persons legally bound to registered enterprises did not represent their total work forces, as officials acknowledged.[80] Many of the hired workers were peasants from crown and former Church estates who worked seasonally to supplement their rural earnings. Nearly two-thirds of them, however, were privately owned serfs and domestics whose masters either allowed or, frequently, arranged their employment. In fact, the second category comprised about 60 percent of all the serfs hired

Table 6 Registered Textile Manufactories in Moscow in 1771, before the Plague

Type	Number	Number of looms	Bondaged males	Bondaged females	Total bondaged personnel
Woolens	20	567	4,372	1,691	6,063
Silks	41	1,286	2,502	1,338	3,840
Linens	7	863	1,440	492	1,932
Totals	68	2,716	8,314	3,521	11,835

Source: *Opisanie*, pp. 587–95.

Table 7 Growth of Hired Labor at Moscow's Registered Manufactories, by Social Origin[a]

Years	Total hired	Private serfs	Household serfs	Economic[b] peasants	Crown peasants	Burghers and *raznochintsy*
1738–44	627	206	45	160	106	110
1745–52	1,107	453	88	251	206	109
1753–62	2,615	1,285	329	571	259	171
1763–69	4,144	1,570	793	1,161	440	180
1770–79	5,205	2,417	1,040	1,378	216	154

[a]M. N. Artemenkov, "Sotsial'nyi sostav naemnykh rabochikh," pp. 154–76.
[b]Peasants formerly belonging to ecclesiastical institutions; with the final secularization of Church estates in 1764, they came under the jurisdiction of the Collegium of Economy—thus their name.

by registered enterprises in Moscow between 1738 and 1779.[81] These statistics counted labor at registered manufactories only; the steady growth of nondecreed enterprises drew upon a much larger labor pool. The expanding demand, small investment requirements, and simple technology involved in cloth fabrication attracted merchants, artisans, and peasants alike. Female peasants and urban dwellers such as soldiers' wives found ample demand for their spinning and weaving skills in Moscow's textile workshops, which mainly produced cheap, fashionable wares like silk ribbons, scarves, and handkerchiefs.[82]

From 1762, moreover, official policy and practice favored hired labor, whether free persons or noble-provided serfs. Preference for hired labor stemmed from the redirection of state economic policy, launched under Elizabeth and Peter III, away from monopolies and privileges toward the expansion of opportunities and the involvement of broader elements of society in trade and industry. Catherine's government extended the new policy by promoting export- and civilian-oriented industries.[83] The state gradually ceased supplying registered industry with declassed elements, and by Peter III's decree of March 29, 1762, which Catherine confirmed four months later, nonnobles were prohibited from purchasing peasants for industrial labor.[84] Protests by *fabrikanty* to the Collegium of Manufactures and at the Legislative Commission proved unavailing. In fact, the collegium's own nakaz censured the *fabrikanty* for their obstinate dependence on bondaged labor, urging that since many enterprises were already operating exclusively with hired labor, all could do so.[85]

Catherine thought the same and quietly withdrew another form of patronage from registered industry. While in Moscow in April 1767 she secretly directed the Collegium of Manufactures to end its suppression of nondecreed enterprises.[86] Catherine reversed the previous policy covertly so as to avoid immediate outcry from the *fabrikanty;* she knew well the antagonism existing between the two kinds of industry. Just a year before, in March 1766, an attempted search for an illegal workshop in Pokrovskoe had ignited violence. A crowd stoned the detachment of police and soldiers sent to confiscate the suburban enterprise, beat senseless the merchant and house-serf who had informed the authorities, and expelled the intruders. This incident repeated almost exactly another near the same suburb 2 years earlier.[87] Although Catherine sent troops to punish the recalcitrant suburbanites and ordered the Moscow police to take Pokrovskoe under their jurisdiction, she also dispatched Policemaster-General Nikolai Chicherin to investigate the cause of the violence.[88]

The outburst at Pokrovskoe evidently made a double impression on the Empress. It fortified her already low opinion of the Muscovite masses, and dramatized the government's ambivalent role in the conflict between decreed and nondecreed industry. Moreover, the supposedly illegal enterprise proved to be operating as an artisan shop by permission of the Moscow Municipal Administration, and further investigation disclosed hundreds of similar enterprises. A survey of the adjacent communities of Preobrazhenskoe, Semenovskoe, and Pokrovskoe discovered in the first two alone textile fabrication at 162 houses with 416 looms, two-thirds of them operated by newly arrived peasants.[89] Although the findings for Pokrovskoe itself are not known, its peasant-artisan population operated at least as many looms as its two neighbors. In 1771, the Collegium of Manufactures issued licenses for 172 looms in Pokrovskoe, 81 in Preobrazhenskoe, and 70 in Semenovskoe, but noted that 321 persons had failed to renew the one-year licenses obtained in 1769–70 for 1,170 looms. Many of the latter were assumed to be still operating and, therefore, were operating illegally. Of the delinquent looms, 400 had been in Pokrovskoe, 245 in Preobrazhenskoe, and 139 in Semenovskoe. By 1773, a total of 232 individuals held licenses for 818 looms in Pokrovskoe.[90]

Clearly, these findings persuaded Catherine and her advisers that it was both futile and foolish for the Collegium of Manufactures to hinder the growth of nondecreed enterprise on behalf of the *fabrikanty.* The impressive expansion of small-scale textile manufacturing in Moscow demonstrated a desirable alternative to the big state-related enterprises that seemed to have outlived their usefulness. Partial legalization of nondecreed industry in 1767 further boosted its growth, so that official statistics for 1773 counted 745 workshops operating 2,680 looms—nearly as many as the registered mills had had before the plague (table 6). No doubt others were working without licenses.[91]

As a result of these economic trends and policy changes, Moscow's textile industry exhibited a dual character on the eve of the plague. If the city still sheltered many large enterprises that produced for state needs and for export, it was sprouting a host of small-scale producers favored by the newly emergent economic policy. Nearly all of these textile workshops operated in the small wooden residences that dotted Moscow's periphery. Like most local dwellings, they were crowded. Twenty-three persons worked at one messuage, according to the survey of Preobrazhenskoe in 1766, and 10 or more was quite common. Packed with raw materials and finished goods, littered with scraps, and frequently communicating with suppliers and customers —many workshops furnished semifinished products to the larger mills—such residential enterprises could have concealed hordes of rats and fleas. They also could conceal plague. Small wonder the plague first showed itself in Moscow in 1770 in one of these suburbs.[92]

Moscow's big textile mills reproduced on a larger scale all the negative qualities of the workshops; their concentration of greater numbers of people in such conditions invited infection all the more. Not only were these cloth manufactories large individually, averaging 172 bondaged workers and their dependents each, but several combined into huge production complexes. Indeed, 5 giant agglomerations dwarfed all the other textile enterprises in the city. The largest center of cloth fabrication in Moscow bore an appropriate name: the Big Woolen Court (*Bol'shoi sukonnyi dvor*). Founded as a state enterprise in 1705, the Big Woolen Court had been transferred in 1720 to a company of *fabrikanty;* the prominent merchants Il'ia Dokuchaev, Mikhail Gusiatnikov, Vasilii Surovshchikov, and Grigorii Likhonin managed the plant in 1770. Its output—mainly "soldier cloth" and kersey, a rough material used for lining and padding—went to the Uniform Office of the Chief War Commissariat. Little ever reached the open market, as was true of the produce of most woolen mills in Russia. Imports and peasant production supplied the finer grades of cloth for civilian consumption. Wedded to military demand for coarse fabrics, the registered woolen industry could not compete in the civilian market. When military procurements diminished during periods of peace, such as in 1762–68, most "decreed" woolen mills fell upon hard times. The resultant unemployment of their bondaged workers, few of whom had other means of subsistence, sharpened Moscow's social problems and worried the police, who foresaw unrest among the manufactory workers, "so audacious and inclined to intolerable acts in public." In 1762, a protest at the Big Woolen Court prompted a senate order to flog eighty-two workers and apprentices. Predictably, the bondaged workers often deserted, and their disorders made the Zamoskvorech'e notoriously unsafe.[93]

Of the 3,260 persons bound to the Big Woolen Court in 1770, its last year of normal operation, only 1,150 men and 250 women actually worked full-time at the main site, using 140 looms. The rest of the people attached to the factory included 1,092 housewives, 220 boys, and 36 elderly persons. Some may have worked part-time at the mill or elsewhere. About 400 toiled at the woolen enterprise formerly owned by Ivan Poluiaroslavtsev, located on the Yauza River east of the Kremlin, which Dokuchaev and his partners had purchased in 1768. Another hundred labored at their 5 fulling mills outside the city.[94]

Besides employing a huge labor force, the Big Woolen Court was an invitation to the plague through crowding and location. About 700 workers and

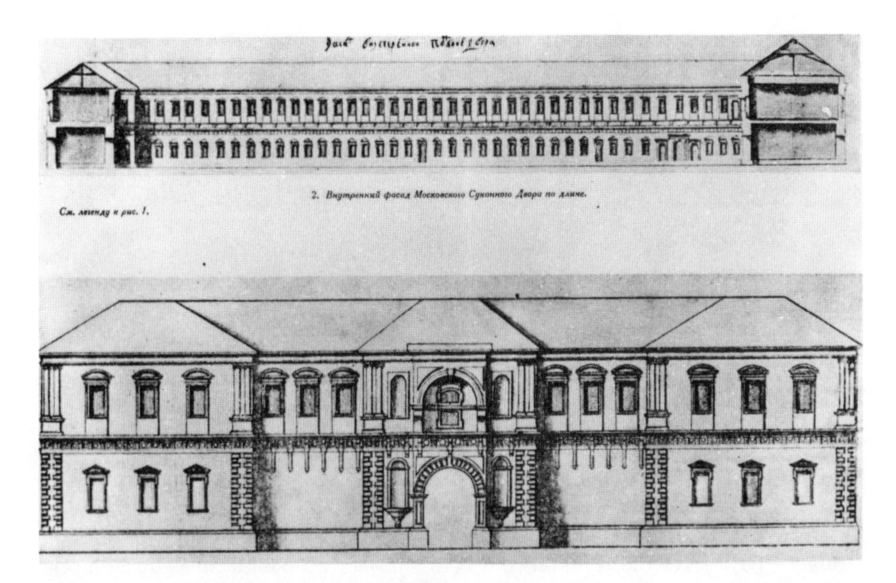

Figure 3 Façades of the Big Woolen Court in Moscow in 1746: interior (*top*) and exterior (*bottom*), facing northeast. From S. G. Tomsinskii, ed., *Moskovskii sukonnyi dvor* (Leningrad, 1934), p. 249.

dependents lived permanently at the plant in 1771. Its main building, a massive hollow rectangle (364 × 182 feet) situated near the Big Stone Bridge across the Moskva from the Kremlin, stood amid a densely inhabited area that offered ideal conditions for rat infestation. The 2-storey brick building contained spinning, weaving, dyeing, and finishing shops, as well as numerous storerooms and workers' quarters (Fig. 3). Many employees and their families resided in wooden dormitories at nearby Tsaritsyn Meadow. The rest lived throughout the city in privately owned or rented quarters, often mere corners of single rooms. Some worked at home.[95] By the 1760s, the mill ceased spinning yarn for kersey and purchased it from workshops in and around Moscow.[96] Although the main building was built of brick, much of the interior was made of wood, as were the numerous, dilapidated auxiliary buildings nestled inside and outside the giant rectangle. Rats and fleas would have found abundant food and shelter in the factory's storerooms, the pantry and kitchen areas of the workers' quarters, and the littered interior courtyard. The huge grain market at adjacent Bolotnaia Square guaranteed the presence of myriad rodents. In addition to heavy traffic from shipments of cloth and deliveries of raw materials, crowds congregated across the street at the city's main liquor warehouse. Thousands of people living and working in close quarters, in a busy commercial-industrial district, in close proximity to a veritable rodent heaven: the Big Woolen Court presented an ideal environment to support an epidemic of bubonic plague.

Figure 4 Façades of the Kadashevskii Court, formerly the mint, in eighteenth-century Moscow. Printed in *Istoriia Moskvy*, 2:29.

Four other production centers furnished similarly perilous conditions. About 500 yards south of the Big Woolen Court sprawled the old mint (*Monetnyi dvor*), a giant brick structure that housed 4 woolen mills. Colloquially named the Kadashevskii Court, these merchant-operated mills together had 140 looms and 964 bondaged workers, 364 of whom were living there permanently in 1771. Another cluster of 4 silk enterprises operated across the river in Kitai-gorod at the old Ambassadorial Court (*Posol'skii dvor*). With 4 related operations located in the suburbs, they employed 572 bondaged and 141 hired workers operating 390 looms. Some 484 of these people permanently resided at the Ambassadorial Court in 1771.[97] Ivan Tames's linen mill, located in the Khamovniki section just south of Zemlianoi Gorod on the left bank of the Moskva, resembled "a little town," remarked a visitor in 1743. Its 580 bondaged males and 264 looms occupied nearly 30 buildings over an area of 2 square blocks. Tames, a russified Dutchman who had achieved noble status and the title of "director," hired additional workers, mainly the serfs of large landowners, and owned more than 100 serfs himself. On the eve of the plague, 708 persons bound to the enterprise or its owner and 254 hired workers were living at the manufactory.[98]

Similar in size was the Admiralty's sailcloth mill, also known as the Weaving Court (*Khamovnyi dvor*), which stood next to the Yauza in Preobrazhenskoe. Built in 1696, the giant mill supplied the new Russian fleet and later produced canvas for export. By 1771, the brick enterprise had 1,170 bondaged personnel (704 males and 466 females) and 500 looms. Few of the women worked at the manufactory, but most of them lived there, and many doubtless did spinning and weaving for nearby workshops. Because of its size, remote location, military organization, and state ownership the Admiralty mill was the single manufactory in Moscow with its own infirmary, permanently staffed by a surgeon from 1764.[99]

These 5 centers of textile fabrication represented more than half of the bondaged people (6,446 workers and dependents) and productive capacity (1,434 looms) of Moscow's registered cloth industry in 1771 (table 6). Centralized in structure and operation, heavily dependent on bondaged labor, they concentrated thousands of people at a few, mainly central, locations. Most important, these production complexes housed a total of at least 3,680 workers and dependents on their premises, in cramped quarters, or nearby in equally crowded dormitories and cottages.[100] They also maintained frequent contacts with smaller textile enterprises inside and outside Moscow and obtained large quantities of raw and semifinished materials from the surrounding guberniias and from abroad. Nearly all silk was imported, and as late as 1770 the Big Woolen Court received considerable raw wool from the Ottoman Empire.[101] The big mills offered, in short, perfect entries for the introduction of plague from outside Moscow. Because of their locations, their enormous work forces, and their dual role as production centers and industrial barracks, they could also spread disease over the city.

Reform and Removal of Urban Industry

The health hazards of industry in Moscow evoked official concern long before plague struck. The government's inability to alter the situation illustrated the complexities of reforming basic features of the city. From the start of her reign Catherine and several advisers accused industrial enterprises of imperiling public health and exacerbating the city's many social problems: overpopulation, inflation, fire hazards, pollution, crowded housing, urban sprawl, deforestation of the hinterland, beggary, labor unrest, and crime. A senate report of 1762 deprecated the growing number of manufactories and workshops, the influx of workers and artisans, and the resultant pollution. "Not only at these manufactories and workshops but even on the streets where these manufactories and workshops stand, great uncleanliness occurs," the report explained, "and from some manufactories and workshops, such as tanneries and the like, there is an unhealthy air. And since here within the city the august procession of Your Imperial Majesty is taking place and may in the future, so such uncleanliness from the manufactories and workshops might not be harmless."[102] So formulated, the matter elicited Catherine's decree of 23 October 1762, prohibiting new industry in Moscow and Petersburg.

The proposal to restrict industrial growth in Moscow also appealed to Catherine because it might work in two directions at once, lessening the old capital's social problems and, conceivably, spurring economic advance elsewhere. Entrepreneurs might locate new enterprises in provincial towns, which could supply convenient sites, cheaper provisions and raw materials, and abundant labor; while the new industry would provide employment opportunities and spread prosperity.[103] The Empress took the idea one step further. Around 1762 she privately summarized the disadvantages of textile manufactories in Moscow and contemplated transferring them to suitable provincial towns; "the workmen would be more industrious and the towns would flourish."[104]

The idea of relocating Moscow's manufactories rested squarely upon cameralist political economy. Bielfeld, for one, censured the location of big enterprises in large cities. Textile mills that use cheap materials, employ many workers, and produce common cloth, he affirmed, "*ought to be located in provincial towns, where victuals are abundant, where working hands are therefore cheaper, and where there are not many distractions.*" Only workshops that employ few workers, require expensive materials, and cater to changing fashion should be allowed in capital cities. These rules appeared so commonsensical to Bielfeld that he declined to explicate their rationale. Justi also opposed the concentration of industry in large cities, citing the deleterious effects upon provincial towns.[105]

Others adopted Catherine's desire to transfer industry from Moscow to the provinces. In January 1765, the Collegium of Manufactures reformulated the idea in response to a report that the Big Woolen Court was sustaining losses. The collegium generalized the difficulties of Moscow's largest textile mill into a plan to relocate all enterprises producing the coarser kinds of fabrics. That in fact meant the larger manufactories, with their mass of unfree semiskilled workers, the social element deemed most dangerous to public order, as Bielfeld hinted. Workers who were "capable and of orderly behavior" might remain in the city as fabricators of fine cloth. Relocation would apply to "other Moscow manufactories at which a large number of bondaged people work, and [which] are found in similar circumstances." Although this proposal was forwarded to the Empress in February 1765, its economic and legal implications combined to postpone action.[106]

The economic dimension worried Catherine, as she confided to Procurator-General Alexander Viazemskii on 15 December 1765, her concern about the Chief War Commissariat's intention to purchase only 150,000 *arshin* (one *arshin* equals 28 in. or 71 cm.) of standard-width woolen cloth in 1766, less than one-quarter of the amount taken in 1765 and nearly a million *arshin* less than the usual annual requirement. Could the registered woolen industry survive such a cutback when the Big Woolen Court, the largest supplier, had been declining for several years? "As this matter is extremely important not only in itself, but even more for the consequences that will result from it,"

Catherine directed the senate to intervene.[107] In early 1766, the authorities resolved to curtail procurements gradually, but in 1767 the state purchased less than 16 percent of the 1,419,000 *arshin* of soldier cloth produced.[108] Similar economic pressures beset the sailcloth industry; in 1766, the Moscow Admiralty Office received orders to investigate whether its sailcloth mill could produce fabrics of sufficient quality to be sold on the open market.[109] Moscow's big textile mills were struggling to adapt to a peacetime, competitive economy.

The idea of removing manufactories from the capitals, a notion that Catherine pursued in Petersburg in 1766, reappeared when she revisited Moscow in 1767.[110] Possibly at the Empress's instigation, an unidentified adviser submitted an "opinion" expounding the economic arguments against large manufactories and extolling the advantages of small-scale industry. Big manufactories were harmful, this observer reasoned, because they employed inefficient bondaged labor, produced wares of low quality, and impaired agriculture and crafts by pulling labor off the land. Like the cameralists, Catherine's adviser seasoned his economic critique with moral strictures. He disparaged large manufactories as dens of "every iniquity and depravity," inhibitors of normal population growth, and incubators of social unrest.[111] Impressed with arguments that crystallized vague sentiments in her own *Great Instruction* to the forthcoming Legislative Commission, the Empress advised the Collegium of Manufactures to make the "opinion" the basis of its nakaz.[112] When, moreover, the collegium evidently responded with some defense of large-scale industry, Catherine refuted its views. Decrying "the multiplication of big agglomerations at which hundreds of cultivators work, to the great loss of husbandry," she insisted that "since the purchase of villages [with serfs] for manufactories exhausts husbandry, so it ought to be prohibited."[113]

The Collegium of Manufactures dutifully appended the aforementioned "opinion" to its nakaz. Still, it raised the practical problem of what to do with the people legally bound to the large manufactories and dependent upon them for subsistence, but left the Legislative Commission to resolve this thorny issue. The collegium's nakaz also recommended the removal of certain workshops, especially tanneries, contrasting Kazan favorably to Moscow in this regard. But it ignored the impact of industry upon public health and merely opposed crafts "that make great filth and a certain ugliness."[114] The police nakaz advocated the removal of tanneries, too, and the prohibition of locating them upstream from settlements, "in order not to cause harm to the health of the inhabitants through the stinking smell and the uncleanliness of the waters." The police likewise favored relocation of crafts unwholesome because of smell, noise, or fire hazard.[115] All these criticisms stressed, then, the impropriety of industry in Moscow, and several cited its potential threat to public health.

Even so, the proposal to remove large manufactories was not immediately implemented. By 1767, Catherine better appreciated the intricate social and economic issues posed by the removal of big manufactories from Moscow. Keeping the end in sight, she pursued it gradually by force of example. She therefore reaffirmed the ban on new industry in Moscow, a prohibition that the Moscow nakaz heartily endorsed, but which had hardly been enforced since 1762.[116] Thenceforth no exceptions were to be permitted. In 1769, for example, the senate investigated the consumption of wood by chemical enterprises near Moscow and blocked the establishment of a vitriol plant in the Klin district, fearing the effect on wood prices in the old capital.[117]

Then too, Catherine's secret quasi-legalization of nondecreed industry in April 1767 foreshadowed eventual transfer of large manufactories out of Moscow. Freed from administrative harassment, small-scale industry could prove its superiority to the big mills and show *fabrikanty* the advantages of relocation, dispersal of operations, and conversion to hired labor. Expansion of the textile workshops might also absorb some labor formerly employed at the big manufactories. If some workers declined to accompany their enterprises to the provinces, and if the relocated mills required fewer hands, redundant workers might still find employment instead of burdening Moscow's rudimentary welfare services. The small size of the workshops and their diffusion among the suburbs would forestall a repetition of the social abuses spawned by the centrally situated big mills. Furthermore, because the labor legislation of 1762 precluded *fabrikanty* from purchasing new bondaged workers, and because bondage to factory labor was hereditary only for those "eternally committed," natural attrition would gradually dispose of such laborers at the enterprises of any *fabrikanty* who refused to relocate or to emancipate their unfree workers.[118] Within a couple of decades Moscow would be rid of the large manufactories and their peculiar species of bondaged labor.

If textile workshops multiplied in greater Moscow after 1767, wartime exigencies soon modified the newly liberalized industrial policy. In late 1769, the government declared all textile enterprises subject to the same tax per loom—temporarily doubled to two rubles to help finance the war—and empowered the Collegium of Manufactures to collect it by licensing all looms in workshops and homes.[119] This fiscally inspired measure threatened to undermine the comparative advantages of small-scale production. Meanwhile large-scale production benefited from the renewed military demand after 1768, which temporarily recouped the leverage of the big textile producers in their dealings with the imperial government.[120] So the proposal to remove such enterprises hung in abeyance, only to reappear with heightened urgency during the plague crisis of 1771.

Even as the plague crept into Moscow the imperial authorities undertook to reduce the ranks of *fabrikanty*. The senate ordered on 22 November 1770, and the Collegium of Manufactures moved to implement three weeks later, the abolition of all manufacturing privileges not consonant with the policy of assisting only the initial establishment of entirely new industries.[121] This redefinition would have quashed the privileges of most *fabrikanty*, equalizing them in status with the rest of the townspeople, as the Moscow nakaz advocated.[122] The crisis of 1771 postponed implementation of the new policy, but only briefly. Ironically, the rapid growth of textile workshops in the suburbs in the late 1760s, a phenomenon that Catherine hoped would ameliorate some of the city's economic and social problems, actually enhanced the local disease potential. It augmented the population and, more menacingly, promoted wider distribution of many conditions favorable to the propagation of plague.

Hospitals, the Foundling Home, and Slaughter Pens

Besides efforts to alleviate health-related economic and social conditions in Moscow, the first decade of Catherine's reign witnessed attempts to ameliorate the threat of disease by enlarging public health facilities. While historical precedent and cameralist theory suggested the means, the matter took on urgency when Catherine's son and heir presumptive, Grand Duke Paul, became dangerously ill en route to Moscow for her coronation. Apparently recovered by mid-September 1762, the eight-year-old Grand Duke suffered an alarming relapse at the end of the month. Paul's illness so dismayed Catherine, who vividly recalled her own bouts with disease in Moscow, that she vowed to dedicate a new hospital to his recovery.[123] In June 1763, the Empress founded Paul's Hospital (*Pavlovskaia Bol'nitsa*), Moscow's first permanent public hospital. Enlarged and rebuilt several times, it still functions. The new facility had only 25 beds and a 3-man staff when it opened on 14 September 1763, in a converted house on the southeastern outskirts. Four years later it moved to a new wooden building in the same area and expanded to 50 beds. Financed entirely by the Empress, Paul's Hospital offered free treatment for the curable poor of both sexes. It released about 28 persons per month in 1770–71, three-quarters of them males. The mortality rate was not announced and is not known.[124]

The Foundling Home that Catherine approved for Moscow in 1763 signified her concern about the abandonment and high mortality rate of infants. It provided a lying-in hospital for unwed and destitute mothers and, from 1768, employed a full-time physician. Opened on 21 April 1764 (Catherine's birthday), the home received 523 babies by the end of the year. The number of infants delivered to the home from Moscow and the neighboring region increased annually to a peak of 1,237 in 1769. For the period to 1770, the official yearly mortality rate (however understated) never dropped below 24 percent, and in 1767 an outbreak of smallpox pushed it past 98 percent. This appalling toll caused the Foundling Home to begin sending several hundred infants to villages for nursing, but the mortality among this group regularly exceeded 50 percent. Meanwhile, births at the lying-in hospital rose from 14 in 1764 to 162 in 1770.

Dr. Charles de Mertens, brought from Vienna in 1767 to supervise medical services at the Foundling Home, used the new Sutton–Dimsdale method to inoculate many of the older children, beginning in 1768. Mertens's contract obligated him to provide medical advice and prescription drugs to the poor without charge, but so many sought these services that the directors of the home opened a public pharmacy near the Varvarskie Gates in 1769. Catherine granted liberal sums to the Foundling Home, nearly 550,000 rubles through 1770, and her example encouraged gifts of smaller amounts from private donors. Archbishop Amvrosii, head of the Church in Moscow, patronized the home and served on its governing council. The three-storied Foundling Home, built in 1764–72 overlooking the Moskva just downstream from the Kremlin, was the first nongovernmental and secular public edifice in Moscow to be built of brick. It symbolized the government's long-term concern for the reconstruction of the city's center and a new interest in public welfare.[125]

In November 1762, the Empress ordered a special house established for the maintenance of the insane of both sexes at the expense of their relatives. The construction of this facility was postponed, however, so the Andreevskii Monastery served as an asylum instead. A poorhouse was opened in Moscow around 1765, but neither its size nor its location is known. In the 1760s, the state supported in Moscow about a thousand persons in various almshouses at churches, monasteries, and conventual houses (*podvor'e*). The annual budget for the maintenance of these people was barely 15,000 rubles, hardly adequate for subsistence. None of these institutions provided regular professional medical care.[126]

Considering these initiatives, it may seem odd that Catherine ignored the General Infantry Hospital in Lefortovo overlooking the Yauza. Two facts may explain the Empress's neglect. First, as a military institution its needs took a backseat to the glaring lack of civilian medical services. Second, it had recently undergone a major expansion. With only 200 beds at mid-century, the hospital became terribly overcrowded, handling as many as 1,474 patients in July 1755. In such conditions, the death rate soared. The large numbers of wounded from the Seven Years' War worsened the situation. Although one brick and several wooden annexes were added by 1759, the hospital still had only about 800 beds to accommodate more than 1,300 patients. Yet plans for further expansion aroused objections. Its propinquity to the Golovin Palace, where Empress Elizabeth liked to stay when visiting Moscow, could threaten the sovereign's health; for spring winds might waft "the considerable bad smell" right into the imperial court. Apprehensive, Elizabeth wished to move the hospital to a remote location.[127]

The War Collegium therefore commissioned state architect Dmitrii Ukhtomskii to design a new multipurpose medical and welfare facility that could treat a thousand patients and house invalids, orphans, and foundlings. Ukhtomskii's project, a set of 4 buildings that would have required 10 years and cost almost 1.4 million rubles, proved to be overly ambitious and ill-timed; the Seven Years' War crippled Russian finances, and it was never built. Nevertheless, the project foreshadowed Catherine's welfare reforms of the 1760s. In response to renewed criticism of the General Infantry Hospital in 1765, the Medical Collegium proposed to replace it with a new brick structure on the Moskva below town, but the plan foundered from lack of funding and bureaucratic buckpassing. Although the hospital was not moved, several wooden annexes were transferred to the Vvedenskie Hills, about a mile northeast of Lefortovo in Semenovskoe. The Vvedenskie Hills annex comprised 4 wooden barn-like structures for 150 to 170 patients each and 2 barracks for the hospital attendants and their families. These barracks would be the first recognized site of plague in 1770.[128]

Beyond these medical facilities, more substantial Muscovites could hire private physicians. The number of practitioners was limited, however, and their state duties took precedence. In Moscow in March 1771, there were only 14 doctors of medicine, 35 surgeons, about 60 surgical students (appendix 1-2), 6 apothecary shops, and a few barbers and midwives—scarcely 100 more or less qualified practitioners. Vienna, a metropolis of comparable size, was served by some 300 practitioners and 20 hospitals.[129]

The Moscow nakaz disclosed in 1767 that some Muscovites remained dissatisfied with the recent efforts to expand public health facilities. Its compilers believed much more should be done; they wished to institute some of the proposals of the Petersburg and the police nakazy. The first supplement to Catherine's own *Great Instruction,* published in St. Petersburg in February 1768, showed the Empress was thinking along the same lines. While Catherine favored police measures against "those *common* Maladies which increase among the People, as well as those which are *contagious,*" the Moscow nakaz cited the dangers of communicable disease, "especially among the lower orders," in requesting additional public hospitals where "persons of both sexes may be treated, the penniless poor at state expense." To lessen infant mortality and deaths from childbirth, the nakaz requested greater numbers of certified midwives and suggested assigning 4 to 6 in each district. Moscow's "great extent and populousness" required greater numbers and better territorial distribution of apothecaries, physicians, and free surgeons. Like Catherine, the Moscow nakaz favored charity for the deserving poor and endorsed an institution for the insane. These proposals demonstrate that some Muscovites knew very well what their city lacked in the sphere of public health.[130] Encouraged by Petersburg's expressed desire to consider local needs directly, and perhaps as a result of the low level of civic consciousness then prevalent in Russian society, the Moscow nakaz left reform to the higher authorities. Scant local initiative emerged to resolve Moscow's social problems before the plague.

Catherine, for her part, continued to ponder Moscow's problems upon returning to Petersburg in January 1768. Two proposals reaffirmed her aspirations and apprehensions. Irritated by the lack of a comfortable palace in Moscow, "where we endured various kinds of anxiety for a whole year," the Empress decided to construct a new Kremlin palace. She commissioned the grandiose plan of Vasilii Bazhenov to transform the Kremlin into a neoclassical showplace as part of the general reconstruction of both capitals. In July 1768, Catherine created an office in Moscow to supervise construction and authorized Bazhenov to spend 50,000 rubles on an elaborate model. Site clearance and foundation work began in 1770. Despite estimates that the project would cost upwards of 20 million rubles, the Empress urged Bazhenov onward, even when state finances faced extraordinary demands from the Turkish war.[131] Concurrently mobilization caused the transfer of most of the Moscow garrison. Aroused by reports of growing disorders in Moscow, Catherine proposed to organize a "police corps" which, recruited from servants of the nobility and maintained at their masters' expense, would bolster local security. Either this militia never materialized or it soon lapsed; none existed on the eve of the plague.[132] By 1770, Catherine had not forgotten Moscow's manifold problems, but they did not become urgent until magnified a thousandfold by the plague.

A few Muscovites remained painfully aware of the local perils to health, as evidenced in a petition submitted to the Moscow Policemaster Chancery in October 1770. The petitioners, three prominent residents of the fifth district on the west side of the city outside the Zemlianoi Val—Lieutenant-General Ivan Yurlov, Major-General Prince Elisei Amilakhorov, and first-guild merchant Nikita Bumazhnikov—complained that some nearby slaughter pens were producing "all sorts of exceedingly stenchful air," potentially harmful to public health. The Moscow nakaz, it will be recalled, had recommended the removal of slaughterhouses from the city and the designation of remote areas for the disposal of organic wastes. Evidently this recommendation had not been fully implemented. The petitioners described how dogs and birds fed upon the accumulation of ordure, blood, and entrails, remnants of which bespattered the orchards and kitchen gardens of the neighborhood. The situation had become especially dangerous because "during the present summer season from such stenchful air (God preserve us) and from the aggravated stink our domestics have been subject to extremely frequent illnesses and weakness, and it is to be hoped that a visitor to the city may not receive some infection or harm to his health from the fetid suffocating heat." Citing the police regulations of 1722 that prohibited slaughterhouses in residential areas, the petitioners urged their removal.[133]

On 29 November 1770, the Moscow police obliged the five provincial merchants who operated the slaughterhouse to clean up the filth and to sprinkle it with lime "at the very earliest time and certainly right now without waiting for the winter frosts." They were to cease slaughtering cattle at the site, and the owners were to move the enterprise. This incident apparently prompted the Moscow police, with the approval of Policemaster-General Chicherin, to propose on 16 March 1771, that all slaughterhouses be removed from the city. The reason for their relocation was the filth they caused, "as well as the stenchful smell, from which it is extremely possible that illnesses multiply." A week earlier, in fact, the police had discovered an epidemic in the heart of Moscow. On 13 April 1771, the Moscow chief of police resolved to call in all those who operated slaughterhouses in the city and order them to remove their operations within four weeks. It is not certain whether this order was ever executed.[134]

The slaughter of cattle, no matter how insanitary the conditions it produced, could not cause an epidemic of bubonic plague in Moscow or anywhere else. Still, this case illustrated what filth the city accumulated, filth that would have attracted rodents as well as dogs and vultures. Equally remarkable was the disclosure that the weather in Moscow in October 1770 was summer-like, and that as late as 29 November winter had yet to arrive. Frosts ordinarily appear in Moscow by late September and continuous cold by mid-October.[135] Obviously, the last 4 months of 1770 were extraordinarily mild. Muscovites rightly suspected that disease might accompany such unseasonably warm weather, but they could not know it would be bubonic plague.

PART II

The Course of the Epidemic

CHAPTER FOUR

Origins and Outbreak of the Plague (Spring 1770–Winter 1770/71)

Contemporaries believed that the plague came to Moscow in 1770 from Constantinople through the Danubian Principalities, Poland, and the Ukraine. Nobody may ever know precisely where the epidemic started, for there were several possibilities. Enzootic both in the Balkans and the Middle East, plague frequented those regions well into the nineteenth century.[1] The decades before 1770 recorded nearly annual outbreaks, several of which affected southern Poland and approached Russian territory. Natural foci of plague evidently existed along the Black and the Caspian seas and also in the Caucasus. In theory, plague could originate within Russian borders, arrive by avenues other than the Danubian Principalities, or strike several regions simultaneously from different sources. In practice, covert spread over any great distance would be most unlikely.

That the epidemic began on Ottoman territory seems probable, however, because Constantinople constantly harbored and periodically spread plague. The Ottoman imperial capital and giant emporium suffered outbreaks in 1765 and 1768.[2] Newspaper reports attributed rioting in Constantinople in November 1769 to "the increasing pestilential contagion."[3] Across the Aegean Sea the port of Smyrna, described as "the Magazine of all Asia," sustained plague annually throughout the period 1757–72, the local French consulate classifying seven of those sixteen manifestations as "very severe." Plague raged there from February to October 1769 and doubtless afflicted other Ottoman localities.[4] The Ottoman declaration of war on Russia in October 1768 entailed enormous transfers of men and supplies into Bulgaria and the Danubian Principalities, where the Turks ravaged widely. Early in 1769, the Crimean Tatars raided the Ukrainian steppes, but bitter frosts stopped them short of Elizavetgrad.[5] Either these war-related activities or ordinary commerce could have introduced plague-infected rats and infective fleas into the Danubian Principalities, if they were not there already.

Widespread sickness weakened the huge Ottoman army that slogged northward beyond the Danube and the Dniester in 1768–69. The ill-supplied soldiery ate bread baked from mouldy flour, "black as dirt," from which many died within 10 days. These maladies later turned into the plague, a Turkish official believed.[6] The European press circulated similar accounts. "An epidemical distemper has broke out among the Ottoman troops, which has carried off great numbers of them," maintained a dispatch of 18 February 1769, and a communiqué from Constantinople reiterated that "the change of air and diet, and the badness of the water, has occasioned a great many disorders among the troops, particularly the bloody flux, which carries off a prodigious number of men."[7] Plague might have been among the diseases which, together with the cold, rainy weather that washed out the bridge over the Dniester, forced the Turks to abandon Moldavia in September 1769.[8]

The Russian occupation of Moldavia and Wallachia, in the fall and winter of 1769–70, introduced additional foreign elements into those plague-enzootic regions. Lest the Russian troops be infected by Turkish prisoners or deserters, General Rumiantsev advised General Christopher von Stoffeln, commander of the division in Moldavia, to institute medical inspections. Part of Stoffeln's troops spent the winter in Jassy quartered among the townspeople. Other detachments occupied Bucharest and burned many villages along the Danube. In conjunction with the floods and the early winter, these operations might have disturbed the local ecological equilibrium; foraging and requisitioning activities also multiplied contacts with the local population. Hence the Russian occupation forces inevitably contracted bubonic plague when it appeared that winter. Suspicious cases of disease cropped up in Wallachia at the end of 1769. "From the pestilential distemper no further dangers have been observed," Rumiantsev informed Catherine on 12 January 1770, obviously relieved, "and our troops have entered Focsani as before."[9] So, when foreign gazettes speculated about epidemics among the Russian armies, Catherine denied the story to Voltaire with a jest, and the Russian press denounced it as slanderous provocation.[10]

Whatever the epidemic's point of origin, extraordinary weather conditions facilitated its spread. During these years Europe and the Middle East experienced drastic changes of season: a short summer, early winter, and early spring in 1769–70, a late fall and late spring in 1770–71, and copious rainfall throughout. Floods and famine, epizootics and epidemics resulted from these meteorological disturbances—possibly a product of volcanic dust veils in the atmosphere and intense sunspot activity.[11] Food prices soared throughout central Europe, and outbreaks of ergotism occurred in France and northern Europe.[12] If plague afflicted some Wallachian localities in the summer and fall of 1769, the early winter temporarily arrested broader outbreaks. Just as floods in the fall disrupted the delivery of supplies, so the early spring of 1770 renewed the inundation, the rivers of the Danubian region thawing by late January. Warm, moist weather persisted throughout the spring.[13] All these circumstances revived the previous year's incipient epidemic, which infiltrated Jassy by mid-March.

When the Russian military practitioners first noticed unusual mortality at Jassy, they debated whether it was ordinary "putrid fever" (typhus) or the dread "pestilential distemper." Few had seen plague before, and they were accustomed to meet typhus in such circumstances. Indeed, typhus and other fevers probably were present. Apparently the early victims displayed a misleading melange of symptoms, but showed few buboes, the best-known sign of plague. The medical professionals undoubtedly assumed that panic would ensue should they prematurely declare the malady to be pestilential.

From Jassy on 18 March 1770, Dr. Ivan de Theyls informed Dr. Georg von Asch, at Rumiantsev's headquarters in the Podolian village of Maly Latichev, that he and two local physicians had examined cases of sickness and death among the soldiery and the townsfolk. All three designated the sickness "epidemic putrid malignant fever" and recommended segregating the sick outside the town. They did not term the disease plague, but 2 weeks later Theyls wrote that the town apothecary, his wife, and aunt had all died in March from "the local contagious disease" and that "the dangerous diseases" were continuing.[14] Despite the threat, General von Stoffeln hesitated to leave Jassy, while the Moldavian boyars entreated his protection against the Turks. Fearful that disease might delay the spring campaign, Rumiantsev ordered Stoffeln out on 27 April, the day before the practitioners finally decided it must be plague. When Rumiantsev received the news on 6 May he reported that the practitioners at Jassy, "after reviewing the causes of the sicknesses and of the sudden death of many people, found on them plain signs of this fatal infection." From 25 April through 1 May a total of 43 soldiers and 93 townspeople perished there. New outbreaks were reported near Focsani, in Bucharest, and among some cossacks recently arrived at Khotin.[15]

Plague at Khotin, a big Turkish granary and entrepôt, posed a dual threat, because Rumiantsev made that town the site of his main supply magazines and the chief assembly point for the spring offensive.[16] An epidemic there might confound military operations and follow the supply routes northward. Rumiantsev therefore instituted a cordon on both sides of the Dniester at Khotin to inspect all wayfarers and wares coming from Moldavia. Reassuring Catherine that the epidemic had not reached the empire's borders, he urged similar precautions around Kiev. To resolve doubts about the nature of the disease, Rumiantsev dispatched Dr. Gustav Orraeus to Jassy.[17]

A native of Russian Finland, experienced military physician, and the first Russian citizen to receive an M.D. from the Medical Collegium, Dr. Orraeus found no clear signs of plague at Khotin on 7 May. Two days later in the village of Botosani en route to Jassy, however, Orraeus beheld a devastated community. His own convoy fled at the sight. The local Russian commandant told him that plague had come from Jassy 2 months before and had killed 800 of the 2,000–3,000 population in 6 weeks. The rest had decamped

Map 4 Progress of the plague from Moldavia to Moscow, 1770–71.

to the mountains. One-third of the Russian garrison also had perished, and half that number were still sick. At Jassy on 10 May, Orraeus witnessed further horrors. Half the civilian and military population was sick or dead. Yet no precautions had been taken, for Stoffeln refused to believe in the plague until one of his servants fell ill. Orraeus immediately established separate lazarets for plague victims, for doubtful cases, and for convalescents. He insisted on evacuating the troops from town, which Stoffeln reluctantly ordered on 20 May. The General himself camped at a large vineyard, where his servants soon began to sicken and where, on 29 May, he also died.[18]

Convinced that the disease was plague, Dr. Orraeus briefly described it for the guidance of others. His clinical picture represented the first authoritative account in Russian of its symptoms, a description widely distributed in subsequent months.

> This disease always begins with great pain in the head. At the same time almost everybody infected by it feels nauseated, yet with few does vomiting happen by itself. Soon the sick fall into very great despondency, feel anxious, and have a very great heat, to which delirium is joined with the majority. Buboes and carbuncles sometimes come out from the very beginning of the disease, and in this case the disease does not continue long; yet sometimes they show themselves within 12 to 24 hours, counting from the onset of the disease. On the third, fourth or at most on the fifth day the buboes suppurate or dissolve, while the carbuncles begin to separate themselves from the healthy part, in which cases there is the best hope for recovery or, on the contrary, the sick die. A large part of the sick completely come to their senses several hours before the end, say that they feel better, even go so far as to ask to eat. At death or soon afterwards the places around and on the very buboes and carbuncles become bluish and darken, while under the skin dark spots quickly spread in great profusion. The most powerful infection of this disease proceeds from the dead and particularly from their clothing. But there are many examples that some suddenly die after having incautiously merely lain upon or firmly touched the bed or clothing of the dead. Of our sick infected by the plague, one can calculate that a third recover; but of the local inhabitants, much the greater part die of it, because their relatives in this case immediately abandon them, besides which they do not take any medicine.[19]

Predictably, the epidemic mainly affected the townspeople. The Russian occupation forces suffered less not because they were healthier or cleaner but because they generally lived farther from the local house-rat population and because their sick received at least nursing care. Dr. Orraeus and some Russian surgeons discerned two types of plague, fast and continual, and sought to treat victims with "strengthening" remedies of acidic mineral and vegetable bases. They vetoed bloodletting, mercurial compounds, and traditional antipoison drugs, such as Theriac. They recommended bathing buboes with vinegar, then applying cataplasms of linseed oil and saffron, and advised lancing carbuncles before applying salves. But when the Medical Collegium provided James's Powders, an antimonial nostrum, Asch hesitated to prescribe it until proper dosage could be determined.[20]

To protect the field army, which crossed the Dniester at Khotin during the second week of May, Asch instructed the regimental surgeons to segregate the troops from the civilian population and warned against any contact with persons, livestock, or merchandise from "suspect places." Field surgeons stationed at outposts were to have vinegar, gunpowder, and sulphur on hand for the fumigation of dispatches, which should be handled with tongs while being purified. As a preventive, the troops should take spirits of vitriol mixed in their drink. "If it happens, God save us," concluded Asch's instructions, "that a person sick from pestilence with a bubo, spots, [or] carbuncles approaches an outpost, he should be ordered to retire without delay and told that, if he does not withdraw quickly, then he will be shot. But in case such a sick man does appear, it must be reported immediately."[21] Dr. Asch still hoped the epidemic would not prove to be pestilential, but Orraeus's reports from Jassy soon disabused him of that notion. On 23 May, Asch informed the Medical Collegium that plague was raging in Moldavia and demanded at least 6 more doctors, 10 surgeons, and 20 surgeon's mates.[22] Perhaps Asch's precautions helped shield Rumiantsev's field forces from infection, but armies on the march have little to fear from plague. Indeed, while the epidemic filtered northward, Rumiantsev won dazzling victories at the battles of Larga and Kagul on 7 and 21 July, respectively.[23]

If the field army largely escaped the plague, its garrisons and supply services did not. The sanitary cordon around Khotin could not prevent an outbreak there in late May that exhibited the same puzzling character as at Jassy. On 10 June fatal cases of spotted fever began appearing at the main field hospital. Plague with buboes, boils, stripes, and carbuncles followed 6 days later, afflicting 200 of the 1,702 patients. Dr. Maksim Baranovich and staff-surgeon Christian Grave informed Asch on 26 June of the critical situation at the Khotin field hospital. The sick "had especially severe pain in the head, anguish in the heart, lost their minds, became delirious, and ran about; and those who were very anguished and lost their minds, they also lost their lives; for those who, after the severe headache and anxiety, a bubo or dark spot appeared, they sometimes still had a hope to be healthy again." The practitioners separated the sick from the healthy, sending the former to a special camp where surgeon Karl Argilandr treated them. The dead were buried in their clothing in graves 7 feet deep. Nevertheless, the epidemic continued to spread, which Baranovich and Grave blamed on the widespread pilferage of the effects of plague victims. Panic reigned at Khotin. Those assigned to convey the sick to the isolation camp sometimes abandoned them en route, "so that it's impossible to know who died from where." The surgeons at the field hospital remained healthy, but half the surgeon's mates were ill. Baranovich and Grave complained that the sick at Khotin were poorly fed, owing to an ineffective contract with the Jewish merchant Wolf; thus "misfortune is multiplying misfortune."[24]

This last report hinted at the plague's four primary means of transmission. First, it followed the army's supply system, which operated through contracts with magnates and merchants.[25] Rats and fleas could easily hide in and feed upon grain shipments, or in the gunny sacks of returning empty wagons. As early as 29 June Rumiantsev reported plague in the Polish localities of Bar and Brailov, the site of Russian supply depots, where several Jews died and others were sick.[26] Indeed, plague ravaged southeastern Poland, striking some 47 towns and 275 villages. Some contemporaries estimated the death toll as high as 300,000, but that inflated figure must include deaths from all causes as well as thousands of fugitives from civil war, famine, and floods.[27] Still, certain localities suffered heavily. Vinnitsa and its environs lost 382 Christians and 146 Jews to plague in 1770–71, and about twice as many in 1772. In the Polish Ukraine, several "wizards" were executed or exiled for allegedly inciting pestilence or failing to ward it off.[28] Second, in any given locality the plague spread epizootically.

The third mode of spreading the disease was in the personal effects of travelers, refugees, troops, and prisoners. In the Danubian Principalities, the native population frequently abandoned their homes to avoid the infection. No doubt many slipped past the cordons that Rumiantsev hastily instituted in May. Refugees allegedly carried the plague into Transylvania, where 18 villages were hit. Of 1,624 recorded sick, 1,204 perished.[29] Russian troops evidently propagated the infection by looting the effects of the dead and taking such booty home or selling it to local peddlers or campfollowers. Moreover, once the First Army began to maneuver, in June and July, the number of sick and wounded rapidly increased. Rumiantsev lost over 11,000 of his 40,000 men to disease in 1770. Many were sent to Khotin and thence into southern Poland and the Ukraine, the same route taken by the plague.[30]

The fourth method of conveying the disease was ordinary commerce, which continued between the Danubian Principalities and their northern neighbors, despite the wartime conditions. As Asch's instructions of 17 May demonstrated, the medical authorities particularly feared raw wool, cotton, and hides as potential "plague goods." The cordon guards on the Dniester and along the Moldavian-Polish-Ukrainian border were instructed to inspect and fumigate all cargoes from the southwest. But it is one thing to proclaim a sanitary cordon, quite another to enforce one. Some merchants and smugglers must have circumvented the checkpoints, bribed their way past them, or reached Russian territory even before the cordons were activated. Austria and Prussia also set up sanitary cordons, encroaching on Polish territory in the process. Vienna, Berlin, Warsaw, and Danzig all anxiously followed the epidemic. Sweden, Denmark, and Britain instituted precautions too. Fortunately for north-central Europe, the plague moved eastward instead, probably deflected more by cool weather than by cordons.[31]

Catherine first mentioned the epidemic on 25 May 1770, when she approved Rumiantsev's countermeasures and urged him to continue military operations.[32] Although the Empress withheld precautions on Russian territory, the peril to the army caused her to dispatch the empire's foremost authority on plague—Dr. Johann Lerche. A Prussian from Potsdam, Dr.

Lerche (M.D., Halle, 1730) had served in Russia nearly forty years and had distinguished himself during the plague of 1738–39. Before his appointment as Petersburg city-physician in 1763, he had held high posts in the Medical Chancery and assisted in the formation of the Medical Collegium. Catherine personally promoted him to collegial councilor, the sixth rank, in 1764 for squelching an epidemic in Finland. Dr. Lerche left Petersburg posthaste on 28 May 1770.[33]

Overtaking the Second Army on 20 June as it moved to besiege Bender, Dr. Lerche detected no trace of plague and approved General Panin's orders to isolate the troops from the local population, most of which had fled anyway. When the army began siege operations in mid-July, however, several deaths with plague symptoms occurred. The victims were not regular soldiers, but a woman—either a local inhabitant or a campfollower—and several cossack auxiliaries who had plundered local habitations. Panin at once banned Wallachians from his camp and moved the civilian sector further away from the troops. Advised that the cossacks had carried the disease to Khotin in May, Panin and Lerche segregated the entire cossack regiment. No further victims were reported. Plague may well have been enzootic around Bender or have regularly arrived there in grain shipments. The locality suffered frequent outbreaks up to the mid-1760s. But plague did not interrupt the bloody siege of 1770, which captured the fortress on 16 September.[34]

Dr. Lerche left Bender on 12 August for Jassy, where he found the plague over by 18 August. Since 18 May some 1,500 sick had entered the pesthouse; only 150 remained, and most of the others had died. Losses among the native population could not be determined, because so many had fled. Dr. Lerche rode into Khotin on 28 August. The epidemic had largely ceased there too, but continued among some soldiers loading winter uniforms at the supply magazines, which had not been aired since the plague began. These cases offered further evidence, as Lerche recognized, that the epidemic was following the army's supply lines.[35]

Weather conditions favorable to plague continued as well. An avid meteorologist, Dr. Lerche recorded weather data wherever he went. His observations confirmed that the summer of 1770 was consistently warm and wet. June had eighteen rainy days, a high of 85° F., and a mean of 66°. While Lerche was at Bender from 14 July to 12 August, it rained almost daily and the thermometer reached 89°, with a mean of 68° for the entire period. At Jassy in late August, the temperature hit 95° amid frequent showers. The heat declined at Khotin in September, with a high of only 55° F. for the month, but half the days were rainy.[36] As Lerche traveled toward Kiev in early October, he noted that the roads had dried, "while we still had beautiful warm autumn days."[37]

The mortality from plague was somewhat lower at Khotin than at Jassy, probably because the town was smaller and the Russian garrison had left sooner. Nevertheless, several army practitioners died there, and on 10 August staff-surgeon Grave reported the death of Dr. Baranovich "after a four-day fever with spots."[38] Ill and exhausted himself, the fifty-nine-year-old Grave requested leave to retire, having served in the military corps for 38 years. His medical colleagues certified his ailments: chronic nephritis, cramps, arthritis, shortness of breath, headache, and "profound hypochondria." Rumiantsev and Asch endorsed Grave's plea on 30 August, and he arrived in Petersburg on 10 December to petition the Medical Collegium for discharge and a pension. While processing Grave's petition, the collegium authorized him to attend to his domestic affairs in Moscow. The Medical Collegium formally discharged Grave on 5 January 1771, recommending that the War Collegium award him a pension, but the military authorities rejected the request on grounds that they had no orders to provide such pensions.[39] Barely 2 months after retirement, Grave would fight plague again, this time in Moscow.

Grave's experience illustrated the pressures Russian medical professionals encountered during the plague and the Russo-Turkish war. Some broke under the strain. Many died. In fact, Asch attributed the death of at least 15 to plague between March and August 1770.[40] Worried about the plague's advance, Asch sent copies of his instructions of 17 May to Dr. Sila Mitrofanov at the field hospital in Kiev and described plague symptoms for his brother Peter, a physician in private practice in Moscow.[41]

Not only doctors on the scene feared the epidemic's mobility. From Khar'kov in mid-June, Governor Evdokim Shcherbinin informed Catherine of rumors that plague had crossed the Dniester. He instituted a cordon across the Zaporozhian steppe and asked the senate to send one doctor and sufficient surgical personnel.[42] A month later Lord Cathcart, the British ambassador, heard that the army had avoided the "Epidemical Distemper" and commented that "it would indeed be very unfortunate if the same disorder were according to reports to extend itself to other Territorys."[43] Similar speculation appeared in the European press. "There is no doubt of every precaution being taken to prevent the spread of that distemper," declared a communiqué of 4 August from Vienna, "but it is apprehended that it will hardly be possible to keep it out of Poland on account of the troubles in that kingdom, which will render all the precautions made use of on such occasions abortive." And the same commentator predicted: "The Russian armies will likewise find it very difficult to escape this distemper, on account of the indispensable communication which the carrying of provisions occasions."[44] By contrast, the official Russian press reprinted accounts of the plague's ravages in the Ottoman Empire, while remaining silent, until late 1770, about its spread into Poland.[45]

These rumors and reports finally goaded Catherine into instituting precautions along the southwestern frontier. Her confidential directive of 27 August informed the governor-general of Kiev that "infectious fevers" in the Danubian Principalities had penetrated Polish territory and might afflict the army besieging Bender. The authorities at Kiev should establish quarantines "without great publicity" so as not to provoke "untimely vain uneasiness in the public."[46] But before these orders reached Kiev, even before they were written, plague infested the city.

Plague at the *Podol* and in the Ukraine

In striking Kiev and its hinterland in 1770–71, the plague foreshadowed events in Moscow. It catalyzed nearly identical reactions in both cities, the main differences stemming from Kiev's smaller size and the plague's shorter visitation. A city of about 20,000 people, Kiev guarded the Polish border and functioned in 1769–70 as the principal staging area within the empire for the Turkish campaign. Large military magazines and a big field hospital were located there. Like Jassy and Khotin, Kiev was at once a fortress, a riverine city, an inland port, a transportation hub, and a marketing center. A few small silk-weaving enterprises constituted the only local industry, but most of the civilian population engaged in crafts and commerce. The many cathedrals, monasteries, shrines, and seminaries attracted flocks of Orthodox pilgrims and students from eastern Europe and the Balkans. Built largely of wood, Kiev consisted of 3 separate sections: the old upper city, the Pecherskaia Fortress, and the *Podol.* The civilian population and commercial activities were concentrated in the *Podol,* literally "the bottomland," a notoriously dirty and dense heap of small wooden houses and shops crouched along the low-lying bank of the Dnieper River. The upper city, enclosed by a wall, overlooked the *Podol* from heights stretching back from the river. On a bluff 2 miles away, the Pecherskaia Fortress and suburbs quartered the garrison, the guberniia chancery, the field hospital, and the main grain magazine.[47]

Kiev was no more unified administratively than physically. The governor-general and the guberniia chancery supervised the city and its environs in theory only. In practice, an elected municipal council and prefect (*voit*) administered the merchant-burgher community; Church authorities managed the numerous ecclesiastical institutions, which controlled large tracts inside and outside the city; and various commanders oversaw the garrison, the reserves and recruits for the field armies, the supply depots, and the field hospital. Wartime conditions and Kiev's frontier situation further muddled lines of authority and overlapping jurisdictions. Consequently, nobody in authority noticed the plague when it quietly arrived in mid-summer 1770.[48]

By early July, *Y. pestis* entered Kiev the same way that it crossed southern Poland, presumably in the goods and baggage of merchants, troops, refugees, or travelers. The opening of the spring campaign had occasioned greatly increased traffic between Russia, the Ukraine, and southern Poland, multiplying the carriers and avenues that might bring infected rodents and infective fleas across the lengthy Russo-Polish border. Wagons and packhorses could traverse the 300 miles from Khotin in 4 to 6 weeks. As the pestilential agents rode northward, they touched off outbreaks in Polish villages, so that when Dr. Lerche traveled from Khotin to Kiev in early October he heard reports of plague all along the way.[49] Furthermore, the weather in Kiev that summer and fall offered ideal conditions for the propagation of plague. Mild temperatures, winds from the south, and ample rainfall prevailed until Christmas.[50] The Dnieper only froze solid on 8 January 1771.[51]

At Kiev, the epidemic developed slowly and surreptitiously, just as it had elsewhere. Bunge, the local apothecary, remembered that in August 1770, before anybody in Kiev suspected plague, "a malignant putrid fever with petechiae" erupted, and the presence of plague was "notorious" by 1 September, the date from which the local authorities later calculated the death toll.[52] Nevertheless, Governor-General Fedor Voeikov only acknowledged the danger on 9 September.[53] This sequence of events repeated the start of the outbreaks at Jassy and Khotin. When suspicious cases occurred among the civilian population, Kiev's few military practitioners failed to detect them for several weeks and then argued whether the malady was really plague.[54] Fearing to incite panic, disrupt the military campaign, and paralyze commerce, the city administration delayed reporting in hopes that the epidemic would prove to be a false alarm. Equally fearful and poorly informed about the plague's spread into Poland, the Petersburg authorities provided no forewarning. Many doubted that plague could appear so far north at that late season. The same doubts and fears would reappear in Moscow.

The Kiev authorities finally became alarmed on 2 September when three persons suddenly died with fever and spots in a house in the *Podol.* The next day somebody in another house succumbed with the same symptoms and, when similar victims appeared nearby, Dr. Mitrofanov and Dr. Poletika concluded by 7 September that it must be plague. Nobody knew how the disease got to Kiev. Whatever the specific source of the disease, the dense merchant-burgher population of the *Podol* suggested that trade was the means of introduction; while its cramped wooden housing and low-lying, riverfront location made the community an ideal receptor. The houses were so close together that the infected ones could not be burned, as standard practice prescribed. Belatedly aroused, the authorities on 7 September sent Dr. Mitrofanov with one surgeon and 50 soldiers to seal off the *Podol.* They established a lazaret outside town for the infected and a quarantine station on an island in the Dnieper for doubtful cases.[55]

These countermeasures seemed successful at first. Voeikov wrote Catherine on 11 September that the disease, confined to the *Podol,* was already diminishing; on 28 September he relayed Dr. Mitrofanov's assurances that no more than 50 persons had died in the *Podol* of all causes and that the epidemic there would soon end. Since no daily mortality figures have been found for the outbreak at Kiev, either these optimistic reports sought to allay fears, or the epidemic suddenly exploded in early October. Bunge recalled that 110 persons died in a single day at the height of the epidemic, apparently in late October or early November.[56]

If the chaotic administration of Kiev obstructed timely detection of the epidemic, its paltry medical resources compounded the confusion. Ambiguous symptoms, lack of medical assistance, concealment of the stricken, and Dr. Mitrofanov's own inexperience probably caused him to underestimate the death toll. When Dr. Lerche arrived in Kiev on 13 October, he found that while most of the sick presented buboes and petechiae, many also died without markings within 24 hours.[57] Sporadic cases of septicemic plague would have been exceptionally difficult to diagnose at the start of the epidemic, as twentieth-century experience has confirmed. The lone physician in Kiev before Lerche's arrival (Dr. Poletika's duties kept him at Vasil'kov most of the time), Dr. Mitrofanov had little assistance. One staff-surgeon, 4 surgeons, a few surgeon's mates, barbers, and surgical students were all the medical cadres available. Several were old and sick; one died at the end of October.[58] The rapidly intensifying epidemic quickly overwhelmed Kiev's medical resources. Focusing upon the outbreak at the *Podol,* Mitrofanov and Voeikov discovered cases in the upper city by 12 September and around the Pecherskaia Fortress a week later. Panic drove hundreds of people from the city. To avoid being sent to the pesthouses and quarantines, where people were dying en masse, many inhabitants secretly buried their dead in courtyards and gardens. Soon the authorities found 10 to 20 corpses on the streets every day. People were dumping the dead at night, it was assumed, to conceal where the plague had struck.[59]

On 3 October Voeikov admitted that plague had enveloped the city. The cordon had failed to contain the initial outbreak, he explained, either because of the upper town's proximity to the *Podol* or because of clandestine intercourse between the inhabitants, whose "deep simplicity and stubborness" made them scorn precautions. Neither the nobility nor the wealthier merchantry had contracted the disease, which claimed all its victims among the common people.[60] To be sure, Voeikov did not mention that the nobility and merchantry had largely fled. Contrary to Voeikov's explanation, the interval between the outbreak in the *Podol* and those elsewhere doubtless mirrored the gradual progress of the rat epizootic. No matter how vigilantly the cordon guards interdicted human movement within the city, rats and fleas spread the disease unmolested. Perhaps too, the constant military and civilian traffic imported plague into the different sections of Kiev at different times.

The death toll continued to climb even after Dr. Lerche's arrival on 13 October. Kiev began to disintegrate. At the height of the plague, in late October or early November, a crowd accosted the municipal administration, threatening violence unless the quarantine regulations were relaxed. The protestors were pacified, however, by promises to cease sending people to the island quarantine and to relocate it in a suburban monastery. Perhaps a fortuitous decline in mortality calmed this explosive situation, for a hard frost chilled the city on 5-15 November.[61] Less than a year later similar circumstances in Moscow would provoke bloody riots. During the time of maximum peril, incidentally, Voeikov left Kiev for a nearby village, where he stayed about 10 days, returning by 23 November.[62] Fortunately for him, his absence coincided with the plague's abatement, or so he informed Petersburg. The next year a briefer absence amid more desperate circumstances would cost the governor-general of Moscow his career.

The plague in Kiev receded in December and ended by early January 1771, which recorded a low temperature of −20° F.[63] Total mortality from the pestilence, officially reported as 3,180, included 1,565 males and 1,615 females. Dr. Lerche remarked that children and pregnant women had been especially susceptible. In terms of social and juridical categories, 892 victims were military servitors and their dependents, 61 were clergy and churchmen, whereas 2,229 were townspeople, cossacks, and *raznochintsy.* The *Podol* and the Pecherskaia Fortress shared the bulk of the victims, with 1,175 and 1,546 dead, respectively; the upper town lost only 461. These totals reflected the greater population density and the economic preeminence of Kiev's commercial and military sections. By contrast, when plague resurged the following summer it caused a total of 449 fatalities, 367 in the Pecherskaia Fortress. Contemporaries believed that the city lost 4,000 to 6,000 dead to plague in 1770-71, but these figures counted many refugees. In May 1771, the prefect of Kiev reported that more than 500 presumed plague victims had since returned in good health.[64]

Plague struck the hinterland at the same time as the city. Dr. Lerche thought that refugees from Kiev, seminary students in particular, infected the countryside.[65] If some did, they were not the main progenitors; the epidemic spread gradually, conveyed by commerce and rodents as much as by refugees. For example, 2 men and 4 women died suddenly at the Roslovitskoi mill on 22 September 1770. Mills were highly vulnerable because of their attraction for rodents and their contacts with other localities. Plague raged in the village of Zhiliany from 1 October to 9 November 1770, killing 101 persons. Here the disease exhibited its characteristic household incidence in claiming a priest, his wife, mother-in-law, and daughter.[66] At the village of Voitovka, the sudden mortality made people suspect a local Uniate priest of sorcery. Denunciations by the priest's wife and cook incited a mob that beat him senseless and then buried him alive.[67] Many communities in Kiev guberniia experienced the epidemic; statistics collected in 1772 attributed a total of 2,819 deaths to plague in 1770-71.[68]

The news of plague at Kiev provoked consternation in St. Petersburg on 19 September. That very day Catherine dispatched couriers with orders to institute a cordon around the Ukraine. To safeguard Petersburg from the epidemic's advancing due north, Dr. Christian Pecken, an experienced member of the Medical Collegium, left to organize quarantines in the

Smolensk region.[69] Special precautions were taken at Riga too, where Governor-General Georg von Browne forbade the frontier guards to admit "Jews from abroad, in whom great danger subsists," expelled all Jews from the city until the plague ended in Poland, and advised the Kurland authorities to do the same.[70] Jews were suspected of spreading plague because of their involvement in the cloth and rag trade. Although the Duke of Kurland also ordered all Jews to leave temporarily, gentry resistance apparently delayed compliance and provoked Russian threats to execute the order by military force. Not all Jews were expelled, for Catherine personally allowed one Benjamin Beyer to stay in Mitau. In any event, Petersburg's fears for the Baltic Provinces soon subsided. On 1 October, Catherine informed Browne that the cool fall season made quarantines unnecessary at the ports of Livland, and on 12 October she approved his withholding the border quarantines so as not to halt commerce.[71]

From 21 September onward, the Empress's council, a conclave of 7 statesmen charged to coordinate policies related to the Turkish war, assumed responsibility for the antiplague campaign. To stop the epidemic at Kiev, they ordered Voeikov to dismantle or burn infected houses, arrange for mail to bypass Kiev, and insure that nobody pass through or leave the city without medical inspection.[72] To Voeikov's colleague in Glukhov, Major-General Prince Platon Meshcherskii, Catherine's decree of 19 September called for bolstering the cordon along the Polish frontier and closing the border temporarily. The Empress dispatched two surgeons to assist Meshcherskii.[73]

Upon receiving Catherine's instructions on 27 September, General Meshcherskii made an inspection tour toward the Polish border. From Nezhin on 25 October he relayed mixed news. The "infectious diseases" in Poland were declining with the onset of cold weather, but on 14 October plague was reported at Pereiaslav, near Kiev. A local cossack who worked in Kiev died suddenly at home, followed the next day by his four-year-old son with the same symptoms. Alarmed, the Pereiaslav authorities removed the family from town and burned their house and belongings. Meshcherskii dispatched a fusilier captain with orders to close the town. He also directed Dr. Paulsohn in Glukhov to assist Pereiaslav and headed that way himself. In Nezhin on 20 October, however, Meshcherskii got word that only one more member of the afflicted family had died in quarantine. Meanwhile, at the nearby hamlet of Skoptsy 4 persons died within 5 days after brief illnesses. Although the examining surgeon thought the victims died of fever, troops surrounded Skoptsy and confined the families of the dead to a quarantine, where 2 more perished.[74]

More worrisome were cases in Chernigov on 21 October and in Kozelets on the 23rd, which showed the epidemic following the main routes northward. Meshcherskii urgently requested more medical assistance. There were but 5 surgeons in the whole of Malorossiia guberniia, he lamented, one of whom was ill and another blind from old age. Only one of the 2 surgeons sent from

Petersburg had arrived; the other had fallen ill before departure. Other towns desperately needed practitioners too; "because of their deficiency not only is there nobody to give aid in necessary cases, but there is nobody to recognize the details of the sickness."[75] By the end of October, no new cases occurred in the four afflicted localities except for Chernigov, where one appeared on 19 October and where 10 of those in quarantine died within a week.[76]

Even before Catherine read these dispatches she resolved to send a special representative to the Ukraine. She chose Major of the Life Guards Mikhail Shipov, a protégé of her favorite, Grigorii Orlov, and a participant in her seizure of the throne. Entrusting deputies with special commissions was a well-tested device of government to cope with emergencies. Frequently it also manifested the sovereign's dissatisfaction with local officialdom, as Catherine's instructions made clear. She told Shipov he should coordinate the antiplague policies, insuring that all traffic from Poland underwent the established quarantine and medical inspection. Recruits sent to Kiev for assignment to the field armies must not enter the town, but stay in nearby villages before going directly to the front. General Efim Sievers, in charge of recruiting and supply operations in Kiev, should carefully regulate the distribution of uniforms and munitions. If plague threatened any supply depots, shipments should be suspended at once and the suspect magazines sealed.[77]

Major Shipov arrived in the Ukraine at the end of November 1770 and conferred with Voeikov and Sievers at the village of Brovary. They agreed to strengthen the cordons. Responding to pleas for more medical assistance, the Medical Collegium in December sent 4 surgeons and 3 newly promoted surgeon's mates. A month later Catherine assigned 6 more surgeons to Major Shipov. The plague demonstrated as never before the urgent need for medical professionals in the newly incorporated southern territories. Major Shipov stayed in the Ukraine nearly 4 years directing efforts against scattered outbreaks of disease.[78] Just as he reinforced the cordon around Kiev, however, the plague reached Moscow.

Plague at the Vvedenskie Hills

At the end of August, Catherine confessed that "the condition of Moscow disturbs me greatly, for besides sickness and fires, there is much stupidity there."[79] On 19 September she directed Governor-General Saltykov of Moscow to establish a checkpoint at the river crossing at Serpukhov, where a surgeon should examine and fumigate everybody arriving from the Ukraine. A week later Saltykov reported dispatching a Guards captain and company of soldiers along with the surgeon.[80] Hardly had this cordon been ordered than it was violated. On 4 October the voevoda chancery in Kashira, about 30 miles east of Serpukhov on the Oka River and 70 miles south of Moscow, separately interrogated two peasants without passports who had recently come from Kiev. "Both in the upper town in Kiev, and the *Podol*," they declared, "as well as in all the other suburbs a pestilential distemper is really afflicting the people, and it began this year from the middle of the month of July, and it appears on a person in various places as dark and red spots equal in size to a *poltinnik* [half-ruble coin about the size of a U.S. fifty-cent piece] or less: whoever receives a dark spot dies, while from the red they recover." This testimony showed how the plague looked to ordinary people and suggested that some in Kiev perceived it long before the authorities did. The men were not sick then, and they said they had not been. While traveling northward to visit relatives, they had been refused lodging if they said they came from Kiev, so they began telling people they were from Nezhin.[81]

This report convinced Saltykov, who forwarded it to Catherine on 11 October, that for some time people had been fleeing northward from Kiev. Fugitive recruits and refugees were conveying goods and other effects away from impested localities without hindrance. To interdict such movement, Saltykov proposed a whole cordon of checkpoints in the towns of Moscow guberniia, but regretted the lack of personnel to staff the enterprise. On 8 November he wrote Catherine that plague had hit Sevsk and was approaching Moscow guberniia. Since the epidemic might spread further with the hordes of prisoners daily arriving from the south, Saltykov reiterated the need for medical inspection on all roads leading to Moscow.[82] The outbreak at Sevsk, about 250 miles south of Moscow, involved a steward and his family from Kiev, and 2 members of a merchant household that gave them lodging. Eight persons died there between 25 October and 11 November. Seventy miles closer to Moscow, the town of Briansk and the community of Kozel sustained an outbreak even earlier, losing 8 persons to infection from 6 October to 16 November. Disease hit the Briansk Postdrivers Community later but harder, 32 persons dying there in 6 weeks, from 1 November to 16 December.[83] This last instance hinted again that the plague followed the commercial routes northward to the empire's commercial-industrial capital.

Increasingly dismayed at the plague's relentless advance, Catherine on 14 November sent Saltykov 6 Guards officers to head a broader cordon on the southwestern border of Moscow guberniia. These checkpoints and quarantines were to be manned by one surgeon and several soldiers, supplemented by shifts of sentries recruited from the local population. Saltykov began implementing the scheme on 23 November. The surgeons received detailed, secret instructions from the Moscow city-physician on 22 November enjoining them to be alert for spotted fever, buboes, and carbuncles.[84]

Events soon exposed the cordon's porosity. On 13 December, Saltykov reported that the Moscow police had halted 2 Greek merchants and one Russian steward bringing textiles from Nezhin. None had any proof of having been inspected along the way, so Saltykov concluded that they had taken secondary roads around checkpoints. He proposed to quarantine the mer-

Figure 5 Portrait of Catherine II in about 1765, engraving by W. Dickinson from the painting by Ericksen in the collection of Baron Thomas Dimsdale. Reproduced in I. N. Bozherianov, *Nevskii Prospekt* (St. Petersburg, 1901), 1:176–77.

Figure 6 Portrait of Field Marshal Count Peter Semenovich Saltykov (1698–1772), governor-general of Moscow during the plague. Reproduced in V. P. Nikiforov and A. V. Pomarnatskii, *A. V. Suvorov i ego sovremenniki* (Leningrad, 1964), K-228.

chants and to burn their goods as having come from "the most dangerous places." This incident elicited a police order of 17 December forbidding the sale of all Turkish goods in Moscow. Once again, all the authorities' good intentions were in vain. Saltykov reported an epidemic in Moscow on 22 December 1770.[85]

Just as happened at Jassy, Khotin, and Kiev, plague stole into Moscow imperceptibly. The huge city's teeming population, sprawling layout, and thriving commerce guaranteed that a few more deaths would hardly be noticed. Plague bacilli must have entered Moscow no later than early November. By mid-November (allowing 2 weeks for a rat epizootic to develop) suspicious disease began appearing among attendants of the General Infantry Hospital, housed in the wooden annex at the Vvedenskie Hills about a mile from the main hospital. Meanwhile, Moscow basked in a prolonged Indian summer, the latest weather anomaly of a year that saw public prayers for rain in May and again for clear weather in July.[86] The petition of several Muscovites against slaughterhouses cited summer-like weather in October and frosts had yet to arrive at the end of November. Winter would not keep the plague out of Moscow.

Most likely, *Y. pestis* entered Moscow in raw wool and silk from Ottoman territory, as many contemporaries came to believe.[87] Several circumstances support this possibility. The cordon established to protect Moscow guberniia in October, and strengthened in November, did not regulate all movement of people and goods, as the incidents with the refugees from Kiev and with the Greek merchants demonstrated. It must have been even less effective earlier. Most of Moscow's flourishing textile industry depended upon imported materials and consisted of small spinning and weaving operations conducted in suburban residences. The Vvedenskie Hills contained textile enterprises, as did the adjacent suburbs along the Yauza.[88] The hospital attendants and their families might have come in contact with infected raw textiles at the nearby workshops, which probably employed some of the womenfolk. In fact, someone might have been weaving silk in their crowded, wooden, and presumably rat-infested communal residences. Among the articles found there and subsequently burned were 8 pounds of raw silk.[89]

Whatever the source of disease at the Vvedenskie Hills, the city authorities only learned of it a month after the fact. Such delay recalled earlier phases of the epidemic elsewhere. The disease emerged sporadically in an isolated subgroup of suburban society; its limited incidence and confusing symptoms made practitioners and officials hesitant to believe it was really plague. Moreover, conflicts of jurisdiction and of personality deepened the confusion.

Sometime in mid-December, Dr. Afanasii Shafonskii, senior physician at the Moscow General Infantry Hospital, discovered unusual symptoms—high fever with "large spots, carbuncles, and buboes"—among the hospital attendants at the Vvedenskie Hills annex. Inasmuch as most of the stricken soon died and their cohabitors began to sicken, Dr. Shafonskii segregated the sick and asked Dr. Andrei Rinder, the Moscow city-physician, to review the matter in consultation with the other physicians. Rinder twice visited the site, examined the sick, and approved the precautions already taken. He did not think the malady was plague, however, and did not report it. Neither did General Andrei Famintsyn, the military inspector of the hospital, with whom Dr. Shafonskii was on bad terms because of his petty tyrannies and constant interference in professional affairs. Meanwhile, Shafonskii closed the hospital premises to outsiders. When 3 more attendants developed similar symptoms and quickly perished, Shafonskii informed Rinder in writing on 21 December that since 18 November as many as 10 attendants had died with alarming symptoms. He demanded that the other doctors in Moscow convene forthwith to identify the disease. In response, Dr. Rinder ordered the other physicians to assemble that afternoon.[90]

While the physicians arranged to meet, the police got wind of the affair. On 20 December, a dead body was found in the ninth district near the General Infantry Hospital. Evidently the corpse bore no unusual signs, but as the law required a post-mortem in such cases, the district police officer, Captain Moltrekh, conveyed the body to the General Infantry Hospital, which he found closed. Moltrekh informed his superior, Chief of Police Nikolai Bakhmetev, who told him to find out why the hospital had been shut. The following day police inquiries disclosed rumors of unusual mortality at the hospital. When Captain Moltrekh interviewed Shafonskii, the doctor confirmed the epidemic. Two more attendants had died that very day, he admitted, with signs of infection. Captain Moltrekh told Bakhmetev, who immediately summoned General Famintsyn for an explanation. But the General professed to know nothing of the matter and even suggested it might be false. Bakhmetev then personally visited Dr. Shafonskii, who had just informed the Medical Office, and learned that since 17 November 14 persons had died with suspicious symptoms and 2 more lay dangerously ill. The dead had been buried with lime under 7 feet of earth. Just back from showing Prince Henry of Prussia around the suburban estate of Kuskovo, Governor-General Saltykov received Bakhmetev's report of these developments on 22 December, the same day the doctors met to consider the epidemic.[91]

In answer to Dr. Rinder's summons of 21 December, 8 physicians rode out with him to the General Infantry Hospital the next day to hear Shafonskii's description of the disease, which he cautiously termed a "foul, putrid, infectious fever." Three of the consulting physicians confirmed Shafonskii's diagnosis, apparently after examining the sick. Though none had seen plague in recent years, they signed a statement proclaiming that the disease must be considered pestilential. Their recommendations were to isolate the hospital from the rest of the city and to place Dr. Shafonskii in charge of antiplague measures there. This report was signed by all 8 physicians.[92] But Dr. Rinder neither signed their report nor accepted their identification of the disease. He "pronounced it to be merely a putrid fever; an opinion which he maintained both in conversation and in writing."[93] Thus began a lengthy, sporadic debate that divided the Moscow medical community.

Saltykov forwarded these reports to Catherine on 22 December and began implementing the doctors' suggestions. Three days later he wrote the Empress that troops had sealed off the hospital and the annex. Having isolated the infected site, he forecast a quick end to the outbreak. He rejected Dr. Mertens's idea of interdicting all access to Moscow as both unnecessary and impracticable. Too many goods, foodstuffs, and munitions had to pass through Moscow to maintain commerce, provision the city, and supply the armed forces; the metropolis simply could not be quarantined from the rest of the empire.[94]

Quarantine did not become necessary, for this initial eruption soon abated, almost certainly because winter belatedly chilled Moscow at the end of December. On 4 January 1771, Saltykov reported all well at the hospital and in the city. He ordered all practitioners to report any cases of sickness, describing their symptoms, and Archbishop Amvrosii enjoined the clergy not to bury anyone without police certification of the cause of death. General Famintsyn had still not explained his failure to alert the authorities sooner. Famintsyn mentioned, however, that during the last thaw many Muscovites had suffered from various fevers, some of them accompanied by spots, as well as bronchial complaints and other ordinary diseases.[95] It is not clear what season Famintsyn meant, whether the spring of 1770 or some later thaw, perhaps in the late fall or early winter following brief frosts. Saltykov's own dispatches of early 1771 indicated that continuous cold had only recently arrived, and he attributed much of the epidemic's decline to that fact.[96] Dr. Mertens recalled that "the cold had set in later this year than usual; the weather was very damp and rainy until the end of December, when a hard frost came on, and continued through the remainder of the winter."[97] South of Moscow in the country, Andrei Bolotov bewailed the autumn of 1770 as "a very bad and inconstant one": snows, thaws, rains, and frosts alternated throughout November and crippled travel by carriage or sleigh.[98] Modern knowledge of the behavior of the flea carriers of *Y. pestis* confirms the likelihood of cold weather causing a plague epidemic to wane, whereas the unusually late winter of 1770–71 and the warm, moist conditions that preceded it clarify why the disease could reach so far north at such a late season.

By 15 January 1771, Saltykov reported the end of the epidemic at the Vvedenskie Hills. Twenty-seven persons in all contracted the disease, of whom only 5 survived. Saltykov's knowledge came secondhand, he admitted. Except for Dr. Shafonskii and two surgeon's mates confined to the hospital, none of the other practitioners had observed the epidemic firsthand. Even Dr. Rinder consulted with Shafonskii from a distance across a bonfire, for which reticence the latter rebuked him. Shafonskii accused Rinder of failing to clarify the nature of the disease at its height. Once it was over, he complained, there was nothing to see and nobody to question. Saltykov assured Catherine that the checkpoints around Moscow were functioning as ordered, and that many persons were arriving on leave from the army. The danger seemed past. "Winter has set in pretty well, which helps a lot; spring is dangerous in such a huge city [where] the building is cramped, there are many horses, from which there is manure and all sorts of filth; it wouldn't be bad when spring comes for people to leave for their estates."[99] Three weeks later, on 7 February, Saltykov reaffirmed the end of the threat. As further precautions, with the approach of spring, he wished to remove all sick persons to monasteries outside town and to expel all vagrants. In this same dispatch, Saltykov sent Catherine accounts of the epidemic compiled, at his request, by Shafonskii and Rinder. "Although these are not very agreeable among themselves," Saltykov understated, "still they are not without doubt."[100]

Rinder vs. Shafonskii

The initial appearance of plague in Moldavia and the Ukraine confused the local medical practitioners, few of whom had ever seen the disease. Dr. Lerche, the acknowledged plague expert, arrived only after the epidemic declared its character. Rinder and Shafonskii reopened the debate in the aftermath of the Moscow outbreak. Their debate exhibited divergent conceptions of plague that produced contradictory analyses and practical advice which, contemporaries believed, yielded fatal consequences. Employing hindsight and fallacious assumptions about bubonic plague, contemporaries, and later Russian commentators, derided Rinder's willful ignorance and lauded Shafonskii's foresight.[101] Perhaps their debate involved more than divergent views of plague; professional jealousy may have excited personal antagonism. At any rate, their careers before 1771 followed opposite patterns that amounted to a generation gap.

Fifty-six years old, Andrei Andreevich Rinder (1714–71) was a russified German born Franz Andreas Rinder, the son of a clergyman near Nuremberg, who earned his M.D. at tiny Altdorf University in 1736, shortly before entering Russian service. He spent 28 years as the single doctor in remote Orenburg guberniia and headed Orenburg's new hospital. During those decades Rinder lost his first wife, remarried, and fathered a son. Professionally, he fought various epidemics, studied local plant resources, and gained permission in 1764 to examine surgical apprentices for promotion to surgeon's mates. Weary of frontier life, Rinder secured the lucrative post of Moscow city-physician and director of the Medical Office in 1765. His new financial security provided a house for 1,000 rubles in a fashionable neighborhood of Zemlianoi Gorod. In 1769, his son Yakov, an "Orenburg native of the Russian nation," received a state scholarship for medical study at

Strasbourg, where he earned the M.D. in 1778. After decades of drudgery in obscurity Dr. Rinder had just begun to enjoy some professional status.[102]

At age thirty, by comparison, Afanasii Filimonovich Shafonskii (1740–1811) had already achieved extraordinary professional standing as an exemplar of the new contingent of Slavic doctors. The son of a Ukrainian cossack official, who sent him abroad for university training in 1756, he earned degrees in law from Halle, philosophy from Leyden, and medicine from Strasbourg. Upon returning to Russia in 1763, Shafonskii served as physician for the foreign colonists along the lower Volga, then briefly as chief field doctor with the army, before becoming senior doctor of the Moscow General Infantry Hospital at the end of 1769.[103] His career looked as rapid and easy as Rinder's had been slow and tortuous. One may speculate that with so little in common the young, cosmopolitan Ukrainian and the elderly russified German would have little sympathy for each other's views on any subject, much less for allegations of negligence in the detection of plague on the premises of Shafonskii's hospital on the outskirts of Rinder's municipal jurisdiction.

On 27 January, Dr. Rinder gave Saltykov his appraisal of the outbreak at the Vvedenskie Hills annex. Even though his conclusions proved erroneous, he recorded revealing information about the plague's arrival. He denied that the epidemic had really been pestilential, reasoning that plague could not originate in a northern situation like Moscow's, but must be imported from the south. Rinder found no evidence of such importation. Moreover, he doubted that the disease had been highly infectious. Thus, attendant Afanasii Strigin fell ill with fever on 12 December. On the fourth day of Strigin's illness, while hospitalized in the main (brick) building, he developed carbuncles and black spots near the elbow and on the nape of the neck. On the sixth day, he died, along with his wife, who had been suffering from high fever without external marks. Nevertheless, the 80 other patients in their ward remained free of infection. "*And so this* single circumstance sufficiently proves that this disease cannot be acknowledged as the real pestilential distemper."[104] Rinder erred, of course, in supposing that plague spreads directly from person to person and in assuming that the sick attendant contracted the disease at the main hospital, where no epidemic ever developed.

In addition, Rinder inadvertently offered evidence that the disease was not confined to the hospital annex.

> Recently I was obliged to examine in one eminent house a woman who had a high fever and, with it, carbuncles on one arm and leg: although the woman died of this disease, still I could not acknowledge her as a case of the pestilential distemper; inasmuch as she did not infect the other people found in that room, which would certainly have occurred had the carbuncles been of that sort, but now the aforementioned house to this day, thanks be to God, has been free of all infections.[105]

If, on the contrary, this incident actually involved plague, then it pointed to cases elsewhere in Moscow by mid-January 1771.

The symptoms of the disease also struck Rinder as unlike plague, just as they had puzzled other observers.[106] He had not seen a case firsthand for many years; therefore, like most of his contemporaries and most physicians in the twentieth century, he had to rely on textbook descriptions. Rinder found neither the buboes nor the carbuncles to be infectious, remarking that both symptoms might signify venereal disease, bedsores, or mumps. Here one should recall the diverse preliminary diagnoses of the 7 cases in New Mexico in the 1960s. "A foul, putrid and infectious fever," the disease could not be plague above all, Rinder concluded, because only 20 of the 25 persons afflicted had died within the span of a month; true plague would have killed more people much faster, many in a day or two. He concurred with continued precautions at the hospital annex, but thought the main hospital might safely reopen, since no cases had occurred there for more than 40 days.

Rinder speculated that the infection had originated from substandard housing conditions. Both the infected structures were one-room dormitories: low, cramped, filthy, stuffy, and crowded (about 25 persons per room). Such conditions could easily spoil the air and corrupt the blood, thereby causing an epidemic. Fear of plague would have worsened matters. Besides, "at the beginning of the sickness the necessary supervision was neglected, and treatment might also have helped." These last remarks were obvious jibes at Dr. Shafonskii and General Famintsyn. Rinder also criticized the fumigatory fires that Catherine had prescribed. Because "the air in Moscow and around it is good, healthy, pure and not filled with any contagious vapors," the pyres merely alarmed the public unnecessarily when danger was already past.[107]

Rinder's views disclosed one variant of the dominant miasmatico-contagionist theory of epidemic disease. He thought plague originated from a miasma which, once it enveloped a locality, then spread by interpersonal contact. Perhaps inspired by the myth of Moscow's clean air in the wintertime, he reasoned that natural conditions militated against the development of a generalized miasma, whereas the behavior of the malady showed it did not spread easily or widely. Much of Rinder's explanation seems reasonable even now. Yet he did not closely observe the course of the brief epidemic, nor did he correlate its behavior with the preceding unusual weather.

Although Dr. Shafonskii believed in the same miasmatico-contagionist theory, on 5 February he handed Saltykov a refutation of Rinder's report, based on close observation. Buboes, carbuncles, and petechiae were not sufficient to confirm a diagnosis of plague, he admitted; but when they appeared in conjunction with very high mortality—more than half the sick dying within 6 days—when they afflicted healthy persons nearby, and when plague raged in neighboring areas, then one should suspect the worst. All these conditions held true for the outbreak at the Vvedenskie Hills, which Shafonskii recounted in detail. He disputed Rinder's contention that the disease could not have reached the hospital annex from outside. The attendants lived "in an open place," Shafonskii remarked, "and both egress for them and access to them by various people were always open, so that it could happen that something infected reached them." He believed that 2 soldiers from Khotin, who visited the attendants in November 1770, must have sold them something contaminated.[108]

Shafonskii questioned Rinder's attempt to minimize the scope of the epidemic. Its incidence should be measured not in terms of the entire hospital, he urged, but only in relation to the 2 infected barracks, where more than half of the residents had perished. Concerning the attendant treated at the main hospital, Shafonskii suggested that his case had not provoked others because of the precautions taken. He rejected Rinder's picture of confusing symptoms, noting that bedsores do not occur in the groin. Venereal disease may cause buboes, he admitted, but they are not usually accompanied by high fever and other symptoms; besides, many of the stricken were too young to be suspected of venereal disease. Nor did Shafonskii accept Rinder's linkage of the outbreak to housing conditions. Other attendants lived in similar quarters, he observed, but contracted no infectious disease.[109] Here Shafonskii scored a telling point. The miasmatic hypothesis could not account satisfactorily for spatial irregularity in the generation or distribution of plague.[110]

Shafonskii also recommended reopening the main hospital and maintaining precautions at the annex. Those attendants still sick should be transferred to the Vvedenskie Hills to avoid the possibility of their causing a recurrence of the epidemic at the main hospital. The moist air of springtime might be dangerous, "for in warm weather perhaps the contagion will renew itself."[111] If the plague had disappeared entirely, this debate would have remained purely theoretical, but Shafonskii's worst apprehensions would be confirmed sooner than anyone suspected.

CHAPTER FIVE

Official Negligence, Medical Incompetence, or Another False Alarm? (January–May 1771)

The disease at the Vvedenskie Hills annex baffled officials in Petersburg as much as it did the physicians and people of Moscow. In response, the imperial government publicly announced precautions for all of European Russia and, mindful of the plague's possible revival, investigated additional countermeasures. Still, the abrupt subsidence and limited incidence of the outbreak combined with the onset of intense cold to muffle most apprehensions. Like Dr. Rinder, many wondered whether plague had caused the alarm in the first place. So when disease stealthily revived in Moscow in early 1771 nobody discerned the fact until it became too menacing to ignore or conceal. Extra alarming as a result, this second outbreak galvanized frantic reactions in Moscow and Petersburg, reactions that energized broader precautions under new administrative and medical leadership. The disease and the weather continued their eccentric behavior, however, regenerating controversy in both capitals.

Confirmation of the epidemic at the Vvedenskie Hills reached Petersburg by 27 December 1770, when the council approved Saltykov's recently instituted precautions and recommended further safeguards for the rest of the empire, Petersburg especially. An empire-wide announcement should urge people to adopt the countermeasures that the government had begun implementing covertly 4 months earlier. On 30 December, Count Nikita Panin reviewed the proposed proclamation, which the council endorsed and Catherine signed the following day. Printed on 3 January 1771, the imperial proclamation was distributed to all government and Church institutions for announcement to the public.[1]

Catherine's proclamation exploded the previous policy of silence and secrecy, but glided over obvious contradictions. Blaming "the brutish and negligent Turks" for spreading the "infectious pestilential distemper," the Empress recounted how plague had ravaged Polish territory "for some time past" and "had been about to burst through Our borders as well; but through quick countermeasures and the Lord's mercy it is already being quickly curtailed everywhere." To reinforce the cordon from the Ukraine to Livland, Catherine prohibited the import of clothing and personal apparel from the Danubian Principalities and Poland. Wayfarers could enter the empire only at designated places, on pain of confiscation of their goods and exemplary punishment as trespassers. These restrictions would protect the empire, the proclamation concluded, so that neither cupidity nor ignorance would cause anybody to become "a betrayer of the Fatherland" and "an author of general misfortune."[2]

Anyone reading between the lines of this pronouncement must have suspected that plague had already invaded. Many certainly knew about the ravages in the Ukraine and the threat to Moscow guberniia. On 9 January, the senate therefore publicly admitted that infection had crossed the Polish border, reaffirmed the ban on textile imports from Poland, and acknowledged the cordon protecting Moscow guberniia. Three days later, moreover, the senate informed all governors that owing to plague in the southern guberniias, they must ensure that "the evil not spread into the very bosom of Russia and its capital cities." Wherever pestilence appeared, the authorities should isolate the locality, burn infected houses and furnishings, and kill dogs and cats; "for this pernicious distemper spreads more from contact with infected bodies and articles than from the air, as has been proved by many experiences." None of these pronouncements cited the outbreak in Moscow, doubtless in the hope that it had already ended, as Saltykov reported on 15 January.[3]

In Petersburg, the foreign embassies soon got wind of the alarm. Police in the capital had recently charged all householders to report sickness immediately, the Austrian *chargé d'affaires* observed on 24 December, forwarding unconfirmed reports of plague in the army and around Moscow. A week later he confirmed the Moscow outbreak, then noted on 7 January that the scare was waning. The French envoy heard about plague in Moscow by 31 December and a week later forecast that it might cause the Russians to moderate their peace terms with the Turks.[4]

As before, neither of the official gazettes acknowledged plague anywhere in the empire. Both intermittently reported the end of the epidemic in Poland and the continuing eruptions in Turkey.[5] For foreign consumption the imperial government waxed optimistic. "The Apprehensions of Plague being in the Army at Bender, or in the Ukraine, are at an End," proclaimed a dispatch from Petersburg to the *London Gazette* in late January. "That fatal Distemper never reached either of those Places. What gave Rise to the Report was, that a Spotted Fever raged in several Places, which had the Appearance of the Plague." A month later the Russian ambassador in London announced that "there is not (thank God) the least Appearance of any infectious Distemper, either in Moscow, Livonia, Estonia, Ingria, or in the adjacent Provinces; and. . .the Measures taken to prevent its being introduced into them, leave not the least Reason to apprehend, in future, any Danger from it." The foreign press generally explained the plague's demise by the extraordinarily severe winter in northern Europe. Navigation into the Baltic, for example, remained closed as late as 20 April; "it has not been known to be so long shut up since the Year 1740."[6]

While publicly radiating optimism at the start of 1771, Catherine privately appreciated the possibility of plague's recrudescing in the springtime. To counter that eventuality, on 6 January she delegated senators Volkov and Teplov to draft a comprehensive statute of antiepidemic precautions. Their inquiry quickly revealed both the shortcomings of previous Russian legislation and the difficulties of adapting foreign antiplague institutions. "The expanse of your empire is unparalleled by all other Christian powers," they informed Catherine. "Nor do its towns, villages, and hamlets bear great similarity to the towns and communities of other lands. Its borders are contiguous for a huge distance with lands in which the pestilential distemper occurs extremely often." Therefore, Volkov and Teplov recommended a threefold defense against plague: a permanent system of border quarantines, precautions in case an epidemic threatened from abroad, and emergency measures to combat actual outbreaks. To design these institutions they suggested study of the Austrian sanitary cordon against Turkey and of the maritime quarantines of Venice, Holland, and England. They also requested assistance from state councilor Timofei von Klingshtet and Dr. Christian Pecken, presumably because both had firsthand knowledge of European antiplague procedures.[7]

This initiative could not produce a sanitary statute immediately, but it assembled ideas and principles that shaped Russian policies in 1771 and after. Among the materials collected was a Russian translation of an unsigned memorial, apparently submitted by a south Slav officer in Russian service who had witnessed plague in Dalmatia in 1764–65. The author probably composed his recommendations in the fall of 1770, for he mentioned rumors of plague at Kiev. Accordingly, he advocated a cordon along the Dnieper, described the workings of quarantines, and stressed the danger of transmission by money and paper. Nationwide prayers for deliverance from pestilence would serve a dual purpose, inspiring the people and informing them how to behave. "If the infection has already increased greatly," the author confided, "then it is not necessary to allow residents out of their own house; for this disease is communicated like the smallpox by touch and by contact, and it never, as some fools claim, subsists either in the air or in food, as one may say about many kinds of fevers and bloody fluxes."[8] Unfortunately, the isolation measures that helped against smallpox had little effect upon plague.

Although Dr. Pecken was not recalled from Smolensk, someone presented in German a 12-point program that advocated public acknowledgement of plague, reasoning that secrecy would impede countermeasures. Border quarantines should rebuff anybody from suspect places. In the capitals and large towns, the police should register foreigners immediately, reporting severe illness forthwith. People should lay in supplies for 6 months and dispatch superfluous servants to the country, in order to lessen crowding "in cramped rooms and in enclosed air, as the spread of infectious diseases is greatly increased thereby, and to avert them later, when such diseases have already become established, will be too late." Medical cadres should be temporarily increased to inspect the sick immediately and to report weekly to the police. Quarantines should be prepared outside towns. Travelers to the interior must carry bills of health, and couriers from the army should undergo special precautions.[9] Combining foreign norms and Russian tradition, this program reiterated many of the precautions already instituted. Of course, effective precautions presumed efficient administration, public cooperation, and clear identification of plague.

If these administrative preparations gradually allayed Petersburg's concern, Catherine still monitored the situation in Moscow throughout January and February. To block reinfection from the Ukraine, the Empress suggested that Saltykov limit entry to a few main roads, turning back persons without loads. She proposed more bonfires of juniper and other aromatic substances. Through police officials Catherine asked Dr. Mertens about instituting at the General Infantry Hospital the "cool regimen" that Dimsdale used for smallpox inoculations. She also demanded to know why General Famintsyn had not reported the epidemic sooner. (Whatever Famintsyn's explanation—perhaps he blamed his enemy Dr. Shafonskii—he kept his post at the hospital.) Saltykov should cultivate public confidence, Catherine urged: "God's mercy for us is great; we must firmly rely on His omnipotent and manifest bounties, so that this sword will pass without smiting us." On 31 January, the Moscow police received authorization to build quarantines outside town, but construction had not yet begun a month later when Bakhmetev visited Petersburg to confirm the epidemic's end.[10]

Naturally, the rapid disappearance of disease from the hospital annex augured well. On 22 February, Catherine approved ending the quarantine of the main hospital and burning the two wooden barracks at the Vvedenskie Hills, but she rejected Saltykov's proposal to remove everybody hospitalized in Moscow to monasteries outside town. The Empress believed there were too few practitioners to scatter patients far and wide. Saltykov executed Catherine's orders on 28 February and reported all secure on 7 March, inquiring whether the spring livestock drives from the Ukraine should undergo quarantine.[11]

As anxiety melted in Moscow, however, Petersburg harkened to alarms in the south. The past year's experience finally convinced the Medical Collegium that the empire faced genuine plague.[12] So when doctors Dahl, Francia, and Rozhalin dismissed plague-like symptoms at Kremenchug and near Elizavetgrad in late 1770 and early 1771 as "sporadic distemper," the

Medical Collegium rejected this euphemism and ordered immediate precautions.[13] Subsequent reports must have reinforced the collegium's new-found convictions. From Kremenchug on 9 March, Dr. Sava Gorgoli, a Greek from Nezhin (M.D., Halle, 1763), lambasted the gullibility of his medical colleagues and the obstructionism of the commandant for denying the local existence of plague. Stained and singed from being dipped in vinegar and passed over flames, Gorgoli's report accused the local field surgeons of willful obfuscation, of calling carbuncles, for example, "anthraces" (i.e., stripes). He later denounced the Kremenchug authorities for falsifying diagnoses to hide pestilential symptoms.[14] Such incidents impressed greater vigilance upon the Petersburg authorities as spring approached. In contrast to the concurrent debate in Moscow between Rinder and Shafonskii, incidentally, Gorgoli's tribulations showed that a practitioner's ethnic origin bore scant relation to his success or failure in diagnosing plague.

Erratic weather heralded the rediscovery of pestilence in Moscow. Just as the late winter of 1770–71 facilitated the plague's arrival, so a slight thaw in late February and early March presaged its resurgence. At Kiev, for example, Dr. Lerche recorded a high of 58° F. on 7 February, and his assistant in Petersburg witnessed temperatures above freezing on seven of the first ten days of March. The winter weakened in Moscow, too, after a blizzard postponed the Foundling Home's benefit lottery on 27 January.[15] "As presently the summer season is approaching," Governor Yushkov proposed on 9 March to ban in Moscow guberniia the traditional practice of burying unclaimed corpses once yearly in a common grave, "so that from those dead bodies there not be bad air and danger therefrom."[16] That same day the police discovered unusual mortality in central Moscow.

Infection at the Big Woolen Court

The new epidemic unleashed intense anxiety because it followed so soon after the first outbreak and because its location directly menaced the whole city. Furthermore, it implicated the textile industry and recalled events at the hospital annex by eluding discovery for reasons that smacked of incompetence or connivance on the part of industrial administrators and medical examiners alike. Thus, without alerting the city authorities, Dr. Rinder and staff-surgeon Friedrich Roeslein inspected the Big Woolen Court as early as 30 January. Roeslein revisited the manufactory on 1 March and the operators called in surgical operator Heinrich Engel on 7 March, but none of these inspectors reported any deaths or unusual symptoms and Rinder kept their findings to himself.[17] Moreover, although the Collegium of Manufactures, on 10 February, ordered all manufactory operators to report any sickness among their employees, nobody mentioned disease at Moscow's largest enterprise.

Eventually rumor took wing. On 2 March, the collegium cryptically demanded that the Big Woolen Court report immediately—"for a certain need tomorrow"—how many persons resided at the manufactory and how many lived outside in their own homes or rented quarters. Only 4 days later did Il'ia Dokuchaev and his partners submit the information. Office records listed a total of 2,528 workers and dependents: 730 living at the mill, 1,516 in hired lodgings in town, and 282 in their own dwellings. The operators cited neither sickness nor death among these people, and the collegium did not comment upon their delay in responding or take any immediate action. All these inspections and inquiries appeared strangely shortsighted, if not criminally negligent, when the police summoned Dr. Kas'ian Yagel'skii to the Big Woolen Court on 9 March.[18]

At first the stewards and workers answered Dr. Yagel'skii's inquiries reluctantly, professing to have kept no tally of sickness or death. Office records disclosed, however, that since 1 January at least 113 persons employed or residing at the manufactory had died; 16 others were presently sick there. Mortality had recently worsened, the workers admitted, with 3 to 7 victims each day, most of whom expired within a span of four days from fever accompanied by dark spots and, on many, pustules. Yagel'skii himself observed similar symptoms on an unburied corpse. Of the 16 persons then ill at the manufactory, moreover, Yagel'skii found that more than half had contracted a "putrid fever" with spots, some as large as a silver ruble (about the size of a U.S. silver dollar). One woman in bed with high fever had buboes on both thighs. Another had a painful swelling in the armpit.

The workers blamed the disease on the Christmas visit of a sick woman, apparently also a textile worker, related to the wife of their fellow employee Aleksei Ostaf'ev. Afflicted with a swelling below the throat, the visitor soon died and her hostess succumbed shortly afterward. The dead visitor formerly resided in the parish of St. Nicholas in Kobylsk, in the ninth district, at the house of the church caretaker. Investigation later confirmed that everybody in the house had died. That parish was located just across the Yauza from the General Infantry Hospital and embraced at least one registered textile manufactory. But nobody discerned the possible link between textile-working in the suburbs and the new outbreak. Indeed, despite Yagel'skii's findings, he declined to name the disease without consulting other practitioners, but he told the police it must be considered dangerous. The police quietly isolated the manufactory on the night of 9–10 March.[19]

Dr. Yagel'skii's discovery provoked suspicion and recrimination as to how an epidemic in central Moscow could go undetected for more than 2 months when extraordinary vigilance was supposedly in force. Inasmuch as Dr. Rinder was responsible for public health, tardy recognition of the disease compromised his competence and credibility. Furthermore, the previously unreported medical inspections and industrial inquiries pointed to bureaucratic inertia, faulty coordination, and high-level connections as in-

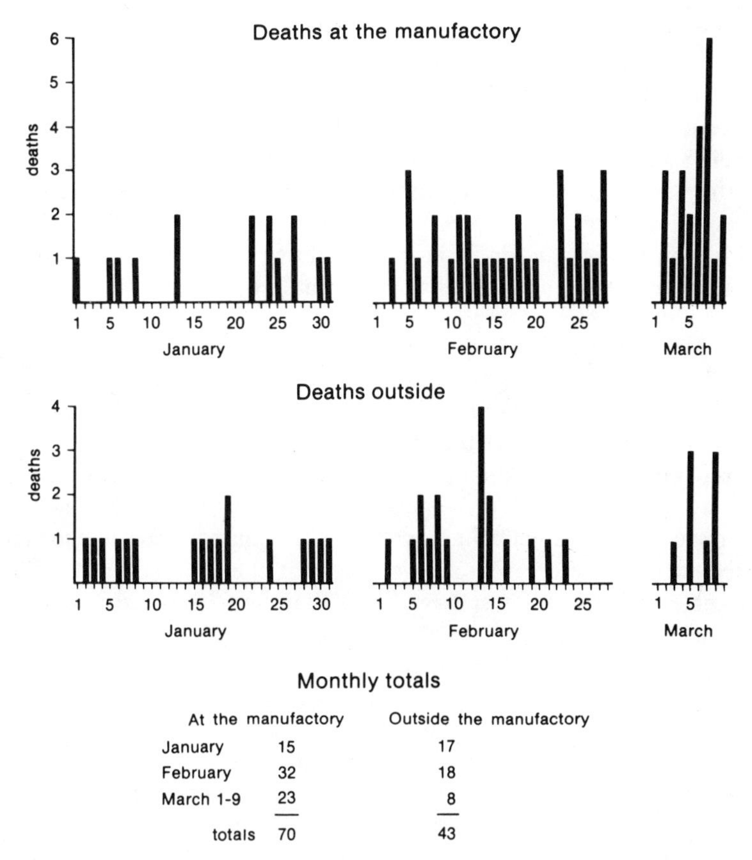

	At the manufactory	Outside the manufactory
January	15	17
February	32	18
March 1-9	23	8
totals	70	43

Graph 1 Deaths of persons attached to the Big Woolen Court, 1 January–9 March 1771. (*Source:* TsGADA, f. 277, op. 12, d. 488: 8–16.)

stitutional culprits behind the failure to uncover the epidemic sooner. Several factors mitigated Rinder's own culpability. The operators and workers obviously concealed the rising mortality which, by their own admission, became manifest by late February. Apparently the disease exhibited confusing symptoms at the start, just as it had done elsewhere in the previous year. Finally, "a gangrenous ulcer on the leg" incapacitated Rinder at the end of February, just as the disease flared forth. His illness and death (from plague?) on 21 April 1771, left the medical community leaderless at a critical moment.[20]

Circumstances other than human failure may partly explain the authorities' late perception of the epidemic. Tabulation of the 113 deaths through 9 March (graph 1) reveals a gradual rise in mortality, nearly 40 percent of the victims perishing outside the manufactory. Scattered deaths among the families of the many workers who lived outside the Big Woolen Court would not necessarily implicate the huge mill itself. Few of the victims were obviously related. Ivan Fedorov, a weaver, lost an eight-month-old son on 10 January and a ten-year-old daughter on 30 January. The burial of both bodies "in the field" suggested that their afflictions looked infectious. Four children of the deceased Efim Drozdov all died within 5 weeks of each other, between 8 January and 13 February. All were buried at the Church of St. John the Baptist on Volkhonka Street, directly across the river from the Big Woolen Court. Another weaver, Egor Skorniakov, succumbed on 3 January and his grown son, Ivan, on 28 January. Both were interred at the Church of the Annunciation of the Most Holy Virgin in Berezhki, on the western edge of Zemlianoi Gorod.[21]

If the 43 victims outside the manufactory were buried where they resided (as can be confirmed for Egor Skorniakov), then one can understand why the operators might not learn of their deaths for some time.[22] Multiple deaths in a few families would have seemed routine, too, inasmuch as many of the victims were children or infants, the fraction of the population with the highest death rate at all times. Had the death toll outside the manufactory become known sooner, it need not have provoked commotion, for it betrayed no marked increase before March. Considering, then, that the Big Woolen Court held jurisdiction over nearly 1,800 persons living throughout the metropolis, 43 deaths spread irregularly over 3 months hardly betokened plague as commonly conceived at the time.

By contrast, the spiraling death rate on the premises of the Big Woolen Court demanded a different explanation. Clearly, the 15 deaths there in January exceeded the norm, prompting the inspection by Rinder and Roeslein on 30 January. Yet the mortality happened so sporadically, as graph 1 shows, that no more than 2 persons perished on any day in January and no more than 3 in February. Only in late February did the daily toll become consistently high. For the whole period since 1 January, however, the abnormal death rate doubled and redoubled, removing nearly 10 percent of the mill's residents by 10 March. The sharp rise in mortality after 22 February, with 34 deaths recorded through 9 March, probably reflected the temporary thaw that accelerated the rat epizootic.

Compared to the scattered deaths outside, the mortality at the Big Woolen Court also displayed a much clearer familial incidence. Working and living together amid the crowded, rat-infested conditions compounded the chances of infection for the manufactory's 730 residents. Carpenter Dmitrii Ostaf'ev, for instance, lost his wife and one daughter on 11–12 February. Possibly they were related to the Ostaf'evs who hosted the sick woman thought to have introduced the disease. On 23 February, three Grigor'ev boys, evidently brothers, all died. Two worked at loom no. 40 and one at no. 42. Evdokeia Grigor'eva, perhaps their grandmother, succumbed on 9 March. Closely related to the Grigor'evs' fate was the death on 14 February of Akilima Alekseeva, who worked at loom no. 42. Her husband Grigorii, a comber at no. 40, expired on 28 February, and 2 of their daughters died on 7 March. Two other Alekseevs perished on 3 and 9 March, respectively, but their surname was so common that one may not presume a relation of kinship.[23]

Even so, given the crowded conditions at the manufactory, surprisingly few of its residents contracted the infection. People usually expected higher death rates among manufactory workers because of their poor living and working conditions, as well as their generally "intemperate" conduct. Indeed, retired General Peter Panin speculated that it might not be plague, "but the fevers which occur among these filthy and impudent people living and working in a great throng, having infected the air in cramped rooms, might have turned into putrid and infectious ones with spots."[24] Thus it required 2 months of erratically rising mortality, culminating in multiple daily deaths over 2 weeks, to demonstrate an epidemic at the Big Woolen Court.

Apprised of Dr. Yagel'skii's findings, Governor-General Saltykov directed the Medical Office to investigate. On 11 March, doctors Erasmus, Shafonskii, Shkiadan, and Pogoretskii accompanied Yagel'skii back to the manufactory, where they examined 8 dead and 21 sick. Since Yagel'skii's first visit, 10 more persons had died at the mill, 2 of them in the physicians' presence. If the most recent deaths came from among the 16 sick whom Yagel'skii saw on 9 March, then about 15 new cases had appeared within 2 days. Both the sick and the dead exhibited dark spots of various dimensions and swellings behind the knee, below the collarbone, under the arm, in the navel and the groin. Some of those without external marks were hot, delirious, and prostrated; others complained of headache, anguish, nausea, and diarrhea. One worker noted that the the dead had perished within one to 7 days, falling ill in various rooms among the healthy.[25]

That evening a medical consilium convened to appraise the threat. Joining the 5 physicians who had visited the manufactory were doctors Mertens, Veniaminov, Zybelin, and Lado, the last of whom had recently arrived in Moscow. Illness prevented Rinder, Kuhlemann, and Asch from attending. Dr. Yagel'skii summarized the situation: since 2 March 32 persons had died at the Big Woolen Court, 17 others were sick there, and 10 had perished outside. All agreed that they were facing an epidemic, but nobody specifically connected it to the earlier outbreak. Nonetheless, they knew how quickly that alarm had subsided and what confusion it had triggered. "This disease is a putrescent, communicable, and infectious one," they informed Saltykov, "and from several symptoms and circumstances, very closely resembles the pestilential distemper."[26] In short, the doctors hesitated to label it plague.

If the medical consilium puzzled over the origin and identity of the disease, it unanimously advocated immediate, stringent precautions. Everybody at the Big Woolen Court should be removed from the city and the manufactory sealed with all its contents; the sick should be separated from the healthy, and both should receive medical attention. A search should be made for other cases and they should be removed as well. The dead should be buried outside town in deep graves in their clothes. Whatever the disease was, it should be treated as plague.[27]

That same day Saltykov also received recommendations from the Collegium of Manufactures. Fedor Sukin, the collegium's officious vice-president, complained that nobody had alerted his agency to the trouble; he conveniently forgot his own inquiry of 2 March. Apprehending danger from closure of the mill, Sukin wondered who would oversee the 668 persons then locked inside. There might also be danger from the sick, who had been taken to a brick building adjacent to the old Kamer Collegium and the spirits warehouse, "where there is a great throng of people." If the epidemic spread, Sukin urged evacuating the sick and their belongings to a quarantine outside the city. In the event that hundreds of workers were confined to the mill, no shortage of subsistence could be allowed, "in order that this multitude, being subjected to danger and finding itself in one place without work or supervision, not undertake some audacity when, even without that, these folk are with difficulty restrained from a dissolute life." Strict quarantine measures, as the cameralist thinker Justi commented, could incite hunger and unemployment that might endanger public order more than plague itself.[28] This dilemma vexed the Russian authorities throughout 1771.

On 12 March, Saltykov presented all these proposals to the senate, which quickly designated the Ugreshskii Monastery in the suburbs as a pesthouse for the sick and Sitnikov's empty manufactory as a quarantine for healthy persons from the Big Woolen Court. The senate directed the police, the Collegium of Manufactures, and the Medical Office to cooperate in containing the epidemic on the basis of the precautions announced in January. With grave foreboding, Saltykov dispatched a courier on 13 March to tell Catherine the baleful news.[29]

Emergency Evacuation and Investigation

The city authorities rushed to execute the senate directives of 12 March. Their initial efforts faltered, however, from a lack of vigorous leadership and of clear medical guidance. After discussing the situation with Saltykov on 13 March, Peter Panin lamented that "this old man," ill-informed and incoherent, "has already declined in vital powers" just when a clear head and firm hand were essential to preserve order in an unruly metropolis that contained but a single, widely dispersed regiment of troops.[30] Seventy-one years old, Saltykov sorely missed Chief of Police Bakhmetev, who returned from Petersburg only on 22 March. In the interim, the police and the Collegium of Manufactures fumbled over who was responsible for what. Neither agency possessed the manpower or the experience necessary to manage a complicated city-wide emergency. Nevertheless, they hastily prepared to evacuate the Big Woolen Court, ordering that quarantine facilities in the suburbs be fenced. Inside the manufactory, stewards recorded those present and soaked the list in vinegar before handing it out to a police officer who, after drying the paper in smoke, initiated the evacuation.[31] This census disclosed more than 600 persons at the mill—twice as many as Sitnikov's house could accommodate—so the authorities commandeered Balashov's empty manufactory in the suburbs east of the Yauza. On 13 March, the Collegium of Manufactures charged the operators to provide everything for the quarantine, including 15 barrels of lime, 20 shovels, and "four hooks for dragging the dead to burial."[32]

That night the police quietly evacuated the Big Woolen Court. Nine soldiers and 6 stewards remained behind to fumigate and guard the premises, blocking some underground passages from the manufactory to the riverbank. These passageways and the preevacuation census convinced the authorities that some clothworkers had evaded removal. The day after the evacuation, in fact, the police caught 30 fugitives from the manufactory, all of whom were consigned to the Balashov quarantine. Of the 730 persons who resided at the Big Woolen Court on 1 January 1771, about 90 had died there by 14 March, when 533 went into quarantine and 27 entered the pesthouse. So at least 80 former residents remained at large, besides those living outside who had visited there before the epidemic had been discovered and the enterprise closed. It was feared that these people might infect the rest of the city. Although the senate decreed medical inspection of everybody attached to the manufactory, this could not be accomplished at once because nobody knew the addresses of the 1,800 workers and dependents who lived outside the mill. The district police therefore began canvassing their bailiwicks on 14 March in search of vagrant clothworkers and to learn the whereabouts of everybody connected with the stricken manufactory.[33]

This task became more urgent as dangerous cases appeared elsewhere. In the fourth district on the western edge of Moscow, for example, police inspection discovered two apprentices from the Big Woolen Court who, married to sisters, lived with their wives and mother-in-law in the same house. Matrena Matveeva, the wife of one apprentice, had left the manufactory on 9 March and suddenly sickened on 12 March. Dr. Yagel'skii found her prostrated, vomiting, and delirious. Small spots appeared the next day. The doctor foretold larger spots and the police quoted his conclusion: "it is possible without doubt to think that this sickness of hers is of the same kind as that which occurred at the manufactory, and in order that this evil not afflict her other relatives and not spread from them over the city (God preserve us), he demands that both the sick woman and her household relatives be separated from the city inhabitants right away." Simultaneously, word arrived from the sixth district, in the northwestern section of Zemlianoi Gorod, that on 11 March a sick man from one Saltykov's household had approached a barrier-guard asking to be taken to the police station. He died while being driven there. The corpse showed many small dark spots, "somewhat larger than with ordinary fever," Dr. Yagel'skii reported. Police in the twelfth district, which embraced the eastern half of Zamoskvorech'e, reported the sudden death of Vasilii Mikhailov, a house-serf belonging to Yakov Khitrovo. Residing at the house of a soldier's widow, Mikhailov perished soon after returning from his master's on 11 March. The deceased had been sick with a fever for several days, Dr. Yagel'skii discovered, "and therefore very small spots are found on the body, such as are usual in several fevers."[34]

Presenting these cases to the senate on the evening of 14 March, the police and the Collegium of Manufactures complained that the Medical Office had not yet sent practitioners to inspect the stricken. Dr. Yagel'skii alone could not continue making rounds night and day. The local authorities also requested guidance in handling apparently healthy persons at infected houses. Should the healthy be left alone in such cases, or should everybody in a stricken dwelling be removed to a quarantine, as Yagel'skii urged?[35] So long as there were few cases, this issue seemed secondary, but once many large houses became infected it took on crucial importance and disrupted popular cooperation with local administrative action, undermining public order.

The Moscow authorities believed that their precautions required professional medical guidance to be effective. Yet the Medical Office had apparently ignored the epidemic for weeks, still hesitated to identify the disease, and seemed reluctant to mobilize against the threat. Only on 15 March did Dr. Rinder assign surgeons Margraf and Val, with 2 apprentices each, to supervise the Ugreshskii pesthouse and the Sitnikov quarantine. Rinder excused his failure to discover the disease and to attend the consilium of 11 March; he had, he declared, already ordered 3 doctors and 3 surgeons to inspect the people from the Big Woolen Court. The following day, however, the senate learned that surgeon Val had fled, surgeon Pegelau had refused to serve because of illness, and doctors Shkiadan and Pogoretskii had only consented to make inspections at their own convenience. By the time the senate heard this news, on 16 March, it received 2 more reports of clothworkers found sick in the city. Concurrently, the police brought 8 more persons to the quarantine and 2 to the pesthouse, which had also received 4 sick from the quarantine and recorded one death. Sukin reported 29 persons at the pesthouse, 13 of them healthy; 3 had died. Faced with a growing medical emergency, the senate summoned all doctors and surgeons to a meeting on 17 March.[36]

Nevertheless, the senate recognized the practical difficulties of instituting medical surveillance in spacious and populous Moscow. The Medical Office was ordered to provide additional medical professionals—a chief practitioner, 2 assistants, and several surgical auxiliaries—for adjacent pairs of the city's 14 police districts. These district medical inspectors were supposed to inform the police immediately "about those newly stricken with extraordinary diseases." They should periodically consult together at the Medical

Office to decide the nature of the diseases and to transmit their findings to the senate. The police, for their part, should inform the population which practitioners were assigned to their district, so that householders could summon medical assistance and daily inform the district police about the condition of anybody sick on the premises.[37]

About 40 medical practitioners met with the senate on 17 March. Conspicuously absent was Dr. Rinder. Although the city-physician continued to sign orders and correspondence of the Medical Office in subsequent weeks from his death bed, he took no part in the antiepidemic campaign. The senate charged the assembled practitioners to obey government orders for the duration of the emergency. They were reminded that all medical professionals in Russia practiced by permission of the state, which could command their service in time of need. The senate arranged with the Medical Office for the assignment of 20 practitioners as district medical inspectors. These men were to begin their duties at once.

In reply, the practitioners all expressed their willingness to serve; several said they had already contacted the police. They suggested, however, that neither Dr. Mertens nor Dr. Kuhlemann perform inspections because of their responsibilities at the Foundling Home and Paul's Hospital, respectively. They admitted doubts as to whether the disease was "pestis" or not, citing their previous definition of the "distemper." They also acknowledged their need for a leader to replace the ailing Rinder.[38] After the practitioners departed for their new assignments, the senate excused Mertens and Kuhlemann from inspections. To resolve doubts about the disease, the senators decided that the doctors should consult Dr. Rinder, at home if necessary, considering "what exactly is the disease that has afflicted the clothworkers and have they really devised the proper precaution against it?" The doctors should communicate their conclusions at once.[39]

Besides instituting medical inspection and seeking a professional explanation of the disease, the city authorities adopted other countermeasures. Vice-President Sukin worked out a division of responsibilities whereby the police sought out sick persons from the Big Woolen Court and delivered them to the quarantines or the pesthouse, while the Collegium of Manufactures investigated sanitary conditions at other manufactories and supervised the quarantine facilities. Both agencies worked overtime, their meetings sometimes lasting past midnight.[40] Although none of the other registered enterprises showed signs of infection, the collegium exhorted their operators to maintain cleanliness, avoid crowding, fumigate daily with smouldering juniper, and keep the workers off the streets, especially during the traditionally drunken Easter holidays. Similar concern focused upon the throng of clothworkers in quarantine; they might threaten public order, Sukin warned, unless discipline was strictly enforced. Accordingly, he had those detained at the Balashov and Sitnikov quarantines divided into male and female associations (*arteli*), assigned to separate quarters. The stewards and senior workers were authorized to punish violators of the rules with bread and water for minor infractions, deprivation of food for major offenses. Regarding the corporal punishments ordinarily used to uphold discipline, secret instructions enjoined the stewards to employ only the lightest blows "and to beware above all that from beating no sickness befall those punished."[41] A dual rationale pervaded this proviso: welts from beatings might conceal symptoms of disease, further confusing the task of the medical inspectors, and it was widely believed that strong emotions, such as fear and anger, could induce sickness.[42]

Simultaneously, the Collegium of Manufactures energetically pursued the chief suspect in the importation of infection—Turkish wool. While inspecting the manufactories for signs of filth and overcrowding, collegium members traced and impounded stocks of Turkish wool. Still apprehensive, the senate sought verification of the information supplied by the manufacturers, so the collegium interviewed several Greek merchants engaged in the wool trade. Although the Greeks corroborated various sales, they could not document most transactions beyond the amounts sold and the date of delivery. Stymied, the collegium confessed its inability to account for all Turkish wool brought to and from Moscow in previous months; clothmakers in other towns used the imports, too, as did the many workshops in and around Moscow, and additional stocks must be in merchant hands. The authorities concluded that wool made into cloth was harmless, since it had been handled, combed, and washed.[43] Nevertheless, all cloth at the Big Woolen Court was stored in a special barn, with grates over the windows to allow air circulation, and nobody was allowed to inspect it until the emergency had passed. The Collegium of Manufactures arranged for provincial mills to fill the Big Woolen Court's state contracts, stipulating that none of the cloth be brought to Moscow.[44]

During the last weeks of March, the senate adopted several related precautions. The local jails were checked for signs of disease. President Grigorii Protasov of the Chief Municipal Administration found no cause for alarm about the 200 prisoners held at the Moscow Municipal Administration. Of 538 inmates under the Investigatory Branch and in jails of the Guberniia Chancery, Governor Yushkov reported only 17 sick, none with dangerous symptoms and most able to walk. Sanitary precautions were taken—fresh sand spread on the floor and juniper burned to sweeten the air—the jailers were to report new cases of illness at once, and a surgeon would visit more frequently. The local almshouses received similar attention. With 1,380 persons in 38 facilities across the city, the Collegium of Economy sent inspectors to check for sickness and to enforce cleanliness and daily fumigation. While the Collegium of Economy regretted that no practitioners served under its jurisdiction, the Main Palace Chancery had 202 persons from its almshouses inspected by surgeon Zurburg, assigned to the Admiralty's sailcloth manufactory, before sending them in late March to crown estates. In early April, the Collegium of Economy likewise packed off to provincial villages and monasteries hundreds of its charges, apparently everyone who could walk. Public begging was strictly forbidden, of course, and vagrants were expelled from the city.[45]

Meanwhile, the police reaffirmed the prohibition on selling Turkish wares and extended it to the sale of old clothes, especially at the rag market beyond the Voskresenskie Gates near the Neglinnaia. The public baths were closed, fumigatory fires were renewed, and burials were forbidden within the city. Cleanliness was to be observed in all public places and commercial establishments.[46] Slaughterhouses were to be moved outside Moscow.[47] When a clothworker died at a tavern in the eleventh district, all taverns were inspected for disease, particularly those in the suburbs, "where there is usually a great throng of people because of the closeness of the residences." Laborers at the Foundling Home and Moscow University also were examined, but no unusual sickness was found at either place.[48]

Medical Debates and Doubts

Amid these administrative precautions the establishment of regular medical inspection in each city district led to the discovery of new cases of suspicious disease. The widening infection insistently posed three fundamental questions: Was the malady plague, and if so, how far had it spread and how could it be arrested? Resolution of these issues lay squarely with the professional medical community. Charged by the senate on 17 March to define the disease, the physicians assigned to the districts began inspections the next day. Since Dr. Rinder was too ill to direct the Medical Office, Dr. Erasmus replaced him on 20 March and ordered the district medical inspectors to consult together twice weekly. Simultaneously, he issued instructions on how to examine the sick and the dead. Surgeons should first ascertain whether the affliction looked infectious. If the surgeon found swollen glands, buboes, or broad infectious spots, "that is, Anthony's Fire" (painful reddish inflammation, often associated with ergotism), then he should summon the doctor. Corpses should be treated in like manner, but must not be dissected. Physicians should keep careful count of everybody examined, in order to present precise data at the consilia.[49]

The district medical inspectors held their own impromptu consilium on 19 March. The police had just reported three incidents: the previous afternoon in the tenth district near the Rogozhskaia Entryway a man "was walking, collapsed, and died"; several deaths happened at the Balashov quarantine the same day; and a woman fell ill in the tenth district where she lived at the house of a clothworker. "In order, therefore, to be in a position to recognize the nature of the disease with confidence," doctors Pogoretskii, Veniaminov,

Zybelin, Lado, Yagel'skii, and staff-surgeon Adrian Tatarinov jointly examined these cases. Afterward the 6 medical inspectors observed:

> In the 10th district in Rogozhskaia the body of the man who had suddenly died on the street near the entryway appeared to have been enfevered for some time and has on the stomach a dark swollen spot the size of a ruble, also on the right shoulder a spot covered with a dark scab the size of a half-ruble, and small dark spots all over the body with a slight swelling of the glands in the left groin. In that same district in Alekseevskaia near the Church of Martin the Confessor was examined a sick factory woman who lives with workers of the Big Woolen Court and fell ill in the house of a factory worker the day before yesterday. She has on the stomach an ugly suppurated abcess around which the edges are infected with Anthony's Fire, on the groin a large red bubo, also on the left kneecap a dark spot the size of a silver five-copeck piece, and behind both knees some bluish elongated [spots]. Of the three dead bodies at the Balashov manufactory, one has been found completely covered with dark spots of various sizes, while the others are clammy and bluish without spots. Furthermore, the factory worker brought to us from Sitnikov's, where he fell ill with a severe fever the day before yesterday, was found in great weakness and on him a dark spot has appeared near the sacrum, around which are pustules. All these dead bodies and the two live ones are acknowledged by us as infected with a dangerous disease, exactly the same as at the Big Woolen Court.[50]

These findings and 2 other sudden deaths on 19 March—a clothworker at a tavern in the eleventh district and a clothworker's baby at the Sitnikov quarantine—stunned the senate. Obviously, the police had not located everybody exposed to the disease at the manufactory, the senators concluded, whereas the case at the Sitnikov quarantine showed the epidemic was still spreading. Quickly and quietly the police and the Collegium of Manufactures should find and quarantine suspect clothworkers; the doctors should check for other cases at Sitnikov's.[51] Concurrently, an authoritative visitor corroborated, independently, the district medical inspectors' conclusions. En route from Jassy to Petersburg, Dr. Gustav Orraeus stopped briefly in Moscow and, at Saltykov's order, inspected 3 patients at the Balashov quarantine on 19 March. Their symptoms showed "an infectious disease, the actual signs of the pestilential distemper: a bubo, carbuncles, and dark spots." Orraeus declared that plague had definitely invaded Moscow.[52]

Meanwhile, Dr. Yagel'skii entreated the police to remove everybody associated with the Big Woolen Court, no matter where they lived, "so that otherwise there might not ensue terror, unrest, and God forbid, harm to the whole city." But the police and the Collegium of Manufactures boggled before this task, citing an earlier senate order to quarantine for 7 days only those who had left the manufactory since the outbreak. Because the 7-day period had already passed for the 1,800 clothworkers and their dependents still living in Moscow, the police and the collegium argued against their removal, except for those who cohabited with known carriers of disease. As before, the local authorities foresaw the practical and logistical problems of large-scale evacuation. Hundreds of clothworkers would swamp the quarantines, inviting disease and disturbance, "and all the more publicity will ensue from the echo among the people."[53]

The police daily informed the senate of persons quarantined, of deaths at the quarantines and the pesthouse, and of suspicious cases elsewhere. Everything indicated the outbreak was continuing.[54] As disturbing symptoms cropped up in different districts, the senate on 21 March demanded that the Medical Office promptly assemble all physicians who had witnessed the disease more than once, plus doctors Shafonskii and Orraeus, to decide the essence of the infection and to prescribe countermeasures. Before the doctors could meet, however, Dr. Orraeus left for Petersburg and Chief of Police Bakhmetev finally returned on 22 March, determined to halt the confusion.[55]

Bakhmetev found Moscow "in extreme unrest; thus almost all the nobility not detained here by their duties have left the city for the districts." Controversy stirred the commotion. Neither the people nor the practitioners could agree whether the disease was dangerous. Nonplussed at the practitioners' disunity, Bakhmetev tried to hire knowledgeable Greeks. None came forward. Then he consulted staff-surgeon Grave, who had seen hundreds of plague victims at Khotin in 1770. Grave told Bakhmetev he had not yet seen any pestilence in Moscow. Since beginning service as a district medical inspector, he had examined 3 corpses, none of which bore the least sign of real plague (but he had missed the inspectors' consilium on 19 March). Within an hour after talking with Grave, however, Bakhmetev sent him to check 3 newly reported cases. Thereupon Grave abruptly reversed himself. He swore that one of the stricken would not live 3 more hours, and he was right. "The disease and symptoms attested by him," Bakhmetev reported, "are found to be exactly the symptoms of the pestilential distemper, and that very kind which was at Khotin in the hospital under his supervision."[56]

Trusting Grave's competence, Bakhmetev had him inspect other cases, which further confirmed his amended diagnosis. "It is also his opinion," wrote Bakhmetev, "that it has already been here about four months and that in consequence of the local climate and the countervailing cold its strength has greatly waned, hence it displays a weaker action than in a warm climate." At the quarantine, Bakhmetev, who assumed sole direction of the antiepidemic campaign on 24 March, reported 16 newly ill on 26 March and 4 dead. Cases elsewhere persuaded him that the disease had infected persons not connected with the Big Woolen Court and who lived on the other side of the river. Did this portend a major epidemic? Bakhmetev declined any prediction.[57]

By contrast, Saltykov despaired over Grave's appraisal. He quoted Grave to Catherine on 23 March as saying "that distemper is a most foul one, the very same as was at Khotin, and extremely dangerous, and that it is now showing itself rarely because of the frosts, which do not permit it to spread, but as soon as it becomes warm and the rivers melt, then one must expect the utmost calamity." Evacuation of the clothworkers could not save Moscow, Saltykov reasoned; they had distributed pestilence too widely, "and almost all the city is already infected, whereas with the opening of spring it will be even more and no means remain to eradicate this distemper, for it has spread to all districts of the city, and many have begun to leave Moscow to save themselves, indeed I hope that everybody without duties here will depart." Moscow's population started to shrink as officials and practitioners urged the nobility to leave for their estates earlier than usual. Grave privately warned Prince Mikhail Dolgorukii of the danger and advised his family to depart before the spring thaw. The Dolgorukii family left on 24 March and spent the rest of the year at their suburban estate, "Volynskoe," 4 miles outside Moscow. Hundreds of other noblemen did likewise.[58]

Pressed by the senate for guidance, the Medical Office called a consilium on 23 March. Erasmus, Shafonskii, and Mertens joined the district medical inspectors to review developments since the evacuation of the Big Woolen Court. At the pesthouse, surgeon Margraf reported having received 48 sick since 14 March, of whom 21 had died, 10 still showed dangerous symptoms (3 of them were recovering), and the others either had noninfectious maladies or were aged and infirm. Full information was lacking as to mortality and morbidity at the quarantines, which then housed a total of 730 persons, i.e., 200 more than the initial contingent from the manufactory. About 1,700 clothworkers and their dependents remained in town. The district medical inspectors associated all suspicious cases with the manufactory, a conclusion that contradicted the views of Saltykov and Bakhmetev. Furthermore, the Collegium of Manufactures confirmed that no other registered enterprises were infected. After considering this evidence the doctors made two recommendations to the senate. First, they reaffirmed their definition of the disease as "a putrid, infectious, and contagious one, and according to several symptoms and circumstances it very closely resembles the distemper." Second, as the disease seemed to be confined to the Big Woolen Court, all of its employees and their dependents should be removed from Moscow forthwith, while the weather remained cold.[59]

These answers appeared maddeningly equivocal to Saltykov and the senate, in view of the unequivocal advice they had lately received from Orraeus and Grave. They accepted the consilium's endorsement of wholesale evacuation on 23 March, but instead of wallowing in doubt, they finally demanded on 26 March that the doctors name the disease. The consilium responded the same day. Their previous opinions had only omitted the popular name of the disease, they explained; "and as now it is specifically demanded of the consilium, so it does not call it otherwise than the pestilential distemper." Most of the Moscow medical elite had made up their minds at last.[60]

On 31 March, the doctors compiled supplementary precautions that they cautiously designated "An Opinion Designed for the Preservation of the City from the Disease That Has Appeared" (they still hesitated to speak of plague in public). Eleven physicians declared that "the disease which has shown itself does not subsist in the air, but proceeds solely from communication and contact with the sick and with infected articles; however, foul air and the use of bad food, in addition to other causes, greatly facilitate infection." They suggested the following precautions to protect the public: (1) maintain cleanliness in all public and private places "from which filth and stench issue forth, and also drain putrid marshy places"; (2) bury refuse and carrion outside town away from thoroughfares, without lime, and dispose of all dead bodies in like fashion; (3) observe cleanliness in large public buildings frequented by many people, and avoid crowding and overheating such structures; (4) insure that all edibles sold be fresh and not putrified; (5) set out fumigatory pyres in public places, using aromatic wood instead of the dung burned heretofore; (6) keep residences clean, dry, and moderately heated, avoid overcrowding single rooms, separate the sick from the healthy, open windows whenever possible, and purify the air with vapors from vinegar, juniper berries, burning gunpowder, or sulphur.[61] Derived from miasmatico-contagionist assumptions, these measures embodied traditional practices used against plague since at least the fourteenth century. Dr. Erasmus sought additional guidance by writing the Medical Collegium on 4 April for the observations of infectious disease that practitioners had submitted the previous year.[62]

If Moscow's medical professionals all agreed upon the need for precautions, they did not all believe the epidemic was plague. Unlike the outbreak in December, which every doctor but Rinder had immediately called pestilential, the new epidemic openly perplexed some and privately confused others—hence their two-week delay in naming the malady.[63] Their uncertainty hinged upon several factors. Except for Dr. Shafonskii and staff-surgeon Grave, none of the practitioners resident in Moscow had recently seen a case of plague. (Grigorii Yakhontov, a surgeon who witnessed the Ukrainian epidemic thirty years earlier, died in Moscow on 28 May 1771, allegedly of plague; apparently nobody consulted him during the debates in March and April.)[64] All had read and heard about plague, of course, and the secondhand nature of their knowledge probably muddled their conceptions. Most knew that plague could present different symptoms. Yet even the very experienced Grave had difficulty diagnosing the first cases he encountered in Moscow. Some thought plague was not so much a discrete affliction as the most virulent stage of a general infective process. "Military surgeons were particularly apt to credit the transformation of epidemic diseases into one another, since in wartime several epidemics commonly flourish side by side." Many associated plague with typhus; the two diseases do in fact possess certain etiological and nosological similarities. As typhus was more common than plague in eighteenth-century Europe, familiarity alone may account for physicians' more benign notions of "putrid fever" as compared to "pestilential distemper." For most practitioners, plague implied, above all, extremely high and sudden mortality. They generally assumed that it happened mainly in warm climates and seasons.[65] The new outbreak seemed to contradict all these assumptions.

Dr. Rinder had employed these popular conceptions to dismiss plague as the agent of the mortality at the Vvedenskie Hills. Evidently, he maintained this view till his death on 21 April, and his doubts influenced practitioners and officials alike. At least 2 other doctors paraded their misgivings. On 26 March, when the medical consilium defined the disease as plague, Dr. Johann Kuhlemann submitted his dissent separately to the senate, which forwarded both views to Petersburg on 29 March. He reviewed his reasoning in detail for the consilium on 31 March. An M.D. of Göttingen in 1753, Kuhlemann served 23 years in the army, acted as personal physician to Field Marshal Saltykov, and headed Paul's Hospital since 1765. Presumably his views carried special weight with his old comrade-in-arms, Count Saltykov. Dr. Georgii Shkiadan filed his own brief dissent on 31 March.[66]

Both Kuhlemann and Shkiadan admitted they had never seen plague before, but they questioned its presence on the basis of experience, logic, and recent observations. If it were really plague, they argued, then large-scale mortality should have followed the initial outbreak at the Big Woolen Court. Cold weather alone could not long arrest pestilence among a multitude of people living in close quarters, "especially in such great filth and in rooms of a great degree of warmth." Infectious diseases such as smallpox and plague were known to have occurred in the wintertime. Shkiadan noted that not many had died at the manufactory and that those stricken there had displayed various symptoms, some suffering from ordinary illnesses. "External symptoms can deceive," cautioned Kuhlemann, "but the mode of transmission, its spread, and the whole course of the disease in general, ought to persuade us completely what characteristic name to give it." He thought it was a typhus-like fever, very similar to plague but less infectious. He had often seen such "putrid infectious fever" among soldiers in winter quarters and among ill-nourished common people. Such infection could easily arise at a place like the Big Woolen Court, "given the extraordinarily poor maintenance of these people in food, especially with their horribly filthy mode of life, where the stench of their quarters was almost unbearable to dumb animals."

Kuhlemann and Shkiadan both supported the measures suggested by the medical consilium on 31 March. But Kuhlemann urged caution, "in order that society not be driven to anxiety." He feared the consequences, for Moscow and for the empire, of prematurely declaring the disease to be plague.[67] Thus, Kuhlemann and Shkiadan recapitulated Rinder's views in his earlier debate with Shafonskii. Since neither served as a district medical inspector, and since Kuhlemann missed the first consilium on 11 March, their arguments might be discounted as based on limited experience and faulty observation. But when the next few weeks witnessed the abrupt subsidence of the epidemic, their doubts seemed vindicated.

Not that such disputes were peculiar to Moscow in 1771. With the virtual disappearance of plague from western Europe after the Marseilles epidemic of 1720–22, and from Russia after the epidemic of 1738–39, medical professionals became "increasingly unfamiliar with plague and ever more reluctant to diagnose it positively. Disputes about the true nature of the early cases became a regular feature of each new epidemic. No name in medicine sounds so ominous as plague; none is so charged with mass emotion."[68]

Senator Eropkin and the Plague's Remission

The consternation in Moscow dismayed Catherine when she heard the news on 17 March. She replied icily to Saltykov's dispatch, inquiring what precautions had been taken about the cloth produced at the Big Woolen Court. The news arrived too late to be presented to the council that day, which discussed certification of vessels from Danzig and their inspection at Reval and Kronstadt. At the same time the Empress ordered the Medical Collegium to assemble all court physicians, doctors, and staff-surgeons in the capital for the purpose of resolving the Rinder–Shafonskii dispute about the disease at the hospital annex. In President Cherkassov's presence, the Petersburg medical elite should evaluate the controversy and decide, "was that sickness genuinely the real infection?" Before Catherine considered the latest eruption, she wished to clarify the earlier outbreak. Unfortunately, the conclusions of her medical advisers have not been found. Probably their views were divided and indecisive, as one can deduce from the hearsay collected by foreign diplomats in Petersburg and from subsequent discussions, reactions, and policies.[69]

Catherine's council discussed Saltykov's report on 21 March. Astonished, some councilors questioned the Governor-General's competence in view of his belated recognition of the danger. Count Saltykov was too old to cope with another, larger emergency, they argued; preservation of the city should be entrusted to somebody else. Others advocated a compromise: Bakhmetev and others could assume executive responsibility under Saltykov's general supervision. Awaiting developments, the Empress took no action for a few days. But Saltykov's next report about the further spread of the disease impelled Catherine to intervene. On 25 March, the Empress dictated a program of countermeasures, most of which the Moscow authorities had already adopted. Her most important prescription, however, changed the leadership of the program. The Empress tactfully told Saltykov that his general responsibility for the whole city precluded his supervision of the short-term precautions that Bakhmetev would implement; so she commissioned a well-connected imperial official in Moscow, Lieutenant-General and Senator Peter Dmitrievich Eropkin (or Erapkin), to coordinate public health policies for the duration of the emergency. Saltykov retained supreme command; he and Bakhmetev were to provide whatever resources Eropkin needed to suppress the epidemic. Thus did Catherine conciliate her venerable friend Count Saltykov, while bringing forward a younger, more energetic administrator.[70]

The Empress granted Eropkin direct authority over all the practitioners and quarantines in Moscow. She also authorized him to select his own staff from local officialdom, appointing one deputy for each of the 14 police districts and as many more as he needed. Intended to supplement the police and the district medical inspectors, these so-called district supervisors (*chastnye smotriteli*) would enable Eropkin "to survey all the city at a glance." Catherine borrowed this novel institution of medical police either from cameralist literature or from the foreign antiplague legislation that Teplov and Volkov had collected. A translated fragment of an Austrian statute of 1763 enumerated the duties of local officials under a health council.[71] Whereas Justi warned that practitioners by themselves did not know enough and should always be assisted by police and judicial officials, Bielfeld called for the police to cooperate with a medical council in fighting epidemics.[72]

Catherine's anguish over the pessimistic, irresolute reports from Moscow climaxed at the end of March. In appointing Eropkin, she provided against the worst contingency. Should calamity threaten, Eropkin might order a special levy of townspeople, "at least from the best of their servants; but do not undertake this, however, without extreme necessity." Then too, the Empress shuddered lest the infection continue northward from Moscow. In Petersburg on 25 March, Governor Jakob Sievers of Novgorod guberniia urgently ordered checkpoints on the roads leading to the imperial capital. At the council session of 28 March, the Empress proposed a whole series of emergency measures, the force of which was to isolate Moscow and to ban all unauthorized movement to and from the city. Muscovites would purchase provisions at special police-supervised markets outside town. The clergy of Moscow and neighboring eparchies would organize public prayers, provided by the Holy Synod, for deliverance from pestilence, and would exhort the population to follow the government's precautions. A network of quarantine stations on major roads would protect Petersburg, reinforced by three successive checkpoints on the main highway from Moscow. Formulated in Catherine's decree of 31 March, this emergency program combined various proposals.[73] The proposals for markets outside Moscow and for public prayers apparently stemmed from the memorandum submitted by the south Slav officer serving in the south.

Having approved the program for use only as a last resort, the council suggested appointing a "special personage" in Petersburg with a mandate like those given Eropkin in Moscow and Shipov in the Ukraine. By publicizing

Figure 7 General and Senator Peter Dmitrievich Eropkin, the official in charge of the antiplague campaign in Moscow from March 1771 to the end of the epidemic and the chief "savior" of the city from the Plague Riot of mid-September 1771. Reproduction courtesy of the Graphics Department, State Historical Museum in Moscow.

the precautions, this official would inspire public confidence and thereby protect the empire's foreign and domestic commerce. The Empress quickly chose Lieutenant-General Count Jakob Bruce, who consulted with the council on 31 March. As concerned implementation of the emergency program in Moscow, however, the council urged Catherine to allow Saltykov and Eropkin to act as circumstances required. Subsequent events would demonstrate that the councilors did not doubt the prudence or practicality of the measures envisaged. Like the Moscow authorities, Catherine's councilors puzzled at the doctors' disputes and on 28 March called in Dr. Orraeus for an explanation. He assured them the disease was the same infection he had witnessed in Moldavia. Accompanying Orraeus, Governor Yushkov of Moscow guberniia confirmed the practitioners' disagreements.[74]

The emergency program of 31 March reflected Catherine's worst nightmares, but her fears soon faded. On 3 April, she decided to halt all work on the new Kremlin palace, "so long as talk will persist in Moscow about the appearance of signs of a supposed pestilential contagion." Nothing should be razed or built, she instructed the project's overseer, "and do not work by digging anything in the ground at all, until the alarm of this misadventure shall completely pass not only in the city itself, but even in adjacent localities." Catherine already had doubts about the disease, which she conceived in miasmatico-contagionist terms, one variant of which traced pestilence to subterranean sources.[75]

Not content with preventive measures, the Empress wrote Saltykov on 2 April, proposing a medical experiment. A capable surgeon, someone "above the usual prejudices of their craft," should select several hopelessly infected persons for special treatment. Housed in cool, dry quarters, the sick should be given cold water with vinegar to drink and be rubbed with ice at least twice a day. The patients' progress would determine the frequency of the ice massages. Only the Empress should be informed of the results of these secret experiments. A month later Catherine transmitted 500 rubles via Saltykov to surgeon Margraf for applying the treatment to one patient, who recovered. Though Margraf kept a journal of his activities, he declined to judge the procedure, which would later be known as *Remedium antipestilentiale Catharinae Secundae.*[76] Catherine's undertaking represented another application of Dimsdale's "cool regimen" and epitomized the optimistic, activist view of plague therapy that evolved in Russia throughout the eighteenth century.

At Moscow, meanwhile, Senator Eropkin took command of the antiplague campaign on 31 March. He began recruiting district supervisors and, with Bakhmetev, continued the recently modified policies. Within 3 weeks, the police removed nearly 1,000 clothworkers and dependents to the Simonov, Danilov, and Pokrovskii monasteries. The village of Troitskoe-Golenishchevo served as a final quarantine facility for persons released from the pesthouses. By 7 May, Eropkin reported that only 202 persons from the manufactory remained at large; 2 weeks later the total had dwindled to just 95.[77] Believing the disease confined to the clothworkers, Eropkin asked the medical consilium, on 31 March, whether, if other houses became infected, seven days' confinement to a separate room would adequately safeguard healthy persons at a stricken dwelling. The physicians advised that such houses should be isolated and the infected rooms aired for at least 2 weeks. The total period of detention might vary according to specific circumstances, and the doctors urged that belongings at suspect dwellings be aired and smoked. Lime should not be used for burials, they advised, because it produced noxious fumes that might "harm the air more."[78] The medical consilium favored a policy of limited, flexible, and selective quarantine. Except for the clothworkers and their dependents, only the sick would be removed from their habitations. The situation did not yet require wholesale evacuation, compulsory quarantine, or destruction of suspect dwellings and belongings.

Indeed, meeting with the senate, on 6 April, Eropkin and Saltykov postponed indefinitely Catherine's emergency program of 31 March. Their reasoning was simple: the expected crisis had waned. Mortality and morbidity remained steady at the two pesthouses. From 30 March through 3 April, fourteen persons died at the Ugreshskii and Simonov pesthouses, where twelve others fell ill. No further cases had been found in the city. Still, Eropkin announced the assignment of district supervisors, who should accompany the district medical inspectors to examine any suspicious cases. If dangerous symptoms were found, the supervisors should dispatch the victims, their clothes and moveable property, to the Ugreshskii pesthouse. After fumigating the infected rooms, sentries would be stationed at the house to prevent anybody from leaving for two days, while the occupants were watched for signs of disease. On the third day, the supervisor should visit again and either declare the house free of danger or consign the remaining inhabitants to quarantines or pesthouses. Finally, the district supervisors were to report daily the number of sick and dead to Eropkin.[79]

At the same meeting, the senate accepted Eropkin's suggestion to print 300 copies of the doctors' recommendations of 31 March for public and private precautions. Worried about security, Saltykov won senate approval to bring in troops from invalid units in the provinces. Spring floods delayed mustering the troops until May, however, by which time they were no longer needed, or so Muscovite officialdom thought.[80]

Saltykov and Eropkin based their postponement of drastic measures on another significant source: the mortality statistics collected by the parish clergy. Archbishop Amvrosii discussed these data with the secular authorities before forwarding them to Catherine on 7 April via Grigorii Teplov. The parish registries disclosed a generally low mortality rate that showed no tendency to increase and which included a low proportion of "sudden" deaths. For the period of 1 January–4 April 1771, the clergy recorded 1,614 deaths: barely 17 per day. Just 26 of these deaths had occurred "suddenly," but only 5 since 23 March, when the general evacuation of the clothworkers began. In compliance with the Archbishop's order of late December 1770, the cause of death was specified for all who had succumbed "suddenly." Of the 26 suspicious cases through 4 April, 10 abruptly perished "from an unknown cause," but a marginal notation commented: "these have been examined by doctors, and no marks appeared." None of the clergy assigned to the quarantines and pesthouses had fallen ill. Moreover, the priest at the Vvedenskie Hills reported that from 26 December 1770, through 6 March 1771, only 7 of the 207 persons isolated there had died, 3 of them infants with smallpox. "And therefore it seems there is no doubt," Amvrosii concluded, "from which one might become so acutely apprehensive and fear the infection, which (God preserve us) leaves far greater mournful traces in such cases."

Citing the practitioners' doubts, Amvrosii advocated patient vigilance. He even declined Saltykov's order of 4 April to institute public prayers for deliverance from pestilence, according to the text received from the Holy Synod. The Archbishop justified his refusal by informing Teplov that no crisis was at hand and that such proclamations would incite widespread "despondency, desperation, and the very worst consequences. This tocsin will be the same as or even much more frightening than a fire." Besides, the clergy were offering daily prayers for salvation from "noxious air, ruin, and death-dealing pestilence." Everybody believed the incident would end like the scare at Vvedenskie Hills, Amvrosii asserted, which arose solely from the doctors' perplexity. Time reinforced such views, as Eropkin compiled another register on 14 April, which listed 42 dead and 28 sick (13 of whom were recovering) at the quarantines in the period 4 April through 13 April. From Petersburg on 18 April, Teplov wrote Amvrosii of Catherine's satisfaction with his advice and actions.[81]

Other Muscovites seconded Amvrosii's sentiments. "About the plague I cannot report to you anything new," Prince Vasilii Golitsyn wrote his brother on 8 April, "[except] that the general rumor on the street claims there's no trace of it, wherein I am persuaded, because several liberties have been granted and precautions abandoned; and the disease is already called not plague but another sort of infection: such smoking as there was when you were here has been curtailed as well as such similar measures of precaution." Ten days later the same observer declaimed: "Our plague has entirely passed and I hope there will soon be free exit and entry to Petersburg, and great squabbles are going on; the commanders against the doctors, and the doctors against the commanders, because it never had been [here]." Indeed, General Famintsyn praised Dr. Rinder's probity to the Medical Collegium and censured Dr. Shafonskii for "claiming something doubtful to be indubitable." Dr. Mertens later lamented that "Almost every body believed that the physicians who had called the disorder the plague, had imposed on the public; others entertained doubts on the subject."[82]

All this reassuring news fortified a cautious optimism in Petersburg. On 11 April, Catherine authorized the senate to announce that although Moscow had reported no further deaths at the Big Woolen Court "from the infectious fever with spots" (she still avoided calling it plague), quarantine regulations would continue in force on all roads leading to Petersburg. Issued 8 days later, this proclamation sought to assure merchants that so long as they circumvented Moscow and secured documentation attesting to the safe origin of their shipments, cargoes would not be delayed in transit. Two weeks earlier Lord Cathcart relayed Nikita Panin's assurances that "all apprehensions with respect to the pestiferous Quality of the Fever at Moscow were at an End; which is since confirmed from all hands."[83]

The Empress's council heard repeated reassurances that all was well in Moscow; so when Eropkin reported no new cases by 21 April, the councilors wished to publish the news and to lift the precautions. Catherine still hesitated, doubly cautious after 2 alarms in 3 months. But after a few more weeks of favorable reports even the Empress relaxed. Whoever said the plague was in Moscow lied, she wrote Frau Bielcke in mid-May, blaming the scare on some instances of "putrid fever and spotted fever." The quarantine precautions were merely intended to forestall panic and to teach people a useful lesson, Catherine confided to her friend in Hamburg.[84]

In retrospect, the persistence of extraordinary weather accounted for much of the plague's fitful behavior from January to May 1771. But people at the time failed to make such correlations. If some assumed that winter curtailed the outbreak at the Vvedenskie Hills annex, nobody deduced the eruption at the Big Woolen Court from the preceding thaw. Perhaps the furor of the occasion diverted attention until the resumption of winter in late March postponed the plague again. A howling blizzard surprised the Tula region south of Moscow on 26 March, the day before Easter. In Moscow, too, "the weather continued cold until the middle of April," Dr. Mertens remembered, "in consequence of which the contagion became more fixed and inactive, attacking only those who dwelt with the infected."[85] In fact, winter gripped Moscow until early May, an anonymous diarist recording a heavy snowfall on 1 May and severe frosts the next 2 days. Peter Panin wrote his brother from Moscow on 3 May that "the first of May a completely new and amazing winter dropped in on us."[86] In conjunction with freezing temperatures from late March to early May, evacuation of the Big Woolen Court must have short-circuited the development of a major epidemic by separating several thousand particularly vulnerable persons from a primary focus of infection.

Assuredly, the disease became less visible. Moscow's administrators and physicians assumed that true plague would cause an immense, sudden rise in mortality. Since nothing like that had happened through May 1771, they decided the visitation had been a freak occurrence. Daily and monthly mortality statistics were not compiled carefully in Moscow at the time, as those from the parish registries showed, nor did anybody know the city's normal mortality rate. Furthermore, a subsequent collation of the death toll for 1771 revealed a very gradual increase, from 744 to 778 deaths in April and 840 to 878 in May to 1,099 in June. The daily rate oscillated from a range of 25 to 47 in April to 40 to 70 in June.[87] Such wide variations from day to day overshadowed the slight monthly increase, explicable as the normal upward trend of springtime.[88] Had this picture of slowly climbing mortality been known at the time, it would hardly have alarmed anyone, least of all observers anticipating an imminent cataclysm.

Had the Moscow authorities foreseen a broader epidemic, they could not have done much more than they did to forestall it. The doctors' failure to detect and to identify the disease earlier paled in significance, then, before the inexorable eruption. The single known measure that might have saved some lives was mass evacuation, an expedient that the more mobile elements of the population began to adopt in March, with official blessing. When Eropkin assumed control of public health policy, he had 500 tickets printed to certify the good health of persons allowed to leave for Petersburg. Departure elsewhere required no special authorization. By 3 May, Eropkin had nearly expended the supply of tickets and asked for 700 more.[89] As Moscow's population departed, the rising mortality among those who stayed behind gained ominous overtones. Even so, a city of several hundred thousand people could not be entirely evacuated overnight. Massive evacuation could not last long and also risked infecting the hinterland, as the sequel would show.

CHAPTER SIX

A Pestilential Summer (April–September 1771)

Perplexed by 2 pestilential alarms within 3 months, Muscovites must have wondered what warm weather might bring after the freeze of early May. The summer of 1771 proved to be extraordinarily long, warm, and moist—ideal conditions for the propagation of plague.

In certain respects, the gradual resurgence of infection recapitulated the 2 previous outbreaks. Moscow's third visitation evaded early detection and definition. Despite the sanitary surveillance instituted in March, neither Eropkin nor his subordinates became alarmed until late June; even then their suspicions crystallized so slowly that another month passed before they renewed extraordinary precautions. The efficiency of their surveillance was limited, to be sure, by Moscow's sprawling layout and loose administration. While primary attention focused upon the pesthouses and quarantines, vigilance elsewhere may have lapsed temporarily in the expectation that all danger was past by mid-June. The departure of many noble households and the rapid subsidence of the epidemic in April, coupled with the medical community's doubts, undermined belief in the need for extraordinary precautions. Officials and practitioners assumed they could arrest any recurrence, just as they had done twice before.

Yet the new upsurge differed from its immediate predecessors in 2 crucial particulars: no distinct focus emerged—no center like the hospital annex or the Big Woolen Court—and no clear-cut symptoms became evident at the start. Plague revived in such a protean manner that nobody in Moscow or Petersburg grasped the magnitude of the menace. When they finally perceived it, the metropolis was already beginning to disintegrate, and the local authorities argued with Petersburg about the best means to save the situation.

As it was generally known that warm temperatures somehow favored infection, many emergency measures remained in force into the summer. Indeed, the plague of 1770 in Moldavia had reaffirmed the disease potential of springtime, an epidemiological lesson that doctors Shafonskii and Orraeus and staff-surgeon Grave all impressed upon officialdom in Moscow and Petersburg. Temporarily in charge of public health in Moscow, Senator

Eropkin appreciated the danger of recrudescence amid the accumulated filth that spring would unveil. Even today the frenetic annual spring clean-up in Moscow uncovers so much debris that one can imagine the greater cogency of such fears in the less hygienic eighteenth century. Eropkin therefore strove to perfect the network of sanitary surveillance while cold weather lasted. On 16 April, he entrusted supervision of the isolation facilities to Dr. Yagel'skii and staff-surgeon Grave. Both were to examine personally all doubtful cases throughout the metropolitan area.[1] If spring regerminated the disease, Eropkin hoped to nip it in the bud instead of belatedly discovering a pestilential creeper.

Intermittent frosts assisted these precautions until mid-May, when spring abruptly stripped away Moscow's protective coating. Muscovites quit lighting their stoves on 12 May. "With us, glory to God, the season became very nice four days ago," Prince Vasilii Golitsyn exulted from Moscow on 17 May. Spring and summer arrived almost at once, Dr. Mertens remembered, as temperatures stayed "very warm" until mid-June.[2] No meteorological readings have been found for that spring in Moscow, but one can infer its general weather patterns from those at Petersburg and Kiev. The freeze at the start of May was Peterburg's last of the winter, and merchant Ivan Tolchenov observed that the barge traffic from central Russia to Petersburg proceeded faster than usual in May and June because of the higher water level from frequent rains. Dr. Lerche at Kiev recorded consistent heat and showers in May with a high of 97 ° F. on the 19th, a mean of 65 ° for the whole month, and 15 rainy days. June in Kiev had 21 days of rain and the temperature reached 88 ° on the 14th, the monthly mean rising to 66 °.[3]

Moist, moderately warm weather greeted Dr. Lerche at Moscow on 13 July. After his arrival it rained 3 days in a row, precipitation dampening 11 of the last 18 days of July. Southeasterly winds pushed the high to 90 ° on 24 July, with a mean temperature of 72.5 ° and mean barometric pressure of 29.14 inches for the month. Similar conditions reigned outside Moscow. Peter Panin, writing from his Petrovskoe estate in mid-August, bewailed "the bad weather that has continued unceasingly since the very middle of July" and hoped it would end soon. Yet frequent, heavy rains persisted into autumn. Lerche recorded precipitation on 26 days of August, designated rainfall as "copious" on half those occasions, and noted virtually continuous showers over 10 days, 19-28 August. Concurrently, temperatures gradually declined, with a high of 84 °, a low of 45 °, and a mean of 64.5 ° for the whole month. Westerly winds prevailed and barometric pressure remained low, 29.10 inches being the mean. In September, 20 days were wet, 9 "copiously." High temperature for the month was 72 ° on 8 September, with a low of 30 ° on the 20th and a mean of 51 °, while the barometric mean rose to 29.73 inches.[4]

This extraordinary weather gave rise to an extraordinary epidemic. The late, short, and hot spring, abruptly succeeding the frigid weather that predominated in Moscow from late March through early May, would have restrained the spread of plague until mid-June, for temperatures above 80° F. and below 50° check the disease. Thenceforth, the constantly moist, moderately warm weather steadily accelerated the plague. As will be seen, the coincidence and persistence of these natural conditions into October 1771 largely determined the chronological course of the Moscow epidemic and partly governed its territorial scope.

The late spring allowed Eropkin time to ponder how to release the quarantined clothworkers without endangering public health and order anew. This problem reopened an old dilemma. During the previous decade the authorities had drawn upon a variety of precedents and immediate problems to advocate the removal of large manufactories from Moscow; but practical difficulties and renewed demand for military textiles had postponed direct action. Inasmuch as the socioeconomic deficiencies of the Big Woolen Court had specifically inspired this proposal in the 1760s, its recent visitation of infection reemphasized the dangers that such enterprises could inflict upon the metropolis. Furthermore, the epidemic partly resolved the dilemma by temporarily evacuating most of the clothworkers. To return them directly to the site of the outbreak seemed imprudent and inopportune. Miasmatico-contagionist premises reinforced Eropkin's apprehension that the summer heat might activate the crowded, insanitary conditions at the Big Woolen Court and regenerate pestilence. Accordingly, he asked the senate on 19 May to consider permanently transferring the Big Woolen Court to a safer site and to investigate other manufactories similarly situated, especially those at the former Ambassadorial Court in Kitai-gorod. On 27 May, the senate requested pertinent data from the Collegium of Manufactures and any previous legislation concerning the relocation of manufactories. Even before the Moscow authorities debated the issue, Catherine's council in Petersburg inquired on 16 June as to the feasibility of moving the Big Woolen Court to "another more convenient place."[5]

The Collegium of Manufactures responded on 13 June, and the senate heard its report a week later. Acknowledging the absence of direct legal precedent for the removal of industry, and noting the operators' reluctance to relocate voluntarily, the collegium retrieved its own project of 25 January 1765, which had proposed transfer of the Big Woolen Court and kindred enterprises. Even though that project had never been adopted, the rationale behind it had motivated legislation in 1767–70 that aimed at the gradual dispersion of large-scale urban industry to the provinces and its conversion from bondaged to hired labor. To the economic, social, environmental, and security concerns of the 1760s, could now be added the recently dramatized health hazards of the 1770s. Nevertheless, the senators in Moscow hesitated to evict the manufactories summarily; they simply postponed the matter.[6] Their procrastination assumed that the issue need not be decided upon at once and that Petersburg must authorize any relocation.

All the same, since Catherine had not yet approved release of all the quarantined clothworkers, the senate and the Collegium of Manufactures arranged to keep them away a while longer. The operators agreed to employ some workers at their fulling mills outside Moscow or at other manufactories, allowing still others to seek their own subsistence. These arrangements were to be temporary, for two or three months, until the fate of the manufactory was settled. On 8 June, the operators pledged to receive the released workers on condition that the police publicly proclaim them free of infection—a conclusion already certified by the medical consilium on 2 June —so that Muscovites would accept them as tenants, employees, and neighbors. The senate approved this plan on 20 June. Within ten days Catherine granted permission and Eropkin released 629 persons from the Pokrovskii and Troitskoe quarantines. More than 800 others remained at the Danilov, Simonov, and Pokrovskii monasteries, but the Ugreshskii pesthouse contained a mere handful of sick.[7]

Both in Moscow and Petersburg the authorities cautiously dismantled the other precautions. Moscow's public baths reopened on 12 May. City officials also watched for unusual mortality in the countryside. On 30 May, the senate informed Catherine about sickness at a village owned by Bakhmetev in the Klin district of Moscow province. A staff-surgeon had inspected the sick there, of whom he found 26, "but on all of them there are not any marks suggestive of an infectious disease, and the greater part of them are finding relief after the previous high fever." The senate only reported the incident to forestall rumors. Whatever the disease was, it did not look dangerous.[8]

Persuaded that the threat had passed, Catherine's council approved partial release of the quarantined clothworkers on 6 June, halved the quarantine period on the Moscow-Petersburg highway on 13 June, advocated removal of most checkpoints around Petersburg and free passage of goods from Moscow on 16 June, and endorsed the release of more quarantined workers on 20 June. A week later the council even allowed cloth from the Big Woolen Court to be shipped to the army and the Chief Commissariat, provided it was washed and aired for 6 weeks beforehand. Still wary, Catherine finally accepted this proposal on 19 July, but stipulated that the people who cleansed the cloth should undergo an additional quarantine of 6 weeks. Her caution proved prophetic, for signs of infection began surfacing in the Moscow suburbs by mid-June.[9]

Sudden Death in the Suburbs

Evidently the disease never died out entirely between March and June, when temperature extremes temporarily inhibited the activity of the bacillus and hampered its flea and rat vectors. In the suburbs, meanwhile, several peculiar cases hinted at the plague's survival and surreptitious progress preparatory to a major outburst. These incidents attested to the ambiguous symptoms and confusing disease circumstances that befuddled Moscow's practitioners during the lull between pestilential storms.

On 7 April, staff-surgeon Grave inspected a dead local overseer at the police station in the second district and found that the man had expired suddenly with a bubo in the right armpit. At mid-day, Grave examined in the eleventh district the corpse of Maksim Petrov, a merchant who had dropped dead, "and it turned out that this Petrov had suddenly died from the sickness called apoplexy, that is a stroke, and no suspicious symptoms appeared." That evening, however, Dr. Yagel'skii investigated the sudden death of a servant in the ninth district. The absence of external marks prompted another diagnosis of apoplexy, a condition that may resemble septicemic plague. A fourth suspicious case came to light the same day in the Olkovets area of the thirteenth district, between Pokrovskoe and Krasnoe Selo, where merchant Ivan Molchanov "died unexpectedly." Witnesses told Dr. Shafonskii that Molchanov fell ill on 2 April with a pain in the side, but the physician found no external symptoms. The neighboring ninth district yielded another corpse on 12 April, a male of about 50 in ragged clothing, with obvious signs of infection: petechiae on the arms, legs, and back.[10]

Other sinister deaths hit these suburban communities from mid-April onward. On 14 April, Grave looked over an old man, unidentified and found dead of apparent apoplexy near a tavern in Pokrovskoe. Two days later an aged couple died in Pokrovskoe without visible signs of infection, and 2 other persons suddenly expired that day in the same district. Although the latter 2 corpses appeared "safe" to Yagel'skii, they were buried with their beds and clothing, and the death room was smoked with juniper for 2 days. On 1 May, Dr. Shafonskii inspected a peasant who had suddenly died at the house of merchant Ivan Abrosimov, proprietor of a hat-making enterprise, near the Foreign Suburb. Death was attributed to epilepsy, a diagnosis which, like apoplexy, would not exclude the possibility of plague.[11]

Two deaths in May disclosed connections with central and suburban textile enterprises, connections of the sort that might have infected some of the previous merchant victims too. Tikhon Alekseev, an employee of Grigorii Serikov's woolen manufactory, expired precipitously in the eleventh district on 4 May after complaining of head pains. Grave classified him as a victim of apoplexy.[12] Even more alarming was the sudden demise of an apprentice from Gusiatnikov's linen manufactory in the adjacent twelfth district, Pavel Anosov, who perished the evening of 15 May, while visiting Samarin's woolen mill at Krasnoe Selo. The multiple cases in that locality in recent weeks, the implication of two textile enterprises in one death, and the onset of warm weather a few days earlier all caused the authorities to investigate.

The police reported Anosov's death the next morning, 16 May, to district supervisor Kliucharev, who informed Eropkin that afternoon. Obviously apprehensive, Eropkin ordered Shafonskii to check the corpse and the site at once. Shafonskii rode over to Krasnoe Selo the same evening. Anosov's relatives and other eyewitnesses told Shafonskii that the deceased had arrived the afternoon of 15 May. Anosov started walking from Zamoskvorech'e, he told his hostess, but became so weak en route that he hired a cart. Upon arrival he insisted that he was not drunk, just exhausted. He stretched out to rest in the courtyard and died before dark. Careful not to touch the corpse, Shafonskii estimated Anosov's age at more than 70, and observed many dark spots on the back and sides, one on the leg and a bloated belly. Death resulted from a circulatory failure, Shafonskii decided, brought on by old age, an advanced case of scurvy, and some signs of putrid fever. He reasoned that Anosov must have felt vigorous the day of his death to have walked such a distance and suggested searching the residence for other cases, to determine whether the dead man had long been sick or had suddenly faltered.[13]

At Eropkin's order, Grave inspected the other residents at the site of death. In the house, which stood apart from the manufactory, Grave examined 11 men, 4 women, and 4 children; none seemed sick. Still, a sentry was detailed to keep them inside until Eropkin authorized their release. Grave then visited Gusiatnikov's linen manufactory in the twelfth district, where Anosov had resided. The owner and one workman declared that the deceased had been over eighty and had long suffered from scurvy. They mentioned that Anosov, when very ill, would not stir from his bed over the peasant-style stove and had recently burned his back in several places. None of the other workers appeared ill. No further cases were reported at either manufactory in the next few weeks, so perhaps the aged Anosov did not die of bubonic plague after all. Yet his fatal odyssey illustrated the human links between Zamoskvorech'e, where the plague erupted earlier, and the northeastern suburbs, where it first appeared and would reappear. This case also demonstrated the crowded living conditions characteristic of suburban Moscow, 19 persons inhabiting a single house, the few rooms of which, like the mill itself, must have been built of wood. Then, too, Anosov's burns recalled the Russian penchant for overheating dwellings in winter, a custom that may have nursed plague foci through the winter of 1770–71. Burn marks could have obscured other, clearer symptoms of plague.[14]

Two days later, on 19 May, a peasant blacksmith died in Pokrovskoe after a single day's illness. Relatives of the deceased told Grave that he had suffered from diarrhea for more than a week, for which he had been drinking brandy. In Grave's estimation, the victim died of inflamed innards. "On the body, except that the back and legs and arms are completely flushed from the stoppage of inflamed blood, no signs of infectious disease appeared."[15] Considering the location of this case and the symptoms described, one may question Grave's diagnosis, for plague symptoms may resemble intoxication.

Cases such as these suggested that bubonic plague survived the unfavorable weather conditions of late spring in several localities. Their scattered distribution presaged a wider epidemic once auspicious natural conditions returned. In mid-June, the conjunction of warmth and humidity inaugurated a summer of pestilence.

On 16 June, Eropkin noted lingering infection at the Ugreshskii pesthouse and, 2 days earlier, 7 persons "newly sick with signs of infectious disease" had arrived from the Simonov quarantine. The outbreak at the Big Woolen Court still weighed upon Eropkin's mind and kindled fears that overcrowding the Simonov Monastery had regenerated disease "from the closeness of the air." On 21 June, he therefore proposed transferring several hundred persons from the Simonov to the Danilov quarantine, the inmates of which were moved to the village of Troitskoe before their final release. By 26 June, the Danilov facility had received 350 clothworkers from the Simonov quarantine. With sickness persisting at the latter, Eropkin removed another 280 persons to the Pokrovskii Monastery on 8 July, leaving only 206 at the Simonov quarantine.[16]

More ominous than flare-ups at the isolation facilities was a succession of sinister incidents in 2 widely separated localities that immediately captured Eropkin's attention. On 22 June, a serf living at the house of merchant Ivan Akonnishnikov in the sixth district suddenly died. Yagel'skii and Grave determined that the victim perished on the third day "from a putrid fever with spots called petechiae of varied size almost all over the body." The corpse was buried with the usual precautions; those living in the same room were temporarily confined to their quarters under observation. The next day, moreover, Dr. Pogoretskii reported 2 other sudden deaths at another house in that district. The wife of an economic peasant and a female house-serf died of putrid, spotted fever acting within 4 days. As before, Eropkin had sentries keep the remaining residents indoors. When a third person expired there with the same symptoms 10 days later, a woman who shared the rooms was taken to a quarantine and all portable belongings were burned.[17]

By 25 June, another peasant was reported ill at Akonnishnikov's house. Dr. Pogoretskii diagnosed the malady as "severe fever with spots." Eropkin evacuated the victim and his cohabitors, under cover of darkness, to the Simonov quarantine. Their movable property was burned, the house was aired and smoked. A day earlier in the adjacent fifth district, Dr. Pogoretskii witnessed a case of multiple death and sickness. At the house of battalion soldier Semen Ivanov beyond the Presnia River in the parish of St. Nicholas the Wonderworker, the doctor found a dead soldier's wife and child. The woman had succumbed in 5 days to a putrid fever with spots, but the infant bore no marks. Ivanov himself died shortly afterwards, he and his aunt having fallen ill with fever, headache, delirium, dark spots, and vomiting. Eropkin ordered the sick woman and anybody else living there to be taken to the Simonov quarantine, their effects burned, and the house fumigated.[18]

Simultaneously, calamity struck across town in Preobrazhenskoe. On 23 June, Eropkin got word that 4 persons had perished suddenly at a house which merchant Vasilii Petrov rented from a deacon for use as a workshop producing silk ribbons. Three peasant workers and Petrov's wife died within 48 hours of each other. None of the victims had been ill more than 3 days, Dr. Yagel'skii estimated; in each case "death proceeded from a powerful putrid fever." A fifth worker expired there on 23 June and Petrov's own death the next day left the workshop empty. All 6 corpses were interred in a field, "and as this occurrence is extraordinary," Eropkin informed the senate, supervisor Kliucharev helped Dr. Yagel'skii burn all the belongings left at the site. A sentry prevented anybody entering the room while it was aired. These precautions did not protect the people living in other rooms, however, and on 5 July a woman became the house's seventh casualty. Eropkin evacuated the 8 persons who shared her room to the Troitskoe quarantine. At the very end of June the death with similar symptoms of a young son of the Petrovs at another house in Preobrazhenskoe, where he must have fled from his parents' household, completed the ruin of the Petrovs, their employees, and their immediate neighbors.[19]

The deaths linked to the Petrovs' workshop underscore several epidemiological relationships. The connection between Moscow's textile industry and the importation and distribution of plague—a connection foreshadowed in both earlier outbreaks and in the scattered cases in April and May—stands out. Preobrazhenskoe and the adjacent suburbs teemed with peasant-manned textile workshops. Operating without licenses, many of these small enterprises escaped regulation and taxation by the municipal and industrial authorities. Thus Petrov purchased one-year licenses for 7 looms in January 1770, but failed to renew them more than a year later, though his enterprise continued in production. In this delinquency, Petrov was only one of 321 individuals and 1,171 looms once known to the authorities.[20] No doubt similar enterprises, never licensed, operated clandestinely in suburban residences. Some operations probably moved from one house to another to avoid detection and because of changes in ownership. Because the workshops had effectively removed themselves from the jurisdiction of the Collegium of Manufactures, that agency had not inspected them after the outbreak at the Big Woolen Court.

Procurement of raw materials and subcontracts with other textile enterprises—some clothworkers and their dependents at the larger manufactories also worked at home and at other workshops—tied such enterprises to the larger economy of the metropolitan area. One may hypothesize that *Y. pestis* reached the Petrovs' workshop in a bale of silk directly from a southern supplier, or indirectly from another local or provincial textile enterprise. "In what manner the contagion got among these people could not be ascertained," Dr. Mertens mused later. "Perhaps, through the negligence of the Centinels, they had some communication with the persons under quarantine; or had become infected by bringing into use clothes and other effects, which the last-mentioned persons might have concealed under ground before their removal to the quarantine-hospital."[21]

This outbreak demonstrates again the importance of housing conditions in the genesis of a plague epidemic. The structure afflicted was obviously crowded: at least 8 persons working and living in one room, 9 in another.

Most if not all of the house was used as dwellings. Although nobody recorded the number of rooms, it probably did not exceed 3. Ownership by a deacon implied modest size, in view of the clergy's generally limited means and the small houses they owned in that area in 1775: 49 messuages with 98 rooms. As a further example of the small houses in Preobrazhenskoe, a fire there in February 1772 destroyed 2 shops and 10 messuages with 21 rooms.[22] The house in which the Petrovs lived was almost certainly built of wood and, hence, easily accessible to rats. If infective fleas arrived with a shipment of silk, they could have quickly infected the workers and residents of the one-room workshop and then reached the other room somewhat later, either borne there by rats or on transferred property.

Finally, this instance showed how the authorities' well-intentioned countermeasures backfired. Confining people to a crowded, plague-infected house was tantamount to a death sentence. Burning the belongings of the deceased and removing the portable property of the quarantined to storehouses, moreover, caused people to conceal the sickness and to flee from confinement to their residences or removal to quarantine. Eropkin's failure to inform the public of these policies and his attempts to camouflage such activities by performing them at night, when people were forbidden to venture out, aggravated popular fears. Such fears, in turn, undercut cooperation with the authorities, stymied their attempts to trace the incidence of disease, and (they feared) propagated it more widely.

Aside from the likelihood that frightened Muscovites hid many new instances of infection, multiple cases with suspicious symptoms remained few and widely scattered until late July, beclouding perceptions of the emergent epidemic. The daily mortality rate displayed no marked rise as it hovered between 35 and 65 for most of the month (graph 2). At any rate, Eropkin had probably received partial figures over several days and had either misread their significance or discounted them as erroneous. Well into July, the periodic reports from the parish clergy disclosed no cause for alarm, either. While nobody knew what the usual mortality rate in Moscow was, everybody expected some increase during the summer "fever season." Dr. Mertens later estimated the normal death rate at 10 or 15 per day, remarking that even when putrid fever was prevalent in 1769-70, the daily toll did not exceed 30.[23]

Thus Eropkin and his medical advisers, though concerned about the reappearance of infection, withheld broader precautions until the threat became clearer. Criticism of the precautions taken in March and April must have encouraged their vacillation. Eropkin steadily reported suspicious cases, but he did not announce them publicly or restrict entry or exit. Only departure to Petersburg required certification, and on 4 July Eropkin requested 700 more tickets of safe passage "because of the great number of persons departing from Moscow as well as passing through." To supplement the local surgeons, Eropkin commandeered the services of Danilo Samoilovich, who had stopped in Moscow en route from the Danubian Provinces to his new post at Orenburg.[24]

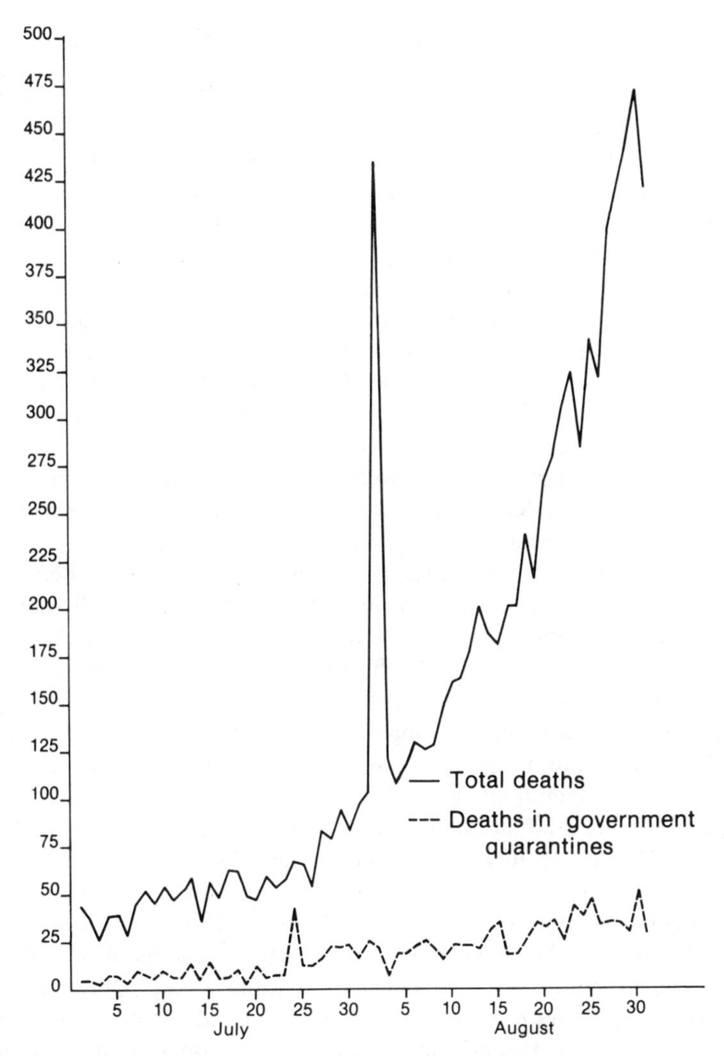

Graph 2 Daily mortality, 1 July–31 August 1771. (*Source:* TsGADA, f. 199, d. 151, pt. 1, no. 1: 140v.–141.) These statistics, evidently gathered from parish registers, were not available to Moscow officials at the time in collated form.

The Petersburg authorities learned of the possible recrudescence on 30 June and immediately reinstituted the checkpoints and three-week quarantine period for travelers and cargoes from Moscow. Four days later they extended precautions against goods from Poland and the Danubian Principalities. Worried about the heartland, Catherine hastily dispatched Dr. Lerche from Kiev to Moscow. The empire's preeminent plague expert arrived in Moscow on 13 July, just in time to witness an explosive epidemic.[25]

The Medical Consilium and Renewed Precautions

At first the new epidemic's territorial advance overshadowed its numerical increase and distressing symptoms. Six of the 14 districts had registered cases of infection by 19 July, when Eropkin asked the senate for two more assistants "as presently here in town in several districts persons are being found sick from fever with spots." Three days earlier he had requested supplemental funds for the growing numbers of persons in quarantine. Given Moscow's crowded housing and the scattered incidence of the disease, the newly instituted practice of removing the healthy as well as the sick from stricken houses inevitably multiplied the quarantined population. Since the Ugreshskii pesthouse contained up to 100 sick on 21 July, Eropkin began sending all new cases to the much larger Simonov Monastery. Consequently, the death toll at the quarantines edged upward to a daily high of 14 on 15 July—double or triple the rate observed from April through June.[26]

By late July, the epidemic started exploding. Following a steady upward trend from 7 July, mortality throughout the city jumped from 53 to 82 on 26–27 July and rose to 97 on the last day of the month (graph 2). Before July ended, sudden death or suspicious illness had stricken every district, and most registered multiple cases. Deaths at the isolation facilities ballooned to 42 on 24 July, triple the previous high. Total mortality reported that month surpassed the June figure by 60 percent.[27] Furthermore, the medical inspectors encountered ever more alarming symptoms with ever greater frequency.

For almost a month, the disease concealed its character; victims exhibited vague and diverse symptoms, much like those seen at the Big Woolen Court six months earlier and in Moldavia the previous year. For example, at Eropkin's order, on 15 July Dr. Kuhlemann and Dr. Lado examined those sent to the Simonov Monastery. Lado's conclusions have not been found, but his senior colleague rejected suspicions of plague and repeated his contention that the disease must be "a most malignant species of spotted fever." Buboes and "so-called carbuncles," which some practitioners had reported, did not alarm Kuhlemann; he dismissed them as accidental symptoms or simple "sores." Unlike true plague, he argued, the disease spread more from "vapors emanating from the sick than through direct contact." Kuhlemann boasted that he risked taking some pulses through a membrane of cow-gut soaked in vinegar, even checked a few bare-handed, so certain was he that it could not be plague.[28] His findings recalled the medical debates of the spring and probably reactivated Eropkin's own doubts.

The Moscow practitioners could now call upon Dr. Lerche's experience and authority. Lerche, however, did not decide it was plague until 24 July. That day he accompanied Shafonskii, Yagel'skii, and Grave to inspect some cases in Pokrovskoe, the site of several puzzling deaths since April. These localities must have harbored some of the first foci, for the victims displayed more advanced symptoms. At Pokrovskoe and in a nearby village, Lerche and his colleagues examined two dead women afflicted with dark spots. Visiting adjacent Krasnoe Selo, they inspected a peasant and a girl, both of whom had been sick for 2 days with headache and prostration. Both had buboes in the groin; the girl had dark spots all over and a carbuncle of the sacrum, "which signs show a dangerous and infectious disease." This medical team also visited the Ugreshskii and Simonov pesthouses, checking about 60 patients in all.[29]

That same day supervisor Kliucharev heard about a corpse in the house of the widow Rudakova, also in the thirteenth district, with whom some Old Believer girls had been living. A girl's body was discovered in a loft bound up in matting and buried under brushwood. Dark marks and a bubo in the groin persuaded Shafonskii that the victim had died of infection. Rudakova testified that her boarder had perished in 4 days, and confessed her own attempt to conceal the corpse. Shafonskii returned to Pokrovskoe and observed a fourteen-year-old girl who had just succumbed after 3 days' illness. Her corpse also displayed dark spots, and the merchant landlord of the house looked "dangerously ill and has a bubo under the left armpit."[30]

These cases marked the first multiple discovery since the spring of the best known sign of plague, the bubo. Only toward the end of July did the medical inspectors regularly find buboes—perhaps because they began looking for them. As Dr. Mertens summarized the symptoms for that period: "The sick, as well as the dead bodies, exhibited large purple spots and vibices; in many there were carbuncles and buboes. Some died suddenly, or in the space of 24 hours, before the buboes and carbuncles had time to come out; but the greatest number died on the third or fourth day." By mid-August, however, "buboes and carbuncles were more frequent than they had been in July." The daily reports to Eropkin from the district medical inspectors confirm Mertens' picture of the changing symptoms encountered in late July and early August.[31] In conjunction with the epidemic's sporadic and scattered incidence, the belated emergence or detection of characteristic symptoms delayed early diagnosis of the disease.

Eropkin finally reconvened the medical consilium on 26 July. In reviewing the situation, Dr. Lerche joined all the local physicians except Kuhlemann and Shkiadan, neither of whom attended this meeting. Indeed, Shkiadan had left Moscow on 21 July and returned only on 9 August. In contrast to the earlier disputes, this time the consilium unanimously and unequivocally declared the disease to be plague. Anticipating Eropkin's doubts, the consilium cited recent findings and leaned on Lerche's expertise. The doctors explained the timely abatement of the 2 previous outbreaks as a consequence of the countermeasures undertaken; "but at present, according to examinations coming in to the consilium from many district doctors, after reviewing and discussing these with those same doctors who have carefully examined the dead and the sick in their district," they concluded that infection had enveloped the city. They described the affliction "from its symptoms, its rapid course, and its death-dealing consequences" as "extremely dangerous" and threatening "great harm to the whole of society." Repudiating any practitioners who still denied that the disease was pestilential, the physicians urged Eropkin not to believe any such assurances. These conclusions received vigorous endorsement from the venerable Dr. Lerche. After inspecting some 60 cases in the course of a few days he "had witnessed and with horror and sorrow acknowledged them all subject to a dangerous and infectious disease with symptoms such as buboes, carbuncles, and dark spots, and without any doubt confirmed the disease as the real pestilential distemper."[32]

The consilium then advocated a broad program of countermeasures, but warned that "all precautions, in such a populous and spacious city as Moscow, are subject to many difficulties." Foremost must be an improved system of registering the sick and the dead. Though people were supposed to inform the district supervisors of all deaths that occurred within a span of 4 days, and though the clergy were obliged to issue burial permits for all corpses, these prescriptions merely encouraged concealment. Besides, accurate registration of all sudden deaths could not be the sole measure of plague. "Experience has sufficiently proved that this disease does not strike everyone equally, but some sooner and others later." To supplement the network of surveillance, inspectors should be chosen from the upper strata of townspeople and from the house stewards of the nobility, to visit daily every 10 or 20 houses in their neighborhoods. They should compile lists of local residents and check the health of each every day. "Through such daily inspections not only is it possible to learn the condition of the inhabitants and the infected houses, but no sick or dead person can be hidden."[33]

To bury the dead outside town and to convey the sick and the suspect to isolation facilities on the periphery, the doctors advised recruiting 4 separate groups of workers: one to remove the dead, another to bury them, a third to transport the sick to the pesthouses, and a fourth to quarantine healthy persons from infected houses. When not working, all these people must live in special houses under guard, to prevent contacts with the public. As before, stricken houses should be fumigated and aired; the immediate belongings of victims should be burned and any valuable movable property stored. To minimize interpersonal contacts, the medical consilium recommended closing the public baths, restricting liquor sales to purchases through a window or door, suspending the sale of used clothes, and prohibiting concourses at eating establishments, "especially in Kitai-gorod at the Synod Choristers where there is great crowding and a great stench."[34] Sentries should enforce all these countermeasures, the doctors concluded, "and if, according to these precautions and those previously given by the medical consilium, everything will be exactly and strictly observed, then the consilium hopes that this disease can be stopped."[35]

Eropkin presented the consilium's program to the senate on 28–29 July. Still perplexed about the identity of the infection, the senators instructed the

Medical Office to poll those practitioners who denied the malady was pestilential. Kuhlemann and Shkiadan submitted their opinions on 6 and 10 August, respectively. After Kuhlemann restated his doubts on the basis of his visit to the Simonov pesthouse on 15 July, he confessed the limitations of his observations, complained of chronic rheumatism and weak vision, and conceded Lerche's authority. Shkiadan acknowledged Lerche's expertise, too, and quoted the testimony of Dr. Lado. Although the senate demanded that the Medical Office also solicit any doubts from surgeons, no other practitioners in Moscow challenged the consensus of the medical consilium.[36]

After conferring with Eropkin and Saltykov, the senate approved most of the consilium's program. If the epidemic worsened, another quarantine might be built outside town, and to assist in burying the dead, convicts might be drafted for duty. All "idle and vagrant villagers" in the city, except for provisioners and victualers, carpenters and stonemasons, should be sent back to their rural abodes by the police, who should warn people against sheltering outsiders.[37] Nevertheless, the senate declined to expand medical surveillance for fear that multiplication of local inspectors would burden Muscovites unnecessarily and promote greater personal contact and wider infection.

The Moscow authorities forwarded this modified program to Petersburg on 2 August, along with the consilium's opinion of 26 July. Should the situation worsen, the senators vowed to adopt Catherine's emergency plan of 31 March. That program, which had not been implemented because of the quick subsidence of the second outbreak, envisaged closing Moscow and regulating all departures by a cordon 20 miles away. If the Moscow authorities had withheld Catherine's emergency program in April for fear of inciting alarm, they now postponed it for a different reason: fear of a subsistence crisis. Muscovites were already restive, "the more so as because of an utterly unfounded rumor about the prohibition of anybody entering or leaving Moscow, which continued no more than two hours, and when nothing was seen being delivered to the markets, then discontent was detected among the people."[38]

The proposals of the medical consilium, as adopted by the Moscow authorities and announced by the district supervisors at the start of August, constituted a cautious response to the emerging epidemic.[39] Founded as these precautions were on faulty epidemiology, they would not have arrested the plague even if perfectly implemented. In practice, their implementation encountered greater obstacles than anyone foresaw. To execute the program would obviously require extensive cooperation between the city administration, the medical professionals, and the population. Yet recent events yielded no promise of such cooperation. Quite the contrary: Moscow's medical and administrative leadership was showing disarray, many Muscovites were decamping, and the municipal economy was decaying. Portents of disaster multiplied as July turned into August.

Two incidents in late July foretold some of the ways Muscovites would react to the impending crisis. On 21 July, parishioners from the Arbat section entreated Dmitrii Mikhailov, archpriest of the Krutitskii Archbishopric Cathedral, to lead a procession with the cross and icons on Sunday, 24 July, offering public prayers against disease. Mikhailov fulfilled their plea, but when the Moscow Synodal Office learned of the proceedings a day afterward, Archbishop Amvrosii inquired who had authorized the procession and mentioned that clergymen of the Rogozhskaia and Tverskaia drovers' communities had requested the same rite. Within a week the Church hierarchy decided to welcome such initiatives, even arranging a procession at the Kremlin's Assumption Cathedral on the Feast of the Assumption (15 August). On 2 August, the Synodal Office ordered public prayers against pestilence read in all churches. For this purpose, Amvrosii retrieved the special prayers printed in April but never released, distributing them to 450 churches and monasteries by 18 August. This activity demonstrated that Muscovites perceived the threat at the same time that Eropkin and the doctors did. Their initial reaction was to seek divine aid, an initiative that the parish clergy and the Church hierarchy both endorsed. Nevertheless, the religious processions that occurred with increasing frequency in August soon elicited criticism from the medical community and city administration, which suspected them of propagating infection and pandering to superstition. This clash of popular mores and medical administrative opinion intensified as the epidemic mounted.[40]

Eropkin personally felt the plague's hot breath on 30 July, when an orderly fell sick in a tent near his house, with "black spots called petechiae on his body, a carbuncle on the leg, and a bubo painfully beginning in the armpit." The patient was sent to the Simonov pesthouse. As the case occurred so close to Eropkin's house, where he constantly received his subordinates, the senator feared for himself and his staff. Fatigued, harried, and chronically ill, Eropkin requested a month's leave from his duties. When Catherine and her councilors received Eropkin's plea on 8 August, along with the first full reports of the deteriorating situation in Moscow, they insisted that he remain on duty. The Empress assured Eropkin that his leadership could not be spared and evidently awarded him a substantial sum, while urging him to cleanse his house. She also assigned senator Mikhail Sobakin to be his chief deputy. Until Sobakin arrived in Moscow on 17 August, however, Eropkin directed the antiplague campaign alone. These pressures were but a foretaste of the trials ahead.[41]

The Plague's Progress

Despite Eropkin's bid for relief, the senate's reimposition of precautions, and the physicians' new-found unanimity in identifying the disease, the epidemic baffled them all until the third week of August. Only then did its mushrooming manifestations dispel all hopeful doubts. If no single indicator convinced Eropkin that calamity had seized the metropolis, a whole series of alarms signalled its tightening grip: an accelerating death rate, multiple cases in many districts, and infection of noble households, industrial enterprises, and Moscow's environs.

The upsweep of mortality plotted in graph 2 was not, it must be repeated, quite so evident to Moscow officialdom. Had such data been known, it is doubtful that they would have inspired greater concern any sooner. Nobody then or now could believe that 435 people died on 2 August: a patently inflated statistic that must have subsumed figures for several days, if it was not simply a copyist's error. Anyone could see that mortality had risen well above normal by August. Yet the death toll climbed rather gradually until 17–23 August, when it shot from 200 to 323 and a week later hit 470. That was the kind of rampant mortality that people expected of real plague. Hence, one anonymous resident saw the epidemic entering the critical stage after 17 August.[42] Although Eropkin monitored the growing death toll throughout August, he interpreted it in a manner that scaled down the epidemic. On 9 August, for instance, he counted 79 deaths from infection in 5 days, i.e., about 16 per day; while for 9–16 August the toll amounted to 189, a daily average of only 24.[43] For 14 August alone, he privately estimated 170 deaths from all causes, as compared to a total of 186 entered for that date in graph 2; but he attributed only 40 deaths to "the aforementioned disease," which he thought had recently killed not less than 16 persons per day.[44] Throughout August, then, Eropkin sharply differentiated the rise in overall mortality from the slowly increasing number of plague victims. Indeed, on 31 August he reported 207 deaths from "dangerous disease" and 615 from "other diseases" in the past 48 hours, but then deduced massive concealment and misdiagnosis because, only a week before, the ordinary daily mortality had not surpassed 50. Similar uncertainty induced the senate to ask the police, on 9 September, for the mortality from natural and pestilential causes in July and August and, if possible, the monthly toll since the start of the year.[45]

More daunting than the rising death count were the abandoned corpses that speckled the streets with greater frequency and the multiple cases of infection that began to appear every day in half or more of the districts.[46] On 15 August, Eropkin calculated that 200 houses had been stricken, including 40 noble households. By infecting new territory and striking houses of the well-born, the epidemic punctured hopes that, like both of the earlier outbursts, it might be confined to poor people and poor districts. For example, by 11 August inspectors discovered 4 dead and 9 sick at the house of Countess Ekaterina Saltykova in the first district, and by 29 August 4 more cases appeared in 2 of her houses in other districts. The victims, all servants, all displayed plague symptoms.[47] Eropkin was particularly shocked to learn on

11 August that the wife of Privy Counselor Fedor Knutov had collapsed with 2 carbuncles of the sacrum at her residence in the second district. Doctors Zybelin and Erasmus confirmed her affliction, which they blamed on a purchase of old clothing and a shawl. Removed to a pesthouse, the lady died on 14 August. Eropkin offered her husband the choice of entering a quarantine or remaining home under guard; he stayed home and survived, but several of his servants died.[48] Indeed, this case anticipated Eropkin's subsequent doubts about the efficacy of compelling the sick and the suspect to enter extramural quarantines. By 10 August, about 200 persons were in the quarantines, where the mortality showed no drastic rise, and Eropkin hoped that the cooler weather of recent days would reinforce such isolation procedures.[49] Unfortunately, temperatures declined only slightly amid constant showers, and the plague skyrocketed.

On 24 July, just as the doctors decided the disease must be plague, Eropkin ordered the Collegium of Manufactures to check the workers at 2 registered textile mills, Kliuev's in the seventh district and Kolosov's in the ninth, where sudden deaths had been reported the day before. These incidents provided the first inkling that manufactories, like the workshops already stricken, also might become hotbeds of infection. Consequently, the Collegium of Manufactures undertook inspection of all registered enterprises on 26 July.[50]

During the next 2 weeks at least 8 other textile manufactories in 5 different districts reported infection, most registering more than one incident. Several cases occurred at 2 of the city's largest enterprises, Tames's linen mill in the fourth district and the Admiralty's sailcloth manufactory in Preobrazhenskoe.[51] By 18 August, in fact, an Admiralty official reported the death of 118 workers and dependents since 13 July; another 97 were still sick.[52] Other statistics for the first 3 weeks of August confirmed the mounting peril: a total of 75 casualties at 13 enterprises, not including the Admiralty mill. Like Eropkin, the manufactory operators attributed most of these losses to noninfectious diseases, admitting only 13 deaths from infection at 6 enterprises; but the magnitude of the mortality and the march of events belied that distinction.[53]

The situation worsened so rapidly that on 17 August Eropkin and Saltykov asked the senate to close all manufactories temporarily.[54] Implementing this order encountered immediate difficulties. About half of the 4,000 workers affected had no refuge once their employers shut down; they were legally and economically bound to the manufactories, where many also resided. Unlike many hired peasant workers, they had neither masters nor villages to return to. The same problem arose for those people, mainly women arrested for vice, whom the authorities consigned to temporary labor at manufactories. A quick survey disclosed 184 of them, only 37 of whom could be sent away.[55]

In consultation with the senate and the operators, Sukin made various dispositions for the different categories of workers. After medical inspection of everybody at the enterprise, hired workers were given passports to return to their villages. Entrepreneurs who owned villages or operated enterprises elsewhere were encouraged to transfer their Moscow employees thither. Bondaged laborers who lived in town were allowed to leave the premises. For those with nowhere to go and no other resources, the operators provided food, shelter, and subsistence money, while keeping them off the street and listing them by name for Eropkin's information. Fearful that sick workers might overflow the isolation facilities, the senate proposed that the operators establish special quarantines of their own. This proposal resulted in several communally organized quarantines that gradually supplemented and, in some instances, supplanted the despised government facilities. Toward the end of August, several groups of entrepreneurs founded quarantines, as did a few individuals.[56] A quarantine for workers from the Kadashevskii Court was organized at Tsaritsyn Meadow, a very dangerous location because of its proximity to the grain market at Bolotnaia Square.[57]

All these measures removed many workers from Moscow and provided for the idled ones left behind. About 400 persons stayed at the Kadashevskii Court, for example, and Tames's mill housed 681 workers in 126 rooms. By contrast, the employees of Kolosov's silk manufactory went several ways: 36 left for his silk enterprise in Yaroslavl and 30 for his village of Batyevo, 186 remained in their homes or apartments in Moscow, and 59 stayed at the Ambassadorial Court or at the owner's homes in the seventh district and on the Yauza in the ninth district. Concurrently, the raging epidemic consumed greater numbers of workers at manufactories and workshops alike.[58] Others died on the streets or at home, many in crowded corners of single rooms. In the period 25 August–16 November, for example, Anna Nosyreva's woolen manufactory at the Kadashevskii Court lost 151 workers and dependents, at least two-thirds of whom perished at home. Sixteen of these victims were married and succumbed together; many of the others also were related.[59] Indeed, the plague inflicted countless family tragedies. Peter Nikitin, an apprentice of Sakharov's hat manufactory, who lived in his own house in the tenth district, came to work sick with headache and fever on 29 August and dolefully recounted how his wife had failed to return from a religious procession 3 days before. He died 2 days later.[60]

The Moscow authorities also took alarm at the plague's invasion of the hinterland and worried about another incursion from the Ukraine. Like the infection of industry, the plague's entry into Moscow's environs was not immediately apparent to Eropkin and his subordinates. Their delayed recognition stemmed from faulty reporting—the network of district supervisors did not encompass many suburbs before 20 August—from the general consternation, and from lack of liaison with the various agencies that administered different suburban communities. In any event, given the haphazard growth of the city, nobody knew exactly where Moscow ended and the countryside began. Several cases finally compelled attention to the epidemic's extraurban dimensions.

On 29 July, the senate proposed dismantling Andronovka, a newly built village of economic peasants east of Moscow near the Vladimir Road, where a suspicious corpse had been brought from the Rogozhskaia Drovers' community. Worried that the district supervisors could not watch the village, the senate had earlier suspected it of harboring thieves and brigands. Because the place came under the jurisdiction of the Collegium of Economy, the senate had to consult the appropriate authorities before ordering its removal. In the interim, disease proliferated there and in other suburban villages.[61]

The senate learned of another, more serious outbreak on 8 August. While inspecting the Ugreshskii pesthouse on 4 August, Dr. Yagel'skii heard from an officer on guard there and from Prince Peter Makulov, overseer of the facility, about unusual mortality in nearby Sluzhnaia Slobotka. All 3 officials went there at once and found 3 dead and 4 sick in 2 houses. Informed that 6 others had recently died in the same rooms, Yagel'skii concluded that "one may assume that they died of the same infectious disease." The neighbors must have known the disease was infectious, Yagel'skii observed, because the adjacent houses had been evacuated and barred. Indeed, the villagers admitted that the same thing had been happening, unreported, in neighboring hamlets. Yagel'skii forecast further deaths if such concealment continued. Prince Makulov reported cases elsewhere. In nearby Kopat'e, "one house has died out, but they do not know how many people, while in the hamlet of Tokarevo 6 persons [died] in one house in a short time, whose dead bodies were buried in a separate place away from the other dead."[62]

The senate directed the Collegium of Economy and Governor Yushkov to institute the antiepidemic measures prescribed by the senate instructions of 9 January. Both the collegium and the governor investigated the afflicted locality. The local government agent, Captain Voeikov, denied concealing the outbreak, explaining that he only heard of it on 4 August and was about to report it when Yagel'skii and Makulov appeared. Inspection of Tokarevo confirmed the death of 7 persons in one house within 5 days. Even so, neighbors avowed that the deceased had been ill 10 to 12 days, and the attending surgeon affirmed that 4 "died of a severe fever, but three infants from smallpox." Kopat'e yielded no more suspicious cases. Yet 3 subsequent visits to Tokarevo revealed 8 more deaths in the same house within 12 days, through 19 August. Residence outside Moscow offered scant protection and conferred no immunity upon crowded households struck by plague.[63]

On 8 August, the senate received word of an incident 60 miles away. From the checkpoint at Borovsk, Captain Bulgakov reported on 3 August that the local voevoda had called surgeon Ivan Shtelin to inspect a corpse outside the town. They discovered a male body with "dark spots on the chest, swelling below the left arm and in the groin, and a dark wound on the same left arm." From caution, they buried the body in a deep pit remote from habitations and burned the dead man's clothes, the cart he had traveled in, and the horse harness. They also quarantined the driver who had transported the deceased, whose identity they investigated. Inquiries at nearby Rebushenskaia brought forward Nikita Savelev, father of the deceased, who said his son Timofei had woven ribbons in Moscow suburb of Pokrovskoe. Alarmed at the thought of diseased persons leaving the city without medical inspection, the senate inquired where the dead Savelev had lived in Moscow. But by the time the Borovsk voevoda chancery received this inquiry on 6 September, the Moscow authorities were no longer interested in the answer. The immediate lesson was clear: refugees from Moscow might carry pestilence afield.[64]

Barely a week later, on 17 August, the Moscow authorities learned of the plague's reappearance at Nezhin in the Ukraine. In the period 16–26 July, more than 100 persons at Nezhin fell ill with "fevers, including several of the usual ones, while the rest are putrid and with spots, and seventeen with carbuncles and buboes." Dr. Paulsohn, the only physician in the region, declared the maladies to be extremely infectious. More than 40 died in a lazaret outside Nezhin and up to 15 in town. In all, Nezhin in the period 16 July–3 August registered more than 400 sick, 34 with carbuncles and buboes; 250 died. The town was closed, but the plague raged until November and supposedly killed 4,594 persons. The senate reacted to this threat by prohibiting the importation into Moscow guberniia of all goods from Nezhin.[65]

If all these danger signals left Eropkin irresolute, Dr. Lerche joined the baleful chorus on 19 August with a detailed explanation of the burgeoning crisis. He assailed the authorities and the people alike for spreading the epidemic by their failure to follow the medical consilium's program. Thus, the stricken had not been detected or isolated in time: "almost all of them have been shown to us no sooner than after their death, despite the fact that they had been ill for several days and that meanwhile the healthy persons around them could infect others through intercourse with the people; from all of this entire houses have died out in various places." Fearful of confinement to infected quarters or of removal to quarantines, people were propagating the disease by fleeing with their belongings. Others concealed the dead and then hauled them at night to different places. The plague also spread by means of the people's adherence to traditional burial ceremonies and the interment of the dead in parish cemeteries in town. Lerche insisted that the clergy exhort their parishioners against these dangerous practices. Those employed to remove the sick and the dead were broadcasting pestilence too, the doctor believed. Instead of being lodged in isolated quarters when off duty, they were allowed to wander about. Their constant intercourse with infected persons and articles practically guaranteed infection, the more so as many lacked protective clothing; "thus many of them have already fallen ill and died." Also, the police lacked sufficient personnel, horses, and carts to handle the multiplying number of victims, not to mention fumigating infected houses. Lerche suggested better wages as an incentive for the people discharging these essential duties.[66]

All these failings obstructed a clear perception of the epidemic's scope, Lerche complained: "Unfortunately this disease has already been so diffused in Moscow that it really is not known which houses still remain free of it." His solution was to summon the people to help themselves. The public—more particularly "the vulgar people, especially in those districts of town where several houses have already been infected"—must regularly air, wash, and fumigate all personal belongings. Special supervisors should oversee this campaign. The imminent arrival of cool autumn weather, heralded by recent showers, also would help. The common people, Lerche reiterated, must be warned against overheating their quarters. He recommended vinegar for sniffing and for bathing the face. Fumigatory bonfires might be used as well. If people diligently observed all these precautions, Lerche predicted that with God's aid the plague would soon wane.[67]

Imploring Eropkin to adopt these measures forthwith, Lerche suggested several departures from previous policy. To appease people's repugnance for the system of compulsory quarantine, the sick and their families should be promised compensation for lost property. Surely, the nobility and the better-off citizenry whom God had spared from pestilence, Lerche reasoned, would succor their less fortunate neighbors. Special rewards should be provided for medical professionals quarantined with the stricken, 8 of whom had already perished. Practitioners drafted from private practice also ought to be specially rewarded. Lerche's proposals essentially repeated the medical consilium's program of 26 July, stressing the urgency of a comprehensive program of emergency measures.[68] But his prescriptions underestimated the obstacles blocking implementation of wider precautions, obstacles that loomed ever larger as the plague erupted.

All these tremors delineated a city-wide crisis that caused Eropkin to take emergency measures. On 19 August, he expanded sanitary surveillance by assigning 6 Guards officers and 6 practitioners to the main suburban communities. In effect, Moscow was now subdivided into 20 districts served by 30 medical professionals. Simultaneously, the district supervisors selected decurions (*desiatskie*) to compile registers of neighborhoods and report mortality therein—the very device that the senate had previously rejected as too burdensome. To cope with the flood of reports, the senate assigned Eropkin 12 more clerks. To ease the load on his office, he delegated 2 clerical assistants to each district supervisor on 29 August. Furthermore, Eropkin and his newly arrived deputy, Senator Sobakin, divided the city between them, each assuming over-all responsibility for half the districts.[69] In another effort to expedite daily tabulation of mortality and morbidity, Eropkin, on 23 August, introduced a standardized form that summarized each day's cases in both halves of the city, listing the district and house, the persons sick or dead, the attending practitioners, and the symptoms observed. These rationalized reporting procedures only confirmed the epidemic's explosive incidence, steepening the upward sweep of the mortality curve in the last week of August (graph 2). So many houses were infected that the police could not spare sentries to guard them all; thus on 25 August Eropkin ordered stricken houses left unguarded but barred against entry.

The crisis soon overwhelmed Eropkin's undermanned staff, forced as they were to govern the metropolis in place of the regular administration, most branches of which had halted normal functions by 20 August.[70] The General Infantry Hospital, Paul's Hospital, the Foundling Home, and the infirmary at the Admiralty complex in Preobrazhenskoe all ceased admissions for fear of infection.[71] The death of 2 boarding students at the local garrison school occasioned its closure on 25 August.[72] Because many clerical students and their parents had already died, rector Feofilakt of the Slavo-Greco-Latin Academy warned on 31 August that resumption of classes would expose others to "extreme danger"; so the academy followed the example of Moscow University and posponed fall classes indefinitely. On 7 September, the Church authorities also ordered the monastic clergy not to leave their refuges except in extreme need. To minimize outside contacts, they should select one member to make purchases.[73]

Guards Captain Alexander Sablukov, new supervisor of the eleventh district in Zamoskvorech'e, chronicled the city's dissolution as the population departed. "There's nobody to borrow money from," he observed on 22 August; "for almost all the gentlemen have driven out to the villages." In command of 1,000 messuages, he dealt with 300 persons daily. Police personnel were dragging out the dead with iron hooks. On 30 August, Sablukov commented that "the distemper has enormously increased, and there are no means to exterminate it completely, and even the medics aver that it cannot be expunged until the onset of frosts." The exodus accelerated. "The people are leaving hour by hour," he noted on 1 September: "all the craftsmen, bakers, piemakers, all sorts of peddlers and the like are scattering about the villages. From my district in 6 days about 700 persons have left; before departure the doctors inspect them and issue bills of health." All the law courts closed by 5 September.[74] Thenceforth Moscow drifted toward disaster.

St. Petersburg vs. Moscow

While Eropkin improvised efforts to save the plague infested city, Catherine dictated extraordinary measures, ordering Moscow officialdom, on 20 August, to institute immediately her emergency program of 31 March. The Empress vetoed the use of convict labor to remove the sick to quarantines and restricted its application to burial duties only. She also decreed that willful concealment or abandonment of plague victims would be punished by condemnation to hard labor. To buttress security, Catherine assigned Eropkin 6 officers and 100 soldiers of the Velikolutskii Regiment stationed near Moscow and authorized recruitment of a "police battalion." Paid up to 1 1/2 rubles per month, fed and clothed at government expense, the volunteers could serve in small groups as cordon guards on all roads around Moscow. Eropkin was told to erect barriers where no natural obstacles delimited Moscow from the countryside. He should maintain, even strengthen, the quarantines. "The inhabitants of infected houses, whatever their status, are to be taken out of the city, but tell the eminent to go to their estates, undergoing quarantine twenty miles from the city." Catherine empowered Eropkin to requisition any personnel and money he needed. He might also close the local rag market and prohibit all petty trade, except in foodstuffs and other necessities. Finally, he should summon all householders to observe three sanitary rules: to air enclosed rooms daily, to fumigate personal belongings as often as possible, and to use cold saltwater and vinegar for drinking and washing.[75]

Catherine warned Eropkin about the possible expansion of "these pernicious diseases," and before her council, on 25 August, she reiterated her hope that it was not really plague. The Empress recalled the implication of industry in the epidemic and asked Procurator-General Viazemskii to look into the possibility of removing large manufactories from Moscow. On 31 August, Viazemskii proposed that several enterprises be transferred from Moscow, particularly woolen and linen mills, dyeworks and tanneries.[76]

Since the imperial government had not publicly acknowledged the epidemic, the official press ignored it. Consequently, the meager news that filtered abroad reflected Petersburg's own doubts and denials. "The Reports of the Plague, or a Distemper resembling it, being at Moscow, are without Foundation," the official *London Gazette* declared, on the basis of a Petersburg dispatch of 27 August. "It is true there is a Fever there, which the poor Patients conceal to the last Extremity, for fear of being sent by the Police to the Pest-Houses, which makes them appear to die suddenly. The Government have nevertheless taken Precautions against its spreading." On 6 September, the same source again denounced all rumors of plague.[77] A week later, however, another report from Petersburg declared plaintively: "We are still in the most cruel uncertainty as to the nature of the malady which reigns at Moscow."[78]

British envoy Cathcart championed, if he did not originate, these denials. On 26 August, he declared that plague had never reached Moscow, but admitted that "many principal Inhabitants have deserted the Town, and the Government have from complicated reasons of Policy, established a Quarantine."[79] By contrast, the Austrian Ambassador first mentioned the outbreak on 3 September, puzzling over Petersburg's secretiveness.[80]

Catherine's emergency directives arrived in Moscow on 25 August, but the senate discussed them only 5 days later. Such delay in considering direct orders from the sovereign betokened doubts about the efficacy of the emergency program. Eropkin and Saltykov implemented some of the orders that they had anticipated. On 23 August, the senate prohibited departure from the city at night and interdicted all imports except edibles. But when the formation of a police battalion was announced, on 26 August, no more than 10 men volunteered for duty, Eropkin remarked, "because at present Moscow is sparsely populated as compared to former times."[81] Thus emerged an unforeseen consequence of the practice, pursued throughout the summer, of encouraging healthy persons to leave the city. Indeed, Dr. Mertens reckoned that in August the population had shrunk by almost half, to 150,000. After closing the rag market, suspending petty trade, and forbidding peddlers to hawk wares door-to-door, Eropkin published Catherine's 3 sanitary rules and had the district supervisors obtain signatures from householders signifying compliance.[82]

On 30 August, the senate finally responded to Catherine's emergency program. Its report took so long to prepare that Eropkin had to hold the courier overnight. Both Eropkin and Saltykov sent letters supporting the senate's report, which they knew would bewilder the Empress, for it proposed to cease compulsory extramural quarantines, theretofore the basis of all antiepidemic measures. The senators argued that forcible removal of all inhabitants of stricken houses had proved to be self-defeating. It not only stimulated widespread flight and concealment of the sick, but overcrowded the ill-provisioned quarantines, compromising their effectiveness and inciting popular feeling against them. The senators proposed to remove only the obviously sick; everybody else might remain at home, if they chose, so long as they stayed indoors for 16 days. Such a policy would defuse popular discontent and forestall "all the disorders and audacities now perceptible among the people," some of whom had begun to take their own precautions. Saltykov and Eropkin both averred that all Muscovites would applaud the abolition of compulsory quarantines.[83]

In opposing Catherine's desire to close the city, the senators employed similar logic. Sprawling over a tremendous expanse, lacking exterior walls and barely fortified, Moscow could not possibly be closed. If it were, hunger would soon result and rioting might follow. Vendors of foodstuffs had already dwindled to a quarter of the usual number. Shortages of food, fodder, and firewood were also appearing because of the cordons that prevented entry and examined those who departed. But fugitives continually bypassed the checkpoints and spread pestilence. "The people have already become so desperate and terrified," Saltykov concluded, "that on the roads they do not admit anybody into their houses or sell anything; the quarantines are burdensome to the local people above all, and the checkpoints have already been threatened several times." The daily mortality toll surpassed four hundred, Eropkin exclaimed, swamping the ability of practitioners to certify the dead and to visit the sick. He therefore requested permission to stop medical inspection of the dead. He and Sobakin ceased submitting the daily figures to the senate by the start of September, when Sobakin resigned after several servants died at his town house.[84]

Moscow's proposals infuriated Catherine. Interrupting the council session of 5 September, the Empress led discussion of the reports and, 3 days later, the council endorsed a vehement rejoinder. In the interim, their anguish deepened at the news of apparent plague cases on the road from Pskov to

Petersburg and in a hamlet of Novgorod guberniia; while on 6 September Governor Yushkov confirmed that many districts around Moscow were infected. The epidemic seemed to be moving northwestward, for the governor of Novgorod guberniia reported suspicious sicknesses in the Staraia Russa district on 7 September. After dispatching orders to Moscow on 9 September, Catherine and her councilors approved the text of an "exhortatory manifesto" to the people of Moscow 3 days later.[85]

Petersburg repudiated Moscow's proposals with outraged disbelief. Reaffirming the quarantines and cordons, Catherine rejected the difficulty of implementing both policies as insufficient grounds for their abolition. If the people dreaded the quarantines, she opined, then it was the authorities' fault for their insistence upon segregating entire houses. "Perhaps it is not the quarantines, but this superfluous severity that makes the Moscow inhabitants despair." On only 2 points would the Empress concede: those who immediately reported infection in their dwellings might themselves decide whether to enter a quarantine or to remain sequestered in their houses for 16 days; and the practitioners might cease inspecting the dead. Otherwise the Petersburg authorities insisted that their emergency program be followed exactly. They feared no dearth in Moscow, believing that the city had food reserves and that precautions would facilitate deliveries. Still they authorized Saltykov and Eropkin to restrain food vendors from leaving and, in the event of hunger, to levy supplies from the countryside. Sending Catherine's manifesto to inspire the Muscovites, the Petersburg authorities trusted that God's clemency would spare the old capital. One thousand copies of this proclamation were dispatched on 13 September. Before Catherine's exhortation reached Moscow, however, Muscovites took matters into their own hands.[86]

CHAPTER SEVEN

The Plague Riot (September 1771)

The plague raced through Moscow in early September 1771. Twice delayed since the epidemic's start in late 1770, pestilence finally overtook the metropolis and prepared its collapse. Thus the first 2 weeks of September witnessed the climax of a deadly competition among the swiftly accelerating epidemic, the frenzied efforts of Muscovites to escape it, and the attempts of local authorities to buy time in the hope that cooler weather would slow the onrushing cataclysm. Try as Eropkin and his associates might to contain the competition, they faced terrible odds against the combined forces of rampant confusion and capricious weather, catastrophic pestilence and incipient panic. Events occurred so rapidly that the Petersburg authorities, several days and several hundred miles removed from the action, could only react to the results. In fact, the crisis proved that the Moscow authorities knew the city and its people better than did Catherine and her councilors.

By early August, the Moscow authorities foresaw violence if popular horror of pestilence impeded the delivery of necessities. Their fears worsened throughout August as the metropolitan economy rapidly disintegrated. To forestall a subsistence crisis, Eropkin and his colleagues began modifying the regime of compulsory quarantines, providing for workers idled by the closure of manufactories, and allowing masses of people to leave the city. On 31 August, the day after the senate reiterated grave apprehensions in its proposals to Catherine, it heard distressing confirmation from Chief of Police Bakhmetev. He discounted Governor Yushkov's report of crowding at Moscow's markets and rejected his proposal to establish special exchange points beyond the city limits—even farther away, that is, than Catherine's plan to locate them outside the Zemlianoi Val. Police reports and personal inspection, Bakhmetev declared, disclosed no crowding at local markets. On the contrary, the number of vendors had recently decreased, in response to rumors that Moscow was closed. Because shortages and high prices had already curtailed supplies of firewood and hay, the police had stopped monitoring deliveries for fear of discouraging vendors en route to market. The proposal for special markets struck Bakhmetev as unworkable and likely to burden the majority of the population who, lacking horses, could not hire transport because "extremely few" cabmen still remained in town. This impediment alone might cause greater shortages and higher prices, exacerbating hardships. Crowding was unlikely at the regular markets, Bakhmetev concluded, because the population was diminishing and largely comprised "those who possess no means to leave Moscow and those who daily buy at the markets all necessities for the satisfaction of their residence here." Harkening to Bakhmetev's worries, the senate ordered him to check prices and supplies during the next trading days, 2 and 4 September. On 9 September, the senate heard Bakhmetev's report of the 5th that reiterated the perilous deficit of provisions.[1]

Equally worrisome was the intensifying revulsion against the system of compulsory quarantine. Nobody, it was rumored, returned alive from the isolation facilities. Although the authorities discontinued medical inspection of the dead, on 2 September they reaffirmed the requirement to examine every instance of sickness, regardless of symptoms. False testimony about or simulation of illness was punishable by 15 days' labor at the quarantines or with the neighborhood decurions. Despair aggravated popular distrust of physicians, many of whom were foreigners and strangers to the bulk of the population. Acute animosity arose over the authorities' exhortation to proscribe traditional religious practices, such as washing and kissing the deceased, administering the last rites, accompanying the dead for burial in local churchyards, and making penitential processions. In response to Dr. Lerche's censure of these practices, Eropkin had the district supervisors announce on 5 September that no one should touch the dead, whose coffins should be nailed shut immediately. On 13 September, Archbishop Amvrosii instructed the clergy to administer the sacraments with the utmost caution.[2] All these official precautions violated the traditional religious responses to pestilence. Accustomed to find comfort in Orthodox ritual, the common people of Moscow felt abandoned and, bereft of leadership, turned their accumulating fury against the practitioners and the heartless machine of quarantine regulations.

Two incidents confirmed the explosive potential of panic-stricken people trapped in the plague-ridden metropolis. The first began in the suburb of Lefortovo on 29 August; the second, in the center of Moscow 3 days later. The senate learned of both on 2 September. When Dr. Shafonskii, surgeon's mate Vasilii Korobovskoi, and Guards Captain Semen Volotskii inspected Lefortovo on 29 August, a crowd threatened the lives of the practitioners for allegedly dispensing harmful powders to attendants at the General Infantry Hospital. Additional hostility emerged when Shafonskii detailed Korobovskoi to examine the sick wife and dead baby of hospital attendant Kozlov. Lieutenant Aleksei Kaftyrev, commissar of the hospital, reproached the practitioners for entering the community without his permission, upbraided them for needlessly posting sentries and consigning people to quarantines, and promised Kozlov that his wife would not be inspected or removed.

Captain Volotskii quieted the confrontation by soliciting samples of the powders in question, but he informed Eropkin of the incident and requested authority to punish the ringleaders. Otherwise, he wrote, "I face danger entering these suburbs for inspections of those who are sick, dead, and dangerously ill from the infectious disease." Shafonskii attributed the incident to the drunken waywardness of Kaftyrev, a long-time antagonist at the hospital, and to the desire of the hospital attendants, confined to their posts, to return to their residences in Lefortovo. Whatever the personal motives behind the protest, it plainly reflected the prevalent fears. Since most Muscovites could see no benefit from medical attention or quarantine, they began to turn on the practitioners as the authors of their misery and to resist removal to quarantines. Better to die at home, many reasoned, than in crowded medical dungeons.

The imbroglio at Lefortovo flared anew on 1 September, when Captain Volotskii sent Sergeant Ivan Lepenitskii with a soldier and a convict to inspect the house and seal the effects of a dead widow. Ensign Rodion Elokhov, a local resident, abused Sergeant Lepenitskii and his subordinates "with all sorts of vile words." Elokhov's shouting attracted a concourse of various people, soldiers and their lackeys. Lepenitskii, they shrieked, had been sent by the devil, not by any captain; and they resented outside interference in their communal affairs. After these threats, Elokhov left to rally resistance. He soon returned at the head of a mob and assaulted Sergeant Lepenitskii with a cane. Fortunately for the beleaguered sergeant, Captain Volotskii sent in troops who extricated him from danger. Cheated of its prey, the mob heaped abuse on Lepenitskii's rescuers, "explaining that they allegedly wish to kill them, instead of helping anything," Volotskii reported. The plague and the precautions had exhausted people's patience, so that innocuous incidents such as these easily burst into violence. Then too, the unrest in Lefortovo demonstrated a certain neighborhood feeling of autonomy, like that manifested in the violence at nearby Pokrovskoe in 1766—communal sentiments that the city authorities unwittingly violated by their emergency intervention into the suburbs.

In response to these disorders, the Moscow authorities on 2 September resolved to punish the ringleaders at once. They confined Lieutenant Kaftyrev on bread and water for 2 weeks, handed over Ensign Elokhov for investigation by a military court, and had the police seek out the other participants, publicly lash them, and obtain pledges of good conduct. Analysis by the Medical Office disclosed nothing harmful in the drugs, so Elokhov and his accomplices were punished as ordered. Kaftyrev, however, underwent investigation for more than 2 years, while remaining on half-pay, until the senate finally acquitted him for lack of evidence.[3]

The second violent incident occurred near Red Square on 1 September. Police Lieutenant Savel'ev, assigned to enforce the prohibition against trade in old clothes, found storage bins for such goods at Red Square and near the Neglinnaia, where rag markets were traditionally held. He ordered the Moscow Municipal Administration to send an agent to seal the bins. But when Savel'ev and the municipal agent tried to attach the seals, they collided with Trifon Burukhin, a soldier from the Synodal Office engaged in the rag trade. A crowd surrounded the newcomers and "from behind the people he threw a stone at the aforementioned Lieutenant Savel'ev; however, it did not hit him, but fractured the skull of a soldier in his corps." Although Burukhin was captured, Savel'ev reported that one of his four men died and complained that he lacked sufficient force to suppress the rag trade. In forwarding Savel'ev's report to the senate on 2 September, Bakhmetev lamented that he could not spare anybody else for such duties. The senate assigned 8 soldiers to the police and ordered the Synodal Office to publicly lash the offending soldier, which sentence was executed on 12 September. Trifon Burukhin died 2 days later, either from the punishment or the plague.[4]

This clash further attested to the tension rapidly building among Muscovites. It was significant that soldiers participated in the violence, as they had done at Lefortovo a few days before. Their involvement signified a dangerous decline of security throughout the city. Obviously, the authorities were not receiving the necessary popular support. The police were too few to supervise everything, for many had perished or entered quarantines. Of 427 men employed by the Moscow police in 1771, a total of 242 died before the year ended. The lowest ranking police personnel endured the heaviest losses. Thus, 128 of 180 carters succumbed, along with 63 of 72 chimney sweeps, 8 of 10 craftsmen, 5 of 11 copyists, 12 of 24 scribes, 8 of 20 mounted dragoons, and 2 of 4 drummers.[5] Eropkin also sensed the growing potential for violence and the diminishing human resources to combat it. Most of the Velikolutskii Regiment had been withdrawn to villages 20 miles away from Moscow. On 31 August, Eropkin sent Catherine a register of military personnel under his command that listed 470 men, of whom 34 had recently died. The plague decimated Moscow's security forces almost as fast as the rest of the population.[6]

Fearful of wider disorders, the Moscow authorities sought to calm people by altering the quarantine regime, even before Catherine could consider their proposals of 30 August to that end. As the skyrocketing mortality and morbidity overwhelmed the city's practitioners and security forces, the senate recommended other measures of self-help. At Eropkin's suggestion, the senate on 1 September resolved to call upon representatives of the Moscow merchantry to organize special quarantines and pesthouses; the police announced the same invitation to various suburban communities. President

Mamonov of the Moscow Municipal Administration accompanied several merchants to the senate session of 7 September, where they pledged to construct a pesthouse for their brethren. Their motives in undertaking the project were made quite clear: "just as they will thereby protect themselves from the affliction of this disease, so they will also preserve themselves from removal to the quarantines established by the Senate."[7]

That same day Eropkin presented the senate with a petition from Old Believer merchants and burghers living near Preobrazhenskoe. Like the other merchants, they proposed to institute a communal quarantine at their own cost, "but only in order that all of them be freed from inspections by doctors and commanding officers." Two of the petitioners, Pimen Alekseev and Ivan Prokhorov, were then admitted into the senate chamber and informed that they might construct the facility, so long as they guarded, staffed, provisioned, and administered it without state aid. The senate insisted that medical and police inspection of the quarantine must continue twice weekly, as the Empress had ordered, but conceded that the petitioners' houses would no longer be subject to entry. Alekseev and Prokhorov accepted this stipulation, so the senate endorsed their undertaking. This venture grew into a major center of the Old Belief, the Preobrazhenskoe Cemetery. Another Old Believer community established similar institutions at Rogozhskoe.[8]

On 7 September, the senate also received a petition from representatives of the Lutheran and Catholic congregations of the Foreign Suburb to set aside a burial ground for them at the Vvedenskie Hills. This request received lower priority than the others, probably because fewer people were involved. Concurrently, the senate approved Eropkin's proposal to close down and seal off the Admiralty's sailcloth mill in Preobrazhenskoe, which had been a hotbed of disease since mid-summer, but had not been closed with the other manufactories because of its suburban location and its independence from the Collegium of Manufactures. Orders closing the huge mill went out on 9 September.[9]

Eropkin worked to dispel suspicion of the government quarantines by other means. On 8 September, he released 101 persons from isolation at Troitskoe-Golenishchevo and, 5 days later, discharged 42 from the quarantine at the Kaluga Gates. Catherine applauded these actions and reminded Eropkin that nobody should be quarantined more than 6 weeks, a term that could be shortened for persons living in separate rooms from plague victims. In the quarantines, the Empress reiterated, the sick and the healthy must be separated, without crowding either group. When Catherine reaffirmed these procedures on 17 September, she could not know that events in Moscow had already made her suggestions superfluous.[10]

Eropkin labored to continue inspection of the sick and removal of the dead. Confronted by a critical shortage of manpower, the Senator drafted 280 manufactory workers to serve in the districts. By 12 September, 10 manufactory operators furnished Eropkin with 375 men who, for wages of six copecks per day, were used to guard buildings, to convey the sick to quarantines, and to haul out the dead for burial. As an extra incentive, workers who agreed to assist with the direct handling and treatment of the sick received 10 copecks a day. This recruitment of workers finally implemented the mobilization of the population envisioned in Catherine's emergency program of 31 March, since the formation of a volunteer "police battalion" had proved abortive a few weeks earlier. The authorities also continued to employ several hundred convicts as gravediggers. Like the police employees, these convicts sustained exceptionally high losses during the plague; some 300 perished by early October—about 85 percent of those drafted.[11]

Even as the epidemic outran the capabilities of Moscow's medical community, some practitioners assisted the authorities in publicizing personal precautions. On 6 September, the *Moskovskie vedomosti* (which continued to appear regularly, but shrank in size in September) carried an advertisement for a newly issued "Short Description of the PESTILENTIAL CONTAGION and of the Means That Protect against It, with an Appendix about a Concentrated Spirit of Vinegar." Published by the Moscow University Press, this tract was a translation from the German of Benjamin Schwartz, city-physician at Danzig. Its prescriptions were conventionally eclectic.[12] At the same time, Dr. Lerche and Dr. Yagel'skii both compiled medical advisories, which the senate approved for publication on 1 September. Ten days later Eropkin distributed 500 copies of each to the district supervisors and the clergy for public announcement. Upon receiving 10 copies, Archbishop Amvrosii immediately asked Eropkin to print 300 more for general distribution.[13]

Both Lerche and Yagel'skii summoned the public, "more particularly the common people," to help themselves. Lerche simply excerpted several practical measures from the advice he had given Eropkin on 19 August, urging everybody to air out and to fumigate personal belongings and habitations. If Muscovites adopted these precautions, cooler weather might save the situation. "The cold autumn air that is approaching can greatly facilitate the beneficial effect of airing things out, even sooner than has been expected, for experiences in other places have repeatedly proven that cold in the open air quickly extinguishes the pestilential poison in infected articles." To assist nature, "the common folk must be exhorted, above all, not to heat the room very hot at the present season."[14]

Dr. Yagel'skii employed strict contagionist premises to persuade the common people of the necessity for personal precautions and to denounce false conceptions of the disease. "The sickness called the distemper. . . is now actually present in our city," he declared, "and it does not subsist in the air, as the common folk think and therefore name this sickness the contagion [*perevalka*], but spreads from one person to another solely from close intercourse and contact, both with articles that are infected by the most subtle poison of this sickness and with persons sick and dead from the same sickness." Accordingly, the surest defense was to avoid communication and contact with infected articles, places, or persons; "but inasmuch as the common folk do not observe this, so therefore this misfortune is occurring almost exclusively among them."

To reassure supervisors, priests, gravediggers, and others whose duties entailed communication with plague victims, Yagel'skii dismissed exaggerated notions of instantaneous infection. Some persons fell ill soon after the "poison" entered the blood; others remained outwardly healthy as much as ten days after exposure. The disease could show diverse symptoms, many of which commonly denoted simple putrid fevers. One should suspect plague only when, in addition to fever symptoms, the patient experienced sudden prostration and exhibited dark spots, lesions, or swollen glands. If anyone "of the common sort in a house" showed these symptoms, then his cohabitors should avoid touching the victim and remove him to separate quarters, preferably in a detached hut, barn, or storage room. "These are the methods essential both for the preservation of oneself from this sickness and consequently for the deliverance of oneself from removal to a quarantine."

In the absence of professional medical care, plague patients should be given acidic and cooling food and drink. *Spiritus Nitridul'tsis* (Sweet Spirit of Niter, an alcoholic solution of ethyl nitrite used as a sudorific and diuretic) and Peruvian bark (*Khina-dekhina*) might help if properly used. Sweating should be encouraged and mild emetics employed in case of nausea, but bloodletting and weakening drugs must be avoided. Whenever possible, healthy persons should leave infected places. If unable to leave, they should stay calm, keep clean, and eat properly. For drinking, bathing, and fumigating, people should use vinegar "of the four thieves or, best of all, bezoar vinegar." (Vinegar of the Four Thieves was a mixture of vinegar with camphor, various herbs, and spices that was supposedly devised during the Marseilles epidemic of 1720. Bezoar stones, concretions from the digestive tracts of various animals, were traditionally believed to have magical or medicinal properties.) If all these precautions were followed, Dr. Yagel'skii felt certain that they "will do much good for people."[15]

The significance of Lerche's and Yagel'skii's advice lay less in specifics, all of which were entirely conventional, as in their urging Muscovites to take individual precautions in order to avoid consignment to the government quarantines. Furthermore, both advisories aimed to encourage the people at large. They represented an effort on the part of the authorities, cognizant of the imminent crisis, to calm the people with practical, humane advice.

Of course, the upper strata of the population had been acting upon such advice for some time, and thousands continued to forsake Moscow. "A great many people are leaving from my district," Captain Sablukov remarked on 8 September: "they are all walking and driving to the villages, and in a house no more than three persons remain, while in the houses of the nobility only single caretakers are left." As Dr. Yagel'skii affirmed, so Sablukov confirmed on 12 September, that not everybody caught the plague; "the officers and the other gentlemen staying in Moscow are healthy." Three days later Sablukov still held out hope for the city: "with great impatience we await winter, which can be the best medicine against the plague."[16]

Those few officials, noblemen, and merchants who remained in Moscow took extraordinary precautions. Thus Ivan Beloglazov, steward of the local office of metallurgical tycoon Nikita Akinfievich Demidov, then absent on a European tour, described Moscow on 5 September as "almost half-empty." From Demidov's Moscow properties, most servants and employees, women and children above all, were evacuated to suburban estates. Stewards oversaw cleanliness and precautions in the Moscow houses. For fumigatory and disinfection purposes, they procured juniper and incense, "regular vinegar and of the four thieves." Those staying in Moscow were kept indoors, Beloglazov informed his employer, and given food prepared at home. The gates were locked and guarded, and nobody could leave without special permission. Persons allowed out had to bathe with vinegar, undergo fumigation, wear amulets with camphor, and avoid touching outsiders. To encourage the 12 workers guarding Demidov's town house, they received daily 3 glasses of wine fortified with garlic and wormwood. With government offices, state and private manufactories all closed, some 75,000 workers were said to be unemployed, but the police had forbidden all public gatherings; "and in one word everything has been extinguished, yet since the danger first started to rage for the most part among the common people, it has been ordered not to have any communication with them." To the Petersburg office, Beloglazov commented that same day: "we are living between life and death."[17]

Despite the efforts of officialdom and individuals, the pestilence inexorably spread (graph 3). By 12 September, Moscow lay prostrate, as both Archbishop Amvrosii and Governor-General Saltykov acknowledged. The Archbishop informed the Holy Synod that day of the many monks and churchmen who had died in the city's monasteries. Since nobody survived at the Krestovozdvizhenskii Monastery, Amvrosii begged Eropkin for a sentry to safeguard the valuables there. At Amvrosii's own consistory in the Kremlin's Chudov Monastery, 8 persons had fallen ill, died, or entered quarantines. Most of the conventual houses in Moscow had closed because of the infection. Indeed, Eropkin advised Amvrosii himself to leave for the nearby Pererviinskii Monastery, "whither I have made it my intention to set out," the Archbishop reported. But he never left Moscow.[18]

On 12 September, Saltykov described the calamity for Catherine. The daily death toll was up to 835, including 60 corpses abandoned on the streets; hundreds more were being buried secretly. Economic exchange had virtually stopped as multitudes fled or isolated themselves. "There is nothing to feed the craftsmen, there is no work, in the shops and foodstuff rows there are no buyers, there are no grainstores, and nothing in reserve, it is unsafe from hunger." Government had ceased. Both Eropkin and Sobakin had detected infection among their servants. Sickness had also affected Saltykov's

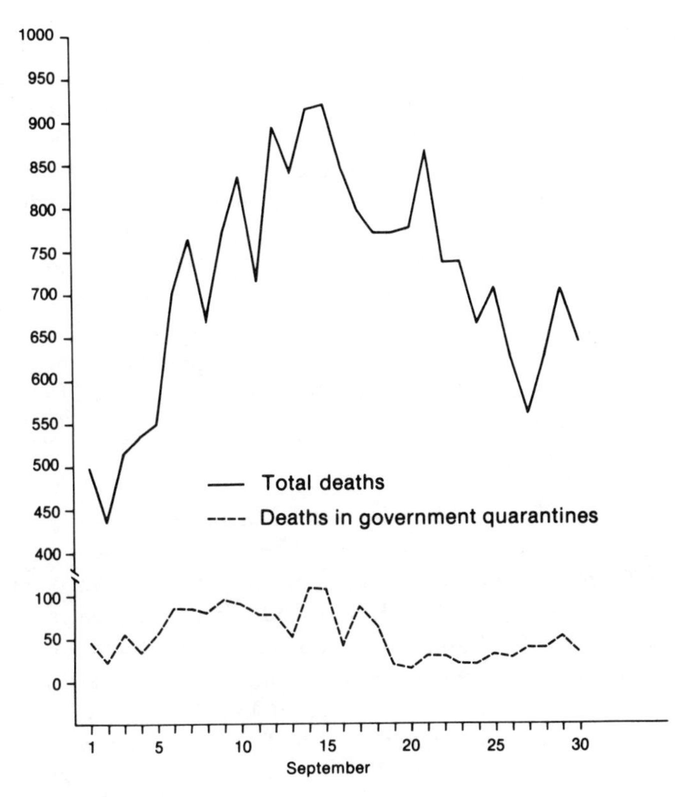

Graph 3 Daily mortality in September 1771. (*Source:* TsGADA, f. 199, d. 151, pt. 1, no. 1: 141.)

chancery, "and people are dying in all the houses around me as well, and I sit alone behind locked gates apprehending my own misfortune." The epidemic had engulfed Moscow's environs too. Saltykov concluded that nothing more could be done and asked permission to leave "during this evil time, until it can become calm from the approaching cold season." He saw Eropkin's efforts as useless, even harmful: "all these district supervisors are spreading the disease further by their own movements and by sending others; it has already so intensified that all measures to stop it are unworkable." Since "nothing terrifies everyone so much as the quarantines," the government should halt the policy of compulsory quarantine and allow people to take their own precautions, as the manufactory operators, merchants, and Old Believers were already doing.[19]

With this agonizing appraisal Saltykov enclosed a summary of mortality statistics for the period from mid-March through 12 September. These registered 2,275 deaths in the pesthouses and quarantines from infectious disease, 17,109 deaths "shown from other diseases," and 665 "dead bodies found on the streets," for a total mortality of 20,049. An interpolation in another hand, undoubtedly Saltykov's, explained the subtotals by commenting that "although by the register it is shown as other diseases, but all those are also infectious, for the number is extraordinary." Two days later Saltykov left Moscow on 14 September, even before his dispatch reached Petersburg.[20]

Unluckily for Saltykov, the events subsequently called the "Plague Riot" (*Chumnyi bunt*) erupted the evening of the day after he drove out to "Marfino," his estate just north of Moscow. On Thursday, 15 September, the official daily mortality count reached 920 in the half-empty city (graph 3). Rioting exploded that very evening. The outbreak should not have surprised the Moscow authorities, in view of the tremulous portents of the previous 3 weeks. Yet in this instance, as before, the violence originated from a seemingly innocuous source.

A Miracle and a Murder

In early September, people began assembling at the Varvarskie Gates in the wall at the eastern edge of Kitai-gorod. From these gates, Varvarka Street, named after St. Varvara (and renamed Razin Street in 1933), ran westward through mixed residential and commercial sections of Kitai-gorod before debouching into the shopping stalls and mud of unpaved Red Square. Above the Varvarskie Gates hung an icon of the Virgin known as the God-Loving Mother of God (*Bogoliubskaia Bogomater'*), which became the subject of miraculous tales.[21] The holy picture attracted special notice when an old woman, after listening to prayers led by a priest of the nearby Church of All Saints, donated 15 copecks to a sentry stationed at the Varvarskie Gates toward the purchase of a lamp to light candles to the icon. Others passing by began to stop and offer prayers. Two supplicants, Savelii Biakov, a soldier of the Semenovskii Guards Regiment, and Il'ia Afanas'ev, a worker at a gold-braid manufactory, brought a lamp to hang before the image. So many supplicants gathered that 5 priests arrived to lead the prayers. Biakov, Afanas'ev, and Peter Ivanov, an economic peasant, started collecting alms to buy a silver cover (*riza*) for the icon, which, they averred, could heal the faithful. According to Biakov, Afanas'ev maintained that he and his sick mother had both obtained relief after praying to the icon; Ivanov also attested to its wonderful powers.[22]

Given the intense religiosity of the Russian Orthodox population in Moscow, with its "forty times forty" churches, the popular veneration of icons, and the desperate circumstances of early September, it is hardly surprising that many Muscovites sought solace in religious ritual. Whether Afanas'ev and his comrades cynically exploited the situation, or simply expressed an elemental desire for salvation in the only forms they knew, remains problematical. In any event, their actions elicited a wide response.

Figure 8 The Varvarskie Gates in the wall of Kitai-gorod in central Moscow; watercolor of the eighteenth century, reproduced courtesy of the Graphics Department, State Historical Museum in Moscow.

Tales of the miraculous icon flew about the city. One version, attributed to Afanas'ev, recounted how the Virgin had appeared to him in a dream complaining of neglect by the people. Enraged at this negligence, Christ resolved to punish the unfaithful with a rain of stones, but His Mother persuaded Him to soften the punishment to a 3-month pestilence. Constant devotion to the icon, it was assumed, would save the faithful from this terrible judgment.[23]

Crowds flocked to pay homage to the icon, blocking passage through the Varvarskie Gates. Within 2 days they collected more than 200 rubles toward the silver cover.[24] Naturally this assemblage in the heart of Moscow frightened the authorities, who believed it might spread pestilence and threaten security. Archbishop Amvrosii, who remained in Moscow despite his vow to leave, regretted especially the role of the clergy in the affair. He believed that some priests without parishes—crossroads clerics as they were familiarly known—were taking advantage of the situation to pander to popular superstitions.

For more than 3 years, Amvrosii had worked to suppress the activities of Moscow's innumerable unemployed clerics, just as the secular administration strove to eliminate beggary and vagabondage. In February 1768, within a month of Amvrosii's installation as archbishop, he forbade clergymen to gather at the Spasskii crossing, the traditional place of assembly for such clerics between St. Basil's Cathedral and the bridge leading over the moat in front of the Kremlin's hallowed Spasskie (Savior's) Gates.[25] To rid Moscow of unemployed clergy, the Archbishop in 1770 tried to regulate the hiring of clerics without parishes, to assign some to provincial parishes, and to expel the rest. In February 1771, he inveighed against public drunkenness among the clergy—a notorious vice of the crossroads clerics in particular—established a schedule of fines for unseemly conduct, and obliged all clergymen to sign pledges acknowledging receipt of the order. Yet some clerics flouted all these policies. On 20 April, a Church official seized 39 illicit clerics at the Spasskii crossing. When the Archbishop's consistory reaffirmed the prohibition on hiring unregistered clerics without parishes and ordered the police to arrest clerical vagabonds, some refractory priests or secular impostors roamed the streets with alms boxes declaring themselves to be "convicts of the consistory." On 21 June, Amvrosii demanded that the police arrest these clerical beggars.[26]

The unsanctioned activities of the clergymen at the Varvarskie Gates seemed doubly dangerous amid the plague. As well as violating hierarchical discipline, they infringed the ban on public assemblies, lent leadership to the restive population, and (many assumed) propagated the plague. From the perspective of these clerics and their multitudinous flock, of course, they were seeking deliverance through time-honored means, and the very failure of medical and administrative measures to alleviate their distress bespoke the need for alternative efforts. Even without the devastating epidemic, the common people of Moscow had ample cause for complaint about the inefficient, arbitrary administration of the city, the lack of welfare services, and the dominance of the nobility, the military, and the top strata of the merchantry. The plague aggravated all these social deficiencies and disparities by afflicting poor people most of all.

The rank-and-file parish clergy, among whom marriage was obligatory, harbored special grievances. They resented the government's draft of military recruits from churchmen and their sons in 1769 as part of the mobilization for the Turkish war. Since Amvrosii and Eropkin had supervised this unpopular levy in Moscow, they incurred great enmity from the clerical estate.[27] The final secularization of Church estates in 1763-64 closed several monastic institutions, for reasons of economy, and made all clergymen more than ever dependent on the state for their livelihood. Nevertheless, the salaries of the parish clergy were so paltry that priests and deacons found themselves compelled to seek larger than legal fees for the performance of rituals such as baptism and marriage, and to solicit alms from the faithful, although the law forbade that practice. The constraints imposed on clerical functions because of the plague—burial of the dead outside the city, avoidance of crowding at Church services, restraint in administering the sacraments, prohibition of penitential processions—all struck hard at the clergy's social functions and slender income and, joined to their considerable losses to disease, drove some to desperation.[28] Little wonder, then, that the discovery of a "miracle" at the Varvarskie Gates attracted clergy from all over the city, or that some of them nursed grudges against the Archbishop. Amvrosii's vigorous support of the antiepidemic campaign, his reputation as a strict administrator, his partly foreign background and education (he was half-Moldavian and half-Ukrainian and had studied at the Kiev Academy and in Poland) all added to his unpopularity.[29]

Eropkin, left alone in charge of the city after the departure of Saltykov and the other senators, conferred with Amvrosii on the best means to disperse the concourse at the Varvarskie Gates. They obviously sensed the danger of provoking the people and sought to proceed discreetly. On 15 September, the Archbishop twice sent emissaries to the Varvarskie Gates, summoning all but 2 of the priests there to report to the consistory. Evidently Amvrosii hoped to remove potential troublemakers from the scene and to prepare the way for the dispersal of the crowd by removing the icon. Whatever his aim, his summons went unheeded. Indeed, this action revived speculation among the crowd to the effect that Amvrosii intended to seize the icon, confiscate the money collected, and give it to the Foundling Home, of which he was a patron. These tales ignited consternation among the crowd and tempered a resolve to "defend" the wonder-working image.

This resolve was heightened when, about five o'clock, as dusk descended over the city, some unidentified priest arrived at the gates and informed Biakov, Afanas'ev, and Yakov Lunin, an eighteen-year-old soldier of clerical background performing guard duty, that Amvrosii was coming with soldiers to take the icon and the money chest in which alms were being collected. "Upon hearing this, the people raised a commotion," Lunin testified later, "and cried out that 'we will not give up either the image or the money, we are putting our last rag toward its decoration in order to make a silver cover and in return to receive healing from the dangerous disease, but the archbishop wishes to give the money to the Foundling Home'." Biakov and Afanas'ev also advised the crowd not to yield the money, complaining that "we are laboring and collecting, but he will take it; and after this," Lunin recalled, "the assembled people stayed to await the archbishop in order not to give up the money."[30]

Perhaps Amvrosii did not perceive that the money was an even more delicate matter than the icon, representing as it did the efforts of the people to contribute to their own salvation. Either he did not know that the money chest already bore a seal and was under guard, or he did not recognize the legitimacy or sufficiency of these measures, which garrison-officer (*Platsmaior*) Vereshchagin had undertaken on his own initiative. From 12 September onward, Major Vereshchagin made daily visits to the Varvarskie Gates to check on the safekeeping of the money, which he feared might be stolen or misused by the collectors. With Governor Yushkov's permission, he ordered the sentry at the gates not to hand over the money to anyone without a written order. Vereshchagin expected, apparently, that Amvrosii would decide what to do with the money, and that the Archbishop would then send instructions or come himself. But Amvrosii did not come in person, and the official he sent, Peter Stepanov, maintained subsequently that his orders were not to remove either the icon or the money, but simply to affix a consistory seal to the money chest and assign a sentry to guard it.

In view of the prior activities of Major Vereshchagin and Amvrosii, however, it seems likely that Stepanov either had secret orders to remove the icon and the money, or had been sent to prepare the way for their removal. For, if one believes Vereshchagin's testimony, Amvrosii and Eropkin must have known about the measures already taken to secure the money. No doubt they intentionally waited until evening, when darkness covered the city, before sending Stepanov and six soldiers. Central Moscow's 600 street lamps scarcely brightened the city in the best of times, but the death of so many police personnel and other city employees must have left most lamps unlighted that September. If Amvrosii and Eropkin hoped the crowd would be more docile after dark, they badly miscalculated.[31]

Sometime after eight o'clock that evening, Peter Stepanov, priest Fedor Sergeev, and a detail of 6 soldiers arrived at the Varvarskie Gates to execute Amvrosii's orders, whatever they were. Stepanov and his party foresaw trouble because of the size of the crowd. They also knew the assemblage was angry with the Archbishop, because earlier that day it had refused to release priests in response to his summons and had even threatened his emissaries. When Stepanov reached the gates, however, he saw before the icon "a multitude of people, who were standing quietly, and there was no noise of any kind." He explained his orders to Corporal Lunin, the sentry, and examined the seal on one of the two money chests. As he did this, several bystanders crowded around him. Two of them wore uniforms, Stepanov recalled, while others were dressed in frock coats and kaftans "better than from the common people," so that he took them to be merchants or servants of noble families. They asked him why he had come and what his instructions were. When Stepanov started to answer and showed his questioners the consistory seal, "at that same time all the rabble there raised a commotion, shrieking to beat him to death."

Terrified, Stepanov tried to save himself by displaying the seal, shouting that if the people opposed his sealing the money chests, he would depart. But just as he was edging away, Corporal Lunin yelled out to the crowd that he had already torn the seal on one of the chests. "For which a multitude of people," Stepanov testified, "suddenly rushed upon him, they began to beat and, after beating, they bound him and put him under the guard of sentries guarding the chests," who defended the prisoner against further molestation. As Stepanov was being assaulted and bound, he recalled, others sounded the tocsin on the bells of the churches nearby.[32]

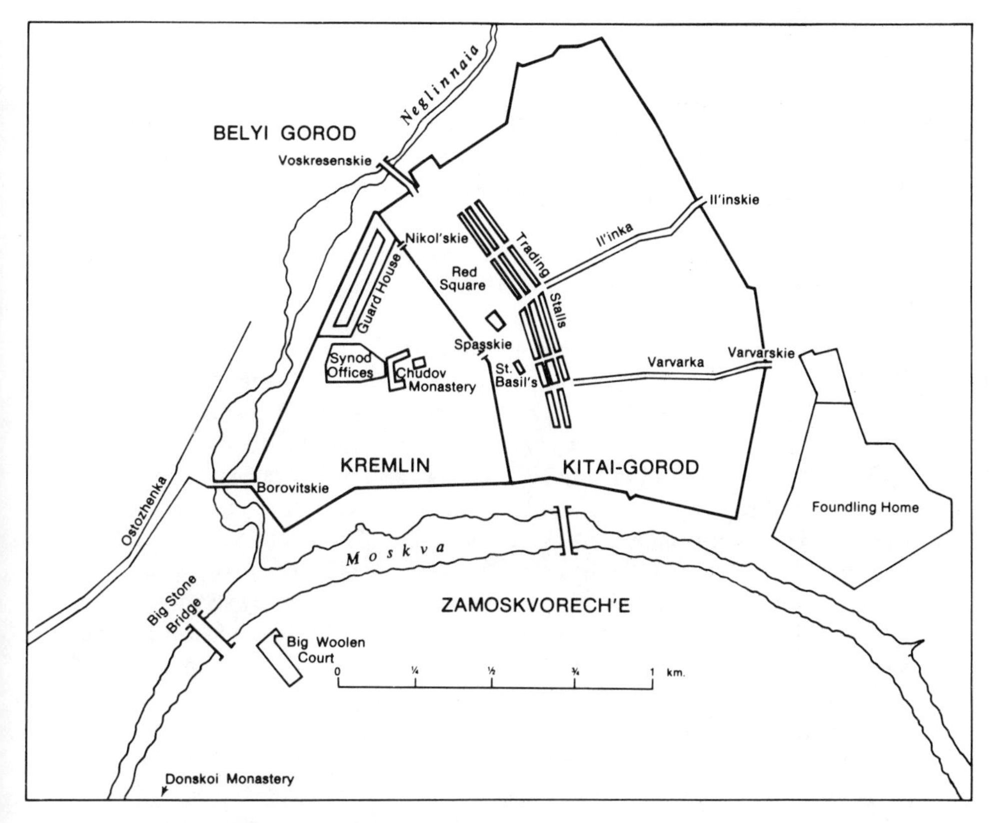

Map 5 Locations of the Plague Riot in Moscow.

Corporal Lukin, by contrast, gave a somewhat different account of these events. After Stepanov tore off the seal, he cried out to the soldiers with him that they had accomplished their mission. The crowd responded by yelling, "pillagers, beat them all to death!" People began throwing stones and attacking Stepanov and the soldiers. In the melee, Corporal Lukin suffered a head wound, a broken arm, and injuries to both legs, "from which he fell down senseless and regained consciousness the next day, being in the sentrybox, and what happened there afterwards, he knows nothing."[33]

When the tocsin split the mournful silence on the evening of 15 September, thousands poured into the streets. They found nobody to oppose them and soon discovered that the city lay at their mercy. Desperate and disgruntled, the lower layers of Moscow society seized their chance to attack a regime that seemed bent on annihilating them between the jaws of pestilence and compulsory quarantine. Thus, sexton Anton Ivanov, after spending the entire day at the Varvarskie Gates, visited two taverns on the way home. When he heard the churchbells clanging and ran out onto the street he saw "a huge multitude of people, some of whom were running toward the Varvarskie Gates, while others came running from thence with news, screaming that they are robbing the Mother of God and telling those they met: run fast and don't let them." At the gates Ivanov joined "a great fight between the people and the soldiers." He grabbed a club, and catching sight of police Captain Batiushkov, "struck him first, and after him they began to beat up others as well."[34]

Like sexton Ivanov, thousands rushed toward the center of town. When Chief of Police Bakhmetev arrived on the scene, he discovered a throng at the Varvarskie Gates extending along both sides of the wall all the way to the Il'inskie Gates (a distance of about 400 yards) and numbering, he estimated, about 9,000 persons. Many wielded clubs. Too numerous for the police to control, the crowd ignored Bakhmetev's admonitions to disperse and his assurances that whoever had threatened the icon and the money, said to exceed 1,000 rubles, would be punished by law. As the Police Chief rode away in search of Eropkin, he met another phalanx of several thousand running from Belyi Gorod through the Voskresenskie Gates into Kitai-gorod and Red Square. They followed "a bearded muzhik in blue padded overalls"—probably a priest, Bakhmetev thought—"who was constantly screaming the following words at the top of his lungs: 'Hurry, lads, to stand up for the Virgin Mother of God and don't let the Mother of God be pillaged!' " Bakhmetev placed the man under guard in a sentrybox and reported to Eropkin, who told the Police Chief that he could not spare any men to contain the disturbance. On the way back to Kitai-gorod, Bakhmetev looked for the man in the blue overalls, only to find some battered sentries but no prisoner. The rampaging crowd manhandled four police officers and three dragoons. Powerless, Bakhmetev withdrew and either left town temporarily or barricaded himself at home.[35]

Then the multiplying crowd, part of which may have come from a nearby tavern, turned upon the main target of popular wrath. "All the rabble in a multitude of voices shrieked out," recalled sexton Ivanov, " 'Let's go after the archbishop, beat him to death, and plunder the monastery.' " Knots of people rushed down Varvarka Street into Red Square, broke into the unguarded Kremlin, and began looting the Archbishop's residence in the Chudov Monastery. Some found winestores in the cellar—the monastery leased the space to wine merchants—and interrupted their pillaging to get drunk and liberally distributed the confiscated liquor, which was commonly thought to protect against pestilence. Yet the authorities' restrictions on sales at taverns, together with the closure of some drinking establishments as the municipal economy decayed, had decreased the supply of spirits just when people thought them most needed. (That very day the Kamer Collegium reported that 86 of its employees had fallen ill since the end of August and that 20 had died.) Drink increased and further inflamed the crowd.[36] The rioters ransacked the Chudov Monastery, looted or destroyed all its furnishings, even

Figure 9 The Plague Riot; watercolor by E. E. Lissner, date unknown (1930s ?), now in the Museum of the History and Reconstruction of the City of Moscow.

broke the window frames as well as the glass. Down from ripped featherbeds and pillows coated the area. But they failed to find their quarry. They mistook Amvrosii's younger brother Nikon for the Archbishop and nearly killed him on the spot; he went mad and died two weeks later. Apprised of the attack beforehand, Amvrosii left the Kremlin for the Donskoi Monastery.[37]

Some of the crowd spent the night in the Kremlin, some dispersed with their booty. Sexton Ivanov started home about midnight and en route ran into police officer Ishutin, who tried to arrest him. Ivanov resisted, "struck Ishutin with a staff," but was overpowered and taken to the guardhouse.[38] The police made little headway against the multitude, however, and the next morning when Brigadier Fedor Mamonov attempted to admonish those still pillaging the Chudov Monastery, they downed him with a barrage of stones from which he barely escaped alive. Later the local commandant, the Georgian Prince Afanasii Gruzinskii, approached the mob, but had to flee before a hail of stones and brickbats.[39] "And so all over Moscow," remarked one eyewitness, "serfs, Old Believers, drovers, manufactory workers, clerks, battalion soldiers, and part of the cannoneers—all were walking the streets with loot and threatening the lives of the well-born."[40] Some rioters broke open the quarantines, releasing those isolated at the Danilov Monastery and at the facility on the Serpukhov Road; others tried to free the convicts held at the Investigatory Branch and pillaged the house of Dr. Mertens, who was away at the Foundling Home at the time. Some looked for other medical

Figure 10 The murder of Archbishop Amvrosii by a mob in Moscow on 16 September 1771. Print of unknown origin, reproduced in L. Ia. Skorokhodov, *Materialy po istorii meditsinskoi mikrobiologii v dorevoliutsionnoi Rossii* (Moscow, 1948), p. 47.

practitioners to attack. Surgeon Danilo Samoilovich barely escaped from one such party, while several doctors left Moscow. Still, the rioters did not forget Amvrosii, and about ten o'clock Friday morning, 16 September, a large contingent left the Kremlin to search for him.[41]

Those stalking the Archbishop reached the Donskoi Monastery about noon that day, just as he was preparing to leave town. They scaled the walls and searched for Amvrosii in the main church. They found him hiding in a choir loft behind the iconostasis and dragged him outside to an open area near a sentrybox. Denouncing him as a Jew—an unusually strong condemnation in Orthodox "Holy Russia"—they assaulted him with clubs and iron bars. More than 500 persons were there, testified Vasilii Andreev, age thirty, a serf who admitted bludgeoning the Archbishop.[42] Two tavern-keepers—Ivan Dmitriev, a twenty-year-old Moscow second guild merchant, and Fedot Parfenov, a thirty-year-old state peasant from the cannoneers' suburb at the town of Kashira—acknowledged participating in the murder, but Parfenov later claimed he was drunk and denied direct complicity.[43] So enraged were the assailants that they tormented Amvrosii for nearly 2 hours. "They pierced the eyes, cut up the face, pulled out the beard, stabbed the chest, broke the

Figure 11 Stone cross erected on the spot where Archbishop Amvrosii was killed, just outside the Donskoi Monastery in Moscow; reproduced in A. Shamaro, "Gibel' arkhiepiskopa," *Nauka i religiia* 11(1971):60.

bones. In a word, his body was a single wound."[44] Archpriest Peter Alekseev recorded the gruesome end: "Having beaten [him] to death, they withdrew a little, fouling the air with their tongues; noticing, however, that the right hand made a movement to wave, they betook themselves to beat about the head with staves for a time; having withdrawn some again, they saw that the sacred sufferer shrugged his shoulders, so they beat a third time until some Churchman, a servant of the devil's church, dealt the last blow, cutting away some of the head, which part remained hanging over one eye."[45] Amvrosii's bloody corpse lay undisturbed until the next day because the clergy, left leaderless by his demise, feared to incite another paroxysm of popular rage by removing it. On the iron gates of the Chudov Monastery, some vengeful Muscovite scrawled Amvrosii's epitaph: "And his memory perished with a roar!"[46]

Suppression and Subsidence

By the late afternoon of 16 September Eropkin had assembled about 130 officers and soldiers. With 2 fieldpieces they set out from Ostozhenka Street, southwest of the Kremlin, and as they marched toward the citadel Governor Yushkov joined them. When Eropkin's detachment entered the Kremlin at the Borovitskie Gates, the rioters within signaled their comrades outside to sound the alarm.[47] Those manning the bells, reported Peter Alekseev, persisted until troops tore them away with bayonets.[48] Eropkin found "more than one thousand drunk" still pillaging the Chudov Monastery, so he sent detachments with a cannon each to block the Spasskie and Voskresenskie Gates, thereby preventing those outside from reinforcing their comrades within. Apparently, Eropkin tried once more to disperse the rioters by exhortation; he received a staff in the chest and a stone on the kneecap for his efforts. Then he gave orders to fire on the crowd. The troops began to scatter the mob with cannon- and musketfire, bayonets, sabers, and pikes.[49] "O, my God," exclaimed an eyewitness, "what a terrible and sorrowful spectacle of the fatherland: those drunk did not remember who stabbed them; others, from mercy, had arms and legs broken, and were bound and put in the cellar."[50]

Driven from the Kremlin, the rioters regrouped on Red Square and summoned reinforcements by ringing the churchbells. Large parties advanced toward the Voskresenskie and the Spasskie gates armed with pikes, clubs, and axes. The officers urged them to desist and fired blanks over their heads. Undaunted, the rioters charged the line of troops on the Spasskii Bridge and momentarily seized the single cannon there. But the cannoneers retreated with their slowmatches, the infantry halted the onslaught with bayonets, and grapeshot from the recovered cannon routed the attackers. Desperation animated some rioters. "That night one well-known merchant fighter hurled himself at a cannon with only bare fists, but was suddenly repelled by grapeshot. Another, named Kobyla, fell upon 3 bayonets and, tearing himself away from them, still possessed enough strength to strike one noncommissioned officer, but then fell at his conquerer's feet run through by a 4th bayonet." The fighting lasted almost four hours. As the rioters ran away, however, some shouted threats of revenge: "We're drunk now, but tomorrow we shall see." Others called to spectators on the roofs: "Why are you sitting, come on with us."[51]

Exactly how many were killed and wounded in the affray remains uncertain. Eropkin informed Catherine on 18 September that at least 100 had died in the Kremlin and 249 had been arrested, many of them wounded. Four days later he amended these figures, reducing those killed to 78 and increasing the number arrested to 279; his own forces lost 19 wounded, one of whom died.[52] Other estimates varied from 150 to 1,000.[53] Among the nearly 300 persons investigated for involvement in the rioting, 56 were found to be wounded, but the cause, time, and venue of their injuries were rarely specified.[54] No doubt other wounded escaped detection, despite the authorities' efforts to track them down, and the crowd must have carried many casualties away. With thousands of people rushing about in a confined area, many must have suffered injuries from accidental collisions. Obviously, many more persons participated in the violence and looting, or witnessed it as bystanders, than these few statistics indicate. Clearly, too, confusion and terror and darkness caused most observers to inflate the proportions of the violence.

Despite the Kremlin battle, another crowd assembled the very next morning opposite the Spasskie Gates. The mood was not riotous, however, and some asked to parley with a Guards officer. But Governor Yushkov refused to send out anybody for fear that the crowd sought hostages to bargain for the release of the captive rioters. Spokesmen for the crowd then shouted several demands: release those under guard, cease taking people to quarantines, bury the dead in churchyards, release everybody from quarantines and destroy the facilities, reopen the public baths, expel the doctors and surgeons from the city, and allow entry into taverns. They wanted Saltykov to pardon the rioters and sign their demands.[55] Although these points hardly amounted to an articulated "antifeudal program," as some Soviet commentators have asserted, the demands illustrated widespread rejection of the official anti-epidemic policies.[56] On only one point did the authorities agree with the mob: compulsory quarantine should be ended. But Eropkin and his associates had favored that policy for several weeks, hopeful that it would avoid violence.

The crowd also demanded, according to some accounts, that Eropkin be handed over for execution as the author of the disaster—a procedure reminiscent of the riots in Moscow in 1648, 1662, and 1682.[57] Eropkin himself reported no such threat, but his dispatch of 19 September to Catherine mentioned rumors to that effect, which made him request temporary removal from his post as a gesture to pacify discontent.[58] When the crowd failed to disperse by noon, after repeated admonitions from Yushkov and Bakhmetev, Eropkin led cavalry out of the Nikol'skie Gates and, suddenly appearing behind the assemblage at the Spasskie Gates, coordinated attacks from 2 sides. Several persons were captured or cut down, while the rest fled headlong. Just then Saltykov returned from his estate to relieve the exhausted Eropkin. Later in the afternoon the Velikolutskii Regiment arrived, 800 men strong, and replaced Eropkin's bone-weary force.[59]

In the tense days after the riot's suppression, Saltykov wrote Catherine several letters filled with forebodings of renewed violence and continuing conspiracies. He urged swift retribution to bring the people to their senses and felt certain that somebody had instigated the rioting. Probably the Old Believers, Saltykov opined, since they had long opposed the quarantines, and he thought that only the schismatics were capable of desecrating the Archbishop's apartments and chapel.[60] The rioters must have been organized, Saltykov informed Catherine on 21 September,

> for not only in Moscow, but in the district some of these miscreants dressed as soldiers are going through crown and economic estates, showing decrees supposedly sent from the guberniia chancery, and ordering the priests to read them before the people; they are forcing the elders and electmen to sign, that as soon as they hear the tocsin or cannonfire in Moscow, they will hasten to Moscow with clubs and staves, and it is rumored that they are drinking indecently along the highways and assembling to pillage and burn in Moscow; indeed, here in Moscow there are also some such idlers, who likewise are going around spreading tales and orders, several of whom have already been caught by local watchmen.[61]

In fact, such reports proved exaggerated. No further notable instances of violence occurred, and the government investigation of the Plague Riot failed to uncover any concerted leadership, conspiracy, or organization. Some contemporaries believed that the rioters secretly arranged to sound the alarm bells and even mentioned printed notices to that effect, although none have been found or described.[62] All those investigated denied prior knowledge of the outbreak; most said they acted "from hearsay alone."[63] Other than some clerical animosity against Amvrosii and perhaps 24 hours' forewarning of his alleged intention to seize the icon, nothing revealed any conscious planning behind the rioting. Rather, the plague provided an environment conducive to violence, which unpredictable circumstances ignited spontaneously. The official investigation condemned Vasilii Andreev and Ivan Dmitriev to death for the murder of Amvrosii, but then underscored the lack of evidence of a conspiracy by ordering two other rioters selected by lot to be executed.[64] Even before the investigation was completed, Catherine concluded that the riots had been an unpremeditated, elemental upheaval with "neither head nor tail, an accidental affair entirely."[65] The Empress never admitted Petersburg's contribution to the policies that helped provoke crisis.

Of the 313 persons examined by government investigators, 261 were found to be only peripherally involved in the rioting. The investigating commission interrogated at length 15 persons accused of inciting the outbreak or participating in the murder of the Archbishop. Forty others were found guilty of involvement in the rioting and the pillaging of the Chudov Monastery.[66] Obviously, some rioters and pillagers must have escaped arrest; just as obviously, many of those arrested must have been bystanders, not active participants. These statistics suggest, then, that the rioting was by no means a massive, organized movement with an articulated program, "antifeudal" or otherwise. It caused some property damage and loss of life because the authorities were unprepared for an emergency and reacted rather slowly. Once confronted with minimal military force, the rioters quickly dispersed.

Who were the rioters? Eropkin singled out "boyar people [i.e., house serfs], merchants, clerks, and manufactory workers, and especially the schismatics." Saltykov echoed Eropkin's indictment and also cited the garrison soldiers, quoting the architect Bazhenov, who implicated the retired soldiers of the Kremlin guard: "they rioted and pillaged more than anybody else."[67] A month after the riots Grigorii Orlov reviewed the troops in Moscow and found them all thoroughly "corrupted"; "for their obedience and discipline are—word for word—like the plague." In Moscow, soldiers forgot their duty. "Almost all of them have their own messuages; all engage in trade; nobody looks after them; they have intermixed with the manufactory workers and other inhabitants, yet the worst of it is that they fear the police less."[68] According to Ivan Beloglazov, the rioters were "vulgar people consisting of every status, and for the most part of manufactory workers." Peter Alekseev thought the riot stemmed from "the evil rabble, from manufactory workers, serfs, merchants, retired soldiers, and other *raznochintsy.*"[69]

Table 8 Social Origins of Alleged Rioters

Legal category	Number
Servants (serfs)	172 (173)[a]
Economic peasants	26
Merchants	26
Soldiers	25[b]
Manufactory workers	13 (14)[a]
Clergy and Church servants	11
Artisans	10
Government clerical workers	9
Crown peasants	9
State peasants	6
Police employees	3
Miscellaneous	1
Total	311 (313)

[a]One person was listed as a servant of manufactory operator Ivan Tames.
[b]Includes one "soldier's wife" and one "soldier's daughter."
Source: A. Zertsalov, comp., "O miatezhakh v gorode Moskve i v sele Kolomenskom, v 1648, 1662 i 1771 gg., " *Ch. OIDR*, bk. 3 (1890), 372–417.

Some Soviet commentators have seized upon these scraps of evidence to support the view that "proletarian" elements played an important role in the Plague Riot.[70] Considering Moscow's population at the time and the temporary closure of its many manufactories and workshops, it would have been amazing if no workers had been involved. Yet the violence erupted so suddenly, spread so rapidly, lasted so briefly, and occurred in such murky circumstances that the accounts of eyewitnesses require cautious appraisal. Though subject to some of the same limitations, the evidence generated by the official investigation of the rioting fleshed out, statistically, the bare observations of contemporaries.

The social origins of the 313 persons arrested and investigated for alleged participation in the rioting may be tabulated as in table 8. These statistics confirm the impressions of contemporaries that the dominant social group involved in the rioting comprised household serfs. Like other social definitions of the time, "servants" denoted a legal category rather than a definite socioeconomic status and function; thus some of the persons listed as servants may actually have worked at occupations other than domestic service. From the 1760s onward, growing numbers of household serfs hired themselves out or, more commonly, were hired out by their masters to manufactories in Moscow, especially to textile mills. Other "servants" may have engaged in small-time trade or produced handicrafts outside the artisan corporations. Similar qualifications apply to the other statuses listed in table 8.

Still, even allowing for some misclassification and overlapping categories, the number of obviously proletarian elements seems quite small. Of the 13 workers interrogated, only 2—Il'ia Afanas'ev, one of the instigators of the alms collection at the Varvarskie Gates, and Dmitrii Zarubai, a twenty-year-old employee of Tames's linen mill—were directly implicated in the disorders. The other 11 workers interrogated were listed with those 261 persons arrested for suspected pillaging or because of their presence near the site of the violence. Yet many of these persons fell afoul of the authorities quite casually. For example, the steward at Gusiatnikov's linen mill turned in Peter Yakovlev, a twenty-five-year-old employee, for leaving on 17-18 September to drink in the taverns. Police arrested a textile worker of the Big Woolen Court, Fedor Andreev (age forty), near the Varvarskie Gates the evening of 16 September with wounds on his nose and cheek. Another worker of the same enterprise, eighteen-year-old Ivan Tikhonov, was captured the same evening, allegedly with stones and clubs in his possession, but he denied the charges. That few workers participated in the violence is scarcely surprising, for they constituted a minor segment of Moscow society in general. Also, the authorities had arranged to remove many idled workers from the city and to provide subsistence for those who had no place to go.[71]

Contemporaries understood clearly the dominance of household serfs in the violence. With the departure of most of the upper and middle strata of Moscow society, the weakening of the city's inadequate security forces, and the virtual collapse of the urban economy, household serfs and urban peasants comprised the bulk of the population. Their housing conditions and mode of life exposed them to the brunt of the pestilence, which in turn subjected them to the brutal regime of compulsory quarantine. They were too numerous and too amorphous a group to petition the authorities for special treatment, as the manufactory operators, merchants, and Old Believers had done. At the same time, they found themselves cut adrift from their social moorings with the departure of their masters and the disruption of Moscow's minimal welfare services. That the Church hierarchy should also abandon them seemed the final blow. So they sought deliverance by means of the miraculous icon, and when the authorities tried to tamper with that, too, their desperation burst into fury.

If a soldier and a manufactory worker devised the miracle, serf domestics rushed to "defend" it and to attack its supposed antagonist, Archbishop Amvrosii. Of the 40 persons considered most guilty of pillaging the Chudov Monastery, 28 were household servants. Also implicated were 3 soldiers—a deserter and 2 members of the Moscow garrison—3 artisans, 2 merchants, 2 economic peasants, one manufactory worker, and a police official. At least 29 of the 40 were less than thirty years old, 21 of whom were serf domestics; 2 were eleven-year-olds.[72] Far from a proletarian outbreak, the Plague Riot mainly involved youthful serf domestics. Conspicuously absent were noblemen, civil officials, military and police officers.

Just as the outbreak of rioting signaled the peak of mortality in Moscow on 15 September, so the violence abruptly subsided in the next few days as the death foll began to decline. The official daily mortality count dropped from 777 on 20 September, when Dr. Lerche recorded a temperature of 30° F. and some Muscovites relit their stoves for the winter, to 643 at the end of the month (graph 3). The day before subfreezing temperatures struck, Ivan Beloglazov commented that "the plague, although it continues, still it has become lighter from the cold air that set in." The simultaneous abatement of unrest and of pestilence comforted officialdom twofold. "The previous quiet reigns," Captain Sablukov observed on 22 September. "The weather is becoming colder, so we hope that God will soon extinguish the plague too."[73] Thus the advent of cooler weather, the saving chill that many had prayed for since late August, arrived a few weeks too late to defuse the desperate circumstances that triggered the Plague Riot. Less than a year before, at Kiev, timely frosts had cut off an incipient crisis of the same kind. By contrast, Moscow's longer, more puzzling exposure to plague generated stronger, less tractable tensions. But those tensions eased soon after the Plague Riot. "Here it is so peaceful and quiet in town," Bakhmetev remarked on 22 September, "that one can say it has almost never been so earlier."[74] The violence of mid-September seemed to mark a break in Moscow's case of pestilential fever. Even so, nobody knew how much longer the plague would last, nor how much farther it might spread before continuous cold neutralized its "poison."

CHAPTER EIGHT

The Orlov Mission and the Plague Commission (September 1771–January 1772)

The Plague Riot dramatized the disasters that unchecked pestilence could inflict on the Russian Empire. To Catherine and her councilors, Moscow's sudden, violent collapse signified a breakdown of imperial authority in the heartland and the bankruptcy of their piecemeal antiplague efforts. The volatile situation demanded an immediate, revised response from Petersburg. Indeed, this crisis captured Catherine's full attention for several months and haunted her long afterward. Pressured to act, the Empress hastily improvised a special mission to Moscow to restore order and precautions in concert with a medical administrative council.

As the reports from Moscow worsened, Catherine felt agitated, even ill; "my whole left side aches from head to toe." But on 10 September her spirits rose in the belief that "the distemper at Moscow, glory to God, has begun to decline." She still placed hope in her proclamation dispatched on 13 September "for the city of Moscow alone, in order to make the people, if possible, reasonable."[1] On 15 September, however, her council heard Count Bruce present Eropkin's report that up to 600 persons were dying each day. Two days later the councilors blanched at Saltykov's plea for permission to leave the plague-ridden metropolis. Catherine had already resolved to dispatch "a trusted personage" from Petersburg with full authority to save Moscow "from utter ruin." While the councilors considered whom to send, they endorsed Saltykov's release for the duration of the crisis and placed Eropkin in charge until Petersburg's plenipotentiary arrived.[2] Although Catherine granted Saltykov's wishes, in private she fumed at his ill-timed departure, the more so as she had just received word of the violence at Lefortovo three weeks earlier. The Empress suspected that Saltykov had ignored the danger until it was too late, and then, just when unruly Moscow most needed firm direction, "the old dotard" left "to divert himself with his hounds."[3] Catherine vented her anxiety on the hapless Saltykov, still unaware of the rioting that Eropkin had already suppressed.

Amid this turmoil, Count Grigorii Orlov volunteered to lead the emergency mission to Moscow. Catherine's lover for almost a decade, Grigorii Orlov enjoyed exceptional status as reflected in his multiple titles, offices, and honors. More important, everyone respected his commanding presence and decisive coolness during crises. While his brother Aleksei and other aristocrats were winning military laurels against the Turks and the Poles, Grigorii had remained at court, eager to show his mettle. As Lord Cathcart recorded Orlov's sentiments the day before his departure:

> he was convinced the greatest misfortune at Moscow was the panic which had seized the highest as well as the lowest, and the bad order, and want of regulations arising from that cause. . . . He said plague or no plague he would go tomorrow morning: that he had long languished for an opportunity to do some signal service to the Empress and his country, that such an opportunity seldom fell to the share of private men, and never without risk, that he hoped he had found one, and that no danger should deter him from endeavouring to avail himself of it.[4]

Orlov conferred separately with Catherine and her council on Wednesday, 21 September, before leaving for Moscow that evening. A considerable entourage accompanied him. Two were prominent senators: Aleksei Mel'gunov, president of the Collegium of Commerce, and Vsevolod Vsevolozhskii, oberprocurator of the senate. Aleksei Shcherbachev, chief administrator of the Postal Chancery, and Vasilii Baskakov, vice-president in the Chancery of Wardship for Foreigners, joined Dr. Gustav Orraeus and Major-General Ivan Davidov, with officers and men from the four Guards regiments, to complete the mission. The council approved Catherine's temporary grant of full authority to Orlov.[5]

Catherine supplied Orlov with a proclamation, ostensibly the product of her own hand, for she spent 20–21 September sequestered in the Winter Palace. "Seeing the most lamentable state of OUR city of Moscow and that a great number of people are dying from the infectious diseases," Catherine declaimed, "WE would OURSELVES have considered it the duty of OUR calling to hasten thither, if this OUR expedition would not have entailed considerable disorder and confusion in the important affairs of OUR empire because of the present circumstances of war." Whether Catherine seriously intended to visit the site of the plague may never be known—but it seems unlikely. Her councilors certainly tried to dissuade her, citing the danger to her person and the possible damage to Russian foreign and domestic policy. Commissioning a special representative offered a well-tested alternative. Furthermore, Orlov's intimate relationship with Catherine underscored the importance of the mission. Besides empowering Orlov to use to use whatever resources necessary to surmount the crisis, Catherine provided for greater flexibility. She authorized him "to abolish whichever of the institutions made there that seem either inappropriate or not useful, and to establish anew everything that he finds facilitating the general good." Recent reports had shaken Catherine's confidence in the previous policies and made her contemplate modifications such as those suggested by the Moscow authorities.[6]

Soon after Catherine watched Orlov gallop off toward Moscow, the news of the rioting shocked Petersburg. On 22 September, the day after Orlov departed, he met a courier from Moscow about a hundred miles from Petersburg. As the rider carried the latest reports, Orlov unsealed his dispatches and learned of the violence. In breaking the news to Catherine, he reassured her that, despite the muddy road, he would make all haste to reach the riot-torn metropolis. He also requested authority to detach 100 men from the artillery depot for service in Moscow, asked how to handle the captive rioters, and acknowledged his own fears. "Most of all it frightens me that this willful infection has so spread that I suppose there is no way to end it, except that God send a cold spell."[7]

This awful news reached Catherine on 23 September. She appeared at court that day, the ninth anniversary of her coronation, obviously crestfallen. "She is said to be infinitely hurt by the misfortunes of her subjects in Moscow, and the dastardly behaviour of the nobility, and people in power, who have left the city, and abandoned it to every sort of calamity," observed Lord Cathcart. Four days later he commented: "She is much affected with these calamities, and cannot, though she endeavours, conceal it."[8]

Catherine first acted to restore order to the old capital. Incensed at "such an outrageous occurrence in Moscow," she authorized Orlov to convene a special commission to investigate the disorders and to punish the culprits. Composed of the senators in Moscow, all military officers and civilian officials of the first 5 ranks, and 2 or 3 eminent clergymen, the commission should interrogate the captive rioters and then conduct a public investigation and trial—public, presumably, in the sense that the commission would represent the interests of both the government and the responsible elements of Moscow society. The guilty should be punished publicly too, Catherine insisted, "in order that all the people might see and be particularly assured that, just as on the one hand Our concern for their welfare is indefatigable and unquenchable, so on the other We do not wish to permit such a villainous sedition, which shakes the entire general tranquillity." To forestall further trouble the Empress urged Orlov to renew the search for "the means of precaution and preservation from the infection among the perplexed people." She directed that the Kremlin be secured at once, purged of any suspicion of infection, and closed to ordinary traffic.[9]

As another measure to alleviate the situation, the Empress on 24 September secretly ordered the senate departments in Petersburg to arrange the removal of all large manufactories from Moscow, which Eropkin and others had blamed for introducing the epidemic and for aggravating the violence.[10] Simultaneously, Catherine aimed at minimizing both the local and foreign impact of the catastrophe. She charged the Petersburg postmaster to burn all letters from Moscow that described the events as a riot, and she anxiously inquired whether the tranquillity after the riot had proved to be lasting. Dispirited, Catherine lamented that "the eighteenth century is playing pranks everywhere, even though it's lauded above its predecessors."[11]

On Monday, 26 September, the Empress visited her council, which she had not attended for three weeks, to condemn the irresponsible conduct of the Moscow authorities. Those who had left the city must return at once, she ordered. Those responsible for the Archbishop's murder should be punished according to the law; the rioters should be enrolled in the army. Despite Catherine's anger at Moscow officialdom, she and her councilors recognized that her manifesto of 9 September, which assailed government and people alike, ought not be published in the aftermath of the rioting. Yet they knew they could not intercept it. As it happened, circumstances conspired to postpone the publication and to alter the form of Catherine's manifesto.[12]

To quash rumors, the Petersburg authorities publicly acknowledged the Moscow tragedy in a supplement to the *Sanktpeterburgskie vedomosti* on 27 September. Just as the Russian government intended, foreigners in the capital relayed this account abroad.[13]

Through this pronouncement, the imperial government tried to play down the violence, to explain the continuation of pestilence by the lack of public cooperation, and to blame the rioting on vaguely defined criminal elements. Naturally, there was no mention of any threat to Petersburg, no hint of the governmental collapse in Moscow, nor a word about the Orlov mission, although all of these matters were already widely known. After admitting the crisis, the Petersburg authorities tensely awaited the outcome of Orlov's mission and the arrival of cold weather. Catherine rapidly recovered her composure, yet still felt ashamed of the governmental breakdown. As she confided to a friend on 20 October: "We have spent a month in circumstances like those that Peter the Great lived under for thirty years. He broke through all difficulties with glory; we hope to come out of them with honor."[14]

Restoring Order and the Municipal Economy

In the immediate aftermath of the rioting, before the Orlov mission reached Moscow, Eropkin and Saltykov labored to restore order, to reimpose the antiplague precautions, and to investigate the riot. Like Catherine and Orlov, they saw all three tasks as interrelated: ending disorder and punishing its instigators would calm the situation and curtail the epidemic, whereas speedy investigation of the captive rioters might reveal undisclosed motives and movers behind the violence. The Moscow authorities knew what to do, but their own disarray and the decay of the municipal economy hampered their efforts. Indeed, Eropkin felt so drained after the ordeal of suppressing the riot that he asked again for temporary relief from his duties. Sick, wounded, and exhausted from sleepless nights and constant tension, he collapsed for a day or two worrying that "a crowd of miscreants" might murder him. As director of the antiplague policies, Eropkin recognized that he attracted the same kind of animosity as the late Amvrosii; so he assured Catherine that his removal would quiet "the agitated people who possess no true reasoning about anything."[15] No local official could replace Eropkin at that critical juncture, however, and he administered Moscow until Orlov arrived.

The Moscow authorities feared further violence above all. Since the police had already proved inadequate, the Velikolutskii Regiment stood guard around the Kremlin. On 22 September, President Protasov of the Main Municipal Administration undertook a voluntary levy of militia from the merchantry, to protect the trading stalls against pillagers and to keep order in the merchant suburbs. Occasional incidents continued to spur apprehension. On the night of 26–27 September, for instance, unidentified assailants lurking in Maria's Grove (*Mar'ina roshcha*), on the north edge of town, forcibly freed a group of convicts transporting corpses for burial. Eropkin requested more troops to tighten the security of such convoys, but persisted in using convicts to transport and to bury the dead. In another effort to forestall violence, the senate, on 23 September, alerted the Tula arms manufactory against selling firearms to any "suspicious persons." The next day the senate cautioned Muscovites not to believe rumors inciting violence and threatened to arrest anybody propagating seditious sentiments.[16]

Meanwhile, Eropkin reorganized the antiepidemic campaign. His new deputy, Senator Mikhail Pokhvisnev, replaced Senator Sobakin and assumed primary responsibility for half of the city's 20 districts. While endeavoring to reinstitute the precautions disrupted by the rioting, both men supported the modified quarantine policies begun a few weeks earlier. On 19 September, Eropkin assured Catherine that he was following her orders to discontinue the evacuation of whole houses in favor of isolating only the rooms of the stricken, and he denied any maltreatment or negligence on the part of local medical practitioners. The common folk harbored "a most intense hatred" of physicians, Eropkin explained, and still refused to take medicines or to believe the disease was really plague. Similar beliefs spawned stories of live burials. Eropkin refuted the rumors and reported that the district supervisors had strict instructions, recently reaffirmed, to separate the living from the dead. He also reassured the Empress as to the fate of those persons whom the mob had released from the quarantines on the Serpukhov Road and at the Danilov Monastery. The first group was not dangerous from a medical point of view, for all had recently arrived from another quarantine; the second group, although about 130 still bore wounds, had all been well fed and treated, and 64 had already returned voluntarily. The quarantines were functioning smoothly, nobody had been detained for more than six weeks, and 150 persons had just been released.[17]

The Moscow authorities also looked into new locations for additional quarantines. On 19 September, the senate considered Sukin's report about possible sites. The senators vetoed several on various grounds—proximity to a stinking tallow manufactory, propinquity to an imperial palace, and sickness among nearby inhabitants—approved one site beyond the Danilov Monastery, and ordered others investigated. To enlighten the public about the means of self-preservation, the authorities resumed distribution of the printed medical advisories written by Lerche and Yagel'skii. Eropkin asked the clergy in particular to explain these tracts to the common folk. He also authorized publication of a similar tract by Dr. Erasmus, but Orlov later countermanded this as superfluous.[18]

Amid these efforts to regain control after the rioting, the local authorities faced a quandary in how to handle Catherine's manifesto of 9 September. Of course, when the printed copies arrived on 19 September, nobody in Moscow knew that Petersburg had already reconsidered the matter and wished the proclamation withheld. The timing of its appearance was certainly unfortunate, for it undercut the confidence of Eropkin and his associates, their nerves already cruelly taxed by the prolonged emergency. Taken aback by the Empress's outraged response to criticism of quarantine policy, the Moscow authorities were equally apprehensive about her reaction to the rioting and embarrassed at their own disarray. Consequently, Eropkin waited four days before discussing the dilemma with Saltykov and Pokhvisnev. They did not dare to ignore a direct order from the sovereign, but, recognizing the fragility of their newly restored authority, they accepted Eropkin's suggestion that the police announce a modified version of Catherine's manifesto.[19]

Issued on 24 September, the Moscow version of the proclamation omitted all explicit criticism of administrative abuses in quarantine operations. It simply called for implementation of the concessions Catherine had already authorized. Muscovites must immediately report all cases of sickness to the district supervisors, so that medical practitioners could inspect the afflicted and isolate them if necessary. This precaution would actually protect others, the manifesto explained, "for an infected person, if he be quickly separated from the healthy, cannot harm them at the start, but if he stays among them 48 hours, the corruption of his disease can attain perfection and also infect all those living with him." Persons reporting sickness in their residences would have the choice of entering a quarantine or remaining isolated at home for 16 days. Those who concealed sickness, however, "will ineluctably be taken off to a quarantine as persons unconcerned and negligent of themselves."[20] Thus the Moscow authorities reworked Catherine's ill-timed manifesto to suit their own purposes and unforeseen circumstances.

When Grigorii Orlov entered Moscow, about 5 P.M. on 26 September, the Plague Riot had run its brief course, the local authorities had regrouped, and the crisis had largely subsided. Still the situation looked desperate to Orlov, who sent Catherine a bleak assessment the day after his arrival, apparently based on conversations with Eropkin and Saltykov. Though the epidemic appeared to be declining, "despondency has mastered the hearts of all inhabitants, and some have been brought to desperation; yet the people scorn all rules of reason and do not use any kind of precautions, leaving everything to the will of God." Doubtful whether the city could be saved, Orlov promised Catherine that he would employ every reasonable method to that end. He also requested that Senator Dmitrii Volkov, the veteran administrator, come from Petersburg to help resuscitate the Moscow administration.[21]

Orlov quickly moved to investigate the riots. On 29 September, he announced the formation of an investigating commission under Procurator Sergei Rozhnov, of the Moscow Synodal Office, who began his duties that very morning. Later in the day, Saltykov left Moscow for his estate, never to return.[22] Orlov officially assumed control of Moscow on 30 September, when he published Catherine's edict authorizing his mission and issued a personal announcement. Orlov's declaration articulated the thinking of Petersburg and Moscow officialdom in blaming the epidemic on the people's own negligence. At first, Muscovites refused to believe the disease was plague, and then "with a raging of the Evil, succeeded Fear, Despondency and wild Despair, Passions as destructive in their Nature and Effects, as productive of the Wrath of our most munificent Creator." Orlov chastised Muscovites for superstitious fatalism and passivity; "an utter neglect of the most obvious Precautions has been the horrible bane of the common People, and, highly criminal before our Allbountiful creator, they have imputed their own Omission, i.e., Negligence to the Will of Fate alone."[23]

Orlov's endorsement of the conventional precautions followed strictly contagionist assumptions: "this poisonous Distemper exists not in the Air, but proceeds merely from the Contact or Communication of the Bodies infected." Therefore, "we must avoid all infected and infectuous Bodies, as we would avoid certain Death; and consequently, in all such Circumstances as the present, abstain, as much as may be from the Touch and Communication." Yet his announcement insisted that precautions need not imperil subsistence. Foodstuffs would not transmit the infection if properly cooked and provided that buyers and sellers avoided direct contact. People should regulate their own purchases. "There are many Houses full of Servants only, in which neither Death nor Sickness has happened, merely because they were carefull, and one of the most sensible and cautious was sent to purchase Provisions of all kinds for the rest." Orlov's pronouncement ended with vague promises of reward if the precautions were followed. "Then will the Government with pleasure share in the general Dangers seeing the good Success and Fruits of its Endeavours," and then Catherine, "who feels our Distress with

Figure 12 Aleksei and Grigorii Orlov, oil painting by Jean Louis de Veilly, late 1770s (?), reproduced by courtesy of the Graphics Department, State Historical Museum in Moscow.

compunctive Sorrow," would "pour down her Benefactions." Failure to adopt the precautions would, by contrast, "draw down upon Us the Vengeance of the most high."[24]

If Orlov's rhetoric scarcely deviated from previous official pronouncements, he displayed greater energy and ingenuity in demonstrating the state's concern for public welfare. To the senate, on 30 September, he proposed two new policies, to arrange subsistence for the many artisans hurt by the economic dislocation, and to provide everybody with vinegar for prophylactic purposes. Senator Mel'gunov coordinated deliveries of vinegar; Senator Pokhvisnev organized assistance for the artisans. A week later Orlov reminded the senators of the continuing shortage of vinegar, and they resolved to obtain 3,250 gallons from the Tver provincial chancery. This consignment only reached Moscow on 17 November, however, when demand had slackened. Mel'gunov set a price ceiling of 10 copecks per gallon, arranged free supplies for hospitals and quarantines, and ordered the Kamer Collegium to distill vinegar from beer for the disinfection of tax monies. By 5 December, Mel'gunov reported that Moscow had adequate supplies of vinegar—enough, in fact, to send some to outlying districts. This matter exemplified the attention to detail of Orlov and his subordinates, as well as their grasp of psychological appeals, for vinegar enjoyed high esteem as a disinfectant. Increasing supplies of that vital commodity advertised the government's effort to help people help themselves.[25] "In highest fashion amongst us now are various vinegars, horseradish, and garlic," commented one Muscovite on 16 October, "and people have gone so far that, despite the arrival of necessary supplies, one can obtain only a bit of plain vinegar. It seems to me that we live in a cemetery and not with the living in a town."[26]

Providing for Moscow's large contingent of unemployed artisans entailed other difficulties. By 3 October, the senate appointed Peter Vyrubov and Prince Evgenii Amilakhorov to arrange purchase of wares that artisans could not sell on the open market. Vyrubov and Amilakhorov immediately rented a house in the third district, belonging to Princess Praskov'ia Shakhovskaia, where needy artisans could dispose of their wares twice a week throughout the day. Fourteen soldiers guarded the house, four watchmen inspected it, and two merchants appraised the articles received. Beginning on 8 October, Amilakhorov and Vyrubov disbursed more than 4,000 rubles to 1,647 persons over the next seven weeks. The operation continued until funds ran out on 26 January 1772, by which time nearly 4,000 persons had received about 9,500 rubles. Since 9 of the guards fell ill and entered quarantines, Grave supervised fumigation of the wares, which were eventually given to the Foundling Home. As with vinegar supplies, on this occasion the authorities exhibited exemplary innovation and efficiency to ameliorate significant economic and social disruption.[27]

Concurrently, Sukin arranged care for children orphaned or abandoned during the epidemic, inasmuch as the Foundling Home had ceased admissions. Urged on by the senate, Sukin took over two houses as a shelter and as a reception point and quarantine. By 9 October, a staff of 31 was ready to receive the orphaned. Orlov sent an icon with bread and salt to open the institution with prayers. When the first infants arrived the next day, however, they were refused admittance because the district supervisors had not certified the absence of parents and relatives. Still, three were accepted later that day, and by 18 October the senate worried about overcrowding the facility. It even empowered Sukin to commandeer an unfinished entertainment hall being built by the Frenchman Lyon. Acceptance of infants ceased on 29 November, apparently because of declining supply and appalling mortality: 163 of the 371 children taken since 10 October had died. After some wrangling, the Foundling Home accepted the surviving children.[28] This attempt to succor orphans illustrated a short-term application of the government's longstanding desire to foster population growth by lowering the rate of infant mortality.

To employ unskilled workers and to extirpate "idleness, the author of every evil," Orlov instituted a public works program that paid men 15, and women 10, copecks per day to deepen the ditch of the Kamerkollezhskii Val.

Workers with their own tools received an additional 3 copecks daily. Mel'gunov supervised this effort for about two months, spending 740 rubles by 27 December. Soon Orlov expanded the program to include digging canals that would drain marshes into the sluggish Neglinnaia and repairing the main highways around Moscow. Both projects were designed to employ the peasantry of the Moscow district. Both continued long after Orlov and the plague had left Moscow, for the city authorities saw the benefits of reducing beggary and vagrancy, lessening congestion, and improving transportation and communications. About 20,000 rubles were expended by mid-1773, and the program served as a prototype for public works elsewhere in the empire. Finally, for Moscow's "great multitude of beggars, especially old women," the authorities provided temporary shelter and subsistence at the Ugreshskii Monastery, but still denied the necessity of beggary. By late November, this institution housed 147 beggars.[29]

Orlov's activities in the first weeks of October implemented the general policy of assisting the poorer people to cushion the effects of the epidemic. In principle, this was the same policy that Eropkin and Saltykov had advocated. In practice, it proved more successful because Orlov enjoyed Catherine's confidence and exercised complete control over more manpower and money.[30] Nevertheless, Orlov apprehended the potential for renewed violence. On 3 October, he informed Catherine of his decision to delay military recruitment in Moscow and Moscow province. Recruiting levies always provoked tension—a whole cycle of folksongs lamented the enrollment of young men for 25 years' service—and the Moscow authorities wished to avoid funneling throngs of recruits into the impested city.[31] Simultaneously, Orlov ordered the Moscow guberniia chancery to comb provincial jails for convicts to serve as gravediggers in Moscow. On 2 October, Eropkin complained that since more than 300 convicts had perished from these duties, the continuing high mortality necessitated doubling the number of gravediggers. Although the provincial authorities were ordered to rush healthy convicts to Moscow, few responded. To encourage the convict gravediggers, Eropkin promised a lightening of their sentences and raised their daily pay from 6 to 8 copecks.[32]

Orlov also worked to restore order through the ecclesiastical authorities. The Church's most immediate needs were to reinstitute clerical discipline and to replace Amvrosii, whose consistory had ceased functioning a week before his death. The Moscow Synodal Office investigated Amvrosii's death, inventoried lost and damaged Church property, and transferred several monks of the Chudov Monastery seen drunk in public. On 21 September, the Moscow consistory instituted daily prayers for the late Archbishop throughout the eparchy. As temporary hierarch in Moscow, the Holy Synod assigned Archbishop Gennadii of Suzdal eparchy. Before he arrived, however, Orlov staged a splendid funeral for Amvrosii at the Donskoi Monastery on 4 October, an occasion he used to publicize his appeals for individual precautions and for public cooperation with the authorities. The prefect of the Moscow

Academy delivered a funeral oration that upbraided Muscovites for resisting Church and state and for their fatalistic, superstitious negligence in the face of pestilence. Printed copies of this oration in Russian and German were widely distributed in subsequent weeks.[33] On 25 October, acting on orders from the Holy Synod, Archimandrite Varlaam of the Donskoi Monastery proclaimed a forty-day vigil in memory of Amvrosii and anathematized his murderers.[34] Thus Orlov and his assistants endeavored to refurbish governmental authority in Moscow. Yet they knew their authority might topple unless they obtained a broader measure of cooperation to stem the epidemic.

Organizing the Plague Commission

The Orlov mission, though well equipped to conquer the administrative chaos in Moscow, confronted stiffer challenges in mobilizing the medical community and the people against the plague. Uncertainty still troubled the authorities. Indeed, Orlov evidently shared Catherine's lingering doubts about the nature of the disease. On 30 September, he publicly called it pestilential, but privately asked the medical community how it was propagated. The practitioners were to describe its symptoms, course, and treatment. Orlov solicited their recommendations for individual precautions, which, he stressed, "must be simple and easily put into practice."[35]

These questions evoked contradictory responses. Dr. Mertens, for instance, denied any corruption of the atmosphere, yet noted the diversity of symptoms and the role of natural conditions. Convinced that the temperature of the air "disposes the human body more or less to receive the contagion; and. . . renders the pestilential miasm more or less violent," Mertens "hoped the frost would not only weaken the contagion, but in great measure destroy it."[36] This reasoning puzzled the authorities all the more because, despite cooler weather in early October, the daily death toll hovered between 600 and 700 (graph 4).

Perplexed at the epidemic's persistence, Orlov had Senator Volkov reconvene the medical community on 6 October in the presence of Eropkin, Baskakov, and Dr. Orraeus. The administrators praised the 23 practitioners in attendance for their medical advisories, but blamed their earlier disputes for confusing the public. Even their published precautions, Orlov charged, bewildered "unenlightened people" because of different wording and emphases—hence his decision to withhold Dr. Erasmus's recently authorized tract. To compile "a single brief, clear, and understandable prescription for the common people," Orlov demanded unequivocal answers to four basic questions: Was the disease "the pestilential distemper?" Did it infect people through the air or by contact with the infected? What would protect one against it? Were there means to treat the afflicted?[37]

The practitioners responded unanimously that all evidence proved the disease was "the real and incontrovertible pestilential distemper." Since the brief medical debate two months earlier, the epidemic's awesome eruption had buried all doubts. The majority of the local medical community, particularly those most actively engaged against the disease, had consistently asserted its pestilential character, and their views had received weighty confirmation from Lerche and Orraeus. Besides, neither Kuhlemann nor Shkiadan, the main dissenters from the majority view, attended this meeting. The conclave reiterated, moreover, that "this disease does not subsist in the air, and the air does not infect people, but solely contact and communication alone," the several modes of which were explained.[38]

Each practitioner prescribed traditional methods for individual precautions, such as bodily cleanliness, dietary moderation, fumigation and ventilation of habitations, avoidance of crowding and of infected articles, persons, and places. Dr. Yagel'skii urged that the clergy inform people "clearly and precisely" about the disease. People should use Sweet Spirit of Niter; "for this medicine protects well against this disease, and the people will thereby possess assurance and encouragement that medicine will protect against disease, and so they will have a calm spirit and will wish for treatment." If the common people did not shun contact and communication with sources of infection, Dr. Shafonskii averred, then all other precautions would be ineffectual. The stricken must be isolated at once and, upon death or recovery, their personal effects must be burned. On 7 October, the same group recommended conventional therapies: drinking warm water with vinegar or fruit juice to encourage perspiration, inducing vomiting, reducing fever with cool drinks and compresses, using plasters on buboes to promote suppuration, and applying pitch or garlic to carbuncles.[39]

These consultations led Orlov immediately to revise the institutional structure and leadership of the antiplague campaign. A select group of 3 administrators (Volkov, Eropkin, and Baskakov) and 5 practitioners (Orraeus, Shafonskii, Yagel'skii, Grave, and Samoilovich) launched the new effort by recommending the city-wide reintroduction of compulsory isolation in extramural quarantines or pesthouses for everybody thought to be infected. Thenceforth the district supervisors should permit quarantines in private residences only when the householder could guarantee separate, secure quarters. "From the other infected houses, however, which comprise an extremely small number of rooms or only one, everybody must be removed without fail to the prevention houses immediately upon the appearance of infection." This proposal repudiated the modified quarantine policy that the Moscow authorities had adopted a month earlier in their efforts to avert social disruption. The continuing epidemic convinced Orlov and his advisers of the urgent need for stricter precautions. To allay public repugnance toward the isolation facilities, they should all have storehouses for the safekeeping of movable property. To relieve overcrowding, 10 more pesthouses should be organized on the periphery of town. The quarantines should accept only suspect persons; the pesthouses would take the stricken, separating seriously ill patients from convalescents, and treat them all as recommended.[40]

Moscow's new leadership perceived the risks involved in the program of compulsory evacuation to extramural facilities. That policy had largely provoked the riots, and many officials also believed that it had failed mainly for lack of public cooperation. To implement the controversial program, therefore, while refurbishing administrative authority, Orlov created, on 11 October, the Commission for the Prevention and Treatment of the Pestilential Infectious Distemper.

The Plague Commission, as the institution will be termed hereafter, originated from a marriage of central and local initiatives. Catherine may have extracted the notion from the foreign and domestic legislation on antiplague precautions that Teplov and Volkov began assembling at the start of 1771. Filed among these materials an untitled and undated memorandum, evidently drafted by the Empress, proposed a permanent special commission "for the preservation of human health." Because infectious disease ranked high among health hazards, this commission should fashion a statute consolidating previous precautions and conduct observations "to make new contrivances and improvements." Catherine obviously had Moscow in mind when she remarked: "experience teaches that, no matter what measures are taken for the people's benefit, but if neither special persons nor an office apply solicitude so that everything prescribed be actually executed and every new supplement effected, then even the institutions will be vain ones." Thus the proposed commission should insure timely detection and efficient suppression of epidemics.[41]

If the Empress formulated this memorandum to guide policy in Moscow, she borrowed the idea of a public health council either from Austria's centralized network of medical surveillance or from cameralist theory.[42] Possibly Volkov brought the idea to Moscow at Catherine's oral command. But then the Moscow authorities could have espoused the project on their own, building upon cameralist recommendations or adapting the policies of communal self-help that they had championed since late August. Whoever provided the initiative, particular circumstances in Moscow dictated the foundation and composition of the Plague Commission. The new institution was designed to supplement temporarily the city's regular administration and to rally the medical community. Composed of eminent representatives of Moscow and Petersburg officialdom and society, the council coordinated local and central initiatives while sharing responsibility for unpopular policies.

Two facets of the commission betokened policy changes. First, its very name signified a more active orientation—treatment as well as prevention—against a more definite target—bubonic plague. There could be no further doubt about the disease's identity. Second, its membership exemplified an effort to unite officials, medical professionals, and public representatives in a joint antiplague campaign. Orlov and his advisers built the commission around the eight officials and medical practitioners who had drafted the proposals for revised policies. The chairman was Senator Eropkin, the man best acquainted with recent policies, who was assisted by Vasilii Baskakov, one of Orlov's deputies from Petersburg. Senator Volkov headed the nonmedical administrative arm, the so-called Executive Commission, which included Chief of Police Bakhmetev and Fedor Borisov, a supervisor of the rebuilding of the Kremlin. Almost as soon as the commissioners started meeting they enlisted Prince Peter Makulov, the retired Moscow official who had administered the quarantines under Eropkin. The 5 medical commissioners represented the main ranks of their profession: doctors Gustav Orraeus, Afanasii Shafonskii, and Kas'ian Yagel'skii, staff-surgeon Christian Grave, and surgeon Danilo Samoilovich. Each possessed recent and extensive, firsthand knowledge of plague. All had substantial professional experience.[43]

The inclusion of 2 public representatives distinguished the Plague Commission from its immediate local predecessors, Eropkin's antiplague organization and the medical consilium. Archpriest Alexander Levshin of the Assumption Cathedral, the senior member of the Moscow Synodal Office, represented the Church and the clergy. An influential component of Moscow society, the clergy traditionally mediated between government and people, proclaiming official decrees from the pulpit. Pestilence had disrupted the ecclesiastical administration and decimated the clergy, already deranged by the Plague Riot and the prohibition of religious processions. Appointing a clergyman to the commission demonstrated officialdom's desire to restore clerical morale and to appeal to the public through the Church.

Similar calculations motivated the selection of Luka Dolgov, a prominent Moscow wholesale merchant. Wealth and eminence had enabled Dolgov to build a mansion on Bol'shaia Meshchanskaia Street and to be the first merchant to sign the Moscow nakaz of 1767. Six of his 10 daughters married noblemen, and Dr. Zybelin and the architect Vasilii Bazhenov were among his sons-in-law. In 1775, Dolgov himself received a patent of nobility for his service against the plague.[44] His participation in the commission provided a link to the mercantile community, portions of which had adopted antiepidemic measures even as many merchants fell victim to the plague. Together with Archpriest Levshin, Dolgov acted as a public observer-adviser of the new antiplague campaign.[45]

The Plague Commission assumed jurisdiction over all medical practitioners, apothecary shops, quarantines, and pesthouses. It met daily at eleven o'clock in the Kremlin to apportion duties among its members. All business was transacted by majority vote and recorded in a daily journal; otherwise paperwork was kept to a minimum. The commission also controlled the district supervisors, who received direct authority over the police in order to avoid overlapping functions and loss of time. It computed the daily toll of sick, dead, and convalescent, reporting the data each day to the senate and Orlov. With a mandate to "maintain the order, tranquillity, and welfare of the city," the Executive Commission implemented the orders of the Plague Commission and fulfilled general police functions. Its members patterned their procedures after those of the parent body and met in adjacent rooms at the same time. The public instructions to both commissions ended with a thundering condemnation of administrative abuses reminiscent of Catherine's unfortunate manifesto of 9 September, which blamed much of the crisis on official negligence, timidity, and weakness. "Every kind of injustice, extortion, assaults and bribery always hateful before God and forbidden by the laws, will be sought out now as capital crimes, without any mercy or personal considerations."[46]

Renewal of the Antiplague Campaign

Faithful to the urgency that created the Plague Commission, it first met on 12 October. The commissioners assembled almost daily for the next 12 months and then gathered frequently until the institution was dissolved in 1775. The Plague Commission immediately considered a multitude of matters. Its first session, for instance, directed the Executive Commission to collect wastepaper and household furnishings discarded near the Zemlianoi Val. Apprehensive lest disease spread from infected articles, the commission warned that the collectors should wear protective clothing; they must not touch suspect material barehanded but use long-handled hooks to form piles for burning. The district supervisors should also collect and burn such trash. In addition, the commission solicited information about the local barbers with a view "for some use of them." It formally accepted Eropkin's files and assigned Dr. Yagel'skii to institute medical precautions for the commission itself. Before adjourning, the commissioners discussed where the new pesthouses should be established, reviewed the quarantines, and considered precautions for persons and goods entering and leaving Moscow. Finally, they received a proposal for the fumigation of infected houses and merchandise from one Frosard, a Swiss formerly in French service.[47]

Within a few days, the commission's workload multiplied as it rejuvenated the antiplague campaign. By 16 October, a clerical staff of 19 assisted the commissioners in their efforts to establish and staff the new pesthouses and quarantines.[48] Yagel'skii, Shafonskii, and Samoilovich were delegated to seek convenient sites for isolation facilities. They looked for large houses with 10 or more rooms on the outskirts of town, near pure water, and which could be divided into separate sections. On 18 October, Yagel'skii and Samoilovich each reported 2 possible sites, while Orraeus won approval of his model plan for the institutions. Shafonskii recommended the Lefortovo and Marly palaces as capable of sheltering 500 and 200 sick, respectively. Prince Makulov also found a promising site at the Pokrovskii Monastery, and Orlov volunteered his house on Voznesenskaia Street as a special facility "for the wellborn."[49]

In the end, 2 large new pesthouses were established at the Pokrovskii Monastery and the Lefortovo Palace, with a third, smaller one for noblemen and officials at the merchant Perepletchikov's house near the Donskoi Monastery. New quarantines at the Marly Palace and the Archbishop's house both served the Lefortovo pesthouse. The pesthouse at the Simonov Monastery continued to function, along with the quarantines at the Danilov Monastery, the Serpukhov and Kaluga gates, and Troitskoe-Golenishchevo.[50] Noting that at least 106 priests had died by 25 October, the Synodal Office petitioned through commissioner Levshin for a special quarantine for the clergy. The commission opened Orlov's house to clergy as well as noblemen, since few of the nobility had appeared there. The various communal quarantines maintained their operations under the general supervision of the commission. Entire houses of Old Believers had died out, so Eropkin feared that the schismatics might spread pestilence by using household belongings from stricken residences to furnish their quarantines. Orlov therefore ordered such property stored until the epidemic passed.[51]

Staffing the isolation facilities taxed the Plague Commission's energies far more than locating suitable sites. Orraeus proposed that a doctor, staff-surgeon, or surgeon have full authority to administer each pesthouse, which should deploy a minimum of one attendant for 10 patients, one barber per 50, one surgeon's mate per 100, and one surgeon per 200. A doctor should be assigned if the sick exceeded 200. With males and females separated, the sick should be grouped according to the degree of their affliction. Convalescents might be used as attendants in case of necessity. The senior medical practitioner, who should visit the sick twice daily, would guide the actual treatment and care provided by the surgeons and surgeon's mates, who should protect themselves from infection and maintain "a jolly and brave spirit."[52]

In view of the administrative collapse and violence of mid-September, the widespread animosity toward medical professionals, and the swollen death toll, many practitioners hesitated to volunteer for quarantine service. Hence the commission reviewed all medical personnel on 16 October, soliciting their service in return for 50 percent higher pay and promises of financial reward and professional promotion. Practitioners were warned that if nobody volunteered, compulsory assignments would follow. Yet the commissioners excused several practitioners: Dr. Lerche because of his age and infirmity, Dr. Asch from sickness, all those already serving on the commission, at pesthouses and quarantines, and the staffs of the Foundling Home and Paul's Hospital. Of 39 practitioners approached, the great majority declined to volunteer. Most cited other duties or ill health. Several said they would serve, but preferred not to. At least one physician, Dr. Shkiadan, could not be found in Moscow. Another practitioner, staff-surgeon Tatarinov, was censured for failing to appear for service; his excuse that he had not been summoned was rejected as inadequate.[53]

Only a few medical men volunteered. On 19 October, Dr. Pogoretskii offered to serve wherever needed. So did 4 men not on the commission's list: Peter Libgolt, a nonscholarship surgical student; Veniamin Knol, a foreign apothecary apprentice; and 2 barbers, the brothers Nikita and Ivan Morozov. Several days later, 6 more barbers asked for assignments. Dismayed at the medical community's paltry response, Orlov directed the commission to offer double salaries, guarantees of further reward, and pensions of one-half salary to widows and orphans of practitioners who died during the emergency. Although a few more volunteers turned up, the commission sought to transfer surgical personnel from the Foundling Home, Paul's Hospital, Sukin's shelter for orphans, the General Infantry Hospital, and the town of Kaluga. It even requested some of the 9 surgeons then with Major Shipov in the Ukraine. The deficit of medical practitioners became larger as several fell ill or perished at the isolation facilities.[54]

On 23 October, the commission issued a general reassignment of the practitioners who prosecuted the final phase of the antiplague campaign in Moscow: 8 doctors, 6 staff-surgeons, 13 surgeons, 10 surgeon's mates, 3 surgical students, one apothecary's apprentice, and 8 barbers—a total of 49 medical professionals outside the commission. The 5 practitioners on the commission itself all practiced quite actively between sessions. They eventually persuaded Dr. Lerche to oversee the medical staff at the quarantine for the nobility and enlisted surgeon Margraf's wife to inspect women who wished to leave Moscow. Some other practitioners rendered service privately. Understandably, the commissioners chastised practitioners who avoided their assignments and those who had denied that the disease was plague. Dr. Shkiadan suffered on both counts.[55]

The Plague Commission resolved on 20 October to have the Executive Commission seek out Dr. Shkiadan and surgeon Luka Golts for service in the districts. After summoning them three times without result, the commission requested, on 26 October, that the senate get the guberniia chancery to look for them outside Moscow. A day later, the commission lost all patience after discovering that Dr. Shkiadan had shirked his duties since the spring and that he had disputed the pestilential nature of the disease. The commissioners found that Shkiadan had been absent from Moscow since 25 August, allegedly attending his sick wife until 18 September, when all medical and administrative personnel had been ordered back to duty; but even then he had not returned. Instead of jailing the doctor for negligence and insubordination, the commission assigned him to the Simonov pesthouse to observe plague firsthand. This assignment served a second purpose, too, because surgeon Golts, the only other practitioner at the pesthouse, barely spoke Russian.[56]

Some commentators have cited such incidents to accent nationalistic antagonism within the Moscow medical community. The patriotic Slavic practitioners, they contend, led the antiplague campaign, whereas many foreigners fled or served half-heartedly.[57] But this simplistic interpretation collapses upon examination. The great majority of Moscow's practitioners, most of whom were Russian citizens whatever their place of birth, fulfilled their duties faithfully throughout the emergency. Considering the catastrophic situation, extraordinarily few cases of dereliction of duty came to light. The few known instances did not divide neatly along national or ethnic lines. On 23 October, for instance, when the Plague Commission learned of the flight of one staff member, petty clerk Andrei Voitov, it ordered the Executive Commission to find fugitive and to employ him as a hospital attendant. Petty clerk Dmitriev, reported absent overnight, was sent to assist Dr. Pogoretskii at the Lefortovo pesthouse. In response to Sukin's complaint about the desertion of barber Ivan Kuznetsov from the orphans' shelter, the commission, on 12 November, ordered the fugitive apprehended and fined. The next day the commission acted on a complaint of Captain Volotskii against district supervisor Zinov'ev, who had declined to hospitalize Volotskii's sick relative despite repeated entreaties. The commissioners appointed one Krechetnikov over Zinov'ev, with orders to use him frequently for inspection of the sick so that he might learn his job better. Surgical apprentice Polushkin, condemned to serve at the Lefortovo pesthouse in December for theft at an infected house, was pardoned two months later for zealous service.[58] Although the foregoing incidents were neither numerous nor typical of the time, they showed that no rank, profession, or nationality exercised a monopoly of cowardice, incompetence, or negligence amid the terrifying circumstances.

Beyond the expansion of isolation facilities and the mobilization of more medical professionals, the commission followed traditional policies of treatment and prophylaxsis. It endeavored mainly to improve the implementation, coordination, and communication of the antiplague measures already agreed upon. On 16 October, the commissioners enlarged the network of district supervisors to 27 by subdividing 7 of the most populous inner-city districts. Orlov provided additional officials to survey the new districts for purposes of determining the number of residences, the total population, and which houses were infected.[59] Appalled at the consistently high mortality, the commissioners abolished all distinctions among causes of death; all corpses were to be buried outside the city in specially appointed cemeteries, without any funeral processions or ceremonies. The district supervisors must arrange speedy interment of all the dead, providing free transport and coffins if necessary. Violators would be punished by compulsory service as hospital attendants or gravediggers. To soften this affront to traditional funeral practices, Orlov ordered construction of special chapels at the suburban cemeteries, so that Muscovites could mourn their dead. To encourage people to seek treatment, he arranged that upon release from quarantines married persons would receive 10 rubles, and the unmarried 5, in addition to new clothes. Because the poor comprised the bulk of those quarantined, these incentives should have been quite attractive, for clothes represented considerable value in a traditional society. Indeed, Dr. Shafonskii believed that a few people even feigned illness to get the money and clothes.[60]

The authorities continued to discover instances of apparent concealment. From the eleventh district, supervisor Shapkin and staff-surgeon Tatarinov reported, on 24 October, having inspected 3 persons with buboes, 3 with carbuncles, and one without marks. These cases convinced the examiners that nobody had reported the sickness for more than a week. The Plague Commission concurred, "for all medical men assert that the dangerous disease begins first with pain in the head, anguish, vomiting, and weakness. And then only after some days do the pestilential marks come out on the body." So the commissioners recommended a public announcement, with signatures from heads of households pledging compliance, that whenever somebody felt nauseous he should be isolated and the district supervisor informed at once. While awaiting examination (the assumption of delay offered mute testimony to the disarray) the sick were to be treated with simple remedies, such as vinegar and cranberry, which a commission publication of 20 October urged people to obtain. Persons responsible for, or cognizant of, concealment of the sick would be consigned to quarantines. In the case at hand, however, the commissioners opted for Catherine's rule of 9 September, allowing persons who lived with the sick to enter a quarantine or to sequester themselves for 16 days. Two days later the commission reaffirmed the obligation of everybody to apprise the district supervisors immediately of all cases of death.[61]

This problem persisted even as the epidemic waned. On 15 November, the senate publicly concluded that "the infection has already greatly diminished." As hope for salvation rose, however, so must the authorities' vigilance. "The madness of hiding the sick has reached such a degree," the senate explained, "that there are many examples of infected persons having died, but still nothing was declared about them. . . . people excuse themselves by saying that the deceased, without being sick, suddenly died. But as this cannot be, the deceit only increases the crime, inasmuch as in such cases those in the same room were more subject to infection in every manner." The senate also decried the laggardness of Muscovites who only brought persons for treatment when already half-dead and beyond hope of recovery. If the afflicted were hospitalized promptly, the senate insisted, "if not all, then at least the far greater number might recover very quickly and soon return to society." Like most of the commission's orders, this edict was to be read in all churches twice a week.[62]

Apparently, the Moscow authorities kept no statistics about cases of concealed sickness or death. Given the imperfect administrative machinery at their disposal, uncertain medical knowledge, and lack of public cooperation, concealment would have been difficult to detect in any event. Physicians and officials worried, moreover, that corpses interred clandestinely might regenerate disease. On 24 December, the senate authorized rewards of 10 rubles for the disclosure of concealed sickness or hidden bodies, and 20 rubles for the apprehension of persons guilty of stealing effects of the dead or selling used clothes. By the spring of 1772, search teams discovered nearly a thousand secretly interred corpses. Several dozen persons were arrested for looting or trafficking in stolen goods or used apparel.[63]

Looting of deserted houses threatened public health, security, and property, so the Executive Commission hastened to implement a senate edict of 12 October threatening death on the spot for "such godless persons and foes of the human race." On 17 October, the commission reviewed the case of 4 looters who, with 5 accomplices, had pillaged 3 abandoned houses in Preobrazhenskoe and Pokrovskoe. Both the police and the Executive Commission favored the death penalty for the culprits. But the senate ruled that, since the crime was committed before the issuance of its edict, the guilty should be flogged, placed in irons, and used to bury plague victims. Before the sentence could be executed, however, 2 of the condemned became infected and entered a pesthouse. When the other 2 were taken to receive their punishment, one "collapsed and began to expire, a surgeon's inspection disclosing a bubo in the groin." So only one of the 4 suffered the sentence immediately, and the plague may have killed the others. On 12 December, Bakhmetev complained about lax security at the quarantines, from which 2 infected looters escaped in irons.[64] No doubt many looters avoided detection altogether.

Movement within and between city districts inspired fears that squatters might rekindle pestilence. The commission therefore charged the district supervisors to maintain surveillance of all residents, warning them not to shelter outsiders or to depart without permission. General Matvei Martynov complained that in the seventh and fifteenth districts, among 143 houses of deceased artillery personnel, 34 were inhabited by "various kinds of people: manufactory workers, serfs, soldiers, merchants and peasants, some of them relatives of the deceased, but others are complete outsiders who should not be there." The commissioners deplored the danger and recommended that the senate consign the offenders to quarantines and dismantle the suspect houses before burning them.[65]

For similar reasons, the health authorities took pains with the clergy. The ban on public processions remained in effect, and for the holy day of the Virgin of Kazan, on 22 October, the authorities arranged to keep the procession small. They also limited the length of prayers offered at the Varvarskie Gates and watched that only accredited clerics ministered there. The Plague Commission enjoined the Church authorities not to transfer clergy to parishes vacated by disease and not to allow services in infected churches. Indeed, clergymen were told to stay home as much as possible. Catherine explained these arrangements as necessary because "our churches are small, everybody prays standing, and there is usually much crowding."[66]

The epidemic also provoked a secondary massacre. The Plague Commission ordered the destruction of dogs and cats from infected houses, as well as strays, "inasmuch as the pestilential poison can remain in their fur for a very long time, and in running from house to house they transmit this disease to healthy houses, so therefore the dogs of such houses, except those that have been chained, ought to be killed too."[67]

To prevent the regeneration of plague, a prospect that increasingly worried the authorities as people started returning to Moscow, the Plague Commission investigated methods of fumigating infected buildings. Yagel'skii and Grave compiled instructions for fumigators, while Samoilovich tested various compounds. The formula of the Swiss Frosard was rejected when he refused to live in a house treated with it, but the commission accepted one from St. Nicolaz, a lecturer at Moscow University, who later received 1,000 rubles for his invention. Samoilovich fumigated the clothing of several plague victims with this powder and then arranged for healthy convicts to wear the cleansed apparel for 15 days. None of the convicts became ill, so the commission, on 10 December, published the recipes of three officially approved powders, all sulphur-based, and launched a systematic fumigation campaign. Fumigation teams devoted special attention to churches, manufactories, and public buildings, treating 6,161 structures with 9,987 rooms by 9 April 1772. The commission considered fumigation so important that when apothecary Meyer was denounced for altering some ingredients, the medical members burned the "false powders," fined Meyer and assigned him to serve at a pesthouse for 10 days, and warned all apothecaries against his example.[68]

Although the medical community entertained no further doubts that the disease was pestilential, practitioners still labored under a keenly felt burden of ignorance. The Plague Commission therefore pursued a dual policy of instruction and consultation. For public consumption, it published, on 20 October, a brief description of treatment and prophylaxsis "for the use of the common people in particular," which repeated the medical advice the practitioners had given Orlov privately. The commission's advisory was more widely distributed than its predecessors. "The success of these prescriptions has been so useful up to the present," announced the senate, on 15 November, "that everywhere people wish to have these leaflets."[69]

From the medical community, however, the Plague Commission solicited guidance and information. All practitioners were asked to file brief weekly reports describing the symptoms most frequently encountered and the actions of the disease. An Armenian tract extolling the antipestilential properties of balsam was translated. To assist practitioners, the commissioners ordered excerpts "from the writings of various experienced doctors and surgeons," and for purposes of rendering them into Russian they consulted the Russian translations of Heister's *Anatomy* and Platner's *Surgery.* On 20 October, the commission sent practitioners printed copies of Dr. Orraeus's tract, "A Brief Advice How to Recognize the Pestilential Distemper as well as to Treat and Preserve against It." Orraeus recognized three types of plague:

two degrees of "tranquil distemper" and one "rapidly fatal" kind, the last probably denoting septicemic plague. His suggestions for treatment varied according to the type encountered, but were entirely traditional. He insisted that his advice came not from books, but from "many experiences" in Moldavia and "here in Moscow." He claimed no special authority and invited others to devise better methods. Nevertheless, the day before endorsing Orraeus's tract, the commission rebuffed Pogoretskii's request for medical books by remarking that there was no time for theory at a pesthouse, "but one must employ actual practice."[70]

Mindful of past dissension within the medical community, the Plague Commission censured insubordination and criticism of its policies. On 27 October, the commissioners protested that their request for weekly reports had elicited just one response—a scornful reproach from Dr. Erasmus. The temperamental Erasmus, whose authority as acting city-physician the Plague Commission had superseded, advised checking the Simonov pesthouse instead of bothering the district medical inspectors. Descriptions of the disease were useless, he asserted, as scarcely 3 percent of the afflicted survived. Summoning Erasmus before the commission, the medical members remonstrated that he had reported only 3 cases in his own district. Inflated statistics, the commissioners exhorted Erasmus, could damage commerce if they became known to the public. When Erasmus shouted that none of the 50 sick in the foreign suburb had recovered, he was reprimanded for "effrontery as well as for false exaggeration of the degree of the disease." Then the commission ordered the doctor imprisoned on bread and water or punished in some other appropriate manner. The actual punishment must have been brief or even waived, for Erasmus returned to duty by 16 November.[71]

At the end of October, the commission finally received some other medical commentaries.[72] Dr. Zybelin, for example, reported, on 24 October, that "petechiae are found extremely rarely at present; carbuncles are still evident on many, but more rarely than formerly, and everywhere for the most part only buboes in the armpits and groin." The usual symptoms seemed less painful and less dangerous, and some victims were treating themselves. "Some say that, having applied pitch to the bubo, and some supplement that with minced garlic, they produced an ulceration and thus seemed to be healthier. Still others, having experienced symptoms at the start analogous to the present disease, recovered the next day and then, two weeks later, the distemper actually appeared on them." Zybelin could not decide whether such delayed cases indicated another disease, a belated reaction to infection, or subsequent reinfection.[73] None of the commentators made any momentous discoveries, but their observations provided much data for later analysis.

The Plague Commission monitored practitioners' activities as best it could. On 14 October, for instance, the commissioners became outraged at a report that 16 of 19 plague patients had died under the care of one Shlage, an impromptu foreign practitioner. "As from this it is evident that this Shlage

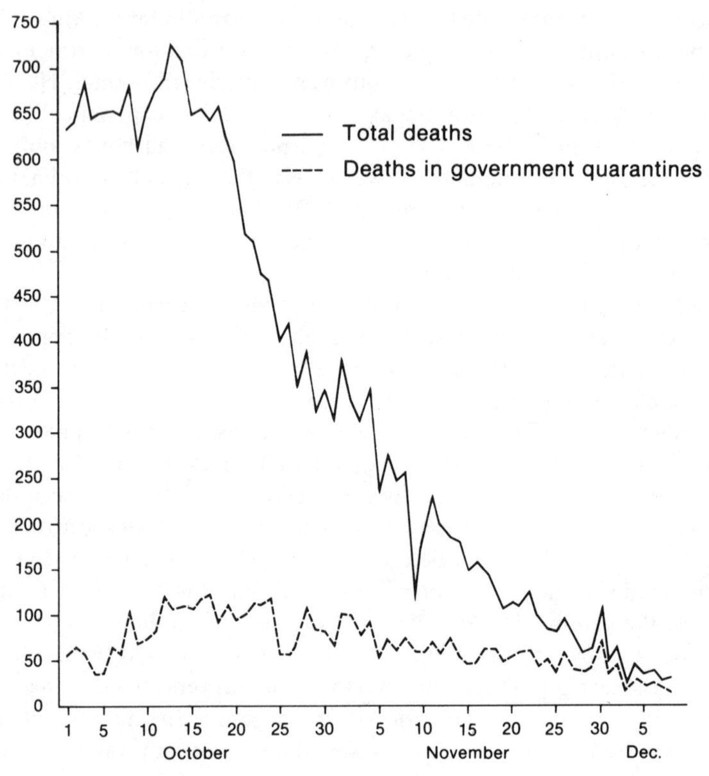

Graph 4 Daily mortality, 1 October–8 December 1771. (*Source:* TsGADA, f. 199, d. 151, pt. 1, no. 1: 141v.-142.)

does not possess the ability to heal, so he should now and henceforward be removed from that occupation and be forbidden either to treat or to sell medicaments." Overly zealous and unsupervised treatment also worried the commission. It advised the district supervisors, on 14 November, of the dangers of bloodletting and directed them to enjoin the barbers in their districts, under threat of "cruel punishment," not to bleed patients "at the present pestilential time." Should phlebotomy be judged necessary in a particular case, a doctor or surgeon must approve the procedure. Two days later the commission heard Dr. Shafonskii's report of the tests he made on plague patients of certain powders recommended by staff-surgeon Tode. Shafonskii concluded that the powders—perhaps the celebrated James's Powders that had been tried in Moldavia in 1770—were ineffective and unsafe because they caused vomiting and diarrhea as well as the desired perspiration. Pending determination of particular usage and dosage, the commission withheld printed prescriptions for the substance.[74]

If a few practitioners incurred the commission's displeasure, others received its praise. On 16 November, the commissioners lauded Dr. Frantz Meltzer's administration of the Pokrovskii pesthouse, where the previous day only 4 of 183 patients had died. They thanked Meltzer, who had only enjoyed limited rights to practice, and promised to reward his zeal.[75] The commission also supported petitions seeking compensation for property lost by practitioners at quarantines and for the heirs of surgical personnel, some 20 of whom perished in the epidemic.[76] On balance, the Plague Commission successfully mobilized the Moscow medical community in support of a broadly conceived, vigorously prosecuted antiplague effort, which happened to coincide with the plague's decline.

The Arrival of Winter and Orlov's Departure

Contrary to widespread expectation, neither the restoration of order nor the renewal of precautions arrested the runaway epidemic. Through 19 October, the daily death count stayed above 600 (graph 4). Furthermore, evacuation of all the sick and the suspect merely increased mortality at the pesthouses and quarantines, where 2,626 deaths were recorded in October, as compared to only 499 persons released. In town and at the isolation facilities, October registered 17,561 deaths, a monthly loss only exceeded by September's 21,401. Orlov's public optimism lapsed into private despair on 18 October, as he confessed to Catherine his failure to check the pestilence, "although there is a weak hope for a lessening of it."[77]

Just after Orlov admitted failure, however, winter finally delivered Moscow. Temperatures gradually declined from a high of 62° F. on 4 October. The first snow fell on the night of 20–21 October, a heavy snowfall followed on 29 October, and hard frosts set in the next day. Intense cold in November and December abruptly terminated the prolonged rainy season that had accompanied the height of the plague. After a big snow on 6–7 November, Muscovites began using sledges and the Moskva froze solid.[78] According to Dr. Lerche's observations, the mean temperature dropped from 40.5° in October to 13.5° in November, and then stayed at 12.5° in December, with a low of −12° on the 29th. The freeze deepened early in 1772, as Lerche recorded a low of −19° on 10 January.[79] Together with the die-off of rats, which are far more susceptible than humans to bubonic plague, temperatures below 50° F. break the chain of infection by causing the fleas to become inactive.

As plotted in graph 4, over-all mortality in Moscow declined almost as fast as the temperature. Within two weeks, 18–31 October, the daily toll dropped from 658 to 312. The downward trend reached 120 on 9 November, before rebounding to 230 two days later. Thereupon the decline resumed more slowly until, after a brief upswing at the close of November (Lerche recorded a high of 37° on 3 December), daily mortality fell below 30 for the first time since early July. The 5,235 deaths registered in November constituted less than one-third of October's terrible toll, and the total of 805 in December fell short of some monthly losses for nonplague years.[80]

By contrast, the death rate at the isolation facilities diminished more slowly. November's toll slightly exceeded September's, for example (1,769 vs. 1,640), and combined with the October total of 2,626 to surpass by a margin of almost two to one the number of persons released during the same period. These statistics prompted Orlov to lament, on 16 November, that the plague was not waning as rapidly as hoped.[81] Even as the epidemic ended, in December, more people died at the isolation facilities than were released; 486 of 1,965 patients succumbed, but only 334 had been released through 18 December. Indeed, of the 12,565 persons quarantined in state facilities between April 1771 and March 1772, 8,133 perished. No wonder Muscovites cringed at the mention of quarantines.[82]

The plague's course and symptoms changed too. "The disorder, which a short time before had terminated on the second or third day, now kept on to the fifth or sixth," Dr. Mertens noticed. "Neither those large purple spots, which we have before described, nor carbuncles, were by any means so frequent as they had been; buboes were now almost the only tumors found upon the infected." In fact, "several persons who had the plague were but slightly indisposed, and walked about though they had buboes upon them." A mild attack, probably of so-called *Pestis minor,* struck Dr. Pogoretskii on 21 October, but he soon recovered sufficiently to resume service at the Lefortovo pesthouse.[83]

Word of the plague's decline reached Catherine by 20 October, when she privately exulted that the death count had already fallen by half—a slight anticipation of the trend shown in graph 4. After further reports confirmed winter's onset and Orlov's success, the Empress decided to recall him and to permanently replace Saltykov by appointing Prince Mikhail Volkonskii governor-general of Moscow.[84] A prominent aristocrat who had backed Catherine's seizure of the throne, Prince Volkonskii (1713–89) enjoyed solid credit at court and had occupied high positions in the new regime. After a difficult stint as ambassador to Poland he had recently returned to Petersburg. In dispatching Volkonskii to Moscow on 6 November, Catherine gave him detailed instructions to continue Orlov's policies. The new Governor-General also received orders to redouble precautions against a recurrence of plague in the spring.[85]

Before leaving, Orlov presided over the trial of the captive rioters. The special court that convened in the Kremlin's Facetted Palace on 31 October and 2–5 November failed to discover any conspiracy, but condemned Vasilii Andreev, a house serf, and Ivan Dmitriev, a Moscow merchant, to death for murdering the Archbishop. Two other house serfs, Aleksei Leont'ev and Fedor Deianov, were selected by lot for execution from a group of 64 adult

Figure 13 The Orlov Gates in Tsarskoe Selo (present-day Pushkin), photograph by the author, 1971.

men implicated in the rioting. The other 62 were sentenced to be knouted, their nostrils torn with tongs, and then sent to hard labor. Ten minors were condemned to be beaten with rods; 89 lesser suspects were to receive lashings. The court released 142 persons without corporal punishment. All these sentences were executed on 11 November. Andreev and Dmitriev were hanged at the Donskoi Monastery, Leont'ev and Deianov were hanged on Red Square, and the other punishments were staged at different public squares. Savelii Biakov and Il'ia Afanas'ev, the originators of the "miracle" at the Varvarskie Gates, were also condemned to be knouted, clapped in irons, and exiled. The police punished Biakov publicly on 25 November, but Afanas'ev's sentence was postponed because he had been quarantined; perhaps he died before receiving his punishment.[86]

Before Orlov departed for Petersburg on 22 November, he conferred extensively with Prince Volkonskii, who had arrived a week earlier. Orlov had the senate allocate 50,000 rubles for Volkonskii to exterminate the last of the plague.[87] After exempting Orlov from much of the quarantine en route to Petersburg, Catherine triumphantly received him at court the evening of

4 December. She commemorated his exploit with a gold medal, a marble medallion, and a triumphal arch at Tsarskoe Selo.[88] Concurrently, Volkonskii delivered her reward to Eropkin: a cavaliership in the order of Saint Andrew, 20,000 rubles, and permission to retire from state service. At first, Eropkin refused the money, but when the Empress insisted, he finally accepted and gratefully rescinded his retirement. By contrast, Catherine ordered the retirement of Count Saltykov on 7 November, noting that "the poor man has outlived his glory." The plague ruined Saltykov's long, distinguished career; he died a year later. The Empress was dissatisfied with Chief of Police Bakhmetev, too, and replaced him with Nikolai Arkharov in January 1772.[89] The year-long epidemic wrought a considerable turnover at the top and the bottom of Moscow's administration.

Neither the Orlov mission nor the Plague commission saved Moscow from the plague's fury. Nonetheless, both together aided in the restoration of order, the revival of the economy, and the renewal of precautions on a broader scale. Although the epidemic killed nearly as many Muscovites after the Plague Riot as before, Orlov and the commission effectively demonstrated the imperial government's concern for the stricken metropolis, enabling the Moscow authorities to survive catastrophe without further shocks. As Samuel Swallow, British consul-general in Petersburg, concluded on 29 November: "There is reason to believe the operations of these Commissions, together with the Frost continuing, have greatly contributed to the decrease of the Disease, as it manifestly has, to the maintaining good Order and Tranquility within the City."[90] The commission's efforts would have seemed positively spectacular if cold weather had arrived earlier. Had the brief frosts of September been longer and stronger, they might have cut off the epidemic in Moscow sooner and blocked its spread into the provinces.

CHAPTER NINE

The Plague in the Provinces and the Threat to Petersburg (August 1771–August 1775)

Plague afflicted many localities en route to Moscow and then menaced all of central Russia. If commercial intercourse facilitated importation of *Y. pestis* to the Russian heartland, then Moscow's functions as the primary inland entrepôt threatened reexportation of plague to the rest of the empire, and even abroad. Apprehension that the disease might spread outward from Moscow perturbed the Petersburg authorities as early as August 1771. Their anxiety mounted steadily in September and October as reports confirmed the infection of Moscow guberniia and suspicious cases appeared as close as Novgorod guberniia. Countering plague in the provinces therefore became an important task of the Orlov mission. Behind the policies of Orlov and the Plague Commission, and the other precautions that the Plague Riot elicited from the imperial government, loomed the ultimate fear: Would the rampant epidemic reach Petersburg itself? Nobody could know how much farther the mysterious disease might travel, or whether it might fade away in one place only to break out elsewhere.

While Moscow's constant exchange of people, merchandise, and raw materials with the hinterland provided multiple avenues of expansion for pestilence, the demographic circumstances of central Russia afforded ample reception points in the form of a dense, substantially urbanized population. On the eve of the plague the 11 provinces of Moscow guberniia contained about 4.6 million residents—nearly one-fifth of the empire's total population.[1] Compared to the rest of European Russia, moreover, both a higher proportion and a greater absolute number of the people of Moscow guberniia lived in towns. In 1762, the third national census enumerated a taxable urban male population of about 90,000 in the guberniia. Though this figure constituted only 3.64 percent of the guberniia's male population, several provinces held significantly higher proportions. Moscow province led, with 20,478 taxable urban males, or 5.16 percent of its total male population. Other sizable urban agglomerations occurred in Tula province, with 14,418 taxable males (4.2 percent); Kaluga province with 13,414 (4.1 percent); and Yaroslavl province with 13,248 (3.97 percent).[2] The capitals of these three provinces all boasted substantial commercial, manufacturing, and artisan communities. Tula was a metal-fabricating center; Kaluga and Yaroslavl both housed textile mills and supported extensive commerce.

These statistics by no means revealed the actual level of urbanization of the greater Moscow region. They took no account, for example, of population increments and movements after 1762. Yet the growth of Moscow itself in the 1760s indicated accelerating urban migration. If Moscow's rate of population increase surpassed that of most provincial towns, one may reasonably infer that some of the trends swelling the metropolis boosted population in the hinterland as well. In 1771, the urban population of Moscow guberniia must have considerably exceeded the figure of 1762. Counting both males and females, temporary and unregistered urban residents, and untaxed groups, such as the nobility, the clergy, and the dependents of military recruits, a figure of 10 percent may still underestimate the urbanized population of that region.[3]

Moscow guberniia also embraced thousands of villages and hamlets. The census of 1762 classified almost 96 percent of the population as peasants, though that juridical definition did not mean that they engaged only in agriculture.[4] Some villages were composed almost entirely of craftsmen.[5] In Moscow and its neighboring provinces, subsequently known as the central industrial region, many peasants worked in urban occupations at least part of the year. Most rural Russian peasants lived in compact communities. A typical village comprised from a dozen to several hundred houses strung out along one or more tracks. The only communal building would be a church, if the village were large enough to have one. Russian peasant huts, built entirely of wood, usually had a single living room warmed by a large corner oven.[6] Family units tended to be large, with married sons often living with parents and grandparents. The high birthrate concealed a high deathrate, especially for infants, and communicable disease was commonplace. Because Russian villages were as vulnerable as towns to rat infestation, they could and did suffer outbreaks of plague, sometimes severe ones. But their smaller populations, dispersed locations, and the easy possibility of flight rendered the countryside much safer than urban areas during the epidemic of 1771. Pneumonic plague could have compromised such relative security, but it seems not to have appeared in the Russian Empire in 1770–72.

Throughout the plague, Moscow's ambiguous boundaries and sprawling layout blurred the epidemic's extra-urban incidence. Orlov complained to Catherine that "heretofore it has been difficult to distinguish what is Moscow from what is a village, and who lives on the basis of which rights, but especially the suburbs surrounding Moscow: these are places that can never be put in order if they are not removed."[7] Since plague apparently entered Moscow through the suburbs, it could spread outward just as easily. The streams

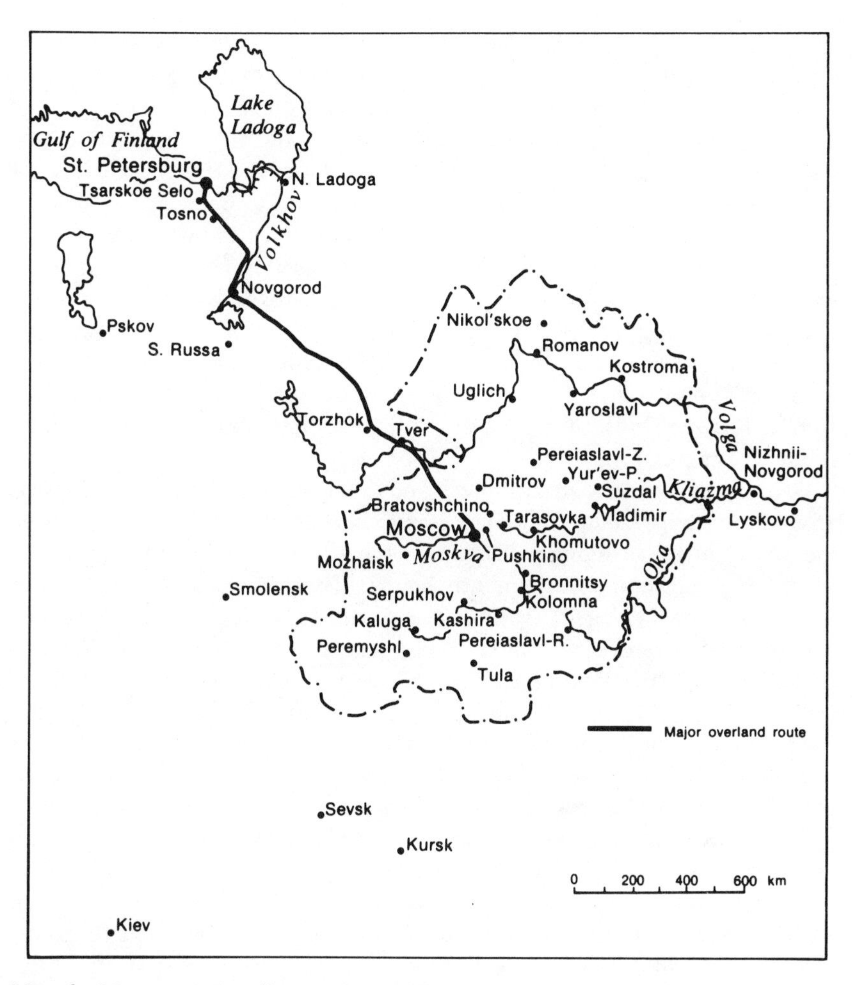

Map 6 Moscow Guberniia and Central Russia.

of people leaving the city, whose numbers reached tidal proportions by late August, guaranteed that disease would follow.

Concern about the epidemic's territorial expansion motivated the imperial government to reinstitute full quarantine precautions along the Moscow-Petersburg highway on 2 August. All travelers from Moscow had to obtain bills of health from Eropkin. By 8 August, moreover, the Petersburg authorities endorsed the removal of a village of economic peasants on the edge of Moscow near the Vladimir Road, fearing infection there. The deteriorating situation finally prompted Catherine, on 20 August, to order the immediate implementation of her emergency program of 31 March, which relied upon a series of cordons to isolate Moscow from its hinterland.[8] This was the program that the Moscow authorities protested as both dangerous and impossible to enforce. By mid-August they knew what Petersburg did not: Moscow's environs were already infected. "Many inhabitants living here are departing, and sick persons are leaving Moscow," Saltykov and Eropkin informed the senate on 23 August, "but it is not possible to observe all this at the gates, for even at night many ride and walk away, wherefore as one can see from reports this disease has also appeared in several villages and hamlets."[9]

At the time, tradition sanctioned the efficacy of flight from plague-infected localities. Throughout August the Petersburg and the Moscow authorities encouraged such migration, particularly on the part of the nobility; those going to provincial estates could depart after medical inspection only. The authorities hoped this policy would relieve overcrowding. Once plague sprouted outside Moscow, however, the Petersburg authorities shuddered for the rest of the empire.

By early September, the Empress and her councilors knew that districts around Moscow were infected. The council session of 12 September reviewed the matter of the economic village near the Vladimir Road, the removal of which they had endorsed a month before. The councilors decided not to remove the whole village, only those houses within the Kamerkollezhskii Val. To prevent future encroachment on city territory, they ordered a ditch dug around the village and threatened to evict any more peasant settlers. Catherine signed the order implementing this measure on 23 September, the day she learned of the Plague Riot. In conjunction with her remembrance of the disturbances of 1764 and 1766 at Pokrovskoe, the recently reported near riot at Lefortovo, and Orlov's blanket indictment of the suburban settlements, this incident convinced the Empress that Moscow's suburbs offered havens "for thieves and crimes and criminals."[10]

On 15 September, the council heard another report from Governor Yushkov about the further spread of the epidemic into the districts around Moscow. In response, the council directed military couriers to bypass Moscow and stipulated a six-week quarantine for anybody leaving the metropolis thenceforth.[11] Events confounded these prescriptions. The cordon 20 miles away from Moscow could not intercept all the refugees then clogging the roads. And when the Plague Riot convulsed the metropolis in mid-September, the possibility of halting the exodus lapsed for several weeks. In practice, the Moscow authorities ceased monitoring departures until early October. The collapse of authority in Moscow redoubled fears in Petersburg that fugitives from the violence might spread rebellion as well as plague to the hinterland. Because measures to isolate Moscow had manifestly failed, Petersburg undertook additional precautions in the provinces.

The Petersburg senate departments prescribed local precautions to all governors and voevodas on 25 September; they were to adopt protective measures in cooperation with the marshal elected by the local nobility. Each rural community should post guards to insure that "no common or vulgar people" entered the settlement and that wayfarers stayed in special lodgings outside the village or bypassed it altogether. If wayfarers needed provisions, the villagers should provide them from afar, without touching the buyers, and receive the money in wooden bowls filled with kvas. Householders should maintain fumigatory fires at home and at both ends of the main street. Since the voevodas and marshals of the nobility could not personally supervise these precautions everywhere, they should subdivide each district into small sectors and delegate authority to reliable members of the resident nobility. Thus the plague highlighted deep-seated deficiencies of provincial administration: the lack of security and the rudimentary mechanisms of governmental authority on the local level. To alleviate the sudden crisis, Petersburg improvised a supplement to local government by mobilizing portions of the provincial nobility, an institutional expedient subsequently elaborated and incorporated into national legislation.[12]

By the time local authorities received these instructions, the plague was already raging outside Moscow. The coincidence of widespread population migration and territorial expansion of the epidemic confirmed contagionist assumptions that infected Muscovites were carrying pestilential "poison" to the countryside. The peasants thought so too, if one is to believe Saltykov's report of 30 August that villagers around Moscow were shunning outsiders.[13] Popular practice may have anticipated the senate warning of 25 September against contacts with strangers and wayfarers. Ivan Tolchenov, a young merchant from Dmitrov, about 70 miles due north of Moscow, observed that since

> the dark [common] people began to scatter to nearby towns and villages and some of them were themselves already infected, while others carried off clothing and other things impregnated with that death-dealing poison, so the infection multiplied among many towns and villages, and especially the villages that lie close to Moscow lost more than half their inhabitants. In Dmitrov too this evil encroached, although not very strongly, yet 40 persons died from it and the greater part of them in houses which either received belongings from Moscow or relatives arrived without having taken precautions.[14]

As Tolchenov intimated, some refugees from Moscow may have carried infective fleas or infected rats in their belongings. It seems probable, however, that contemporaries overestimated the role of human carriers and that plague spread out from Moscow just as it had crept in: through the established trade routes and through extension of the rat epizootic to rural areas. The summer harvest may have increased and concentrated the number of rats and other susceptible rodents in many villages around Moscow.

The Plague's Incidence in the Countryside

Three main variables determined the incidence of plague in Moscow's hinterland: distance from the metropolis, density of population, and duration of the disease as governed by its time of arrival and local weather conditions. To be sure, these factors subsumed others, such as the economic infrastructure and communications linking Moscow and the localities, the particular demographic composition of individual communities, and the efficacy of governmental and individual precautions. Predictably, the epidemic struck hardest at the communities nearest Moscow and traveled farthest to several populous commercial centers. Since the disease migrated primarily under human auspices, it reached different communities at different times and with different results.[15] Over-all mortality statistics will demonstrate trends for the region as a whole, which the analysis of selected localities can qualify and specify. Even so, one must be prudently skeptical about the accuracy of the death toll that contemporaries reported for the provinces. Distance, confusion, and the dearth of medical and administrative personnel in the countryside all hindered the accurate collection of full mortality data.

The epidemic began infecting suburban villages in the summer of 1771. It spread farther and faster in the fall, but then receded almost as rapidly in the winter, surviving briefly into 1772 in a few instances. In contrast to Petersburg's frantic reaction, the Moscow authorities paid scant heed to these developments until early October, absorbed as they were in battling catastrophe in the capital. Once order returned to the metropolis, however, its rejuvenated administration began monitoring the plague's incidence in Moscow guberniia. On 10 October, the senate sent Petersburg a summary of 75 incidents reported since August that yielded 236 deaths attributed to plague, 223 abandoned corpses dead from unknown causes, and 97 dangerously ill. These figures barely scratched the surface; 9 days later the senate registered more than 300 infected localities, two-thirds of them in the Moscow district. By mid-November, in fact, Governor Yushkov reported that 502 localities had lost 12,686 persons to pestilence.[16]

With the plague's sharp decline in Moscow, the senate, on 10 December, appointed Senator Mel'gunov overlord of a concerted antiplague campaign in the Moscow district. Mel'gunov divided the district into 12 sectors, assigning each an official to inspect all villages and to supervise precautions. These emissaries burned abandoned houses, dismantled houses where persons had died, and aired and isolated other stricken houses for 40 days. The Plague Commission could spare only 5 surgical personnel to assist Mel'gunov, and several of them served in the district quite briefly.[17] By the end of January 1772, before Mel'gunov left for Petersburg, his organization had checked 2,207 villages with 16,330 houses. In the 967 villages reportedly infected, 5,357 houses suffered 25,979 deaths. The 12 district inspectors forwarded a final report six weeks later, which added 12 more infected places and raised the death toll to 26,006. They also counted 930 peasants who died of plague while in Moscow.[18] Later that year the Moscow guberniia chancery estimated the district's losses at 34,402, a total that included 3,239 suburban inhabitants and 1,997 peasants temporarily in Moscow.[19]

Table 9 Deaths in Moscow Guberniia, 1769–73

Province	1769	1770	1771	1772	1773
Moscow	16,696	15,537	52,869	13,862	15,565
Yaroslavl	4,439	4,007	8,942	4,756	5,128
Pereslavl-Zalesskii	3,517	3,064	5,927	3,817	4,570
Vladimir	3,396	3,070	5,458	3,424	3,786
Pereslavl-Riazanskii	3,552	3,356	4,655	3,640	3,671
Uglich	2,794	2,946	4,380	2,881	3,194
Kostroma	2,592	2,324	3,081	2,605	2,746
Tula	2,818	2,419	3,041	2,525	2,729
Kaluga	2,863	3,138	3,012	2,425	2,994
Suzdal	2,290	1,990	2,446	2,266	2,544
Yur'ev-Pol'skii	791	716	1,208	783	932
Totals	44,748	42,567	95,019	42,984	47,759

Source: TsGADA, f. 199, d. 385, pt. 2, no. 10: 1–9v.

Allowing for some faulty reporting, then, the plague killed about 25,000 persons in the Moscow district in 1771–72, nearly half the total of 52,869 recorded in Moscow province in 1771 (table 9). If 15,500 deaths are subtracted as the province's normal annual mortality, then Moscow province lost about 37,000 people in the epidemic, two-thirds of them from the Moscow district. The 15 other districts of Moscow province together registered only about 12,000 deaths attributable to plague in 1771. If several thousand provincial peasants died while in Moscow, many of those who succumbed in Moscow province must have been refugees from the metropolis. Assuming a total population of 600,000 for Moscow province outside the capital, the epidemic killed barely 6 percent of the rural population.[20] If, moreover, the Moscow suburbs are excluded from the rural total because of their urban character, the plague's provincial inroads appear even less consequential.

By the same token, those communities closest to the metropolis generally suffered the heaviest losses. Proximity to Moscow implied involvement in the urban economy and earlier exposure to plague. Particularly prone to import infection were the many textile-working villages northeast of Moscow. In fact, Mel'gunov's inspectors found that plague had visited 564 of 1,188 villages in the northeastern quadrant of the Moscow district.[21] If the mortality statistics compiled by Yushkov and Mel'gunov sketch the plague's impact on the Moscow district as a whole, one must doubt their accuracy in relation to specific communities. The duration and mortality attributed to plague in specific places should be viewed as only approximations. Since the provincial authorities began restricting movement rather late, many peasants must have abandoned their villages beforehand. Besides, the noblemen mustered to oversee local precautions generally relied for their information on local village elders, who may have deliberately exaggerated losses so as to decrease the government's demands for taxes and recruits. Probably they often marked down all deaths for the period, whatever the cause, to plague alone.

To cite some examples, the economic village of Pushkino, just northeast of Moscow, allegedly lost 537 of 629 inhabitants in the period from 17 August to 28 October 1771, after a peasant from Moscow brought his wife an infected doll.[22] Several other circumstances implicated the textile trade in this outbreak. Two peasants from Pushkino operated silk looms in the nearby villages of Khomutovo and Tarasovka, from both of which several peasants also worked textiles in the Moscow suburbs.[23] Plague supposedly afflicted Tarasovka 2 days before Pushkino, killing 221 of 277 inhabitants from 15 August to 1 November, while Khomutovo reportedly lost 338 of 479 inhabitants between 2 September and 12 December.[24] Just down the road from Pushkino another satellite of the Moscow market, the state village of Bratovshchino, suffered a similarly disastrous outbreak; 387 of 612 inhabitants allegedly perished in 10 weeks, from 18 August to 5 November.[25] Whether the plague arrived in textile shipments or the belongings of refugees, it disrupted all these villages. Yet these mortality figures undoubtedly included many who survived the epidemic by temporary flight. For example, the peasants of Pushkino fled en masse. The Moscow authorities learned in late August that "many healthy inhabitants of that village, having left their homes, went off secretly at night for residence in the woods, great fears of death are entertained, and those who bury the dead have taken to bed themselves, but now that they have been forced to bury them, they wish henceforth to leave all houses and to run away secretly like ghosts."[26] Whatever the mortality at Pushkino in 1771, the village suffered no permanent loss of population or industry.[27]

Officials received contradictory reports about the plague in some localities. Andronovka, an economic hamlet on the eastern edge of Moscow, supposedly lost 312 of 464 inhabitants between 5 August and 10 October; but another report listed a death toll of 253 for the period from 3 August to 24 November, when 56 of 67 houses became infected and 8 died out.[28] Both estimates probably overstated the actual mortality. The same held true of the suburban state village of Izmailovo. According to one account, the epidemic visited there from 25 August to 14 December, killing 203 persons and striking 36 of 163 houses, 4 of which died out. But another report maintained that the epidemic began almost 3 weeks earlier, on 6 August, and removed 230 out of a total population of 859.[29] Very likely, many deaths in these suburban communities were counted more than once, the Moscow authorities including them in the city's toll, while the provincial administrators credited them to the countryside. Evidently, this happened to Pokrovskoe, the big textile-working crown "village" inside the city limits, which reportedly lost 1,174 from a registered male population of 2,527. No estimate was given as to when plague began there, probably because everybody assumed that it coincided with the Moscow epidemic.[30]

As shown in table 10, plague exerted a selective impact on the different kinds of villages in the Moscow district. Size and density of population ac-

Table 10 Deaths from Plague in the Moscow District in 1771-72

Type of community	No. of infected villages	Total population	Deaths	Mortality rate
Economic villages	288	60,097	11,429	18.8%
Crown estates	112	29,703	7,097	23.9
Stables villages	26	5,508	889	16.1
Private landowners	429	65,237	9,751	14.0
Totals for the Moscow district	855	160,545	29,106	18.1
Rural peasants temporarily in Moscow		32,237	1,997	6.1
Total for Moscow district and peasants temporarily in Moscow		192,782	31,163	16.1

Source: TsGAg.M, f. 636, op. 2, d. 57: 206-207.

counted for some of the variation. Thus, the crown estates, surpassing the others in average population, endured the highest proportional loss—more than 23 percent. At the other extreme, the more numerous and less populated estates of private landowners lost only 14 percent of their inhabitants. In between, were the economic and palace stables villages with plague losses of 19 and 16 percent, respectively. About 2,000 peasants temporarily in Moscow perished there as well, but they represented barely 6 percent of their fellow villagers.

Reports about the source of local outbreaks varied considerably. Some were very specific: "on 23 September from a visitor from Moscow"; "at the start of September from a priest of that village, but it is unknown what he got it from"; "on 7 September from the purchase of a fur coat in Moscow"; "on 15 August from those who drove from the village to a gristmill where the dangerous disease was present"; "in August from recruits coming from Moscow." Others ignored the question, blamed unknown causes, or cited "the will of God."[31] If the indictment of persons from Moscow seems generally plausible, one should believe it in a general sense.

Contemporary observers blamed the plague's inroads into the countryside upon the lack of precautions. "The Moscow disease," Count Alexander Vorontsov wrote Grigorii Orlov from his estate near Vladimir, "has been conveyed to many districts, which is not surprising when one considers, first, the ignorance and carelessness of our rabble as well as their greediness for belongings of the dead. While from one direction many unhealthy folk had dispersed from Moscow; in the district towns not only the simple folk but even the better ones had no conception of this infectious disease, hence one can judge what measures were adopted for averting it."[32]

As in Moscow earlier, the imposition of precautions also caused trouble in the provinces. "The local folk are in the utmost despondency," Vorontsov observed, "first from the danger of imprudent death (for the most part they are without any of the necessary precautions for averting it) and on the other hand from the fact that they have been deprived of any occupation and cannot sell their produce. Open communication from one place to another has ceased in this locality; yet this is all the more painful for the common folk in that it has come at a time when the recruiting levy and the collection of the capitation taxes are approaching."[33] To minimize personal contacts through commercial intercourse, local authorities received orders to transfer fairs to secure locations. But, to avoid man-made dearth in villages without tillage, officials and landowners were to provide for the delivery of staples.[34]

Understandably, refugees from Moscow sometimes met a hostile reception in the provinces. Many died on the roads from hunger, exposure, and diseases other than plague. For example, officials at Mozhaisk recorded an adult male, "an arrival of unknown origin and status found dead 8 September on the main road from Moscow." Countless tragedies occurred such as that which befell the family of Agrafena Verbovskaia, a noblewoman with a bill of health from Moscow who was stopped at the checkpoint outside Mozhaisk. Verbovskaia arrived with her brother, one daughter, and 3 servants. After spending the night there in the field, they entered a quarantine where "they began to die on September 14 and it ended, that is everyone died, on October 20."[35] Leaving Moscow could be as dangerous as staying there amid the plague.

Plague in Yaroslavl, Kaluga, Tula, and Nizhnii-Novgorod

Table 9 indicates that at least 5 other provinces of Moscow guberniia recorded unusual mortality in 1771. The death toll in Yaroslavl province, for example, more than doubled that of 1770. One might assume heavy losses in Yaroslavl, a busy commercial-industrial town on the Volga 170 miles north of Moscow; for its riverine location and expansive economy, considerable population and cramped wooden housing all invited the importation of plague.[36] Indeed, some textile workers evacuated from Moscow may have brought the disease to the area.[37] News of plague at Yaroslavl, on 21 October, shocked officials in Petersburg and Moscow alike. Fearful of plague's spreading along the Volga routes, the Petersburg authorities blamed administrators in Yaroslavl for neglecting the precautions prescribed by the senate on 25 September, which they reaffirmed at length. On 8 November, Grigorii Orlov dispatched a newly arrived practitioner from Petersburg, Dr. Matthew Halliday, with surgeon's mate Johann Mikel to combat the Yaroslavl epidemic.[38]

When Dr. Halliday reached Yaroslavl, on 12 November, he found a small epidemic and utter confusion in town, a larger epidemic and great consternation in the district and province. Within a week the city authorities reported 22 houses infected, 8 of which had died out with 20 victims; at the other 14 residences 42 persons had perished and 43 remained quarantined on the premises. Since Halliday's arrival 10 persons had died of plague and 72 were ill with other diseases, "especially from the continuing smallpox." In the district, more than 80 localities had reportedly lost 1,073 persons. Dr. Halliday attempted to institute an antiplague campaign in Yaroslavl, but he soon became frustrated by the footdragging of the local authorities. Fortunately, while his frustration waxed the epidemic waned.[39]

On 3 December, Halliday reported that only 9 persons had died of plague in Yaroslavl during the past 2 weeks; 2 had recovered, 5 houses had been declared free of infection, and 5 others had been placed under guard. Although the district authorities had reported 103 localities infected through 22 November, plague had already ceased in many. Nevertheless, Halliday censured the Yaroslavl authorities for refusing to evacuate the sick and the suspect to isolation facilities outside town, complained that peasants were mixing with the townspeople at the local markets, and lamented the shortage of medical assistance. City-surgeon Rugan had left to assist Governor Yushkov, privately practicing surgeon Govii had gone to inspect recruits in the Poshekhona district, and surgeon Shtok had responsibility for the thousands of clothworkers at Savva Yakovlev's huge mill outside town. Except for surgeon's mate Mikel, there was nobody to supervise quarantines or pesthouses. Halliday expressed "extreme apprehension" that "these obstacles not hinder the complete cessation of the infectious disease in the local city and district at the presently convenient cold season."

A week later, Halliday's worries lifted as winter snuffed out the epidemic. He finally affirmed the end of the plague in Yaroslavl and its district on 19 January 1772 and left for Moscow several weeks later.[40] Yet his earlier allegations of official negligence, together with Petersburg's fears of a rebirth of pestilence, prompted Catherine to assign a special deputy to the Yaroslavl region. From Moscow the senate dispatched retired Major-General Peter Krechetnikov to Yaroslavl on 1 January 1772.[41] Only one plague-related incident disturbed Krechetnikov's mission, which lasted through the next fall.

Like the plague in Moscow, the outbreak in Yaroslavl exacerbated the problems of urban industry based upon bondaged labor. On 23 March, a group of Yakovlev's clothworkers petitioned for their release from compulsory residence at the manufactory. The petition, presented by a delegation of 35 workers and signed by more than 50, charged that Yakovlev had used the plague as an excuse to transfer workers from their homes in town, making them live at the mill and buy provisions from the factory stores at inflated prices. Although the plague had ended without touching the mill, Yakovlev refused to allow workers into town, and even arrested one man the others sent. All work ceased while the men presented their grievances.

General Krechetnikov arrested the delegation for assembling illegally and ordered the other workers to resume work. Meanwhile Yakovlev acknowledged his actions, which he had not reported to any officials, but declared that his aim was to safeguard his employees and his mill, a concern justified by their deliverance from the disease. He and Krechetnikov pacified the aroused workers by promising their release if the spring passed without any recurrence of plague, lowering prices at the factory stores, and allowing some workers to visit town. Most of the petitioners received a lashing before their release. The 4 who wrote the petition were publicly flogged, and 3 clerical workers who assisted them were fired.[42]

In duration and mortality, the plague at Yaroslavl proved to be quite limited for a town of more than 10,000. One summation registered 99 deaths for the period from 12 September to 4 December 1771, but another listed only 93 for a period 6 weeks longer, from 15 July to 18 November.[43] Diseases and conditions other than plague must have caused some of those 90-odd deaths. Dr. Halliday mentioned the presence of smallpox, which in some cases could have been mistaken for plague. Moreover, the outbreak exhibited a narrowly residential incidence: 99 deaths in only 29 houses, 9 of which were emptied by 36 deaths. All but 3 of the infected houses belonged to burghers, *posadskie,* which implied small size, crowded conditions, and wooden construction. In age the victims ranged from 90 to 2 weeks. If the plague killed few residents of Yaroslavl, it wiped out more than 20 entire families.[44] The relatively small death toll suggests that *Y. pestis* reached Yaroslavl late in the fall, too late for a bigger rat epizootic or epidemic because of the timely onset of winter.

The heavier losses in Yaroslavl district, where almost two thousand deaths were reported from more than a hundred localities, may indicate that plague hit some areas earlier and lasted somewhat longer, or simply that rural observers padded their totals. For instance, among 38 economic villages of the district reporting 525 deaths from pestilence, most dated the outbreaks to September. The hamlet of Antonovskaia in the Edomskaia region supposedly lost half its 67 inhabitants from 12 August to 19 November. Elsewhere in Yaroslavl province, the town of Romanov sustained a small epidemic beginning on 26 August that killed 90 persons by 2 December, while the postal station across the river lost 52 of 139 inhabitants between 24 July and 17 November. Postal stations would naturally have been early recipients of plague-infected merchandise following established routes.[45]

Following the tardy response in Yaroslavl itself, precautions in the province began even later and exposed similar deficits of administrative and medical personnel. The Yaroslavl provincial chancery only started organizing surveillance of the district on 11 November. In the Edomskaia region, which embraced 233 villages and hamlets, 16 resident nobles were enlisted in late November. They received various instructions from Moscow and Petersburg, including extracts from the memorial that somebody with experience in Dalmatia had submitted in 1770. Within a month, 3 of these nobles were relieved of their duties because of illness or absence, and at the end of January 1772 neither replacements nor any redivision of duties had been made.[46] No medical professionals assisted these local supervisors. Furthermore, the peasantry sometimes resisted the imposition of precautions.

Major Bulygin, administrator of economic estates in one sector of Yaroslavl district, denounced the village of Nikol'skoe for harboring Ivan Kniazev, a peasant who had returned from Moscow in early November with two sons, both registered as merchants in the metropolis. Either incited or cowed by Kniazev, a meeting of the village commune rejected Bulygin's demand for documentation of the newcomers' right to enter the area. Two weeks later, when troops arrived from Yaroslavl to enforce the prohibition against receiving unauthorized outsiders, the culprits had vanished.[47] This incident elucidates some of the complications that local officials encountered in attempting to regulate movement in the countryside.[48] One can imagine, too, the villagers' own conflicting urges in that situation: should they shelter some of their own former neighbors, or reject them as potential plague-carriers?

The mortality data of table 9 suggest that plague brushed the provinces of Pereslavl-Zalesskii, Vladimir, Pereslavl-Riazanskii, and Uglich, but no large outbreaks afflicted any of them. In the case of Kaluga, a town of about 15,000 southwest of Moscow, a combination of distance, season, and good fortune averted all but trifling losses: 59 dead in town and 58 dead in the district, 52 of the latter in a single village.[49] Like Yaroslavl, Kaluga's economic and administrative importance magnified the threat of plague. Therefore, the Moscow authorities reacted strongly, on 11 November, to a report from cordon guards at Kaluga that three weeks earlier a resident merchant from Peremyshl had died with his wife, 2 children, and a household worker; 6 other occupants of the house had been quarantined. With only an old surgeon to oversee the town and the cordon checkpoint (the Plague Commission had recalled surgeon Valerian to Moscow), Orlov detailed Dr. Christian Wendrich (M.D., Erlangen, 1766) and surgical apprentice Georgii Klein to Kaluga.[50] While in Kaluga for almost a year, Dr. Wendrich saw few cases of plague, reporting the death on 25–26 December of 2 merchants in the same house, one of whom had allegedly donned clothes brought from Moscow that summer. Only a few more suspicious deaths occurred before the epidemic ceased in early January 1772, but Dr. Wendrich lambasted the Kaluga municipal administration for lack of cooperation, a complaint which, like Halliday's in Yaroslavl, elicited general orders from Petersburg that municipal administrators must assist voevodas and governors in suppressing the epidemic.[51] Reactions to the plague in these provincial towns illustrated the same weaknesses of urban administration as seen in Moscow: shortage of trained personnel, overlapping jurisdictions and confused chain of command, lack of local initiative and responsibility.

As described by Andrei Bolotov, a noble landowner, plague caused great fear in Tula province. Living on the family estate in the Kashira district some 80 miles south of Moscow, Bolotov began hearing rumors of pestilence in late 1770. Visitors from Moscow assured him that everybody was eating garlic and wearing it in amulets. "Concerning plague we all still had then a shadowy and not entirely correct conception," Bolotov recalled, "and imagined it as incomparably more dangerous than it was in fact. We did not think otherwise than that wherever it struck it left not a single person alive, for everyone held such an opinion about the pestilential contagions that had visited Russia in early times; yet this most of all amazed and terrified us, and led to desperation."[52] These comments offer valuable glimpses into popular attitudes toward plague. Although Bolotov was better educated and informed than most provincial residents, he shared the widespread, exaggerated notions of pestilence based on tradition and hearsay. Plague had last visited the Tula region in 1654, an event that would have seemed ancient history to most Russians in 1771. Bolotov and his neighbors dimly perceived that, located as they were near the main highway from Moscow, plague might come their way. But when nothing confirmed the rumors they were soon forgotten.[53]

During the Easter celebrations at the end of March 1771, apprehension revived over the outbreak at the Big Woolen Court. All the roads from Moscow, travelers said, were jammed with the vehicles of noble families hastening to their provincial seats. Yet once again the danger lapsed. Recurrent rumors throughout the summer received no confirmation, either. Indeed, the very fact of the plague's remaining riveted to Moscow contradicted its supposedly incredible virulence. All the more alarming, therefore, was a report of early September that one muzhik had suddenly died at a nearby estate and that another, having come from Moscow, lay near death. Dumbfounded, Bolotov contemplated fleeing, but delayed in the hope that the story would prove to be false. It did. Another alarm a few days later also proved unfounded. As September lengthened, however, the constant rumors unnerved Bolotov. He apprehended plague in his own household when his mother-in-law developed an ugly inflammation of the leg upon returning from a visit to a neighbor whose mother had just arrived from Moscow.[54] Bolotov's mother-in-law apparently recovered, but amid this state of awful anticipation word of the Plague Riot arrived on 21 September. Sometime in the next few weeks, Bolotov heard about the precautions for localities ordered by the senate on 25 September. With other noblemen, he arranged the patrols, inspections, and pyres that those precautions entailed.[55]

On 27 September, Bolotov learned about another supposed plague victim. A young parish priest denounced his senior colleague for administering the last rites to a niece of Prince Gorchakov, who, having fled from Moscow to a local village, died soon afterward with suspicious symptoms. The old priest had secretly buried the body in the churchyard. Bolotov was as much outraged at the priest as he was afraid of the consequences. "Naturally one had to conclude that he buried the prince's niece, who died of plague, for nothing

Table 11 Deaths Recorded in Tula Province, 1769–75

Year	Deaths
1769	2,818
1770	2,419
1771	3,041
1772	2,525
1773	2,729
1774	2,899
1775	3,533

Source: TsGADA, f. 199, d. 385, pt. 2, no. 10: 1, 3, 5, 7, 9, 11, 15.

other than a huge payment," Bolotov reasoned. Indeed, Bolotov warned the obstinate priest of the risks and threatened to denounce him to the archbishop. "But the priest did not even hesitate at these threats, but continued his pernicious craft and, to our extraordinary amazement, he was saved from the plague, although he had contact with many plague victims and not only brought them to church and conducted funerals, but even personally buried them."[56]

This episode may support an interpretation quite the reverse of Bolotov's. It demonstrated the steadfastness of one clergyman in deliberately violating the ban on burying suspected plague victims in parish cemeteries. Custom and compassion could outweigh community fears and governmental prohibitions. By itself, the monetary motive imputed by Bolotov seems implausible to explain the priest's behavior. That he survived need occasion no surprise either. Whatever his contacts with the sick, he would have been no more susceptible to plague than anybody else, and perhaps less so than most peasants, if he did not farm and lived in better quarters. Probably, the priest lived through the epidemic because it barely affected the area. Bolotov never recorded a confirmed case in his own district, and the mortality for that period (table 11) also indicated that Tula province suffered very little loss from its population of about 350,000. Three servants from Moscow supposedly brought plague to Tula, but the town and the adjacent munitions manufactory recorded only 32 deaths from a population of more than 18,000 in the period from 2 September to 9 November. The Tula district registered only 39 deaths from plague in 7 localities.[57]

Bolotov chronicled 2 other popular responses to plague. Furious at the local priest's conduct, the Bolotov family traveled to a neighboring parish to celebrate the holy day of the Virgin's Veil on 1 October and, upon returning home, they joined the entire village in a procession of the cross on 3 October. The crowd carried icons around the village and then blessed the waters of a local pond. "There we prayed and after the blessing of the waters, kneeling, we delivered our most fervent prayers to the Almighty, and I do not think that we ever again prayed with such sincere zeal as at that time." Afterward Bolotov invited everybody for dinner before they accompanied the icons out of the village.[58]

Similar religious responses occurred all over central Russia. At Dmitrov, for example, Ivan Tolchenov witnessed frequent processions around the various parishes on Sundays and three around the entire town. The people of Yaroslavl celebrated their deliverance with religious processions and festivities every July, a custom that lasted well into the nineteenth century. As in Moscow, however, such processions sometimes worried the local authorities. An official at the village of Bronnitsy complained that, despite the epidemic in the Kolomna district, the local priests "permit folk from all sides into church for prayer and go with icons to various adjacent places, and through these people coming to Bronnitsy and going with icons to adjacent places they can introduce that disease." Like Bolotov's priest, the clergy in Bronnitsy denied any danger from their actions and refused the orders of lay officials to desist. Nevertheless, upon appeal to the Moscow Synodal Office, the Church authorities directed Archbishop Feodosii to make the Bronnitsy clergy obey the government's antiplague precautions.[59]

A superstitious response also figured in Bolotov's account. In their haste to flee, some people discarded possessions along the road, which gave rise to the notion that somebody was deliberately broadcasting pestilential "poison." "For amongst the dark people there took root then," Bolotov remarked, "a most hellish superstition and pernicious prejudice: that if people wish the plague to end someplace, then it is necessary to throw some plague-infected thing onto the road and then if somebody picks it up and takes it home, the plague will break out there afresh but will end in the former place." Because of this belief people allegedly shunned abandoned clothes and other articles, just as the authorities counseled. This episode unveiled a variant of an idea often linked to plague in other countries—the notion of a conspiracy of poisoners.[60] To judge from Bolotov's experiences, the plague's psychological impact exceeded its physical ravages. Unlike some religious reactions to the plague in Poland and the Ukraine, rural Russia recorded no instances of witchcraft as the supposed source of infection.

Outside Moscow guberniia, plague traveled eastward to the region around Nizhnii-Novgorod. On 1 September, the acting police chief reported 3 suspiciously sudden deaths in the house of drover Semen Nedonoskov: the owner's wife, a retired soldier's wife, and the latter's young son. City-surgeon Pel ascertained that the deceased had been seized by a violent infectious fever that left dark spots. Nedonoskov's wife had been engaged in the rag trade, so authorities theorized that she had received something infected from Moscow. She had been sick for 3 days, her tenants for only 24 hours. After sealing off the house and burning its contents, the authorities used 3 female convicts to bury the dead. The convicts and those left in the house were quarantined. None of the quarantined caught the disease, and all were released after 40 days' detention. As in Yaroslavl, Kaluga, and Tula, the epidemic in Nizhnii-Novgorod caused limited mortality; by 2 December only 140 persons had died among a population of about 10,000.

More cases appeared outside the city. A report of 20 September brought surgeon Pel to the village of Lyskovo and neighboring hamlets, where he discovered 2 persons dead from "fever with spots." A month later, the mortality reached 20 per day. Pel revisited the area, confirmed the disease as dangerous, and surveyed 5 villages and 4 hamlets. Three of these communities supposedly lost more than 10 percent of their residents in the period from 30 August to 21 December 1771. Lyskovo, a center of the Volga grain trade and the most populous point, with a registered population of 3,729, sustained the heaviest loss, with 403 deaths. Some of those listed as dead had probably fled. Whatever the actual mortality, these outbreaks remained isolated, and the advent of winter caused them to abate by 6 November, when Governor Andrei Kvashin-Samarin belatedly reported the epidemic to the senate. The Governor postponed the fall recruiting levy until mid-November and asked for one doctor, 3 surgeons, and several surgeon's mates with appropriate medicaments to be assigned to the guberniia. "Although there is one surgeon with the battalion and here in the city," explained Kvashin-Samarin, "still he is not unneedful of the advice of others, especially concerning such a disease as he happened to see for the first time, and furthermore it is impossible for him to oversee the city and residences fifty miles or more distant, besides which, without informed persons, untrue reports must come to me about these diseases." In March 1772, the Plague Commission sent Dr. Halliday and a surgeon's mate to check the situation in Nizhnii-Novgorod, where, although the epidemic had already ended, they stayed until the fall.[61]

All these provincial outbreaks disclosed the deficiencies of public health in the countryside. Even when medical professionals were available they often received little support. During the plague at Kolomna, for example, surgeon Fedor Smirnov complained that the citizenry refused to report the sick, declined to take medicine, and threatened to kill him. Surgeon Ivan Povanarius at Pereslavl-Riazanskii confessed his inability to diagnose a malady that left blue spots on its victims. By contrast, the Plague Commission praised surgeon Andrei Minne at Tula for his vigorous efforts against the epidemic.[62] The plague illuminated some of the enormous tasks confronting Russia's emergent medical profession, tasks that multiplied as the empire expanded.

Trepidation in Petersburg

In St. Petersburg, the imperial government reacted to the expansion of the epidemic with special intensity. As the empire's "new" capital, seat of the court, and leading port, Petersburg faced a threefold threat from the plague. It might paralyze the government, undercut military operations abroad, and ruin Russia's foreign trade. Furthermore, the Plague Riot inflamed Catherine's animus against Moscow and ignited fears for the security of her beloved, Europeanized imperial capital. Perhaps she sensed that Petersburg, despite its European façade, harbored many of the same conditions that caused the plague in Moscow.

The second largest city of the empire, with a population of about 150,000,

Petersburg straddled the delta of the Neva River, which periodically flooded the low-lying metropolis. Beyond a modicum of official buildings and mansions of the aristocracy, the new capital encompassed numerous quarters of traditional wooden, one- and two-storied houses in which the working population lived cramped together. Thousands of peasant workmen flocked to the city during the spring to fall shipping and building seasons. Because Petersburg stood amid an area of marginal agriculture, it depended upon food shipments from the interior, especially grain, much of which moved through Moscow. Sizable merchant communities in both capitals managed the large-scale commerce between them. And since both cities were centers of the imperial administration, couriers shuttled back and forth.[63] Lest the multiplicity of Petersburg's links to the interior convey plague to the northwest, the authorities undertook elaborate precautions.

The pestilential menace to northwestern Russia emerged in mid-summer 1771 and persisted deep into autumn, reinforcing Petersburg's reaction to events in Moscow. On 23 July, Governor Sievers reported infection in 4 localities of Novgorod guberniia. Catherine's councilors heard Major Shipov's report of recurrent plague in Kiev, Nezhin, and Novorossiia guberniia on 11 August; they learned of suspected cases near Pskov and in two villages of Novgorod guberniia on 5 and 12 September. At the council session of 21 September that approved the Orlov mission, Count Zakhar Chernyshev, head of the War Collegium, recommended washing in vinegar all goods brought to Petersburg from the interior. Merchandise that could not be washed should be withheld. Chernyshev's proposal received tentative approval, but the councilors showed greater concern about possible infection from the palace stables. Although master of the horse Lev Naryshkin assured the council that he made weekly surveys of health among the stables servitors, the councilors ordered them checked daily and urged medical inspection of their dependents too. Catherine approved these arrangements on 26 September, when she visited the council to vent her fury over the Plague Riot and suggested medical inspection of other administrators and their subordinates. The councilors agreed to consult with the city authorities at their next meeting.[64]

The subjects of mail and money also provoked anxiety. On 23 September, the Empress ordered the senate to have couriers from the south bypass Moscow. A week later the senate forbade all governmental offices in Petersburg (except the Foreign Affairs, War, and Admiralty collegiia) to receive couriers directly from Moscow. Messengers were to stop at Torzhok, where emissaries from Petersburg would take their dispatches. Mail from infected localities was to be handled with tongs, and all thread or linen binding carefully removed and burned. All letters should then be pricked full of holes, dipped in vinegar, and dried out over fumigatory fires. Tax monies delivered to Moscow were to be left there; those for Petersburg would pass through Tver, where the various financial administrations would establish temporary facilities.[65] On 27 October, Catherine commissioned Governor Sievers to oversee the operations at Tver, which temporarily functioned as virtually a substitute capital for Moscow. Sievers organized quarantine and fumigatory operations at Tver in November, before General Mansurov arrived from Moscow to head medical surveillance of the area.[66]

At the council's invitation Policemaster-General Nikolai Chicherin and Prince Alexander Golitsyn, the governor-general of St. Petersburg, attended the session of 29 September to explain what precautions they were taking. Since both bemoaned the difficulty of implementing security measures and complained of being shorthanded, the council assigned 6 commissars to reinforce surveillance of the metropolitan area. The council also solicited their opinion about the placement of checkpoints on all roads to Petersburg. In response, Chicherin won the council's approval, on 3 October, for a program of individual precautions, proclaimed in Russian, German, French, and Finnish on 10 October.[67]

Still leery of calling the epidemic pestilential, the police proclamation referred to "a disease infectious to people" that had appeared in Moscow "some time ago" and "presently still continues." To supplement the checkpoints on all roads to Petersburg, the police commanded "each local householder and resident" to observe a plethora of precautions concerning the reception of visitors and strangers, the fumigation of baggage, and the inspection of all cases of sudden death and febrile disease. In particular, the police warned about infection from cloth, furs, and skins, especially old clothes sold by peddlers.[68]

This public acknowledgement of the danger led the Petersburg authorities to implement strict precautions. The Holy Synod, for example, had its staff sign the edict and submit to medical inspection. Still anxious, Catherine interrupted the council, on 17 October, to announce that growing public apprehension necessitated additional measures to forestall economic disruption. Lengthy discussion produced agreement to institute a cordon around Petersburg, whereby all arrivals would undergo a further brief quarantine. In addition, provincial governors should keep people away from Petersburg, citing possible food shortages as a pretext. A stern edict forbade bypassing the checkpoints. Satisfied with these proposals, the Empress noted that Petersburg had adequate provisions, and she proposed to hire 20 doctors and 40 surgeons abroad.[69]

Catherine's own worries about Petersburg lasted until late October, when she dictated special protection for Tsarskoe Selo, the imperial estate south of the capital. Checkpoints guarded the main roads, barriers blocked others, and nobody could enter without documentation from the cordon guards or after sundown. The palace and gardens were kept locked, and an officer was assigned to enforce security throughout the area. Meanwhile, the Petersburg police discovered a few instances of suspicious sickness and had staff-surgeon Nilus and surgeon Remer examine all cases of sudden death. Nilus inspected a corpse in the quarters of the Izmailovskii Guards Regiment on 28 October and concluded that the deceased had perished "with a putrid yellow fever, but no dangerous marks are present on the body." Two days later he examined another male corpse, apparently a laborer, but found no signs of beating or infection and registered the death *"from diarrhea."* Either the Empress or the Policemaster-General, who reported to her weekly, underlined this diagnosis to affirm the nonpestilential symptoms; both remembered the disputed diagnoses early in the Moscow epidemic. Worrisome, too, were more reports of plague in the Ukraine and the Kuban, whence it had reached Taganrog and the lower Don.[70]

All these anxieties began subsiding by 31 October, however, when Catherine informed her council that the epidemic in Moscow had significantly declined. Concurrently, Petersburg's weather grew colder. Frosts occurred on 20, 26, 29–30 October, and continuously from 6 November onward. Reassured, the council vetoed a proposal, on 7 November, to isolate Petersburg guberniia with checkpoints and barriers of felled trees. Instead the councilors endorsed suspension of quarrying at Tosna, about 40 miles from Petersburg, in order to block an influx of workmen from the provinces.[71]

While Petersburg rejoiced at the advent of winter and the waning of plague in Moscow, the authorities still reacted precipitously to a report of unusual mortality near Novaia Ladoga in the Novgorod district. On 6 December, Count Bruce dispatched Guards Captain Kologrivov and surgeon Shlefokht to investigate. Arriving on the scene within 24 hours, Captain Kologrivov discovered that local officials had already cordoned off the hamlet of Melekse, where 19 persons had reportedly died in 6 houses since early October. Although nobody had perished or sickened for the past 2 weeks and none of the neighboring hamlets seemed infected, 2 peasants from Melekse working elsewhere were both quarantined. Of the 6 houses afflicted, 2 stood empty and the other 4 housed 20 persons in quarantine. The peasants had all been ordered to freeze out their huts and their clothes and to fumigate everything.

Surgeon Shlefokht questioned the parish priest and the peasants, who ascribed the mortality to "various diseases, from which at the start of the disease there was pain in the head, shivering in the legs, and fever over-all; but not one of them died in less than four or more than seven, nine, or eleven days, of whom one was an old man and one was an infant." Except for one woman buried in the field, the peasants had interred all the dead in the churchyard. Two women had died in childbirth, the priest reported, and 9 victims had received the last rites. Though Melekse was barely a mile from the main summer road, the route used in the winter was almost 14 miles away. These facts and the continuous frosts calmed fears about wider transmission of the unidentified disease.[72] Whatever the origin of this outbreak, it claimed few lives and spread no farther. Novgorod guberniia as a whole registered 25,650 deaths in 1771, as compared to 16,775 in 1769, 16,624 in 1768, and 18,945 in 1766, the nearest years for which comparable data have been found. The higher death toll in 1771 did not stem from plague alone; 993

deaths were attributed to smallpox, 1,000 to fevers, and so forth. Poor harvests in 1769–70 also may have raised the mortality.[73]

In short, plague never got very close to Petersburg. Still the threat provoked deep public and private concern, as William Richardson, tutor to Lord Cathcart's children, wrote from Petersburg on 3 December 1771: "Vinegar is burnt in great quantities in every house; and the utmost attention is paid to the health of the lower ranks. Yet it is not very pleasant to be within two or three days journey of so dreadful a neighbour."[74] Human precautions did not save Petersburg so much as its northern location, distance from Moscow, and the timely advent of winter.

The plague threatened to impair the flow of international trade through the maritime metropolis. Foreign nations might embargo exports from Russia, damaging Petersburg's economy and augmenting the empire's plague-related losses. Markets lost temporarily might be forfeited forever. A decline in customs collections, one pillar of state finance, would strain Russia's already depleted treasury. The economic pressure of the Turkish war, which increased government efforts to stimulate exports and to replace many imports, made Petersburg extremely sensitive to the potential commercial disruption. Fears for the export trade occasioned the system of quarantines adopted in the spring of 1771 and revived that summer.

Before the council on 19 September, Count Nikita Panin, head of the Collegium of Foreign Affairs, raised the threat to foreign trade and, by extension, to Russian foreign policy in general. To protect Russian credit abroad, Panin forwarded a proposal from Baron Fredericks, the court banker, who mentioned the Dutch ambassador's desire that Russia provide bills of health for the cargoes of all departing ships. The council endorsed this proposal as "extremely necessary."[75] After reporting on 20 September that the epidemic "is an acknowledged and confirmed plague," British ambassador Cathcart had consul-general Swallow inquire of Count Münnich, chief of the customs-house, about the precautions taken with goods from the interior. The next day Münnich certified that all merchandise conveyed to Petersburg that year had undergone quarantine en route. Thus reassured, Cathcart informed London that Swallow would continue to grant bills of health to departing British ships, "the City as well as Cronstadt being entirely free from any Contagious or Pestilential Disorder." Nevertheless, "the total stagnation of Business in Moscow" might cripple internal trade, Cathcart warned, and force Russian merchants to default on their obligations to foreign firms.[76]

Inquiries from foreign envoys worried Panin so much that he urged the council, on 26 September, to decree a double quarantine for all products brought to Petersburg for export, with all containers to be unpacked and aired en route. This precaution should be published in the main gazettes abroad. The councilors found Panin's idea "extremely useful," and Procurator-General Viazemskii announced having made similar proposals to the senate. These discussions resulted in the publication of a senate edict, on

14 October, expressly intended to inform foreign merchants of the precautions applied to all goods brought to Petersburg. The regulations entailed a 5-day quarantine for grain, 2 or 3 weeks for other goods, and medical inspection of all persons transporting merchandise. The *Sanktpeterburgskie vedomosti* printed this edict on 11 November and its German edition on 13 December. Foreign representatives supplied translations to their governments.[77]

Notwithstanding these Russian efforts, news of the plague provoked apprehension when it finally filtered abroad. British reactions were unusually complicated because of the conflicting interests of British merchants in Russia and the royal government in London. Ambassador Cathcart and consul-general Swallow, for example, both reflected the opinion of the British Factory—the influential community of British merchants in Petersburg—in their efforts to dissuade the British government from quarantining cargoes from Russia. Before 20 September, Cathcart had consistently accepted Russian assurances that the disease was not plague, and on 11 October he eagerly reported its decline. Nonetheless, Cathcart feared the crisis might cause famine, damage commerce, and handicap Russia's prosecution of the Turkish war. Through mid-November, the British envoy argued against any quarantine, but on 8 November the King in council proclaimed a quarantine upon all imports from Russia.[78]

Predictably, the British Factory staunchly opposed the new quarantine. A prominent merchant in his own right, consul-general Swallow led 15 firms in protesting the quarantine. Airing cargoes, they argued, could damage such products as hemp, flax, and linen. In any event, few goods from Moscow had been loaded at Petersburg since mid-August, and those loaded had already passed quarantine. None of the thousands of workmen sorting and packing hemp and flax at Petersburg had fallen ill that autumn. The British merchants concluded that "no danger is to be apprehended from any Cargoes ship'd from hence this season, the Navigation of which is now entirely closed by the setting in of the Winter."[79]

Despite such assurances, the royal government maintained its quarantine until 10 September 1772. In a speech to Parliament on 21 January 1772, George III cited the plague's subsidence; nevertheless, he proclaimed, "I must recommend it to you not to suffer our Happiness, in having been hitherto preserved from so dreadful a Calamity, to lessen your Vigilance in the Use of every reasonable Precaution for our Safety."[80] Lord Suffolk admitted to Cathcart the inconvenience of the quarantine, but explained the government's thinking that "any Danger of the Plague must over ballance all other Considerations; and till the Distemper is totally eradicated, there can be no other Assurances of Safety." Since the press reported that Denmark, Sweden, and the Dutch Republic had adopted precautions, Britain's commercial interests in northern Europe dictated the same course. The Russian government's credibility appeared suspect, Suffolk explained: "And the

Pains taken to propagate a Persuasion, that the Plague was not at Moscow, when it was raging there, will perhaps, from the Doubts that will be entertained of all subsequent Accounts, prolong the Quarantines." Like the Russian authorities, British officials apprehended renewed plague in the spring of 1772.[81]

In the end, plague never reached Britain or northwestern Europe in 1771–72. Anglo-Russian trade sustained little direct loss, but the damage to Russian merchants and to some of their British creditors may have aggravated the credit crisis of 1772, which threatened several British firms in Petersburg. Perhaps the plague added to a slight commercial depression at Petersburg in 1772, when the number of ship arrivals amounted to 500, as compared to 662 in 1771 and 676 in 1773. At any rate, Russian commerce soon recouped any losses.[82]

Last Sparks and Lingering Fears

Occasional sparks of apparent plague kindled continual fears of its recrudescence in subsequent years, so antiplague precautions in Russia far outlasted those abroad. In Moscow, the authorities concluded that plague had virtually ended in mid-January 1772. Governor-General Volkonskii wished to reopen government offices after the offering of public prayers, and the Plague Commission prepared to release some of its staff. But on 27 January a soldier's widow turned up with fever and a swelling in the groin. As chairman of the Plague Commission, Eropkin considered the case so suspicious that he personally observed Dr. Yagel'skii's examination of the woman. Doctors Erasmus and Pogoretskii supported Yagel'skii's diagnosis that the symptoms did not signify plague, but had resulted from a cold and chronic impairment of the circulation. Apparently the patient recovered. Meanwhile Catherine wrote Volkonskii to withhold public prayers until the second week of Lent, by which time the fumigation campaign should have decreased the danger. Her caution appeared prudent when the Plague Commission confronted a more alarming case one week later.[83]

On 2 February, Dr. Veniaminov observed plague symptoms on a servant woman and sent her to the Lefortovo pesthouse where commissioners Shafonskii and Samoilovich described her the next day as prostrated and speechless, with carbuncles on the thigh and sacrum. Dr. Pogoretskii found the patient feverish, unconscious, and "with abcesses on which the skin has died." This last description confused the Plague Commission, which demanded a fuller explanation from Pogoretskii. Moreover, the commission requested that the Executive Commission punish the district official who had failed to bring the patient directly to the pesthouse. Apparently the victim soon died. This and the previous case caused the Plague Commission to revoke its release of several district medical inspectors and prompted a resolution of

16 February that if other doubtful cases appeared, the district medical inspectors should not send them to a pesthouse until a commissioner verified the affliction. Both incidents also induced Catherine's decision, on 20 February, to postpone the public prayers indefinitely.[84]

Lest pestilence recur in the spring from the thousands of corpses buried around Moscow, the authorities hastily arranged for at least 2 more feet of earth to be heaped over all fresh graves. To discover bodies interred secretly, the Plague Commission on 27 February doubled the reward for the disclosure of such burials, true reports of which would receive 20 rubles each. That same day the senate reaffirmed decrees against beggary because of the fear that the "great number" of villagers seeking alms in Moscow would increase crowding and crime and, by settling in abandoned houses, renew the plague.[85] The district supervisors also received orders that when dismantling or fumigating infected residences their subordinates should check the courtyards for clandestine graves and concealed belongings. Foreseeing the discovery of many bodies, the Plague Commission and the Executive Commission decided, on 1 March, that in the case of unburied corpses and well-preserved burials, the bodies should be taken to cemeteries outside town so long as cold weather lasted; decayed corpses would be left in place and the graves covered with two more feet of dirt and, if the householders desired, with a row or two of bricks.[86]

During the next several months, hundreds of bodies were discovered throughout Moscow, especially in clusters in the suburbs. For example, 12 unburied corpses were found in the house of manufactory operator Stepan Kalinin at the Vvedenskie Hills. The Plague Commission welcomed these discoveries and, to encourage the removal of bodies before spring, reminded the district supervisors, on 15 March, that householders need not fear fines or other costs for the reburial of bodies discovered on their premises. Simultaneously, the commission adopted protective measures for the burial teams, who should wear gloves and clothes of oilcloth, keep vinegar-soaked paper in their noses, ears, and mouths, disinter corpses either early in the morning or in the evening when the air was cold, and burn the sleds or carts used to haul the dead.[87]

With spring approaching, the Plague Commission suggested reimposing quarantines on departures from the city, warning suburban inhabitants against receiving outsiders, removing any trades that produced "rotten air," and admitting only certified persons and cargoes. The senate also recommended that, since all infected manufactories had been fumigated, their operators should resume production and maintain close supervision of the workers. "As the snow has already begun to melt now from the warm air of spring, and the earth has started to show itself," the Plague Commission, on 28 March, called upon the district supervisors to collect, remove, and burn all clothes and furs found on the streets. On 6 April, Eropkin reported that Moscow seemed secure, "and the weather has continued to be very clear and healthy." Although more than 200 corpses had been reburied, none of the gravediggers had become infected, which proved, Eropkin concluded, that "this poison has lost its power." On 10 April, the Plague Commission and the Executive Commission jointly agreed to continue all precautions, but not to adopt any more for the time being.[88]

Confidence grew in Moscow well into the summer of 1772. In August, however, 2 incidents caused consternation. On 5 August, the police requested an autopsy upon the body of a sixty-year-old house servant who had dropped dead. The absence of specific external symptoms, in combination with evidence of urinary infection and circulatory failure, made Dr. Shafonskii attribute death to apoplexy.[89] A week later a far more frightening case appeared. On 12 August, surgeon Zurburg found dark spots all over Filip Detkov, an orderly to the widowed Sara Scott, whose family had been staying at the house of Colonel Yakov Berents in the ninth district. Sixty years old, Detkov had felt weak and feverish for a week. Dr. Shafonskii confirmed Zurburg's finding on 13 August. That same day both the Plague Commission and the Executive Commission hastened to neutralize the danger.[90]

Eropkin had commissioners Yagel'skii and Samoilovich investigate further, while Volkov directed precautions on the spot. Within an hour, Volkov had removed Detkov to the nearby General Infantry Hospital, burned his belongings, confined under guard those who had attended him, transported the Scott family and a neighboring French family to the Marly quarantine, and evacuated adjacent residences. Volkov personally checked these precautions every day thereafter. In the meantime, Yagel'skii and Samoilovich questioned everybody around and examined Detkov, who remained conscious. The medical examiners all agreed that the disease was not plague, but ordinary "putrid fever with spots." Five days later, Volkonskii informed Catherine that "the danger has already passed"; Detkov was recovering and there were no signs of infection in Moscow or its district, where all precautions remained in effect. Lauding these "strong safeguards," the Empress asked Volkonskii to report "more often, so long as doubt remains" and suggested halting excavation for the new Kremlin palace if such digging "will spoil the present autumn air." The scare ended on 24 August with the release of Detkov, fully recovered, and of all those quarantined, none of whom had become ill.[91]

The end of these false alarms eventually convinced the Moscow authorities of the plague's demise. Indeed, Eropkin declared, on 10 October, that "there do not now remain any traces that might in any way incur doubt about the disease formerly here." With the onset of another winter, Catherine finally authorized the senate to proclaim the end of the epidemic with a *Te Deum* in Petersburg on 15 November and another in Moscow on 24 November. All government offices in Moscow reopened on 1 December 1772. Although the Plague Commission continued to function, execution of its policies devolved upon the regular police. Travelers and cargoes to Petersburg, if certified as coming from plague-free districts, were no longer subject to quarantine. The cordon around Moscow lapsed at the same time, but checkpoints were left at Serpukhov, Sevsk, and Kursk to guard against epidemics from the Ukraine. Sporadic, localized outbreaks in the south, where Russian forces stayed active until the victorious peace with the Turks in the summer of 1774, delayed the abolition of the Plague Commission and all internal quarantines until August 1775. Thus ended the special antiplague precautions instituted five years earlier.[92]

The ravages in the provinces and the short-lived threat to Petersburg magnified the epidemic's impact. Millions of people in thousands of communities experienced some dimension of the plague, from its death-dealing visitations to its demoralizing and disruptive threats. Fortunately for Petersburg and the countryside of central Russia, the epidemic spread outward from Moscow so erratically that it reached many communities too late in the autumn to cause major damage. The timely onset of winter saved much of central Russia from sharing the Moscow calamity. Yet the plague's wide scope, high mortality, and persistence in the south, fostered apprehension in Russia for decades. The epidemic disclosed the perennial shortage of medical professionals in the provinces, which constituted one measure of Russia's incomplete modernization. Because of the peculiar nature of plague, however, this deficit of practitioners in the countryside had little effect on the epidemic's rural incidence. Paradoxically, the plague caused more damage in the more modern, urbanized, and industrialized sectors of the Russian economy and society.

PART THREE

The Epidemic's Impact and Consequences

CHAPTER TEN

The Plague's Impact on Moscow

The plague left multiple imprints on Moscow. Foremost among its immediate effects was the awesome mortality. The yearlong epidemic killed tens of thousands of Muscovites directly and indirectly, drove away tens of thousands, and caused massive unemployment by disrupting the municipal economy and closing most manufacturing enterprises, government offices, educational institutions, and entertainment facilities. Fear of infection also kept away many visitors, vendors, and buyers, deepening the economic dislocation. As in the hinterland, so in the metropolis plague was unpredictable; certain social groups, occupations, and neighborhoods suffered more heavily than others. In the absence of precise mortality figures and full census data, one can only venture some general correlations about the epidemic's demographic impact. Moscow's experience with plague was also reflected in city planning, welfare institutions, and national administrative reforms.

How many people died of plague in Moscow and the rest of the Russian Empire in 1770–72? The Plague Commission, while acknowledging that its figures were incomplete, computed a death toll of 56,900 for Moscow from April 1771 to March 1772 and 1,000 bodies discovered afterward.[1] To this total one should add about 200 deaths at the Vvedenskie Hills and the Big Woolen Court from November 1770 through March 1771. To be sure, some of the deaths in the spring and winter did not stem from plague directly; ordinary causes accounted for part of the mortality. Disregarding the outbreaks before April 1771, one may deduct at least 5,800 deaths as Moscow's ordinary mortality for the period April–December, based on the average monthly losses recorded in the nonplague years of 1773–74. This would yield a net total of 52,300 deaths from plague in Moscow. Of course, this estimate excludes concealed deaths and deaths of refugees in the provinces. Eyewitnesses generally reported higher totals. Dr. Lerche estimated 60,000 deaths in Moscow and at least 30,000 in the hinterland, while Dr. Mertens reckoned 80,000 deaths in town and about 100,000, counting losses in the hinterland. Whereas Catherine herself mentioned a toll of 100,000 for Moscow—perhaps meaning greater Moscow—Samoilovich cited the commission's estimate for the city and added 75,398 plague deaths reported elsewhere in the empire,

Table 12 Vital Statistics for Moscow Guberniia and Moscow Province, 1769–75

Moscow Guberniia			
Year	Births	Deaths	Marriages
1769	82,825	44,748	30,773
1770	82,506	42,567	32,307
1771	79,829	95,019	24,226
1772	82,681	42,984	30,758
1773	79,343	47,759	28,080
1774	92,569	46,973	30,475
1775	88,778	46,862	31,704
Moscow Province			
Year	Births	Deaths	Marriages
1769	28,275	15,696	8,477
1770	27,333	15,537	9,344
1771	24,904	52,869	5,245
1772	26,010	13,862	9,293
1773	26,004	15,565	8,326
1774	30,396	14,671	7,871
1775	28,670	15,745	8,575

Source: TsGADA, f. 199, d. 385, pt. 2, no. 10: 1–15v.

some of which evidently occurred after 1772, for a grand total of 133,299.[2] All these observers probably overestimated the actual toll, particularly losses in the provinces. In sum, discounting the commission's estimate for Moscow and the census data for Moscow guberniia for 1771 (table 12) by 10 percent, one obtains a net figure of about 100,000 plague deaths in central Russia, half of them in Moscow, and a total of about 120,000 for the entire empire. These figures seem reasonable estimates in the light of modern epidemiology and in view of the plague's spasmodic course.

Without mortality data for Moscow by age and sex, one can only estimate the plague's long-range demographic effects. Outside the city, figures for the hinterland (table 12) showed a drop in births in 1771 of 9.3 percent in Moscow province and 3.9 percent in Moscow guberniia, with marriages declining by almost 44 and 25 percent, respectively. Although marriages and births remained slightly below preplague levels in 1772 and 1773, deaths dropped to the preplague level within a year and then slightly exceeded it in 1773–75. In Moscow guberniia, males comprised 52 percent of the deaths in 1771, about half of the victims being less than ten years old or more than fifty (table 13). If the same proportions held true for the smaller female population of greater Moscow, then the plague's effect on population replacement would have been quite modest. To offer a hypothetical example: if plague killed 20 of every 100 persons in Moscow in 1771, and if 9 of those 20 were females, then only 4 or 5 would have been of childbearing age—hence the slight impairment of population reproduction.[3] Just as plague caused Moscow's death rate to soar in 1771, so the next year deaths and births both declined sharply until they returned to "normal" in 1773–75, which together registered more

Table 13 Ages of Male Deaths in Moscow Guberniia, 1770-74

Ages	1770	1771	1772	1773	1774
1-10	5,080	9,787	5,151	4,926	4,162
11-20	1,628	6,185	1,589	1,999	1,962
21-30	2,025	6,211	1,800	2,195	2,386
31-40	2,112	6,750	1,929	2,259	2,523
41-50	2,531	5,152	2,415	2,886	3,121
51-60	2,816	4,898	2,648	3,194	3,326
61-70	3,143	5,046	3,299	3,647	3,680
71-80	2,218	3,763	2,780	3,092	2,913
81-90	1,066	1,571	1,273	1,419	1,454
91-100	288	418	369	457	420
101 +	19	30	21	12	25
Totals	22,926	49,811	23,274	26,086	25,972

Source: TsGADA, f. 199, d. 385, pt. 2, no. 10: 4, 6, 8, 10, 12.

Table 14 Births and Deaths in Moscow, 1771-75

Year	Deaths	Births
1771	56,672	unknown
1772	3,592	1,510 (9 months only)
1773	7,195	3,989
1774	7,527	3,395
1775	6,559	2,108

Source: Opisanie, pp. 620-22.

than twice as many deaths as births (table 14). The unusually low death toll in 1772, albeit obviously understated, stemmed from the smaller postplague population and from the smaller proportion of young and old, the population groups most vulnerable to a subsistence crisis.

The age-specific mortality for males in Moscow guberniia in 1771 revealed disproportionate losses of adolescents and young adults, ages 11 to 50. This group accounted for 48.7 percent of all deaths, as compared to only 36.1 percent in 1770 and 33.2 percent in 1772. Yet the general rise of the death rate in 1771 obscured the fact that mortality among those aged 11-50 tripled and almost quadrupled among those aged 11-40; whereas the very young and the elderly lost barely 40 percent more than in 1770 and 1772. However shaky the statistical base of this age-specific incidence, it parallels the pattern observed in several plague epidemics in seventeenth-century Britain.[4] In the case of Moscow's hinterland, the disproportion may be partly explained by the large number of temporary residents in the metropolis—migrant male adults without their families—and by the lesser involvement in the metropolitan economy of women, children, and old people. Adult males were presumably at greater risk because of their wider sphere of activity outside their residences and because of their more limited possibilities to leave the city. The population of Moscow itself probably experienced a similar age-specific and heavily male mortality from the plague. At least the mortality and morbidity reported to Eropkin from late June through August 1771 indicated a predominance of adult males, as did the heavy losses of bondaged manufactory workers.[5] "The young and robust were more liable to become infected than elderly and infirm persons," observed Dr. Mertens; "pregnant women and nurses were not secure from its attacks. Children under four years of age were much less readily infected, but when they were, they exhibited the worst symptoms."[6]

In any event, Moscow's loss of population in 1771 reinforced the established pattern of in-migration, which replaced the plague victims rather quickly. In 1774–75, births in Moscow guberniia surpassed the preplague level by almost 10 percent and were almost twice as high as the death toll in both years (table 12). Visiting Moscow in 1775, Catherine found it less populous than before the epidemic, but she was surprised at its rapid recovery; in fact, the metropolis apparently regained the preplague level of population by the early 1780s.[7] The registered male population of Moscow province, including the city, increased from 395,744 in 1762 to 443,092 in 1782.[8] Thus, natural increase and migration recouped the plague losses within a decade. This process repeated the experience of several British towns in the seventeenth century and may have been common to most urban outbreaks in early modern Europe.[9]

Because no one knew how many people were in Moscow when the plague began, nor how many left during the epidemic, proportional death rates remain quite problematical. Dr. Mertens calculated that the population had dwindled from more than 250,000 to only 150,000 by August 1771, a figure which, when compared to the official death toll of 51,465 from August to November (table 14), implied a death rate of 34.3 percent. Three-fourths of the population fled, according to Lerche, but Lord Cathcart forwarded an anonymous report from Moscow that set the mortality at 60,000 out of a population of 300,000, or 20 percent.[10] Whether plague killed 2 or 3 of every 10 persons in Moscow in 1771, it exterminated much higher proportions of particular social groups, occupations, and neighborhoods.

In Russia, as elsewhere, plague spared the social elite, a phenomenon that impressed contemporaries. "Amid so great a number of deaths," observed Mertens, "I think there were only three persons of family, a few of the principal citizens, and not more than three hundred foreigners of the common class, who fell victims to the plague; the rest consisted of the lowest order of the Russian inhabitants."[11] The survival of Orlov and his entourage, despite continual exposure, convinced Catherine that "in general this disease proceeds only among the common people; persons of quality are exempt either because the precautions they have taken preserve them, or because that is the nature of the disease itself." Plague simply accentuated the usual pattern of infectious disease, Lord Cathcart explained.[12]

Very few noblemen died in Moscow during the plague. After the death of Madame Knutova in early August, her husband stayed at home until late October when, sickness continuing on the premises, he asked to enter the quarantine for nobility along with 3 servants.[13] Evidently he survived. By contrast, Lieutenant-Captain Kozlov reportedly succumbed to plague and his wife moved outside to the bathhouse, but Dr. Pogoretskii found neither fever nor swelling although she complained of pain in the armpits and "disturbed" blood. Pogoretskii prescribed some medicine and recommended that Kozlova return to the house, where she seems to have recovered.[14] Senator Sobakin, who resigned as Eropkin's deputy because of plague among his servants, also survived.[15] Only one of the district supervisors, all of whom were noblemen-officials, died amid the epidemic. Kliucharev of the thirteenth district perished in early October 1771, ostensibly of plague, although his age and previous health were not reported.[16] Aleksei Morsochnikov, supervisor of the eighth district, underwent quarantine at home for a month when 3 servants and his son Ivan, a retired ensign who lived in an apartment in the same house, fell ill with suspicious symptoms. Two of the sick servants were sent to the Simonov pesthouse and the third died in a separate storeroom. Upon inspecting Morsochnikov's son, surgeon Margraf discovered a bubo in the groin, but neither headache nor prostration, and concluded that the affliction might be venereal. Apparently both Morsochnikovs survived the ordeal.[17] The Kamer Collegium reported that one of its administrators, Bushuev, died of plague with his servants and that another, Beshentsov, abandoned his house after 12 successive deaths there and, rebuffed by relatives, camped outside town in a tent.[18]

If the professional medical community included a representative group of Moscow noblemen by service, then the lowest ranks of the service hierarchy suffered the greatest loss. About 20 practitioners succumbed to plague, but not one doctor (excluding Rinder) or staff-surgeon and just a few surgeons. The victims were mainly surgeon's mates, surgical students, and schoolboy attendants (appendix 2).[19] Like the nobility as a whole, the upper strata of the medical community were protected from plague by better living conditions, greater mobility, and smaller numbers than their professional inferiors. Doctors were not expected to treat plague victims; they supervised treatment by surgical personnel. Most of the medical victims in Moscow were surgical auxiliaries assigned to the pesthouses. On the eve of the plague, the nobility probably comprised no more than 4 percent of Moscow's population, a proportion that fell much lower during the epidemic, when the landed nobility and many officials left for provincial estates. If a few died en route, many more arrived safely and survived the plague's scattered incidence in the countryside. Also, warfare abroad caused considerable numbers of noble officers to be absent from central Russia for most of the period. It is scarcely surprising then that plague killed so few nobles in Moscow. This pattern, which was largely a product of population density, housing conditions, and differential mobility, held true all over early modern Europe.[20]

The same calculus accounted for the epidemic's differential impact on the clergy and the merchantry. Beyond Archbishop Amvrosii's extraordinary death, very few leading clerics and merchants fell victim to the scourge. Of 164 unmarried members of the first-guild merchantry who might have continued their families through marriage, only 7 perished from plague.[21] Luka Dolgov, the prominent merchant on the Plague Commission, had to cease attending its meetings for three days because of a sick servant girl at his house, but her illness proved to be noninfectious and he quickly resumed his duties.[22] Hardly any manufactory operators contracted the plague. By contrast, the parish clergy and lesser merchants died in large numbers. More than 100 clergy perished or disappeared in the plague, which infected at least 106 of Moscow's 269 parishes.[23] The parish clergy's cheap, crowded housing and wide social contacts made them especially vulnerable. In 1772, the Moscow merchantry petitioned the government for relief from tax and service obligations, citing the previous year's loss of 4,244 registered merchants from a total of 10,123 males. Another, later petition counted the loss as 4,055 of 10,177 merchants, 71 of 281 registered artisans, and 36 missing.[24] Perhaps these statistics overstated the merchantry's losses, but the fourth national census in 1782 confirmed the plague's disastrous impact on hundreds of merchant families and recorded widespread transfers of provincial and foreign merchants—many Old Believers from former Polish territory—to replenish the mercantile community in Moscow.

To cite some examples, the Gostinaia Sotnia listed 355 males and females in 1762, but only 208 twenty years later; the census-takers attributed the death of 48 persons to plague.[25] The population of Barashkaia Sloboda fell from 694 in 1762 to 519 in 1784, with 202 deaths blamed on the pestilence.[26] The Krasnosel'skaia Sotnia lost even more, declining from 587 persons in 1762 to 351 in 1782, the plague having killed 176.[27] The 206 households of the Sadovaia Bol'shaia Sloboda in 1782 reported 208 deaths from the plague, but the unit's preepidemic population is not known.[28] Individual families endured multiple losses. Thus Matrena Okonnishnikova, a merchant's widow, died in the epidemic, along with one son, 2 grandsons, and a daughter-in-law. Andrei Bogodel'nikov and his wife both succumbed, in addition to 3 sons, 2 grandsons, 2 nephews, and 2 nieces.[29] These cases could be multiplied a thousandfold. The crowded housing of ordinary merchants, coupled with their constant accessibility to potentially infected merchandise and raw materials, made them exceptionally vulnerable to plague. Moreover, in Russia the merchant estate included many shopkeepers, artisans, peddlers, and other smalltime traders—low status social groups with higher than ordinary mortality rates. Because of the relatively closed membership of the merchant estate, it depended upon a high degree of self-reproduction; therefore the loss of so many women and children boded ill for the recovery of the Moscow merchantry as a whole. On the other hand, the death of so many merchants opened opportunities for the younger generation and attracted newcomers from provincial towns and from the state peasantry. The plague accelerated the constant turnover of population in the merchant and artisan suburbs of Moscow—a pattern also seen in seventeenth-century British towns.[30]

Several occupational groups of low status—artisans, manufactory workers, drovers, peddlers, garrison troops, soldiers' wives, police personnel, and convicts—all faced the same high risk of infection because of their large numbers, crowded wooden housing, vulnerability to a subsistence crisis, and relative inability to flee. These were the social strata that usually lost the most to disease and dearth, and so the plague's heaviest incidence occurred in districts housing large numbers of these marginal social groups: primarily in selected central locations and the suburbs. As an example of an outbreak in the center of Moscow, the Holy Synod's press in Kitai-gorod lost 196 of 392 workers from 8 May 1771 through 30 January 1772, about 90 percent of the deaths falling in the period August-November. Printers, compositors, and inkers comprised about half the victims, probably a reflection of their high proportion of the work force. Because of the loss of workers, the press resumed operations in February 1772 with only 10 of its 20 machines.[31] Assuming that most of the press workers were housed on the premises from late August, when most government institutions ceased normal operations, their high mortality rate indicated an intense pocket of plague. Many manufactories sustained similar outbreaks.

By contrast, three other institutions sustained very different rates of mortality. Although Moscow University, the Foundling Home, and the Slavo-Greco-Latin Academy were all closed from the summer of 1771 until early 1772, the university and the home lost hardly anybody to plague, but the academy lost 96 of about 275 students and, despite efforts to recruit replacements from the sons of clergymen in the Moscow eparchy, only 196 students were enrolled in January 1773.[32] The high toll from the academy stemmed primarily from the poor housing of its clerical student body; whereas the smaller, mostly upper class enrollment of the university enjoyed safer housing at home and greater opportunities to leave town.

The Foundling Home also escaped the epidemic almost entirely, although it housed nearly one thousand children of humble social origins and several hundred attendants in the very center of Moscow. Dr. Mertens believed that strict isolation measures saved the institution. "Only four workmen, and as many soldiers, who had got over the fences in the night time, were seized at different times; but by immediately separating them from the rest of the house, the disorder was prevented from spreading any farther." Because provisions were stockpiled when admissions were halted at the end of July, the Foundling Home did not share the subsistence crisis that afflicted many poor people in Moscow at the height of the plague. Equally important, the foundlings were housed in a new masonry building that must have been almost rat-free. Since the attendants and maintenance personnel lived in wooden quarters on the grounds or in town, some of them became infected. The mas-

Table 15 Distribution of Housing in Moscow before and after the Plague

Area	1771		1781	
	Messuages	Rooms	Messuages	Rooms
Kremlin, Kitai-gorod and Belyi Gorod	1,399		1,183	8,320
Zemlianoi Gorod (without Zamoskvorech'e)	2,416		1,841	8,254
Zamoskvorech'e	1,967		1,556	5,880
Beyond the Zemlianoi Val	6,776		4,294	12,862
Totals	12,558	35,230	8,874	35,316

Source: Sytin, *IPZM*, 2: 52; register of housing in Moscow in 1781, ORGBL, f. 129, no. 22, d. 5: 1.

ter chimney sweeper constantly smoked a pipe "as an infallible preservative," but after secretly visiting his family in town he collapsed with buboes in the groin and armpit and died within two days. His young apprentice succumbed with the same symptoms soon after.[33] Of course, many children orphaned by the plague died at Sukin's temporary shelter, at the various communal quarantines, or alone in abandoned houses.

A partial measure of the plague's territorial impact on Moscow was registered in the decreasing number of small houses in different areas. In May 1773, when Andrei Bolotov visited Moscow for the first time since the plague, he was stunned: "Many houses still stood empty with broken frames among the windows, and this sight caused my whole soul to shudder even though there was no longer any danger from the distemper."[34] According to the Plague Commission, the epidemic afflicted more than a quarter of all rooms and almost half of all houses; nearly a quarter of all houses were abandoned as a result.[35] Many small dwellings in the suburbs were burned or dismantled as antiplague measures. Accidental fires added to the plague's impact, moreover, as two conflagrations in 1773 consumed 1,231 messuages.[36] Thus a comparison of housing statistics for 1771 and 1781 (table 15) revealed a notable reduction in the number of messuages in the suburbs and significant declines in Zemlianoi Gorod and Zamoskvorech'e. The ratio of rooms to messuages indicated that most of the lost housing consisted of tiny oneroom dwellings. Among the hardest hit suburban districts were the fifth, which lost 598 of 1,589 messuages, the tenth, which dropped from 1,651 to only 859 messuages, and the adjoining ninth and thirteenth districts, which together declined from 1,722 to 1,249 messuages.[37] All these areas had been early foci of infection.

Consequently, the plague reinforced the previous trend in Moscow toward a contraction of the number of messuages and an expansion of their average size as the nobility and the merchantry gained possession of more and more real estate at the expense of small free-holders, suburban communities, and ecclesiastical institutions. Much land came onto the market because of the epidemic, and the higher strata naturally obtained the greater part of such property, a trend that the authorities welcomed, in the hope that it would promote a cleaner, healthier, more orderly, and less crowded metropolis. Many years passed before all the property transfers could be completed and the authorities could auction off land left without heirs.[38]

Economic Repercussions Upon Industry

The loss of approximately one-fifth of Moscow's total population and of two-fifths of the merchant estate severely impaired the municipal economy. If greater in-migration would replenish the population fairly soon, it was harder to replace mercantile skills and capital, always scarce resources in early modern Russia.[39] Provincial merchants needed time to become acclimated to Moscow's economic environment. Meanwhile, the influx of "trading peasants" provided increasingly stiff competition in the marketplace. Besides some temporary tax relief, the government apparently provided no special assistance to the mercantile community, portions of which also incurred losses from the disruption of industry and crafts in greater Moscow.

Plague devastated the city's industry by decimating the labor force, closing most enterprises for at least six months, and depleting liquid and fixed capital. Furthermore, the close connection between large-scale industry and pestilence—an association that the outbreak at the Big Woolen Court and the Plague Riot both seemingly exemplified—revived Catherine's long-held desire to save Moscow from such hazards by transferring big manufactories to the provinces. Even as the plague raged in Moscow in the fall of 1771, Procurator-General Viazemskii began to implement Catherine's confidential directive of 24 September to prepare the removal of large manufactories. On 27 October, the Petersburg senate departments endorsed the project, after reviewing the arguments already advanced against large-scale industry in Moscow: infection, pollution, overcrowding, inflation, and exclusivist economic policies burdensome to society. Indeed, the senators blamed the epidemic on the manufactory operators' negligence and the workers' filthy mode of life. With industrial production suspended temporarily, the time seemed opportune to carry out the Empress's proposal. Orlov advised the same course, and Catherine paraphrased Bielfeld's strictures against large manufactories in big cities when she directed Volkonskii to expedite the matter upon taking charge of the metropolis.[40]

Despite these preparations, Petersburg's project encountered immediate obstacles. Indeed, on 8 November Orlov ordered the Collegium of Manufactures not to announce the senate's authorization of the removal. Orlov did not explain his action, but one may surmise that he postponed the project from fear of provoking tension and augmenting unemployment among Moscow's exhausted, hungry population.[41] At any rate, so many manufactories were infected that none could be safely moved until fumigation and frosts extinguished the danger, a process that lasted until the next spring. By mid-January 1772, the district supervisors listed 66 enterprises as infected, 30 uninfected, and 16 unspecified; thus plague struck at least half, and perhaps as much as two-thirds, of all registered industry in Moscow.[42] Whatever Orlov's explanation, Catherine approved this postponement. Meanwhile, the noble owners of several small enterprises received permission to transfer their operations to the hinterland.[43]

The Moscow authorities soon recognized that wholesale evacuation could not be effected before the spring of 1772; so, to guard against an early recurrence of plague, they decided in mid-March that the remaining manufactories should reassemble their workers and resume operations. "This has been done all the more in order that, should future reconsideration find it necessary to remove them from Moscow," the senate informed Catherine, "then they will be more prepared for that, instead of being scattered as now and having been long accustomed to a wayward life in Moscow, it will be difficult to assemble them, but even harder to keep [them] out of town, as it happened earlier with the beggars that no matter how many times they were taken out of Moscow they always returned again immediately, until finally they were put in the Ugreshskii Monastery under strict guard."[44] By likening industrial workers to beggars, the Moscow authorities unconsciously revealed how the plague had worsened their already low opinion of the city's nascent proletariat.

Evidently at Catherine's behest, the Collegium of Manufactures retrieved the senate's order to investigate removal of the manufactories in late November 1772, when fears of plague officially ceased.[45] At a series of meetings with the collegium in December 1772 and January 1773, the manufactory operators firmly, albeit humbly, protested the proposed removal collectively and individually. Collectively, the *fabrikanty* declined to specify methods of removal; they cited the losses and destruction incurred from the plague and the likelihood that relocation would entail additional, ruinous outlays, inasmuch as provincial towns lacked suitable facilities. "It is known to the State Collegium of Manufactures that at present the manufactories cannot cause overcrowding, and that the greater part of the work is performed in the district by district people, about which we do not dare to prove at length as it is a known fact." The operators left the matter of their privileges to the Empress and purposely avoided naming a price or other compensation.[46]

Besides this collective response, signed by 46 operators, many commented on the issue of relocation as it applied to their own enterprises. Predictably, nearly all opposed the proposal, but they offered a variety of reasons. "Director" Ivan Tames, for instance, recounted his huge investment in the brick linen mill that he had rebuilt at a cost of 50,000 rubles after a fire in 1752, asserted that he had spent 19,000 rubles in 1771 "for the good subsistence and supervision" of his workers, and pleaded that he was too old and ill to move the enterprise, at which he lived. The brothers Matvei and Ivan Evreinov, co-operators of silkweaving mills at the Ambassadorial Court, blamed the plague for killing "almost all" the workers they had trained at considerable expense, and for causing the additional loss of goods and materials ruined or stolen. Already in considerable debt, they could not afford relocation and grumbled that abolition of their privileges would ruin their last source of income. The Dudishkin brothers, who operated silkweaving enterprises in the city and the district, foresaw further losses if they had to relocate their Moscow enterprise and requested that, if it must be moved, the state purchase the plant. Others filed similar requests. Ivan Tatarinov and Aleksei Skorniakov could not relocate their silkweaving enterprise, they argued, because nobody would advance the money, nobody in the provinces could repair their implements, and none of the hired workers who lived in Moscow would follow the mill, preferring instead to concentrate upon their own handiwork, which "differs from manufactories in name only." Other *fabrikanty*, however, denied anything in common between manufactories and workshops and took the occasion to criticize anew the unfair competition of unregistered textile producers. Yet one of the largest woolen producers, Egor Grunt, acknowledged that he had already moved most of his operations to the suburbs or the hinterland and could remove the rest if freed from rental charges.[47]

Separately from the *fabrikanty* as a group, "Ober-director" Vasilii Khastatov negotiated with the Collegium of Manufactures over the disposition of his silk enterprise, which entailed legal complications because of prior debts and the plague's destructive impact. Indeed, Khastatov explained that he had failed to sell the enterprise by June 1771, as ordered by the senate, because he could find no buyer during the plague. The manufactory became infected in September 1771, Khastatov maintained, when 10 workers were drafted as gravediggers. Plague killed 82 of his 111 bondaged workers and exposed the enterprise to theft, "like the other manufactories," because his steward and 2 guards died. The Collegium of Manufactures confirmed all these losses and supported Khastatov's appeal to the senate for a ten-year, interest-free extension of his debt. Apparently the senate did not grant the full ten years, for in 1778 Khastatov petitioned the Empress for another extension, still blaming the plague for his indebtedness. Catherine's decision is not known, but either Khastatov's manufactory failed or was sold off by the 1780s.[48]

The plague's fury discriminated against large enterprises and bondaged labor. Statistics collected by the Collegium of Manufactures confirmed the operators' contention that their enterprises had become fewer and smaller after the epidemic, more dispersed in location and less dependent on bondaged labor. As compared to 12,681 bondaged persons at 113 registered enterprises in greater Moscow in 1771, two years later 79 enterprises employed just 6,187 workers, only 2,752 of whom were bondaged laborers.[49] Thus the plague and its aftermath removed about 30 percent of Moscow's registered industry and almost 80 percent of its bondaged work force. Bondaged workers bore the brunt of the mortality because they predominated in Moscow industry generally and at the larger manufactories especially. Unlike the many hired workers who either left the city or stayed away during the epidemic, most bondaged laborers lived permanently in Moscow—many at their assigned manufactories—and had nowhere to go; thus their higher losses. Moreover, the decline of bondaged vis-à-vis hired labor corresponded to the state's economic policies as reformulated in the 1760s. Small-scale production also recovered more rapidly than the manufactories, with 745 licensed textile workshops operating 2,680 looms in 1773—nearly as many as the registered manufactories had possessed before the plague.[50] By largely disposing of Moscow's sizable corps of bondaged industrial workers, the plague brutally resolved one complex social problem and rendered mass removal of manufactories unnecessary. After such a cataclysm, nobody could accuse the remaining enterprises, which averaged barely 77 workers each, of overcrowding Moscow and endangering public tranquillity.

The city's largest enterprises naturally lost the most victims. At the Admiralty's sailcloth mill in Preobrazhenskoe, for example, 614 of 704 male workers died or disappeared, along with 488 women and 605 children. Crowded housing produced this extraordinary mortality at Preobrazhenskoe, where 183 messuages were dismantled as a result, 54 of them at the Admiralty mill; and of 157 houses of Admiralty workers fumigated, only 9 had as many as 2 rooms each.[51] The loss of 87 percent of the mill's bondaged laborers prompted a petition to the Collegium of Manufactures for replacements from other manufactories, but President Volkov denied the request as illegal and advised the Admiralty to obtain sailcloth from other mills.[52] In January 1772, Catherine inquired whether the Admiralty might transfer the ravaged mill to Novgorod, closer to sources of flax and hemp, and the Admiralty agreed a month later. Because the Admiralty mill was state-owned and operated, its removal threatened no large proprietary interests in Moscow, such as those represented by the enterprises under the Collegium of Manufactures. Besides, the big mill had experienced economic difficulties in the 1760s and was poorly located to supply the Baltic fleet and the export trade. Its removal would also facilitate the integration of Preobrazhenskoe into Moscow as a whole. Despite these incentives, the matter hung in limbo for more than a year, probably because of the continuing confusion in Moscow and, perhaps, footdragging by the Admiralty office there. Finally, on 6 March 1773, the Empress ordered the mill transferred to Novgorod and converted to hired labor. Relocation required several years and much expense before the mill, now half the size of its Moscow predecessor, resumed production in 1780. It maintained a tenuous solvency until liquidated in 1829.[53]

Moscow's 4 other giant manufacturing complexes remained in the city longer because, as a result of the plague, they were no longer very large. The largest enterprise, the Big Woolen Court, absorbed the hardest blow. From a total of 2,734 bondaged persons in 1770, 1,400 of them operating 140 looms,

Figure 14 A photograph of the former Big Woolen Court in Moscow before its demolition in 1937. Reproduced from I. E. Grabar', ed., *Russkaia arkhitektura pervoi poloviny XVIII veka* (Moscow, 1954), p. 259.

the manufactory's principal center shrank to 672 persons, with 332 workers tending just 25 looms in 1772. In the same interval, output plummeted from 164,504 *arshin* to 20,711. The operators asked permission to sell the plant in November 1774, citing the loss of workers in the plague, the impossibility of acquiring bondaged replacements because of the government ban of 1762, and their inability to attract hired labor. Not all of the lost workers perished, of course; some must have seized the opportunity to flee, and 15 were freed from bondage as a reward for hospital service during the epidemic. All the same, the plague directly or indirectly eliminated 76.3 percent of the Big Woolen Court's human capital. Only the continuing demand of the armed forces allowed the mill to survive at a much reduced level until the 1840s. So innocuous was the Big Woolen Court after 1771, that the authorities refused repeated requests from the operators to remove it. The main buildings were finally razed in 1937.[54] Ironically, the enterprise most responsible for suggesting the removal of large manufactories from Moscow was itself never removed.

Similar devastation blighted the other big textile complexes. Tames's linen mill in 1770 had 350 bondaged and 340 hired workers operating 367 looms; by mid-1773 only 153 unfree and 165 hired laborers remained at 259 looms. Output and sales slumped throughout the 1770s, and in the 1790s the head of the firm told an English visitor that during the plague "Thames's house lost 500 men belonging to their Manufactory." Sometime before 1806 the plant ceased to exist.[55] The 4 woolen enterprises at the Kadashevskii Court likewise declined from 132 to 46 looms by 1773, and from 609 bondaged workers to 439, of whom 130 were hired. The economic deterioration lasted for decades. In 1791, a war year, the complex employed only 156 workers, and it was razed in 1812.[56] The silk mills at the former Ambassadorial Court were reduced from 356 looms and 702 workers (141 hired) in 1771 to 255 looms and 438 workers, more than half of them hired, in 1773. Evidently these enterprises were removed soon afterwards.[57] In all, the plague cost the city's 5 largest manufacturing centers 72.8 percent of their bondaged work force and, undoubtedly, the major portion of all the bondaged persons (women and children included) they had controlled in 1771. The government's refusal to replace bondaged labor forced the big enterprises to recruit hired workers or to decline. None ever regained preepidemic size.

While the plague-induced depression of Moscow's large-scale textile industry lasted for several decades, textile workshops took advantage of the demise of the large manufactories. Because textile manufacturing required limited skills already mastered by many peasants, urban migration and rural dispersal of textile enterprises quickly replaced the loss of bondaged labor. The rapid growth of textile workshops and the return of peace after 1774 persuaded the imperial government to remove other restrictions from entrepreneurship. A decree of 17 March 1775 authorized any free person to establish a manufactory or workshop without obtaining permission from any office or paying any special taxes. This enactment made the distinction between registered and unregistered enterprise obsolete, so the Collegium of Manufactures was abolished in 1779.[58] Thus the plague gave a strong boost to the government's recently developed preference for small manufacturing, hired labor, and freedom of enterprise. Nevertheless, although the government did not remove much industry from Moscow, Catherine still reviewed all proposals for new enterprises there. The liberalized policy after 1775 did not negate all the previous prohibitions. As late as 1791, the Empress reaffirmed the formal and informal policies forbidding the establishment of new manufactories in the old capital, and a decree of 1796 reconfirmed the ban on building "fire-using manufactories and workshops" in Moscow guberniia. Those policies were maintained well into the nineteenth century.[59]

The epidemic's impact diminished the duality of industry in Moscow. Disproportionately devastating large manufactories based on bondaged labor, the plague helped reshape the city's industrial structure in the direction that recent government policy favored. The epidemic removed large concentrations of workers from Moscow's central districts, and subsequent industrial development proceeded mainly on the periphery—a trend noticeable even before the plague. In conjunction with market forces and government policy, plague facilitated the dispersal of industry to the hinterland. The frightful experience of 1771 also impressed upon the imperial government the dangers to public health and order from large numbers of filthy, intemperate, and ill-housed workers in metropolitan areas—dangers that industrialization and urbanization could only worsen.[60]

Institutional and Legislative Responses

The plague convinced Catherine still more of the urgent need to reform Moscow. Moreover, the epidemic temporarily curtailed the growth of population, reshaped local industry, and removed many decrepit dwellings, thereby effecting important changes that the authorities had long desired. The turnover that the plague produced in Moscow's leadership eased the adoption of other changes. Accordingly, throughout the 1770s Governor-General Volkonskii and Chief of Police Arkharov enacted many of the reforms formulated in the Moscow nakaz of 1767. Together with the interim ecclesiastical authorities, which the new archbishop of Moscow, Platon Levshin, superseded in 1775, the new city administration also sought to reform the local clergy. Catherine's lengthy visit to Moscow in 1775, from mid-January to early December, facilitated several of these reform measures, and she incorporated certain lessons of the plague into new legislation for the whole empire. In particular, the epidemic heightened the urgency of city planning and welfare reform. All these changes occurred as part of the second phase of intensive domestic reform under Catherine, a period framed on the one side by the end of the Russo-Turkish War and of the Pugachev Revolt in 1774 and, on the other, by the renewal of Russo-Turkish hostilities in 1787. As in the case of the Moscow nakaz and subsequent reforms in the old capital, so the work of the Legislative Commission of 1767-68 and its numerous subcommittees foreshadowed the principal legislation of this period: the Guberniia Reform of 1775, the Police Code of 1782, the charters to the towns and to the nobility of 1785. Reactions to the plague contributed to the first two of these reforms.

Catherine's renewed attempt to reform Moscow actually began with the Orlov mission. Indeed, a few weeks in Moscow persuaded Orlov of the need for basic changes in the relationship of the suburbs to the city proper, in the economic basis of the clergy, and in the composition and discipline of the garrison and the police. "What a people are the local inhabitants," he expostulated to Catherine; "as you look inside their life, their way of thinking, your hair stands on end, and it's amazing that something even more abominable hasn't happened in Moscow!"[61] The Empress's council responded by recommending that Brigadier Neronov replace the aged commandant of Moscow, and Catherine elaborated Orlov's suggestions in her instructions to Volkonskii. Like Orlov, the Empress blamed administrative negligence for allowing the plague to derange the metropolis; so she urged the Governor-General to restore discipline to local government, particularly the Moscow Municipal Administration, and to reestablish respect for authority. As a visible reassertion of authority the Empress ordered that the commandant reside in the Kremlin and the governor-general in the imperial palace at Lefortovo. But when that palace burned down, on 31 December 1771, Volkonskii moved his quarters to the Kremlin for more than a year.

By way of reorganizing the local garrison, Catherine advised Volkonskii to transfer the battalion of retired Guards to Murom as soon as the epidemic ceased. She also echoed Orlov's criticism of the Moscow suburbs. "At present it is difficult to discern the difference between the city and the villages that surround it; from these very villages many furies erupt, to the city's detriment." The villages "should either be united with the city under one law, or be brought into such a state of order that the city not experience evil from them." The occasion was propitious, Catherine urged, to reorganize Moscow's institutions in order to correct the chronic deficiencies revealed by the plague.[62]

As in the case of removing industry, however, implementation of these directives proved to be quite complicated. The continuation of extraordinary precautions until late 1772, in conjunction with the crisis in Poland and the Turkish war, strained the economy so much that fiscal and manpower constraints delayed most domestic reforms until 1775 or later. In the decades after the epidemic, then, institutional changes in Moscow occurred in a sporadic, piecemeal fashion. It is difficult to distinguish the results of the plague from changes that might have happened for other reasons.

In the matter of security, for instance, the new Moscow authorities evidently hired replacements for the local police, while investigating the composition of the local retired Guards battalion.[63] Whatever the fate of the Guards battalion, Volkonskii desired additional security forces for greater Moscow and, citing Eropkin's levy of 1771, he requested permission at the end of 1773 to recruit a special police battalion of hussars. Commanded by retired military officers or active volunteers, the new unit would enroll freeholders from the Ukraine, a region famed for horsemanship, discipline, and martial arts—qualities notably lacking among the common people of Moscow. Three squadrons of hussars, in all 494 officers and men, would serve under the governor-general's personal direction. Volkonskii estimated that the battalion would cost 51,351 rubles the first year and 30,995 annually thereafter. Even though this project appeared amid the furor of the Pugachev Revolt, it does not seem to have won approval, perhaps because of the cost involved and

Catherine's lack of confidence in the political trustworthiness of the Ukrainian militia. Barely a year later, however, Volkonskii again asked for increased security forces in his proposals to Catherine for the general revamping of regional government.[64]

The imperial authorities also maintained the network of noble inspectors in the Moscow district at least until mid-1773, converting it into a general instrument of rural police directed mainly against banditry.[65] This institution served as the prototype for the office of land-captain—a sort of sheriff or justice of the peace elected by the nobility of each district—as formulated in the Guberniia Reform of 1775, which Catherine personally drafted during her visit to Moscow. Indeed, the Empress drew several articles of that reform from the decree of 25 September 1771 appointing noble inspectors in the districts, and from the numerous noble nakazy to the Legislative Commission calling for the establishment of local commissars to oversee security in the countryside.[66] The authorities recognized the unwieldy size of Moscow's 14 police districts and expanded their number to 20 by the 1780s—the same number Eropkin had employed. The crown "village" of Pokrovskoe was incorporated into the city in 1782, by which time several other suburban communities had lost their autonomy. Only in 1806 did all the communities between the Zemlianoi Val and the Kamerkollezhskii Val come under the city's administration.[67]

Concern about slaughterhouses near Moscow also reappeared, despite the order of 1771 to remove them and the actual removal that year of the fishmongers' row from Kitai-gorod. In August 1773, several Moscow merchants complained to the district medical inspectors about a slaughterhouse near their residences in the fifth sector of the Moscow district. The petitioners charged that a cattle plague had broken out there recently. They asked that a senate order of 4 April 1772, for the removal of slaughterhouses near the Petersburg-Moscow highway be extended to their locality. Investigation revealed that the community in question was not only infected, but that a year earlier when a local official brought 10 diseased cows for burial the local inhabitants—notorious for their drunken disorders—had driven him away with curses and threats. Although the senate ordered the slaughterhouses removed on 20 December 1773, it noted the absence of any proof that the order had been implemented.[68] If some slaughterhouses were moved, others remained near Moscow. In 1793, a certain Miliutin, proprietor of a silkweaving manufactory who lived near the Danilov Monastery, petitioned against some adjacent slaughterhouses supposedly built there "years ago" without authorization, the stench from which produced such a "rotten air that one cannot pass by." Nearby peasants supported Miliutin's quest, and the police had the facilities removed.[69]

Another practice initiated during the plague—burial of the dead outside the city limits—was extended from Moscow in 1772 to the rest of the empire. In order that winds would disperse any harmful vapors from the graves, cemeteries were to be surrounded by low walls or fences. In Moscow, the plague mortality led to the construction of 7 new cemeteries for the Orthodox beyond the Kamerkollezhskii Val, the enlargement of the Lazarevskoe Cemetery, and authorization for the two Old Believer cemeteries at Preobrazhenskoe and Rogozhskoe. In 1772, a cemetery for Lutherans and Catholics was established at the Vvedenskie Hills. These cemeteries shaped subsequent settlement patterns and land use outside the Kamerkollezhskii Val, nearly doubling in area by 1887.[70] As an additional product of the epidemic, 6 new churches were built at these cemeteries. Consecrated by January 1773, these churches encountered problems of maintenance and support because they lacked regular congregations, but the Moscow Municipal Administration declined to provide selectmen from the merchantry as guards for the large donations given the new chapels, citing the loss of merchants to plague and their reluctance to serve outside their own parishes.[71]

The Plague Riot made the imperial authorities especially attentive to the conduct of the local clergy. Orlov blamed the parish clergy for causing "much evil," a sentiment that Catherine echoed in censuring Moscow's religious "fanaticism."[72] Nonetheless, Moscow's leaders did not dare to move the popular icon from the Varvarskie Gates; instead they prohibited any large gatherings and supervised the merchant-guards who watched over the money and property that people continued to donate. In December 1771, Fedor Matveev, a priest at the Church of All Saints at Kulishki, was arrested for singing prayers at the Varvarskie Gates without permission. Although he denied the charge, the Church authorities first transferred him to a rural parish and later ordered him defrocked. The same punishment befell deacon Peter Trofimov of the same church for failing to denounce his colleague. The clerical administration became equally aroused at reports of persons impersonating clergymen at the Varvarskie Gates and reciting unauthorized prayers, a handwritten copy of which the hierarchy pronounced "incoherent." The Holy Synod requested that Volkov prevent such gatherings. Furthermore, the secular authorities reacted strongly to a denunciation of Semen Miasnikov, one of the merchants safeguarding donations to the icon, for allegedly stealing some of the money. Under interrogation and whipping, Miasnikov maintained that Volkov had put him in charge of donations—a claim he could not document—and he admitted using 100 rubles for household needs. The Investigative Branch fined Miasnikov 200 rubles, and the Moscow Municipal Administration assigned another merchant to oversee the donations, which as late as 1777 amounted to 815 rubles for the year. Some of this money was spent on a new public hospital.[73]

In cooperation with the Church administration, the secular authorities worked to reorganize the parish clergy. Several small parishes, left without priests after the plague, were consolidated with other congregations. Several decrepit churches were abolished. Like Amvrosii before him, Archbishop Platon sought to reassign superfluous clerics to provincial parishes and to stem the influx of provincial clerics seeking employment in Moscow. In fact, the loss of clergy to plague may have stimulated that very influx. Thus the plague's reduction of clerical cadres in Moscow seems to have been short-lived. Crossroads clerics also soon reappeared.[74] In direct reaction to the Plague Riot, moreover, the Holy Synod reaffirmed the ban on bell-ringing during fights and ordered the parish clergy to check the doors to the belfries of their churches, to equip them with stout doors and locks, and to keep possession of the keys. The icon at the Varvarskie Gates stayed in place until 1842, when it was taken to the nearby Church of All Saints. As late as 1917, public prayers were still offered to the icon once a year on 18 June, but its present location is not known.[75]

The plague, in addition to large fires in 1770 and 1773, opened wide areas of Moscow to the kind of regulated reconstruction that Catherine preferred. Ironically, however, fear of infection also played a part in blocking construction of the grandiose new Kremlin palace that the Empress had commissioned in 1768. By the time of the plague, several buildings, towers, and part of the Kremlin wall had been razed to make space for the new palace, and excavation of its foundations had begun. On 15 March 1771, Catherine contemplated related alterations elsewhere in the Kremlin, such as canalizing the Neglinnaia alongside the west wall, removing the mills along it, and transferring a proposed stable outside the wall across the Neglinnaia. But 3 weeks later, frightened by the outbreak at the Big Woolen Court and apprehensive that digging might release subterranean effluvia, the Empress temporarily halted further excavation in the Kremlin. Little was accomplished in the next 2 years because architect Bazhenov was occupied with other public works. During the brief plague scare of August 1772, Catherine again ordered the foundation work delayed for fear of polluting the air. After Bazhenov finally laid the cornerstone for his masterpiece in July 1773, the Empress suddenly countermanded construction, allegedly because the digging had caused a crack in the historic Cathedral of the Archangel. Russia's financial stringency in 1773–74 undoubtedly influenced Catherine's decision against the costly edifice, but fear of disturbing dormant plague in Moscow's soil also dissuaded her.[76] The project was never resumed.

The epidemic may have speeded completion of a comprehensive plan for the metropolis in 1775. The Commission for the Building of St. Petersburg and Moscow, the state agency in Petersburg charged with drafting plans for all other towns of the empire, proposed in 1774 to establish a Special Department in Moscow under the governor-general for purposes of expediting its planned reconstruction. Approved by Catherine, in March 1774, the Special Department started functioning in Moscow 3 months later and within a year compiled a plan for the city, a project for the regulation of buildings and for the greater production of building materials, and a new institution, entitled the Stone Bureau, for the supervision of construction.

The Moscow plan of 1775, which Catherine approved there on 7 July 1775, drew upon cameralist visions of European cities, the example of Petersburg, the Moscow nakaz of 1767, and Volkonskii's recommendations for rebuilding burned-out sectors. All these elements combined to prescribe a new city of regulated size divided spatially into three parts: the central city *(gorod),* suburbs *(predmest'e* or *Vorstadt),* and the periphery or pasturage *(vygon).* In theory, these divisions would vary in type of construction, the social status and economic function of their residents, and the density of population. The central city would comprise mostly officials, nobles, merchants, and clergy living in brick houses; the suburbs would house artisans, burghers, lesser merchants, and manufactory workers in brick residences or wooden structures on brick foundations; and the periphery would shelter the poorest strata in traditionally wooden housing. Like many city plans, this one was never fully implemented. The Stone Bureau lacked the administrative influence and financial resources needed for the task, and its functions reverted to the police in 1782; but the plan of 1775 previewed many of the changes effected in Moscow before the great fire of 1812. Manufactories were removed from the center, where the proportion of masonry buildings steadily increased. Efforts were made to clean up the Moskva, Neglinnaia, and Yauza rivers, and in 1779 construction began on an aqueduct to bring water from springs outside town.[77] When Catherine revisited Moscow in 1787 she pronounced it greatly improved.[78]

The experience of the plague spurred codification of antiplague precautions and expansion of public health facilities both in Moscow and throughout the empire. The government's reaction found direct expression in the Guberniia Reform of 1775, which represented a legislative response to the prolonged governmental crisis of 1768–75 that subsumed the Russo-Turkish War, the First Partition of Poland, the Pugachev Revolt, and—certainly—the plague. Although historians have often linked the Guberniia Reform to the Pugachev Revolt in particular, the statute itself contained many more articles derived from the plague epidemic. For example, in prescribing duties of the new office of land-captain in each district, the Empress borrowed several provisions from the instructions issued to commissars of Petersburg guberniia during the plague. The senate endorsed the permanent establishment of commissars for Petersburg guberniia in 1774, when Catherine ordered a set of instructions from which she extracted provisions for the office of district inspector, later termed land-captain.[79]

Three articles of the Guberniia Reform spelled out the land-captain's duties during epidemics. In case of "infectious diseases such as fevers with spots, bloody fluxes, and other similar diseases," the land-captain should personally confirm the nature of the malady in cooperation with the district medical practitioner, the parish priest, and at least 2 other witnesses. Should the disease prove to be communicable, it must be reported to the guberniia authorities immediately, with a full description by the attending practitioner, and the sick must be separated from the healthy. "If somewhere in the district the distemper (may the Almighty deign to avert it from His people for eternity) actually occurs, then the land-captain should act by the power of the prescriptions about precautions in the year 1771," which called for the isolation of infected localities and the use of fumigatory pyres. "If there occur somewhere in the district whole communities infected by one dangerous disease, then the land-captain should apply concern and action about the treatment and preservation of the human species."[80] Article 241 provided against cattle plague on the basis of laws issued in 1746, 1771, and 1774, a subject that the Plague Commission had also addressed in 1774.[81] In specifying the duties of the new office of *gorodnichii,* the urban equivalent of the land-captain, three articles repeated those describing the land-captain almost word for word. Yet article 262 constituted a significant insertion, evidently derived from both the plague crisis and the Pugachev Revolt: "The *gorodnichii* shall not abandon the town in any dangerous situation under pain of losing his post and honor."[82] In effect, this legislation extended the general antiepidemic institutions, first codified in the instructions of 1728 to governors and voevodas, to all localities in the person of new civil officials who were to oversee public health in concert with local medical professionals.

For the empire as a whole, the Guberniia Reform regulated the size of guberniias and districts according to population, and dropped the intermediary unit of the province. As a result, the territory of the former Moscow province was redefined as a much diminished Moscow guberniia, the other 10 provinces of which were refashioned into 6 guberniias and parts of 2 others. Several collegiia in the capitals were closed and their functions transferred to the new guberniia administrations. In theory, this administrative reorganization curtailed Moscow's dominance over central Russia and enhanced the relative status of provincial towns—a cameralist axiom that Catherine had long favored.[83]

In the same cameralist spirit, the Guberniia Reform projected public health services and welfare institutions, elaborating proposals voiced at the Legislative Commission. The various welfare provisions of the Moscow nakaz gained cogency from the plague and from the Plague Commission's example. According to the reform, each guberniia and district should employ one doctor and one surgeon, 2 surgeon's mates and 2 surgical apprentices. The district administrator should hire the doctor and surgeon by contract for a stipulated term; they, in turn, would recommend surgeon's mates and apprentices. To consolidate health and welfare services, the Guberniia Reform provided for a Bureau of Public Charity in each guberniia, which would supervise public schools, orphanages, hospitals, poorhouses, asylums, madhouses, work houses, and reformatories. Perhaps the Empress had Moscow in mind when she stipulated that public hospitals for a populous town should be located outside the city limits, downstream from the town, and on an open elevation. Moreover, "it ought to be observed with extreme diligence that the building not be cramped or low, that the rooms be kept clean, and that the air in the rooms be circulated by opening the window at least for a short time." Catherine suggested a model staff and budget for public hospitals, and spelled out their operating procedures in detail.[84]

Even before the Empress finished drafting the Guberniia Reform she decreed the establishment of a new public hospital and poorhouse in Moscow on 12 August 1775. The poorhouse, first organized in one of the quarantine buildings, was later moved to the quarters of the Admiralty's former sailcloth mill in Preobrazhenskoe. The hospital became known after its benefactress as Catherine's Hospital and lasted into the mid-twentieth century at its site in northeastern Moscow. It was built with money donated to the icon at the Varvarskie Gates, supplemented by police funds.[85] William Coxe visited the institution around 1778 and described it as follows:

> The hospital of Catherine is placed in a very wholesome and airy situation in the suburbs,. . . it contains with ease 150 patients, and there is room for 200 patients: the wards for the sick are about sixteen feet square, and contain at most nine patients; each has a separate bed; the rooms are neatly papered; the beds have linen curtains. Each patient is allowed a linen bed-gown, a night-cap, a pair of drawers, stockings and slippers, a tin-mug, a glass-tumbler; a small table is placed between every two beds, with a small bell upon it: each bed has a mattrass, a blanket and coverlet; the sheets are changed once a fortnight, and the linen twice a week. In each room a tin can with a spout at the bottom is fastened against the wall, for washing; for which purpose a large towel is provided, which is changed twice a week: each window has a small ventilator. At the furthest extremity of the court-yard is a hospital for inoculation, capable of containing 200 children.

In Coxe's opinion Catherine's and Paul's hospitals were both "fine institutions; they look more like private houses than hospitals."[86]

A madhouse, work house, and invalid asylum were all opened in Moscow in the late 1770s.[87] Thus, the welfare proposals of the Moscow nakaz finally materialized a decade later. In the interim, the plague had dramatized Moscow's needs so that, once the external and internal crisis abated, after 1774, domestic reform received the highest priority and Moscow became one of its first objects. Through the Guberniia Reform and subsequent legislation, moreover, several policies pioneered in Moscow found broader application. For instance, the Police Code of 1782 made it a criminal offense to threaten public health by spreading infection or selling spoiled provisions.[88]

One cannot measure another dimension of the plague's impact—the terror that haunted some Muscovites for decades. As one observer commented in 1786, the memory of the plague "still causes alarm even today."[89] If plague assisted the reform of Moscow, it aggravated Catherine's aversion for the metropolis. Such prejudice in Petersburg, coupled with Moscow's losses in 1771, may have retarded the old capital's growth until it was extensively rebuilt after the invasion and fire of 1812. Perhaps, too, the plague cultivated a sense of martyrdom in Moscow, fertilizing the growth of romantic and nativist sentiments that Slavophiles could use to attack the cosmopolitanism and modernism of Petersburg.

CHAPTER ELEVEN

Medical Reactions and Debates: Plague Tractates from Russia

The catastrophe of 1771 called into question the efficacy of Russia's developing medical profession and public health institutions. Their failure to ward off disaster demanded explanation and justification, all the more so because of the empire's enhanced exposure to infection through annexation and penetration of plague-enzootic territory in the south. Throughout the epidemic the imperial authorities consulted the medical professionals and mobilized a considerable proportion of them. Together with the Russo-Turkish War of 1768–74, the plague reinforced efforts to recruit medical personnel abroad and to expand medical training at home. For the many practitioners who fought the epidemic, moreover, it posed insistent problems of theory and practice. They pondered its origins and identification, the nature of the disease, and the means of prevention and treatment. The peculiarities of the Moscow outbreak aroused doubts about traditional explanations of plague. Analogous doubts might question the value of medical professionals to the state and society. To vindicate the actions of medical practitioners during the epidemic and to forestall criticism of their role in the formulation of public health policy, some doctors and surgeons seized the occasion to publish reasoned explanations of the cataclysm. Their explanations drew lessons from the tragedy in hopes of averting its repetition; they also expressed intensified commitment to an expansive, activist policy toward epidemic disease. Thus the medical debates about the plague continued long after its end, stimulating medical policies and thought, research and publication in Russia. If medical thinkers from Russia made no great discoveries in the scientific study of plague, they brought the subject to a respectable level of discourse and demonstrated a thorough, frequently critical, knowledge of the lengthy European tradition of plague tractates. Their contributions enlivened that tradition for Russian and European audiences.

Because the plague involved large numbers of medical professionals, it exerted multiple effects upon the profession in Russia. An unprecedented number of practitioners died during the epidemic: about 20 in Moscow, several in the Ukraine, and many more with the armies outside Russian borders.

Those who survived never forgot the experience. Despite these losses and nightmares, both the government and the practitioners agreed that medical professionals had rendered valuable service during the crisis. Both strongly believed that, should plague recur, they must employ even more practitioners against it. Memories of the epidemic, in conjunction with the plague's continuous threat to Russia's new territory in the south, inspired the Medical Collegium to redouble recruitment of professional practitioners. Catherine gave the matter high priority in the Guberniia Reform of 1775, which incorporated several lessons from the plague and required medical professionals for each guberniia and district. The Empress personally assisted in the recruitment of foreign medical practitioners by soliciting candidates from Dr. Johann Zimmermann in Hannover.[1] According to Brückner's tabulation, the number of M.D.'s in Russia rose from 94 in the 1760s to 229 in the 1780s, the Slavic physicians among them increasing from 21 to 34 (table 1). At the same time surgical personnel multiplied commensurately, although their exact numbers remain uncertain. By 1803, about 2,000 medical practitioners of all types served the armed forces and the civilian population. The surgical schools were reorganized in the 1780s and again a decade later; the first one in the provinces functioned temporarily at Elizavetgrad in the Ukraine. To be sure, diverse considerations dictated the need for larger cadres of medical professionals, but the horrors of 1771 injected a new urgency.[2]

Greater numbers of medical personnel found employment in the empire's expanding network of border quarantines, which assumed more definite organization through special statutes of 1786, 1793, and 1800. In fact, the last law codified regulations for land and sea quarantines, provided substantial salaries and retirement benefits for quarantine servitors and their dependents, and projected an annual budget of about 209,000 rubles. By 1803, twelve quarantine offices and ten checkpoints, most of them located along the empire's southern fringe, employed a total of 57 medical professionals and 278 auxiliary personnel. As before, the authorities sent out additional medical cadres against actual emergencies and established internal quarantines if plague crossed the border. This antiplague organization operated throughout the nineteenth century.[3]

By way of encouraging practitioners already in service, the government rewarded those who waged the antiplague campaign. The medical members of the Plague Commission—doctors Shafonskii, Yagel'skii, and Orraeus, staff-surgeon Grave, and surgeon Samoilovich—all received an extra year's salary, attractive service appointments, and promotion in rank: the doctors to collegial councilor (sixth rank) and the surgeons to collegial assessor (eighth rank). Thirty-two other practitioners who served against the plague in Moscow were all rewarded with an extra year's salary (one-half for doctors Shkiadan and Peter von Asch), in addition to the double pay they received during the special service.[4] Dr. Orraeus became the Moscow city-physician in 1772, but retired from service in 1776 to his estate near Petersburg, where he died in 1811. Besides heading the Moscow General Infantry Hospital, Dr. Shafonskii worked for the Plague Commission until its dissolution in 1775 and then succeeded Orraeus as city-physician in 1776. Shafonskii left medical service five years later to enter the judiciary of the newly established Chernigov vicegerency, where he became chief judge before his death in 1811. Dr. Yagel'skii died of tuberculosis in Moscow in 1774.[5] Staff-surgeon Grave lived in retirement in Moscow until at least 1775, when he petitioned the Plague Commission for back pay; the date of his death is not known.[6] Samoilovich, promoted in 1771 to staff-surgeon for the senate, went abroad for advanced medical study in 1776 and received his M.D. from Leyden in 1780. He reentered service with the army in the south in 1784 and later supervised the quarantines along the Black Sea until his death in 1805.[7] Shafonskii, Orraeus, and Samoilovich all figured prominently in the public debates about plague after the epidemic. Had Yagel'skii and Grave lived longer they might have participated in the controversy too. Of the other practitioners who faced the epidemic in Moscow, however, only Dr. Mertens and Dr. Meltzer publicly (and Dr. Pogoretskii privately) joined the discussion. Additional commentaries came from practitioners who had encountered plague in the south.

The debates about plague elicited an outburst of medical theorizing that stimulated the general growth of medical literature in Russia and revitalized the European tradition of plague tractates in a new Russian context. Both phenomena attested to the maturation of European scientific medicine in Russia under state patronage. Before 1700, medical literature in Russia, whether written in Russian or in other languages, developed slowly. As modern science and medicine evolved in western Europe, they only gradually and sporadically reached Muscovy, which had inherited a weak scientific tradition from Byzantium that largely missed "the valuable Islamic and Jewish element which meant so much for the rebirth of learning in the West."[8] The first book to be printed in Muscovy appeared only in 1565, and book publishing grew so slowly that printed volumes remained rare until the eighteenth century. Literacy and education underwent similarly slow advances. Notwithstanding the general medical progress of the Petrine era, the bulk of medical literature available in the middle decades of the eighteenth century still comprised three main categories: foreign works, Russian translations of foreign works, and Russian compilations of foreign and native (often folk) sources, such as leechbooks *(lechebniki)*. None of this medical literature was widely accessible even by mid-century, as evidenced by the efforts of Archiater Kondoidi to bolster libraries at the surgical schools, by Lomonosov's criticism in 1761, and by the deputies' complaints to the Legislative Commission of 1767–68.[9]

Beyond the limited readership for medical literature in foreign languages, the chaotic condition of the Russian language raised many obstacles. Russian had yet to assimilate the language of the new science, despite a flood of borrowing from Europe that began in the sixteenth century. By the second half of the eighteenth century, however, Russian translations of European medical works began to overcome the many terminological deficiencies. Concurrently, larger numbers of Russian citizens, the majority of them from the Ukraine, obtained medical degrees abroad, for which they performed and published, usually in Latin, more or less original research. Foreign doctors at the Academy of Sciences, the 4 surgical schools, and the new medical faculty of Moscow University also produced a growing number of works, mostly in foreign languages. All this spurred publication in Russia. In the period 1761–1800, some 203 separate medical titles appeared in the empire in Russian, as compared to just 5 in the preceding 60 years.[10]

In the 1760s, the Russian medical authorities also began to encourage research and publication. Archiater Mounsey, in 1762, called upon all practitioners to record their most important cases, obviously with a view toward disseminating such information. When reorganizing the medical administration in 1763, moreover, officials and practitioners criticized the Medical Chancery for its failure to foster intellectual exchange and research. The Medical Collegium therefore ordered, in 1764, that all physicians and surgeons should submit "medical histories, that is descriptions of new, rarely encountered, difficult or any other kind of diseases worthy of comment, showing how one has treated them." All practitioners were urged to discuss other medical topics, especially those ignored or inadequately explained in books, and to report all new medicines made from native ingredients. These works could be in Russian, Latin, French, German, English, or Italian, and were to follow the model of the English physicians Sydenham, Pringle, and Huxham. Approved contributions would be considered as a basis for promotion in service, and the best works were to be published in a series under the title of *Russian Medical Commentaries.*[11] By the 1770s, in short, preconditions had matured for the rapid emergence of medical theorizing and publication in Russia. The epidemic of 1771 and the recurrent alarms thereafter guaranteed that plague tractates would bulk large in the new medical literature. Circumstances also favored the publication of the first specifically Russian plague treatises.

Prior to 1770, Russia lacked a native scholarly tradition of writing about plague. The few works that considered the subject were either healing manuals, which simply transmitted traditional ideas, or the Latin and German editions of Dr. Schreiber's treatise on the epidemic of 1738–39. The plague of 1771 amounted to a pestilential baptism for a large segment of Russia's medical practitioners, who were more numerous, better prepared, and more eager to record their experiences than the previous generation had been. Furthermore, the intense state and public interest in the matter increased the incentive for practitioners to formulate and to publish their views. During the epidemic several practitioners submitted their observations to the Medical Collegium for the guidance of others.[12] In Moscow, doctors

Lerche, Yagel'skii, Orraeus, and Erasmus compiled medical advisories to inform the public of antiplague precautions. In Petersburg, the Foundling Home published a compilation of these advisories in 1772.[13] The Plague Commission elaborated these policies, soliciting observations from the district medical inspectors and their assistants. It collected extensive materials on the subject and finished operations in 1775 by issuing a tome that offered a theoretical introduction to plague along with the main government decrees and medical discussions from the time of the epidemic.

During the plague and soon afterward several original and translated treatises appeared in print in the empire. Subsequently, several medical eyewitnesses published extensive commentaries in Russia and abroad, and some public lectures discussed plague and related subjects. In the period 1770–1801, more than twenty other tracts on plague were written in Russia, most of them in Russian and never published. Counting works written in the early nineteenth century based on observations of the eighteenth century, medical professionals in Russia submitted to the Medical Collegium 1,144 works in manuscript, 267 of which concerned infectious diseases; 40 discussed plague.[14] In quantity alone, then, writings about plague constituted a significant portion of Russia's new-born medical literature.

European models for plague tractates materialized in Russia during the epidemic itself and soon thereafter. Peter Fridrich Körber (1732–99; M.D., Erfurt, 1756), a widely experienced physician who had published a book in 1761 about the treatment of common diseases among the Livland peasants, dedicated his *Abhandlung von der Pest* (Reval, 1771) to the Medical Collegium and the governor-general of Estland.[15] A French practitioner at court, Nicholas Gabriel Le Clerc (1726–98), inscribed to the Empress his treatise *De la contagion* (St. Petersburg, 1771).[16] In 1772, Semen Sulima, evidently a Petersburg surgeon, translated into Russian Richard Mead's well-known plague tractate, first published at London in 1720. Sulima acknowledged that his publication was too late to assist the antiplague campaign. "But I am releasing my translation to the public solely in order that, through this small endeavor of my zeal for the Fatherland, I may at least somewhat satisfy the curiosity of my countrymen about that disease which brings all the world such great anxiety."[17] None of these medical writers had seen plague firsthand. All relied upon the long tradition of classical and European medical theories about infectious disease. For example, Körber cited Hippocrates and Galen, Diemerbroeck, Pringle and Chenot, Schreiber and Lerche.[18]

By contrast, Professor Johann Rost (1726–91) presented at Moscow University on 22 April 1772, the first eyewitness retrospective analysis of the epidemic, "that horrible time." The university press published his public lecture in Latin and Russian on the occasion of Catherine's forty-third birthday under the title of "A Word about the Harmful Atmosphere Noticeable in Houses, especially of the Common Folk, and about Expedient Means to Correct It." Perhaps because Rost was not a physician, but a professor of practical mathematics and experimental physics, he took an unusual approach to the problem of housing conditions and their relationship to the plague. In the process, he revealed a thorough knowledge of the relevant scientific literature, including the *Philosophical Transactions* of the Royal Society.[19]

Publication of the Plague Commission's official account in 1775 superseded all previous theorizing about plague in Russian and opened further discussion. Dedicated to Catherine and published at the Moscow University press, this large volume attempted to synthesize traditional theory and recent observations. It immediately occupied a central position in Russian plague literature, epitomizing as it did the collective medical expertise of the prestigious Plague Commission. Its main compiler, Dr. Afanasii Shafonskii, exemplified the new generation of European-trained Slavic physicians and enjoyed great repute because of his intimate knowledge of the Moscow epidemic from its inception. So authoritative was this volume that the government had it reprinted without alteration in 1787. Here subsequent theorists found a lode of documentation that they could mine for their own purposes. Furthermore, its publication signaled official encouragement of plague research and thereby promoted Russia's first public medical debate about plague. This debate also reached European medical circles through the treatises in foreign languages of Franz Meltzer, Charles de Mertens, Il'ia Rutzky, Danilo Samoilovich, Gustav Orraeus, Pieter van Woensel, and Johann Minderer.[20] Mertens's book proved exceptionally popular and soon appeared in German, French, Italian, and English, the last translation including material from Orraeus and Samoilovich.[21] The tractates of Samoilovich and van Woensel also appeared in German and Russian, respectively, the latter with an original preface by a Major Andrei Meyer.[22] Georg von Asch and Matthew Guthrie popularized elements of these debates in 1779 and 1780.[23] Several German physicians with experience in Russia published commentaries in the 1780s.[24] Inside Russia, these debates culminated in the encyclopedic work of Ivan Vien in 1786.[25] Taken together, these treatises inaugurated in Russia a body of theorizing about plague that extended the venerable European tradition of plague tractates.

The treatises themselves, however, continued the medical debates that had accompanied the Moscow epidemic, the peculiar course of which they attempted to explain. Besides saving Russia from another invasion of pestilence, these writers sought to contribute to general European medical knowledge. Plague theorists from Russia took the occasion to adumbrate the activist outlook of the empire's state-dominated medical service.[26] None voiced public doubts about the efficacy of the policies they had applied against the plague. All hastened to blame the failure of those policies on the lack of public initiative and cooperation and to claim credit for partial successes while predicting greater progress. In 1780, Georg von Asch even had a medal struck proclaiming him "Liberator a peste 1770," a claim that evoked protest from Orraeus, who asked for additional reward, and censure from Catherine, who had prohibited the release of unauthorized medals.[27] Some of these medical writers polemicized with plague theorists inside and outside Russia, attempting to rethink the disease's puzzles in the light of the Moscow experience.

Nationalistic feelings, professional tensions, and personal rivalries within the Russian medical community colored several treatises. The publication of Mertens's account outside Russia provoked scornful criticism from Samoilovich, for instance, who not only attacked the Austrian on substantive and methodological grounds, but accused him of exaggerating his own role in the epidemic while belittling the service of native practitioners. Indeed, Samoilovich's publications reek with a perfervid patriotism that facilitated their rediscovery and translation into Russian in the Soviet Union toward the end of the Stalin era. Ironically, many of his writings were in French, and the originals of his few works in Russian about plague attracted little attention, mainly because of their incomprehensible language.[28] Of Ukrainian clerical origins, Samoilovich transmuted a fiery temperament—"always stubborn," a close friend called him—into ardent Russian chauvinism.[29] By dedicating his tractate to Catherine, he evidently hoped to attract her favorable attention, which Mertens had conspicuously enjoyed during his sojourn in Russia (1767-72). In 1781, Samoilovich sent two of his works to Grand Duke Paul, whose service he wished to enter and whose support he sought for appointment to the post of scholarly secretary of the Medical Collegium. Both goals eluded him.[30] A surgeon at the time of the plague, Samoilovich later derided Dr. Mertens, then his senior professionally, for having barely seen the epidemic; he dismissed Mertens's views as unfounded and erroneous because they were not based upon observation. In fact, all traditional theories about plague incurred general disdain from Samoilovich, who rejected them out of hand.[31] In subsequent editions, Mertens denied these charges, cited laudatory official recognition of his service in Russia, and noted that he had never spoken with Samoilovich—a jibe at the latter's previously humble status.[32]

Samoilovich's own tractate, in French, encountered sharp criticism in Russian at the hands of a fellow surgeon and russified citizen of the empire, Ivan Vien (Johann Wien). Born in Moscow of German percentage—"son of a conference secretary"—and non-Orthodox in religion, Vien (c.1748-1809) received his medical training at the Moscow surgical school and the Petersburg Admiralty Hospital, where he must have known Samoilovich in the 1760s. Although Vien never studied abroad or earned a doctorate, he wrote an elaborate tractate in Russian that combined firsthand observation of the plague, which he witnessed in the Ukraine in 1771-74, with an impressive knowledge of previous scholarship in Latin, French, German, English, and Russian. Indeed, the book's citations revealed his familiarity with virtually the entire corpus of plague literature from antiquity to his own time. Dedicated to Catherine, Vien's *Loimologia* was printed by the Academy of

Sciences at her expense; she also approved his petition for an advance on royalties and awarded him the 1,200 copies. The book won Vien the rank of staff-surgeon and the reputation of a leading specialist on plague. In 1793, he became scholarly secretary of the Medical Collegium and served in that post until the collegium was abolished in 1803. During his tenure, he edited the only volume of *Russian Medical Commentaries,* published in Latin in 1805. He also participated in the committee that drafted the new imperial statute on quarantines in 1800. Vien headed an antiplague expedition in the Caucasus in 1804, for which he received the Emperor's thanks and promotion to state councilor (fifth class).[33] All these achievements must have galled his rival Samoilovich.

The careers of Vien and Samoilovich ran parallel in many respects. Beyond a desire to publicize accurate knowledge of plague, however, the two disagreed fundamentally on the subject. Samoilovich's superpatriotism, disparagement of foreign medical practitioners in Russian service, repudiation of traditional plague authorities, and boasts of original and novel insights into the disease, all obviously rankled Vien. He proclaimed that *Loimologia* was intended to offer practical guidance for practitioners and officials and to encourage research into the causes and treatment of plague; but while denying that his book attacked anyone in particular, he used the occasion to debunk several of Samoilovich's views.[34] Nevertheless, unlike Samoilovich's attack on Mertens, Vien's criticism was temperate and scholarly, and he agreed with his rival on several questions. The fate of his book, which deserves to be known as the first comprehensive Russian plague tractate, has been almost the reverse of Samoilovich's work. Respected well into the nineteenth century, *Loimologia* ultimately suffered neglect and disparagement in the twentieth century from the same Soviet commentators who lionized Samoilovich.[35] This is an unfortunate situation because both men and their works merit impartial study in the context of their time. Both personified the hybrid medical elite of late eighteenth-century Russia, an elite that emerged from a complex, continuous fusion of native and foreign elements. If the issue of nationality sometimes divided this elite, it provided intellectual and cultural leavening as well.

The Tractates and the Problems of Plague

Unlike the theoretical treatises of Körber and Le Clerc, and the Russian translation of Mead's work, the tractates published from 1772 onward were all written by men who had personally witnessed the recent epidemic. Personal experience and direct observation, the hallmarks of the best European work on fevers in the eighteenth century, permeated the original plague tractates from Russia too. "To a physician on the scene, an epidemic can sharpen the acuity and at the same time reduce and concentrate the field of attention. Instead of a vague general 'system' which was all-inclusive and could explain everything, we find close attention to a specific field of endeavor. Instead of vagueness, there is more desire for precision. Instead of logical completeness, we find concern for insistent practical details."[36] In thinking about plague, all these writers harped upon observation as the key to understanding the mysterious disease. Most questioned the main theories about plague and sought to modify them on the basis of their own observations and those of their contemporaries. They were influenced by previous theory, to be sure, but endeavored to adapt it to the Russian context, urging the necessity of an activist and optimistic approach to infectious disease. Viewed in the light of medical theories of the time, the epidemic of 1771 spurred medical observers in Russia to ponder three sets of problems about plague. First, they debated its origins and differential incidence in space, time, and social status. Second, they speculated about the nature of the causative agent—was it animate or not? Third, they discussed therapeutics and prevention, and several considered the possibility of inoculation against plague.

Miasmatico-contagionist assumptions shaped the conceptions of plague etiology in all the tractates, just as "vagueness and tautology marked all the discussions of fever" in eighteenth-century European medical theory.[37] Yet this hyphenated formulation allowed considerable flexibility and latitude, accommodating many variations of the three modes of infection delineated in the sixteenth-century treatise of Fracastorius: at a distance (through the air), by contact, and by infected media or fomites.[38] Körber, for example, inclined to miasmatic conceptions, but noted the difficulty of explaining how the air became corrupted. If the air were polluted, he wondered why fumigatory fires of noxious substances were used to cleanse it. Plague might be caused, he suggested, by a poison produced by local conditions, such as putrefying corpses after a battle.[39] Mertens, Orraeus, and Vien all accepted this possibility, too, though they thought it rarely happened; and some authorities clung to cadaveric or soil-poisoning theories as late as the 1890s.[40] Samoilovich, however, denied the phenomenon in general and noted in particular that the Russian field army in the Danubian Principalities had largely escaped from plague despite marching past thousands of corpses in huge common graves.[41]

None of the tractate writers believed in a general miasma, only localized or temporary ones. Most theorists saw direct contact and contact with infected articles as the main modes of transmission, but they thought that plague originated through miasmatic processes. Vien speculated that plague proceeded from air corrupted by a volatile poison akin to an alkaline salt in gaseous form. Such corruption could occur anywhere, he explained, but since heat and moisture speeded the process, southern locales were unusually prolific sites, Egypt and Ethiopia in particular. The inundations of the Nile provided ideal conditions: water, mud, multitudes of dead plants and animals, and hordes of insects—all worked upon by prolonged and powerful sunshine. Unstirred by winds, the air might become shot through with invisible particles of corruption deadly to man. These miasmata could then infest merchandise and persons and be carried elsewhere.[42]

Even contagionists such as Samoilovich and Mertens conceived of the mechanics of interhuman transmission through contact as a micromiasmatic process. A plague victim radiated a magnetic field or toxic "whirlwind" which, Samoilovich opined, mixed with the body's effluvia, penetrated the skin, and corrupted the blood. "When I looked at a patient's tongue," Mertens explained, "I used to hold before my mouth and nose a pocket-handkerchief moistened with vinegar." This makeshift mask implied miasmatic ideas, as Mertens's English translator pointed out. Mertens also admitted that the sick might exhale the pathogenic agent from the lungs or transpire it through the skin. Finally, he consistently linked the Moscow epidemic's vagaries to the changing climatic conditions, an idea that could support either miasmatic or contagionist interpretations. But Samoilovich, who arrived in Moscow after the epidemic's two false starts, criticized the link to weather as miasmatic gibberish.[43]

It has been maintained that physicians of this era generally supported miasmatic notions, whereas laymen usually believed in contagion, trusting the evidence before their eyes.[44] In the plague tractates from Russia, however, no such dichotomy obtained. The single nonphysician scholarly commentator opted for a variant of miasmatic theory. Professor Rost postulated corrupted air as a precondition for plague without attempting to decide the general origin or agent of that corruption. His miasmatic terminology spoke of "the force of the pestilential vapors which spread everywhere [and] struck so many thousands of people with deathdealing poison." Air is like food, he averred: if spoiled it can harm the human body, especially when filled with poisonous substances so subtle that they strike people without being detected by the senses. Two paradoxes emerged from this attempt to understand the Moscow epidemic in miasmatic terms. First, far from being universal in incidence, the disease had afflicted almost exclusively "the lowborn or the rabble"; and second, contrary to conventional expectations that cold weather would end the epidemic, "thousands perished at the coldest time of autumn."[45] Although the latter assertion was not strictly true, it led Rost to some ingenious theorizing.

Corrupted air prevailed in the crowded, filthy quarters of the unwashed poor, which Rost compared to the atmosphere of ships, dungeons, and hospitals—conditions that bred disease, as Pringle and others had demonstrated. In Moscow, popular mores exacerbated the disease potential among the common folk.

> For this sort of people is seized from youth with such a great craving for warmth, that in their chambers they choose to sleep either above the stove or in berths usually located in a very warm place. And often they live two or perhaps even

> three families together in one hut. Therefore the vapors abundantly emanating from them are further multiplied by the influence of food and clothing: the tendency of which [vapors], although it is frequently limited by cold air, yet in a very warm place appointed for sleeping, they emanate and arise in greater force and number. Hence the emergent evil is transformed into an even more grievous one inasmuch as these folk, from want, rarely manifest cleanliness and neatness.
>
> In this manner the air in these places, having become corrupted and laden with harm, is held under the ceiling by the action of the heat of the chamber, where it becomes more harmful and more corrupted, takes on the sharpest acidity, the lightest subtlety, and most intense power of action, whereby it rapidly penetrates the opened sweat pores of those asleep.[46]

Corrupted air alone should not have prolonged the Moscow epidemic, Rost concluded, for experience showed that cold weather curtailed plague. Rather, the overheated air in the huts of the poor, in which the temperature sometimes exceeded 70° F., must have regenerated lethal qualities in "the infectious poison" that extended the epidemic well past the first frosts. To protect against such contingencies, Rost proposed the addition of a ventilating pipe to Russian stoves to circulate the air inside.[47]

In a footnote, Rost also considered the case of the Big Woolen Court. Did plague break out there from infected wool imported from Poland, he wondered, or did it originate from local sources, from "the disorder and unexampled filth of the multitude of people at the mill, who breathed the musty and quite harmful air?" On behalf of a localist miasmatic genesis, Rost remarked that a nobleman had woven cloth from the same wool without ill effect. If bad sanitation were the primary cause of pestilence, then dirty and decrepit Moscow should have experienced outbreaks every year.[48] Rost's analysis offered, in short, a refined explanation of the plague's differential seasonal and social impact, focusing upon housing conditions and the temperature of the microatmosphere of Moscow's small wooden habitations. His ideas exhibited a sophisticated application of miasmatic conceptions, an application that suggested the unexhausted explanatory potential of that venerable notion of infectious disease.

Despite Rost's miasmatic reflections, contagionist interpretations prevailed among most of the plague theorists from Russia. Contagionist arguments took several forms, however, some of which were as critical of each other as they were of miasmatic conceptions. In fact, the polemic among Mertens, Samoilovich, and Vien involved a fundamentally contagionist perspective on the part of all three. They all relied extensively upon the majority view of the Moscow medical community as codified in Shafonskii's tractate for the Plague Commission in 1775. His account followed the medical advisories of 1770–71 in its thoroughgoing contagionism, its criticism of abstract hypotheses, and its advocacy of theory drawn from direct observation. Predictably, this tractate steadfastly defended the government's policies toward the Moscow epidemic.[49]

According to Shafonskii, "the pestilential poison" originated in the hottest regions of Africa and spread elsewhere through contact with infected persons and merchandise. Samoilovich doubted the African origins of plague, but agreed that it spread solely by direct contact with infected persons or objects, a position that Mertens and others upheld for the Moscow outbreak. Contagionists noted that textiles long retained the infection unless aired or cleansed.[50] Plague often struck the Ottoman Empire because the Turks took no precautions about suspect goods or carriers. The disease traveled easily, as the epidemic of 1770–72 had demonstrated, but it seldom visited northern countries, where the common people knew nothing about it and, consequently, disdained precautions. The Russian government had failed to contain the epidemic, Shafonskii insisted, not because it pursued improper policies, but because it received no cooperation from the population; "and especially the common folk, who did not believe in the existence of that dangerous disease and, by not adopting personal caution and rational measures to preserve themselves, fell victim to superstition, obstinance, avarice, and subjected themselves to perdition." Popular disbelief also gained strength from the refusal of some practitioners to acknowledge the disease as plague. Had the people believed in the government's quarantine policies, Shafonskii averred, those precautions would have saved the situation sooner.[51]

Shafonskii followed Orraeus and others in positing two types of plague, fast and continuous. Orraeus later subdivided both into mild and acute varieties, thereby visualizing four varieties. By contrast, Mertens and Samoilovich believed in a single basic type. "Does not the plague," expostulated Samoilovich, "which has been given so many different names, really always remain the same plague?" Vien agreed, but pointed out the diverse effects of the disease in different individuals and, like Meltzer and Samoilovich, he hypothesized that epidemic plague proceeded through three distinct phases characterized by the dominance of certain symptoms.[52] Indeed, based on the Moscow outbreak and those at Kiev and Nezhin, Samoilovich proposed a tripartite periodicity for all plague epidemics. During the first phase, from April to early June 1771 in Moscow, the plague slowly gathered strength until it became "more infectious, more subtle, and more volatile." Then it burst into the second, most lethal phase, which in Moscow lasted from August through early November, whereupon the disease entered the third, declining phase, from December 1771 through March 1772. Buboes predominated during the first and third phases, Samoilovich asserted, whereas carbuncles and petechiae, "most often of a huge size," marked the middle phase. Shafonskii remarked upon the frequency of carbuncles at Moscow in August and September 1771, labeling that symptom a "dark lesion" or "pestilential coal," usually fatal to the afflicted. In the Ukraine, Vien reported a victim with a carbuncle formed from the union of numerous petechiae.[53]

Samoilovich's three-phase theory did not link the plague's behavior to environmental changes; rather, he thought the "pestilential poison" itself underwent autonomous change that governed the succession of phases as manifested in the dynamics of the mortality rate. From this deduction, Samoilovich concluded that in order to halt an epidemic, countermeasures must be instituted at the very start of the plague's first phase. Otherwise the disease would become so virulent and so widespread that the deadly second phase must ineluctably follow. Vien chided such overemphasis on contagion by observing that not everybody in an epidemic became infected, "even though Samoilovich supposes so." This same feature of Samoilovich's theory prompted his chief Soviet biographer to decry its "element of fatalism."[54]

Contagionist theorists offered various explanations of plague's social discrimination. Pestilence could strike anyone, Shafonskii allowed, but the young were more susceptible than the old, women more than men, and "the lower calling more than the eminent." The poor suffered worse owing to negligence, poor diet, domestic filth, overheated habitations, fumes from stoves, avarice, drunkenness, pillaging infected property, and disbelief in the disease's infectiousness.[55] As aware of administrative obstacles and socio-economic imperatives as he was of popular mores, Shafonskii gave a basically cameralist interpretation of the features of Moscow that exposed it to plague. Catherine's policies toward the metropolis before and after the plague revealed her wholehearted agreement with Shafonskii's indictment that "Moscow was circumscribed neither in the arrangement of houses, nor the calling of its inhabitants, nor in the style of domestic life or construction of dwellings, according to the calling and substance of each inhabitant: in this city reigned idleness and luxury which tear asunder that necessary link of general order and public welfare. Is the rapid propagation of the distemper astonishing in such a city?"[56]

Mertens, Samoilovich, and Vien echoed Shafonskii's general explanation of the plague's differential incidence upon society. In Moscow, the poor suffered more, Samoilovich reiterated, because they neglected the elementary precaution of avoiding contacts with infected persons, and because their mode of life exposed them to more frequent contacts with the outside world. Samoilovich cited his own example, together with those of Orlov and Eropkin, Grave and Yagel'skii, to buttress his contention that rational precautions could protect persons closely exposed to plague. Moreover, he believed that these cases disproved the existence of miasmata, for everyone in Moscow breathed the same air.[57] Although not an eyewitness of the Moscow epidemic, Dr. Matthew Guthrie questioned other practitioners about it and accepted Russian assurances that plague "only is communicated *by actual contact,* or the touch." With other contagionists, he used this assumption to explode miasmatic conceptions. "It must be very particularly noticed, that the better classes of society *escaped* to a man, though they inhabited the upper storeys of the houses (to be more insulated and separated from the mob) and it is well known that corrupted, or mephitic air, being much lighter than common air mounts up; so of course if the plague had been communicated by the atmosphere, the inhabitants of the upper storeys could not have escaped it as they did."[58]

Concerning plague's relationship to other infections, the tractates advanced several views. Shafonskii, Mertens, Samoilovich, and Guthrie all thought it was a specific disease, clearly distinguishable from other "putrid fevers." Meltzer denied any connection between human and cattle plague; so did Minderer, who, like Orraeus, first encountered plague in the Danube region. But Orraeus believed that plague was closely related to typhus. Disputing Samoilovich's view that plague and typhus were quite different, Vien saw the issue as a matter of degree only: "no, they are both essentially unfortunate progeny of one mother, that is, corruption."[59]

Questions about the causative agent of plague occupied all of the writers of tractates. All were aware of the germ theory and several considered it critically, but none championed the idea, then in general disfavor throughout the European medical community.[60] Körber dismissed the microscopic germ theory as unproved and implausible. Sulima's translation of Mead's treatise argued likewise. Noting the wide range of symptoms, van Woensel posed the question, "Do the very seeds of the distemper differ, or does this distinction stem from the difference of the infected bodies? I confess my ignorance about the essence of this distemper." In common with many other theorists, Le Clerc acknowledged the controversy over the pestilential agent and speculated about it in confused terms; "the germs of the contagion" showed it to consist "essentially of an acrid and septic venom" that attacked the lymph. "The contagious particles that one calls deleterious miasmata manifest a preference for humidity, and the perspiration of the body seems to be their true element." Similar to an electric spark, these tiny particles could travel great distances and produce violent reactions.[61]

Rost also mentioned the germ theory, citing with approval Richard Bradley's treatise of 1721. Like Le Clerc, however, Rost described the agent variously as "pestilential and death-dealing seeds" and as a "poison." Interested in the mechanism of propagation rather than the nature of the agent itself, Rost saw little significance in whether the substance was organic or not. In the same vein, Meltzer spoke of the "pestilential virus" and of "contagious miasma"; while Mertens called it "the contagion," "the pestilential virus," and "the pestilential germ," and referred to "the terrible activity of its poison"—all of which was standard contagionist terminology. Like Rost, Mertens largely ignored the precise nature of the causative agent as he endeavored to conceptualize "contagion" in mechanistic terms. His correlation of the Moscow epidemic with weather patterns implied that the pestilential agent was nonorganic. None of the plague theorists in Russia detected any connection of plague to rodents or fleas. None mentioned rats in Moscow during the plague. Only Körber remarked offhand that eating "unnatural food" such as cats, rats, and mice might bring on plague.[62]

Samoilovich considered whether plague might stem from microscopic organisms, only to conclude that if the microorganisms found on humans played any role in the genesis or transmission of disease, it must be a secondary one. Still, he envisioned plague's "invisible buds" penetrating the body through the skin and not through the air. In 1784, while fighting plague in the southern Ukraine, Samoilovich undertook some dissections and investigations with a microscope to reconsider the germ hypothesis. This research simply confirmed his previous ideas; "for I found that there are not any insects [i.e., microorganisms], as has generally been thought, either in the air, in articles, or in habitations infected with the pestilential poison, and that this disease nowhere and never infects otherwise than solely through direct contact." Vien likewise denied any life to the infective agent. The germ theories and observations of Kircher and others struck him as unsubstantiated and illogical. If "microscopic worms" or "winged insects" existed at all, Vien reasoned, then they must be merely harbingers, not bearers, of pestilence. Even so, he concluded that to explain the extraordinary infectivity of plague the causative agent must consist of "a most subtle, penetrating material endowed with an extremely powerful reproductive quality."[63] Thus the weak development of microscopy and of staining techniques, together with the dominance of mechanistic-chemical conceptions of infection, deflected European and Russian plague theorists from moving toward microbiological explanations.[64] Nevertheless, in criticizing the germ theory they kept it alive for subsequent generations of researchers.

All the plague tractates from Russia endorsed activist approaches to the disease. The dominant contagionist persuasion led most tractate writers to emphasize quarantine measures. Samoilovich and Vien both favored evacuation of infected localities, but cautioned that officials and medical practitioners must remain behind.[65] Although nobody claimed to have a cure for plague, all rejected fatalistic notions and believed that it should be treated in some fashion. Samoilovich, for example, felt certain that plague could be conquered, boasted that he had saved hundreds of patients in quarantine, and advocated a variety of therapeutic techniques, such as ice massages, emunctories, scarification of buboes, sudorifics, plasters, and (on occasion) bloodletting. "Those who have the plague in its moderate and slow form, may be rescued from death," concluded Mertens, by taking doses of mineral acids and Peruvian bark. But these remedies rarely worked in severe cases, "so that we are compelled to acknowledge, that the plague (under its more violent forms) is of such a malignant nature as not to yield to any medicines with which we are acquainted, howsoever well adapted they may, *a priori*, seem to be for getting the better of this disorder." Mertens denounced "James's Powders" as inferior to ipecacuanha as an emetic and thought "bleeding to be very improper in the plague" except in unusual circumstances.[66]

The activist orientation of plague theorists from Russia found vigorous expression in a debate about inoculation as an antiplague weapon. This idea had been proposed in treatises by Professor Elias Kamerarius (Tübingen,

1721) and by the Hungarian physician Istvan Weszpremi (London, 1755).[67] The analogy with smallpox was particularly likely to appear in Russia, of course, because Catherine's sponsorship of smallpox inoculation in 1768 had publicized that concept throughout the empire. Körber hinted at such an analogy in foreseeing the appearance of a "northern Hippocrates" who might discover, by the end of the century, an antidote to plague like those used against smallpox and the bites of poisonous animals.[68] After the epidemic of 1770–72, several practitioners claimed to have proposed and, in the case of at least 2 claimants, to have successfully demonstrated inoculations against plague. Others commented on the possibility.

Dr. Peter Pogoretskii privately advanced the most ambitious claims in a petition of 1775 to Catherine herself. Besides successfully treating 539 infected persons during five months' service at Moscow's pesthouses, Pogoretskii had sought to forestall the epidemic "by means of inoculation of plague." He described the procedure in rather vague terms:

> I first made the experiment on different animals; then, wishing to ascertain the consequences of this inoculation on people, I began this experiment on myself. I inoculated myself and, knowing all the degrees of the course of this disease, thanks be to God, saved myself from death; and through this exposure of myself, I learned that the method of inoculation can be useful to humanity. Subsequently I inoculated 72 persons with plague, all of whom, aided by the benevolence of the Lord, recovered, and about which I had the good fortune to inform the [Plague] Commission, which recognized my daring and zeal with a special certificate. The details of the method of inoculation, and its value for humanity, I am prepared to explain if it will please YOUR IMPERIAL MAJESTY.[69]

Unfortunately, Catherine's response has not been found and Pogoretskii died in 1780 without ever publishing his "method," which did not become known.

Better publicized, by contrast, was the self-inoculation performed by field surgeon Matthias Dehio at a plague hospital in Bucharest in 1772. Dr. Georg von Asch publicly claimed credit for the exploit, upon his election to the Petersburg Academy of Sciences in October 1779, and his endorsement appeared in the local press, from which Matthew Guthrie relayed it to the British medical community. Dehio intended to protect practitioners by this procedure, Guthrie commented, "perceiving the gentlemen of his profession condemned, in a manner, to death, if punctual in their duty. . . . He produced the disease, by inserting with the point of a lancet, under the epidermis of his arm, matter from a pestiferous abcess, and followed the cold regimen observed in the small pox, as he had imitated its mode of inoculation." Asch acclaimed Dehio's experiment as an application of the diffident proposal of Kamerarius. To those who questioned the efficacy of inoculation by asserting that plague could strike a person more than once, Asch rejoined that inasmuch as the disease occurred in various forms, cases of apparent reinfection might actually involve different varieties. He called for further experiments in plague-ridden regions, cited recent German attempts to inoculate cattle, and attacked the idea of plague's being incurable as an obstacle to necessary experimentation.[70]

Mertens compared plague to smallpox but rejected inoculation on grounds that the disease could infect the same person again—a position that his English translator emphatically reaffirmed in 1799.[71] Yet Samoilovich, like Asch, championed the idea in a separate pamphlet, *Mémoire sur l'inoculation de la peste* (Strasbourg, 1782), and in his larger tractate of 1783. But, unlike Asch, he ignored precedents and maintained that his ideas were entirely original. Indeed, he claimed to have first proposed inoculating some hospital personnel in Moscow in 1771, but admitted that his attempt to test the procedure had foundered upon popular prejudice and other unspecified difficulties. In addition to the analogy with smallpox, his own experiences in Moscow had suggested the idea; he survived three attacks of plague-like fever during the epidemic and never knew a survivor to die from reinfection. Samoilovich explained his own survival, incidentally, as mainly due to timely treatment in the first instance and to his contracting the disease during its last, declining phase in the two latter instances.[72] Apparently, he never actually attempted an inoculation on himself or anybody else, although some commentators have advanced such a claim for him.[73] No corroboration has been found for Samoilovich's claims of priority and originality in recommending inoculation against plague. Orraeus acknowledged that several Moscow practitioners had championed the notion, but he named none and rejected inoculation as illogical and too dangerous to try. Then too, Samoilovich could have borrowed the idea, possibly from Georg von Asch, with whom he had supposedly held "very frequent private conversations" about the plague in Moldavia in 1771.[74]

Irritated by Samoilovich's grandiose claims, Vien pointed out his European predecessors. Neither did Dehio's experimental inoculation convince Vien. The surgeon-inoculator might not have contracted plague at all, but some milder fever; or perhaps Dehio survived, Vien conjectured, owing to an unusually high individual resistance. "All this has not been resolved by this experiment!" Nevertheless, both Vien and van Woensel favored testing inoculations on condemned criminals in future outbreaks.[75] The following decades witnessed no experimental confirmation of the procedure, new commentators inveighed against it, and the idea lapsed until after the plague bacillus was isolated in 1894.[76] Although several kinds of vaccine were developed in the twentieth century, their effectiveness has been limited at best; they are usually employed only in crisis situations. But this is a subject that Soviet plague researchers continue to study, in the tradition of their activist-minded predecessors of the eighteenth century.[77]

The plague of 1770–72 stimulated, then, a vigorous growth of epidemiological theorizing in Russia and, to a lesser extent, western Europe. While rapidly absorbing the long European tradition in this sphere of medical theory, plague theorists from Russia began to contribute their own observations. Their discussion of the germ theory indicated a certain parity with European contemporaries. Although commentators on plague in Russia all rejected the idea of a *contagium vivum*, they knew about it and struggled, however blindly, with its implications. The professional medical community in Russia was much less numerous than its European progenitors, but the training of its top echelon was of comparable quality and produced a small elite with similar intellectual capacities. Their intense interest in controlling plague had the effect of breathing new vitality into old debates, as in their discussions of etiology and pathology, while posing more sharply the possibility of new control measures, such as inoculation. Their debates about plague provided much impetus to medical research in Russia and to the publication of the first modern plague tractates in Russian. If one accepts the contention that in fighting cholera in the 1820s and 1830s the Russian medical profession "was generating ideas and methods comparable to the most advanced in Europe," then similar recognition should be extended to the plague theorists of the last decades of the eighteenth century.[78] By exposing the helplessness of medical science, the plague of 1771 spurred the further development of public health institutions and epidemiological theory. Both would eventually furnish the means to control, if not to eradicate, the nightmare of epidemic plague on Russian-controlled territory.

Conclusions and Comparisons

For Russian history, the reign of Catherine II in particular, the plague of 1770-72 offers a spectacular example of the sudden intrusion of external forces and events. The calamity provoked social disruption in the precipitate extinction of more than 100,000 human beings, the temporary paralysis of economic life, the violent collapse of Moscow during the Plague Riot, and the tragic murder of Archbishop Amvrosii. All these events seemed products of a suprahuman disaster, the outcome of a baleful caprice of an inscrutable nature. Terrifyingly relentless and perplexingly sporadic, the epidemic confounded contemporaries even more than they were surprised by an incursion of plague after decades of relative security. In an age when the social elite of Europe prided itself upon a devotion to reason and to the progressive attainment of secular knowledge leading to human perfection, plague exemplified the persistence of monumental irrationality in nature and society. On the one hand, the epidemic revealed how fragile the social fabric could be under stress and, on the other hand, how resilient society could be in recovering from unforeseen disaster. To explain this resiliency one might play down the scope of the catastrophe and doubt that it was as awful as contemporaries believed. But this study has demonstrated that the Moscow plague was both extraordinarily puzzling and exceptionally intense, whether viewed from the perspective of the eighteenth or of the twentieth century.

Measured by the standard of plague epidemics within Russia, the outbreak of 1770-72 presents regularities and singularities. Like most epidemics after 1350, the disease reached central Russia from the south and, despite efforts to block its arrival and to confine its spread, the worst ravages befell Moscow and its hinterland in the summer and fall, the usual fever season. The coincidence of warfare and plague in the south joined with Moscow's burgeoning commercial-industrial economy to fashion a broad avenue for the northward transmission of infected rats and infective fleas. Much the same thing happened to Moscow in 1570 and 1654. On all three occasions, the wooden metropolis sustained ghastly mortality, but massive flight of the population obscured the exact proportions of the losses in each instance. In 1770-72, the disease was definitely bubonic plague. Neither the symptoms reported nor the monthly mortality totals gave any hint of pneumonic plague, which hardly appeared in Russia between 1450 and 1878.

The territorial sweep and duration of the Moscow epidemic of 1771 conformed to the pattern of plague's incidence after the Black Death in that the outbreak originated outside Russian borders and primarily affected central Russia and the Ukraine. It did not reach either as far northward or as far eastward as the epidemic of 1654–56, but it still encompassed a huge region. Total mortality from plague in 1770–72 may well have surpassed any previous epidemic in Russia, including the Black Death, which afflicted a much less populated and less urbanized realm. In absolute numbers, Moscow lost the most victims to the disease, just as it probably did in 1570 and 1654. Provincial towns and villages suffered less, on the whole, although their proportional losses may have been greater in a few instances. Within Moscow, losses were extremely erratic in terms of neighborhoods and social groups, a pattern that reflected the city's irregular layout and the plague's quixotic emergence. The suburbs were hit hard and many merchants, clergy, and artisans were struck down, but the elite largely escaped through flight.

If most plague epidemics manifest some similarities, Moscow's last visitation in 1771 disclosed several eccentricities. Foremost were the unusually late beginning and the lengthy build-up, from November 1770 to July 1771, preceding the major mortality. Both these features derived from extraordinary weather conditions. The prolonged autumn of 1770 permitted the plague to reach Moscow unseasonably late in the year and prepared for an expanded epidemic by nurturing an extra generation of fleas and rats, which multiplied even faster amid the moist and warm weather of the prolonged summer of 1771. Indeed, the late winter of 1770–71 not only failed to cut off the incipient epidemic, but it perplexed contemporaries by fostering two false starts, while delaying the main event. The Plague Riot of September 1771 endowed the Moscow epidemic with the melancholy distinction of exhibiting Russia's most violent reaction to disease prior to the various cholera riots of the nineteenth century.[1] It may be the only plague on record that resulted directly in the murder of such a highranking prelate as Archbishop Amvrosii. Another distinctive attribute of this epidemic was the role played by the textile industry. As contemporaries deduced, plague probably entered Moscow in shipments of wool or silk and then spread over the metropolis through the network of densely inhabited textile manufactories and the hundreds of small workshops. The epidemic dramatized the dangers of largescale industry in the heart of a metropolis, but its lethal impact on the bondaged labor brutally ameliorated that complex social problem for several decades.

Compared to previous epidemics in Russia, moreover, the plague of 1770–72 witnessed a much more vigorous and sophisticated response from officials and medical practitioners at all levels and in all regions. For that reason alone it left an unusually abundant documentation. In Moscow, the very intensity and scope of these responses tragically complicated the social disorientation and administrative disintegration that sparked the rioting. Yet the Orlov mission and the Plague Commission both represented far more elaborate institutional reactions to epidemic disease than had ever been attempted in Russia. In 1654, by contrast, no medical assistance whatever was provided and officialdom left the metropolis to its fate. Paradoxically, such neglect may have been no more damaging to Moscow than was the antiplague campaign of 1771, as mandated by Petersburg and fruitlessly protested in Moscow before the riots confirmed its dangers.

Within the context of Catherine II's reign, the Moscow plague contributed to the protracted, occasionally acute, crisis of 1768–75—the most complex challenge the Empress had faced since attaining the throne. Indeed, the epidemic itself epitomized the multiple dimensions and complex causality of that crisis by originating from a general subsistence crisis that embraced Europe and the Mediterranean world, entering the empire as a result of warfare and commerce, following the main routes to the marketing and manufacturing metropolis, and radiating outward to scourge the demographic heartland of Russia and to threaten St. Petersburg. In the process, the epidemic prolonged the Turkish war that nurtured it, aggravated the chaos in Poland that led to that country's partition in 1772–73, and burdened the Russian economy with additional pressures that exploded into the Pugachev Revolt of 1773–74.

For Catherine personally, the plague constituted a frightening and frustrating experience. Preoccupied with Polish and Turkish affairs, the Empress did not foresee the pestilential incursion, which nobody could have divined at the time. When the threat drew nearer, however, she sought expert advice, ordered sensible precautions, and kept calm as the epidemic waxed and waned confusingly. From Petersburg, she closely followed the situation and when the Moscow leadership disappointed her, she prepared emergency measures and arranged for Senator Eropkin and Dr. Lerche to coordinate the antiplague campaign. Like everybody else, Catherine was perplexed at the plague's episodic appearances in Moscow and began to suspect incompetence on the part of officials and practitioners alike. The plague's provincial inroads gradually stimulated anxiety for the safety of Petersburg that deepened her perplexity. In these circumstances, news of the Plague Riot almost shattered her composure. Had she not already dispatched Grigorii Orlov to the scene, she might have reacted even more strongly. Her fury at Saltykov's desertion of his post betrayed her mental turmoil, however, just as her order to remove large manufactories from Moscow bespoke an urge to strike out at the impested city's obdurate evils. Orlov's confident leadership and the onset of winter quickly cooled Catherine's enfevered imagination, and her spirits soon rebounded as the plague rapidly faded. Nevertheless, apprehension continued to mark her correspondence with Governor-General Volkonskii in 1772. Plague still weighed on her mind in 1775 as she drafted the Guberniia Reform.

If this apprehension subsided later on, it reappeared in 1783 when plague threatened Russian forces in the Crimea. As Catherine instructed Potemkin, her viceroy in the south: "Please let me know about the continuation or abatement or curtailment of the distemper, it frightens me; I keep worrying lest it creep into Russia through some sort of negligence at the borderposts." A month later she confessed: "the plague frightens me; may God grant you success in guarding your [troops] against it and in ending its visitation in the Crimea."[2] The Empress reacted even more emphatically in 1784 when plague struck the new city of Kherson and the Kremenchug area. "Take a strong hand for the extinction of the Kherson distemper," she advised Potemkin. "Employ the measures taken at the time of the Moscow misfortune: they were so effective that from September to December they extinguished the death-dealing sickness." Rumors of disease in Moscow brought an order for Governor Arkharov to investigate.[3] Though not serious, these outbreaks activated Catherine's memories of the Moscow disaster and reminded her of the plague's lurking peril to the empire.

The Empress saw the plague of 1770–72 as a blot upon the record of enlightenment and progress that she wished to bequeath to posterity. Seeking to accentuate the virtues of optimism and heroism, she liberally rewarded the official saviors of Moscow and commissioned the Orlov Gates, which the Italian architect Antonio Rinaldi constructed at Tsarskoe Selo in 1777–82 (fig. 13). Catherine personally selected inscriptions for this monument. On one side, Orlov's heroism was recounted: "When in 1771 there was in Moscow a pestilence on people and popular disorder, General of Ordnance Count Grigorii Orlov, by his own request received orders to go there, restored order and obedience, provided subsistence and treatment for the orphaned and the poor, and ended the ravages of the distemper through his beneficient institutions." The other side exhibited the last line of Vasilii Maikov's poem on the occasion of Orlov's departure from the city: "Moscow has been delivered from calamity by Orlov" (*Orlovym ot bedy izbavlena Moskva*). Neoclassical in style, the Orlov Gates were built of marble from the Olonets region and remain standing to the present day.[4] A portrait of the Orlov brothers by the court painter Jean Louis de Veilly reflected the same accent on individual heroism amid social calamity; Grigorii stands before a rather indistinct scene of figures collapsing on Red Square (fig. 12). Similar fulsome praise resounded in Maikov's panegyrical poem and in another by Princess Ekaterina Urusova which, albeit ostensibly addressed to Eropkin, rationalized Catherine's decision not to visit Moscow in person and lauded her as "Minerva, Astraea, Mother of the Fatherland, and the Mistress of hearts—Immortality is braiding her crown for Thee."[5]

Once the plague scare passed, Catherine wished to forget the awful experience and did not encourage its public commemoration. During her visit to Moscow in 1775, the celebrations of the peace with Turkey and the triumph over Pugachev predominated. A minor reference to the plague in a medallion-like picture on some temporary triumphal gates, sponsored by the Moscow nobility, portrayed Hercules slaying the seven-headed hydra that spews poison into the air. An official guide explained the picture as related "to the pestilential distemper, the most calamitous actions of which were fortunately averted from us by the wise and indefatigible policies of our dearest Mother of the Fatherland. A godlike affair! for which more than Herculean strength was required." And its slogan proclaimed: "For the Salvation of the People."[6]

In 1782, Dr. Danilo Samoilovich conceived a project for a commemorative mural. His idea was to debunk the horrors of plague and to praise the prudence of governmental policies by depicting practitioners discovering plague symptoms and fearlessly treating the infected. Some scenes would honor the exploits of Orlov and Eropkin. Others would publicize Samoilovich's contagionist ideas through idyllic pictures of peasants working in the fields, some of them placidly watching a burial procession. To refute notions of atmospheric corruption, all this action must unfold under a clear sky, with birds roosting on pesthouses and flying about.[7] When Catherine heard about this venture she did nothing to help, perhaps distressed by the subject and irritated by Samoilovich's importunity. He subsequently published a brochure calling upon the Moscow nobility to sponsor the proposed mural, but it never materialized.[8] Although Catherine sponsored plague tractates such as Ivan Vien's addressed to practitioners, officials, and the literate public, she had no desire to perpetuate memories of the Moscow catastrophe. Unlike the Lisbon earthquake's chilling effect on enlightened thought in western Europe, this official posture of optimism in Russia discouraged artistic, literary, and philosophical speculation about the meaning of natural disaster for social and intellectual progress.[9]

The plague of 1770–72 also affected the evolution of Russia's public health institutions and of the medical profession. Officials and practitioners both interpreted the plague as proof of the need for better precautions and more medical professionals, particularly in civilian capacities and at the local level. Drawing upon criticism voiced at the Legislative Commission of 1767–68 and the policies adopted during the plague, the Guberniia Reform of 1775 provided for an impressive expansion of public health facilities and medical professionals throughout the empire. Civilian medical service gradually ceased to be seen as a secondary career, a mere dumping ground for superannuated military practitioners. The medical professionals themselves took pride in their steadfast service against the plague, and some later looked upon it as a subject for research and reflection, laying the foundation in Russia for a tradition of epidemiological investigation. Confident of their professional preparation and powers of observation, several Russian practitioners felt certain that they had valuable expertise to communicate to the Russian public and to the international medical community. Whatever their private doubts about the efficacy of the policies used against the plague, all agreed publicly upon the need for active medical intervention. All insisted that the disease could be contained and, ultimately, conquered. All argued that medical professionals must lead antiplague efforts, beginning with a greatly improved network of border quarantines. None discerned a medical triumph in the epidemic, but all believed their efforts had helped. Most thought that, had the common people heeded their warnings earlier and followed their precautions better, the plague would have ended sooner and killed fewer.

To look at the Moscow plague from an international perspective, it can be compared to three epidemics of the same general period in three different regions of Europe: the plagues at London in 1665-66, at Marseilles in 1720-21, and at Debrecen in 1739-40. In terms of intensity as manifested in total and proportional mortality, the Moscow epidemic appears most like the London plague (table 16). Both killed about 20 percent of the population in the city proper, peak mortality falling in the period August-October. By contrast, Marseilles and Debrecen suffered higher proportional losses—about 50 and 30 percent, respectively—perhaps because of their smaller sizes, denser populations, and more southerly locations.[10] In Marseilles, plague raged most fiercely in August and September, whereas the greatest mortality at Debrecen occurred from August through November (table 16). The source of the Debrecen outbreak is not known, except that it is supposed to have come from Transylvania. Like the Moscow epidemic, however, those at London and Marseilles have been linked to the cloth trade.[11] Few if any medical practitioners fought the plague at Debrecen, it seems, but substantial contingents of doctors and surgeons battled the disease in London, Marseilles, and Moscow. During the Marseilles plague, indeed, 4 of 12 doctors and 32 of 35 surgeons died—a sharp contrast to London and Moscow where relatively few practitioners succumbed.[12] On the other hand, the Moscow plague stimulated an outpouring of medical theorizing much like the British and French reactions to the epidemic in London and Marseilles.[13] In the amount of government assistance, Marseilles most resembled Moscow, for the royal government took vigorous steps to contain the epidemic and to aid the distressed population. London and Debrecen received more aid from the municipal authorities, perhaps because of better developed traditions of urban self-government.[14]

Violence like the Plague Riot in Moscow did not disrupt the other plague-stricken cities, but some disorders did perturb Debrecen, and strikes hit Marseilles. At Debrecen crowds prevented sentries from quarantining suspect houses, forcibly opened closed residences, and solemnly convoyed the dead to cemeteries. The authorities could not discover the instigators of these practices, which foreshadowed the religious responses observed in Moscow in 1771.[15]

One may speculate that London and Marseilles escaped such violence for quite different reasons in each instance. Plague was no newcomer to London; the metropolis experienced repeated outbreaks throughout the sixteenth and seventeenth centuries. Accordingly, the city authorities evolved regular procedures to cope with disease through the normal organs of administration. If "a spirit of revolt was seething below the apparent calm," as the historian

Table 16 Monthly Mortality in London, Marseilles, Debrecen, and Moscow

Month	London (1665)	Marseilles (1720)*	Debrecen (1739)	Moscow (1771)
April				744
May			72	851
June	590		145	1,099
July	6,137	200	313	1,708
August	17,036	8,000	824	7,268
September	26,230	24,000	2,556	21,401
October	14,375	4,000	3,493	17,561
November	3,449	3,000	998	5,235
December	590		195	805
Totals	68,407	39,200	8,596	56,672

*Monthly estimates from a graph of daily mortality in Biraben, *Les hommes et la peste*, 1: 236.

Sources: Shrewsbury, *Plague in the British Isles*, 462; Robert Horváth, "La statistique de la peste de Debrecen (1739-40) et du choléra de Pest (1831) en Hongrie et leurs conséquences sociales," *Acta Universitatis Szegediensis: Acta Juridica et Politica*, 9, fasc. 4 (Szeged, 1962), 4; *Opisanie*, 601.

Bell maintained, then "it was a great gain that the magistrates, aldermen and parish officers set over the people were those to whom they were accustomed." But then a subsistence crisis did not threaten London in 1665 as much as it did Moscow in 1771.[16] By comparison, Marseilles underwent a subsistence crisis, but may have avoided violence because of the sudden onset and short duration of the plague there, and because, moreover, the royal government immediately rushed many troops and large-scale assistance to the beleaguered port.[17] Moscow and Debrecen both endured longer visitations, received less help from municipal or central authorities, and fell prey more easily to social unrest as a result. Presumably, London and Marseilles were more modern cities than Moscow or Debrecen, which lacked large numbers of autonomous social groups that enjoyed a status between that of the small elite and the mass of the unprivileged.

Perhaps too, the people of London and Marseilles possessed greater confidence in public health officials and medical practitioners than did most Muscovites, who were unaccustomed to seek professional medical assistance from an unfamiliar, heavily foreign medical elite. There was no apparent parallel in London or Marseilles to the widespread animosity toward practitioners seen in Moscow, an animosity that the erratic course of the epidemic further inflamed. None of these comparisons should be pressed too hard, for the present study has endeavored to delineate the peculiar concatenation of circumstances and contingencies that gave birth to the Plague Riot in Moscow—a phenomenon that one would not expect to see repeated the same way at any other time or place. To be sure, plague and other epidemics have provoked violence in various cities before and since the eighteenth century.[18]

Because the Moscow outbreak was the last great epidemic of plague to penetrate the Russian interior, it raises questions about the reasons for the general withdrawal of plague from Europe after the eighteenth century.[19] Of course, all plague epidemics are partly fortuitous, because bubonic plague is not primarily a human disease, and this study has consistently maintained that the plague of 1770–72 originated from a multiplicity of causes: biological, meteorological, military, economic, social, institutional, medical, and personal. The Moscow plague was the extraordinary product of a unique configuration of weather, warfare, and textile weaving in a wooden metropolis. Still, at the risk of generalizing wildly from one unusual outbreak of plague, several trends can be seen as militating against a repetition of the terrible epidemic of 1770–72. For one, weather cycles favorable to plague do not seem to have occurred in central Russia between the 1770s and 1830s.[20] Russia scarcely felt the anomalous weather of 1816, when a disastrously cold summer provoked crisis and distress throughout the western hemisphere.[21] At the same time, colonization and cultivation and land clearance in the southern Ukraine, the middle and lower Volga region, and the northern Caucasus in the late eighteenth and early nineteenth centuries may have protected central Russia by changing the conditions for rodent life in the steppe zone. Marmots, one of the main species afflicted by wild rodent plague, largely disappeared from these regions by the mid-nineteenth century.[22] Perhaps, too, the influx of Norway rats diminished the density of house rats in northern cities, such as Moscow, and, together with the greater separation of cities from the countryside, lessened the proximity of humans to rodents.

The Russian conquest of the north coast of the Black Sea, effected by the annexation of the Crimea in 1783 and further gains by the Russo-Turkish War of 1787–92, may have improved barriers to plague in the form of a more effective maritime quarantine. Russian colonization of the region gradually introduced some of the structural safeguards against plague associated with better living standards: improved housing, separate storage of grain, and better sanitary surveillance.[23] All these changes allowed earlier detection of plague and isolation of the scattered outbreaks that persisted into the early nineteenth century, mainly affecting ports such as Odessa in 1812, 1835, 1837, and 1901–02, Astrakhan and Saratov in 1806–08, and various localities of the Caucasus in 1798–1819 and 1838–43. A sudden outbreak of pneumonic plague struck some villages in Astrakhan guberniia in 1878–79, and sporadic plague recurred east of the Volga and the Caspian as late as the 1930s.[24] If epidemic plague disappeared from the Soviet Union in the late 1930s, the world's largest country still encompasses huge foci of wild rodent plague, which must cause occasional human cases.[25]

The epidemic of 1770–72 ranks as the most destructive visitation of bubonic plague that Russia and Moscow ever encountered. It also represents one of the worst urban disasters of the preindustrial era. The Moscow plague was doubly tragic because contemporaries could not understand its causes, and their best efforts either proved ineffectual or even worsened the calamity, which starkly revealed the limits of medical and scientific knowledge.

APPENDIX ONE

Doctors and Surgeons in Moscow in March 1771

Doctors and Degrees	Service Assignments
1. Andrei Rinder* Altdorf, 1736	Moscow city-physician and head of the Medical Office
2. Peter Veniaminov Leyden, 1764	Medical Faculty, Moscow University
3. Semen Zybelin Leyden, 1764	Medical Faculty, Moscow University
4. Adrian Tatarinov Göttingen, 1768	Moscow University
5. Charles de Mertens Strasbourg, 1758	Foundling Home
6. Kas'ian Yagel'skii Leyden, 1765	Junior doctor, General Infantry Hospital
7. Afanasii Shafonskii Strasbourg, 1763	Senior doctor, General Infantry Hospital
8. Johann Erasmus Jena, 1747	Supervision of midwives
9. Grigorii Shkiadan unknown	Private practice
10. Peter von Asch Göttingen, 1756	Private practice
11. Johann Kuhlemann Göttingen, 1753	Paul's Hospital
12. Peter Pogoretskii Leyden, 1765	Private practice
13. Christian Lado Uppsala, 1763	Private practice
14. Frantz Meltzer Strasbourg, 1769	General Infantry Hospital
15. Johann Maut Leyden, 1760	Private practice

Staff-surgeons

1. Christian Minau	Medical Office
2. Johann Wiel	General Infantry Hospital
3. Heinrich Engel	General Infantry Hospital
4. Friedrich Roeslein	Palace Stables Chancery
5. Johann Hamers	Governor-General Saltykov
6. Johann Fries	Private practice
7. ________ Chemze	Private practice
8. Christian Grave	Retired

Surgeons

1. Ferenz Keresturi	Medical Faculty, Moscow University
2. Karl Timan	Medical Office
3. Grigorii Yakhontov*	________
4. Johann Jonas	________
5. Johann Stelin	________
6. Pavel Mille	________
7. Andreas Rikman	Artillery depot
8. Fedor Figner	Policemaster Chancery
9. Konrad Julius	Secret Branch of the senate
10. Johann Pegelau	Guards Battalion
11. Alexander Zurburg	Admiralty Sailcloth Mill
12. Peter Einbrot	Paul's Hospital
13. Ivan Dir	Velikolutskii Regiment
14. Caspar Mürke	Private practice
15. Friedrich Margraf	________
16. Josif Blandot	________
17. ________ Dubarrei	________
18. ________ Daresku	________
19. ________ Fokht	Foundling Home
20. ________ Zeidel	________
21. ________ Val	________
22. ________ Nagel	________
23. ________ Boernike	Retired
24. ________ Müller	Moscow garrison
25. Luka Golts	Army

Surgeon's Mates

1. Emel'ian Gornik*	General Infantry Hospital
2. Semen Kasagov*	General Infantry Hospital
3. Johann Shaden	General Infantry Hospital
4. ________ Korobovskii	General Infantry Hospital
5. ________ Chepelov*	Retired

*died in 1771

Sources: TsGADA, f. 263, op. 1, pt. 2, d. 1663:21–23v.; TsGAg.M, f. 636, op. 2, d. 5:48–50; *Opisanie*, 244–51, 631–33. Dates and places of degrees are from Rossiiskii, *Istoriia*, and Chistovich, *Istoriia*, app. 10.

APPENDIX TWO

Students at the Moscow Surgical School in 1770–71

Name	Age	Name	Age
1. Ivan Kistenmaker	17	26. Karl Gotlibsen*	18
2. Vasilii Trokhimovskii	21	27. Erazm Strekh	20
3. Andrei Shafronovskii	24	28. Vasilii Goloekevich	21
4. Ivan Prokhorovich	21	29. Il'ia Resh'	21
5. Grigorii Sulima	23	30. Gerasim Protasov*	20
6. Vasilii Sobol'	22	31. Filip Tsyergolts	25
7. Ivan Danilevskii*	22	32. Genrikh Iogan Laurin	20
8. Ivan Anufrievskii*	23	33. Kondratei Zurburg	18
9. Moisei Piatkovskoi	22	34. Peter Malakhov	18
10. Stefan Lekhnitskii	22	35. Vasilii Konstantinovich	19
11. Nikolai Mordovskii	21	36. Grigorii Mokrenets	16
12. Stepan Tsvetkov*	21	37. Ivan Fedorovskii	18
13. Aleksei Smirnov*	21	38. Georgi Klein	20
14. Vasilii Makedonets	20	39. Kondrati Rakovskii	20
15. Zakhar Bredenbek	17	40. Yakov Shtrunts	—
16. Maksim Magerovskii	26	41. Iogan Davyd Mikel	—
17. Grigorii Mokrenets	19	42. Danila Gelshert	—
18. Grigorii Konstantinov	24	43. Yakov Orobevskii	—
19. Johann Friedrich Adam*	20	44. Vasilii Kapustinskii	—
20. Yakov Buderts	20	45. Matvei Yakubovich	—
21. Denis Volchenetskii	20	46. Ivan Velichkin*	—
22. Grigorii Cherniavskii	20	47. Aleksei Nazarov*	—
23. Tikhon Grigorovich	24	48. Gavrila Izmailov	—
24. Afonasii Maslovskii	19	49. Aleksei Teteshkin	—
25. Ivan Vitvinskii*	26	50. Ivan Popov	—

Volunteers

1. Iogan Tsimerman
2. Andrei Rikhter
3. Peter Libgolt
4. Peter Aralychev
5. Martin Zeger
6. Yakov Gaselkvis
7. Veniamin Knol'

Adjunct Students
1. Il'ia Friazinov
2. Zakhar Levashov
3. Nikita Protopopov
4. Grigorii Oleoridskii
5. Nikita Kriukov
6. Alexander Volgemutov

Schoolboys assigned to assist surgical students
1. Lavrentii Evgutov*
2. Aleksandr Atiushev*
3. Ivan Yakovlev*
4. Ivan Petrov*
5. Vasilii Zhurov*
6. Nikita Strigin*

*died in 1771
Source: TsGADA, f. 344, op. 1, bk. 46:74v.-80; *Opisanie*, 631-33.

Abbreviations

AGS	*Arkhiv gosudarstvennogo soveta* [Archive of the State Council]
AKV	*Arkhiv kniazia Vorontsova* [Archive of Prince Vorontsov]
C., *Sochineniia*	*Sochineniia imperatritsy Ekateriny II* [Writings of Empress Catherine II]
Ch.OIDR.	*Chteniia v imperatorskom obshchestve istorii i drevnostei rossiiskikh pri Moskovskom universitete* [Readings in the Imperial Society of History and Russian Antiquities at Moscow University]
CN	*The Chronicle of Novgorod, 1016–1461*
IZ	*Istoricheskie zapiski* [Historical Notes]
Lerche, "Conspectus"	J. J. Lerche, "Conspectus observationum Meteorologicaum a triginta octo annis (XLVII/L) continuatarum potissimum in Ruthenidae, Persiae et Finnlandiae diversis provincis: Observationes meteorologica ab Anno 1729 usque ad Annum 1776-1779 continuata," unpaginated manuscript notebook preserved at the Meteorological Museum of the Main Geophysical Observatory of the USSR in the village of Voeikovo near Leningrad.
Lerche, "Ephemerides"	J. J. Lerche, "Ephemerides Meteorologiae Petropolitane," three unpaginated manuscript volumes held at the Meteorological Museum.
MV	*Moskovskie vedomosti* [The Moscow News]
OPI-GIM	Otdel pis'mennykh istochnikov, Gosudarstvennyi istoricheskii Muzei [Department of Written Sources, State Historical Museum in Moscow]

Opisanie	A. F. Shafonskii, comp., *Opisanie morovoi iazvy, byvshei v stolichnom gorode Moskve s 1770, po 1772 god,...* [A Description of the Pestilential Distemper Formerly in the Capital City of Moscow from 1770 to 1772]
ORGBL	Otdel rukopisei, Gosudarstvennaia biblioteka imeni V. I. Lenina [Department of Manuscripts State Lenin Library in Moscow]
OV	*Osmnadtsatyi vek: Istoricheskii sbornik* [The Eighteenth Century: An Historical Collection]
PB	*Pis'ma i bumagi imperatora Petra Velikogo* [Letters and Papers of Emperor Peter the Great]
PPEE	Ia. Rost, ed., *Vysochaishiia sobstvennoruchnyia pis'ma i poveleniia...Imperatritsy Ekateriny Velikiia, k...Petru Dmitrievichu Erapkinu i...ego doneseniia* [Official and Private Letters and Orders of Empress Catherine the Great to Peter Dmitrievich Eropkin, and His Reports]
PROSP	Public Record Office, State Papers (London)
PSZ	*Polnoe sobranie zakonov rossiiskoi imperii* [The Complete Collection of Laws of the Russian Empire]
RBS	*Russkii biograficheskii slovar'* [Russian Biographical Dictionary]
SA	*Senatskii arkhiv* [Senate Archive]
Samoilovich, *IP*	Danilo Samoilovich, *Izbrannye proizvedeniia* [Selected Works of Danilo Samoilovich]
SIRIO	*Sbornik imperatorskogo russkogo istoricheskogo obshchestva* [Collection of the Imperial Russian Historical Society]
SPV	*Sanktpeterburgskie vedomosti* [The St. Petersburg News]
Sytin, *IPZM*	P. V. Sytin, *Istoriia planirovki i zastroiki Moskvy: Materialy i issledovaniia* [A History of the Planning and Building of Moscow: Materials and Researches]
TsGADA	Tsentral'nyi gosudarstvennyi arkhiv drevnikh aktov [Central State Archive of Old Documents in Moscow]
TsGAg.M	Tsentral'nyi gosudarstvennyi arkhiv goroda Moskvy [Central State Archive of the City of Moscow]
TsGIA-SSSR	Tsentral'nyi gosudarstvennyi istoricheskii arkhiv [Central State Historical Archive of the USSR in Leningrad]
ZhA	"Zhurnal Georgiia Fedorovicha Barona fon Asha v Turetskikh pokhodakh s 1768 do 1775 goda" [The Journal of Baron Georg Fedorovich von Asch during the Turkish Campaigns from 1768 to 1775], Manuscript Department, Niedersächsische Staats- und Universitätsbibliothek, Göttingen.

Notes

Introduction

1. Berton Roueché, "Annals of Medicine: A Small, Apprehensive Child," *The New Yorker*, 10 April 1971, pp. 70-90.
2. William P. Reed et al., "Bubonic plague in the Southwestern United States: A review of recent experience," *Medicine* 29 (1970):480.
3. Norman Howard-Jones, "Kitasato, Yersin, and the Plague bacillus," *Clio Medica* 10 (1975):23-27; David J. Bibel and T. H. Chen, "Diagnosis of plague: An analysis of the Yersin-Kitasato controversy," *Bacteriological Reviews* 40 (1976): 633-51.
4. Reed et al., "Bubonic Plague," p. 469.
5. *New York Times*, 18 July 1976, p. 21; *World Health Statistics Report* 30, no. 2 (1977):157; Charles T. Gregg, *Plague!* (New York, 1978), pp. 194-211.
6. H. H. Mitchell, *Plague in the United States: An Assessment of Its Significance as a Problem Following a Thermonuclear War*, RAND Corporation Study (June 1966); Gregg, *Plague!*, pp. 251-56, 260.
7. Geoffrey Marks and William K. Beatty, *Epidemics* (New York, 1976), pp. 6-11; S. H. Blondheim, "The first recorded epidemic of pneumonic plague: The Bible, I Sam. 6," *Bulletin of the History of Medicine* 29 (1955):337-45.
8. Marks and Beatty, *Epidemics*, pp. 19-28; John Scarborough, "Thucydides, Greek medicine, and the plague at Athens: A summary of possibilities," *Episteme* 1 (1970), pp. 77-90.
9. J. -N. Biraben and Jacques Le Goff, "The Plague in the early Middle Ages," in Robert Forster and Orest Ranum, eds., *Biology of Man in History, Selections from the Annales E.S.C.*, vol. 1, trans. Elborg Forster and Patricia M. Ranum (Baltimore and London, 1975), pp. 48-80.
10. K. F. Meyer, "Pasteurella and Francisella," in René J. Dubois and James G. Hirsch, eds., *Bacterial and Mycotic Infections of Man*, 4th ed. (Philadelphia and Montreal, 1965), p. 675.
11. Ibid., p. 670.
12. Thomas Butler, "A clinical study of bubonic plague: Observations of the 1970 Vietnam epidemic, with emphasis on coagulation studies, skin histology, and electrocardiograms," *American Journal of Medicine* 53 (September 1973):274.
13. Ibid., p. 272.
14. Meyer, "Pasteurella," pp. 672-73.
15. Jack D. Poland, "Plague," in Paul D. Hoeprich, ed., *Infectious Diseases: A Guide to the Understanding and Management of Infectious Processes* (New York, 1972), pp. 1145-46.
16. Meyer, "Pasteurella," p. 671.
17. Arthur J. Viseltear, "The pneumonic plague epidemic of 1924 in Los Angeles," *Yale Journal of Biology and Medicine* 47 (1974):40-41.
18. L. F. Hirst, *The Conquest of Plague* (Oxford, 1953), pp. 30-34, 221-33; Robert Pollitzer, "A review of recent literature on plague," *Bulletin of the World Health Organization* 23, nos. 2-3 (1960):347.
19. Poland, "Plague," p. 1145.
20. Hirst, *Conquest of Plague*, p. 30.
21. Reed et al., "Bubonic Plague," pp. 472-80.
22. Hirst, *Conquest of Plague*, p. 175.

23. Ibid., p. 176.
24. Robert Pollitzer and Karl F. Meyer, "The Ecology of Plague," in Jacques M. May, ed., *Studies in Disease Ecology* (New York, 1961), pp. 461, 465.
25. C. Fordham von Reyn et al., "Epidemiologic and clinical features of an outbreak of bubonic plague in New Mexico," *Journal of Infectious Diseases* 136 (1977):492–93.
26. Hirst, *Conquest of Plague*, pp. 221, 262–75; Gregg, *Plague!*, pp. 87–88.
27. Reed et al., "Bubonic Plague," pp. 468–69; Mitchell, *Plague in the United States*, p. 7.
28. Fordham von Reyn et al., "Plague in New Mexico," pp. 491–93.
29. Hirst, *Conquest of Plague*, pp. 239–46; J. R. Busvine, *Insects, Hygiene, and History* (London, 1976), pp. 34–38, 56–57.
30. S. A. Barnett, "Rats," *Scientific American* 216 (January 1967):79.
31. B. S. Vinogradov and A. I. Argiropulo, *Fauna of the U.S.S.R.: Mammals*, trans. Israel Program of Scientific Translation (Jerusalem, 1968), p. 143.
32. Pollitzer and Meyer, "Ecology of Plague," pp. 447–48.
33. Ernst Schwarz, "Classification, origin and distribution of commensal rats," *Bulletin of the World Health Organization* 23, nos. 2–3 (1970):411–16.
34. Pollitzer and Meyer, "Ecology of Plague," p. 452.
35. Thomas Y. Canby, "The Rat: Lapdog of the Devil," *National Geographic* 152 (July 1977):63, 86.
36. Barnett, "Rats," pp. 78–79, 81.
37. Vinogradov and Argiropulo, *Fauna of the U.S.S.R.*, pp. 145–46.
38. Hirst, *Conquest of Plague*, pp. 239–46.
39. Barnett, "Rats," p. 81; Canby, "The Rat," p. 82.
40. J. F. B. Shrewsbury, *A History of Bubonic Plague in the British Isles* (Cambridge, 1970), p. 17.
41. Pollitzer and Meyer, "Ecology of Plague," pp. 444, 454.
42. Shrewsbury, *Plague in the British Isles*, p. 8.
43. Robert Pollitzer, *Plague* (Geneva, 1954), p. 485.
44. G. I. Twigg, "The role of rodents in plague dissemination: A worldwide review," *Mammal Review* 8, no. 3 (1978):89–96.
45. Shrewsbury, *Plague in the British Isles*, p. 4.
46. Hirst, *Conquest of Plague*, pp. 121, 127–29, 147–48.
47. Bibel and Chen, "Diagnosis of Plague," p. 648.
48. See John Norris's response to the criticism of Michael W. Dols, "Geographical origin of the Black Death: Comment," *Bulletin of the History of Medicine* 52 (1978):112–20.

Chapter One

1. Mirko Grmek, "Ancient Slavic medicine," *Journal of the History of Medicine* 14 (1959):21–22; B. A. Larin, *Russko-angliiskii slovar'-dnevik Richarda Dzhemsa (1618–1619 gg.)* (Leningrad, 1959), p. 123.
2. William H. McNeill, *Plagues and Peoples* (Garden City, N.Y., 1976), pp. 13, 105.
3. Arcadius Kahan, "A Catalogue of Epidemics in Russia," unpublished paper (University of Chicago, n.d.), pp. 1–10. The table appended to Jean-Noël Biraben, *Les hommes et la peste en France et dans les pays européens et méditerranéens*, 2 vols. (Paris, 1975–76), 1:426–30, seems based on outdated information from the works of Sticker and Derbek.
4. William H. McNeill, *Europe's Steppe Frontier, 1500–1800* (Chicago, 1964), pp. 8–9.
5. Chronicle reports of epidemics from the tenth century to 1710 are collected in L. F. Zmeev, *Byloe vrachebnoi Rossii*, bk. 1 (St. Petersburg, 1890), pp. 1–30, and 47 discrete epidemics to 1710 are discussed by V. Ekkerman, *Materialy dlia istorii meditsiny v Rossii* (Kazan, 1884). For a table of epidemics and other calamities from 1124 to 1488, see also Lawrence N. Langer, "The Black Death in Russia: Its effects upon urban labor," *Russian History* 2 (1975):59–61.
6. McNeill, *Plagues and Peoples*, pp. 149–69.
7. F. A. Derbek, *Istoriia chumnykh epidemii v Rossii s osnovaniia gosudarstva do nastoiashchago vremeni* (St. Petersburg, 1905), pp. 2–12.
8. Ibid., pp. 12–13; K. G. Vasil'ev and A. E. Segal, *Istoriia epidemii v Rossii* (Moscow, 1960), pp. 21–25.

9. George Vernadsky, *The Mongols and Russia* (New Haven, 1953), pp. 204–5; Elisabeth Carpentier, "Autour de la peste noire: famines et épidémies dans l'histoire du XIVe siècle," *Annales E.S.C.* 6 (1962): 1062–92.
10. Derbek, *Istoriia chumnykh epidemii*, pp. 21–23.
11. Shrewsbury, *Plague in the British Isles*, p. 3.
12. Vasil'ev and Segal, *Istoriia epidemii v Rossii*, p. 20; N. P. Mironov, "The past existence of natural foci of plague in the Steppes of Southern Europe," *Journal of Microbiology, Epidemiology, and Immunobiology* 29, no. 8 (1958):1193–98; V. D. Fyodorov, "The question of the existence of natural foci of plague in Europe in the past," *Journal of Hygiene, Epidemiology, Microbiology, and Immunology* (Prague) 4, no. 2 (1960):135–41; N. I. Kalabukhov, "The structure and changes of the natural foci of plague," *Journal of Microbiology, Epidemiology, and Immunobiology* 32, no. 5 (1961):877–83; V. V. Kucheruk, "Voprosy paleogenezisa prirodnykh ochagov chumy v sviazi s istoriei fauny gryzunov," in *Fauna i ekologiia gryzunov* (Moscow, 1965), pp. 5–86.
13. John Norris, "East or West? The geographic origin of the Black Death," *Bulletin of the History of Medicine* 51 (1977):1–24.
14. *CN*, p. 145.
15. Derbek, *Istoriia chumnykh epidemii*, pp. 14–21; Langer, "Black Death in Russia," pp. 55–57.
16. Gustave Alef, "The crisis of the Muscovite aristocracy: A factor in the growth of monarchical power," *Forschungen zur osteuropäischen Geschichte* 15 (1970):15–58, esp. 37–40.
17. Lawrence N. Langer, "V. L. Ianin and the history of Novgorod," *Slavic Review* 33 (1974):116–17; V. L. Ianin, *Novgorodskie posadniki* (Moscow, 1962), pp. 193–95.
18. Ekkerman, *Materialy*, pp. 50–51; *CN*, pp. 163–90. See also Lawrence N. Langer, "Plague and the Russian countryside: Monastic estates in the late fourteenth and fifteenth centuries," *Canadian-American Slavic Studies* 10 (1976):351–69.
19. M. Iu. Lakhtin, "Bor'ba s epidemiiami v do-Petrovskoi Rusi," *Russkaia starina* 121, no. 2 (1905):415; Russell Zguta, "The ordeal by water (swimming of witches) in the east Slavic world," *Slavic Review* 36 (1977):226.
20. N. A. Bogoiavlenskii, *Meditsina u pervoselov russkogo severa* (Leningrad, 1966), p. 13.
21. Derbek, *Istoriia chumnykh epidemii*, pp. 21–25.
22. Ibid., pp. 26–30; R. E. F. Smith, *Peasant Farming in Muscovy* (Cambridge, 1977), pp. 118, 120.
23. *CN*, p. 196.
24. Vasil'ev and Segal, *Istoriia epidemii v Rossii*, pp. 36–38; Elinor Lieber, "Galen on contaminated cereals as a cause of epidemics," *Bulletin of the History of Medicine* 44 (1970): 332–45.
25. Ekkerman, *Materialy*, pp. 54–55; Langer, "Black Death," pp. 55, 59–61.
26. *CN*, p. 191.
27. N. A. Bogoiavlenskii, *Drevnerusskoe vrachevanie v XI–XVII vv.* (Moscow, 1960), pp. 113, 178, 257–59; idem, *Meditsina u pervoselov*, pp. 78–80.
28. Arcadius Kahan, "Natural Calamities and Their Effect upon the Food Supply in Russia: An Introduction to a Catalogue," *Jahrbücher für Geschichte Osteuropas*, n.s., 16 (1968), pp. 365–66; Friedrich Prinzing, *Epidemics Resulting from Wars* (London, 1916).
29. Derbek, *Istoriia chumnykh epidemii*, pp. 31–33; Vasil'ev and Segal, *Istoriia epidemii v Rossii*, pp. 38–39.
30. Gustaf Utterström, "Climatic fluctuations and population problems in early modern history," *Scandinavian Economic History Review* 3, no. 1 (1955):3–47.
31. Vasil'ev and Segal, *Istoriia epidemi v Rossii*, pp. 39–42; Ekkerman, *Materialy*, pp. 36–41; Bogoiavlenskii, *Drevnerusskoe vrachevanie*, pp. 228–33.
32. Sigismund von Herberstein, *Notes upon Russia*, ed. and trans. R. N. Major, 2 vols. (London, 1851; reprinted New York, 1961), 2:6–7.
33. Bogoiavlenskii, *Drevnerusskoe vrachevanie*, p. 123; R. G. Skrynnikov, *Oprichnyi terror* (Leningrad, 1969), pp. 69–76.
34. Heinrich von Staden, *The Land and Government of Muscovy: A Sixteenth Century Account*, ed. and trans. Thomas Esper (Stanford, 1967), pp. 29, 46.
35. E. Delmar Morgan and C. H. Coote, eds., *Early Voyages and Travels to Russia and Persia by Anthony Jenkinson and Other Englishmen*, 2 vols. (London, 1886; reprinted New York, 1963), 2:337.

36. Derbek, *Istoriia chumnykh epidemii*, pp. 39-40.
37. V. I. Koretskii, *Formirovanie krepostnogo prava i pervaia krest'ianskaia voina v Rossii* (Moscow, 1975), pp. 117-47; Ekkerman, *Materialy*, p. 46; Smith, *Peasant Farming in Muscovy*, pp. 145-47.
38. Vasil'ev and Segal, *Istoriia epidemii v Rossii*, p. 52.
39. *Pskovskaia pervaia letopis'* (St. Petersburg, 1848), p. 333; N. Ia. Novombergskii, comp., *Materialy po istorii meditsiny v Rossii*, 5 vols. (St. Petersburg and Tomsk, 1905-10), 4:15-18.
40. Lakhtin, "Bor'ba s epidemiiami," p. 421; Novombergskii, *Materialy*, 4:161-63; A. S. Podrazhanskii, "Sanitarno-epidemicheskoe sostoianie zapadnykh oblastei Ukrainy za gody mnogovekovogo poraboshcheniia," in B. D. Petrov et al., eds., *Ocherki istorii meditsinskoi nauki i zdravookhraneniia na Ukraine* (Kiev, 1954), p. 184.
41. Samuel H. Baron, ed. and trans., *The Travels of Olearius in Seventeenth-Century Russia* (Stanford, 1967), p. 118.
42. S. M. Solov'ev, *Istoriia Rossii s drevneishikh vremen*, 15 vols. (Moscow, 1959-66), 5: 629-31; "Akty o morovom povetrii, 1654-55 goda," *Dopolneniia k Aktam istoricheskim, sobrannye i isdannye Arkheograficheskoiu Komissieiu*, 12 vols. (St. Petersburg, 1846-72), 3:446.
43. *Letopistsy poslednei chetverti XVII v.* (Moscow, 1968), p. 182.
44. Derbek, *Istoriia chumnykh epidemii*, pp. 46-50.
45. "Skazanie o postroenii obydennago khrama v Vologde 'vo isbavlenie ot smertonosnyia iazvy'," *Ch. OIDR*, 3 (1893), pt. ii:12.
46. Solov'ev, *Istoriia Rossii*, 5:642; Derbek, *Istoriia chumnykh epidemii*, pp. 51-60.
47. E. Zviagintsev, "Chuma v Moskve v XVII i XVIII vv.," *Istoricheskii zhurnal* 2 (1937):55; A. G. Brikner, "Chuma v Moskve v 1654 godu," *Istoricheskii vestnik* 16 (April 1884):17-22; Sytin, *IPZM* 1:112; David H. Miller, "State and City in Seventeenth-Century Muscovy," in Michael F. Hamm, ed., *The City in Russian History* (Lexington, Ky., 1975), p. 42.
48. Tertius Chandler and Gerald Fox, *3000 Years of Urban Growth* (New York, 1974), pp. 160, 162.
49. Derbek, *Istoriia chumnykh epidemii*, p. 54; B. S. Bessmertnyi, "Opyt istoricheskogo analiza epidemii XIV-XVII stoletii," *Zhurnal mikrobiologii, epidemiologii i immunobiologii* 42, no. 5 (1966):154.
50. Hirst, *Conquest of Plague*, p. 34.
51. Gordon M. Weiner, "The demographic effects of the Venetian plagues of 1575-77 and 1630-31," *Genus* 26, no. 1/2 (1970):41-55.
52. "Akty o morovom povetrii," pp. 517-21; Ivan Vas'kov, *Sobranie istoricheskikh izvestii, otnosiashchikhsia do Kostromy* (Moscow, 1792), pp. 62-63.
53. David H. Miller, "City and State in Muscovite Society: Iaroslavl', 1649-99," Ph.D. dissertation, Princeton, 1974, pp. 168-72.
54. Novombergskii, *Materialy*, 4:163-66; Ia. E. Vodarskii, "Chislennost' i razmeshchenie posadskogo naseleniia v Rossii vo vtoroi polovine XVII v.," in N. M. Druzhinin et al., eds., *Goroda feodal'noi Rossii* (Moscow, 1966), pp. 283-86.
55. Novombergskii, *Materialy*, 2:229, 231-48; vol. 4:176-90, 195-96, 224-26, 276-82.
56. Novombergskii, *Materialy*, 4:290-314.
57. Ibid., pp. 302-8, 315-16.
58. Novombergskii, *Materialy*, 3, pt. 2:36-38; vol. 4:315, 317-64.
59. I. N., "Izvestie o byvshei v Astrakhani morovoi iazve v 1692 i 1693 godakh (Pis'mo k izdateliu)," *Vestnik Evropy* 97 (1809):212-16; Novombergskii, *Materialy*, 3, pt. 2:1-8; vol. 4:368-74, 390-93, 400-5, 440; I. D. Kozubenko and M. T. Koveisha, "Iz istorii meditsinskogo obsluzhivaniia v Taganroge," *Sovetskoe zdravookhranenie* 31, no. 6 (1972):68.
60. Derbek, *Istoriia chumnykh epidemii*, pp. 44-69; Eugeniusz Sienkowski, "Dżuma w Gdańsku w 1709 roku: Studium z dziejów epidemiologii," *Archiwum historii medycyny* 33, no. 3/4 (1970):309-401; R. M. Hatton, *Charles XII of Sweden* (London, 1968), pp. 325-26, 328-30, 441, 517.
61. Vasil'ev and Segal, *Istoriia epidemii v Rossii*, pp. 94-95; *PB*, 9:135, 139, 1219, 1374-75; vol. 10:118, 138-39, 146, 173, 202, 211-12; Novombergskii, *Materialy*, 4:438; M. Iu. Lakhtin, *Meditsina i vrachi v Moskovskom gosudarstve v do-Petrovskoi Rusi* (Moscow, 1907), p. 59.
62. *PB*, 10:343-44, 420, 627, 629; vol. 11, pt. 1:160; Derbek, *Istoriia chumnykh epidemii*, p. 72.
63. Isidorus Brennsohn, *Die Aerzte Estlands vom Beginn der historischen Zeit bis zur Gegenwart* (Riga, 1922), pp. 89-93; *PB*, 11, pt. 2:59, 65, 384.

64. S. S. Mikhailov, *Meditsinskaia sluzhba russkogo flota v XVIII veke* (Leningrad, 1957), pp. 186–91.
65. Derbek, *Istoriia chumnykh epidemii*, pp. 74–77.
66. Ibid., pp. 78–80; Mikhailov, *Meditsinskaia sluzhba*, pp. 191–96.
67. A. I. Iukht, "Torgovye sviazi Astrakhani v 20-kh godakh XVIII v.," in *Istoricheskaia geografiia Rossii XII-nachalo XX v.: Sbornik statei k 70-letiiu professora Liubomira Grigor'evicha Beskrovnogo* (Moscow, 1975), pp. 177–92; A. A. Lisitsyn, *Genezis i landshaftno-ekologicheskie osobennosti Volgo-Ural'skogo prirodnogo ochaga chumy*, diss. abstract (Saratov, 1973), pp. 15–17.
68. Mikhailov, *Meditsinskaia sluzhba*, pp. 206–13.
69. Gov. Ivan von Mengden (Astrakhan) to Supreme Privy Council, 5 September 1727, *SIRIO*, 69:368–69.
70. Col. Savenkov (Tsaritsyn) to Council, 17 January 1728; Mengden to Council, 3 May 1728, *SIRIO*, 79:61, 488–89.
71. Mengden to Council, 24 June and 3 July 1728, *SIRIO*, 84:229, 559–60.
72. Derbek, *Istoriia chumnykh epidemii*, pp. 82–86; Mengden to Council, 28 August 1728; Council order, 13 June 1729, *SIRIO*, 84:561–64; vol. 94:765–66.
73. Derbek, *Istoriia chumnykh epidemii*, p. 84; Vasil'ev and Segal, *Istoriia epidemii v Rossii*, p. 104.
74. N. B. Golikova, *Astrakhanskoe vosstanie 1705–1706 gg.* (Moscow, 1975), pp. 62–63; Chandler and Fox, *3000 Years*, p. 160.
75. Claudius Rondeau to Lord Harrington, 25 November 1738, *SIRIO*, 80:395; *Kabardino-Russkie otnosheniia v XVI–XVIII vv.*, 2 vols. (Moscow, 1957), 2:92, 95; Georg Sticker, *Abhandlungen aus der Seuchengeschichte und Seuchenlehre*, vol. 1: *Die Pest*, pt. 1: *Die Geschichte der Pest* (Giessen, 1908), p. 239.
76. Kahan, "Natural Calamities," p. 372; C. H. von Manstein, *Contemporary Memoirs of Russia from the Year 1727 to 1744* (London, 1856; reprinted London, 1968), pp. 184, 191; Solov'ev, *Istoriia Rossii*, 10:424–25; Gustaf Utterström, "Some population problems in pre-industrial Sweden," *Scandinavian Economic History Review* 2, no. 2 (1954):121, 132.
77. Ia. A. Chistovich, "Morovaia iazva 1738 goda (po offitsiial'nym istochnikam)," *Voenno-meditsinskii zhurnal* 127 (September 1876):72, 74; Manstein, *Contemporary Memoirs*, pp. 184, 192; Solov'ev, *Istoriia Rossii*, 10:437–39.
78. Cabinet of Ministers to Münnich, 20 March 1738, *SIRIO*, 120:243.
79. Wilhelm M. Richter, *Geschichte der Medicin in Russland*, 3 vols. (Moscow, 1813–17; reprinted Leipzig, 1965), 3:325.
80. Manstein, *Contemporary Memoirs*, pp. 216–17; Rondeau to Harrington, 7 October 1738, *SIRIO*, 80:370.
81. Johann Jacob Lerche, *Lebens- und Reise-Geschichte von ihm selbst Geschrieben, und mit Anmerkungen und Züsatzen herausgegeben von Dr. Anton Friedrich Büsching* (Halle, 1791), pp. 138, 141, 146, 155; Egidi's report from Izium, 19 August 1738, *SIRIO*, 124:231–32; Richter, *Medicin in Russland*, 3:236.
82. Lerche, *Lebens- und Reise-Geschichte*, pp. 149, 152–54, 169–76, 183; D. I. Bagalei and D. P. Miller, *Istoriia goroda Khar'kova za 250 let ego sushchestvovaniia* (Khar'kov, 1905), 1:189; Solov'ev, *Istoriia Rossii*, 10:440; Kahan, "Natural Calamities," p. 372.
83. Cabinet of Ministers to Shipov and Trubetskoi, 1 July and 12 September 1738, *SIRIO*, 124:1–13, 229, 305–6; Lerche, *Lebens- und Reise-Geschichte*, pp. 142, 154; Chistovich, "Morovaia iazva 1738 goda," pp. 84, 96, 99; *SIRIO*, 138:541; War Collegium to Senate, 4 August 1740, *SA*, 2:41.
84. V. D. Otamanovskii, "Do istorii meditsini ta apteknoi spravi u Vinnitsi i Vinnits'komu poviti 2. polovini XVIII st.," *Zbirnik pam'iati Akademika Teofil Gavrilovicha Ianovs'kogo*, Vseukrains'ka Akademiia nauk, ed. D. Zabolotnyi et al. (Kiev, 1930), p. 324; Sticker, *Abhandlungen*, 1, pt. 1:246–49.
85. Sticker, *Abhandlungen*, 1, pt. 1:241–52.
86. *SA*, 13:46–47, 92, 102, 114, 128.
87. P. S. Saltykov to C., 23 May 1767, TsGADA, f. 16, d. 328, pt. 1:2–2v.
88. *SA*, 11:322.
89. *SA*, 13:57–58, 66–67.
90. Max Vasmer, *Russisches Etymologisches Wörterbuch*, 3 vols. (Heidelberg, 1950–58), 3:354–55.

91. V. M. Kabuzan, *Zaselenie Novorossii* (Moscow, 1976), pp. 101–19, 276.

92. B. B. Kafengauz, *Ocherki vnutrennego rynka Rossii pervoi poloviny XVIII v.* (Moscow, 1958), pp. 287–317.

93. *PSZ*, 16: no. 12,201 (7 July 1764).

94. Lawrence N. Langer, "The Russian Medieval Town," in Hamm, ed., *The City in Russian History*, pp. 20, 26, 30; Carsten Goehrke, *Die Wüstungen in der Moskauer Rus'* (Wiesbaden, 1968), pp. 65–78, 159–74; Henry L. Eaton, "Decline and recovery of the Russian cities from 1500 to 1700," *Canadian-American Slavic Studies* 11 (1977):220–52.

95. Lomonosov to I. I. Shuvalov, 1 November 1761, in M. V. Lomonosov, *Polnoe sobranie sochinenii*, ed. S. I. Vavilov et al., 10 vols. (Moscow and Leningrad, 1950–57), 6:397–98.

96. Quoted by Bogoiavlenskii, *Meditsina u pervoselov*, p. 72.

97. Carlo M. Cipolla, *Cristofano and the Plague* (Berkeley and Los Angeles, 1973), p. 23.

98. Patriarkh Nikon, *Pouchenie o morovoi iazve* (Moscow, 1655), p. 7v.

99. Lakhtin, "Bor'ba s epidemiiami," pp. 415–18; N. Ia. Novombergskii, *Vrachebnoe stroenie do-Petrovskoi Rusi* (Tomsk, 1907), pp. 321–22, 361–63; Langer, "Black Death," p. 58.

100. Michael W. Dols, *The Black Death in the Middle East* (Princeton, 1977), pp. 109–21.

101. Cabinet of Ministers to Trubetskoi, 8 October 1738, *SIRIO*, 124:316.

102. Novombergskii, *Vrachebnoe stroenie*, pp. 318–23.

103. Carlo M. Cipolla, *Public Health and the Medical Profession in the Renaissance* (Cambridge, 1976), ch. 2.

104. Novombergskii, *Vrachebnoe stroenie*, pp. 324–38.

105. P. E. Zabludovskii, "Razvitie ucheniia o zaraznykh bolezniakh i kniga Frakastoro," in K. M. Bykov, ed., *Dzhirolamo Frakastoro, O kontagii, kontagioznykh bolezniakh i lechenii* (Moscow, 1954), pp. 192–93.

106. "Akty o morovom povetrii," p. 452.

107. Staden, *Land and Government*, p. 40. For social reactions and precautions in Europe, see Biraben, *Les hommes et la peste*, 2:7–185.

108. Staden, *Land and Government*, p. 29.

109. Vasil'ev and Segal, *Istoriia epidemii v Rossii*, p. 78; Cabinet of Ministers' decisions, 19 May and 11 July 1740, *SIRIO*, 138:525–26; vol. 146:259–60; *PSZ*, 8: no. 5, 333 (12 September 1728); Cabinet of Ministers to Shipov, 21 September 1738, *SIRIO*, 124:251–52.

110. Novombergskii, *Vrachebnoe stroenie*, pp. 334, 339, 343–48, 353–55; Lakhtin, "Bor'ba s epidemiiami," 422, 424–26.

111. *PSZ*, 8: no. 5, 333 (12 September 1728); Derbek, *Istoriia chumnykh epidemii*, pp. 80–82.

112. John T. Alexander, "Communicable disease, anti-epidemic policies, and the role of medical professionals in Russia, 1725–62," *Canadian-American Slavic Studies* 12 (1978): 154–69.

113. "Instruktsiia Slobodskoi Ukrainskoi gubernii komisaram 1766 goda," in D. I. Bagalei, comp., *Materialy dlia istorii kolonizatsii i byta Khar'kovskoi i otchasti Kurskoi i Voronezhskoi gubernii* (Khar'kov, 1890), pp. 314–15.

114. Chistovich, "Morovaia iazva 1738 goda," pp. 73, 81–83, 86–96, 98–99; Cabinet of Ministers to Shipov, 30 July 1738, *SIRIO*, 124:102; Lerche, *Lebens- und Reise-Geschichte*, pp. 153–54.

115. Egidi's report of 19 August 1738, *SIRIO*, 124:231–32; John Cook, *Voyages and Travels through the Russian Empire, Tartary, and Part of the Kingdom of Persia*, 2 vols. (Edinburgh, 1770), 1:249–50, 265–69.

116. Chistovich, "Morovaia iazva 1738 goda," pp. 98–99; Richter, *Medicin in Russland*, 3:240–46, 257–58, 583–87; D. M. Rossiiskii, *Istoriia vseobshchei i otechestvennoi meditsiny i zdravookhraneniia: Bibliografiia (996–1954 gg.)* (Moscow, 1956), p. 407; Medical Chancery to Cabinet of Ministers, 24 March and 28 May 1739, *SIRIO*, 126:281, 511; Medical Chancery to Cabinet of Ministers, 7–9 March 1740, *SIRIO*, 138:197–98; Lerche, *Lebens- und Reise-Geschichte*, p. 155.

117. Vasil'ev and Segal, *Istoriia epidemii v Rossii*, pp. 114–15; *SA*, 9:144; Kozubenko and Koveisha, "Iz istorii," p. 71; Ia. A. Chistovich, *Istoriia pervykh meditsinskikh shkol v Rossii* (St. Petersburg, 1883), pp. 615–16; *Opisanie del arkhiva morskogo ministerstva za vremias poloviny XVII do nachala XIX stoletiia*, 10 vols. (St. Petersburg, 1877–1906), 7:126; *SA*, 9:607; Mikhailov, *Meditsinskaia sluzhba*, pp. 198–200.

118. Senate and Medical Collegium correspondence, 1750, 1754-55, 1765, 1770, TsGADA, f. 16, d. 328, pt. 1:228-38; f. 344, op. 1, bk. 43:42-53v; *SA*, 9:271-73, 298-300; vol. 14:239-40, 353-55; Medical Collegium to Senate, 31 December 1765, TsGADA, f. 344, op. 1, bk. 43: 34-37; *PSZ*, 14: no. 10,365 (22 February 1755).

119. *SA*, 13:66-67, 91, 104.

120. Poletika to Medical Collegium, 13 November 1765, TsGADA, f. 344, op. 1, bk. 43: 38-41.

121. Chistovich, *Istoriia*, app. 10:258-66; some of the original documents are now in TsGADA, f. 16, d. 322, pt. 1:272-96.

Chapter Two

1. *Tabeli k otchetu Ministerstva vnutrennikh del za 1803 god* (St. Petersburg, 1804), table N. The figure for 1700 is a rough estimate derived from Brückner, Palkin, Novombergskii, and Richter.

2. Heinz Müller-Dietz, *Der russische Militärarzt im 18. Jahrhundert* (Berlin, 1970), pp. 50-54, 65-72.

3. Cipolla, *Public Health and the Medical Profession*, pp. 70, 74-76; Lester S. King, *The Medical World of the Eighteenth Century* (Chicago, 1958), ch. 1-2.

4. D. M. Rossiiskii, *200 let meditsinskogo fakul'teta Moskovskogo gosudarstvennogo universiteta* (Moscow, 1955), pp. 39-42.

5. Alexander Brückner, *Die Aerzte in Russland bis zum Jahre 1800* (St. Petersburg, 1887), pp. 39-43, 68-69.

6. For a listing of degrees, assignments, service tenure, and salaries of thirty-nine doctors under the Medical Chancery in 1763, see John T. Alexander, "Medical professionals and public health in 'doldrums' Russia (1725-62)," *Canadian-American Slavic Studies*, 12 (1978):133-35.

7. Brückner, *Die Aerzte*, pp. 64-69; Gregory L. Freeze, *The Russian Levites* (Cambridge, Mass., 1977), pp. 52-53, 207-8.

8. Richter, *Medicin in Russland*, 2:416-40; vol. 3:177-97, 210-12, 297-302, 494-508; John T. Alexander, "Medical developments in Petrine Russia," *Canadian-American Slavic Studies* 8, no. 2 (1974):218-21; and idem, "Medical professionals in 'doldrums' Russia, pp. 120-21.

9. B. N. Palkin, *Russkie gospital'nye shkoly XVIII veka i ikh vospitanniki* (Moscow, 1959), p. 3.

10. Mikhailov, *Meditsinskaia sluzhba*, p. 24.

11. S. A. Semeka, *Meditsinskoe obespechenie russkoi armii vo vremia Semiletnei voiny 1756–1763 gg.* (Moscow, 1951), p. 196; Ia. A. Chistovich, "Vrachebnyi personal russkikh armii v Turetskuiu voinu 1769-1774 godov," *Protokoly zasedanii obshchestva russkikh vrachei v S. Peterburge za 1877–1878 god* (St. Petersburg, 1877), pp. 64-65.

12. Cipolla, *Public Health and the Medical Profession*, pp. 79-86; Jean-Pierre Goubert, "The extent of medical practice in France around 1780," *Journal of Social History* 10 (1977): 410-27; *Malades et médecins en Bretagne, 1770–1790* (Rennes, 1974), pp. 78-100, 468-84.

13. Isidorus Brennsohn, *Die Aerzte Livlands von den ältesten Zeiten bis zur Gegenwart* (Mitau and Riga, 1905), pp. 68-70, 447-48; idem, *Die Aerzte Estlands*, pp. 378-80; idem, *Die Aerzte Kurlands vom Beginn der herzoglichen Zeit bis zur Gegenwart*, 2nd rev. ed. (Riga, 1929), pp. 462-64.

14. B. N. Palkin, *Ocherki istorii meditsiny i zdravookhraneniia zapadnoi Sibiri i Kazakhstana v period prisoedineniia k Rossii (1716–1868)* (Novosibirsk, 1967), pp. 21-22, 33-34, 43, 50, 74, 83-84.

15. Richter, *Medicin in Russland*, 2: app. 59, 171-75.

16. Chistovich, *Istoriia*, pp. 1-3, 467-76; Novombergskii, *Vrachebnoe stroenie*, pp. 87-92.

17. Chistovich, *Istoriia*, app. 10:202-5; S. M. Troitskii, *Russkii absoliutizm i dvoriantsvo v XVIII v.: formirovanie biurokratii* (Moscow, 1974), p. 171; V. V. Fursenko, "Delo o Lestoke 1748 goda," *Zhurnal Ministerstva narodnogo prosveshcheniia*, n.s., 38, no. 4 (1912):185-247.

18. Chistovich, *Istoriia*, pp. 85-95, 266-82, 477-507; app. 10:233-35.

19. C., *Sochineniia*, 12:135-36, 263-64, 466.

20. [J. J. Lerche], "Pro-memoria Meditsinskoi kantseliarii," 5 February 1763; idem, plan of Medical Chancery (1763); idem, "Pribavlenie o sposobakh k priumnozheniiu v Rossiiskoi im-

perii osoblivo zh dlia upotrebleniia k voinskoi sluzhbe iskushnykh lekarei" (1763), TsGADA, f. 16, d. 322, pt. 1:140–51.

21. Anon., critique of Medical Chancery, 1763, ibid., pp. 165–68.

22. [A. I. Cherkassov and G. N. Teplov?], "O meditsinskoi kantseliarii," 18 October 1763, ibid., pp. 153–64.

23. *PSZ*, 16: no. 11,964, no. 11,965 (12 November 1763); no. 12,179 (9 June 1764).

24. Chistovich, *Istoriia*, pp. 508–11; app. 10:206, 248–49; Arnold Buchholz, *Die Göttinger Russlandsammlungen Georgs von Asch: Ein Museum der russischen Wissenschaftsgeschichte des 18. Jahrhunderts* (Giessen, 1961), p. 29.

25. Cherkassov to C., 1 May 1764, 1 September 1765, 1 January 1766; Cherkassov to G. N. Teplov, 2 March 1767; Cherkassov to C., March 1768, TsGADA, f. 16, d. 322, pt. 1:197, 226–27, 309, 316.

26. C. to Cherkassov [1766], ibid., pp. 236–36v.; Ia. A. Chistovich, *Ocherki iz istorii russkikh meditsinskikh uchrezhdenii XVIII stoletiia* (St. Petersburg, 1870), pp. 201–9.

27. Chistovich, *Istoriia*, app. 10:243–46, 260–65.

28. C. to Z. G. Chernyshev, N. I. Chicherin, and G. N. Teplov, 19 September 1768, TsGADA, f. 16, d. 322, pt. 1: 315.

29. [Cherkassov and Teplov], "O Meditsinskoi kantseliarii," 18 October 1763, ibid., p. 158.

30. Alexander, "Medical developments," p. 207.

31. *The Unknown Drawings of Nicholas Bidloo, Director of the First Hospital in Russia*, intro. by David Willemse (Voorburg, 1975), pp. 27–32, 50.

32. A. N. Alelekov and N. I. Iakimov, *Istoriia Moskovskogo voennogo gospitalia v sviazi s istorieiu meditsiny v Rossii* (Moscow, 1907), pp. 98, 345–60, 366–72.

33. Alexander, "Medical developments," pp. 208–9, 219–220, and "Medical professionals in 'doldrums' Russia."

34. Alelekov and Iakimov, *Istoriia*, pp. 214, 277–80, 302, 309–11, 373–75, 397–400; Palkin, *Russkie gospital'nye shkoly*, pp. 21, 27–31.

35. Alelekov and Iakimov, *Istoriia*, pp. 90–94, 168–70, 173, 317, 374, 376–83; Palkin, *Russkie gospital'nye shkoly*, pp. 37–38, 46, 56; S. V. Shershavkin, *Istoriia otechestvennoi sudebno-meditsinskoi sluzhby* (Moscow, 1968), pp. 31–72.

36. Palkin, *Russkie gospital'nye shkoly*, pp. 3, 15–18, 30, 52; M. Iu. Lakhtin, *Etiudy po istorii meditsiny* (Moscow, 1902), p. 112.

37. Alelekov and Iakimov, *Istoriia*, pp. 91–92, 103, 112–14, 146, 175, 209–14, 277, 280, 294, 376, 412; Chistovich, *Istoriia*, pp. 47, 116, 252–56, 291, 329.

38. Chistovich, *Istoriia*, p. 117.

39. Ibid., pp. 117–20; app. 10: 254–58; N. Kulibin, in *RBS*, 14:174–76; Alelekov and Iakimov, *Istoriia*, pp. 415–22; S. M. Grombakh, "Petr Ivanovich Pogoretskii (1740–1780) i ego bor'ba za samostoiatel'nost' russkoi meditsinskoi shkoly," *Trudy Instituta istorii estestvoznaniia i tekhniki*, vol. 4: *Istoriia biologicheskikh nauk* (Moscow, 1955):290–314; Palkin, *Russkie gospital'nye shkoly*, pp. 84–85, 225–26; C. to P. S. Saltykov, 16 November 1768, "Pis'ma imperatritsy Ekateriny velikoi k fel'dmarshalu grafu Petru Semenovichu Saltykovu, 1762–1771," *Russkii arkhiv*, bk. 3 (1886):74.

40. Novombergskii, *Vrachebnoe stroenie*, p. 235; Palkin, *Russkie gospital'nye shkoly*, pp. 4–6, 30–31, 48, 55–58, 97, 110, 121, 153, 188.

41. Mirko Grmek, "The History of Medical Education in Russia," in C. D. O'Malley, ed., *The History of Medical Education* (Berkeley, 1970), pp. 303–10.

42. Ibid., p. 306.

43. D. M. Rossiiskii, *200 let meditsinskogo fakul'teta*, pp. 8–36; N. A. Penchko, comp., and G. A. Novitskii, ed., *Dokumenty i materialy po istorii Moskovskogo universiteta vtoroi poloviny XVIII veka*, 3 vols. (Moscow, 1960–63), 1:288–89, 293, 332–33, 340–41, 350, 353–54, 385–86; vol. 2: 6–9, 137, 143, 168–70, 172–73, 183, 311–12; vol. 3: 124, 178, 180–82, 192, 207–8, 225–26, 242, 256, 337, 357, 381, 400. Chistovich, *Istoriia*, app. 10: 121–22, 169–70, 177, 356–61.

44. Rossiiskii, *200 let meditsinskogo fakul'teta*, pp. 23–24.

45. Grmek, "Medical Education in Russia," pp. 310–11.

46. Alexander, "Medical Developments," pp. 204–5; Nicholas Hans, "Russian students at Leyden in the 18th century," *Slavonic and East European Review* 35, no. 85 (1957): 555–56.

47. Palkin, *Russkie gospital'nye shkoly*, pp. 94–97; Hans, "Russian students," pp. 556–57.

48. Heinz E. Müller-Dietz, "Die Anfänge der Stadtphysikats in Moskau und St. Petersburg," *Sudhoffs Archiv* 60 (1976):194-206.
49. Chistovich, *Istoriia*, pp. 554-58; Palkin, *Russkie gospital'nye shkoly*, pp. 171-72.
50. Alelekov and Iakimov, *Istoriia*, p. 430.
51. *PSZ*, 16: no. 11,965 (12 November 1763); no. 12,017 (19 January 1764); no. 12,174 (5 June 1764).
52. Lomonosov, *Polnoe sobranie sochinenii*, 6:396-97.
53. Ibid., pp. 388-91.
54. Richter, *Medicin in Russland*, 3:337-38; Chistovich, *Istoriia*, pp. 317, 339; app. 10:206-7, 356-61; idem, *Ocherki*, pp. 128-84; S. M. Grombakh, *Russkaia meditsinskaia literatura XVIII veka* (Moscow, 1953), p. 81.
55. P. M. Maikov, *Ivan Ivanovich Betskoi: opyt ego biografii* (St. Petersburg, 1904), pp. 111-30, 143.
56. *Nakaz imperatritsy Ekateriny II, dannyi kommissii o sochinenii proekta novago ulozheniia*, ed. N. D. Chechulin (St. Petersburg, 1907), p. 77 (art. 266).
57. *SIRIO*, 43:215-17.
58. *SIRIO*, 43:362; V. N. Bochkarev, "Vrachebnoe delo i narodnoe prizrenie v Rossii XVIII veka: po materialam Zakonodatel'noi komissii 1767 goda," *Sbornik statei v chest' Matveia Kuz'micha Liubavskago* (Petrograd, 1917), pp. 445-68, 479-82.
59. M. T. Beliavskii, "Novye dokumenty ob obsuzhdenii krest'ianskogo voprosa v 1766-1768 godakh," *Arkheograficheskii ezhegodnik za 1958 god* (Moscow, 1960), pp. 397, 423-24; Bochkarev, "Vrachebnoe delo," pp. 466-68.
60. *SIRIO*, 43:7.
61. Bochkarev, "Vrachebnoe delo," p. 455; *SIRIO*, 43:331.
62. *PSZ*, 18: no. 13,045 (10 January 1768).
63. Chistovich, *Istoriia*, app. 10:192-93.
64. Ibid., pp. 560-68; Solov'ev, *Istoriia Rossii*, 13:236-37; Palkin, *Russkie gospital'nye shkoly*, pp. 47-48, 173; A. M. Kopylov, "Iz istorii pervykh bol'nits Peterburga," *Sovetskoe zdravookhranenie* 21, no. 2 (1962):59.
65. Lerche and Chemnitser to Medical Collegium, 8 August 1766, TsGADA, f. 16, d. 322, pt. 1:263-68v.
66. *Nakaz Ekateriny II*, 77.
67. Palkin, *Russkie gospital'nye shkoly*, p. 44.
68. Grombakh, *Russkaia meditsinskaia literatura*, p. 87; Alexander Radishchev, *A Journey from St. Petersburg to Moscow*, ed. Roderick P. Thaler, trans. Leo Wiener (Cambridge, Mass., 1958), pp. 126-28, 131-32.
69. V. O. Gubert, *Ospa i ospoprivivanie*, vol. 1: *Istoricheskii ocherk do XIX stoletiia* (St. Petersburg, 1896), pp. 195-96; Vasil'ev and Segal, *Istoriia epidemii v Rossii*, pp. 169-71.
70. C., *Sochinenia*, 12:42-45, 58, 203, 230, 280; C. to N. I. Panin, 5, 8-9, and 15 May 1768, *SIRIO*, 10:290-94; C. to Friedrich II, 5 December 1768, *SIRIO*, 20:246-48; C. to P. S. Saltykov, 31 May, 27 October, and 9 November 1768, "Pis'ma Saltykovu," pp. 69, 72-74; C. to Voltaire, 6 December 1768, in A. Lentin, ed., *Voltaire and Catherine the Great: Selected Correspondence* (Cambridge, 1974), pp. 52-55; David L. Ransel, *The Politics of Catherinian Russia: The Panin Party* (New Haven and London, 1975), pp. 176-77.
71. Gubert, *Ospa i ospoprivivanie*, pp. 187-91.
72. D. M. Rossiiskii, *Istoriia*, p. 366.
73. Vasil'ev and Segal, *Istoriia epidemii v Rossii*, p. 172; Grombakh, *Russkaia meditsinskaia literatura*, pp. 80-81, 86.
74. John B. Blake, *Public Health in the Town of Boston, 1630–1822* (Cambridge, Mass., 1959), pp. 52-73 et passim.
75. W. J. Bishop, "Thomas Dimsdale, M.D., F.R.S. (1712-1800), and the Inoculation of Catherine the Great of Russia," *Annals of Medical History*, n.s., vol. 4, no. 4 (1932):321-26.
76. Ibid., pp. 327-36; Vasil'ev and Segal, *Istoriia epidemii v Rossii*, pp. 172-75; C. to Saltykov, 9 December 1768, "Pis'ma Saltykovu," p. 75.
77. Hirst, *Conquest of Plague*, pp. 67, 73-75; Richter, *Medicin in Russland*, 3:245-46.
78. L. G. Beskrovnyi, *Russkaia armiia i flot v XVIII veke* (Moscow, 1958), pp. 304-8, 385-97; [Catherine II], "Dopolnenie k instruktsii v voennuiu kommissiiu," 9 November 1762, TsGADA, f. 16, d. 322, pt. 1:139-39v.

79. Alelekov and Iakimov, *Istoriia,* pp. 396–99, 424–39; Cook, *Voyages and Travels,* 2:200–2, 532–33.
80. Müller-Dietz, *Der russische Militärarzt,* pp. 58, 69–71, 76–78.
81. *PSZ,* 16: no. 11,965 (12 November 1763).
82. [Z. G. Chernyshev, A. I. Cherkassov, and G. N. Teplov], "Uchrezhdenie o meditsinskikh sluzhiteliakh," 26 November 1765, TsGADA, f. 16, d. 322, pt. 1:209–25v.
83. Richard Ungermann, *Der Russisch-Türkische Krieg 1768–1774* (Vienna and Leipzig, 1906), pp. 31–32; army assignments, December 1768, in P. K. Fortunatov, ed., *P. A. Rumiantsev,* vol. 2:*1768–1775* (Moscow, 1953), pp. 39–43.
84. Chistovich, "Vrachebnyi personal," p. 67.
85. G. Asch to Medical Collegium, 16 January and 1 May 1769, the latter acknowledging receipt of the collegium's order of 24 March 1769:ZhA.
86. First army assignments, 14 August 1769, *P. A. Rumiantsev,* 2:122–27.
87. G. Asch, journal entries, 11 May, 11 July, 17 August, 17 September, 1 October, 15 October, 26 October, 29 October, 12 November, 19 December 1769; 1 March, 5 March 1770, ZhA.
88. Asch to P. A. Rumiantsev, 29 October 1769, ZhA.
89. C. to Rumiantsev, 13 August 1769; Rumiantsev to N. I. Panin, 18 September 1769; Rumiantsev to Catherine, 22 September, 26 September, 1 October, and 4 October 1769, *P. A. Rumiantsev,* 2:119, 142–47, 150–53.
90. Rumiantsev to C., 18 November 1769, ibid., pp. 182–83.
91. War Collegium to Medical Collegium, 6 December 1770, referring to Rumiantsev's request of 1 December 1769 and Panin's of April 1770, TsGADA, f. 344, op. 1, bk. 44:411v.
92. War Collegium to Rumiantsev, 18 December 1769, *P. A. Rumiantsev,* 2:202–9.
93. P. I. Panin to Medical Collegium, 3 April 1770; C. Dahl to Medical Collegium, 24 March, 14 April, 30 May, 11 June 1770; Medical Collegium order, 27 June 1770, TsGADA, f. 344, op. 1, bk. 44:52–53, 55, 59, 68, 72–83.
94. Erik Amburger, *Beiträge zur Geschichte der deutsch-russischen kulturellen Beziehungen* (Giessen, 1961), p. 37; G. Asch to Medical Collegium, 17 June, 15 July 1770, ZhA.
95. List of fourteen students promoted to surgeon's mate at Petersburg General Infantry Hospital, 18 February 1771, TsGADA, f. 344, op. 1, bk. 43:687; P. I. Panin to Medical Collegium, 21 July 1770; War Collegium to Medical Collegium, 6 December 1770, TsGADA, f. 344, op. 1, bk. 44:93, 404–11; G. Asch to Medical Collegium, 23 May 1770, ZhA.

Chapter Three

1. See G. Teplov's list of Catherine's domestic achievements through 1769, *SIRIO,* 2:275–83.
2. C., *Sochineniia,* 12:39, 42–45, 55, 92, 141–42, 151, 169, 328–35.
3. Marc Raeff, "The domestic policies of Peter III and his overthrow," *American Historical Review* 75 (1969–70):1302–3.
4. C. to Voltaire, 6 October 1771, *SIRIO,* 13:176.
5. *O Vremia!* in C., *Sochineniia,* 1:3–48.
6. John Parkinson, *A Tour of Russia, Siberia, and the Crimea, 1792–1794,* ed. W. Collier (London, 1971), pp. 41, 102.
7. Jacob Friedrich Bielfeld, *Institutions politiques,* 2 vols. (La Haye, 1760), 1:259; Johann Heinrich Gottlob von Justi, *Die Grundfeste zu der Macht und Glückseligkeit der Staaten,* 2 vols. (Königsberg and Leipzig, 1760–61), 1:316, 341–43. The Russian translations are *Nastavleniia politicheskiia Barona Bilfelda,* trans. F. Shakhovskoi and A. Barsov, 2 vols. (Moscow, 1768–75); and I. G. G. Iusti, *Osnovanie sily i blagosostoianiia tsarstv, ili podrobnoe nachertanie vsekh znanii kasaiushchikhsia do gosudarstvennogo blagochiniia,* trans. I. Bogaevskii, 4 vols. (St. Petersburg, 1772–78).
8. Sytin, *IPZM,* 2:196, 221; V. L. Snegirev, *Moskovskie slobody* (Moscow, 1956), pp. 33–34.
9. N. A. Skvortsov, ed., *Materialy po Moskve i Moskovskoi eparkhii za XVIII vek,* 2 vols. (Moscow, 1911–14), 2:618, 799–800. The number of parishes in 1771 is from a Moscow consistory report of 4 April, TsGIA-SSSR, f. 796, op. 52, d. 107:15.
10. K. V. Sivkov, "Nakaz zhitelei Moskvy deputatu Komissii 1767 g. i zakonodatel'naia deiatel'nost' imp. Ekateriny II v 60–80-kh godakh XVIII v.," *Uchenye zapiski Moskovskogo gos. ped. inst. im. Lenina,* 60, fasc. 2 (1949):193–222.

11. For a translation and commentary, see Fr.-X. Coquin, "Un document d'histoire sociale: Le cahier de doléances de la ville de Moscou (printemps 1767)," *Revue historique* 245 (1971):19–46.

12. William Coxe, *Travels in Poland, Russia, Sweden, and Denmark,* 5 vols. (5th ed.; London, 1802), 1:277, 281.

13. Giacomo Casanova, *History of My Life,* trans. W. Trask, 12 vols. (New York, 1966–71), 10:128–29.

14. "Nakaz ot zhitelei goroda Moskvy," arts. 15, 17, *SIRIO,* 93:125–26.

15. Coxe, *Travels,* 1:283–84.

16. Wolfgang Knackstedt, *Moskau: Studien zur Geschichte einer mittelalterlichen Stadt* (Wiesbaden, 1975).

17. S. V. Bakhrushin et al., eds., *Istoriia Moskvy,* 6 vols. (Moscow, 1952–59), 2:429–33, 448–55.

18. F. A. Thesby de Belcour, *Relation ou Journal d'un officier françois au service de la confédération de Pologne, pris par les russes et rélegué en Sibérie* (Amsterdam, 1776), p. 213.

19. John Andrews, *A Collection of Plans of the Capital Cities of Europe, and Some Remarkable Cities in Asia, Africa, and America,* 2 vols. (London, 1771), 2:102.

20. Sytin, *IPZM,* 1:283.

21. E. A. Zviagintsev, "Rost naseleniia v Moskovskikh slobodakh XVIII veka," *Moskovskii krai v ego proshlom,* pt. 2 (Moscow, 1930), pp. 136, 139.

22. Sytin, *IPZM,* 1:100–4, 203–4, 304–5, 316–17, 356; vol. 2:36, 52, 126.

23. V. I. Tsalkin, "Nekotorye itogi izucheniia kostnykh ostatkov zhivotnykh iz raskopok Moskvy," in N. N. Voronin and M. G. Rabinovich, eds., *Drevnosti Moskovskogo kremlia,* Materialy i issledovaniia po arkheologii SSSR, no. 167 (Moscow, 1971), pp. 164–85, discusses no animals smaller than pigs, unfortunately.

24. Sytin, *IPZM,* 1:18–22; vol. 2:387; M. P. Kudriavtsev, "Ispol'zovanie rel'efa mestnosti v russkom gradostroitel'stve na primere Moskvy XVII v.," *Arkhitekturnoe nasledstvo,* 21 (1973):3–13.

25. "Vybrannomu...ot glavnoi politsii deputatu Nakaz...," arts. 350–55, *SIRIO,* 43:353–54; Sivkov, "Nakaz zhitelei Moskvy," pp. 209–12.

26. Arts. 6–7, *SIRIO,* 93:122.

27. Pollitzer, *Plague,* pp. 283, 286–90; Barnett, "Rats," pp. 78–81; Vinogradov and Argiropulo, *Fauna of the USSR,* pp. 143, 145–46.

28. Sytin, *IPZM,* 2:53.

29. Pollitzer, *Plague,* p. 288; Barnett, "Rats," pp. 79, 81.

30. Sytin, *IPZM,* 2:22, 28, 52, 76, 108, 521.

31. "1753–1754 gg. O myshakh v Moskovskom Poteshnom dvortse i o pokupke dlia ikh istrebleniia koshek i pastei," *Ch.OIDR,* bk. 2 (1902), *smes;*:45–46.

32. C., *Sochineniia,* 12:328.

33. Ivan Rost, *Razsuzhdenie o pronitsatel'nom deistvii maleishikh chastits, kotoryia iz tel, osoblivo zhivotnykh, proistekaiut,* trans. from Latin (Moscow, 1765), pp. 3–23.

34. Art. 5, *SIRIO,* 93:121–22.

35. TsGADA, f. 199, d. 367, p. 226; Joseph Marshall, *Travels through Holland, Flanders, Germany, Denmark, Sweden, Lapland, Russia, the Ukraine, and Poland, in the Years 1768, 1769, and 1770,* 3 vols. (London, 1772), 3:159; F. A. Polunin, *Geograficheskii leksikon rossiiskogo gosudarstva* (Moscow, 1773), p. 183.

36. Coxe, *Travels,* 1:282; Bakhrushin, *Istoriia Moskvy,* 2:306; "General'naia vedomost', uchinenaia v Moskovskoi politsii v 1781 godu, o chisle v Moskve nakhodiashchikhsia zhitelei...," ORGBL, f. 129, no. 22 d. 15, 1.

37. Charles de Mertens, *An Account of the Plague Which Raged at Moscow in 1771,* ed. and trans. R. Pearson (London, 1799; reprinted Newtonville, Mass., 1977), p. 25.

38. *PSZ,* 16: no. 11,689 (23 October 1762).

39. *PSZ,* 16: no. 11,649 (20 August 1762); no. 11,661 (3 September 1762).

40. V. A. Bil'basov, *Istoriia Ekateriny Vtoroi,* 3 vols. (Berlin, 1900), 2:163–87; "Dnevnik kurskogo pomeshchika I. P. Annenkova," *Materialy po istorii SSSR* 5 (Moscow, 1957):792–93, 796–97.

41. *PSZ,* 16: no. 11,701 (6 November 1762); B. N. Mironov, "O dostovernosti vedomostei o khlebnykh tsenakh XVIII v.," *Vspomogatel'nye istoricheskie distsipliny* (Leningrad, 1969),

2:252, 258-60; idem, "Statisticheskaia obrabotka otvetov na senatskuiu anketu 1767 g. o prichinakh rosta khlebnykh tsen," in I. D. Koval'chenko et al., eds., *Matematicheskie metody v istoricheskikh issledovaniiakh: sbornik statei* (Moscow, 1972), pp. 89-104.

42. Bielfeld, *Institutions politiques,* 1:63, 66.

43. *PSZ,* 16: no. 11,698 (8 October 1762); no. 11,766 (14 March 1763); no. 11,859 (11 June 1763); no. 12,173 (3 June 1764); no. 12,279 (12 November 1764); C. to Capt. Durnovo, 29 November 1764, *SIRIO,* 7:394-95; *SA,* 15:898-900.

44. C. to N. I. Panin, 3 May 1767, *SIRIO,* 10:186.

45. Art. 234, *SIRIO,* 43:333-34.

46. Arts. 11-14, 16, 26-27, *SIRIO,* 93:123-25, 128-29.

47. Paul Dukes, *Catherine the Great and the Russian Nobility* (Cambridge, 1967), pp. 101-2, 123-24, 137.

48. *SA,* 12:265.

49. Bakhrushin, *Istoriia Moskvy,* 2:452, 476-78, 592, 594; Sytin, *IPZM,* 2:54-55.

50. N. D. Chechulin, *Ocherki po istorii russkikh finansov v tsarstvovanie Ekateriny II* (St. Petersburg, 1906), pp. 320-23.

51. Coxe, *Travels,* 1:281.

52. "Dnevnik Annenkova," pp. 793, 796-97, 799; A. T. Bolotov, *Zhizn' i prikliucheniia Andreia Bolotova,* 3 vols. (Moscow and Leningrad, 1931), 2:188, 215, 221, 233-37, 290-91.

53. F. A. Polunin, *Novyi i polnyi geograficheskii slovar' rossiiskago gosudarstva,* 3 vols. (Moscow, 1788-89), 3:239-40.

54. Justi, *Die Grundfeste,* 1:341; M. Ia. Volkov, "Otmena vnutrennikh tamozhen v Rossii," *Istoriia SSSR* 2 (1957):78-95; idem, "Tamozhennaia reforma 1753-1757 gg.," *IZ,* 71 (1962):134-57.

55. I. A. Tolchenov, *Zhurnal ili zapiska zhizni i prikliucheniia Ivana Alekseevicha Tolchenova* (Moscow, 1974), pp. 31-33, 35-38.

56. Quoted by S. I. Volkov, *Krest'iane dvortsovykh vladenii Podmoskov'ia v seredine XVIII v. (30–70e gody)* (Moscow, 1959), p. 84.

57. G. L. Vartanov, "Kupechestvo gorodov Moskovskoi gubernii vo vtoroi polovine XVIII veka," kand. diss. (Leningrad, 1966), p. 36, 45, 54, 95, 143-57; idem, "Kupechestvo i torguiushchee krest'ianstvo tsentral'noi chasti Evropeiskoi Rossii vo vtoroi polovine XVIII veka," *Uchenye zapiski Leningradskogo gos. ped. inst. im. Gertsena,* kafedra istorii SSSR, 229 (1962):161-96, esp. 189.

58. Vartanov, "Kupechestvo i torguiushchee krest'ianstvo," pp. 190-91; V. I. Semevskii, *Krest'iane v tsarstvovanie Imperatritsy Ekateriny II,* 2 vols. (St. Petersburg, 1901-08), 2:196, 260.

59. E. I. Indova, "Moskovskii posad i podmoskovnye dvortsovye krest'iane v pervoi polovine XVIII v.," in Druzhinin et al., eds., *Goroda feodal'noi Rossii,* p. 480.

60. Zviagintsev, "Rost naseleniia," pp. 147-48.

61. Christopher Becker, "*Raznochintsy:* The development of the word and of the concept," *American Slavic and East European Review* 18 (1959):63-74.

62. Sytin, *IPZM,* 2:28-29, 52, 84.

63. E. A. Beletskaia, N. L. Krasheninnikova, L. E. Chernozubova, and I. V. Ern, *"Obraztsovye" proekty v zhiloi zastroike russkikh gorodov XVIII–XIX vv.* (Moscow, 1961), pp. 41, 43, 45-47.

64. Moskovskii arkhiv Ministerstva iustitsii, *Moskva: Aktovye knigi XVIII stoletiia,* ed. N. Naidenov, 12 vols. (Moscow, 1892-1900), 10:1-3, 12, 22-23, et passim.

65. *Opisanie del arkhiva morskogo ministerstva,* 7:751.

66. C., *Sochineniia,* 12:642.

67. *Moskva: Aktovye knigi,* 10:30, 87.

68. *MV,* 25 March 1771.

69. Arts. 2-3, *SIRIO,* 93:120-21.

70. *PSZ,* 16: no. 11,723 (11 December 1762); Sytin, *IPZM,* 1:295, vol. 2:8-71; N. I. Fal'kovskii, *Moskva v istorii tekhniki* (Moscow, 1950), pp. 157-58.

71. *PSZ,* 13: no. 10,096 (4 May 1753); vol. 16: no. 11,793 (10 April 1763).

72. "Nakaz zhitelei Moskvy," arts. 3-4, *SIRIO,* 93:121; Fal'kovskii, *Moskva v istorii tekhniki,* pp. 173-89.

73. Sytin, *IPZM,* 1:22; M. N. Tikhomirov, *Rossiia v XVI stoletii* (Moscow, 1962), p. 68;

G. P. Latysheva and M. G. Rabinovich, *Moskva i moskovskii krai v proshlom* (Moscow, 1973), p. 182.

74. E. I. Zaozerskaia, *Rabochaia sila i klassovaia bor'ba na tekstil'nykh manufakturakh v 20–60 gg. XVIII v.* (Moscow, 1960), pp. 69-75; V. N. Kashin, ed., *Materialy po istorii krest'ianskoi promyshlennosti XVIII i pervoi poloviny XIX v.* (Moscow and Leningrad, 1935), pp. lix-lxxvi, 247, 257-58; A. L. Shapiro, "Krest'ianskie promysly i manufaktury v Rossii v XVIII v.," *IZ*, 31 (1950):143-53; *SA*, 12:150-67.

75. D. S. Baburin, *Ocherki po istorii manufaktur-kollegii* (Moscow, 1939), pp. 92-93, 137-41, 147-49; I. V. Meshalin, *Tekstil'naia promyshlennost' krest'ian Moskovskoi gubernii v XVIII i pervoi polovine XIX veka* (Moscow, 1950), pp. 47-51.

76. *PSZ*, 15: no. 11,433 (31 January 1762); no. 11,494 (4 April 1762).

77. Meshalin, *Tekstil'naia promyshlennost' krest'ian*, pp. 45, 58; Zaozerskaia, *Rabochaia sila*, pp. 72-73; Bakhrushin, *Istoriia Moskvy*, 2:241-42.

78. A. I. Aksenov, "Moskovskoe kupechestvo v XVIII v. (Opyt genealogicheskogo issledovaniia)," kand. diss. (Moscow, 1974), pp. 104-5, 133-35, 174.

79. Zaozerskaia, *Rabochaia sila*, pp. 88-109; idem, "Manufaktura v Moskve v seredine XVIII veka," *IZ*, 33 (1950):124, 143-45; Baburin, *Ocherki*, pp. 199-200; M. N. Artemenkov, "Promyshlennaia deiatel'nost' krest'ianstva Rossii v XVIII v.," kand. diss. (Leningrad, 1949), pp. 95-140; "Nakaz zhitelei Moskvy," art. 39, *SIRIO*, 93:132.

80. *Opisanie*, p. 601.

81. M. N. Artemenkov, "Sotsial'nyi sostav naemnykh rabochikh Moskovskikh manufaktur v seredine XVIII v.," *Uchenye zapiski Leningradskogo gos. ped. inst. im. Gertsena* 278 (1965), p. 165.

82. Zaozerskaia, *Rabochaia sila*, p. 60; P. G. Liubomirov, *Ocherki po istorii russkoi promyshlennosti XVII, XVIII i nachalo XIX veka* (Moscow and Leningrad, 1947), pp. 113, 115-116, 564, 569, 572-73.

83. S. M. Troitskii, *Finansovaia politika russkogo absoliutizma v XVIII veke* (Moscow, 1966), pp. 56-113; Raeff, "Domestic Policies of Peter III," pp. 1299-1300.

84. *PSZ*, 15: no. 11,490 (29 March 1762); no. 11,638 (8 August 1762). F. Ia. Polianskii, "Zakreposhchenie rabochikh v Rossii XVIII veka," *Vestnik Moskovskogo universiteta*, seriia obshchestvennykh nauk, 11 (1953):86, notes that the Moscow guberniia chancery dispatched 44 men and 9 women to factories, from 1762 to 1769.

85. "Nakaz ot gosudarstvennoi manufaktur-kollegii...," art. 14, *SIRIO*, 43:209-10; Zaozerskaia, *Rabochaia sila*, pp. 238-45.

86. *PSZ*, 18: no. 12,872 (7 April 1767).

87. I. V. Meshalin, comp., *Materialy po istorii krest'ianskoi promyshlennosti*, vol. 2: *Tekstil'naia promyshlennost' Moskovskoi gubernii v XVIII i nachale XIX v.* (Moscow and Leningrad, 1950), pp. 85-107.

88. C. to P. S. Saltykov, 27 March 1766, "Pis'ma Saltykovu," pp. 44-45; Saltykov to C., 20 March 1766, and C. to N. I. Chicherin, 27 March 1766, *SIRIO*, 42:419-21.

89. Artemenkov, "Promyshlennaia deiatel'nost' krest'ianstva," pp. 105-6.

90. Meshalin, comp., *Materialy*, 2:89-103, 105-7, 130-57; Meshalin, *Tekstil'naia promyshlennost' krest'ian*, p. 76.

91. Meshalin, *Tekstil'naia promyshlennost' krest'ian*, pp. 73-76.

92. Meshalin, comp., *Materialy*, 2:92; A. P. Doroshenko, "Rabota na domu v tekstil'noi promyshlennosti Moskvy v seredine XVIII v.," *IZ*, 72 (1972):274-75.

93. Zaozerskaia, *Rabochaia sila*, pp. 87, 373; idem, "Manufaktura v Moskve," p. 139; S. G. Tomsinskii, ed., *Moskovskii sukonnyi dvor* (Leningrad, 1934), pp. 179-89, 230-35, 246.

94. *Moskovskii sukonnyi dvor*, pp. 59-61, 229; *Opisanie*, p. 587.

95. *Moskovskii sukonnyi dvor*, pp. 218, 225, 228-29; Zaozerskaia, "Manufaktura v Moskve," pp. 151-52; idem, *Rabochaia sila*, pp. 360-64.

96. Doroshenko, "Rabota na domu," p. 261.

97. Collegium of Manufactures, register of factories and workers in Moscow, March 1771, TsGADA, f. 263, op. 1, pt. 2, d. 1663:50-51; Collegium of Manufactures, reports of factory inspections, March 1771, TsGADA, f. 277, op. 12, d. 488:220-20v.; *Opisanie*, p. 595.

98. Jonas Hanway, *Account of British Trade over the Caspian*, 4 vols. (London, 1753), 1:92; Zaozerskaia, "Manufaktura v Moskve," pp. 132-33, 140; Artemenkov, "Sotsial'nyi sostav naemnykh rabochikh," pp. 166-68.

99. Zaozerskaia, *Razvitie legkoi promyshlennosti*, pp. 123–42; *Opisanie*, p. 595; *Opisanie del arkhiva morskogo ministerstva*, 7:736, 751.

100. Collegium of Manufactures to Moscow Senate, register of workers living constantly at factories, March 1771, TsGADA, f. 263, op. 1, pt. 2, d. 1663:50–51v.

101. Doroshenko, "Rabota na domu," pp. 269–75; Zaozerskaia, "Manufaktura v Moskve," pp. 138, 140–41; K. A. Pazhitnov, *Ocherki istorii tekstil'noi promyshlennosti dorevoliutsionnoi Rossii: Khlopchatobumazhnaia, l'no-pen'kovaia i shelkovaia promyshlennost'* (Moscow, 1958), p. 312; idem, *Ocherki istorii tekstil'noi promyshlennosti dorevoliutsionnoi Rossii: Sherstianaia promyshlennost'* (Moscow, 1955), p. 39; *Moskovskii sukonnyi dvor*, pp. 238–39.

102. *SA*, 11:276–77.

103. Ibid, p. 277.

104. C., *Sochineniia*, 12:616–17, 785–87.

105. Bielfeld, *Institutions politiques*, 1:259; Justi, *Die Grundfeste*, 1:316, 341–43.

106. Collegium of Manufactures to Moscow Senate, 13 June 1771, summarizing memo of 25 January 1765, TsGADA, f. 263, op. 1, pt. 2, d. 1663:154–55.

107. *SA*, 15:962.

108. *PSZ*, 17: no. 12,558 (30 January 1766); Beskrovnyi, *Russkaia armiia i flot v XVIII veke*, pp. 365–66.

109. *Opisanie del arkhiva morskogo ministerstva*, 8:12, 22.

110. George E. Munro, "The Development of St. Petersburg as an Urban Center during the Reign of Catherine II (1762–1796)," Ph.D. dissertation, University of North Carolina at Chapel Hill, 1973, pp. 246–49.

111. "Mnenie Imperatritsy Ekateriny II o manufakturakh," *Russkii arkhiv*, bk. 3 (1865): 1285–93; A. V. Florovskii, "K istorii ekonomicheskikh idei v Rossii v XVIII veke," *Nauchnye trudy russkogo narodnogo universiteta v Prage* 1 (1928):81–93, esp. 84, 86.

112. *Nakaz Ekateriny II*, pp. 85–86, 89, 149, 157.

113. Catherine II, quoted by Florovskii, "K istorii ekonomicheskikh idei," p. 91.

114. *SIRIO*, 43:204–10.

115. Arts. 230, 376, 378, 380, *SIRIO*, 43:333, 357–58.

116. Art. 12, *SIRIO*, 93:124; *PSZ*, 16:no. 11,761 (18 February 1763); no. 12,242 (15 September 1763).

117. P. M. Luk'ianov, *Istoriia khimicheskikh promyslov i khimicheskoi promyshlennosti Rossii do kontsa XIX veka*, ed. S. I. Vol'kovich, 6 vols. (Moscow, 1948–65), 1:109–10; C. to Senate, 16 September 1769, *SIRIO*, 10:380.

118. Zaozerskaia, *Rabochaia sila*, pp. 195, 211, 219–27, 363; Semevskii, *Krest'iane*, 1:562–63.

119. C., correspondence with Teplov and Volkov about new taxes, 12 February –10 September 1769, *SIRIO*, 10:328–30, 362–77; Meshalin, comp., *Materialy*, 2:107–10, 409–10.

120. *Moskovskii sukonnyi dvor*, pp. 242–43; Beskrovnyi, *Russkaia armiia i flot*, p. 366; Aksenov, "Moskovskoe kupechestvo," pp. 160–61.

121. The senate orders of 22 November and 15 December 1770 concerning the abolition of manufacturing privileges were issued secretly, like the decree of 7 April 1767 partially legalizing workshops, and were never published; they are mentioned in senate correspondence about the removal of factories from Moscow in 1771–72, TsGADA, f. 277, op. 12, d. 699: 2, 71–71v.

122. Art. 39, *SIRIO*, 9:132.

123. Bil'basov, *Istoriia Ekateriny Vtoroi*, 2:165, 173.

124. *PSZ*, 16: no. 11,855 (11 June 1763); N. A. Zhivopistsev, *Bol'nitsa Imperatora Pavla I-go v Moskve: Kratkii ocherk za 150 let eia sushchestvovaniia, 1763–1913* (Moscow, 1914), pp. 3–10, 59, 72; *MV*, 12 February, 5 March, 13 April, 7 May, 4 June, 2 July, 3 August, 7 September, 5 October, 5 November, 3 December, 1770; 1 February, 4 March, 8 April, 3 May, 5 July, 6 September 1771.

125. *PSZ*, 16: no. 11,908 (1 September 1763); P. M. Maikov, *Ivan Ivanovich Betskoi: Opyt ego biografii* (St. Petersburg, 1904), pp. 112–47, 156–62; V. Drashusov, ed., *Materialy dlia istorii imperatorskago Moskovskago vospitatel'nago doma*, 2 vols. (Moscow, 1863–68), 1:17–26, 46, 64–67; pt. ii:1–5; pt. iii:26–27, 35–38, 49–58; Sytin, *IPZM*, 2:15–17.

126. *PSZ*, 16: no. 11,647 (20 August 1762); Bakhrushin, *Istoriia Moskvy*, 2:468–71; Sytin, *IPZM*, 2:19.

127. Alelekov and Iakimov, *Istoriia*, pp. 360–65; A. I. Mikhailov, *Arkhitektor D. V. Ukhtomskii i ego shkola* (Moscow, 1954), pp. 222–23.

128. Mikhailov, *Ukhtomskii*, pp. 223-34, 361 n 293; Alelekov and Iakimov, *Istoriia*, p. 407; Chistovich, *Istoriia*, app. 10:211-13.

129. Senate registers of practitioners in Moscow, March 1771, TsGADA, f. 263, op. 1, pt. 2, d. 1663:21-23v.; V. G. Ruban, *Opisanie imperatorskago, stolichnago goroda Moskvy,...* (St. Petersburg, 1783), p. 53; Paul P. Bernard, "The limits of absolutism: Joseph II and the Allgemeines Krankenhaus," *Eighteenth-Century Studies* 12 (1975-76):198, 203.

130. *Nakaz Ekateriny II*, pp. 102, 148, 150-51; *SIRIO*, 93:122-25.

131. C. to N. I. Panin, 24 January 1768, *SIRIO*, 10:277; Sytin, *IPZM*, 2:47-49; V. Snegirev, *Arkhitektor V. I. Bazhenov* (Moscow, 1937), pp. 55-64.

132. C. to [N. I. Chicherin?] and to P. S. Saltykov, January 1769 (?), *SIRIO*, 10:322-23.

133. Petition to Moscow Policemaster Chancery, October 1770, OPI-GIM, f. 440, d. 683; 116-16v. These documents are copies of the originals made for I. E. Zabelin and preserved among his papers.

134. Police correspondence about the above petition, 29 November 1770-13 April 1771, ibid., pp. 118-20v. But the fishmongers' row was moved elsewhere in 1771. Sytin, *IPZM*, 2:75.

135. N. P. Afanas'ev, *Ocherk meteorologicheskikh nabliudenii i klimaticheskikh uslovii Moskvy* (Moscow, 1896), pp. 14-16.

Chapter Four

1. Werner Hermann, *Beitrag zur Geschichte der Pest in den unteren Donauländern* (Bucharest, 1938), pp. 4-14; Georg Z. Petresco, *Les dernières épidémies de peste dans les pays Roumains au XVIIIe et au XIXe siècle*, 2 pts. (Bucharest, 1934-36), 1:8-29; Pompei Gh. Samarian, *Din epidemiologia trecutuli romanesc Ciuma* (Bucharest, 1931), pp. 4-12; Emile Szejdel, *Histoire de la Peste en Roumanie* (Paris, 1932), pp. 24, 28-29.

2. Sticker, *Abhandlungen*, 1, pt. 1:210-12, 244-46, 250-52.

3. *SPV*, 15 January 1770, citing "Turkish border," 12 December 1769.

4. Francois de Tott, *Memoirs of Baron de Tott*, 4 vols. (London, 1785; reprinted New York, 1973), 4:144; Daniel Panzac, "La peste à Smyrne au XVIIIe siècle," *Annales E.S.C.*, 4 (1973):1090, 1093.

5. *Memoirs of Baron de Tott*, 2:137-38, 147-48, 159-63, 171-80, 234.

6. O. Senkovskii, ed., "Razskaz Resmi-Efendiia, ottomanskago ministra inostrannykh del, o semi-letnei bor'be Turtsii s Rossiei (1769-1776)," *Biblioteka dlia chteniia* 124 (1854):13-15.

7. *Scots Magazine* (Edinburgh) 31 (March 1769):159, citing "Banks of the Danube," February 18; and (August 1769), citing "Constantinople," June 16.

8. Senkovskii, ed., "Razskaz Resmi-Efendiia," pp. 24-25.

9. Rumiantsev to Stoffeln, 30 October 1769; Rumiantsev to C., 15 November 1769; Rumiantsev to Stoffeln, 16 November, 23 November, 29 November, 8 December, 11 December, 26 December 1769; Rumiantsev to C., 12 January, 31 January, 3 February, 14 February 1770; Rumiantsev to Stoffeln, 21 March 1770, in Fortunatov, ed., *P. A. Rumiantsev*, 2:167-72, 180-82, 186-88, 192-93, 197-98, 209-11, 216-17, 220-25, 258-59.

10. C. to Voltaire, 20 March 1770, *SIRIO*, 10:407; *SPV*, 2 April 1770.

11. J. F. C. Hecker, *Geschichte der neueren Heilkunde* (Berlin, 1839), pp. 132-48; H. H. Lamb, "Volcanic dust in the atmosphere; with a chronology and assessment of its meteorological significance," *Philosophical Transactions of the Royal Society of London*, series A, 266 (1970):507-8; D. J. Schove, "The sunspot cycle, 649 B.C. to A.D. 2000," *Journal of Geophysical Research* 60 (1955):128, 136, 139.

12. Wilhelm Abel, *Massenarmut und Hungerkrisen im vorindustriellen Europa* (Hamburg and Berlin, 1974), pp. 199-266, 410-15; George Barger, *Ergot and Ergotism* (London, 1931), pp. 73-77; H. H. Lamb, *Climate: Past, Present and Future* (London, 1977), 2:562-65, 569, 573, 587-89; Christian Pfister, "Climate and economy in eighteenth-century Switzerland," *Journal of Interdisciplinary History* 9 (1978):233-43; Utterström, "Some Population Problems in Pre-Industrial Sweden," pp. 132, 135.

13. Rumiantsev to C., 21 January, 3 February, 14 February, 6 March, 13 March, 6 May, 20 May 1770; Rumiantsev to Stoffeln, 27 April 1770; Rumiantsev's journal of field operations, 14 May 1770, *P. A. Rumiantsev*, 2:222-24, 230, 257, 273, 280-83, 289, 294.

14. Theyls to Asch, 18 March, 3 April 1770, ZhA.

15. Rumiantsev to Stoffeln, 27 April 1770; to General Weisman, commandant of Khotin, 3 May 1770; to C., 6 May 1770, *P. A. Rumiantsev*, 2:273–5, 279–81; Petresco, *Les dernières épidémies*, p. 60.

16. Mikhail Guboglu, "Turetskii istochnik o Valakhii, Moldavii i Ukraine," in A. S. Tveritinova, ed., *Vostochnye istochniki po istorii narodov iugo-vostochnoi i tsentral'noi Evropy*, vol. 1 (Moscow, 1964), pp. 137–45.

17. Rumiantsev to General Essen, commander of supply operations in southern Poland, 28 April 1770; Rumiantsev to C., 6 May 1770, *P. A. Rumiantsev*, 2:275–86.

18. Gustav Orraeus, *Descriptio pestis quae anno MDCCLXX. in Jassia, et MDCCLXXI. in Moscua grassata est* (St. Petersburg, 1784), pp. 1–23, 142–44; Sticker, *Abhandlungen*, 1, pt. 1:253–57.

19. [G. Orraeus], "Perevod: Kratkoe opisanie morovago povetriia poiavivshagosia v Iassakh, po volokhski chuma, po turetski emurchan" (May 1770), ZhA.

20. Asch to Medical Collegium, 25 June, 2 and 3 July 1770, with copies of Orraeus's prescribed treatments, ZhA.

21. G. Asch, "Nastavlenie dlia nabliudeniia v forpostakh, po nyneshnei sumnitel'noi zaraze v otdalennykh mestakh, komandirovannym lekariam neotmenno vsegda ispolniat'," 17 May 1770, ZhA.

22. Asch to Medical Collegium, 23 May 1770, ZhA.

23. Rumiantsev to C., 13 June, 29 June 1770, *P. A. Rumiantsev*, 2:311, 318; Ungermann, *Der Russisch-türkische Krieg*, pp. 96–106.

24. Asch to Baranovich, 21 June 1770; Baranovich and Grave to Asch, 26 June 1770, ZhA.

25. A. N. Petrov, *Voina Rossii s Turtsiei i pol'skimi konfederatami v 1769–1774 gg.*, 5 vols. (St. Petersburg, 1866–74), 2:8–18.

26. Rumiantsev to C., 29 June 1770, *P. A. Rumiantsev*, 2:318.

27. A. Koreshchenko, *Istoricheskii ocherk chumy s 1770 po 1772 god, v iugovostochnoi Evrope* (Moscow, 1854), pp. 21–23; *London Magazine* (May 1771):284; *Daily Advertiser* (London), 28 May 1771.

28. Otamanovskii, "Do istorii meditsini ta apteknoi spravi u Vinnitsi," pp. 323–324; idem, "Goroda pravoberezhnoi Ukrainy pod vladychestvom shliakhetskoi Pol'shi ot serediny XVII do kontsa XVIII veka," unpublished Ph.D. dissertation, 2 vols. (Saratov, 1954), 2:12, 128–29, 179, 219, 444–50.

29. Sticker, *Abhandlungen*, 1, pt. 1:258.

30. Urlanis, *Voiny i narodo-naselenie Evropy*, p. 267; Rumiantsev to C., 3 August 1770, *P. A. Rumiantsev*, 2:264.

31. Albert Sorel, *The Eastern Question in the Eighteenth Century*, trans. F. C. Bramwell (London, 1898; reprinted New York, 1969), pp. 108–9; Herbert H. Kaplan, *The First Partition of Poland* (New York and London, 1962), pp. 118, 126, 129–130; Erik Amburger, *Russland und Schweden 1762–1772* (Berlin, 1934; reprinted Vaduz, 1965), pp. 230–31; Urszula Jonecko and Antoni Jonecko, "Studia nad patentem o kordonie sanitarno-wojskowym ksiestwa Slaskiego z roku 1770," *Archiwum Historii Medycyny* 36 (1973):163–75; John T. Alexander, "British Responses to the Moscow Plague of 1771," in Mertens, *Account*, pp. 17–22.

32. C. to Rumiantsev, 25 May 1770, *P. A. Rumiantsev*, 2:296; *AGS*, 1, pt. 1:48–50.

33. Lerche, *Lebens- und Reise-Geschichte*, pp. 9, 13, 394–99; *SA*, 14:79.

34. Ibid., pp. 403–16, 422, 435.

35. Ibid., pp. 423–36.

36. Lerche, "Conspectus," data from June to 2 October 1770.

37. Lerche, *Lebens- und Reise-Geschichte*, p. 438.

38. Ibid., pp. 430–35; Asch to Medical Collegium, 18 August 1770, ZhA.

39. Correspondence of the Medical Collegium concerning Grave's retirement, 5 August 1770–31 January 1771, TsGADA, f. 344, op. 1, bk. 43:181–83, 198–200v., 203–5, 221–23v., 225–26v., 232, 236–38, 241.

40. Asch journal entries, 10 April, 18 June, 25 June, 8 July, 23 July, 18 August 1770, ZhA.

41. Asch to Mitrofanov, 10 September 1770, ZhA; Asch's undated letter to his brother is quoted in Mertens, *Account*, pp. 1–3.

42. E. A. Shcherbinin to C., 17 June 1770, TsGADA, f. 6, d. 410:481.

43. Cathcart to Wroughton, 16 July 1770, PRO/SP, 91/85: 57v.

44. *London Magazine* (September 1770):491.

45. *SPV*, 25 May, 11 June, 25 June, 20 July, 27 August, 3 September, 17 September, 21 September, 5 October 1770.
46. C. to F. M. Voeikov, 27 August 1770, *PSZ*, 19: no. 13,502.
47. Nikolai Zakrevskii, *Opisanie Kieva* (rev. ed., Moscow, 1868), 1:83-86, 94-95, 103-5, 115; E. A. Gutkind, *Urban Development in Eastern Europe: Bulgaria, Romania, and the U.S.S.R.* (New York and London, 1972), pp. 318-23; Solov'ev, *Istoriia Rossii*, 11:504; S. A. Verkharatskii, "Pervye gorodskie i uezdnye vrachi i pervye bol'nitsy na Ukraine," in B. D. Petrov et al., eds., *Ocherki istorii meditsinskoi nauki i zdravookhraneniia na Ukraine* (Kiev, 1954), p. 131; Chistovich, "Vrachebnyi personal," pp. 68-69.
48. Solov'ev, *Istoriia Rossii*, 14:25-26; A. Andrievskii, "Arkhivnaia spravka o morovoi iazve v g. Kieve v 1770-71 gg.," *Kievskaia starina* 34 (July 1891):308, 313-14.
49. Lerche, *Lebens- und Reise-Geschichte*, pp. 437-38.
50. Johann M. Minderer, *Abermal ein Beytrag zur Kenntnis und Heilung der Pest* (Riga, 1790), pp. 34-35, quoting a letter from his father-in-law, Bunge, an amateur meteorologist and long-time apothecary in Kiev.
51. Weather data in Kiev, 13 October 1770-5 July 1771, Lerche, "Conspectus."
52. Bunge's letter, in Minderer, *Abermal ein Beytrag*, p. 35.
53. Andrievskii, "Arkhivnaia spravka," p. 313; *AGS*, 1, pt. 1:391.
54. Lerche, *Lebens- und Reise-Geschichte*, pp. 442-43.
55. Andrievskii, "Arkhivnaia spravka," 305-6; Mitrofanov to Wedel, apothecary-provisioner at Kiev, 7 September 1770, TsGADA, f. 344, op. 1, bk. 42:223.
56. Voeikov to C., 11 September and 28 September 1770, TsGADA, f. 6, d. 410:460-62; Bunge's letter in Minderer, *Abermal ein Beytrag*, p. 35.
57. Lerche, *Lebens- und Reise-Geschichte*, p. 444.
58. Chistovich, *Istoriia*, app. 10:233; Ia. V. Elchanikov, ober-commandant of Kiev, to War Collegium, 3 November 1770, TsGADA, f. 344, op. 1, bk. 42:612-13v.
59. Lerche, *Lebens- und Reise-Geschichte*, pp. 442-3; Andrievskii, "Arkhivnaia spravka," p. 313.
60. Voeikov to C., 3 October 1770, TsGADA, f. 6, d. 410:463-64v.
61. Lerche, *Lebens- und Reise-Geschichte*, pp. 439, 443-46.
62. Andrievskii, "Arkhivnaia spravka," p. 309; Voeikov to C., 27 October 1770, TsGADA, f. 6, d. 410:465-66.
63. Weather data for January 1771, Lerche, "Conspectus."
64. Lerche, *Lebens- und Reise-Geschichte*, pp. 443-45, 449; Andrievskii, "Arkhivnaia spravka," pp. 312-13.
65. Lerche, *Lebens- und Reise-Geschichte*, p. 443.
66. General registers of plague losses throughout the empire (1772), TsGAg.M, f. 636, op. 2, d. 57:169v., 191-91v., 195v.
67. Ia. Sh., "Ubiistvo upyria v kievshchine vo vremia chumy 1770 goda," *Kievskaia starina* 28, no. 2 (1890):338-40.
68. I. I. Pantiukhov, *Epidemii v Pol'she i Zapadnoi Rossii do kontsa XVIII veka* (Kiev, 1876), p. 20.
69. *AGS*, 1, pt. 1:391; Pecken to Medical Collegium, 18 November 1770, TsGADA, f. 344, op. 1, bk. 43:33.
70. Browne to C., 24 September 1770, TsGADA, f. 16, d. 328, pt. 1:10-11v.
71. C.-von Browne correspondence, 1770-71, *OV*, 3:246-59; *AGS*, 1, pt. 1:391-92.
72. *AGS*, 1, pt. 1:391-93; Voeikov to C., 3 October 1770, TsGADA, f. 6, d. 410:463; C. to Voeikov, 19 September 1770, TsGIA-SSSR, f. 1329, op. 2, d. 112:79-80.
73. C. to Meshcherskii, 19 September 1770, TsGIA-SSSR, f. 1329, op. 2, d. 112:81-82v.; C. to S. M. Koz'min [19 September 1770], *SIRIO*, 42:341-42.
74. Meshcherskii to C., 28 September, 25 October 1770, TsGADA, f. 6, d. 410:470-73, 476; Frantz Wolf, town surgeon in Pereiaslav, to Medical Collegium, 11 October 1770, TsGADA, f. 344, op. 1, bk. 42:45.
75. Meshcherskii to C., 25 October 1770, TsGADA, f. 6, d. 410:471v.-73.
76. Meshcherskii to C., 31 October 1770, ibid., pp. 474-75.
77. C. to Shipov, 1 November 1770, in V. A. Bil'basov, ed., "Morovaia iazva (ukazy i reskripty imperatritsy Ekateriny II)," *Russkaia starina* 80 (December 1893):451-55.

78. Catherine to Shipov, 4 January 1771, 25 September 1774, ibid., pp. 455–56, 464; *AGS*, 1, pt. 1:394; Andrievskii, "Arkhivnaia spravka," pp. 309–10.

79. C. to N. Panin, 25 August 1770, *SIRIO*, 10:436; dated by *Kamerfur'erskii zhurnal 1770 goda*, p. 191.

80. C. to Saltykov, 19 September 1770, "Pis'ma Saltykovu," p. 84; Saltykov to C., 25 September 1770, TsGADA, f. 6, d. 410:100.

81. Kashira voevoda chancery to Moscow guberniia chancery, 4 October 1770, TsGADA, f. 6, d. 410:102–3v.

82. Saltykov to C., 11 October, 8 November 1770, ibid., pp. 101–1v., 104–4v.

83. Death toll from plague at Sevsk and Briansk, TsGAg.M, f. 636, op. 2, d. 57:144v.–45.

84. C. to Saltykov, 14 November 1770, "Pis'ma Saltykovu," pp. 88–90; Saltykov to C., 25 November 1770, TsGADA, f. 6, d. 410:105–6; A. Rinder to surgeon Fedor Smirnov, 22 November 1770, *Opisanie*, pp. 176–79.

85. Saltykov to C., 13 December 1770, TsGADA, f. 6, d. 410:107–7v.; Collegium of Manufactures and Moscow Policemaster Chancery to Moscow Senate, 19 March 1771, referring to police order of 17 December 1770, TsGADA, f. 263, op. 1, pt. 2, d. 1663:142; *AGS*, 1, pt. 1:393–94.

86. Skvortsov, *Materialy*, 2:644.

87. C. to M. N. Volkonskii, November 1771, *SIRIO*, 13:192; Cathcart to Suffolk, 18 November 1771, *SIRIO*, 19:242–43.

88. Meshalin, comp., *Materialy*, 2:130–43, 157; *Opisanie*, p. 608.

89. Saltykov to C., 7 March 1771, with register of articles burned at the Vvedenskie Hills, TsGADA, f. 16, d. 328, pt. 1:111–12v.

90. Shafonskii to Rinder, 21 December 1770; Rinder to Shafonskii, 21 December 1770; Shafonskii to Saltykov, 5 February 1771, *Opisanie*, pp. 180, 205–7, 634–35.

91. Saltykov to C., 22 December 1770; Bakhmetev to Saltykov, 22 December 1770, TsGADA, f. 6, d. 410:108–8v., 111–12.

92. Shafonskii to Saltykov, 5 February 1771; doctors' opinions, 22 December 1770; Rinder to Shafonskii, 22 December 1770, *Opisanie*, pp. 181–83, 207; Medical Office to Saltykov, 22 December 1770, TsGADA, f. 6, d. 410:109–10v.

93. Mertens, *Account*, p. 5.

94. Saltykov to C., 25 December 1770, TsGADA, f. 6, d. 410:113–16v.

95. Saltykov to C., 4 January 1771, ibid., 117–18v.

96. Saltykov to C., 4 January, 15 January 1771, ibid., 117v., 119v.–20.

97. Mertens, *Account*, p. 6.

98. Bolotov, *Zhizn'i prikliucheniia*, 2:497.

99. Saltykov to C., 15 January 1771, TsGADA, f. 6, d. 410:119–20.

100. Saltykov to C., 7 February 1771, ibid., pp. 121–22.

101. S. M. Grombakh, in Samoilovich, *IP*, 2:316–18; A. I. Metelkin, "Bor'ba meditsinskoi organizatsii s chumoi vo vremia Moskovskoi epidemii 1770–1772 gg.," *Zhurnal mikrobiologii, epidemiologii i immunobiologii* 51 (April 1974):143; Vasil'ev and Segal, *Istoriia epidemii v Rossii*, pp. 130–31. A popular historical novel by E. A. Salias (1840–1908), *Na Moskve*, first published in 1879, accents the nationalistic side of the conflict between Rinder and Shafonskii, perhaps reflecting the endemic anti-German sentiment that became epidemic after the Congress of Berlin in 1878.

102. Amburger, *Beiträge*, pp. 59, 81–85, 91, 98, 100, 103, 105–6; Palkin, *Ocherki*, pp. 84–85, 325; *Moskva: Aktovye knigi*, 10:165; petition of Yakov Rinder, December 1769, *Shchukinskii sbornik*, fasc. 3 (Moscow, 1904), p. 357; *RBS*, 16:227.

103. V. A. Nevskii, "A. F. Shafonskii—odin iz pionerov otechestvennoi sanitarii," *Gigiena i sanitariia* 11 (1950):42–45; L. Dagaev in *RBS*, 22:567.

104. Rinder to Saltykov, 27 January 1771, *Opisanie*, pp. 197–99.

105. Ibid., p. 199.

106. Minderer, *Abermal ein Beytrag*, pp. 9–10.

107. *Opisanie*, pp. 200–3.

108. Shafonskii to Saltykov, 5 February 1771, ibid., pp. 204–8.

109. Ibid., pp. 208–9.

110. Hirst, *Conquest of Plague*, p. 68.

111. *Opisanie*, pp. 210–11.

Chapter Five

1. *AGS*, 1, pt. 1:394–95.
2. *PSZ*, 19: no. 13,551 (31 December 1770).
3. *PSZ*, 19: no. 13,552 (9 January 1771); no. 13,556 (12 January 1771); Saltykov to C., 15 January 1771, TsGADA, f. 6, d. 410:119.
4. Seddler to Kaunitz, 4, 11, and 18 January 1771 (NS), *SIRIO*, 109:497–99; Sabatier de Cabres to Choiseul, 11 and 18 January 1771 (NS), *SIRIO*, 143:234–35.
5. *MV*, 1 April 1771; *SPV*, 1 February, 1 March, 26 April, and 3 May 1771.
6. *London Gazette*, 29 January, 23 February, 4 May 1771.
7. A. A. Viazemskii to Volkov and Teplov, 6 January 1771; Volkov and Teplov to C., February–March 1771 (?), TsGADA, f. 16, d. 328, pt. 1:113–17, 122–24, 185–89.
8. Anon., "O predostorozhnostiakh, kotoryia prinimat' dolzhno v takoi zemle, gde nakhoditsia morovaia iazva, dlia umensheniia bedstvii mogushchikh prichinitsia ot onyia; i o predostorozhnostiakh kasaiushchikhsia do pred"uprezhdeniia i otvrashcheniia iazvy v takoi zemle, gde opasaiutsia onyia (perevod)," ibid., pp. 171–80.
9. Anon., "Sredstvo k otvrashcheniiu rasprostraneniiu morovoi iazvy na granitsakh tekh stran i provintsii gde onaia deistvitel'no est': Perevod s nemetskago," ibid., pp. 239–45v.
10. C. to Saltykov, 29 December 1770, "Pis'ma Saltykovu," 92; Bakhmetev to Mertens, January 1771, citing Catherine's order to Chicherin, translated in Charles de Mertens, *Traité de la peste, contenant l'histoire de celle qui a régné à Moscou en 1771* (Vienna and Strasbourg, 1784), pp. 12–13; Senate to Petersburg departments, 31 January 1771, TsGADA, f. 248, op. 113, d. 1605:1; Saltykov to C., 7 March 1771, TsGADA, f. 16, d. 328, pt. 1:111.
11. C. to Saltykov, 22 February 1771, "Pis'ma Saltykovu," pp. 93–94; Saltykov to C., 21 February, 28 February, 7 March 1771, TsGADA, f. 6, d. 410:123–25.
12. Report to Medical Collegium of plague in the Crimea, March 1771, TsGADA, f. 344, op. 1, bk. 44:882; Medical Collegium to Astrakhan Guberniia Chancery, 19 January 1771, and Medical Collegium directives of May 21 and June 18, about the continuing threat of plague near Kizliar, TsGADA, f. 344, op. 1, bk. 46:101–2, 108–8v., 112–13v1; list of persons inspected at Kizliar quarantine, 13 April–15 May 1771; Medical Collegium to Governor Beketov of Astrakhan, 18 May 1771, TsGADA, f. 344, op. 1, bk. 44:594–95v., 835ff.
13. Medical Collegium to Dr. Dahl, 21 February and 24 February 1771, TsGADA, f. 344, op. 1, bk. 43:632–35v.
14. Chistovich, *Istoriia*, app. 10:144–45; Gorgoli to Medical Collegium, 9 March and 19 March 1771, the latter with register of symptoms encountered 17 February–16 March 1771; Medical Collegium resolution, 21 May 1771, TsGADA, f. 344, op. 1, bk. 44:545–46, 839–50.
15. Lerche, "Conspectus," weather data at Kiev in February 1771; Lerche, "Ephemerides," vol. 3: temperatures in Petersburg, March 1771; *MV*, 1 February 1771.
16. Yushkov to Synodal Office, 9 March 1771, TsGADA, f. 1183, op. 1, d. 62:1–2v.
17. Medical Office (Rinder) to Senate, 15 March 1771, TsGADA, f. 263, op. 1, pt. 2, d. 1663:27–28v.; Senate to Medical Collegium, 14 March 1771, TsGADA, f. 344, op. 1, bk. 44:518–18v.
18. V. Kireev, steward of Nosyreva's woolen mill, to Collegium of Manufactures, February 1771, responding to the collegium's order of 10 February, TsGADA, f. 277, op. 12, d. 492:1; resolution of the Collegium of Manufactures, 2 March 1771; Dokuchaev et al. to Collegium of Manufactures, 6 March 1771; register of people attached to the Big Woolen Court in early March 1771 (14 April 1771), TsGADA, f. 277, op. 12, d. 488:1–3, 280.
19. Yagel'skii to Moscow Policemaster Chancery, 9 March 1771, *Opisanie*, pp. 45–46, 212, 619; Sytin, *IPZM*, 1:177; Meshalin, comp., *Materialy*, 2:458.
20. Mertens, *Account*, p. 13; Medical Collegium inquiry, 16 June 1771, TsGADA, f. 344, op. 1, bk. 44:1003.
21. Register of deaths of persons outside the Big Woolen Court, 1 January–9 March 1771 (11 March 1771), TsGADA, f. 277, op. 12, d. 488:8–11.
22. *Moskva: Aktovye knigi*, 10:122.
23. Register of deaths at the Big Woolen Court, 1 January–9 March 1771 (11 March 1771), TsGADA, f. 277, op. 12, d. 488:12–16.
24. P. I. Panin to N. I. Panin, 14 March 1771, ORGBL, f. 222, XV/9:13.
25. Policemaster Chancery to Senate, 12 March 1771, TsGADA, f. 263, op. 1, pt. 2,

d. 1663:lv.; Shkiadan et al. to Saltykov, 11 March 1771, *Opisanie*, pp. 215–16.

26. Policemaster Chancery to Senate and Senate discussion, 12 March 1771, TsGADA, f. 263, op. 1, pt. 2, d. 1663:lv., 5.

27. *Opisanie*, p. 47.

28. Sukin to Saltykov, 11 March 1771; register of persons locked inside the Big Woolen Court, 11 March 1771, TsGADA, f. 277, op. 12, d. 488:6–7, 16v.; Justi, *Die Grundfeste*, 1:250.

29. Senate resolutions, 12 March 1771, TsGADA, f. 263, op. 1, pt. 2, d. 1663:11–14.

30. P. I. Panin to N. I. Panin, 14 March 1771, ORGBL, f. 222, XV/9:13–14v.

31. Joint meeting of Policemaster Chancery and Collegium of Manufactures, 12 March 1771, TsGADA, f. 263, op. 1, pt. 2, d. 1663:37–40.

32. Policemaster Chancery and Collegium of Manufactures to Senate, 14 March 1771, with register of persons removed, ibid., pp. 33v.–35v., 44–44v.; Collegium of Manufactures to V. Surovshchikov, 13 March 1771, TsGADA, f. 277, op. 12, d. 488:95.

33. Register of persons removed, 14 March 1771, TsGADA, f. 277, op. 12, d. 488:117–17v.; Policemaster Chancery to Senate, 15 March 1771; register of persons attached to the Big Woolen Court, 14 March 1771, TsGADA, f. 263, op. 1, pt. 2, d. 1663:31, 36–36v.; resolutions of Policemaster Chancery, 13 March 1771, TsGADA, f. 277, op. 12, d. 488:248–49.

34. Policemaster Chancery and Collegium of Manufactures to Senate, 14 March 1771, TsGADA, f. 263, op. 1, pt. 2, d. 1663:25–26.

35. Ibid., p. 26.

36. Medical Office to Senate, 15 March 1771; register of practitioners assigned to police, 15 March 1771; Policemaster Chancery to Senate, 16 March 1771; Policemaster Chancery to Senate with posting of practitioners, 15 March 1771; Policemaster Chancery to Senate, 16 March 1771; Sukin to Senate, 16 March 1771; Senate resolution, 16 March 1771, TsGADA, f. 263, op. 1, pt. 2, d. 1663:27–28v., 30–32, 82–83, 85–86; Senate to Medical Collegium, 17 March 1771, TsGADA, f. 344, op. 1, bk. 44:524–25.

37. Senate to C., 17 March 1771, TsGADA, f. 263, op. 1, pt. 2, d. 1663:66v.–68v.

38. Senate to C., 17 March 1771; Medical Office to Senate, 17 March 1771, TsGADA, f. 263, op. 1, pt. 2, d. 1663:70, 90–91v.; Senate to Medical Collegium, 17 March 1771, TsGADA, f. 344, op. 1, bk. 44:526–27.

39. Senate discussion and resolutions, 17 March 1771; Senate to C., 21 March 1771, TsGADA, f. 263, op. 1, pt. 2, d. 1663:94–97.

40. Register of sick and dead at registered manufactories, 1 January–14 March 1771 (14 March 1771); Sukin to Senate, 16 March and 18 March 1771; Policemaster Chancery to Senate, 24 March 1771, TsGADA, f. 263, op. 1, pt. 2, d. 1663:52–54, 84–84v., 102, 155v.; Sukin to Collegium of Manufactures, 17 March 1771, TsGADA, f. 277, op. 12, d. 488:161–63.

41. Collegium of Manufactures to steward at Ugreshskii pesthouse, 13 March 1771; persons at Balashov quarantine, 15 March 1771; Collegium of Manufactures to manufactory operators, with signatures attesting compliance, 19 March 1771; Sukin to stewards at Balashov and Sitnikov quarantines, 17 March and 22 March 1771; Senate to C., 24 March 1771; Senate discussion and meeting with manufactory operators, 24 March 1771, TsGADA, f. 277, op. 12, d. 488:97–98, 134–40, 154–59, 164–67, 193–96v., 209v., 217v.–219; Sukin to Senate, 18 March 1771, TsGADA, f. 263, op. 1, pt. 2, d. 1663:102–2v.

42. Ivan Vien, *Loimologia ili opisanie morovoi iazvy*. . . (St. Petersburg, 1786), pp. 187–98; Hirst, *Conquest of Plague*, p. 58.

43. Collegium of Manufactures to operators of woolen mills, 17 March 1771, TsGADA, f. 277, op. 12, d. 488:168; senate meetings, 4 April, 6 April, and order to Collegium of Manufactures, 7 April 1771; Collegium of Manufactures to Senate, 13 April 1771; senate discussion, 3 May 1771, TsGADA, f. 263, op. 1, pt. 2, d. 1663:189–99; Collegium of Manufactures' inquiries about Turkish wool, 8–13 April 1771, TsGADA, f. 277, op. 12, d. 420:1–36.

44. Collegium of Manufactures to Senate, 2 April 1771, TsGADA, f. 263, op. 1, pt. 2, d. 1663:75–76v.

45. Senate to C., 17 March 1771; G. Protasov to Senate, 19 March 1771; Yushkov to Senate with register of sick convicts, 19 March 1771; Collegium of Economy to Senate, 18 March 1771; Main Palace Chancery to Senate, 19 April 1771; Senate resolutions, 21 March 1771; Senate discussion, 30 March 1771; Collegium of Economy to Senate, 12 May 1771, TsGADA, f. 263, op. 1, pt. 2, d. 1663:68v.–71v., 120–21, 125–25v., 129, 145–46, 259, 265.

46. Senate to C., 17 March 1771; Policemaster Chancery to Senate, 19 March 1771; Senate

resolutions, 21 March and 24 March 1771; Senate to C., 28 March 1771, ibid., pp. 71–71v., 142, 148–148v., 205–6v.

47. N. I. Chicherin to N. I. Bakhmetev (Petersburg), 16 March 1771, OPI-GIM, f. 440, d. 683:118–18v.

48. Policemaster Chancery to Senate, 20 and 21 March 1771; Senate resolutions, 21 March 1771; Moscow University to Senate, 22 March 1771, TsGADA, f. 263, op. 1, pt. 2, d. 1663:124, 144, 148v., 152.

49. Medical Office to Senate, 20 March 1771; J. F. Erasmus, "Nastavlenie kakim obrazom osmatrivateli bolnykh, ravno kak i umershikh, po obshchemu sovetu Doktorov meditsiny postupat' dolzhny," trans. N. Bantysh-Kamenskii (20 March 1771), TsGADA, f. 263, op. 1, pt. 2, d. 1663:130–33.

50. Policemaster Chancery to Senate with posting of practitioners, 19 March 1771, TsGADA, f. 263, op. 1, pt. 2, d. 1663:108–9; Pogoretskii et al. to Policemaster Chancery, 19 March 1771, TsGADA, f. 277, op. 12, d. 488:269–69v.

51. Senate to Collegium of Manufactures, 20 March 1771; "Vedomost' o umershikh v Moskve vne karantinov opasnoiu bolezniiu," 20 March 1771, TsGADA, f. 277, op. 12, d. 488:184–87, 272; Senate resolutions, 20 March 1771, TsGADA, f. 263, op. 1, pt. 2, d. 1663:110–11.

52. Orraeus to Saltykov, 19 March 1771; Senate discussion, 24 March 1771; TsGADA, f. 263, op. 1, pt. 2, d. 1663:134, 217.

53. Policemaster Chancery to Senate, 20 March 1771; Policemaster Chancery and Collegium of Manufactures to Senate, 19 March 1771, ibid., pp. 123, 137, 140v.

54. Policemaster Chancery to Senate, 19–23 March 1771, ibid., pp. 122, 124, 144, 157, 167–67v.

55. Senate resolution and order to Medical Office, 20 March 1771, TsGADA, f. 263, op. 1, pt. 2, d. 1663:135–36; Saltykov to C., 23 March 1771, TsGADA, f. 6, d. 410:142v.

56. Bakhmetev to Chicherin, 26 March 1771; Saltykov to C., 23 March 1771, TsGADA, f. 6, d. 410:97–98, 142.v.

57. Bakhmetev to Chicherin, 26 March 1771, ibid., pp. 97–98v.; Senate resolutions, 23 March 1771; Bakhmetev to Senate, 24 March 1771, TsGADA, f. 263, op. 1, pt. 2, d. 1663:168, 173, 270.

58. Saltykov to C., 23 March 1771, TsGADA, f. 6, d. 410:142–43v.; I. M. Dolgorukii, *Sochineniia Dolgorukago (kniazia Ivana Mikhailovicha)*, vol. 2 (St. Petersburg, 1849), pp. 495–97.

59. Medical Office to Senate, 24 March 1771, TsGADA, f. 263, op. 1, pt. 2, d. 1663:159–60; *Opisanie*, p. 51.

60. Medical Office to Saltykov, 26 March 1771; Medical Office to Senate, 31 March 1771; Senate to C., 24 March 1771, TsGADA, f. 263, op. 1, pt. 2, d. 1663:162–63, 209–9v., 251.

61. Medical Office to Senate, 1 April 1771, with enclosure: "Mnenie sluzhashchee k predokhraneniiu goroda ot poiavivsheisia bolezni," ibid., pp. 164–65v.

62. Medical Collegium resolution, 7 April 1771, TsGADA, f. 344, op. 1, bk. 44:540–41v.

63. *Opisanie*, pp. 44, 52; Mertens, *Account*, pp. 13–14.

64. Medical Office to Medical Collegium, 2 June 1771, TsGADA, f. 344, op. 1, bk. 45:89–94; Palkin, *Russkie gospital'nye shkoly*, p. 243.

65. Hirst, *Conquest of Plague*, pp. 67, 74–75.

66. Senate to C., 29 March 1771, TsGADA, f. 263, op. 1, pt. 2, d. 1663:254–55v.; Kuhlemann's opinions, 26 and 31 March 1771; Shkiadan's opinion, 31 March 1771, *Opisanie*, pp. 230–39, 249–50; Chistovich, *Istoriia*, app. 10:194–95; Zhivopistsev, *Bol'nitsa imperatora Pavla I-go*, p. 72.

67. Kuhlemann's and Shkiadan's opinions, 31 March 1771, *Opisanie*, pp. 233–39, 249–50.

68. Hirst, *Conquest of Plague*, p. 76.

69. C. to Saltykov, 17 March 1771, "Pis'ma Saltykovu," pp. 94–95; *AGS*, 1, pt. 1:396; C. to Cherkassov, 17 March 1771, TsGADA, f. 16, d. 328, pt. 1:74; Sabatier de Cabres to Vrillière, 12 and 19 April 1771 (NS), *SIRIO*, 143:268–70; Seddler to Kaunitz, 5 and 12 April 1771 (NS), *SIRIO*, 109:518, 522.

70. *AGS*, 1, pt. 1:396–97; C. to Saltykov, 25 March 1771, "Pis'ma Saltykovu," pp. 95–97; Ransel, *Politics of Catherinian Russia*, pp. 111–12.

71. C. to Eropkin, 25 March 1771, *PPEE*, p. 1; C. to Saltykov, 25 March 1771, "Pis'ma

Saltykovu," pp. 96–97; "O zvanii podchinennoi kommissii o zdravii," translated excerpt from *Beschreibung Infections-Ordnung* (Vienna, 1763), TsGADA, f. 16, d. 328, pt. 1:216–17v.

72. Justi, *Die Grundfeste*, 1:254–55; Bielfeld, *Institutions Politiques*, 1:104–5.

73. C. to Saltykov, 25 March 1771; Catherine's manifesto of 31 March 1771, "Pis'ma Saltykovu," pp. 97–99; Sievers to C., 25 March 1771, TsGADA, f. 16, d. 328, pt. 1:13; *AGS*, 1, pt. 1:397–99.

74. *AGS*, 1, pt. 1:398–400; C. to Bruce, 30 March 1771, TsGADA, f. 10, op. 3, d. 566:7–8 (cf. *SIRIO*, 13:80–81); Catherine's emergency program of 31 March 1771, "Pis'ma Saltykovu," p. 98.

75. C. to M. M. Izmailov, 3 April 1771, TsGADA, f. 10, d. 491:6–7; Hirst, *Conquest of Plague*, 41, 283–92; Vien, *Loimologia*, pp. 81–84.

76. C. to Saltykov, 2 April, 2 May 1771, "Pis'ma Saltykovu," pp. 100–1; [F. W. Margraff], "Dnevnyia primechaniia nad bol'nym goriachkoiu, zlago roda strazhdushchim," *Opisanie*, pp. 365–75; Saltykov to C., 3 May, 6 May 1771, TsGADA, f. 16, d. 328, pt. 1:4–5.

77. Eropkin to C., 31 March 1771, *PPEE*, pp. 8–9; Eropkin to Senate with register, 30 March 1771; Senate resolution, 31 March 1771; registers of persons quarantined, 18 April 1771, TsGADA, f. 263, op. 1, pt. 2, d. 1664:11–11v., 13–14v., 131–34; Eropkin to Collegium of Manufactures, 7 May and 21 May 1771, TsGADA, f. 277, op. 12, d. 488:328, 339.

78. Eropkin to C., 4 April and 14 April 1771, *PPEE*, pp. 20–33; Eropkin to Medical Consilium, 31 March 1771; Medical Consilium to Eropkin, 2 April 1771, *Opisanie*, pp. 243–49; Eropkin to Senate with opinion of Medical Consilium, 8 April 1771; Senate to Policemaster Chancery, 8 April 1771, TsGADA, f. 263, op. 1, pt. 2, d. 1664:58–60.

79. Senate resolutions, 5–6 April 1771; Senate to C., 6 April 1771, TsGADA, f. 263, op. 1, pt. 2, d. 1664:30–35v.; Eropkin to C. with register of deaths, 30 March–4 April 1771 (4 April 1771), *PPEE*, pp. 20–26; assignment of district supervisors and medical inspectors, 6 April 1771, *Opisanie*, pp. 57–58, 249–51.

80. Medical Office to Senate, 1 April 1771, TsGADA, f. 263, op. 1, pt. 2, d. 1663:164–66; Eropkin to Senate with Medical Consilium's "opinion" of 31 March 1771, 6 April 1771; Senate resolution, 8 April 1771; War Office to Senate, 24 March 1771; Saltykov to Senate, 6 April 1771; Senate to C., 11 April 1771, TsGADA, f. 263, op. 1, pt. 2, d. 1664:43–57v., 60; Senate to Petersburg Departments, 8 April 1771, TsGADA, f. 248, op. 113, d. 1605:17.

81. Amvrosii to Teplov, with registers of deaths in Moscow, 1 January–4 April 1771 (7 April 1771); Teplov to Amvrosii, 18 April 1771, TsGADA, f. 18, d. 251:36–42v.; register of deaths at Vvedenskie Hills, 26 December 1770–6 March 1771; register of deaths in Moscow, 1 January–4 April 1771, TsGIA-SSSR, f. 796, op. 52, d. 107:14–15v.; Eropkin to C., 14 April 1771, *PPEE*, pp. 27–33.

82. V. B. Golitsyn to V. B. Golitsyn, 8 April and 18 April 1771, ORGBL, f. Viazemi 94/15:11v., 14–14v.; Famintsyn to Medical Collegium, 12 April 1771, TsGADA, f. 344, op. 1, bk. 44:689v.; Mertens, *Account*, p. 19.

83. *PSZ*, 19: no. 13,594 (11 April 1771); Cathcart to Rochford, 6 April 1771, PROSP, 91/87:170.

84. *AGS*, 1, pt. 1:401–2; C. to Bielcke, 18 May 1771, *SIRIO*, 13:95.

85. Bolotov, *Zhizn' i prikliucheniia*, 2:511; Mertens, *Account*, pp. 18–19.

86. "Zametki neizvestnago vo frantsuzskom al'manakhe, 1771 goda," *Shchukinskii sbornik*, fasc. 6 (Moscow, 1907), p. 38; P. I. Panin to N. I. Panin, 3 May 1771, ORGBL, f. 222, XV/9:15v.

87. Register of deaths in Moscow, April–June 1771, *Opisanie*, p. 620; "Vedomost' o chisle umershikh v gorode i v karentine aprelia s l-go chisla 1771 goda," TsGADA, f. 199, d. 151, pt. 1, no. 1:140–40v.

88. Monthly mortality for 1773–74 in *Opisanie*, p. 621.

89. Copy of bill of health; Senate to Senate typography, 6 April 1771; Senate typography to Senate, 8 April 1771; Eropkin to Senate, 9 April 1771; Senate resolution, 11 April 1771; Eropkin to Senate and Senate order, 3 May 1771, TsGADA, f. 263, op. 1, pt. 2, d. 1664:37–41, 65, 111–12.

Chapter Six

1. Eropkin to Yagel'skii, 16 April 1771, *Opisanie*, pp. 281-84; Eropkin to Senate, 17 April 1771, TsGADA, f. 263, op. 1, pt. 2, d. 1664:90-91.

2. "Zametki neizvestnago," p. 38; V. B. Golitsyn to V. B. Golitsyn, 17 May 1771, ORGBL, f. Viazemi, 94/15:7; Mertens, *Account*, p. 19.

3. Lerche, "Ephemerides," 3: weather at Petersburg in May 1771; Tolchenov, *Zhurnal*, pp. 35-37; Lerche, "Conspectus," weather data in Kiev, May-June 1771; Lerche, *Lebens- und Reise-Geschichte*, p. 454.

4. Lerche, "Conspectus," weather data in Moscow, 13 July-30 September 1771; *Lebens- und Reise-Geschichte*, pp. 455-57; P. I. Panin to N. I. Panin, 15 August 1771, ORGBL, f. 222, XV/9:17.

5. Eropkin to Senate, 19 May 1771; Collegium of Manufactures to Senate, 30 May 1771, TsGADA, f. 263, op. 1, pt. 2, d. 1664:152-53; *AGS*, 1, pt. 1:404.

6. Collegium of Manufactures to Senate, 13 June 1771, with three tables of registered manufactories and workers in the Moscow region, TsGADA, f. 263, op. 1, pt. 2, d. 1664:154-88.

7. Medical Office to Senate with medical consilium's report, 2 June 1771; Senate to C., 10 June 1771; Collegium of Manufactures to Senate, 13 June 1771; manufactory operators' discussion with Collegium of Manufactures, 8 June 1771; Eropkin to Senate, 16 June 1771; Senate resolution, 30 June 1771; Eropkin to Senate, 1 July and 3 July 1771, TsGADA, f. 263, op. 1, pt. 2, d. 1664:201-4, 211, 215-17, 219, 222.

8. Senate to C., 28 July 1771, citing senate report of May 12, TsGADA, f. 263, op. 1, pt. 2, d. 1664:257-57v.; Senate to C., 30 May 1771, TsGADA, gosarkhiv, r. XVI, d. 168, pt. 8:198-98v.

9. *AGS*, 1, pt. 1:403-4; C. to Saltykov, 19 July 1771, "Pis'ma Saltykovu," p. 102.

10. Grave to Eropkin, 7 April 1771; Ivan Domashnev (9th district) to Eropkin, 7 April 1771; Aleksandr Kliucharev (13th district) to Eropkin, 7 April 1771; Eropkin to Shafonskii, and Shafonskii to Eropkin, 7 April 1771; Domashnev and Yagel'skii to Eropkin, 12 April 1771, TsGAg.M, f. 636, op. 1, d. 19:6-14.

11. Grave to Eropkin, 14 April 1771; Yagel'skii to Eropkin, 16 April 1771; Kliucharev to Eropkin, 16 and 17 April 1771; Kliucharev to Eropkin, 1 May 1771; Shafonskii to Eropkin, 1 May 1771, TsGAg.M, f. 636, op. 1, d. 19: 19, 21-23, 27-28; registered enterprises in Moscow in 1771, *Opisanie*, p. 616.

12. Andrei Sokolov (11th district) to Eropkin, 4 May 1771; Grave to Eropkin, 4 May 1771, TsGAg.M, f. 636, op. 1, d. 19:32-33.

13. Kliucharev to Eropkin, 16 May 1771; Shafonskii to Eropkin, 16 May 1771, TsGAg.M, f. 636, op. 1, d. 20:3-4v.; Eropkin to Senate, 17 May 1771, TsGADA, f. 263, op. 2, d. 1710:7.

14. Grave to Eropkin, 17 May 1771; Aleksandr Zinov'ev (12th district) to Eropkin, 17 May 1771, TsGAg.M, f. 636, op. 1, d. 20:5-6.

15. Sergei Urusov (5th district) to Eropkin, 19 May 1771; Grave to Eropkin, 19 May 1771, ibid., pp. 8-9.

16. Eropkin to Senate, 16 June, 21 June, 26 June, and 9 July 1771, TsGADA, f. 263, op. 1, pt. 2, d. 1664:211-14, 239.

17. Eropkin to Senate, 23 June, 24 June, and 4 July 1771, ibid., pp. 8, 10v., 16.

18. Eropkin to Senate, 25 June and 26 June 1771, ibid., pp. 12, 14.

19. Eropkin to Senate, 24 June, 25 June, 30 June, and 6 July 1771, ibid., pp. 9-10, 13, 15, 17-17v.

20. Senate to Collegium of Manufactures, 5 August 1771; register of delinquent workshop licenses, 1769-71 (August 1771), in Meshalin, comp., *Materialy*, 2:130, 133.

21. Mertens, *Account*, p. 20.

22. Sytin, *IPZM*, 2:81; N. P. Arkharov to N. I. Chicherin, 6 May 1772, TsGAg.M, f. 46, op. 7, d. 7722:16-16v.

23. Summary of parish reports, 13-16 July 1771, TsGAg.M, f. 203, op. 755, d. 730:14; d. 731, passim; Mertens, *Account*, p. 21.

24. Eropkin to Senate, 4 July 1771, TsGADA, f. 263, op. 1, pt. 2, d. 1664:225, 229; Samoilovich, *IP*, 2:328.

25. *AGS*, 1, pt. 1:404-5; Lerche, *Lebens- und Reise-Geschichte*, pp. 455-56.

26. Eropkin to Senate, 16, 19, and 21 July 1771, TsGADA, f. 263, op. 1, pt. 2, d. 1664:240, 245, 248.
27. Eropkin to Senate, 7 July–1 August 1771, TsGADA, f. 263, op. 2, d. 1710:16–23, 25–52; registered deaths in June and July 1771, TsGADA, f. 199, d. 151, pt. 1, no. 1:140v.
28. Kuhlemann to Medical Office, 6 August 1771, TsGADA, f. 199, d. 151, pt. 1, no. 1:37–43.
29. Eropkin to Senate, 24 July 1771, TsGADA, f. 263, op. 2, d. 1710:32–32v.; opinion of the medical consilium, 26 July 1771, TsGADA, f. 263, op. 1, pt. 2, d. 1664:266v.–67.
30. Eropkin to Senate, 24 July 1771, TsGADA, f. 263, op. 2, d. 1710:33–33v.
31. Mertens, *Account*, p. 21; Eropkin to Senate, daily reports, 27 July–7 August 1771, TsGADA, f. 263, op. 2, d. 1710:39–72.
32. Opinion of the medical consilium, 26 July 1771, TsGADA, f. 263, op. 1, pt. 2, d. 1664:266–67.
33. Ibid., pp. 267–68.
34. Ibid., pp. 268–68v. A block-deep complex of buildings, the Synod Choristers (*Sinodal'nye pevchie*) lost its special community status and functions in the seventeenth century and was leased out as shops, warehouses, and eating establishments. Sytin, *IPZM*, 1:100, 104; vol. 2:388.
35. Ibid., pp. 268v.–69.
36. Eropkin to Senate, 28–29 July 1771; Medical Office to Senate, 10 August 1771; Shkiadan to Medical Office, 10 August 1771; Senate resolution, 10 August 1771, TsGADA, f. 263, op. 1, pt. 2, d. 1664:273, 276v., 335–36v., 343; Kuhlemann to Medical Office, 6 August 1771, TsGADA, f. 199, d. 151, pt. 1, no. 1:39–41.
37. Senate to C., 2 August 1771, TsGADA, f. 263, op. 1, pt. 2, d. 1664:273–76.
38. Ibid., pp. 276–82.
39. Eropkin to Senate, 4–5 August 1771, TsGADA, f. 263, op. 1, pt. 2, d. 1664:291, 293–94.
40. Moscow Synodal Office to Holy Synod, 27 July 1771; Krutitskii spiritual consistory to Moscow Synodal Office, 3 August 1771, enclosing testimony of Dmitrii Mikhailov and others; resolutions of Moscow Synodal Office, 3, 5, and 17 August 1771; Moscow spiritual consistory to Moscow Synodal Office, 18 August 1771, with register of prayerbooks distributed, TsGADA, f. 1183, op. 1, d. 290:227–37, 250–51v., 257, 290; Lerche, *Lebens- und Reise-Geschichte*, p. 458; Mertens, *Account*, pp. 22–23.
41. Eropkin to Senate, 30 July 1771, TsGADA, f. 263, op. 2, d. 1710:49; Saltykov to C., 2 August 1771, TsGADA, f. 6, d. 410:163–63v.; *AGS*, 1, pt. 1:405–07; C. to Eropkin, 8 August 1771, *PPEE*, pp. 42–44.
42. "Zametki neizvestnago," p. 38.
43. *AGS*, 1, pt. 1:407.
44. Eropkin to P. I. Panin, 15 August 1771, ORGBL, f. 222, XV/9:18.
45. *AGS*, 1, pt. 1:408; Eropkin to C., 31 August 1771, *PPEE*, pp. 68–69.
46. Eropkin to Senate, 4–15 August 1771; Sobakin to Senate, 27 August 1771, TsGADA, f. 263, op. 2, d. 1710:60–98v., 141, 149–50.
47. Eropkin to Senate, 30 July, 5, 11, 17, and 27 August 1771; Sobakin to Senate, 29 August 1771; ibid., pp. 48, 65v., 84–84v., 103, 140, 155.
48. Eropkin to P. I. Panin, 15 August 1771, ORGBL, f. 222, XV/9:18; Eropkin to Senate, 12 and 14 August 1771; Sobakin to Senate, 26 and 29 August 1771, TsGADA, f. 263, op. 2, d. 1710:86, 95v., 138v., 155v.
49. Eropkin to Senate, 10 August 1771, TsGADA, f. 263, op. 1, pt. 2, d. 1664:345.
50. Eropkin to Collegium of Manufactures, 24 July 1771; Collegium of Manufactures to mill operators, late July 1771, TsGADA, f. 277, op. 12, d. 363:1–9.
51. Eropkin to Senate, daily reports, 27 July–18 August 1771, TsGADA, f. 263, op. 2, d. 1710:39, 48, 61, 63–64, 65v., 69, 71–72, 79v., 81v., 88v., 93–93v., 95v., 98v., 99v., 105v., 106, 107v., 111.
52. Eropkin to Senate, 19 August 1771, enclosing report of office of the sailcloth mill to Moscow Admiralty Office (18–19 August 1771), ibid., pp. 109–10.
53. Noninfectious deaths at 13 registered manufactories, 27 July–22 August 1771; deaths from infection at 6 registered manufactories, 31 July–22 August 1771, TsGADA, f. 277, op. 12, d. 371:54–55.
54. Collegium of Manufactures to mill operators, 11 August 1771; Collegium of Manufac-

tures to police, 18 August 1771, TsGADA, f. 277, op. 12, d. 363:20, 22-23; Senate resolution and order, 17 August and 19 August 1771, TsGADA, f. 263, op. 1, pt. 2, d. 1664:387-91.

55. Registers of Moscow manufactories with villages (20 with 1,904 workers) and without villages (60 with 2,132 workers); register of women assigned by Collegium of Manufactures to silk enterprises, TsGADA, f. 277, op. 12, d. 371:44, 53-53v.

56. Collegium of Manufactures to mill operators, 20 and 21 August 1771; Senate resolution, 22 August 1771, TsGADA, f. 263, op. 1, pt. 2, d. 1664:429-30v., 434v.-35; Collegium of Manufactures to groups of mill operators, 25 August and 27 August 1771; Collegium of Manufactures to operators of small enterprises, 29 August 1771; TsGADA, f. 277, op. 12, d. 371:102-2v., 122-28v.

57. Vasilii Kireev (Nosyreva's steward) to Collegium of Manufactures, 24 August 1771, TsGADA, f. 277, op. 12, d. 492:3.

58. Sukin to Senate, 22 August 1771, TsGADA, f. 263, op. 1, pt. 2, d. 1664:426v.; Bogdan Kramer and Ivan Pel' (Tames's stewards) to Collegium of Manufactures, 2 September 1771; Pankrat Kolosov to Collegium of Manufactures (August-September 1771), TsGADA, f. 277, op. 12, d. 371:141-47, 154-58; this last file also contains replies of other mill operators to the Collegium of Manufactures, 19 August-6 September 1771:130-40, 148-52, 163-205.

59. V. Kireev to Collegium of Manufactures, 30 August-22 November 1771, TsGADA, f. 277, op. 12, d. 492:4-15.

60. Mikhail Ivanov (Sakharov's steward) to Collegium of Manufactures, 31 August 1771, TsGADA, f. 277, op. 12, d. 491:2a-3.

61. Eropkin to Senate, 26 July 1771, TsGADA, f. 263, op. 2, d. 1710:36; Eropkin to Senate, 27 July 1771; Collegium of Economy to Senate, 1 August 1771; Collegium of Economy to Senate, 17 March 1771; Senate to C., 2 August 1771; C. to Senate, 8 August 1771; Collegium of Economy to Senate, 19 August 1771; TsGADA, f. 263, op. 1, pt. 2, d. 1664:260-61, 263, 270-72v., 276, 375, 383; *AGS*, 1, pt. 1:405-6.

62. Eropkin to Senate, 5 August 1771; Yagel'skii to Eropkin, 5 August 1771; Makulov to Eropkin, 5 August 1771, TsGADA, f. 263, op. 1, pt. 2, d. 1664:305-7v.

63. Senate resolution, 8 August 1771; Senate to Yushkov, 18 August 1771; Yushkov to Senate, 20 August 1771; Collegium of Economy to Senate, 26 August 1771, ibid., pp. 309-12v.

64. Eropkin to Senate, 6 August 1771; Bulgakov to Eropkin, 3 August 1771; Senate discussion, 8 August 1771; Borovsk voevoda chancery to Senate, 6 September 1771, ibid., pp. 318-20v., 323.

65. Malorossiia Collegium to Senate, 6 August 1771; Senate resolution, 17 August 1771; Senate order, 24 August 1771, ibid., pp. 385-85v., 387-88, 417; total mortality at Nezhin, 12 July-1 November 1771, TsGAg.M, f. 636, op. 2, d. 57:196-96v.

66. Lerche to Eropkin, 19 August 1771, TsGADA, f. 199, d. 151, pt. 1, no. 1:22-25.

67. Ibid., pp. 25-28.

68. Ibid., pp. 24-26.

69. Eropkin to Senate, 19 August 1771, with assignments of practitioners and district supervisors, TsGADA, f. 263, op. 2, d. 1710:112-13v.; Eropkin to district supervisors, 19 August 1771, *Opisanie*, p. 81; Eropkin to Senate, 21 August 1771; Senate resolution, 25 August 1771, TsGADA, f. 263, op. 1, pt. 2, d. 1664:374, 476; Eropkin to C., 29 August and 31 August 1771, *PPEE*, pp. 63, 67-68.

70. Eropkin to Senate, 25-30 August 1771, with daily registers of deaths, 22-30 August 1771; Sobakin to Senate, 24-30 August 1771, with daily registers of deaths, 23-30 August, TsGADA, f. 263, op. 2, d. 1710:125-62; Senate order to government offices, 19 August 1771; Policemaster Chancery to Senate, 25 August 1771; Eropkin to Senate, 24 August 1771, with listing of subordinates (22 men), TsGADA, f. 263, op. 1, pt. 2, d. 1664:391, 458-59v., 461-63.

71. Eropkin to Senate, 30 August 1771, TsGADA, f. 263, op. 2, d. 1710:146v.; Zhivopistsev, *Bol'nitsa imperatora Pavla*, pp. 26-27; Mertens, *Account*, pp. 118-19; Admiralty Office to Eropkin, 18 August 1771, TsGADA, f. 263, op. 2, d. 1710:110v.

72. Yushkov to Senate, 25 August 1771, TsGADA, f. 263, op. 2, d. 1664:478-79.

73. Feofilakt to Synodal Office, 31 August and 5 September 1771; Moscow University to Synodal Office, 2 September 1771; Synodal Office to monasteries, 7 September 1771, TsGADA, f. 1183, op. 1, d. 290:301-3, 306, 308.

74. Sablukov letters, 22 August-5 September 1771, "Moskva v 1771 godu," *Russkii arkhiv* (1866):336.

75. C. to Eropkin, 20 August 1771, *PPEE*, pp. 53–59; C. to Saltykov, 20 August 1771, "Pis'ma Saltykovu," pp. 103–04.

76. C. to Eropkin, 20 August 1771, *PPEE*, p. 54; *AGS*, 1, pt. 1:407; C. to Viazemskii (August 1771?), in A. Smirdin, ed., *Sochineniia Imperatritsy Ekateriny II* (St. Petersburg, 1850), 3:497; Solov'ev, *Istoriia Rossii*, 15:150.

77. *London Gazette*, 21–24 September 1771; 1–5 October 1771.

78. *Weekly Magazine* (Edinburgh), 7 November 1771, citing Petersburg, 13 September.

79. Cathcart to Suffolk, 26 August/6 September 1771, PROSP, 91/88:120–20v.

80. Lobkowitz to Kaunitz, 23 August 1771 (NS), *SIRIO*, 109:578.

81. Senate resolution, 23 August 1771; Policemaster Chancery to Senate, 30 August 1771, TsGADA, f. 263, op. 1, pt. 2, d. 1664:451–51v., 495; Eropkin to C., 29 August 1771, *PPEE*, p. 61.

82. Mertens, *Account*, p. 26; Senate resolution, 25 August 1771; Policemaster Chancery to Senate, 1 September 1771; Moscow Municipal Administration to Senate, 1 September 1771, TsGADA, f. 263, op. 1, pt. 2, d. 1664:471, 507–08v.; Eropkin to C., 29 August 1771, *PPEE*, pp. 60–64.

83. Senate to C., 30 August 1771, *Moskovskii vestnik*, pt. 5 (1829):139–42, 144–48; Eropkin to C., 31 August 1771, *PPEE*, pp. 66–67; Saltykov to C., 30 August 1771, TsGADA, f. 6, d. 410:164–64v.

84. Senate to C., 30 August 1771, *Moskovskii vestnik*, pt. 5 (1829):142–43; Saltykov to C., 30 August 1771, TsGADA, f. 6, d. 410: 164v.; Eropkin to C., 31 August 1771; C. to Eropkin, [ca. 12] September 1771, *PPEE*, pp. 68–69, 79; *AGS*, 1, pt. 1:411–12.

85. *AGS*, 1, pt. 1:408–12.

86. C. to Senate in Moscow, 9 September 1771, *Moskovskii vestnik*, pt. 5 (1829):149–57; C. to Eropkin, 9 September 1771, *PPEE*, pp. 72–78; Stepan Strekalov to C., 9 September and 13 September 1771, TsGADA, f. 263, op. 2, d. 1670:84–85; Catherine's manifesto of 9 September 1771, *SIRIO*, 13:165–66.

Chapter Seven

1. Bakhmetev to Senate, 29 August 1771; Senate discussion, 1 September 1771; Bakhmetev to Senate, 5 September 1771, TsGADA, f. 263, op. 1, pt. 2, d. 1670:15–17, 53.

2. *Opisanie*, pp. 90–91; Amvrosii to clergy, 13 September 1771, in N. P. Rozanov, *Istoriia Moskovskogo eparkhial'nogo upravleniia* (Moscow, 1870), 2, pt. 2:80–81.

3. Eropkin to Senate, 1 September 1771; Volotskii to Eropkin, 2 September 1771; Shafonskii to Eropkin, 29 August 1771; Korobovskoi to Volotskii, 29 August 1771; Lepenitskii to Volotskii, 1 September 1771; Senate resolution, 2 September 1771; Medical Office to Saltykov, 16 September 1771; Chief War Commissariat to Senate, 11 November 1773, Senate decree, 9 December 1773, TsGADA, f. 263, op. 2, d. 1671:1–25v., 61–63.

4. Bakhmetev to Senate and Senate resolution, 2 September 1771; Bakhmetev to Senate, 12 September 1771, TsGADA, f. 263, op. 1, pt. 2, d. 1670:23–25v., 28; P. Viatkin to Moscow Synodal Office, 28 September 1771, TsGADA, f. 1183, op. 1, d. 237:3.

5. Register of past and present personnel of Moscow Policemaster Chancery, 26 January 1772, TsGAg.M, f. 46, op. 7, d. 7722:1v.–3v.

6. S. M. Solov'ev, "Moskva v 1770 i 1771 gg.," *Russkaia starina* 17 (October 1876):202; Eropkin to C., 31 August 1771, *PPEE*, pp. 70–71.

7. Senate discussion and order to Municipal Administration, 1 September 1771; Policemaster Chancery to Senate, 3 September 1771; Municipal Administration to Senate, 5 September 1771; Senate discussion with merchants, 7 September 1771, TsGADA, f. 263, op. 1, pt. 2, d. 1670:18–19, 21–22, 42.

8. Senate meeting with Old Believers, 7 September 1771, ibid., pp. 47–47v.

9. Senate discussion, 7 September 1771; Senate to Policemaster Chancery, 29 September 1771; Admiralty Office to Senate, 13 September 1771, ibid., pp. 43–45, 48–48v.

10. Eropkin to Senate, 8 and 13 September 1771, ibid., pp. 71–77; C. to Eropkin, 17 September 1771, *PPEE*, pp. 82–83.

11. Registers of workers assigned to Eropkin, 7–9 and 12 September 1771, TsGADA, f. 277, op. 12, d. 419:1–13; *Opisanie*, p. 92; Investigatory Branch to Senate, 16 and 21 September

1771; Eropkin to Senate, 2 October 1771; register of convicts assigned as gravediggers, 30 October 1772, TsGADA, f. 263, op. 2, d. 1673:2-9v., 17, 119v.-25.

12. *MV*, 6 September 1771; V. Shvarts, *Kratkoe opisanie morovago povetriia i sredstv ot onago predokhraniaiushchikh, s pribavleniem o kontsentrirovannom uksusnom spirte* (Moscow, 1771).

13. Senate resolution, 1 September 1771; Eropkin to Senate, 10 September 1771, TsGADA, f. 263, op. 1, pt. 2, d. 1670:11-12; Eropkin to Amvrosii, 10 September 1771; Amvrosii to Eropkin, 12 September 1771, TsGADA, f. 1183, op. 1, d. 247:10-11.

14. [J. Lerche], "Primechaniia kollezhskogo sovetnika i shtat fizika gospodina doktora Lerkha" (September 1771), *Opisanie*, pp. 308-09.

15. [K. Yagel'skii], "Doktora Iagel'skago nekotorye primechaniia, v Pribavlenie k nastavleniiam dlia predokhraneniia ot zarazitel'noi bolezni" (September 1771), in ibid., pp. 310-16.

16. Sablukov's letters, excerpted in *Russkii arkhiv* (1866):336-37.

17. Beloglazov to Demidov, 5 September 1771, in B. B. Kafengauz, *Istoriia khoziaistva Demidovykh v XVIII–XIX vv.* (Moscow and Leningrad, 1949), 1:271, 500.

18. Amvrosii to Holy Synod, 12 September 1771, TsGIA-SSSR, f. 796, op. 52, d. 325:1-2.

19. Saltykov to C., 12 September 1771, TsGADA, f. 6, d. 410:165-66.

20. Register of deaths in Moscow through 12 September 1771; Saltykov to C., 19 September 1771, ibid., pp. 167-68.

21. P. V. Sytin, *Iz istorii Moskovskikh ulits*, 2nd. rev. ed. (Moscow, 1952), pp. 65-67.

22. A. Zertsalov, comp., "O miatezhakh v gorode Moskve i v sele Kolomenskom, v 1648, 1662 i 1771 gg.," *Ch. OIDR*, bk. 3 (1890):373-75, 377-78.

23. Ibid., p. 378; D. N. Bantysh-Kamenskii, *Zhizn' preosviashchennago Amvrosiia, arkhiepiskopa Moskovskago i Kaluzhskago, ubiennago v 1771-m godu* (Moscow, 1813), pp. 38-39.

24. Zertsalov, "O miatezhakh," p. 378.

25. I. E. Zabelin, *Istoriia goroda Moskvy*, pt. 1 (Moscow, 1902; reprinted Vaduz, 1969), pp. 614–22.

26. Rozanov, *Istoriia*, 2, pt. 2:62-77. See also A. Vvedenskii, *Kresttsovoe dukhovenstvo v staroi Moskve* (Moscow, 1899), whose interpretation downplays any independent role of the crossroads clerics in the Plague Riot.

27. Rozanov, *Istoriia*, 2, pt. 2:73-74.

28. Freeze, *Russian Levites*, pp. 136, 166.

29. Bantysh-Kamenskii, *Zhizn' Amvrosiia*, pp. 5-11, 32-35, 41.

30. Zertsalov, "O miatezhakh," pp. 372, 374, 376, 382.

31. Ibid., pp. 372, 380-82; Anon., "Opisanie o chume u o byvshem v Moskve narodnom smiatenii 1771 goda," in P. Bartenev, ed., *AKV*, 16:460.

32. Zertsalov, "O miatezhakh," p. 373.

33. Ibid., pp. 374-75.

34. Zertsalov, "O miatezhakh," pp. 376–77.

35. Ibid., pp. 370–71; Bakhmetev's account of the riot (22 September 1771), TsGADA, f. 6, d. 410:7-11; Solov'ev, "Moskva v 1770 i 1771 gg.," pp. 200-02.

36. Sytin, *Iz istorii Moskovskikh ulits*, pp. 66-67; Zertsalov, "O miatezhakh," p. 377; Beloglazov to Demidov, 19 September 1771, in Kafengauz, *Istoriia khoziaistva*, p. 501; Eropkin to Medical Consilium, 13 September 1771; Lerche, Shafonskii, Pogoretskii, and Veniaminov to Eropkin, 14 September 1771, *Opisanie*, pp. 317–19; Kamer Collegium to Senate, 15 September 1771, TsGADA, f. 248, op. 133, d. 1605:86.

37. Anon., "Opisanie o chume," pp. 461-62; Bantysh-Kamenskii, *Zhizn' Amvrosiia*, pp. 46-48.

38. Zertsalov, "O miatezhakh," p. 377.

39. P. Alekseev, "Opisanie Moskovskogo bunta 1771 goda sentiabria 15 dnia," *Russkii arkhiv*, 1863 (2nd ed., 1866):499.

40. Anon., "Opisanie o chume," p. 462.

41. Zertsalov, "O miatezhakh," p. 269; Mertens, *Account*, p. 23; Samoilovich, *IP*, 2:107–8; Lerche, *Lebens- und Reise-Geschichte*, pp. 460-61.

42. Bantysh-Kamenskii, *Zhizn' Amvrosiia*, pp. 49-63; Zertsalov, "O miatezhakh," p. 383; letter to Archbishop Platon in Petersburg from his brother in Moscow, Alexander Levshin, 19 September 1771, GPB, Erm. 355:93; Anon., "Opisanie o chume," p. 463.

43. Zertsalov, "O miatezhakh," pp. 382–86.
44. [F. V. Karzhavin], "O bunte moskovskom ochevidnoe izvestie, nedokonchennoe," in S. R. Dolgova, ed., "Zapiski ochevidtsa o chumnom bunte v Moskve v 1771 godu," *Sovetskie arkhivy* (1976), 6:68.
45. Alekseev, "Opisanie bunta," p. 495.
46. [N. N. Bantysh-Kamenskii?] to Anon., 31 October 1771, "Materialy dlia istorii chumy v Moskve v 1771 godu," in A. P. Barsukov et al., eds., *Pamiatniki novoi russkoi istorii*, 3 vols. (St. Petersburg, 1871–73), 3:309.
47. Anon., "Opisanie o chume," pp. 464–65.
48. Alekseev, "Opisanie bunta," p. 497.
49. Anon., "Opisanie o chume," pp. 465–66; Karzhavin, "O bunte moskovskom," pp. 68–69.
50. Anon., "Pis'mo ochevidtsa o bunte v Moskve vo vremia chumy, 15 i 16 sentiabria 1771 goda i o ubienii arkhiereia Amvrosiia Zertis-Kamenskago," *Deistviia Nizhegorodskoi gubernskoi uchenoi arkhivnoi kommissii*, fasc. 1–8 (Nizhnii-Novgorod, 1890), p. 360.
51. Karzhavin, "O bunte moskovskom," p. 69.
52. Eropkin to C., 18, 22, and 29 September 1771, *PPEE*, pp. 88, 107, 116–17.
53. Karzhavin, "O bunte moskovskom," p. 69; Alekseev, "Opisanie bunta," p. 497; Anon., "Opisanie o chume," p. 466; Anon., "Pis'mo ochevidtsa," p. 360: Saltykov to C., 19 September 1771, TsGADA, f. 6, d. 410:169v.
54. Zertsalov, "O miatezhakh," pp. 388–417.
55. Anon., "Opisanie o chume," p. 467; Karzhavin, "O bunte moskovskom," p. 69.
56. P. K. Alefirenko, "Chumnyi bunt v Moskve v 1771 godu," *Voprosy istorii* 4 (1947):84, 87–89; V. N. Bernadskii, "Ocherki iz istorii klassovoi bor'by i obshchestvenno-politicheskoi mysli Rossii v tret'ei chetverti XVIII veka," *Uchenye zapiski Leningradskii gos. ped. inst. im. Gertsena*, kafedra istorii, 229 (1962):96–98.
57. E. V. Chistiakova, *Gorodskie vosstaniia v Rossii v pervoi polovine XVII veka* (Voronezh, 1975); V. I. Buganov, *Moskovskoe vosstanie 1662 g.* (Moscow, 1964), and idem, *Moskovskie vosstaniia kontsa XVII veka* (Moscow, 1969).
58. Karzhavin, "O bunte moskovskom," p. 69; Beloglazov to Demidov, 19 September 1771, in Kafengauz, *Istoriia khoziaistva*, p. 501; Alekseev, "Opisanie bunta," p. 496; Eropkin to C., 19 September 1771, *PPEE*, pp. 93–96.
59. Karzhavin, "O bunte moskovskom," pp. 69–70.
60. Saltykov to C., 19 September (2 letters) and 21 September 1771, TsGADA, f. 6, d. 410:168–77v.
61. Saltykov to C., 21 September 1771, ibid., pp. 176–76v.
62. Alekseev, "Opisanie bunta," pp. 492, 500.
63. Zertsalov, "O miatezhakh," pp. 377, 384–85, 401–2, 418–20.
64. Ibid., p. 422.
65. C. to A. I. Bibikov, 20 October 1771, *SIRIO*, 13:180.
66. Zertsalov, "O miatezhakh," pp. 388–417.
67. Eropkin to C., 18 September 1771, *PPEE*, p. 85; Saltykov to C., 19 September 1771, TsGADA, f. 6, d. 410:168v., 174v.
68. G. Orlov to C., late October 1771, *SIRIO*, 13:205.
69. Beloglazov to Demidov, 19 September 1771, in Kafengauz, *Istoriia khoziaistva*, p. 501; Alekseev, "Opisanie bunta," p. 491.
70. Bernadskii, "Ocherki klassovoi bor'by," pp. 90, 95–97; Iu. R. Klokman, *Sotsial'no-ekonomicheskaia istoriia russkogo goroda: Vtoraia polovina XVIII veka* (Moscow, 1967), pp. 74–76.
71. Zertsalov, "O miatezhakh," pp. 392–93, 399–401.
72. Ibid., pp. 387–91.
73. Lerche, "Conspectus," Moscow weather in September 1771; "Zametki neizvestnago," p. 38; Beloglazov to Demidov, 19 September 1771, in Kafengauz, *Istoriia khoziaistva*, p. 501; Sablukov, 22 September 1771, *Russkii arkhiv* (1866): 337.
74. Bakhmetev's account, 22 September 1771, TsGADA, f. 6, d. 410:10v.

Chapter Eight

1. C. to N. I. Panin, 10 September and [12 September] 1771, *SIRIO,* 13:166; vol. 42:371.
2. *AGS,* 1, pt. 1:412–13.
3. C. to Saltykov, 20 September 1771, "Pis'ma Saltykovu," p. 105; Senate reports of the incidents at Lefortovo and on Red Square, received in Petersburg on 19 September and heard by the Senate on 21 September 1771, TsGADA, f. 248, op. 113, d. 1605:79–82; C. to A. I. Bibikov, 20 October 1771, *SIRIO,* 13:180–81.
4. A. A. Golombievskii, *Biografiia kniazia G. Orlova* (Moscow, 1904), pp. 1–35; Cathcart to Suffolk, 20 September 1771, *SIRIO,* 19:232–33.
5. *AGS,* 1, pt. 1:414; *Opisanie,* pp. 97–98.
6. *Kamer-fur'erskii tseremonial'nyi zhurnal 1771 goda* (St. Petersburg, 1857), pp. 341–42; C., manifesto issued in Petersburg on 21 September and published in Moscow on 30 September 1771, TsGADA, f. 199, d. 151, pt. 1, no. 1:51 (published in *PSZ,* 19: no. 13,657).
7. Orlov to C. [22 September 1771], TsGADA, f. 6, d. 410:274–74v.
8. C. to Orlov, 23 September 1771, *SIRIO,* 2:286; Cathcart to Suffolk, 23 and 27 September 1771, *SIRIO,* 19:234, 237.
9. C. to Orlov, 23 September 1771, *SIRIO,* 2:286–87.
10. C. to Senate, 24 September 1771, TsGIA-SSSR, f. 1329, op. 2, d. 112:114.
11. C. to Eck, undated notes, [September 1771], *SIRIO,* 13:169–71.
12. *AGS,* 1, pt. 1:414–15.
13. *SPV,* 27 September 1771, supplement; draft of newspaper article with corrections, TsGADA, f. 6, d. 410:12–13; Cathcart to Suffolk, 27 September 1771, *SIRIO,* 19:235–36; Lobkowitz to Kaunitz, 30 September/11 October 1771, *SIRIO,* 109:590–91.
14. C. to A. I. Bibikov, 20 October 1771, *SIRIO,* 13:179–80.
15. Eropkin to C., 19 September 1771, *PPEE,* pp. 93–95.
16. Saltykov to C., 21 September 1771; Protasov to M. Mamonov, president of the Moscow Municipal Administration, 22 September 1771, TsGADA, f. 6, d. 410:176v.–78v.; Eropkin to Senate, 30 September 1771; senate discussion, 4 October 1771, TsGADA, f. 263, op. 2, d. 1678:21, 31–32; Senate to Tula Arms Manufactory, 23 September 1771, with instructions to courier, TsGADA, f. 268, op. 2, d. 1677:1–3, 6; *PSZ,* 19: no. 13,659 (24 September 1771).
17. Eropkin to C., 19, 22 (three letters), and 29 September 1771, *PPEE,* pp. 97–115.
18. Moscow guberniia chancery to Senate, 17 September 1771; Sukin to Senate, 15 September 1771; Senate discussion, 19 September 1771; Senate to Collegium of Manufactures, 27 September 1771; Senate receipt of 500 copies of Lerche's and Yagel'skii's advisories, 23 September 1771; [J. F. Erasmus], "Kratkoe opisanie morovoi iazvy, kakim obrazom onuiu uznavat', i kak sebia i drugikh vo vremia morovoe predokhraniat'," and senate discussion, 19 September 1771, TsGADA, f. 263, op. 1, pt. 2, d. 1670:55, 62–63, 92–95, 98–102v.; Eropkin to Moscow Synodal Office, 24 September 1771; Synodal Office to Moscow Consistory, 27 September 1771, TsGADA, f. 1183, op. 1, d. 247:4–5.
19. Eropkin to Senate, 21 September; senate discussion, 23 September 1771; Senate to Petersburg Senate, 24 September 1771; Policemaster chancery to Senate, 26 September 1771, TsGADA, f. 263, op. 1, pt. 2, d. 1670:87–91, 104–13.
20. *PSZ,* 19: no. 13,660 (24 September 1771).
21. Orlov to C., 27 September 1771, TsGADA, f. 6, d. 410:275.
22. Senate resolution after discussion with Orlov, 29 September 1771; Senate announcement of investigating commission, 30 September 1771; Rozhnov to Senate, 2 October 1771, TsGADA, f. 263, op. 2, d. 1675:1–1v., 3, 8; *AGS,* 1, pt. 1:418.
23. C., manifesto about Orlov's mission, 21 September 1771, *SIRIO,* 13:168–69; Orlov's proclamation, *PSZ,* 19: no. 13,665 (30 September 1771). For the text of Orlov's proclamation, I have used a translation of the time prepared at the British embassy in Petersburg and sent by Cathcart to London on 11 October 1771: PROSP, 91/88:209–10v.
24. PROSP, 91/88:209v.–10v.
25. Senate correspondence with Mel'gunov, Tver provincial chancery, Kamer Collegium, and Moscow guberniia chancery, 30 September–14 December 1771, TsGADA, f. 263, op. 2, d. 1681:1–18.
26. P. Mokeev to A. R. Vorontsov, 16 October 1771, *AKV,* 16:455.
27. Senate correspondence with Vyrubov, Amilakhorov, and Shakhovskaia, 30 September

1771–July 1773, TsGADA, f. 263, op. 2, d. 1680:1–22, 37–61; Executive Commission to Vyrubov and Amilakhorov, 26 October 1771, TsGADA, f. 263, op. 2, d. 1683:16.

28. Senate correspondence with Sukin, 3 October–1 December 1771, TsGADA, f. 263, op. 2, d. 1684:1–30v.; V. Drashusov, ed., *Materialy*, 2:40–43.

29. *PSZ*, 19: no. 13,688 (26 October 1771); senate correspondence concerning public works, 25 October 1771–26 July 1773, TsGADA, f. 263, op. 2, d. 1689:2, 7, 9–11, 16–17, 22, 30–30v., 38, 41, 48–54, 59, 72–74; Orlov to C., October 1771, *SIRIO*, 13:205; *PSZ*, 19: no. 13,697 (15 November 1771); Brigadier Shtok to Plague Commission, 24 November 1771, TsGAg.M, f. 636, op. 2, d. 13:40–40v.

30. The government spent more than 400,000 rubles in Moscow alone, the greater part of it after Orlov's arrival. *Opisanie*, p. ii.

31. Orlov to C., 3 October 1771, TsGADA, f. 6, d. 410:276–76v.; Senate to C., 12 December 1771, TsGADA, r. XVI, no. 168, pt. 8:199–201.

32. Moscow guberniia chancery to Senate, 3 October 1771, TsGADA, f. 263, op. 2, d. 1681:9–9v.; Yushkov to Senate, 30 September 1771; Eropkin to Senate, 2 October 1771; Eropkin's discussion with Senate, 7 October 1771; senate discussion, 23 November 1771, TsGADA, f. 263, op. 2, d. 1673:16–18, 39–40, 74.

33. Moscow Synodal Office to Moscow Consistory, 19 September 1771; Consistory to Synodal Office, 21 September 1771; journal of Synodal Office, 1, 3, 5, 12 October 1771, TsGADA, f. 1183, op. 1, d. 250:7–8v., 19–22, 25–26, 30, 35; Holy Synod to Moscow Synodal Office, 28 September 1771; Synodal Office to Synod, 6 October 1771, TsGIA-SSSR, f. 796, op. 52, d. 337:5–9, 13–14v.; "Slovo skazyvannoe pri pogrebenii Preosviashchennogo Amvrosiia, Arkhiepiskopa Moskovskogo i Kaluzhskago," 4 October 1771, with German translation, TsGADA, f. 199, d. 151, pt. 1, no. 1:56–62v.; *SPV*, 28 October 1771.

34. Journal of Synodal Office, 24 October 1771, TsGADA, f. 1183, op. 1, d. 250:53–54.

35. Orlov to Moscow medical community, 30 September 1771, *Opisanie*, pp. 325–26; English translation in Mertens, *Account*, pp. 78–80.

36. Mertens, *Account*, pp. 83, 93.

37. Orlov to medical community, 6 October 1771, *Opisanie*, pp. 326–28.

38. Medical community to Orlov, 6 October 1771, ibid., pp. 328–29.

39. Medical community to Orlov, 6 and 7 October 1771, ibid., pp. 329–36.

40. Volkov et al. to Orlov, 7 October 1771, ibid., pp. 337–39.

41. [Catherine II?], untitled and undated memo [September 1771?], TsGADA, f. 16, d. 328, pt. 1:118–19v.

42. Bielfeld, *Institutions politiques*, 1:104–5; Justi, *Die Grundfeste*, 1:249–51. For the Austrian model, see Erna Lesky, *Österreichisches Gesundheitswesen im Zeitalter des aufgeklärten Absolutismus* (Vienna, 1959), pp. 118–40.

43. *Opisanie*, pp. 100–01; commission session of 13 October 1771, TsGAg.M, f. 636, op. 2, d. 2:2v.

44. *SIRIO*, 93:134; N. Krasheninnikova, "K voprosu ob atributsii byvshego doma Dolgova na 1-i Meshchanskoi ulitse," *Arkhitekturnoe nasledstvo* (Moscow, 1951), 1:86–93; Aksenov, "Moskovskoe kupechestvo v XVIII v.," pp. 181, 187–88.

45. Samoilovich, *IP*, 2:122n.

46. *PSZ*, 19: no. 13,675 (11 October 1771).

47. Session of 12 October 1771, TsGAg.M, f. 636, op. 2, d. 2:1–1v.; commission (Grave) to district supervisor Kazakov, 14 October 1771, TsGAg.M, f. 636, op. 2, d. 5:2.

48. V. Baskakov, assignment of clerical workers, 16 October 1771, TsGAg.M, f. 636, op. 2, d. 2:30–31.

49. Commission sessions, 13–14, 17–19 October 1771, TsGAg.M, f. 636, op. 2, d. 2:3–4, 7v., 23v., 32v.–35, 39.

50. *Opisanie*, pp. 104–6; assignment of pesthouses and quarantines, 8 November 1771, TsGAg.M, f. 636, op. 2, d. 10:11–11v.

51. Moscow Synodal Office to Levshin, 31 October 1771; extract of Plague Commission journal, 1 November 1771, TsGADA, f. 1183, op. 1, d. 247:84–86; Senate journal, 4 October 1771, TsGADA, f. 263, op.2, d. 1678:30. Registers of churches without services and churches where priests died, 19 October 1771, Skvortsov, *Materialy*, 2:601–8.

52. Orraeus's instructions, 19 October 1771, TsGAg.M, f. 636, op. 2, d. 2:35–35v., 36.

53. Sessions of 15–16, 18 October 1771, TsGAg.M, f. 636, op. 2, d. 2:14, 17–17v., 33v.; practitioners' replies to commission, ca. 20 October 1771, TsGAg.M, f. 636. op. 2, d. 5:48–50.

54. Sessions of 14, 17, 19, 20, 22–23, 27–28 October 1771, TsGAg.M, f. 636, op. 2, d. 2:6v., 24, 39–41v., 45v.–47v., 67–68; sessions of 11–12 November 1771, TsGAg.M, f. 636, op. 2, d. 10:58–59; d. 11:5.

55. Sessions of 23 and 25 October 1771; instructions to Frau Margraf, 1 November 1771, TsGAg.M, f. 636, op. 2, d. 2:47v.–48v., 55v., 59–61; session of 12 November and commission to Lerche, 16 November 1771, TsGAg.M, f. 636. op. 2, d. 11:3–4.

56. Sessions of 20, 23, 26–27, 29 October 1771, TsGAg.M, f. 636, op. 2, d. 2:42v., 48, 63, 65, 67v., 70.

57. S. M. Grombakh, "S. G. Zybelin v bor'be s epidemiei chumy 1771–1772 gg.," *Sovetskoe zdravookhranenie* 6 (1962):87–88; A. I. Metelkin, "Bor'ba meditsinskoi organizatsii s chumoi vo vremia Moskovskoi epidemii 1770–1772 gg.," *Zhurnal mikrobiologii, epidemiologii i immunobiologii* 9 (1974):144–47.

58. Sessions of 23 and 26 October 1771, TsGAg.M, f. 636, op. 2, d. 2:47v., 65v.; sessions of 12–13 November 1771, TsGAg.M, f. 636, op. 2, d. 11:7, 16–16v.; session of 25 April 1772, TsGAg.M, f. 636, op. 2, d. 26:41v.

59. Session of 16 October 1771, TsGAg.M, f. 636, op. 2, d. 2:18–19; commission correspondence with newly subdivided districts, 19 October–1 November 1771, TsGAg.M, f. 636, op. 2, d. 5:51–68v.

60. Sessions of 17 and 23 October 1771, TsGAg.M, f. 636, op. 2, d. 2:22–23, 48v.; *PSZ,* 19: no. 13,680 (15 October 1771); Orlov to C. [23 October 1771], *SIRIO,* 13:205–6; *Opisanie,* pp. 109–11.

61. Sessions of 24 and 26 October 1771, TsGAg.M, f. 636, op. 2, d. 2:51–52v., 64–64v.

62. *PSZ,* 19: no. 13,697 (15 November 1771).

63. *PSZ,* 19: no, 13,722 (24 December 1771), no. 13,768 (27 February 1772); *Opisanie,* pp. 129–30, 138; police investigation of 23 suspected looters, 12 January–3 February 1772, TsGAg.M, f. 46, op. 7, d. 4070.

64. *PSZ,* 19: no. 13,676 (12 October 1771); Executive Commission correspondence about case of looting, 16–21 October 1771, TsGADA, f. 263, op. 2, d. 1678:120–27v.; Bakhmetev to Commission, 12 December 1771, TsGAg.M, f. 636, op. 2, d. 17:48–48v.

65. Session of 23 October 1771, TsGAg.M, f. 636, op. 2, d. 2:48v.–49v.

66. Discussions in Moscow Synodal Office, 17–31 October 1771, TsGADA, f. 1183, op. 1, d. 247:61–62, 121–30v.; C. to Bielcke, 13 November 1771, *SIRIO,* 13:186.

67. Session of 15 October 1771, TsGAg.M, f. 636, op. 2, d. 2:14.

68. Sessions of 17–18, 22, 25 October 1771; St. Nicolaz's proposal, 14 October 1771, TsGAg.M, f. 636, op. 2, d. 2:23, 28–31v., 33, 45, 55, 66v.; session of 12 November 1771, TsGAg.M, f. 636, op. 2, d. 10:64–66v.; Eropkin to G. Orlov, 26 July 1773, TsGADA, f. 16, d. 328, pt. 1, 308–9v.; Samoilovich, *IP,* 2:332–34; *PSZ,* 19: no. 13,715 (10 December 1771), no. 13,736 (12 January 1772); sessions of 14–16 January 1772, TsGAg.M, f. 636, op. 2, d. 23:25–29.

69. Session of 13 October 1771, TsGAg.M, f. 636, op. 2. d. 2:4; *PSZ,* 19: no. 13,683 (20 October 1771), no. 13,697 (15 November 1771).

70. Sessions of 15, 19, 21, 28 October 1771; "Polza ot balsamoi," translation from Armenian by V. Khastatov, 19 October 1771, TsGAg.M, f. 636, op. 2, d. 2:14v., 25–27, 44, 68v.; [G. Orraeus], "Kratkoe uvedomlenie kakim obrazom poznavat' morovuiu iazvu, takzhe vrachevat' i predokhraniat' ot onoi," *PSZ,* 19: no. 13,682 (20 October 1771).

71. Session of 27 October 1771, TsGAg.M, f. 636, op. 2, d. 2:65v.–66; commission to Krechetnikov, 16 November 1771, TsGAg.M, f. 636, op. 2, d. 10:71.

72. Session of 31 October 1771, TsGAg.M, f. 636, op. 2, d. 2:80.

73. Zybelin to Commission, 24 October 1771, as quoted by Grombakh, "Zybelin v bor'be," pp. 88–89.

74. Session of 18 October 1771, TsGAg.M, f. 636, op. 2, d. 2:32v.; commission journals, 14 and 16 November 1771; commission to Kazakov and all district supervisors, 17 November 1771, TsGAg.M, f. 636, op. 2, d. 11:62–63, 79.

75. Session of 16 November 1771; commission to Meltzer, 19 November 1771, TsGAg.M, f. 636, op. 2, d. 11:77–78.

76. Commission journal, 9 November 1771, TsGAg.M, f. 636, op. 2, d. 10:40; sessions of 17–18, 23, 27 January 1772, TsGAg.M, f. 636, op. 2, d. 23:31v.–33, 45, 65; *Opisanie,* pp. 631–33.

77. *Opisanie,* p. 620; register of releases from quarantines, 4 October–20 November 1771, TsGADA, f. 263, op. 2, d. 1678:317; Orlov to C., 18 October 1771, TsGADA, f. 6, d. 410:277.

78. "Zametki neizvestnago," p. 38; Sablukov diary, 7 November 1771, *Russkii arkhiv* (1866):338.
79. Lerche, "Conspectus," weather data in Moscow, October 1771-January 1772; Mertens, *Account,* p. 29.
80. *Opisanie,* pp. 620-22.
81. Ibid., pp. 620, 622; releases from quarantines, 4 October-20 November 1771, TsGADA, f. 263, op. 2, d. 1678:317; Orlov to C., 16 November 1771, TsGADA, f. 6, d. 410:278.
82. *AGS,* 1, pt. 1:426; releases from quarantines, 4-18 December 1771, TsGADA, f. 263, op. 2, d. 1678:390; *Opisanie,* pp. 620-22.
83. Mertens, *Account,* pp. 29-30; Pogoretskii to commission, 21 October 1771, TsGAg.M, f. 636, op. 2, d. 6:39.
84. C. to A. I. Bibikov, 20 October 1771; to senate and S. Koz'min, 4 November 1771, *SIRIO,* 13:180, 182; to Orlov, 3 November 1771, *SIRIO,* 2:288; *AGS,* 1, pt. 1:421-22.
85. C. to Orlov, 5-6 November 1771, *SIRIO,* 2:288; to Volkonskii, 5 November 1771, TsGIA- SSSR, f. 1329, op. 2, d. 112:118-21, published without dating in *SIRIO,* 12:191-96; C. to Volkonskii, 6 and 10 November 1771, *OV,* 1:62-63.
86. Proceedings of the trial in Zertsalov, "O miatezhakh," pp. 364-68, 417-39; *PSZ,* 19: no. 13,695 (10 November 1771).
87. *AGS,* 1, pt. 1:424-25; Orlov to C., 16 November 1771, TsGADA, f. 6, d. 410:278-78v.; Senate journal, 19 November 1771, TsGADA, f. 263, op. 2, d. 1678:212; "Zametki neizvestnago," p. 39.
88. C. to Orlov, 3 December 1771, *SIRIO,* 2:288-89; *Kamer-fur'erskii zhurnal 1771 goda,* p. 423; A. G. Brikner, "O chume v Moskve 1771 goda," *Russkii vestnik* 10 (1884):527-39, demolishes insinuations that Catherine sent Orlov to Moscow hoping to get rid of him altogether.
89. C. to Eropkin, 5 November 1771; Eropkin to C., 21 November and 15 December 1771, *PPEE,* pp. 123-35; C. to Saltykov and to Senate, 7 November 1771, C. to Bielcke, 13 November 1771, *SIRIO,* 13:185-86; C. to Volkonskii, 10 January 1772, *OV,* 1:66-67.
90. Swallow to Suffolk, 29 November 1771, PROSP, 91/88:293v.

Chapter Nine

1. V. M. Kabuzan, *Narodonaselenie Rossii v XVIII-pervoi polovine XIX v.* (Moscow, 1963), pp. 130, 165.
2. V. M. Kabuzan, *Izmeneniia v razmeshchenii naseleniia Rossii v XVIII-pervoi polovine XIX v.* (Moscow, 1971), p. 86.
3. Gilbert Rozman, *Urban Networks in Russia 1750–1800 and Pre-modern Periodization* (Princeton, 1976), pp. 105, 160-80.
4. Kabuzan, *Izmeneniia,* p. 83.
5. Ia. E. Vodarskii, *Promyshlennye seleniia tsentral'noi Rossii v period genezisa i razvitiia kapitalizma* (Moscow, 1972).
6. See Basile H. Kerblay, *L'isba d'hier et d'aujourd'hui: l'évolution de l'habitation rurale en U.R.S.S.* (Lausanne, 1973).
7. G. Orlov to C. [October 1771], *SIRIO,* 13:205.
8. *AGS,* 1, pt. 1:405-7.
9. Senate to St. P., 30 August 1771, quoting report of Saltykov and Eropkin of 23 August, TsGADA, f. 248, op. 113, d. 1605:63.
10. *AGS,* 1, pt. 1:410-11; C. to Collegium of Economy, 23 September 1771, TsGADA, f. 263, op. 2, d. 1678:48-48v.; C., *Sochineniia,* 12:642.
11. *AGS,* 1, pt. 1:412.
12. *PSZ,* 19: no. 13,662 (25 September 1771).
13. See ch. 6, p. 175.
14. Tolchenov, *Zhurnal,* pp. 37-38.
15. For comparison, see Leslie Bradley, "The Geographical Spread of Plague," in *The Plague Reconsidered* (Matlock, Derbyshire, 1977), pp. 127-32.
16. Senate to St. P., 10 October 1771, TsGADA, f. 248, op. 113, d. 1605: 110-12v.; Senate to C., 19 October 1771, TsGADA, f. 6, d. 410:68-72; *AGS,* 1, pt. 1:424.

17. Commission to Mel'gunov, 17 December 1771 and 5 January 1772, TsGAg.M, f. 636, op. 1, d. 48:23, 26; commission session of 7 February 1772, TsGAg.M, f. 636, op. 2, d. 24:9v.

18. Mel'gunov to Senate, 28 January 1772, with enclosures and register; register of mortality in Moscow district, 16 March 1772, TsGADA, f. 263, op. 2, d. 1688:102, 106–8v., 178, 493.

19. Moscow guberniia chancery to Senate, 24 October 1772, with register, TsGAg.M, f. 636, op. 2, d. 57:205–7.

20. Population extrapolated from Kabuzan, *Izmeneniia*, pp. 83, 95; for the administrative division of Moscow province, see Kabuzan, *Narodonaselenie*, p. 180.

21. Mortality in Moscow district from the Kashira to the Petersburg roads, 16 March 1772, TsGADA, f. 263, op. 2, d. 1688:493.

22. Mortality in Moscow district (January 1772?), TsGAg.M, f. 636, op. 2, d. 57:214; *Opisanie*, pp. 76–77; Samoilovich, *IP*, 2:68, 136.

23. Meshalin, comp., *Materialy*, 2:117–18, 131, 135, 137, 142–43, 149–51.

24. Mortality in Moscow district, TsGAg.M, f. 636, op. 2, d. 57:214.

25. Meshalin, comp., *Materialy*, 2:112, 144–45, 250; Volkov, *Krest'iane dvortsovykh vladenii*, pp. 17–18, 31, 40, 123, 126, 141; mortality in Moscow district, TsGAg.M, f. 636, op. 2, d. 57:219.

26. Senate to Petersburg departments, 24 August 1771, citing report to Moscow guberniia chancery, TsGADA, f. 248, op. 113, d. 1605:56.

27. Meshalin, comp., *Materialy*, 2:335; Vodarskii, *Promyshlennye seleniia*, pp. 50, 81–82.

28. Mortality in Moscow district, TsGAg.M, f. 636, op. 2, d. 57:215; Tukhachevskii to Mel'gunov, January 1772, with register, TsGAg.M, f. 636, op. 1, d. 42:20v.; register of closed villages, January 1772, TsGADA, f. 263, op. 2, d. 1688:110.

29. Mortality in Moscow district, TsGAg.M, f. 636, op. 2, d. 57:219v.; registers of closed villages, January 1772, TsGADA, f. 263, op. 2, d. 1688:110.

30. Mortality in Moscow district, October 1772, TsGAg.M, f. 636, op. 2, d. 57:206.

31. Tukhachevskii to Mel'gunov, late December 1771, with registers, TsGAg.M, f. 636, op. 1, d. 42:16–17v., 20–20v.

32. Vorontsov to G. Orlov, *AKV*, 16:449–50, 452.

33. Ibid., pp. 450–51.

34. *PSZ*, no. 13,729 (31 December 1771).

35. Mozhaisk voevoda chancery to Senate, late 1772, with register of plague losses, TsGAg.M, f. 636, op. 2, d. 57:19v.

36. Polianskii, *Gorodskoe remeslo i manufaktura*, pp. 28, 130; Rozman, *Urban Networks*, pp. 167–68; A. I. Suslov and S. S. Churakov, *Iaroslavl'* (Moscow, 1960), pp. 132, 138, 269–70.

37. See ch. 6, p. 169.

38. *PSZ*, 19: no. 13,696 (11 November 1771); Plague Commission journal, 8 November 1771, TsGAg.M, f. 636, op. 2, d. 10:35.

39. Halliday to Plague Commission, 19 November 1771, TsGAg.M, f. 636, op. 1, d. 13:18.

40. Halliday to commission, 3 December 1771; commission discussion, 17 December; commission to Senate and Yushkov, 19 December; Yushkov to commission, 27 December; Halliday to Commission, 10 December 1771, TsGAg.M, f. 636, op. 1, d. 13:23–30; Commission session of 19 January 1772, TsGAg.M, f. 636, op. 2, d. 23:34.

41. C. to Volkonskii, 20 December 1771, *OV*, 1:65; Volkonskii to C., 1 January 1772; Senate to Yaroslavl provincial chancery, 9 January 1772, TsGADA, f. 455, op. 1, d. 608:21–21v., 272–72v.; Senate to C., 10 January 1772, TsGADA, f. 16, d. 328, pt. 1:98–100.

42. A. F. Griaznov, *Iaroslavskaia bol'shaia manufaktura za vremia s 1722 po 1856 g.* (Moscow, 1910), pp. 204–11.

43. Yaroslavl provincial chancery to Senate, late 1772, TsGAg.M, f. 636, op. 2, d. 57:34; Moscow guberniia chancery to Senate, December 1771, TsGADA, f. 16, d. 328, pt. 1:276v.

44. Yaroslavl provincial chancery to Senate, January 1772, with registry of plague deaths, TsGADA, f. 455, op. 1, d. 701:39–41v.

45. Yaroslavl provincial chancery, Romanov voevoda chancery, and Kineshma voevoda chancery to Senate, late 1772, TsGAg.M, f. 636, op. 2, d. 57:120–37v.

46. Yaroslavl provincial chancery to Major Semen Malygin, 11 November 1771; register of noble inspectors and villages in Edomskaia region; Yaroslavl provincial chancery to noble inspectors, 10 December 1771, 3 January 1772, and 31 January 1772, with Senate instruction and assignments in Edomskaia region, TsGADA, f. 455, op. 1, d. 608:1–19v.

47. Yaroslavl provincial chancery with summary of Bulygin's report, 15 November 1771; instructions to Corporal Vasilii Boiarintsov, 17 November 1771; Boiarintsov to Yaroslavl provincial chancery, 26 November 1771, TsGADA, f. 455, op. 1, d. 656:1-4. I am indebted to Daniel Morrison for guidance to these materials.

48. For some other incidents in the Yaroslavl region, see P. Mizinov, *Melochi Iaroslavskoi istorii XVIII i XIX v.* (Yaroslavl, 1895), pp. 62-66.

49. Kaluga provincial chancery to Senate, 31 July 1772, TsGAg.M, f. 636, op. 3, d. 57:178-79.

50. Guards quartermaster Stepan Ergol'skii (Kaluga) to Plague Commission, 28 October 1771; commission discussion, 11 November, and orders to Ergol'skii, 14 November, TsGAg.M, f. 636, op. 2, d. 10:57-59; Chistovich, *Istoriia*, app. 10:120; *Opisanie*, p. 633.

51. Commission to Wendrich, 19 December 1771; Wendrich to commission, late December 1771; commission discussion of Wendrich's report, 31 January 1772, TsGAg.M, f. 636, op. 2, d. 17:42; d. 19:39-39v., 76v.; commission discussions of Wendrich's reports, 6 February, 9 February, 2 March, 24 March, 3 April, 27 April, 16 June, 17 July, 26-27 October 1772, TsGAg.M, f. 636, op. 2, d. 24:8v.-9, 15v.; d. 25:5, 59v.; d. 26:4v., 43; d. 28:22; d. 29:25; d. 32:45v., 47; *PSZ*, 19: no. 13,729 (31 December 1771).

52. Bolotov, *Zhizn' i prikliucheniia*, 2:501-2; vol. 3:16.

53. Ibid., 2:511-12.

54. Ibid., 2:511-12, 527, 529, 532; vol. 3:14, 15.

55. Ibid., 3:18-21, 41.

56. Ibid., 3:46.

57. Tula provincial chancery to Senate, late 1772, TsGAg.M, f. 636, op. 2, d. 57:103-4; Donald H. Van Lare, "Tula Province in the Eighteenth Century: The Deputy Instructions to the Legislative Commission of 1767 as a Source for Local History," Ph.D. dissertation, University of Kansas, 1977, pp. 12, 17-20.

58. Bolotov, *Zhizn' i prikliucheniia*, 3:46-47.

59. Tolchenov, *Zhurnal*, p. 38; Griaznov, *Iaroslavskaia bol'shaia manufaktura*, p. 211; Palace stables chancery to Moscow Synodal Office, 28 November 1771; Synodal Office to stables chancery, 9 December 1771; Feodosii to Synodal Office, 15 December 1771, TsGADA, f. 1183, op. 1, d. 329:1-3, 6.

60. Bolotov, *Zhizn' i prikliucheniia*, 3:48. For European analogues, see Biraben, *Les hommes et la peste*, 2:23-24.

61. Kvashin-Samarin to Senate, 6 November 1771, with register of mortality in district, TsGADA, f. 263, op. 2, d. 1678:241-44; Nizhnii-Novgorod guberniia chancery to Senate, late 1772, TsGAg.M, f. 636, op. 2, d. 57:151-55v.; commission sessions of 7 February, 6 March, 24 March, and 26 October 1772, TsGAg.M, f. 636, op. 2, d. 24:11; d. 25:9, 59v.; d. 32:45v. On the grain trade at Lyskovo, see Kafengauz, *Ocherki vnutrennego rynka*, pp. 79, 84, 88, 140, and Tolchenov, *Zhurnal*, pp. 35, 50, 56.

62. Medical Office to Plague Commission, 7 November; commission discussion, 9 November; Commission to Povanarius, 24 November 1771, TsGAg.M, f. 636, op. 2, d. 10:41-43.

63. Munro, "The Development of St. Petersburg," pp. 28-40, 60-63, 169-234, 275-78, 307.

64. Sievers to C., 23 July 1771, TsGADA, f. 16, d. 785:218; *AGS*, 1, pt. 1:406-10, 412, 414-16.

65. *PSZ*, 19: no. 13,658 (23 September 1771); no. 13,663 (30 September 1771).

66. *AGS*, 1, pt. 1:420-21; Sievers (Tver) to G. Orlov, 9 November 1771; Plague Commission to Sievers, 13 November 1771, TsGAg.M, f. 636, op. 2, d. 10:60-62v.; Mansurov's reports from Tver, 2 December 1771-29 September 1772, TsGADA, f. 6, d. 410:354-85.

67. *AGS*, 1, pt. 1:416-18.

68. Police proclamation, 10 October 1771, with German, French, and Finnish translations, TsGADA, f. 199, d. 151, pt. 1, no. 1:64-68; Russian text in *PSZ*, 19: no. 13,674.

69. Synod order to staff, with signatures of compliance, 19 October 1771, TsGIA-SSSR, f. 796, op. 52, d. 370:5-7; *AGS*, 1, pt. 1:419-20.

70. *PSZ*, 19: no. 13,689 (26 October 1771); Chicherin to C., 30 October and 6 November 1771, TsGADA, f. 16, d. 481, pt. 3:201v., 203; *AGS*, 1, pt. 1:419-20.

71. *AGS*, 1, pt. 1:421-23; Lerche, "Ephemerides," 3: weather data, October 1771-March 1772; C. to Bielcke, 13 November 1771, *SIRIO*, 13:185-86.

72. Kologrivov to Bruce, 8 December 1771, TsGADA, f. 16, d. 328, pt. 1:399-400.

73. Mortality in Novgorod guberniia in 1766, 1768, 1769, and 1771, TsGADA, f. 16, d. 785:61-62, 87-88, 161-62, 213-17v., 223. I am indebted to Robert E. Jones for these data.

74. William Richardson, *Anecdotes of the Russian Empire* (London, 1784; reprinted London, 1968), p. 450.

75. *AGS*, 1, pt. 1:414.

76. Cathcart to Suffolk, 20 September 1771, *SIRIO*, 19:231; Cathcart to Suffolk, 23 September 1771, enclosing Münnich to Swallow, 21 September 1771, PROSP, 91/88:161-63.

77. *AGS*, 1, pt. 1:415, 418; *PSZ*, 19: no. 13679 (14 October 1771), reprinted in *SPV*, 11 November 1771, supplement, and *St. Peterburgischen Zeitungen*, 13 December 1771, TsGADA, f. 199, d. 151, pt. 1, no. 1:71-88; Swallow to Suffolk, 29 November 1771, PROSP, 91/88:291.

78. Cathcart to Suffolk, 11 October 1771, PROSP, 91/88:207v., partially printed in *SIRIO*, 19:238; Cathcart to Suffolk, 14, 18, 21 October 1771, PROSP, 91/88:215v.-16, 228; *London Gazette*, 5-9 November 1771.

79. British Factory to Cathcart, 22 November 1771, PROSP, 91/88:264-65v.

80. *London Gazette*, 18-21 January 1772; 8-12 September 1772.

81. Suffolk to Cathcart, 31 January 1772 and 20 March 1772, PROSP, 91/89:1-3, 116.

82. Richard B. Sheridan, "The British credit crisis of 1772 and the American colonies," *Journal of Economic History* 20 (1960):161-86; A. V. Safonova, "Obshchestvenno-politicheskaia zhizn' Peterburga v 60-70e gody XVIII veka," kand. diss., Leningrad, 1953, p. 84.

83. Plague Commission sessions of 27-31 January 1772, TsGAg.M, f. 636, op. 2, d. 23:64v.-76; C. to Volkonskii, 25 January 1772, *OV*, 1:67-68.

84. Sessions of 4, 6, 13, and 16 February 1771, TsGAg.M, f. 636, op. 2, d. 24:5-5v., 10, 25v., 31v.; C. to Volkonskii, 20 February 1772, *OV*, 1:69.

85. *PSZ*, 19: no. 13,767 and no. 13,768 (27 February 1772).

86. Sessions of 25 February and 1 March 1772, TsGAg.M, f. 636, op. 2, d. 24:46v.-47; d. 25:3-4.

87. Sessions of 13-15 March 1772, TsGAg.M, f. 636, op. 2, d. 25:33v.-37.

88. Plague Commission to Senate, 17 March 1772, and sessions of 28 March and 10 April 1772, TsGAg.M, f. 636, op. 2, d. 25:39-40v., 69v.; d. 26:24; Senate to C., 15 March 1772; Eropkin to Bruce, 6 April 1772, TsGADA, f. 16, d. 328, pt. 1:85-85v., 286-97v.

89. Shafonskii to Policemaster Chancery, 9 August 1772, OPI-GIM, f. 145, d. 86051/3812:37-37v.

90. Plague Commission (Makulov) to Volkonskii, 13 August 1771, OPI-GIM, f. 145, d. 86051/3812:39-39v.

91. Volkonskii to C., 14 and 18 August 1772, f. 16, d. 328, pt. 1:289-90v., 297-97v.; C. to Volkonskii, 22 August 1772, *OV*, 1:79; commission session of 24 August 1772, TsGAg.M, f. 636, op. 2, d. 30:36-37.

92. Eropkin to Bruce, 10 October 1772, TsGADA, f. 16, d. 328, pt. 1:287-87v.; *AGS*, 1, pt. 1:429-32; *PSZ*, 19: no. 13,906 (15 November 1772); no. 13,907 (16 November 1772); no. 13,913 (30 November 1772); no. 13,919 (12 December 1772); no. 13,928 (19 December 1772); no. 13,929 (20 December 1772); no. 13,941 (21 January 1773); *Opisanie*, pp. 153-57.

Chapter Ten

1. *Opisanie*, pp. vii, 620-22.

2. Lerche, *Lebens- und Reise-Geschichte*, pp. 458-59; Mertens, *Account*, pp. 32-33; C. to Grimm, 30 January 1775, *SIRIO*, 23:15; Samoilovich, *IP*, 2:132-34. A Swiss visitor reported 58,091 deaths in Moscow and 91,000 in the provinces for a total of 149,091. Walther Kirchner, ed., *Eine Reise durch Sibirien in achtzehnten Jahrhundert: Die Fahrt des Schweizer Doktors Jakob Fries* (Munich, 1955), p. 36.

3. I owe this suggestion to Arcadius Kahan, "Comments on Some Social Aspects of the Plague Epidemics in 18th Century Russia," unpublished paper (University of Chicago, December 1975), pp. 3-5.

4. Leslie Bradley, "The Most Famous of All English Plagues: A Detailed Analysis of the Plague at Eyam, 1665-66," and Roger Schofield, "An Anatomy of an Epidemic: Colyton, November 1645 to November 1646," both in *The Plague Reconsidered*, pp. 73, 109-19.

5. Eropkin's reports, 22 June-30 August 1771, TsGADA, f. 263, op. 2, d. 1710:8-162. These

scattered reports, which often fail to specify the age or sex of victims, listed approximately 840 men, 520 women, and 134 children as presumed plague victims.

6. Mertens, *Account*, pp. 38-39.
7. C. to Grimm, 30 January 1775, *SIRIO*, 23:15; Coxe, *Travels*, 1:282.
8. Kabuzan, *Izmeneniia*, pp. 71, 83, 95.
9. I. G. Doolittle, "The effects of the plague on a provincial town in the sixteenth and seventeenth centuries," *Medical History* 19 (1975):333-41; Penelope Corfield, "A Provincial Capital in the late Seventeenth Century: The Case of Norwich," in Peter Clark and Paul Slack, eds., *Crisis and Order in English Towns, 1500–1700* (London, 1972), pp. 266-69.
10. Mertens, *Account*, p. 26; *Opisanie*, p. 620; Lerche, *Lebens- und Reise-Geschichte*, p. 458; Cathcart to Suffolk, 22 November 1771, PROSP, 91/88:261v.
11. Mertens, *Account*, pp. 35-36.
12. C. to Bielcke, 13 November 1771, *SIRIO*, 13:186; Cathcart to Suffolk, 18 November 1771, *SIRIO*, 19:242.
13. Plague Commission session of 26 October 1771, TsGAg.M, f. 636, op. 2, d. 2:63-63v.
14. Sessions of 20-21 October 1771, ibid., pp. 41v., 43; Pogoretskii to commission, 20 October 1771, TsGAg.M, f. 636, op. 2, d. 6:38.
15. Zertsalov, "O miatezhakh," p. 366.
16. Eropkin to Senate, 9 October 1771, TsGADA, f. 263, op. 2, d. 1678:52-53.
17. Plague Commission sessions of 19 October, 20 October, 30 October 1771, TsGAg.M, f. 636, op. 2, d. 2:39v., 42, 72; Morsochnikov to commission, 19 October 1771; Pushkin to commission, 19 October 1771, TsGAg.M, f. 636, op. 2, d. 5:20-22; Morsochnikov to commission, 29 October 1771, TsGAg.M, f. 636, op. 2, d. 8:57.
18. Kamer Collegium to Senate, 13 October 1771, TsGADA, f. 263, op. 2, d. 1678:102-3.
19. Lerche, *Lebens- und Reise-Geschichte*, p. 64; Alelekov and Iakimov, *Istoriia Moskovskogo voennogo gospitalia*, pp. 488-89.
20. Carlo M. Cipolla and Dante E. Zanetti, "Pest et mortalité différentielle," *Annales de demographie historique* (1972):197-202.
21. Aksenov, "Moskovskoe kupechestvo," p. 122.
22. Commission sessions of 20 October and 23 October 1771, TsGAg.M, f. 636, op. 2, d. 2:42v., 49v.-50.
23. Skvortsov, *Materialy*, 2:601-13.
24. Petition of Moscow merchantry (1772), OPI-GIM, f. 145, d. 86051/3812: 13v.; Senate to C. and Petersburg depts. (1774?), TsGADA, f. 16, no. 168, pt. 8:35-37.
25. N. A. Naidenov, ed., *Materialy dlia istorii Moskovskogo kupechestva*, 6 vols. (Moscow, 1883-89), 2:10; vol. 3:1-7.
26. Ibid., vol. 2:62-80; vol. 3:148-66.
27. Ibid., vol. 2:10-23; vol. 3:47-48.
28. Ibid., vol. 2, pt. 2:38-42; vol. 3, supplement:1-33.
29. Ibid., vol. 3, supplement:9, 16-17.
30. Zviagintsev, "Rost naseleniia v Moskovskikh slobodakh," pp. 141-42; idem, " 'Kozhevniki' i ikh posadskoe naselenie v XVIII veke," *Staraia Moskva* (Moscow, 1929):109-26, esp. 118; Paul Slack, "The Local Incidence of Epidemic Disease: The Case of Bristol, 1540-1650," *The Plague Reconsidered*, pp. 49-62.
31. Moscow Typographical Office to Holy Synod, 22 November 1771-30 January 1772, TsGIA-SSSR, f. 796, op. 52, d. 419:2-19.
32. Moscow Academy to Synodal Office, 20 March 1772 and 11 January 1773, TsGADA, f. 1183, op. 1, d. 328:3-7, 111v.; S. K. Smirnov, *Istoriia moskovskoi slaviano-greko-latinskoi Akademii*, 2 vols. (Moscow, 1855), 1:181.
33. Mertens, *Account*, pp. 37, 115-20.
34. Bolotov, *Zhizn' i prikliucheniia*, 3:94.
35. *Opisanie*, pp. 605-6.
36. Sytin, *IPZM*, 2:56-57.
37. Sytin, *IPZM*, 2:52-53, 487; ownership and distribution of messuages in Moscow in 1781, ORGBL, f. 129, no. 22, d. 15:1.
38. Sytin, *IPZM*, 2:72-73, 82-86.
39. Kahan, "Comments," pp. 7-9.
40. Petersburg depts. to C., 27 October 1771, TsGADA, f. 16, d. 168, pt. 8:254-60; Peters-

burg depts. to Collegium of Manufactures, 27 October 1771, TsGADA, f. 277, op. 12, d. 699:1-3; Orlov to C., October 1771, quoted by Solov'ev, *Istoriia Rossii* 15:149; C. to Volkonskii, 5 November 1771, TsGIA-SSSR, f. 1329, op. 2, d. 112:121, published with minor variations but without the date in *SIRIO*, 13:196; Bielfeld, *Institutions politiques*, 1:259.

41. Collegium of Manufactures' resolution, 26 November 1772, referring to Orlov's oral order of 8 November 1771, TsGADA, f. 277, op. 12, d. 699:3–4.

42. Plague Commission to Collegium of Manufactures, 6 February 1772, with register of manufactories, TsGADA, f. 277, op. 2, d. 520:1, 3–10.

43. Meshalin, *Tekstil'naia promyshlennost' krest'ian*, p. 81.

44. Senate to C., 15 March 1772, TsGADA, f. 16, d. 328, pt. 1:85–85v.

45. C. to Viazemskii, 1772, *Russkii arkhiv* 3 (1865):632; Collegium of Manufactures' discussion, 26 November 1772, and order to operators, 29 November and 11 December 1772, TsGADA, f. 277, op. 12, d. 699:3–15v.

46. Operators to Collegium of Manufactures, February 1772, TsGADA, f. 277, op. 12, d. 699:19–21, 78–79. See also Baburin, *Ocherki*, pp. 154–56.

47. Operators' replies to Collegium of Manufactures, January-February 1773, TsGADA, f. 277, op. 12, d. 699:79v.–82, 86–88, 94–94v., 97, 99–100v.

48. Khastatov to Collegium of Manufactures, 1 March and 27 June 1772; collegium's inventory of mill, 26 July 1772; Senate to collegium, 15 March 1773; Khastatov to C., 23 October 1778, TsGADA, f. 277, op. 12, d. 671:1–4v., 10–14, 20–31v., 38–38v., 98–101v.; "Vedomost' o predpriiatiiakh legkoi promyshlennosti, 1778 g.," in L. G. Beskrovnyi and B. B. Kafengauz, eds., M. T. Beliavskii and N. I. Pavlenko, comps., *Khrestomatiia po istorii SSSR: XVIII v.* (Moscow, 1963), pp. 312–17.

49. Collegium of Manufactures to Volkonskii and Volkov, 18 February 1773, TsGADA, f. 277, op. 12, d. 699:72–77v.; manufactories in Moscow before the plague, *Opisanie*, pp. 606–20.

50. Meshalin, *Tekstil'naia promyshlennost' krest'ian*, pp. 71–77.

51. Ibid., p. 81; register of deaths in Moscow and district (late 1772), TsGAg.M, f. 636, op. 2, d. 57:206; register of houses dismantled in suburbs, January 1772; houses of the Admiralty mill fumigated in Preobrazhenskoe, May 1772, TsGAg.M, f. 636, op. 2, d. 60:42v.–43; d. 64:2v.–5v.

52. Solov'ev, *Istoriia Rossii*, 15:150.

53. I. V. Meshalin, "Promyshlennost' g. Novgoroda v XVIII veke," *Novgorodskii istoricheskii sbornik*, fasc. 7 (Novgorod, 1940):45–47; C.'s memo, 6 March 1773, *SIRIO*, 13:316–17; M. Murzanova, "Na Moskovsko-Novgorodskoi parusnoi fabrike (1696–1772–1829 gg.)," *Arkhiv istorii truda v Rossii*, bk. 2 (1921):1–7.

54. Tomsinskii, *Moskovskii sukonnyi dvor*, pp. 20–21, 25–39, 99, 229, 242–43, 247; Sytin, *IPZM*, 1:216.

55. "Vedomost' o predpriiatiiakh," p. 318; register of manufactories in Moscow under the Collegium of Manufactures (1773), TsGADA, f. 277, op. 12, d. 699:112; Artemenkov, "Promyshlennaia deiatel'nost' krest'ianstva Rossii," pp. 129–30; Parkinson, *A Tour*, p. 105; Sytin, *IPZM*, 2:391.

56. "Vedomost' o predpriiatiiakh," p. 306; register of woolen output in Moscow, 1791, TsGAg.M, f. 16, op. 1, d. 827:3–3v.; Sytin, *IPZM*, 1:114; V. A. Kondrat'ev and V. I. Nevzorov, eds., *Iz istorii fabrik i zavodov Moskvy i Moskovskoi gubernii (konets XVIII–nachalo XXv.): Obzor dokumentov* (Moscow, 1968), pp. 8, 52.

57. "Vedomost' o predpriiatiiakh," pp. 312–13; Sytin, *IPZM*, 2:75; Bakhrushin et al., *Istoriia Moskvy*, 2:356. At least one of these mills was removed in 1780 to the Dmitrov district; see Griaznov, *Iaroslavskaia bol'shaia manufaktura*, p. 464.

58. Meshalin, *Tekstil'naia promyshlennost' krest'ian*, pp. 81–85; *PSZ*, 20: no. 14,295 (17 March 1775); Baburin, *Ocherki*, pp. 157–60, 165–68.

59. C. to A. A. Bezborodko (n.d.), and A.A. Prozorovskii to C., 14 April 1791, TsGADA, f. 16, d. 555, pt. 2:172–75; Luk'ianov, *Istoriia khimicheskikh promyshlov*, 1:109–10.

60. G. S. Isaev, *Rol' tekstil'noi promyshlennosti v genezise i razvitii kapitalizma v Rossii, 1760–1860* (Leningrad, 1970); Meshalin, *Tekstil'naia promyshlennost' krest'ian*, pp. 91–160, 246–54; Reginald E. Zelnik, *Labor and Society in Tsarist Russia: The Factory Workers of St. Petersburg, 1855–1870* (Stanford, 1971), pp. 23–29.

61. Orlov to C. [October 1771], *SIRIO*, 13:205.

62. *AGS*, 1, pt. 1:420–21; C. to Volkonskii [5 November 1771], *SIRIO*, 13:191–96; Volkon-

skii to C., 1 January 1772, TsGADA, f. 16, d. 328, pt. 1:273–75; C. to Volkonskii, 29 January 1773, *OV*, 1:89.

63. Register of retired Moscow Lifeguards Battalion, filed among materials dated 1770–74, TsGADA, f. 14, d. 51, pt. 2:59–76v.

64. Volkonskii to C., 20 December 1773, TsGADA, f. 16, d. 555, pt. 2:49–62v.; Volkonskii to C., 1775, *SIRIO*, 5:122–27.

65. D. Balashev to Volkonskii, "Vedomost' o Moskovskom uezde," 31 December 1772, OPI-GIM, f. 145, d. 86051/3812:1–1v., 57–57v.

66. M. M. Bogoslovskii, "Dvorianske nakazy v Ekaterininskuiu komissiiu 1767 goda," *Russkoe bogatstvo* 6–7 (1897):46–83, 136–52.

67. Sytin, *IPZM*, 2:56, 122–23, 126.

68. Petition to commission for the supervision of precautions in Moscow district, 14 August 1773, with senate and guberniia chancery correspondence, TsGAg.M, f. 636, op. 1, d. 200:1–3v.

69. Sytin, *IPZM*, 2:336.

70. Ibid., pp. 49–51.

71. Skvortsov, *Materialy*, 1:146–51; vol. 2:587–88; I. E. Zabelin, ed., *Materialy dlia istorii, arkheologii i statistiki goroda Moskvy*, 2 vols. (Moscow, 1884–91), 2:1029–30.

72. Orlov to C. [October 1771], *SIRIO*, 13:205; C., *Sochineniia*, 12:642.

73. Skvortsov, *Materialy*, 2:474–76; Zabelin, *Materialy*, 2:1023–26, 1037.

74. Sytin, *IPZM*, 2:188; *PSZ*, 19: no. 13,764 (20 February 1772); no. 13,946 (7 February 1773); Skvortsov, *Materialy*, 2:636–38; Rozanov, 2, pt. 2:101–5, 326–27.

75. Synod order about security of belfries, 5 October 1771, TsGIA-SSSR, f. 796, op. 52, d. 349:1–2; repeated in Moscow in 1774, Skvortsov, *Materialy*, 2:374; [D. I. Zhuravlev], *Moskovskaia Ekaterininskaia gorodskaia bol'nitsa, rodonachal'nitsa gorodskoi i obshchestvennoi meditsiny 1776–1926, iubileinyi sbornik* (Moscow, 1929), p. 23; N. A. Geinike et al., eds., *Po Moskve: Progulki po Moskve i eia khudozhestvennym i prosvetitel'nym uchrezhdeniiam* (Moscow, 1917), p. 639.

76. Sytin, IPZM, 2:48–49, 51; Snegirev, *Arkhitektor Bazhenov*, pp. 59–70.

77. *AGS*, 1, pt. 2:693–94; T. Efimenko, "Iz istorii gorodskogo zemleustroistva vremeni Ekateriny II," *Zhurnal Ministerstva narodnogo prosveshcheniia*, n.s. 54 (December 1914):280–315; Sytin, *IPZM*, 2:57–188.

78. C. to Paul, 10 June 1787, in A. F. Bychkov, ed. *Pis'ma i bumagi imperatritsy Ekateriny II khraniashchiiasia v imperatorskoi Publichnoi biblioteke* (St. Petersburg, 1873), p. 29.

79. N. P. Pavlova-Sil'vanskaia, "Sotsial'naia sushchnost' oblastnoi reformy Ekateriny II," in N. M. Druzhinin et al., eds., *Absoliutizm v Rossii* (Moscow, 1964), pp. 473–74.

80. *Uchrezhdeniia dlia upravleniia gubernii vserossiiskoi imperii* (St. Petersburg, 1775), arts. 238–40.

81. A. Shafonskii, "Kratkoe nastavlenie kakim obrazom skotskoi padezh otvrashchat' " (Moscow, 1774), in *Opisanie*, pp. 588–98.

82. *Uchrezhdeniia dlia upravleniia gubernii*, arts. 241, 260–63.

83. Iu. V. Got'e, *Istoriia oblastnogo upravleniia v Rossii ot Petra I do Ekateriny II*, 2 vols. (Moscow, 1913–41), 2:261.

84. *Uchrezhdeniia dlia upravleniia gubernii*, arts. 24, 70, 386, 394, 411–12.

85. Sytin, *IPZM*, 2:206, 278, 309; Zabelin, *Materialy*, 2:1032–37; Zhuravlev, *Moskovskaia Ekaterininskaia bol'nitsa*, pp. 9–40.

86. William Coxe, *Account of the Prisons and Hospitals in Russia, Sweden, and Denmark, with Occasional Remarks on the Different Modes of Punishments in Those Countries* (London, 1781), pp. 19–21.

87. Sytin, *IPZM*, 2:97–98; Sivkov, "Nakaz zhitelei Moskvy," pp. 216–22.

88. *PSZ*, 21: no. 15,379 (8 April 1782), arts. 232, 274.

89. Vien, *Loimologia*, p. 35.

Chapter Eleven

1. Amburger, *Beiträge*, pp. 37–39, 238–51.

2. Alelekov and Iakimov, *Istoriia*, pp. 506–12; Brückner, *Die Aerzte in Russland*, pp. 13, 68;

Palkin, *Russkie gospital'nye shkoly*, pp. 3, 168–70, 172; Müller-Dietz, *Ärzte im Russland*, pp. 93–102; *Tablei k Otchetu Ministerstva vnutrennikh del za 1803*, table N.

3. *PSZ*, 20: no. 16,390 (6 May 1786); vol. 23: no. 17,131 (7 June 1793); vol. 26: no. 18,476 (7 July 1800); *Tabeli k Otchetu za 1803;* Vasil'ev and Segal, *Istoriia epidemii v Rossii*, pp. 380–97.

4. Eropkin to C., 18 March 1773, with register of practitioners' rewards, TsGADA, f. 16, d. 328, pt. 1:306–7, 332–33, 340v.–41.

5. Chistovich, *Istoriia*, app. 10:246–247, 307–8, 364; V. A. Nevskii, "A. F. Shafonskii—odin iz pionerov otechestvennoi sanitarii," *Gigiena i sanitariia*, 11 (1950):42–45.

6. Grave to commission, 16 September 1775, OPI-GIM, f. 145, d. 86051/3812:11–12.

7. Grombakh in Samoilovich, *IP*, 2:337–404.

8. W. F. Ryan, "Science in medieval Russia: Some reflections on a recent book," *History of Science* 5 (1966):54–55.

9. Alelekov and Iakimov, *Istoriia*, pp. 376–80; Bochkarev, "Vrachebnoe delo," pp. 466–71.

10. H. Leeming, "Polish and Polish-Latin medical terms in pre-Petrine Russian," *Slavonic and East European Review* 42 (1963):89–109; Grombakh, *Russkaia meditsinskaia literatura*, pp. 26, 54–64, 273–80.

11. Palkin, *Russkie gospital'nye shkoly*, pp. 118–21. This decree of 8 March 1764 was sent to surgeon Grigorii Bakaevskii on 13 June 1771, TsGADA, f. 344, op. 1, d. 45:448–49v.

12. The archives of the Medical Collegium listed 29 compositions concerning plague dated 1738–1801, but the archivists in Leningrad and Moscow could not find any of these for me in 1975. For the register of titles, see TsGIA-SSSR, f. 1294, Inventarnaia opis' no. 1, 1738–1823 gg., sect. III, 'Sviazka soderzhashchaia raznyia zapiski o morovykh iazvakh 1738 po 1801-yi god," pp. 10–12v. Other sources refer to additional unpublished works, such as Dr. Mitrofanov's composition in Latin and Russian detailing the methods he used at Kiev in 1770–71 and Ivan Vien's "Brief Outline of the Kiev Pestilential Distemper and of the Method of My Treatment, Sent to the Medical Collegium in German in 1772." Mitrofanov to Medical Collegium, 13 January 1771, TsGADA, f. 344, op. 1, bk. 43:617v.; list of Vien's manuscript and published works (1804), TsGIA-SSSR, f. 1297, op. 1, bk. 71:309.

13. *Kratkoe predokhranitel'noe spoznanie o zarazitel'noi iazve* (St. Petersburg, 1772).

14. Palkin, *Russkie gospital'nye shkoly*, pp. 121, 130–32, 257–58.

15. Rossiiskii, *Istoriia*, pp. 420, 437, 614; Brennsohn, *Die Aerzte Estlands*, p. 242; Peter Fridrich Körber, *Abhandlung von der Pest und andern hinraffenden Seuchen samt den dawider dienenden Präservations- und Heilungsmitteln* (Reval, 1771).

16. Rossiiskii, *Istoriia*, pp. 424, 437; Nicolas Gabriel Le Clerc, *De la contagion, de sa nature, de ses effets, de ses progrès, et des moyens les plus surs pour le prévenir et pour y remedier* (St. Petersburg, 1771), pp. 2–3v.

17. *O morovoi iazve, sochineniia Richarda Meada, Aglinskago doktora, s nemetskago perevel Semen Sulima* (St. Petersburg, 1772), v. On Mead's treatise, see Charles-Edward Armory Winslow, *The Conquest of Epidemic Disease* (Princeton, 1943; reprinted New York, 1967), ch. 10.

18. Körber, *Abhandlung*, pp. A4–A5, 73, 78, 80, 86.

19. Iogan Ioakim Iuliii Rost, *Slovo o vrednom vozdukhe v zhilishchakh osoblivo prostago naroda primechaemom i o sredstvakh udobnykh k popravleniiu onago*, trans. from Latin (Moscow, 1772), pp. 3–5, 8, 22–23.

20. Frantz Karl Meltzer, *Beschreibung der Pest von 1770 bis 1772 in Moskau* (Moscow, 1776); Charles de Mertens, *Observationes de febribus putridis, de Pest, & c.* (Vienna, 1778); Helias Rutzky, *Dissertatio inauguralis medica de Peste* (Strasbourg, 1781); D. Samoilowitz, *Mémoire sur la peste, qui, en 1771, ravagea l'Empire de Russie, sur-tout Moscou, la capitale* (Paris, 1783); Gustavus Orraeus, *Descriptio pestis quae anno MDCCLXX, in Jassia, et MDCCLXXI in Moscua grassata est* (St. Petersburg, 1784); Pieter van Woensel, *Mémoire sur la peste, dans lequel on prouve qu'il est possible d'exterminer de dessus del la terre le germe. . .* (St. Petersburg, 1778); Johann Martin Minderer, *Abermal ein Beytrag zur Kenntniss und Heilung der Pest, Aerzten und Wundärzten bei der russisch-Kaiserlichen Armee gewidmet* (Riga, 1790).

21. *Beobachtungen der faulen Fieber, der Pest und einiger andern Krankheiten* (Göttingen, 1779); *Traité de la peste, contenant l'histoire de cette qui a régné à Moscou en 1771*, rev. trans. from Latin (Vienna and Strasbourg, 1784); *An Account of the Plague Which Raged at Moscow in 1771*, trans. Richard Pearson (London, 1799). Rossiiskii mentions but does not cite an Italian translation (p. 671).

22. D. S. Samoilowitz, *Abhandlung über die Peste welche 1771 das Russische Reiche, besonders aber Moskau, die Hauptstadt, verheerte, Nebst dagegen gebrauchten Mitteln,* trans. A. F. Bohme (Leipzig, 1785); *Razsuzhdenie o morovoi iazve, sochinennoe P. fon Vunzelem, doktorom vrachebnyia nauki, Perevedennoe s frantsuzskago na Rossiiskii iazyk i umnozhennoe osobennym na onoe predisloviem Riazhskago pekhotnago polku premier-maiorom i trekh uchenykh v Rossii obshchestv chlenom Andreem Meierom* (Moscow, 1791).

23. "Discours sur l'avantage ou les lumières que les Sciences ont acquises à l'occasion des guerres; particulierement sur la peste; prononcé par le Baron George d'Asch à l'assemblee publique de l'Academie Impériale des Sciences de St. Petersburg le 12 d'Octobre 1779," manuscript section, Niedersächsische Staats- und Universitätsbibliothek, Göttingen, Codex Asch 188a; "Observations on the plague, quarantines, & c. in a letter from Dr. Matthew Guthrie, physician at St. Petersburg, to Dr. Duncan," *Medical Commentaries* (Edinburgh) (1781-82), 8:345-63.

24. Such as P. J. Ferro, *Von der Ansteckung der epidemischen Krankheiten, und besonders der Pest* (Leipzig, 1782); J. C. Ringebroig, *Von der Pest, ihren Ursachen, Zufällen, Behandlung und Sicherungsmitteln* (Leipzig, 1783), and J. A. Dolst, *Observationes nonnulae de peste* (Jena, 1784). See the discussion in Hecker, *Geschichte der neueren Heilkunde,* pp. 96-99, 583-607.

25. Ivan Vien, *Loimologiia ili opisanie morovoi iazvy, eia sushchestva, proizshestviia, prichin, porazheniia i proizvodstva pripadkov, s pokazaniem obraza predokhraneniia i vrachevaniia seia skorbi* (St. Petersburg, 1786).

26. V. D. Otamanovskii, "Otechestvennye lekari-novatory vtoroi poloviny XVIII v., sozdavshie bolee progressivnoe napravlenie v lechenii chumy, i rol' ikh kak zachinatelei natsional'noi terapii," *Trudy Saratovskogo meditsinskogo instituta,* vol. 10, fasc. 1 (Saratov, 1958):5–42.

27. Chistovich, *Istorii,* app. 10:71-72; Grombakh in Samoilovich, *IP,* 2:361-62; Müller-Dietz, *Ärzte im Russland,* pp. 80-91.

28. Grombakh in Samoilovich, *IP,* 2:402.

29. A. M. Shumlianskii to I. V. Rutskii, 28 June 1783, in S. I. Vavilov et al., eds., *Nauchnoe nasledstvo* (Moscow, 1951), 2:449-50.

30. Ibid., pp. 449-50, 486; Grombakh in Samoilovich, *IP,* 2:346–50, 363-67.

31. Samoilovich, *IP,* 2:22, 93, 189-90, 278.

32. Mertens, *Traité de la peste,* pp. v-xxviii.

33. There is no biography of Vien. This sketch mainly relies upon his service record of 1803-1805 in TsGIA-SSSR, f. 1297, op. 1, bk. 73:199v.-201; bk. 71:285-321v.; Vien to C., 1786, TsGADA, gosarkhiv, r. XVII, no. 124:1-2.

34. Vien, *Loimologia,* unpaginated preface.

35. Grombakh in Samoilovich, *IP,* 2:434–47; A. Ia. Skorokhodov, *Materialy po istorii meditsinskoi mikrobiologii v dorevoliutsionnoi Rossii* (Moscow, 1948), pp. 46–51.

36. King, *Medical World,* p. 154.

37. Ibid., p. 127.

38. Winslow, *Conquest of Epidemic Disease,* ch. 7.

39. Körber, *Abhandlung,* pp. 74-80, 82-86.

40. Mertens, *Account,* pp. 109-10; Orraeus, *Descriptio pestis,* pp. 160-67, 183, 196; Vien, *Loimologia,* pp. 69-90; Hirst, *Conquest of Plague,* pp. 283-92.

41. Samoilovich, *IP,* 2:20.

42. Vien, *Loimologia,* p. 30.

43. Samoilovich, *IP,* 2:14-16, 67, 95-96, 140; Mertens, *Account,* pp. 35, 38, 83.

44. Winslow, *Epidemic Disease,* pp. 181-82.

45. Rost, *Slovo,* pp. 6-11.

46. Ibid., pp. 15-21.

47. Ibid., pp. 22-27.

48. Ibid., p. 31.

49. *Opisanie,* pp. ii-iv, viii, 1-3.

50. Ibid., pp. 2-3; Samoilovich, *IP,* 2:18-19; Mertens, *Account,* pp. 81-83, 93.

51. *Opisanie,* pp. ii, v-viii, 4.

52. Ibid., p. 14; Mertens, *Account,* with summary of Orraeus's views, pp. 46-48, 65-72; Samoilovich, *IP,* 2:144; Vien, *Loimologia,* pp. 224-51; Meltzer, *Beschreibung,* pp. 16-21, 49.

53. Samoilovich, *IP,* 2:13-14, 71-72, 146-50; *Opisanie,* pp. 10-11; Vien, *Loimologia,* p. 242.

54. Vien, *Loimologia*, p. 160; Grombakh in Samoilovich, *IP*, 2:429–30.
55. *Opisanie*, p. 16.
56. Ibid., pp. vi–vii.
57. Mertens, *Account*, pp. 34–36, 38–39; Vien, *Loimologia*, pp. 198–212; Samoilovich, *IP*, 2:47–54, 141–43.
58. Matthew Guthrie, remarks on the plague in Moscow in 1771, in "Supplemental Tour of Taurida" (1804-1805), British Museum, Additional Manuscripts, no. 14,388, fols. 195–97. My thanks to K. A. Papmehl for the loan of this material.
59. *Opisanie*, pp. 1, 5, 9–10; Mertens, *Account*, pp. 42–44; Samoilovich, *IP*, 2:144–46, 168, 176; Guthrie, "Observations," pp. 357, 359; Meltzer, *Beschreibung der Pest*, p. 10; Minderer, *Abermal ein Beytrag*, p. 23; Orraeus, *Descriptio Pestis*, pp. 194–96; Vien, *Loimologia*, p. 120.
60. Hirst, *Conquest of Plague*, pp. 73–86; Richard H. Shryock, "Germ theories in medicine prior to 1870: Further comments on continuity in science," *Clio Medica* 7 (1972):81–109, esp. 99.
61. Körber, *Abhandlung*, p. 81; Sulima, tr. *O morovoi iazve*, p. 49; [Woensel], *Razsuzhdenie o morovoi iazve*, pp. 58–59; Le Clerc, *De la contagion*, pp. 31–32, 34–37, 40, 46.
62. Rost, *Slovo*, pp. 13, 23; Meltzer, *Beschreibung*, pp. 4–5, 13, 15; Mertens, *Account*, p. 26, 29–30, 100; Körber, *Abhandlung*, pp. 76, 79. For the rather confused classical and European ideas and terminology for infection, see Owsei Temkin, "An Historical Analysis of the Concept of Infection," in *The Double Face of Janus and Other Essays in the History of Medicine by Owsei Temkin* (Baltimore and London, 1977), pp. 456–71.
63. Samoilovich, *IP*, 1:53–65; vol. 2:14–17; Vien, *Loimologia*, pp. 90–96, 136. On Athanasius Kircher (1602-80), see Winslow, *Epidemic Disease*, ch. 8.
64. S. L. Sobol', *Istoriia mikroskopa i mikroskopicheskikh issledovanii v Rossii v XVIII veke* (Moscow and Leningrad, 1949), pp. 398–402.
65. Samoilovich, *IP*, 2:195–96; Vien, *Loimologia*, pp. 277, 291–92.
66. Samoilovich, *IP*, 2:178–87; Mertens, *Account*, pp. 86–92.
67. Hirst, *Conquest of Plague*, pp. 440–41; Asch, "Discours sur l'avantage," p. 11.
68. Körber, *Abhandlung*, p. 95.
69. Pogoretskii to C., November 1775, TsGADA, f. 10, gosarkhiv, d. 553:1–1v.
70. Asch, "Discours sur l'avantage," Codex Asch 188a, 3–12, esp. 7; Russian translation in *SPV*, no. 88, 29 October 1779:747–50, 755–58; Guthrie, "Observations," pp. 348–49, 361–62.
71. Mertens, *Traité*, pp. 64–68; Mertens, *Account*, pp. viii–ix.
72. Samoilovich, *IP*, 2:31, 58–59, 67–68, 74–76, 81–84, 284–306.
73. Areta O. Kowal, "Danilo Samoilowitz: An eighteenth-century Ukrainian epidemiologist and his role in the Moscow plague (1770–72)," *Journal of the History of Medicine and Allied Sciences* 27 (1972):434, 442; *Materialy nauchno-prakticheskoi konferentsii, posviashchennoi 225-letiiu so dnia rozhdeniia vydaiushchegosia otechestvennogo epidemiologa Danily Samoilovicha 19–21 iiunia 1969 g.* (Nikolaev, 1969), pp. 16, 25. But S. M. Grombakh long ago noted that Samoilovich himself never claimed to have done an inoculation. See Grombakh in Samoilovich, *IP*, 2:422–25.
74. Samoilovich, *IP*, 2:37; and Grombakh in Samoilovich, *IP*, 2:433.
75. Vien, *Loimologia*, pp. 373–78; Woensel, *Razsuzhdenie*, pp. 74–78. Yet Woensel's Russian translator also rejected the idea of inoculations on convicts as inhumane (p. 22).
76. Walther Kirchner, "The Black Death: New insights into 18th century attitudes toward bubonic plague," *Clinical Pediatrics* 7 (1968):434, 436.
77. Pollitzer, *Plague and Plague Control in the Soviet Union*, pp. 57–268.
78. Roderick E. McGrew, *Russia and the Cholera, 1823–1832* (Madison, 1965), p. 147.

Conclusion

1. McGrew, *Russia and the Cholera*, pp. 50–51, 67–74, 106–117, 122; Nancy M. Frieden, "The Russian cholera epidemic, 1892-93, and medical professionalization," *Journal of Social History* 10 (1977):544–47; Vasil'ev and Segal, *Istoriia epidemii v Rossii*, pp. 247–49, 388.
2. C. to Potemkin, 13 June and 20 July 1783, *SIRIO*, 27:265, 270.
3. C. to Potemkin, 25 April, 5 May, 17 May, 28 May, 3 October and 15 October 1784; C. to P. A. Rumiantsev, 3 October 1784; C. to A. A. Bezborodko (1784), *SIRIO*, 27:333–36, 339–40,

344, 346. For an eyewitness account of the plague at Kherson, see "Zapiski nemetskago vracha o Rossii v kontse proshlago veka," *Russkii arkhiv*, bk. 1 (1881):33-36.

4. C., proposed inscriptions, n.d., *SIRIO*, 13:293; A.N. Petrov, *Pushkin: dvortsy i parki*, 2d. ed. (Leningrad, 1969), pp. 80-81; [V. I. Maikov], "Pis'mo ego siiatel'stvu grafu Grigor'iu Grigor'evichu Orlovu, na otbytie v Moskvu vo vremia byvshiia v nei zarazitel'noi bolezni, dlia istreblenyia onyia," printed copy (St. Petersburg, 1771?), TsGADA, gosarkhiv, r. 10, no. 446.

5. *Pis'mo Petru Dmitrievichu Eropkinu, sochinennoe kniazhnoi Ekaterinoi Urusovoi v Moskve* (Moscow, 1772), printed copy in TsGADA, f. 199, pt. 1, no. 1:206v.-07v.

6. *Opisanie oboikh vnov' postroennykh triumfal'nykh vorot*. . . (Moscow, January 1775), unpaginated.

7. D. S. Samoilovich, *Nachertaniia dlia izobrazheniia v zhivopisi presechennoi v Moskve 1771 goda morovoi iazvy, kotoroe predlagaet khudozhnikam Danilo Samoilovich* (St. Petersburg, 1795; Nikolaev, 1802), reprinted in Samoilovich, *IP*, 1:75-84.

8. Grombakh in Samoilovich, *IP*, 2:395-97.

9. Barbara W. Maggs, "Eighteenth-century Russian reflections on the Lisbon earthquake, Voltaire and optimism," *Studies on Voltaire and the Eighteenth Century*, ed. Theodore Bestermann (Banbury, 1975), 137:7-29.

10. Jean-Noël Biraben, "Certain demographic characteristics of the plague epidemic in France, 1720-1722," *Daedalus* 97 (Spring 1968):538, 541; Robert Horváth, "La statistique de la peste de Debrecen (1739-40) et du choléra de Pest (1831) en Hongrie et leurs conséquences sociales," *Acta Universitatis Szegediensis: Acta Juridica et Politica* 9, fasc. 4 (Szeged, 1962):4, 6.

11. Horvath, "La statistique de la peste," p. 6; Biraben, "Demographic characteristics," p. 536; Shrewsbury, *Plague in the British Isles*, pp. 368, 462; W. G. Bell, *The Great Plague in London in 1665* (London and New York, 1924), p. 246.

12. Bell, *The Great Plague*, pp. 35, 86-89, 96-98, 206; Biraben, "Demographic characteristics," p. 538. But another commentator reports that 3 of 17 physicians and 31 of 97 surgeons died at Marseilles, while of those practitioners sent elsewhere in the region only 9 of 72 perished, 5 of the victims being surgeons; these figures are more like those for Moscow. Shelby T. McCloy, *Government Assistance in Eighteenth-Century France* (Durham, N.C., 1946), p. 144.

13. Charles F. Mullett, *The Bubonic Plague and England* (Lexington, Kentucky, 1956), pp. 236-97. See also E. A. Hammond and Claude C. Sturgill, "A French plague recipe of 1720," *Bulletin of the History of Medicine* 46 (1972):591-97.

14. McCloy, *Government Assistance*, pp. 139-57; Bell, *The Great Plague*, pp. 68-70, 82-86; Horvath, "La statistique de la peste," pp. 6-7.

15. Horvath, "La statistique de la peste," pp. 6-7; Biraben, "Demographic characteristics," p. 537.

16. Bell, *The Great Plague*, pp. 123-24, 173-75. See also Andrew P. Trout, "The municipality of Paris confronts the plague of 1668," *Medical History* 17 (1973):418-23.

17. Ch. Carriere, M. Courdurie, and F. Rebuffat, *Marseille ville morte: la peste de 1720* (Marseilles, 1968), p. 95; McCloy, *Government Assistance*, pp. 140-42, 147-49.

18. Mullett, *The Bubonic Plague*, pp. 98, 118; Bartolomé Bennassar, *Recherches sur les grandes épidémies dans le Nord de l'Espagne à la fin du XVIe siècle* (Paris, 1969), p. 59; Charles E. Rosenberg, *The Cholera Years* (Chicago, 1962), pp. 33, 119, 203-05.

19. Biraben, *Les hommes et la peste*, 1:105-11.

20. Kahan, "Natural calamities," p. 373; Lamb, *Climate: Present, Past and Future*, 2:562-65.

21. John D. Post, *The Last Great Subsistence Crisis in the Western World* (Baltimore and London, 1977), pp. 7, 21, 55.

22. Fyodorov, "The question of the existence of natural foci of plague in Europe in the past," pp. 138-40; Mironov, "The past existence of natural foci of plague in the steppes of Southeastern Europe," pp. 1194-1197.

23. Post, *Last Great Subsistence Crisis*, pp. 137-40.

24. Derbek, *Istoriia chumnykh epidemii*, pp. 212-385; Vasil'ev and Segal, *Istoriia epidemii v Rossii*, pp. 226-46, 391-96; E. I. Lotova and Kh. I. Idel'chik, *Bor'ba s infektsionnymi bolezniami v SSSR 1917-1967* (Moscow, 1967), pp. 258-62.

25. Pollitzer, *Plague and Plague Control in the Soviet Union*, p. 401. A recent Soviet dissertation summary notes, however, the occurrence of four plague epizootics in the Caspian region in 1961-67. Lisitsyn, *Genezis i landshaftno-ekologicheskie osobennosti*, p. 43.

Selected Bibliography

I. Research Aids and Specialized Bibliographies

Besides the titles listed below, extensive bibliographical coverage of plague epidemics worldwide and in Europe and the Mediterranean may be found in the surveys by Georg Sticker, vol. 1, pt. 1:423-538, and by Jean-Noël Biraben, vol. 2:186-413.

Anisimov, P. I., Anisimova, T. I., and Koneva, Z. A., eds. *Chuma: Bibliografiia otechestvennoi literatury, 1740–1964*. Saratov, 1968.

Catalogus Librorum Academiae Caesaraeai Medico-Chirurgicae. St. Petersburg, 1809.

Frari, A. A. *Della Peste e della Pubblica Amministrazione Sanitaria*, vol. 1. Venice, 1840.

Grimsted, Patricia K. *Archives and Manuscript Repositories in the Soviet Union: Moscow and Leningrad*. Princeton, 1972.

Kondrat'ev, V. A., and Nevzorov, V. I., eds. *Iz istorii fabrik i zavodov Moskvy i Moskovskoi gubernii (konets XVIII-nachalo XX v.): Obzor dokumentov*. Moscow, 1968.

National Library of Medicine, U.S. Public Health Service. *Index Medicus*.

Petrov, B. D., ed., and Matskina, R. Iu., comp. *Istoriia razvitiia meditsiny i zdravookhraneniia v Rossii: Obzor dokumental'nykh materialov*. Moscow and Leningrad, 1958.

Pollitzer, Robert. *Plague and Plague Control in the Soviet Union: History and Bibliography through 1964*. Bronx, N.Y., 1966.

Putevoditel' po fondam lichnogo proiskhozhdeniia otdela pis'mennykh istochnikov Gosudarstvennogo istoricheskogo muzeia. Moscow, 1967.

Rossiiskii, D. M. *Istoriia vseobshchei i otechestvennoi meditsiny i zdravookhraneniia: Bibliografiia (996–1954 gg.)*. Moscow, 1956.

Shmidt, S. O., ed., and Gaisinskaia, L. I., comp. *Gosudarstvennyi istoricheskii arkhiv Moskovskoi oblasti: Putevoditel'*. Moscow, 1961.

Shumilov, V. N., comp., and Bakhrushin, S. V., ed. *Tsentral'nyi gosudarstvennyi arkhiv drevnikh aktov: Obzor dokumental'nykh materialov po istorii g. Moskvy s drevneishikh vremen do XIX v.* Moscow, 1949.

Valk, S. N., and Gedin, V. V. *Tsentral'nyi gosudarstvennyi istoricheskii arkhiv SSSR v Leningrade: Putevoditel'*. Leningrad, 1956.

The Wellcome Institute of the History of Medicine. *Current Work in the History of Medicine: An International Bibliography*. London, 1954 to the present, quarterly.

II. Archival Sources

Gosudarstvennaia biblioteka im. V. I. Lenina. Rukopisnyi otdel (Moscow).
f. 222 Panina
f. 129 Kiselevy
f. 94 Viazemy
Gosudarstvennaia publichnaia biblioteka im. M. E. Saltykova-Shchedrina. Otdel rukopisei (Leningrad).
Ermitazhnoe sobranie, No. 355
Gosudarstvennyi istoricheskii muzei. Otdel pis'mennykh istochnikov (Moscow).
f. 145 M. N. Volkonskii
f. 440 I. E. Zabelin
Meteoroligicheskii muzei Glavnoi geofizicheskoi observatorii im. A. I. Voeikova (Voeikovo).
J. J. Lerche manuscripts (uncatalogued)
Niedersächsischen Staats- und Universitätsbibliothek in Göttingen. Handschriftenabteilung.
Codex Asch 198
Public Record Office (London).
State Papers, Russia 91/85-92
Tsentral'nyi gosudarstvennyi arkhiv drevnikh aktov (Moscow).
f. 6 gosarkhiv
f. 10 gosarkhiv
f. 16 gosarkhiv
f. 199 Portfel' Millera
f. 248 Pervyi departament Senata
f. 263 Piatyi departament Senata
f. 277 Manufaktur-kollegiia
f. 344 Meditsinskaia kollegiia
f. 455 Iaroslavskaia provintsial'naia kantseliariia
f. 1183 Moskovskaia sinodal'naia kontora
Tsentral'nyi gosudarstvennyi arkhiv goroda Moskvy (Moscow).
f. 46 Kantseliariia Moskovskogo gradonachal'nika
f. 203 Moskovskaia dukhovnaia konsistoriia
f. 205 Krutitskaia dukhovnaia konsistoriia
f. 636 Komissiia dlia predokhraneniia i vrachevaniia ot morovoi iazvy

III. Contemporary Newspapers and Periodicals

Annual Register (London)
Daily Advertiser (London)
London Gazette
London Magazine

Moskovskie vedomosti (Moscow)
Sanktpeterburgskie vedomosti (St. Petersburg)
Scots Magazine (Edinburgh)
Weekly Magazine (Edinburgh)

IV. Published Sources

"Akty o morovom povetrii, 1654-1655 goda," *Dopolneniia k Aktam istoricheskim, sobrannye i izdannye Arkheograficheskoiu komissieiu* 3 (1848):442-521.

Alekseev, P. "Opisanie Moskovskago bunta 1771 goda sentiabria 15 gnia," *Russkii arkhiv* 1 (1863; reissued 1866):491-99.

Andrews, J. *A Collection of Plans of the Most Capital Cities of Every Empire, Kingdom, Republic and Electorate in Europe and Some Remarkable Cities in the Other Three Parts of the World*. London, 1772.

Arkhiv gosudarstvennago soveta, vol. 1, pts. 1-2. St. Petersburg, 1869.

Bagalei, D. I., comp. *Materialy dlia istorii kolonizatsii i byta Khar'kovskoi i otchasti Kurskoi i Voronezhskoi gubernii*. Khar'kov, 1890.

Bantysh-Kamenskii, N. N. (?) "Materialy dlia istorii chumy v Moskve v 1771 godu," *Pamiatniki novoi russkoi istorii* 3 (1873):303-10.

Baron, Samuel H., ed. *The Travels of Olearius in Seventeenth-Century Russia*. Stanford, 1967.

Beliavskii, M. T., ed. "Novye dokumenty ob obsuzhdenii krest'ianskogo voprosa v 1766-1768 godakh," *Arkheograficheskii ezhegodnik za 1958* (Moscow, 1960):387-430.

Bidloo, Nicholas. *The Unknown Drawings of Nicholas Bidloo, Director of the First Hospital in Russia*. Edited by David Willemse. Voorburg, 1975.

Bielfeld, Jacob Friedrich. *Institutions politiques*. 2 vols. La Haye, 1760.

Bolotov, A. T. *Zhizn'i prikliucheniia Andreia Bolotova*. 3 vols. Moscow and Leningrad, 1931.

Catherine II. "Mnenie imperatritsy Ekateriny II o manufakturakh," *Russkii arkhiv* 3 (1865):1285-93.

________. "Morovaia iazva (ukazy i reskripty imperatritsy Ekateriny II)," ed. V. A. Bil'basov, *Russkaia starina* 80 (1893):449-64.

________. *Nakaz imperatritsy Ekateriny II, dannyi kommissii o sochinenii proekta novogo ulozheniia*. Edited by N. D. Chechulin. St. Petersburg, 1907.

________. "Pis'ma imperatritsy Ekateriny Velikoi k fel'dmarshalu grafu Petru Semenovichu Saltykovu, 1762-1771," *Russkii arkhiv* 9 (1886):5-105.

________. *Sochineniia imperatritsy Ekateriny II*. Edited by A. N. Pypin. 12 vols. St. Petersburg, 1901-7.

________. *Sochineniia imperatritsy Ekateriny II*. Edited by A. F. Smirdin. 3 vols. St. Petersburg, 1849-50.

________. *Uchrezhdeniia dlia upravleniia gubernii vserossiiskoi imperii*. St. Petersburg, 1775.

________. *Vysochaishiia sobstvennoruchnyia pis'ma i poveleniia blazhennoi i vechnoi slavy dostoinoi pamiati gosudaryni imperatritsy, Ekateriny Velikiia, k pokoinomu Generalu Petru Dmitrievichu Erapkinu i vsepoddaneishiia ego doneseniia*. Edited by Ia. Rost. Moscow, 1808.

[Chebotarev]. *Istoricheskoe i topograficheskoe opisanie gorodov Moskovskoi gubernii s ikh uezdami*. Moscow, 1787.

The Chronicle of Novgorod, 1016–1461. Translated by Robert Mitchell and Nevill Forbes. London, 1914.

Cook, John. *Voyages and Travels through the Russian Empire, Tartary, and Part of the Kingdom of Persia*. 2 vols. Edinburgh, 1770.

Coxe, William. *Account of the Prisons and Hospitals in Russia, Sweden, and Denmark*. London, 1781.

———. *Travels in Poland, Russia, Sweden, and Denmark*. 5 vols., 5th ed. London, 1802.

"Doklad Senata imperatritse Ekaterine II po povodu ee rasporiazhenii o morovoi iazve v Moskve v 1771 i reskript imperatritsy na etot doklad," *Moskovskii vestnik*, 1829, pt. 5:139–157.

Dolgorukii, I. M. "Zapiski kniazia Ivana Mikhailovicha Dolgorukago," *Sochineniia Dolgorukago (kniazia Ivana Mikhailovicha)*, vol. 2. St. Petersburg, 1849.

Drashusov, V., ed. *Materialy dlia istorii imperatorskago Moskovskago vospitatel'nago doma*. 2 vols. Moscow, 1863–68.

Drimpelman, E. W. "Zapiski nemetskago vracha o Rossii v kontse proshlago veka," *Russkii arkhiv* 1 (1881):32–51.

Guboglu, Mikhail, ed. "Turetskii istochnik 1740 g. o Valakhii, Moldavii i Ukraine," in A. S. Tveritinova, ed., *Vostochnye istochniki po istorii narodov iugo-vostochnoi i tsentral'noi Evropy* 1 (Moscow, 1964):131–61.

Guthrie, Matthew. "Observations on the Plague, Quarantines, etc. in a Letter from Dr. Matthew Guthrie, Physician at St. Petersburgh, to Dr. Duncan," *Medical Commentaries* 8, pt. 2 (1781-82):345-63.

Hanway, Jonas. *An Historical Account of British Trade over the Caspian Sea*. 4 vols. London, 1753.

Heinrich von Staden. *The Land and Government of Muscovy: A Sixteenth Century Account*. Edited and translated by Thomas Esper. Stanford, 1967.

Justi, Johann Heinrich Gottlob von. *Die Grundfeste zu der Macht und Glückseligkeit der Staaten*. 2 vols. Königsberg and Leipzig, 1760–61.

Kabardino-russkie otnosheniia v XVI–XVIII vv. Edited by N. A. Smirnov and U. A. Uligov. 2 vols. Moscow, 1957.

Kamer-fur'erskii tseremonial'nyi zhurnal, 1770–71. St. Petersburg, 1859.

[Karzhavin, F. V.] "Zapiski ochevidtsa o chumnom bunte v Moskve v 1771 godu," ed. S. R. Dolgova, *Sovetskie arkhivy* 6 (1976):66–70.

Kirchner, Walther, ed. *Eine Reise durch Sibirien in achtzehnten Jahrhundert: Die Fahrt des Schweizer Doktors Jakob Fries*. Munich, 1955.

Körber, Peter Fridrich. *Abhandlung von der Pest, und andern hinraffenden Seuchen samt den dawider dienenden Praeservations- und Heilungsmitteln*. Reval, 1771.

"Kopiia svedeniia Senatu ot Sinoda, ob ubiistve arkhiepiskopa Amvrosiia, 29 sentiabria 1771 goda," *Sbornik starinnykh bumag, khraniashchikhsia v Muzee P. I. Shchukina* 8 (1901):53–54.

Lappo, F. I., and Samsonov, V. I., eds. "Dnevnik Kurskogo pomeshchika I. P. Annenkova," *Materialy po istorii SSSR* 5 (1957):661–823.

Le Clerc, Nicolas Gabriel. *De la contagion, de sa nature, de ses effets, de ses progres, et des moyens les plus surs pour la prévenir et pour y remédier*. St. Petersburg, 1771.

Lerche, Johann Jakob. *Lebens- und Reise-Geschichte von ihm selbst geschrieben, und mit Anmerkungen und Zusätzen herausgegeben von Dr. Anton Friedrich Büsching*. Halle, 1791.

Lomonosov, M. V. *Polnoe sobranie sochinenii*, vol. 6. Edited by S. I. Vavilov et al. (Moscow and Leningrad, 1952).

Manstein, C. H. von. *Contemporary Memoirs of Russia from the Year 1727 to 1744*. London, 1856; reprinted London, 1968.

Marshall, Joseph. *Travels through Holland, Flanders, Germany, Denmark, Sweden, Lapland, Russia, the Ukraine, and Poland, in the Years 1768, 1769, and 1770*. 3 vols. London, 1772.

Materialy dlia istorii Moskovskago kupechestva. Edited by N. N. Naidenov. 6 vols. Moscow, 1883–87.

[Mead, Richard]. *O morovoi iazve, sochineniia Richarda Meada, Aglinskago doktora*. Translated by S. Sulima. St. Petersburg, 1772.

Meltzer, Frantz Karl. *Beschreibung der Pest von 1770 bis 1772 in Moskau*. Moscow, 1776.

Mertens, Charles de. *Traité de la peste, contenant l'histoire de celle qui a régné à Moscou en 1771*. Vienna, 1784.

———. *An Account of the Plague Which Raged at Moscow in 1771*. Translated by Richard Pearson. London, 1799; reprinted Newtonville, Mass., 1977.

Meshalin, I. V., comp., Kashin, V. N., and Sivkov, K. V., eds. *Materialy po istorii krest'ianskoi promyshlennosti XVIII i pervoi poloviny XIX v*. 2 vols. Moscow and Leningrad, 1935–50.

Minderer, Johann Martin. *Abermal ein Beytrag zur Kenntniss und Heilung der Pest*. Riga, 1790.

Ministerstva vnutrennikh del. *Tabeli k otchetu Ministerstva vnutrennikh del za 1803 god*. St. Petersburg, 1804.

Moskovskii arkhiv Ministerstva iustitsii. *Moskva: Aktovye knigi XVIII stoletiia*. 12 vols. Moscow, 1892–1900.

Nikon, Patriarch. *Pouchenie o morovoi iazve*. Moscow, 1655.

Novombergskii, N. Ia., comp. *Materialy po istorii meditsiny v Rossii*. 5 vols. St. Petersburg and Tomsk, 1905–10.

"O morovoi iazve v Moskve," *Arkhiv kniazia Vorontsova* 16 (1880):449–69.

Opisanie del arkhiva morskago Ministerstva za vremia s poloviny XVII do nachala XIX stoletiia. 10 vols. St. Petersburg, 1877–1906.

Orraeus, Gustav. *Descriptio pestis quae anno MDCCLXX in Jassia, et MDCCLXXI in Moscua grassata est*. St. Petersburg, 1784.

Osmnadtsatyi vek: Istoricheskii sbornik. Edited by P. I. Bartenev. 4 vols. Moscow, 1868–69.

Over, A. I., comp. *Materialy dlia istorii Moskovskikh bol'nits grazhdanskogo vedomstva*. Moscow, 1859.

Parkinson, John. *A Tour of Russia, Siberia, and the Crimea, 1792–1794*. Edited by W. Collier. London, 1971.

Penchko, N. A., comp., and Novitskii, G. A., ed. *Dokumenty i materialy po istorii Moskovskogo universiteta vtoroi poloviny XVIII veka*. 3 vols. Moscow, 1960–63.

"Pis'mo ochevidtsa o bunte v Moskve vo vremia chumy, 15 i 16 sentiabria 1771 goda, i o ubienii arkhiereia Amvrosiia Zertis-Kamenskago," *Deistviia Nizhegorodskoi gubernskoi uchenoi arkhivnoi kommissii*, fasc. 1–8 (1890):358–61.

Polnoe sobranie zakonov rossiiskoi imperii. First series, 45 vols. St. Petersburg, 1830.
Polunin, F. A. *Geograficheskii leksikon Rossiiskago gosudarstva*. Moscow, 1773.
———. *Novyi i polnyi geograficheskii slovar' Rossiiskago gosudarstva*. 3 vols. Moscow, 1788-89.
Richardson, William. *Anecdotes of the Russian Empire*. London, 1784; reprinted London, 1968.
Rost, I. I. *Razsuzhdenie o pronitsatel'nom deistvii maleishikh chastits, kotoryia iz tel, osoblivo zhivotnykh, proistekaiut*. Moscow, 1765.
———. *Slovo o vrednom vozdukhe v zhilishchakh osoblivo prostago naroda primechaemom i o sredstvakh udobnykh k popravleniiu onago*. Moscow, 1772.
Ruban, V. G. *Opisanie imperatorskago stolichnago goroda Moskvy*. St. Petersburg, 1782.
P. A. Rumiantsev, vol. 2:*1768–75*. Edited by P. K. Fortunatov. Moscow, 1953.
Russkii biograficheskii slovar'. 25 vols. St. Petersburg, 1896-1913; reprinted New York, 1962.
Rutzky, Helias. *Dissertatio inauguralis medica sur de Peste*. Strasbourg, 1781.
Sablukov, A. A. "Moskva v 1771 godu," *Russkii arkhiv* 4 (1866):329-39.
Samoilovich, D. S. *Izbrannye proizvedeniia*. 2 vols. Edited by O. I. Karakhanian and B. S. Bessmertnyi. Moscow, 1947-50.
Sbornik imperatorskago russkago istoricheskago obshchestva. 148 vols. St. Petersburg, Moscow, Iur'ev, and Petrograd, 1867-1916.
Senatskii arkhiv. 15 vols. St. Petersburg, 1888-1913.
Senkovskii, O., ed. "Razskaz Resmi-Efendiia, ottomanskago ministra inostrannykh del, o semi-letnei bor'be Turtsii s Rossiei (1769-1776)," *Biblioteka dlia chteniia* 124 (1854):1-78.
Shafonskii, A. F., comp. *Opisanie morovoi iazvy, byvshei v Moskve s 1770 po 1772 god*. Moscow, 1775.
Shvarts, V. *Kratkoe opisanie morovago povetriia i sredstv ot onago predokhraniaiushchikh, s pribavleniem o kontsentrirovannom uksusnom spirte*. Moscow, 1771.
"Skazanie o postroenii obydennago khrama v Vologde 'vo izbavlenie ot smertonosnyia iazvy,' " *Chteniia v Obshchestve istorii i drevnostei rossiiskikh* 3 (1893), pt. 2:i-x, 11-21.
Skvortsov, N. A. *Materialy po Moskve i Moskovskoi eparkhii za XVIII v*. 2 vols. Moscow, 1911-14.
Tiul'pin, Mikhail. *Letopis' o sobytiiakh v g. Tveri Tverskogo kuptsa Mikhaila Tiul'pina 1762–1823 gg.* Edited by V. Kolosov. Tver, 1902.
Tolchenov, I. A. *Zhurnal ili zapiska zhizni i prikliuchenii Ivana Alekseevicha Tolchenova*. Edited by N. I. Pavlenko. Moscow, 1974.
Tomsinskii, S. G., ed. *Moskovskii sukonnyi dvor*, Krepostnaia manufaktura v Rossii, vol. 5. Leningrad, 1934.
Tott, Francois de. *Memoirs of Baron de Tott*. 4 vols. London, 1785; reprinted New York, 1973.
[Van Woensel, Pieter]. *Razsuzhdenie o morovoi iazve, sochinennoe P. fon Vunzelem*. Translated by Andrei Meyer. Moscow, 1791.
"Vedomost' o predpriiatiiakh legkoi promyshlennosti, 1778 g.," in Beskrovnyi, L. G., and Kafengauz, B. B., eds., *Khrestomatiia po istorii SSSR: XVIII v.* (Moscow, 1963), pp. 305-26.
Vien, Ivan. *Loimologia ili opisanie morovoi iazvy, eia sushchestva, proizshestviia,*

prichin, porazheniia i proizvodstva pripadkov, s pokazaniem obraza predokhraneniia i vrachevaniia seia skorbi. St. Petersburg, 1786.
Zabelin, I. E., ed. *Materialy dlia istorii, arkheologii i statistiki goroda Moskvy*. 2 vols. Moscow, 1884-91.
"Zametki neizvestnago vo frantsuzskom al'manakhe, 1771 goda," *Shchukinskii sbornik* 6 (1907):38-39.
Zertsalov, A., ed. "O miatezhakh v gorode Moskve i v sele Kolomenskom v 1648, 1662 i 1771 g.," *Chteniia v Obshchestve istorii i drevnostei rossiiskikh* 3 (1890):1-439.

V. *Secondary Works*

Abel, Wilhelm. *Massenarmut und Hungerkrisen im vorindustriellen Europa*. Hamburg and Berlin, 1974.
Afanas'ev, N. P. *Ocherk meteorologicheskikh nabliudenii i klimaticheskikh uslovii Moskvy*. Moscow, 1896.
Aksenov, A. I. "Moskovskoe kupechestvo v XVIII v. (opyt genealogicheskogo issledovaniia)." Kand. diss., Moscow, 1974.
Alefirenko, P. K. "Chumnyi bunt v Moskve v 1771 godu," *Voprosy istorii*, 1947, no. 4:82-88.
Alelekov, A. N., and Iakimov, N. I. *Istoriia Moskovskogo voennogo gospitalia v sviazi s istoriei meditsiny v Rossii (1707-1907 gg.)*. Moscow, 1907.
Alexander, John T. "British Responses to the Moscow Plague of 1771," introduction to reprint of Mertens, *Account*, pp. 1-39.
________. "Catherine II, Bubonic Plague, and the Problem of Industry in Moscow," *American Historical Review* 79 (1974):637-71.
________. "Communicable Disease, Anti-epidemic Policies, and the Role of Medical Professionals in Russia, 1725-1762," *Canadian-American Slavic Studies* 12 (1978): 154-69.
________. "Medical Developments in Petrine Russia," *Canadian-American Slavic Studies* 8 (1974):198-221.
________. "Medical Professionals and Public Health in 'Doldrums' Russia, 1725-1762," *Canadian-American Slavic Studies* 12 (1978):116-35.
________. "Plague in Russia and Danilo Samoilovich: An Historiographical Comment and Research Note," *Canadian-American Slavic Studies* 8 (1974):525-31.
Amburger, Erik. *Beiträge zur Geschichte der deutsch-russischen kulturellen Beziehungen*. Giessen, 1961.
Amundsen, Darrel W. "Medical Deontology and Pestilential Disease in the Late Middle Ages," *Journal of the History of Medicine and Allied Sciences* 23 (1977):403-21.
Andreevskii, A. "Arkhivnaia spravka o morovoi iazve v g. Kieve v 1770-1771 gg.," *Kievskaia starina* 24 (1891):304-14.
Appleby, Andrew B. *Famine in Tudor and Stuart England*. Stanford, 1978.
Artemenkov, M. N. "Naemnye rabochie Moskovskikh manufaktur v 40-70-kh godakh XVIII v.," *Istoriia SSSR*, 1964, no. 2:133-44.
________. "Promyshlennaia deiatel'nost' krest'ianstva Rossii v XVIII v." Kand. diss., Leningrad, 1949.
________. "Sotsial'nyi sostav naemnykh rabochikh Moskovskikh manufaktur v sere-

dine XVIII v.," *Uchenye zapiski Leningradskogo. gos. ped. inst. im. Gertsena* 278 (1965):154-76.

Baburin, D. S. *Ocherki po istorii manufaktur-kollegii*. Moscow, 1939.

Bakhrushin, S. V., et al., eds. *Istoriia Moskvy*. 6 vols. Moscow, 1952-59.

[Bantysh-Kamenskii, D. N.] *Zhizn' Nikolaia Nikolaevicha Bantysh-Kamenskago*. Moscow, 1818.

———. *Zhizn' preosviashchennogo Amvrosiia, arkhiepiskopa Moskovskogo i Kaluzhshogo, ubiennogo v 1771 godu*. Moscow, 1813.

Barger, George. *Ergot and Ergotism*. London, 1931.

Barnett, S. A. "Rats," *Scientific American*, January 1967.

Becker, Christopher. "*Raznochintsy*: The Development of the Word and of the Concept," *American Slavic and East European Review* 18 (1959):63-74.

Beletskaia, E. A., Krasheninnikova, N. L., Chernozubova, L. E., and Ern, I. V. *"Obraztsovye" proekty v zhiloi zastroike russkikh gorodov XVIII-XIX vv*. Moscow, 1961.

Belilovskii, V. A., and Gamaleia, N. F. *Chuma v Odesse*. Odessa, 1903.

Bell, Walter G. *The Great Plague in London in 1665*. London and New York, 1924.

Benesch, W. "The Use of Wood as a Building Material in Pre-Modern Russia: Its Extent and Potential Cultural Implications," *Cahiers d'histoire mondiale* 8 (1964): 160-67.

Bennassar, Bartolomé. *Recherches sur les grandes épidémies dans le nord de l'Espagne à la fin du XVI-e siècle*. Paris, 1969.

Bernadskii, V. N. "Ocherki po istorii klassovoi bor'by i obshchestvenno-politicheskoi mysli Rossii v tret'ei chetverti XVIII v.," *Uchenye zapiski Leningradskogo gos. ped. inst. im. Gertsena* 229 (1962):3-160.

Bernard, Paul P. "The Limits of Absolutism: Joseph II and the Allgemeines Krankenhaus," *Eighteenth-Century Studies* 9 (1975-76):193-215.

Beskrovnyi, L. G. *Russkaia armiia i flot v XVIII veke*. Moscow, 1958.

Bessmertnyi, B. S. "Opyt istoricheskogo analiza epidemii XIV-XVII stoletii," *Zhurnal mikrobiologii, epidemiologii i immunobiologii*, 1966, no. 5:153-57.

Bibel, David J., and Chen, T. H. "Diagnosis of Plague: An Analysis of the Yersin-Kitasato Controversy," *Bacteriological Reviews* 40 (1976):633-51.

Bil'basov, V. A. *Istoriia Ekateriny Vtoroi*. 3 vols. Berlin, 1900.

Biraben, Jean-Noël. *Les hommes et la peste en France et dans les pays européens et mediterranéens*. 2 vols. Paris, 1975-76.

———. "Certain Demographic Characteristics of the Plague Epidemic in France, 1720-1722," *Daedalus* 97 (1968):536-45.

———, and Le Goff, Jacques. "The Plague in the Early Middle Ages," in R. Forster and O. Ranum, eds., *Biology of Man in History* (Baltimore and London, 1975), pp. 48-80.

Bishop, W. J. "Thomas Dimsdale, M.D., F.R.S. (1712-1800) and the Inoculation of Catherine the Great of Russia," *Annals of Medical History*, n.s., 4 (1932):321-38.

Blake, John B. *Public Health in the Town of Boston, 1630-1832*. Cambridge, Mass., 1959.

Blondheim, S. H. "The First Recorded Epidemic of Pneumonic Plague: The Bible, I Sam. VI," *Bulletin of the History of Medicine* 29 (1955):337-45.

Bochkarev, V. N. "Vrachebnoe delo i narodnoe prizrenie v Rossii XVIII v. po mate-

rialam zakonodatel'noi komissii 1767 goda," *Sbornik statei v chest' M. K. Liubavskago* (Petrograd, 1917):442-89.
Bogoiavlenskii, N. A. *Drevnerusskoe vrachevanie v XI-XVII vv*. Moscow, 1960.
________. *Meditsina u pervoselov russkogo severa*. Leningrad, 1966.
Brennsohn, Isidorus. *Die Aerzte Estlands vom Beginn der historischen Zeit bis zur Gegenwart*. Riga, 1922.
________. *Die Aerzte Kurlands vom Beginn der herzoglichen Zeit bis zur Gegenwart*. 2nd ed. rev. Riga, 1929.
________. *Die Aerzte Livlands von den ältesten Zeiten bis zur Gegenwart*. Mitau, 1905.
Brown, John H. "A Provincial Landowner: A. T. Bolotov (1738-1833)." Ph.D. dissertation, Princeton, 1976.
Brückner, Alexander. [Brikner, A. G.] "Chuma v Moskve v 1654 godu," *Istoricheskii vestnik* 16 (April 1884):5-22.
________. *Die Aerzte in Russland bis zum Jahre 1800*. St. Petersburg, 1887.
________. "O chume v Moskve 1771 goda," *Russkii vestnik* (1884), no. 9, 5-48; no. 10, 502-68.
Buchholz, Arnold. *Die Göttinger Russlandsammlungen Georgs von Asch: Ein Museum der russischen Wissenschaftsgeschichte des 18. Jahrhunderts*. Giessen, 1961.
Busvine, J. S. *Insects, Hygiene and History*. London, 1976.
Butler, Thomas. "A Clinical Study of Bubonic Plague: Observations of the 1970 Vietnam Epidemic with Emphasis on Coagulation Studies, Skin Histology and Electrocardiograms," *American Journal of Medicine* 53 (1973):268-76.
Canby, Thomas Y. "The Rat: Lapdog of the Devil," *National Geographic* (July 1977): 60-87.
Carpentier, Elisabeth. "Autour de la peste noire: famines et épidémies dans l'histoire du XIVe siècle," *Annales E.S.C.*, 1962, no. 6:1062-92.
Carriere, Ch., Courdurie, M., and Rebuffat, F. *Marseille ville morte: la peste de 1720*. Marseilles, 1968.
Chandler, Tertius, and Fox, Gerald. *3000 Years of Urban Growth*. New York, 1974.
Chistovich, Ia. A. *Istoriia pervykh meditsinskikh shkol v Rossii*. St. Petersburg, 1883.
________. "Morovaia iazva v 1738 g. (po offitsiial'nym istochnikam)," *Voenno-meditsinskii zhurnal* 127 (September 1876):71-100.
________. *Ocherki iz istorii russkikh meditsinskikh uchrezhdenii XVIII stoletiia*. St. Petersburg, 1870.
________. "Vrachebnyi personal russkikh armii v Turetskuiu voinu 1769-1774 gg.," *Protokoly zasedanii Obshchestva russkikh vrachei v Sanktpeterburge za 1877-1878* (St. Petersburg, 1877):55-69.
Cipolla, Carlo M. *Cristofano and the Plague: A Study in the History of Public Health in the Age of Galileo*. Berkeley and Los Angeles, 1973.
________. *Public Health and the Medical Profession in the Renaissance*. Cambridge, 1976.
________, and Zanetti, Dante E. "Pest et mortalité différentielle," *Annales de demographie historique 1972* (Paris and La Haye, 1972):197-202.
Clark, Peter, and Slack, Paul, eds. *Crisis and Order in English Towns, 1500-1700*. London, 1972.
Clemow, Frank G. "Plague Epidemics in Russia: Some Historical Notes," *Indian*

Medical Gazette (September 1898):331-36; (October 1898):363-68.

Clendenning, Philip H. "Dr. Thomas Dimsdale and Smallpox Inoculation in Russia," *Journal of the History of Medicine and Allied Sciences* 28 (1973): 109-25.

Coquin, Fr.-X. *La grande Commission législative 1767-1768: Les cahiers de doléances urbains (Province de Moscou)*. Paris and Louvain, 1972.

———. "Un document d'histoire sociale: Le cahier de doléances de la ville de Moscou (printemps 1767)," *Revue historique* 245 (1971):19-46.

Derbek, F. A. [Dörbeck, Franz] *Istoriia chumnykh epidemii v Rossii s osnovaniia gosudarstva do nastoiashchego vremeni*, Seriia doktorskikh dissertatsii, dopushchennykh k zashchite v Imperatorskoi voenno-meditsinskoi akademii v 1904-1905 uchebnom godu, no. 14. St. Petersburg, 1905.

Desaive, J.-P. et al. *Médecins, climat et épidémies à la fin du XVIIIe siècle*. Paris and La Haye, 1972.

Dols, Michael W. *The Black Death in the Middle East*. Princeton, 1977.

Doolittle, I. G. "The Effects of the Plague on a Provincial Town in the Sixteenth and Seventeenth Centuries," *Medical History* 19 (1975):333-41.

Doroshenko, A. P. "O sushchnosti sotsial'no-ekonomicheskikh otnoshenii v ukaznoi legkoi promyshlennosti Moskvy v 1730-1760-e gody," *Uchenye zapiski Moskovskogo oblastnogo ped. inst. im. Krupskoi*, vol. 74, Trudy kafedry istorii SSSR, fasc. 5 (1958):3-69.

———. "Rabochaia sila v ukaznoi legkoi promyshlennosti Moskvy v 1730-1760 gg.," *Istoriia SSSR*, 1958, no. 5:144-67.

———. "Rabota na domu v tekstil'noi promyshlennosti Moskvy v seredine XVIII v.," *Istoricheskie zapiski* 72 (1972):259-75.

Dubasov, I. I. "Chuma i Pugachevshchina v Shatskoi provintsii," *Istoricheskii vestnik* 13 (1883):113-35.

Dukes, Paul. *Catherine the Great and the Russian Nobility*. Cambridge, 1967.

Dyer, Alan D. "The Influence of Bubonic Plague in England 1500-1667," *Medical History* 22 (1978):308-26.

Efimenko, T. "Iz istorii gorodskogo zemleustroistva vremeni Ekateriny II," *Zhurnal Ministerstva narodnogo prosveshcheniia*, n.s. 54 (1914):280-315.

Ehrard, J. "Opinions médicales en France au XVIII-e siècle: La peste et l'idée de contagion," *Annales E.S.C.*, 1957, no. 12:46-59.

Ekkerman, V. *Materialy dlia istorii meditsiny v Rossii: Istoriia epidemii X-XVIII vv.* Kazan, 1884.

Fal'kovskii, N. I. *Moskva v istorii tekhniki*. Moscow, 1950.

Flinn, Michael, ed. *Scottish Population History*. Cambridge, 1977.

Florinskii, V. M. "Materialy dlia izucheniia chumy," in N. F. Vysotskii, ed., *Sbornik statei o chume* (Kazan, 1879) 1:1-30.

Florovskii, A. V. "K istorii ekonomicheskikh idei v Rossii v XVIII v.," *Nauchnye trudy russkogo narodnogo universiteta v Prage* 1 (1928):81-93.

Fordham von Reyn, C., et al. "Epidemiological and Clinical Features of an Outbreak of Bubonic Plague in New Mexico," *Journal of Infectious Diseases* 136 (1977):489-94.

Freeze, Gregory L. *The Russian Levites: Parish Clergy in the Eighteenth Century*. Cambridge, Mass., 1977.

Fursenko, V. V. "Delo o Lestoke 1748 goda," *Zhurnal Ministerstva narodnogo prosveshcheniia*, n.s. 38 (1912):185-247.

Fyodorov, V. N. "The Question of the Existence of Natural Foci of Plague in Europe in the Past," *Journal of Hygiene, Epidemiology, Microbiology and Immunology* (Praha), 4 (1960):135-41.

Goehrke, Carsten. *Die Wüstungen in der Moskauer Rus': Studien zur Siedlungs-, Bevölkerungs- und Sozialgeschichte*. Wiesbaden, 1968.

Gol'denberg, P., and Gol'denberg, B. *Planirovka zhilogo kvartala Moskvy XVII, XVIII i XIX vv*. Moscow and Leningrad, 1935.

Gol'denberg, P. I. *Staraia Moskva*. Moscow, 1947.

Golikova, N. B. *Astrakhanskoe vosstanie 1705-1706 gg.* Moscow, 1975.

Golombievskii, A. A. *Biografiia kniazia G. Orlova*. Moscow, 1904.

Gottfried, Robert S. *Epidemic Disease in Fifteenth Century England: The Medical Response and the Demographic Consequences*. New Brunswick, N.J., 1978.

Goubert, Jean-Pierre. *Malades et médecins en Bretagne 1770-1790*. Rennes, 1974.

________. "The Extent of Medical Practice in France around 1780," *Journal of Social History* 10 (1977):410-27.

Gregg, Charles T. *Plague! The Shocking Story of a Dread Disease in America Today*. New York, 1978.

Griaznov, A. F. *Iaroslavskaia bol'shaia manufaktura za vremia s 1722 po 1856 g.* Moscow, 1910.

Grmek, M. D. "Ancient Slavic Medicine," *Journal of the History of Medicine and Allied Sciences* 14 (1959):18-40.

________. "The History of Medical Education in Russia," in C. D. O'Malley, ed., *The History of Medical Education* (Berkeley, Los Angeles, and London, 1970), pp. 303-27.

Grombakh, S. M. "P. I. Pogoretskii i ego bor'ba za samostoiatel'nost' russkoi meditsinskoi shkoly," *Trudy Instituta istorii estestvoznaniia i tekhniki* 4 (Moscow, 1955): 290-314.

________. *Russkaia meditsinskaia literatura XVIII veka*. Moscow, 1953.

________. "S. G. Zybelin v bor'be s epidemiei chumy 1771-1772 gg.," *Sovetskoe zdravookhranenie*, 1962, no. 6:85-89.

Gubert, V. O. *Ospa i ospoprivivanie*, vol. 1: *Istoricheskii ocherk do XIX stoletiia*. St. Petersburg, 1896.

Gutkind, E. A. *Urban Development in Eastern Europe: Bulgaria, Romania, and the U.S.S.R.*, International History of City Development, vol. 8. New York and London, 1972.

Haigh, Basil. "Design for a Medical Service: Peter the Great's Admiralty Regulation (1722)," *Medical History* 19 (1975):129-46.

Hamm, Michael F., ed. *The City in Russian History*. Lexington, Ky., 1975.

Hannaway, Caroline G. "The Société Royale de Médecine and Epidemics in the Ancien Régime," *Bulletin of the History of Medicine* 46 (1972):257-73.

________. "Veterinary Medicine and Rural Health Care in Pre-Revolutionary France," *Bulletin of the History of Medicine* 51 (1977):431-47.

Hans, Nicholas. "Russian Students at Leyden in the Eighteenth Century," *Slavonic and East European Review* 35 (1957):551-62.

Hecker, J. F. C. *Geschichte der neueren Heilkunde*. Berlin, 1839.

Heilbronner, Hans. "The Russian Plague of 1878-79," *Slavic Review* 21 (1962):89-112.

Hermann, W. *Beitrag zur Geschichte der Pest in den unteren Donauländern*. Inaugu-

ral-Dissertation. Bucharest, 1938.
Hirst, L. F. *The Conquest of Plague: A Study of the Evolution of Epidemiology*. Oxford, 1953.
Horvath, Robert. "La statistique de la peste de Debrecen (1739–40) et du choléra de Pest (1831) en Hongrie et leurs conséquences sociales," *Acta Universitatis Szegediensis: Acta Juridica et Politica*, 9, fasc. 4 (1962):3–18.
Howard-Jones, Norman. "Fracastoro and Henle: A Re-Appraisal of Their Contribution to the Concept of Communicable Diseases," *Medical History* 21 (1977):61–68.
———. "Kitasato, Yersin and the Plague Bacillus," *Clio Medica* 10 (1975):23–27.
Imhof, Arthur E., and Larsen, Øivind. *Sozialgeschichte und Medizin*. Oslo and Stuttgart, 1975.
Iukht. A. I. "Torgovye sviazi Astrakhani v 20-kh godakh XVIII v.," *Istoricheskaia geografiia Rossii XII-nachalo XX v.: Sbornik statei k 70-letiiu professora Liubomira Grigor'evicha Beskrovnogo* (Moscow, 1975), pp. 177–92.
Jonecko, Urszula, and Jonecko, Antoni. "Studia nad patentem o kordonie sanitarno-wojskowym ksiestwa Slanskiego z roku 1770," *Archiwum Historii Medycyny* 36 (1973):163–75.
Kabuzan, V. M. *Izmeneniia v razmeshchenii naseleniia Rossii v XVIII-pervoi polovine XIX v*. Moscow, 1971.
———. *Narodonaselenie Rossii v XVIII-pervoi polovine XIX v*. Moscow, 1963.
———. *Zaselenie Novorossii (Ekaterinoslavskoi i Khersonskoi gubernii) v XVIII-pervoi polovine XIX veka (1719–1858 gg.)*. Moscow, 1976.
Kafengauz, B. B. *Istoriia khoziaistva Demidovykh v XVIII–XIX vv.*, vol. 1. Moscow and Leningrad, 1949.
———. *Ocherki vnutrennego rynka Rossii pervoi poloviny XVIII*. Moscow, 1958.
Kahan, Arcadius. "A Catalogue of Epidemics in Russia." Unpublished paper, University of Chicago, n. d.
———. "Comments on Some Social Aspects of the Plague Epidemics in Eighteenth Century Russia." Unpublished paper, University of Chicago, 1975.
———. "Natural Calamities and Their Effect upon the Food Supply in Russia: An Introduction to a Catalogue," *Jahrbücher für Geschichte Osteuropas*, n. s., 16 (1968):353–77.
———. "Social Aspects of the Plague Epidemics in Eighteenth-Century Russia," *Economic Development and Cultural Change* 27 (1979):255–66.
Kalabukhov, N. I. "The Structure and Changes of the Natural Foci of Plague," *Journal of Microbiology, Epidemiology, and Immunobiology* 5 (1961):877–83.
Kaplan, Herbert H. *The First Partition of Poland*. New York and London, 1962.
Keele, Kenneth D. "The Sydenham-Boyle Theory of Morbific Particles," *Medical History* 18 (1974):240–48.
Khanykov, Ia. V. *Ocherk istorii meditsinskoi politsii v Rossii*. St. Petersburg, 1851.
King, Lester S. *The Medical World of the Eighteenth Century*. Chicago, 1958.
Kiparisova, A. "Proekt Pavlovskoi bol'nitsy v Moskve," *Arkhitekturnoe nasledstvo*, 1 (1951):119–26.
Kirchner, Walther. "The Black Death: New Insights into 18th Century Attitudes Toward Bubonic Plague," *Clinical Pediatrics* 7 (1968):432–36.
———. "Zur Geschichte der Pest in Europas: Ihr letztes Auftreten im russischen Heer," *Saeculum* 20 (1969):82–92.

Kirikov, S. V. *Izmeneniia zhivotnogo mira v prirodnykh zonakh SSSR: Stepnaia zona i lesostep'*. Moscow, 1959.

Klokman, Iu. R. *Sotsial'no-ekonomicheskaia istoriia russkogo goroda: Vtoraia polovina XVIII veka*. Moscow, 1967.

Knabe, Bernd. *Die Struktur der russischen Posadgemeinden und der Katalog der Beschwerden und Forderungen der Kaufmannschaft (1762–1767)*. Berlin, 1975.

Knackstedt, Wolfgang. *Moskau: Studien zur Geschichte einer mitteralterlichen Stadt*. Wiesbaden, 1975.

Kopylov, A. M. "Iz istorii pervykh bol'nits Peterburga," *Sovetskoe zdravookhranenie*, 1962, no. 2:57-59.

Koreshchenko, A. O. *Istoricheskii ocherk chumy s 1770 po 1772 god v iugo-vostochnoi Evrope*. Moscow, 1854.

Kowal, Areta O. "Danilo Samoilowitz: An Eighteenth-Century Ukrainian Epidemiologist and His Role in the Moscow Plague (1770-72)," *Journal of the History of Medicine and Allied Sciences* 27 (1972):434-46.

Kozubenko, I. D., and Koveisha, M. T. "Iz istorii meditsinskogo obsluzhivaniia v Taganroge," *Sovetskoe zdravookhranenie* (1972) no. 6:67–71.

Kucheruk, V. V. "Voprosy paleogenezisa prirodnykh ochagov chumy v sviazi s istoriei fauny gryzunov," *Materialy po gryzunam*, fasc. 7: *Fauna i ekologiia gryzunov*, ed. A. N. Formosov, Moskovskoe obshchestvo ispytatelei prirody: Materialy k poznaniiu fauny i flory SSSR, n. s., Otdel zoologicheskii, fasc. 40 (Moscow, 1965), pp. 5-86.

Kudriavtsev, M. P. "Ispol'zovanie rel'efa mestnosti v russkom gradostroitel'stve na primere Moskvy XVII v.," *Arkhitekturnoe nasledstvo* 21 (1973):3–13.

Kupriianov, V. V. *K. I. Shchepin—doktor meditsiny XVIII veka*. Moscow, 1953.

Lakhtin, M. Iu. "Bor'ba s epidemiiami v do-Petrovskoi Rusi," *Russkaia starina* 2 (1905):414–27.

________. *Etiudy po istorii meditsiny*. Moscow, 1902.

________. *Meditsina i vrachi v Moskovskom gosudarstve v do-Petrovskoi Rusi*, Uchenyia zapiski imperatorskogo Moskovskogo universiteta, meditsinskogo fakul'teta, fasc. 10 (Moscow, 1907).

Lamb, H. H. *Climate: Present, Past and Future*, vol. 2: *Climatic History and the Future*. London and New York, 1977.

Langer, Lawrence N. "The Black Death in Russia: Its Effects upon Urban Labor," *Russian History* 2 (1975):53-67.

________. "Plague and the Russian Countryside: Monastic Estates in the Late Fourteenth and Fifteenth Centuries," *Canadian-American Slavic Studies* 10 (1976):351–69.

Latysheva, G. P., and Rabinovich, M. G. *Moskva i Moskovskii krai v proshlom*. Moscow, 1973.

Lauber, Jack M. "The Merchant-Gentry Conflict in Eighteenth-Century Russia." Ph.D. dissertation, University of Iowa, 1967.

Lesky, Erna. *Österreichisches Gesundheitswesen im Zeitalter des aufgeklärten Absolutismus*. Vienna, 1959.

Lieber, Elinor, "Galen on Contaminated Cereals as a Cause of Epidemics," *Bulletin of the History of Medicine* 44 (1970):332–45.

Lisitsyn, A. A. *Genezis i landshaftno-ekologicheskie osobennosti Volgo-Ural'skogo*

prirodnogo ochaga chumy. Dissertation summary, Saratov, 1973.
Liubimenko, Inna. "Vrachebnoe i lekarstvennoe delo v Moskovskom gosudarstve," *Russkii istoricheskii zhurnal*, 1917, bk. 3-4:1-36.
Liubomirov, P. G. *Ocherki po istorii russkoi promyshlennosti XVII, XVIII i nachalo XIX veka*. Moscow and Leningrad, 1947.
Luk'ianov, P. M. *Istoriia khimicheskikh promyslov i khimicheskoi promyshlennosti Rossii do kontsa XIX veka*. 6 vols. Moscow, 1948-65.
McCloy, Shelby T. *Government Assistance in Eighteenth-Century France*. Durham, N.C., 1946.
McGrew, Roderick E. *Russia and the Cholera, 1823-1832*. Madison and Milwaukee, 1965.
McNeill, William H. *Europe's Steppe Frontier*. Chicago, 1964.
———. *Plagues and Peoples*. Garden City, N.Y., 1976.
Maikov, P. M. *Ivan Ivanovich Betskoi: Opyt ego biografii*. St. Petersburg, 1904.
Marks, Geoffrey, and Beatty, William. *Epidemics*. New York, 1976.
Meshalin, I. V. "Promyshlennost' g. Novgoroda v XVIII veke," *Novgorodskii istoricheskii sbornik* 7 (1940):39-47.
———. "Promyshlennost' Rossii vo vtoroi polovine XVIII v. i ee territorial'noe razmeshchenie," *Izvestiia vsesoiuznogo geograficheskogo obshchestva* 73 (1941):259-68.
———. *Tekstil'naia promyshlennost' krest'ian Moskovskoi gubernii v XVIII i pervoi polovine XIX v.* Moscow and Leningrad, 1950.
Metelkin, A. I. "Bor'ba meditsinskoi organizatsii s chumoi vo vremia Moskovskoi epidemii, 1770-1772 gg. (po arkhivnym materialam)," *Zhurnal mikrobiologii, epidemiologii i immunobiologii* 51 (1974):142-47.
Meyer, K. F. *Disinfected Mail*. Holton, Kansas, 1962.
———. "Pasteurella and Francisella," in Rene J. Dubois and James G. Hirsch, eds., *Bacterial and Mycotic Infections of Man* (4th ed., Philadelphia and Montreal, 1965), pp. 659-97.
Mikhailov, A. I. *Arkhitektor D. V. Ukhtomskii i ego shkola*. Moscow, 1954.
Mikhailov, S. S. *Meditsinskaia sluzhba russkogo flota v XVIII veke: Materialy k istorii otechestvennoi meditsiny*. Leningrad, 1957.
Miller, David H. "City and State in Muscovite Society: Iaroslavl, 1649-1699." Ph.D. dissertation, Princeton, 1974.
Mironov, N. P. "The Past Existence of Natural Foci of Plague in the Steppe of Southern Europe," *Journal of Microbiology, Epidemiology, and Immunobiology* 29 (1958):1193-98.
Mitchell, H. H. *Plague in the United States: An Assessment of Its Significance as a Problem Following a Thermonuclear War*. RAND Corporation Study, n. p., 1966.
Mizinov, P. *Melochi Iaroslavskoi istorii XVIII i XIX v. (po delam, khraniashchimsia v arkhive Iaroslavskoi gubernskoi arkhivnoi komissiia)*. Iaroslavl, 1895.
Mordovtsev, D. "Chuma v Moskve v 1771 g.," *Drevniaia i novaia Rossiia*, 1875, no. 5: 6-19; no. 6:104-28; no. 9:78-80.
Müller-Dietz, Heinz E. *Ärzte im Russland des achtzehnten Jahrhunderts*. Esslingen/Neckar, 1973.
———. "Die Anfänge der Stadtphysikats in Moskau und St. Petersburg," *Sudhoffs Archiv* 60 (1976):194-206.

———. *Der russische Militärarzt im 18. Jahrhundert*, Bericht des Osteuropa-Instituts an der Freien Universität Berlin, Reihe Medizin, vol. 90 (Berlin, 1970).

———. "Die wirtschaftlichen Verhältnisse russischer Truppenärzte um 1770," *Forschungen zur osteuropäischen Geschichte* 25 (1978):271-82.

———. "Informatii de interes medico-sanitar cu privire la principatele dunarene in vremea razboiului ruso-turc din 1768-1774," *Din traditiile medicinii si ale educatiei sanitare* (Bucharest, 1978):109-18.

Mullett, Charles F. *The Bubonic Plague and England: An Essay in the History of Preventive Medicine*. Lexington, Ky., 1956.

Munro, George E. "The Development of St. Petersburg as an Urban Center during the Reign of Catherine II (1762-1796)." Ph.D. dissertation, University of North Carolina at Chapel Hill, 1973.

Murzanova, M. "Na Moskovsko-Novgorodskoi parusnoi fabrike (1696-1772-1829 gg.)," *Arkhiv istorii truda v Rossii*, 1921, no. 2:1-7.

Nechaev, V. V. *Chuma 1771 goda v Moskve*. Moscow, 1911.

Nevskii, V. A. "A. F. Shafonskii—odin iz pionerov otechestvennoi sanitarii," *Gigiena i sanitariia*, 1950, no. 11:42-45.

Norris, John. "East or West? The Geographic Origin of the Black Death," *Bulletin of the History of Medicine* 51 (1977):1-24.

Novombergskii, N. Ia. *Vrachebnoe stroenie do-Petrovskoi Rusi*. Tomsk, 1907.

"O chume 1692 g. v Astrakhani," *Vestnik Evropy* 47 (1809):212-16.

Opochinin, E. N. "K istorii chumy," *Istoricheskii vestnik* 33 (1888):201-4.

Orlovskii, P. "K istorii chumnoi epidemii v Kieve 1770-1771 gg.," *Kievskaia starina* 57 (1897):445-59.

Otamanovskii, V. D. "Do istorii meditsini ta apteknoi spravi u Vinnitsi i Vinnits'komu poviti 2. polovini XVIII st.," *Zbirnik pam'iati Akademika Teofila Gavrilovicha Ianovs'kogo*, ed. D. Zabolotnyi et al. (Kiev, 1930), pp. 322-38.

———. "Goroda pravoberezhnoi Ukrainy pod vladychestvom shliakhetskoi Pol'shi ot serediny XVII do kontsa XVIII veka." Ph.D. dissertation, 2 vols. Saratov, 1954.

———. "Otechestvennye lekari-novatory vtoroi poloviny XVIII v., sozdavshie bolee progressivnoe napravlenie v lechenii chumy, i rol' ikh kak zachinatelei ratsional'noi terapii," *Trudy Saratovskogo meditsinskogo instituta* 10, fasc. 1 (1958):5-42.

Palkin, B. N. *Ocherki istorii meditsiny i zdravookhraneniia zapadnoi Sibiri i Kazakhstana v period prisoedineniia k Rossii (1716-1868)*. Novosibirsk, 1967.

———. *Russkie gospital'nye shkoly XVIII veka i ikh vospitanniki*. Moscow, 1959.

———. "Vozniknovenie meditsinskoi kantseliarii v XVIII veke i pervyi period ee deiatel'nosti," *Sovetskoe zdravookhranenie*, 1974, no. 4:63-66.

Pantiukhov, I. I. *Epidemii v Pol'she i zapadnoi Rossii do kontsa XVIII veka*. Kiev, 1876.

Panzac, Daniel. "La peste à Smyrne au XVIIIe siècle," *Annales E.S.C.*, 1973, no. 4: 1071-93.

Pastukhov, B. N. "The Epizootic and Epidemic Situation in the Natural Foci of Plague in the USSR and the Prophylactic Measures Taken," *Bulletin of the World Health Organization* 23 (1960):401-4.

Pavlova-Sil'vanskaia, N. P. "Sotsial'naia sushchnost' oblastnoi reformy Ekateriny II," in N. M. Druzhinin et al., eds., *Absoliutizm v Rossii* (Moscow, 1964), pp. 460-91.

Pazhitnov, K. A. *Ocherki istorii tekstil'noi promyshlennosti dorevoliutsionnoi Rossii: Khlopchatobumazhnaia, l'no-penkovaia i shelkovaia promyshlennost'*. Moscow, 1958.

———. *Ocherki istorii tekstil'noi promyshlennosti dorevoliutsionnoi Rossii: Sherstianaia promyshlennost'*. Moscow, 1955.

Petresco, G. Z. *Les dernières épidémies de peste dans les pays Roumains au XVIIIe et au XIXe siècle*. Bucharest, 1934.

Petrov, A. N. *Voina Rossii s Turtsiei i pol'skimi konfederatami v 1769–1774 gg.* 5 vols. St. Petersburg, 1866–74.

Petrov, B. D. et al., eds. *Ocherki istorii meditsinskoi nauki i zdravookhraneniia na Ukraine*. Kiev, 1954.

Pfister, Christian. "Climate and Economy in Eighteenth-Century Switzerland," *Journal of Interdisciplinary History* 9 (1978):223–44.

Poland, Jack D. "Plague," in Paul D. Hoeprich, ed., *Infectious Diseases: A Guide to the Understanding and Management of Infectious Processes* (New York, 1972), pp. 1141-48.

Polianskii, F. Ia. *Gorodskoe remeslo i manufaktura v Rossii XVIII v.* Moscow, 1960.

Pollitzer, Robert. "A Review of Recent Literature on Plague," *Bulletin of the World Health Organization* 23 (1960):313–400.

———. *Plague*. Geneva, 1954.

———, and Meyer, Karl F. "The Ecology of Plague," in Jacques M. May, ed., *Studies in Disease Ecology* (New York, 1961), pp. 433-501.

Post, John D. *The Last Great Subsistence Crisis in the Western World.* Baltimore and London, 1977.

———. "Meteorological Historiography," *Journal of Interdisciplinary History* 3 (1973):721–32.

Prinzing, Friedrich. *Epidemics Resulting from Wars*. London, 1916.

Pyliaev, M. E. *Staraia Moskva*. St. Petersburg, 1891.

Raeff, Marc. "The Domestic Policies of Peter III and His Overthrow," *American Historical Review* 75 (1969–70):1289–1310.

———. "The Well-Ordered Police State and the Development of Modernity in Seventeenth- and Eighteenth-Century Europe: An Attempt at a Comparative Approach," *American Historical Review* 80 (1975):1221–43.

Ransel, David L. *The Politics of Catherinian Russia: The Panin Party*. New Haven and London, 1975.

Reed, W. P., Palmer, D. L., Williams, R. C., and Kisch, A. L. "Bubonic Plague in the Southwestern United States: A Review of Recent Experience," *Medicine* 49 (1970):465–86.

Richter, W. M. *Geschichte der Medicin in Russland*. 3 vols. Moscow, 1813–17; reprinted Leipzig, 1965.

Rosen, George. "Cameralism and the Concept of Medical Police," *Bulletin of the History of Medicine* 27 (1953):21–42.

Rossiiskii, D. M. *200 let meditsinskogo fakul'teta Moskovskogo gosudarstvennogo universiteta*. Moscow, 1955.

Rothenberg, Gunther E. "The Austrian Sanitary Cordon and the Control of Bubonic Plague: 1710–1871," *Journal of the History of Medicine and Allied Sciences* 28 (1973):15–23.

Rozanov, N. *Istoriia Moskovskogo eparkhial'nogo upravleniia*. 3 vols. Moscow, 1869–71.

Rozman, Gilbert. *Urban Networks in Russia 1750–1800 and Premodern Periodization*. Princeton, 1976.

Safonova, A. V. "Obshchestvenno-politicheskaia zhizn' Peterburga v 60–70e gody XVIII veka." Kand. dissertation, Leningrad, 1953.

Samarian, P. G. *Din epidemiologia trecutuli Romanesc Ciuma*. Bucharest, 1932.

Sbornik posviashchennyi 150-letiiu Klinicheskoi bol'nitsy Moskovskogo gosudarstvennogo universiteta (b. Novo-Ekaterininskoi bol'nitsy). Moscow, 1926.

Schultheiss, Emil, and Tardy, Louis. "Short History of Epidemics in Hungary until the Great Cholera Epidemic of 1831," *Centaurus* 11 (1967):279-301.

Selwyn, S. "The Hiatus in Medical Microbiology throughout the Eighteenth Century," *Acta Congressus Internationalis XXIV Historiae Artis Medicinae*, vol. 2 (Budapest, 1976), pp. 759-69.

Semeka, S. A. *Meditsinskoe obespechenie russkoi armii vo vremia Semiletnei voiny 1756–1763 gg*. Moscow, 1951.

Semevskii, V. I. *Krest'iane v tsarstvovanie imperatritsy Ekateriny II*. 2 vols. St. Petersburg, 1901-08.

Shershavkin, S. V. *Istoriia otechestvennoi sudebno-meditsinskoi sluzhby*. Moscow, 1968.

Shrewsbury, J. F. D. *A History of Bubonic Plague in the British Isles*. Cambridge, 1970.

Shryock, Richard H. "Germ Theories in Medicine prior to 1870: Further Comments on Continuity in Science," *Clio Medica* 7 (1972):81–109.

Sieńkowski, Eugeniusz. "Dzuma w Gdańsku w 1709 roku: Studium z dziejów epidemiologii," *Archiwum Historii Medycyny* 33 (1970):309–401.

Sil'vai, K. I. "Deiatel'nost' vengerskikh vrachei v Rossii vo vtoroi polovine XVIII veka," *Sovetskoe zdravookhranenie* 2 (1961):77–83.

Sivkov, K. V. "Nakaz zhitelei Moskvy deputatu komissii 1767 g. i zakonodatel'naia deiatel'nost' imp. Ekateriny II v 60-80-kh godakh XVIII v.," *Uchenye zapiski Moskovskogo gos. ped. inst. im. Lenina*, 60, fasc. 2 (1949):193–222.

Skorokhodov, L. Ia. *Materialy po istorii meditsinskoi mikrobiologii dorevoliutsionnoi Rossii*. Moscow, 1948.

Slack, Paul, et al. *The Plague Reconsidered: A New Look at Its Origins and Effects in Sixteenth and Seventeenth Century England*. Matlock, Derbyshire, 1977.

Slesarchuk, G. I. "Vedomosti k Moskovskim atlasam kak istochnik po istorii promyshlennosti Moskvy kontsa XVIII v.," in Druzhinin et al., eds., *Goroda feodal'noi Rossii* (Moscow, 1966), pp. 498–505.

Smith, R. E. F. *Peasant Farming in Muscovy*. Cambridge, 1977.

Snegirev, I. M. *Moskva—podrobnoe istoricheskoe i arkheologicheskoe opisanie goroda*. 2 vols. Moscow, 1865–73.

Snegirev, V. *Arkhitektor V. I. Bazhenov*. Moscow, 1937.

Snegirev, V. L. *Moskovskie slobody*. Moscow, 1956.

Sobol', S. L. *Istoriia mikroskopa i mikroskopicheskikh issledovanii v Rossii XVIII veka*. Moscow and Leningrad, 1949.

Solov'ev, S. M. *Istoriia Rossii s drevneishikh vremen*. 15 vols. Moscow, 1959-66.

________. "Moskva v 1770–1771 g.," *Russkaia starina* 10 (1876):189–204.

Stahnke, Joachim. *Anfänge der Hebammen-Ausbildung und der Geburtshilfe in Russland*. Inaugural dissertation. Berlin, 1975.
Sticker, Georg. *Abhandlungen aus der Seuchengeschichte und Seuchenlehre*, vol. 1: *Die Pest*, pt. 1: *Die Geschichte der Pest*. Giessen, 1908.
Suslov, A. I., and Churakov, S. S. *Iaroslavl'*. Moscow, 1960.
Sytin, P. V. *Istoriia planirovki i zastroiki Moskvy: Materialy i issledovaniia*. 3 vols. Moscow, 1950–72.
———. Iz istorii Moskovskikh ulits. 2d ed. rev. Moscow, 1952.
Szejdel, Émile. *Histoire de la peste en Roumanie*. Paris, 1932.
Taradin, I. P. "Materialy po istorii meditsiny v Voronezhskom krae XVII, XVIII i nachale XIX stoletiia," *Trudy Voronezhskogo universiteta* 4 (1927):479–617.
Temkin, Owsei. "An Historical Analysis of the Concept of Infection," in *The Double Face of Janus and Other Essays in the History of Medicine by Owsei Temkin* (Baltimore and London, 1977), pp. 456–71.
Troitskii, S. M. *Russkii absoliutizm i dvorianstvo v XVIII v.: formirovanie biurokratii*. Moscow, 1974.
Tsvetkov, M. A. *Izmenenie lesistosti Evropeiskoi Rossii s kontsa XVII stoletiia po 1914 god*. Moscow, 1957.
"Ubiistvo upyria v Kievshchine vo vremia chumy 1770 goda," *Kievskaia starina* 28 (1890):338–40.
Ungermann, Richard. *Der Russisch-Türkische Krieg 1768–1774*. Vienna and Leipzig, 1906.
Urlanis, B. Ts. *Voiny i narodo-naselenie Evropy*. Moscow, 1960.
Utterström, Gustaf. "Climatic Fluctuations and Population Problems in Early Modern History," *Scandinavian Economic History Review* 3 (1955):3–47.
———. "Some Population Problems in Pre-Industrial Sweden," *Scandinavian Economic History Review* 2 (1954):103–65.
Van Lare, Donald H. "Tula Province in the Eighteenth Century: The Deputy Instructions to the Legislative Commission of 1767 as a Source for Local History." Ph.D. dissertation, University of Kansas, 1977.
Van Zwanenberg, David. "A 'Singular Calamity'," *Medical History* 17 (1973):204–7.
———. "The Last Epidemic of Plague in England? Suffolk 1900–1918," *Medical History* 14 (1970):63–74.
———. "The Suttons and the Business of Inoculation," *Medical History* 22 (1978): 71–82.
Vartanov, G. L. "Gorodskie iarmarki tsentral'noi chasti Evropeiskoi Rossii vo vtoroi polovine XVIII v.," *Uchenye zapiski Leningradskogo gos. ped. inst. im. Gertsena* 194 (1958):137–68.
———. "Kupechestvo gorodov Moskovskoi gubernii vo vtoroi polovine XVIII veka." Kand. dissertation, Leningrad, 1966.
———. "Kupechestvo i torguiushchee krest'ianstvo tsentral'noi chasti Evropeiskoi Rossii vo vtoroi polovine XVIII v.," *Uchenye zapiski Leningradskogo gos. ped. inst. im. Gertsena* 229 (1962):161–96.
———. "Moskovskoe i inogorodnee kupechestvo vo vtoroi polovine XVIII v.," *Uchenye zapiski Leningradskogo gos. ped. inst. im. Gertsena* 278 (1965):272–89.
Vasil'ev, K. G., and Segal, A. E. *Istoriia epidemii v Rossii: Materialy i ocherki*. Edited by A. I. Metelkin. Moscow, 1960.

Vinogradov, B. S., and Argiropulo, A. I. *Fauna of the U.S.S.R.: Mammals.* Israel Program of Scientific Translations. Jerusalem, 1968.

Viseltear, Arthur J. "The Pneumonic Plague Epidemic of 1924 in Los Angeles," *Yale Journal of Biology and Medicine* 47 (1974):40-54.

Vodarskii, Ia. E. "Chislennost' i razmeshchenie posadskogo naseleniia v Rossii vo vtoroi polovine XVII v.," in N. M. Druzhinin et al., eds., *Goroda feodal'noi Rossii* (Moscow, 1966), pp. 271-97.

________. *Naselenie Rossii v kontse XVII-nachale XVIII veka.* Moscow, 1977.

________. *Promyshlennye seleniia tsentral'noi Rossii v period genezisa i razvitiia kapitalizma.* Moscow, 1972.

Volkov, S. I. *Krest'iane dvortsovykh vladenii podmoskov'ia v seredine XVIII v.* Moscow, 1959.

Vvedenskii, D. *Kresttsovoe dukhovenstvo v staroi Moskve.* Moscow, 1899.

Weiner, Gordon M. "The Demographic Effects of the Venetian Plagues of 1575-77 and 1630-31," *Genus* 26 (1970):41-57.

Willemse, David. *António Nunes Ribeiro Sanches—élève de Boerhaave—et son importance pour la Russie,* Supplements to *Janus,* vol. 6. Leiden, 1966.

Williamson, Raymond. "The Germ Theory of Disease: Neglected Precursors of Louis Pasteur (Richard Bradley, Benjamin Marten, Jean-Baptiste Goiffon)," *Annals of Science* 11 (1955):44-57.

________. "The Plague of Marseilles and the Experiments of Professor Anton Deidier on Its Transmission," *Medical History* 2 (1958):237-52.

Winslow, Charles-Edward A. *The Conquest of Epidemic Disease: A Chapter in the History of Ideas.* Princeton, 1943; reprinted New York and London, 1967.

Zakrevskii, N. *Opisanie Kieva,* vol. 1. Rev. ed., Moscow, 1868.

Zaozerskaia, E. I. "Manufaktura v Moskve v seredine XVIII veka," *Istoricheskie zapiski* 33 (1950):123-57.

________. "Le salariat dans les manufactures textiles russes au XVIIIe siècle," *Cahiers du monde russe et sovietique* 6 (1965):189-222.

________. *Rabochaia sila i klassovaia bor'ba na tekstil'nykh manufakturakh v 20-60 gg. XVIII v.* Moscow, 1960.

________. *Razvitie legkoi promyshlennosti v Moskve v pervoi chetverti XVIII v.* Moscow, 1953.

Zhivopistsev, N. A. *Bol'nitsa imperatora Pavla I-go v Moskve: kratkii ocherk za 150 let eia sushchestvovaniia, 1763-1913.* Moscow, 1914.

[Zhuravlev, D. I.] *Moskovskaia Ekaterininskaia gorodskaia bol'nitsa, rodonachal'nitsa gorodskoi i obshchestvennoi meditsiny 1776-1926, iubileiny sbornik.* Moscow, 1929.

Zmeev, L. F. *Byloi vrachebnoi Rossii,* bk. 1. St. Petersburg, 1890.

Zviagintsev, E. A. "Chuma v Moskve v XVII i XVIII v.," *Istoricheskii zhurnal* 2 (1937):52-59.

________. "Rost naseleniia v Moskovskikh slobodakh XVIII veka," *Moskovskii krai v ego proshlom,* pt. 2 (Moscow, 1930), pp. 125-48.

________. "'Kozhevniki' i ikh posadskoe naselenie v XVIII veke," *Staraia Moskva,* bk. 1 (Moscow, 1929), pp. 109-26.

Index

The Johns Hopkins University Press

This book was composed by Britton Composition Company and printed on 50-lb. Eggshell Offset Cream by Universal Lithographers.

Library of Congress Cataloging in Publication Data

Alexander, John T
Bubonic plague in early modern Russia.
(The Johns Hopkins University studies in historical and political science; 98th ser., no. 1)
Bibliography: pp. 353-71
Includes index.
1. Plague—Russia—History. 2. Public health—Russia—History. 3. Epidemiology—Russia—History.
I. Title. II. Series: Johns Hopkins University.
Studies in historical and political science;
98th ser., no. 1.
RC179.R8A43 614.5'73'20947 79-3652
ISBN 0-8018-2322-6